MAINSTREAMS IN INDUSTRIAL ORGANIZATION

STUDIES IN INDUSTRIAL ORGANIZATION

Volume 6

Mainstreams in Industrial Organization

Book I. Theory and International Aspects

edited
by

H.W. de Jong

University of Amsterdam, The Netherlands

W.G. Shepherd

University of Michigan at Ann Arbor, U.S.A.

SPRINGER-SCIENCE+BUSINESS MEDIA, B.V.
1986

Library of Congress Cataloging in Publication Data

Mainstreams in industrial organization.

(Studies in industrial organization ; 6)

1. Industrial organization--Congresses.
2. Managerial economics--Congresses. 3. Trade
regulation--Congresses. 4. Industry and state--
Congresses. I. Jong, H. W. de. II. Shepherd,
William G. III. Series.
HD29.M25 1986 338.6 86-12345

ISBN 978-94-017-0495-3 ISBN 978-94-017-0493-9 (eBook)
DOI 10.1007/978-94-017-0493-9

PREFACE

The present two volumes contain the essays and part of the discussions as presented at the conference on Mainstreams in Industrial Organization, held at the University of Amsterdam, 21–23 August 1985. The thema was chosen because the field of studies commonly designated "industrial organization" in the Anglo-Saxon countries, or "market theory" in Continental Europe, has experienced important alterations during the past decade.

Partly this reflects changing theoretical views inside the field, in which shifts in the core concepts have occurred and different emphasis is laid on time-honoured views and results. Partly, critical views have been voiced from outside the field. As in all open scientific debate, they have to be weighed and, if necessary, taken into account. Partly also, divergent developments in thinking between the Anglo-Saxon, European and Japanese areas need to be considered, because both the problems and the ways of approaching them still differ.

The variety of views, theories and results is testimony to the vitality of this field of economics; variety is generated by the creative endeavours, from which the chaff is being beaten out by critical discussions. That is especially true for the concept of competition itself, which industrial organization economists are debating intensively.

But it should not be thought that the participants lack a common understanding. As this conference brought forward again, the economists assembled here share the view that the study of the market economy needs a measure of realism in order to be worthwhile. Realism involves taking note of market situations as well as market processes, of recognizing entrepreneurial actions as well as power games, of modelling behaviour as well as investigating empirical evidence, of looking for shifts in explanations of what occurs as well as for policies that need to be widened or trimmed. Negatively, such realism rejects "l'art pour l'art" theorizing as well as pure empiricism or description.

Such a program is strewn with difficulties, as a reading of the two volumes brings out. No useful purpose is served by denying that industrial organization means to study very complex phenomena. It should nevertheless encourage industrial organization economists to persevere in their efforts, for amidst useless shells many valuable pearls can be found.

The editors are grateful, both to the organizing institutions – the University of Amsterdam and the Universities of Michigan and Massachusetts – for their support and to the economists who presented papers and who took part in the lively discussions. They also invite readers from a wider audience to join in the experience, which shows that industrial organization economists do not represent a single orthodoxy or "school". For a school of thinking has some resemblance to a cartel: it easily degenerates into predictable behaviour and the blocking of new initiatives.

The pairing of views on five different themes, contained in these volumes, should therefore be a challenge to readers to contribute themselves the innovations required in this fascinating field in the coming decades. If that occurs the highest hopes of the conference's organizers will be fulfilled.

W. G. SHEPHERD
University of Michigan

H. W. DE JONG
University of Amsterdam

CONTENTS

BOOK II. Policies: Antitrust, Deregulation and Industrial

Part III. Antitrust Policy

Part IV. Deregulation

Part V. Industrial Policy

LIST OF CONTRIBUTORS

Walter Adams, Associate Professor of Economics and Law, The University of Michigan, Ann Arbor, Michigan, U.S.A.

Kenneth D. Boyer, Professor of Economics, Michigan State University, East Lansing, U.S.A.

Richard E. Caves, Professor of Economics, Harvard University, Cambridge (Mass), U.S.A.

Gunnar Eliasson, President, The Industrial Institute for Economic and Social Research (IKI), Stockholm, Sweden.

Eleanor M. Fox, Professor of Law, New York University, New York, U.S.A.

Chris Green, Professor of Economics, McGill University, Ottawa, Canada.

Ann M. Hendriks, Assistant Professor of Economics, Tufts University.

Dennis C. Gribbin, Economist, The Monopolies Commission, London, U.K.

Henk W. de Jong, Professor of Economics, University of Amsterdam, The Netherlands.

Eberhard Kantzenbach, Professor of Economics, University of Hamburg, President of Monopol Kommission, West Germany.

William Kingston, John Good Senior Lecturer (Innovation), Trinity College, Dublin, Ireland.

Remo Linda, Economist, Commission of the European Communities, Brussels, Belgium.

Stephen Martin, Assistant Professor of Economics, Michigan, Maryland, U.S.A.

Dennis C. Mueller, Professor of Economics, University of Maryland, Maryland, U.S.A.

Takao Nakao, Professor of Economic, Doshisha University, Kyoto, Japan.

H. Odagiri, Professor of Economics, University of Trukuba, Sakura, Japan.
Jacques Pelkmans, Professor of Economics, European Institute of Public Administration, Maastricht, The Netherlands.
Frederic M. Scherer, Joseph Wharton Professor of Political Economics, Swarthmore College, U.S.A.
William G. Shepherd, Professor of Economics, University of Michigan, Ann Arbor, U.S.A.
Mike A. Utton, Professor of Economics, University of Reading, U.K.

BOOK I

THEORY AND INTERNATIONAL ASPECTS

PART I. THEORY

1. ON THE CURRENT STATE OF KNOWLEDGE IN INDUSTRIAL ORGANIZATION

F. M. Scherer*

My task in this paper is to provide a broad overview on recent developments in our understanding of industrial organization economics. This seems a particularly propitious time for perspective-taking, since, it seems to me, industrial organization is at a stage of intellectual crisis not unlike what occurred in astronomy during the period we now call the Copernican Revolution. In attempting to survey the dimensions of this crisis, I shall focus on four main themes: the relationship between theoretical and empirical work; the breakdown of the 'classical' (i.e., Mason–Bain) structure-conduct-performance paradigm; the tension between static and dynamic models; and the sharply disparate schools of thought emerging on the economics of mergers and takeovers.

I. THEORY AND EMPIRICAL WORK

As I perceive the scene in both Europe and America, industrial organization economics is characterized now by a state of affairs like that just before Johannes Kepler went to Prague in the year 1600. To motivate the analogy, the reader may recall that Kepler was greatly influenced by the views of Copernicus, who had concluded, both from the manifest failure of the Ptolemaic system as a basis for calendar-setting and from his own (empirical) observations, that the planets, including Earth, rotated about the sun. Unlike Copernicus, Kepler was first and foremost a mathematical theorist. In his early attempts to provide a sound mathematical basis for the Copernican cosmology, he conceived many ingenious models of planetary systems with circular orbits. They were, of course, wrong. It was not until he joined Tycho Brahe in Prague in 1600 that he obtained the unprecedently detailed observational data permitting him to see why the assumption of circular orbits was wrong, and leading him to assume

de Jong, H. W., Shepherd, W. G. (eds) Mainstreams in Industrial Organization
 ISBN 978-94-017-0495-3

elliptical orbits, which were the basis for Kepler's law of motion and ultimately Newton's law of gravitation.

Industrial organization today, to repeat, is in a pre-1600 state. It has long been clear that pure atomistic competition – economists' analogue to the Ptolemaic system – is inconsistent with the observed facts of the world. The crisis has spawned much work by atheoretical fact-gatherers – the modern counterparts of Tycho Brahe – and pure theorists like the Kepler of 1596. Right now, in contrast to the situation four centuries ago, it is the pure theorists to whom the greatest attention and prestige are accorded. Hundreds of bright young theorists sit at their desks and toil away at the latest 'I-O' puzzles, stacking circular orbits within circular orbits to create new models of the economic world. Some may indeed happen upon ellipses. But if I am correct in my choice of an analogy, genuine progress is not likely to be made unless there is fruitful cooperation between the modern-day equivalents of Brahe *and* Kepler – i.e., between those who have the skill to make ever more accurate observations on the real world, and those who can relate the empirical evidence to a better theoretical model of the world.[1]

II. THE BREAKDOWN OF THE S-C-P PARADIGM

Although the Keplers will play a role, let me turn now to our modern-day Brahes – the economists who diligently collect data on such things as industry structure and performance and who seek truth by establishing the relationships among them. Although there were minor precursors, the leader of this school, which dominated industrial organization during the 1960s, was Joe S. Bain. In two major studies (1951, 1956), he found that industry profitability (a measure of performance) was positively and significantly correlated with two indices of industry structure – the seller concentration ratio and a subjectively estimated categorization of the height of barriers to new entry. The largely rudimentary theory motivating and explaining these results implied that high seller concentration facilitated collusion (an aspect of conduct), while high barriers to entry protected the profits of colluding firms from erosion through new entry. Bain's results were enthusiastically received, in part because they reached an economics profession eager to utilize 'new' econometric tools (which actually can be traced back 150 years to the astronomical work of Carl Friedrich Gauss) and partly because the ideological climate of the time favored public intervention to nulify the price-raising effects of monopoly and oligopoly. More than 100 studies in the basic Bain tradition have been carried out, most (but not all) indicating that industry profits, variously measured, rise with industry concentration, variously defined.

Not all scholars shared the interventionist idealogy, however, and it was from an anti-interventionist wing that the first counter-attacks came.[2] The leaders were Yale Brozen of Chicago (1971) and Harold Demsetz of UCLA (1973). They pointed to possible anomalies in the Bainian findings: notably, that the results were sensitive to sample choice; that they might not be stable over time; and most importantly (Demsetz), that what held for the largest sellers in the industry size distribution might not hold for smaller fringe firms, whose profitability appeared insensitive to market structure. I confess to being unimpressed by the attack, partly because I did not belong to the same idealogical school, but mainly because the data analyzed were crude and the statistical methodology primitive. Most scholars shared my skepticism.

My own doubts about the Bainian paradigm were kindled much more effectively by work more directly in the Brahe–Kepler tradition. Although again there were precursors, the first important contributions were by W. G. Shepherd (1972) and Bradley Gale (1972).[3] They used *company*, rather than the traditional industry, data, and they attempted to measure not only the conventional industry concentration ratio, but also the *market shares* possessed by individual firms. What they found was that individual market share was more strongly associated with profitability than concentration. This reinforced the Demsetz query: Why is it that the market share leaders seem to benefit most from structural concentration, however measured? If prices are raised as a result of high concentration and/or high leading firm market shares (which must be correlated), why don't the smaller fringe firms experience equally high profits under the high-price umbrella? There were several possible answers. The most traditional rationalization, emphasized by Shepherd, is that monopoly power is associated more closely with having a high market share – e.g. through opportunities to exploit product differentiation or price discrimination – than with simply being a member of a concentrated industry. The alternative conjecture emphasized by Demsetz is that firms with large market shares are more profitable than firms with small market shares either because there are persistant economies of large scale, so that larger firms enjoy lower unit costs, or because certain firms have come to have lower costs (perhaps by chance, Mancke (1974) observed) and *therefore* grew to have both large market shares and lower costs. Furthermore, the more compelling the advantages of large firms are, i.e., the steeper cost curves are, the more likely it is that firms with large market shares will emerge, implying high concentration, and the more heavily those low-cost firms' profits will be weighted in industry aggregates leading (spuriously) to a correlation between profitability and concentration in cross-industry regression analyses.[4]

Wherever the truth lay, it was clear by 1972 that the world of industries was much more complicated than classical structure-performance regressions had presumed it to be. Nevertheless, a major problem stood in the way of disentangling what was going on. Since the typical large enterprise operates in numerous 'industries', using company-wide market share and profitability averages was like averaging planetary position observations made at differing hours of the night. To progress, we must invent the spherically-mounted sextant (Brahe) and the telescope (improved by Galileo) and use better chronometers. The solution is and can only be obtaining data on the numerous individual lines of business in which companies operate.

On this, U.S. economists have progressed far beyond their European counterparts because we have superior data: the PIMS (Profit Impact of Market Strategies) and the Federal Trade Commission's LB (Line of Business) data sets. With these data, the early findings of Shepherd and Gale have been strengthened. Profitability rises strongly with larger market share; belonging to a more highly concentrated industry adds little or nothing. Let me make the point more strongly: At least for the United States, the many studies that found a positive association between aggregated industry profits and concentration were almost surely spurious, the victims of aggregation biases.

Although there is much more to be learned, the 'state of the art' today is best embodied in a paper already published by Ravenscraft (1983) and in another (still unpublished) paper by Kwoka and Ravenscraft (1984), both based upon Line of Business data. Several findings are relevant. First, as noted already, the effect of concentration fades or turns negative when individual firms' market shares are included as separate variables. Second, the strong positive effect of larger own market share on profitability appears, in ways that have yet to be disentangled fully, to be bound up closely with both economies of large-scale operation and product differentiation advantages. Third, when the sample is divided between leader and follower firms, the effect of increased leader market share is to depress follower firms' profitability in industries with sizeable optimial plant scales, but not in small-plant industries. This almost surely reflects some form of price leadership: either a 'low price preference' strategy for large leader firms or a more sophisticated limit pricing strategy. See Scherer (1980, pp. 156–159, 176–184, and 232–252). Finally, there is evidence that having a relatively large 'number two' firm in the industry tends to introduce rivalry and increase pressure on the leading firm's profits.

These results do not imply the absence of monopoly power. Monopoly power is the power to choose the price that is most profitable. What the new results suggest is that such power is not exercised collectively, but by the leading firm, especially when that firm has a cost or price advantage over its rivals. Then a tradeoff must be made: the leader can set lower prices and achieve lower current profits, gaining (perhaps only slowly) market share relative to its rivals, or it can choose a high-price, high-profit strategy and sustain a smaller market share. In this kind of monopoly structure, a social tradeoff may also be implied. An alternate structure with smaller leading firm market shares may mean high unit costs (although when the leading firm's advantage comes only from product differentiation, this is not necessary). Whether lower prices result from a more fragmented market structure depends upon the extent to which the leading firm's price-raising power (and desire) is constrained vs. the degree to which unit costs are elevated.

It is important to recognize that the explanatory power of these disaggregated regressions (e.g., as reflected in R^2 values) is low both absolutely and in comparison with what has been achieved in aggregated (but biased) industry cross-sectional studies. This undoubtedly means that there are important differences in behaviour that are not captured by simply-quantified structural variables. It also implies the existance of considerable 'noise', in part from more or less random shocks to firms' earnings in particular years and perhaps also from differences in the accounting conventions adopted by diverse firms. On the latter, Fisher and McGowan (1983) have argued (as an offshoot of their work defending IBM from monopolization charges) that the difficulties of establishing true economic rates of return on capital investment are so great that no confident inferences about monopoly power (or anything else) can be drawn from accounting data. Their article is certain to be a spectre that haunts nearly every analysis of market structure and profitability in the future. It is a peculiarly difficult spectre to exorcise, since everyone admits that accounting data are imperfect, and it is virtually impossible to prove the negative proposition that the problems are not so serious as to preclude valid inferences. Much seems to hinge on basic matters of faith,[5] reminding one of the efforts to silence Galileo. Attempts to test the robustness of structure-performance regression results to variations in accounting conventions (e.g., Long *et al.*, 1984) have shown no significant sensitivity. But they have not persuaded the unbelievers, in part because other accounting convention variations remain unexplored. It is clear that much work remains to be done – if one's faith is sufficiently strong to sustain what will undoubtedly be an arduous task.

For good reasons rooted in the literature of econometrics, there has been in recent years a growing insistence that statistical studies of the relationship between market structure and profitability be specified in conformity with a rigorously-derived a priori theoretical model. Most commonly, the model adopted for this purpose is a Cournot–Nash model, sometimes qualified to allow conjectural variations of a non-Cournot type.[6] Cournot models appear to be favored for two main reasons: because they are the most mathematically tractable and richly developed of extant imperfect competition pricing models; and because their implications lead in a substantial class of cases to a clear choice of the Herfindahl–Hirschman index as the relevant measure of aggregated industry structure, in contrast to the more ambivalent guidance of alternative theories. I find this specific choice of models to be quite unfortunate – indeed, a reversion to pre-1600 Keplerism. For one thing, the assumptions are patently implausible for repeated pricing games in all but rare situations (i.e., those with 'consistent' conjectual variations). Business decision-makers playing by the Cournot rules would soon learn that their assumptions are invalid. Second, the Cournot assumption in particular (with a quantity conjectual variation of zero) implies positive monopoly profits for small numbers of sellers even when there are no barriers to entry, which is inconsistent with long-run equilibrium. Third and most important, the Cournot model is a short-run model. It does not allow for strategic behavior – e.g. as the leading firm adopts a price policy that maximizes long-run profits, among other things, shaping the structure of the market within which it will operate in future periods. Since there is considerable evidence that price leaders do commonly price strategically, to insist upon a Cournot formulation because it is mathematically appealing is to fit circles within circles when the true cosmology is elliptical. One hopes that, like Kepler, modern-day industrial organization economists will seek the better data by which their Cournot conjectures can be falsified and change their theoretical schema when they are confronted by contrary results – as seems already evident to me. Unfortunately, recognition is likely to come only slowly, in part because the real cosmos of industry is complex, and also because the quantitative data on industrial structure and performances will never be as reliable even as those collected by Brahe before the telescope became available.

III. STATICS VS. DYNAMICS

One of the largest challenges confronting industrial organization economics at present is to build an adequate, integrated dynamic theory that incorporates not only the mandates of long-run profit maximization, but also the strategies through which firms move toward their goals in an environment characterized by small numbers of meaningful competitors. Much has already been accomplished here, but much remains to be done. Several fields of work must be touched upon with a brevity that belies their importance.

Limit pricing

Limit pricing, or pricing to take into account the consequences of one's actions on the entry of new rivals and the growth of existing rivals, is not a model to fit all industries. If it is to be relevant, there must be a price leader large enough, or with sufficiently strong cost or quality advantages, to believe it can pursue a long-run structure-shaping strategy, *or* a group of rivals whose collusion is sufficiently perfect that long-run considerations take precedence over problems of muddling through the current period. Yet the evidence implying widespread limit pricing behavior has mounted to an impressive level. There are hints of it in the Kwoka-Ravenscraft (1984) results; there is strong evidence from a study by Caves *et al.* (1984) of U.S. dominant firm pricing and market shares in the early decades of the 20th century; and there is support from an unusually sophisticated cross-section analysis (using rather poor data) by Masson and Shaanan (1982). Other evidence comes from quantitative studies of individual industries, e.g., Sultan's study (1975, Chapter 14) of turbogenerators and Yamawaki's analysis (1982) of the United States Steel Corporation's pricing. Much more empirical work, needless to say, remains to be done.

If a limit pricing view of the world is favored over Cournot–Nash perspectives, at least for a sizeable subset of all industries, significant implications follow. For one, market structure can no longer be considered an exogenous variable in studies of price and profit behavior. Rather, simultaneous equation system models will be needed, and the demands on data, already stretched to require disaggregation to the individual line of business level, must be stretched further to cover lengthy time series. Second, there are quite different implications for how industries react to exogenous cost shocks. Assuming constant unit costs, only half of a cost increase is passed on to consumers under pure monopoly, while all of it tends to be passed on under pure limit pricing, with Cournot oligopolies occupying intermediate positions. Whether inflationary shocks are heavily or lightly damped, then, depends upon the market structure and the mode of behavior. Much more research could and should be done to illuminate these differences. Third, the sacrifice of current profits to gain future market position under some limit pricing strategies has important welfare implications that have scarcely been explored. It is probable that an omniscient social welfare maximizer would prefer low price, market share-expanding strategies to the strategies that are associated with the classic 'declining dominant firm'. But the magnitude of the divergence between social and private discount rates is likely to play a critical role, with consequences inter alia for tax policy and capital markets policy.

The impact of foreign trade

The debate over behavioral models also has potentially important implications for our understanding of how international trade adjustments occur. It is well-established statistically that import competition serves as a check on the pricing freedom of domestic monopolies and oligopolies. But much remains to be learned about how that constraint operates. Suppose a nation is running a balance of trade deficit and that, to remedy the imbalance, its currency is devalued. The price of importers' goods can be expected to rise. The 'classical' theory of adjustment assumes either Edgeworth behavior, in which case domestic firms hold their prices constant and gain market share rapidly vis-a-vis importers, or if price equalization occurs, the domestic firms at least ride competitively up their supply curves and gain market share. But if, alternatively, a collusive domestic industry either follows the price lead of importers (who may be the low price-preference suppliers) and passively adjusts quantities to clear the market, or if it pursues a limit-pricing strategy with importers viewed as the most-favored entrants, domestic prices will rise in lock step with the devaluation-induced import price increase and the trade adjustment mechanism's effectiveness will be blunted. Such pricing behavior by the U.S. steel and automobile industries, and probably by others, contributed significantly to America's manifest (and more complex) merchandise trade adjustment difficulties during the 1970s. More recently, many European and Japanese exporters reacted to rising dollar exchange rates by holding their prices in the U.S. roughly constant rather than reducing them, taking their competitive position gains in the form of higher profits rather than deeper market penetration. Much needs to be done to understand these strategy choices better.

Contestability

I would be remiss if I did not mention the theory of contestability, which its co-inventor William Baumol has characterized as 'no less than a unifying theory as a foundation for the analysis of industrial organization' (1982, p. 15). My own evaluation is somewhat less enthusiastic than Professor Baumol's. I view contestability theory as more circles within circles – an aesthetically pleasing creation whose conformity to reality is at best questionable.[7] The essential idea is straightforward. If entrants to an industry can *exit* quickly and with little or no loss of sunk costs, incumbent firms, however monopolistic their structural position may be, are constrained from raising price above the least-cost level by fear of 'hit and run' entry that captures the incumbent's market share and profits. The 'run' part of 'hit and run' entry comes from the exit of new entrants whenever the incumbents respond by reducing their prices to entry-inhibiting levels, only to be 'hit' again if they attempt after exit to raise prices. The theory offers the useful (but not entirely new) insight that the ability of potential competition to constrain incumbents' pricing depends not only upon the 'height' of entry barriers, but also upon how readily entrants can liquidate their investments if the incumbents react in a hostile manner. Its main limitation is the difficulty of finding real-world cases in which liquidation of entry investments is quick and not subject to 'fire sale' losses. Aside from situations in which contracting for a term long enough to amortize special-purpose investments is feasible, the main practical applications are to offering the services of high mobile equipment (such as passenger airliners, trucks, and boats) importing undifferentiated products into relatively small markets from a well-established and flexible foreign production base. Even in the former case, it is clear from the U.S. airline industry experience that the costs sunk in building a reputation are sufficiently large and irretrievable that 'hit and run' entry is not a potent constraint. In my view, the most interesting application is in the area of foreign (or inter-regional) trade, where its implications have scarcely been explored.

Strategic behavior

It is hardly possible to discuss limit pricing, contestability, and the real world of foreign trade without tackling the concept of strategic behavior, i.e., positioning oneself physically or psychologically so as to discourage or thwart actions or reactions by rivals and potential rivals that would, if taken, impair one's own goal attainment. It has long been recognized that if the main impediment to entry on equal terms is the need for a large scale of operation, the successful pursuit by incumbents of an entry-deterring strategy (i.e., a special case of limit pricing) requires a complement of strategic measures to discourage large-scale entrants.[8]

Contestability theory has been offered, but not generally accepted, as a means of dispensing with the theoretically messy problems of strategic behavior. And in foreign trade, it is widely believed that the Japanese have developed new market entry strategies that render the deterrent measures of Geijin incumbents either futile or non-credible.

In recent years there has been an explosion of work, mostly mathematical, on theories of strategic behavior and (especially) entry deterrence. It is unclear whether the main impetus to this explosion came from the demand side, e.g., as the various IBM antitrust cases revealed new and more sophisticated means of combatting new entrants, or from the supply side, as bright young scholars who turned to economics rather than overcrowded mathematics and physics found industrial organization on a fruitful area for demonstrating their model-building skills.

The most interesting work on strategic deterrent behavior has emphasized three notions: 'prepositioning', e.g., investing in reserve capacity so as to keep one's marginal costs on reactive output low and hence enhance one's price war fighting credibility; 'preemption', or being first on the market with a new product, plant, or advertising campaign; and inculcating in rivals' minds the expectation that one might react to an incursion irrationally (e.g., Schelling's 'threats that leave something to chance' (1960, pp. 187–203)). All three have received rich theoretical development. On the empirical side, by far the most important advance is illumination of the role 'first mover' advantages play in building product differentiation. It was once argued seriously that firms could, by spending enough, advertise their way to monopoly power in consumer goods markets. This hypothesis is no longer empirically tenable, its demise explaining inter alia why *all* firms do not choose to advertise their way to monopoly power. The critical new insight is that advertising per se is not sufficient. To be effective in building long-run strategic position, it must be accompanied by something more: usually some element of innovation, either in physical product characteristics or in the characteristics advertising imparts to the product. 'Innovation' here means being the first mover, although there is also a 'fast second' theory explaining why being literally first is not always essential.[9] In any event, it has become clear from several empirical studies that firms who have led some field of product development build up substantial reputational capital that can be exploited in at least three important ways: in the ability to charge premium prices without suffering severe customer defection; in the ability to expand one's customer base at lower advertising costs per unit than firms lacking a first mover reputation; and in the opportunity to race down learning curves before rivals, building market share and securing production cost advantages both through learning-by-doing and conventional scale economies. Once a firm has gained such first-mover advantages, it becomes difficult to displace even though it commands supranormal profits. This set of relationships is almost surely a significant reason why market share and profitability are strongly correlated, although much remains to be done toward sharpening our insights statistically.

Technological innovation

The innovation that yields first-mover advantages is not necessarily technological innovation, although the technological species is an important component and also most important in its own right. Indeed, it is a source of continuing astonishment to me that we industrial organization economists allocate such a large fraction of our intellectual resources to pricing questions and so small a portion to the study of technological change. We have been much too stubborn about acknowledging that Schumpeter (1912, 1942) was right. What matters for economic welfare in the long run is not how finely tuned the resource allocation process is at any moment in time, but how successful we are in creating new production functions and shifting upward the functions for existing products.

Although the comparative allocation of resources has been small, truly remarkable progress has been achieved in understanding how innovation and technological change affect, and are affected by, the economy. One shot that ushered in the revolution was Robert Solow's (1957) article. Confirming Schumpeter's qualitative insight, Solow found that only a small fraction (initially, 13 percent) of the growth in U.S. output per labor hour during the first half of the 20th century could be attributed to capital deepening. The rest he assigned to a 'residual' called 'technical progress'. Since then, we have been working hard to identify and decompose that residual. Among other things, we have found that industrial research and development, or whatever bundle of activities is associated with measured R & D, is a major contributor. My own research (1982), which recognizes that one industry's new products may be used to enhance another industry's productivity, found that moving from the lowest quartile to the highest quartile among R & D-using industries roughly doubles an industry's labor productivity growth rate. There is still much more to be learned here. The concepts are now well-developed; the most severe barrier to progress is the dearth of reliable data. Accurate measurement of productivity, if possible at all, is most urgently needed. In a comparative sense, our productivity data are far worse than the planetary observations with which Copernicus worked, which were greatly inferior to those of Brahe and Galileo. Unless we improve, we may never discover the ellipses.

The current world productivity growth slump poses at least as great an intellectual challenge as the calendar reform problem of the 16th century. This is not a field on which the macroeconomists can be left alone; there is much for industrial organization economists to do. Part of the problem is surely attributable to the macroeconomic shocks generated by the OPEC cartel. But there is surely more to the story. Productivity growth flows from technical change, which is significantly driven by formally-organized research and development activities. In most major nations (excepting Japan), domestic patenting declined absolutely, and real R & D growth rates fell, *before* the OPEC price moves of 1973. See Scherer (1984a). Evidently, there were important seeds of stagnation along with the oil crisis. What was their origin? I would emphasize two hypotheses. One is that, after a period of very rapid R & D growth, we ran into a stage of severely diminishing returns that can be reversed only by replenishing the scientific knowledge base. The other is that many leading industries of major western nations were shocked and demoralized by the rapid technological advances, and ensuing surge of high-technology exports, achieved by the Japanese. With rapid Japanese import penetration, profits fell, and of the two possible reactions to falling new product profits – redouble one's R & D efforts or cut back – the latter was chosen. I don't know whether either of these hypotheses holds much truth, but I do know that the problem is very important, and it is one for whose solution industrial organization economists should have comparative advantage.

The potential dualism of enterprises' reaction to new technological rivalry has been recognized at least since Schumpeter's (1942) book. In recent years there has been a proliferation of high quality theoretical research on the problem of market structure. Despite much work, the dualism persists: rivalry may either accelerate or retard the pace of innovation, depending upon numerous other circumstances. The most recent contributions, however, lead me to wonder whether we have taken a wrong turn.[10] What they seek is an equilibrium solution in which the intensity of each (identical) firm's R & D effort *and* the number of firms are simultaneously determined so as to achieve a zero-profit result. This emphasis on zero-profit innovation equilibria stands Schumpeter on his head. It is like 'seeing' a ballet through a 1/250 second photograph in which the entire Corps de Ballet stands en pointe, without any appreciation for how they got there, in what order, and whether some of the Corps members play a more important role than others. If we are to resume making genuine progress in explaining how the industrial cosmos works, we shall have to devote much more attention to dynamics, strategic pre-positioning, and nomination mechanisms. Because of data deficiencies, this is an area in which empirical work has lagged badly behind theory-building. However, a rich new data base collected by Levin and others (1985) seems an important start toward restoring the balance.

IV. THE ECONOMICS OF MERGERS

Many of the themes explored thus far join in an analysis of the causes and consequences of mergers. Both in the United States and Europe, mergers have precipitated significant industry structure transformations. Mergers can lead to monopoly power. However, most U.S. horizontal mergers of recent decades have joined market shares too small to believe that appreciable changes in price-setting institutions followed; and especially during the merger wave of the 1960s, most American mergers were conglomerate, not horizontal. In 1984, both the United States and the United Kingdom experienced all-time record levels of merger activity, a considerable fraction entailing 'hostile' take-overs of an unwilling victim by an aggressive suitor.

In recent years a new 'Chicago–Rochester school' of merger analysis has become firmly established. Its publications, admirably surveyed by Jensen and Ruback (1983), are extensive. Its methodology is very much in the spirit of my Kepler–Brahe metaphor: rich time series data on movements in stock prices coincidental with merger 'events' are analyzed and juxtaposed with a theory of merger motivations. One might suppose that I would applaud wholeheartedly. Yet I do not, because I believe this new school has failed to accept some important methodological lessons of the Kepler–Brahe–Galileo–Newton revolution.

The central tenet of the new school is that, from the study of stock price behavior around the time of merger events, one can infer that mergers increase economic values and hence efficiency. The argument begins with the observation that a substantial premium over pre-merger prices is usually paid for the acquired firm's common stock shares. From the perspective of the acquired firm's shareholders, this merely reflects the fact that, if their reservation prices were not above prevailing market values, they would not be holding the shares. More interesting is the acquiring firm's motivation for paying a premium. Excluding (too quickly) 'irrational' empire-building motives, the acquiring firm must believe the acquired firm is worth more in its hands than the stock market's valuation.

Why? Chicago–Rochester school members stress efficiency-increase explanations, i.e., as the acquirer brings in more efficient management after takeover or achieves cost-reducing or value-enhancing 'synergies' with the target. Through analyses invoking Demsetz' (1973) argument and suggesting (somewhat inconclusively) that the stock prices of acquired-firm horizontal *competitors* do not rise following a merger event, they reject the hypothesis that increased monopoly power underlay the value enhancements. The hypothesis that merger-makers were simply engaged in a zero-sum game benefitting the stockholders of acquired entities but hurting acquiring firm shareholders is rejected on the basis of evidence that acquiring firm stock prices rose, or at least did not significantly fall, in the merger event time frame.

There are several problems with the Chicago–Rochester story. For one, there is an alternative hypothesis that is consistent with virtually all of the observed stock price behavior surrounding merger 'events': that the stock market undervalued the acquired firm's shares, making the firm an attractive target for acquirers seeking bargains. This alternative is rejected by Chicago–Rochester analysis because it is inconsistent with the efficient markets axiom, i.e., holding that prevailing share prices continually impound all relevant information on firms' economic prospects. The axiom is precisely that, adhered to on the basis of faith rather than demonstrable evidence. In fact, there are important pieces of evidence (e.g., on the values of small-firm shares and closed-end trust shares) squarely inconsistent with it. And even if the efficient markets axiom were true, an undervalued assets theory of merger activity could be applicable if the relevant actors did not *believe* it to be true. Interviews reveal that merger-makers commonly do search for undervalued assets. But such evidence is rejected by Chicago–Rochester scholars as 'unscientific'. The word 'scientific' is reserved for frequent reference to their statistical merger event studies. If Kepler could have interviewed God about what laws of planetary motion He ordained, would he have refrained because it was unscientific? One doubts it. From the extant biographical accounts, Newton probably did talk to God about such matters, or at least, he thought he did.

A serious internal inconsistency in the Chicago–Rochester analysis is the instability over time of the finding that acquiring firm shareholders, benefit from increased share values. Their key result holds consistently only for short periods – e.g., up to 30 days after merger. Several studies extended the time frame to a year after merger and found small negative acquiring firm returns – results Jensen and Ruback (1983, p. 20) characterize as 'unsettling because they are inconsistent with market efficiency'. Longer time horizons show even more drastic anomalies. Thus, if one invested $1,000 in June 1968, at the peak of the U.S. conglomerate merger boom, in each common stock of the 13 most active conglomerate acquirer firms, reinvested all dividends, and sold the portfolio in June of 1974, one would have received $5,669. An equivalent June 1968 investment of $13,000 in the Standard & Poor's 425 industrials portfolio would have yielded $14,340. Something evidently went wrong with market 'efficiency'.

The efficiency inferences drawn by Chicago–Rochester scholars are also inconsistent with a considerable quantity of micro-micro evidence. More detailed studies suggest that relatively few conglomerate mergers yielded appreciable "synergies" other than easier access to financing (a result hard to square with efficient markets axioms). Contrary to the 'inefficient managers displacement' hypothesis, case studies and interviews reveal that acquirers preponderantly seek well-managed companies, not sluggards. Consistent with this, acquired entities in the United States have been shown to be of at least average and probably above-average profitability before merger. Moreover, case studies [e.g., Scherer 1984b] and many periodical reports show that the acquiring companies frequently managed their acquisitions ineptly, failing to solve emerging problems and sometimes aggravating them. Values consequently diminished. One manifestation was the high incidence of sell-off following U.S. acquisitions of the 1960s and 1970s. For every 100 acquisition transactions recorded by the W.T. Grimm Co. during the 1970s, there were 40 sell-off transactions, most the aftermath of an earlier merger.

Again, Chicago–Rochester school members reject such micro evidence as unscientific. Their monolithic focus on a single statistical methodology defies, I believe, the best traditions of science. It is as if Galileo had rejected the use of the telescope, without which he could not have discovered Jupiter's moons – an important confirmation of the Copernican world-view. It is as if Galileo and Newton abjured micro-experiments on the motion of falling bodies, without which Kepler's laws could not have been generalized into the Newtonian system. It is a most unsatisfactory state of affairs. As in other episodes in the history of science, corrective work is underway. It is premature to tell where it will lead. The only thing of which I am certain is that a new paradigm is needed.

V. CONCLUSION

There is an old Chinese curse, 'May you live in interesting times'. For my generation of industrial organization economists, these have been interesting times of gratifying accomplishment. We have learned and unlearned a lot. We have much yet to learn (and unlearn). If I am correct in my continuing metaphor, we shall progress most effectively in the future by heeding the examples of Brahe, Kepler, Galileo, and Newton, maintaining a close interweaving of empirical and theoretical work. This is a course from which we have strayed too far in recent years. In coming years, our renewed motto must be, 'To Prague!'

NOTES

* An earlier German language version of this paper, 'Stand und Perspektiven der Industrieökonomik', was presented at the Ottobeuren Seminar in September 1984. It is being published in the seminar proceedings. The original version was written at the International Institute of Management in Berlin, to which the author is indebted.

1. My focus on Kepler and Brahe is not simply a special case. Consider the two 20th century scientific breakthroughs likely to have the most profound long-run practical consequences. Einstein's special theory of relatively was influenced by the equisitely careful Michelson-Morley experiments, showing the directional invariance of the speed of light; and the ultimate practical consequence of Einstein's work, nuclear fission, came through the careful empiricism of Hahn and Strassmann in Berlin-Dahlem. Watson and Crick were abstract model builders, but without careful chemical work determining the frequency with which bases Guanine and Adenine occurred in DNA, and without Rosalind Franklin's X-ray diffraction experiments, the secrets of the double helix could scarcely have been identified.
2. To perfect my analogy, it would have been helpful if the Ptolemaic system had been overthrown by sun-worshippers. But Protestants and heretics (Galileo) will have to suffice.
3. Strong confirmation comes from more recent work by Dennis Mueller (1983), studying the persistence of firms' profits over time.
4. The likelihood of such a bias was shown in simulation analyses by David Ravenscraft. I summarized his results at the 1979 EARIE meetings. So stubborn is the profession's resistance to unorthodox methodology and the overturning of prevailing paradigms that it took five years for Ravenscraft's basic analysis to be published (1984).
5. For example, the argument that business and financial decision-makers constantly use accounting data, so how can the data be economically meaningless?
6. The leading article currently is by Roger Clarke and Stephen Davies (1982), who, unlike many appliers of the relevant theory, recognize the need to disaggregate to the line of business level.
7. For a relatively sympathetic review, see Spence (1983). For reviews closer to my views, see Brock (1983) and Shepherd (1984).
8. For an excellent survey of the literature, see Geroski and Jacquemin (1984).
9. To the best of my knowledge, my (1967) paper was the first to model the first mover advantage and 'fast second' phenomenon formally.
10. I refer, for example, to Loury (1979), Dasgupta and Stiglitz (1980), and Tandon (1983).

REFERENCES

Bain, Joe S., 'Relation of Profit Rate to Industry Concentration', *Quarterly Journal of Economics* (August 1951), pp. 293–324.

Bain, Joe S., *Barriers to New Competition*, Cambridge, MA: Harvard University Press (1956).

Baumol, William J., 'Contestable Markets: An Uprising in the Theory of Industry Structure', *American Economic Review* (March 1982), pp. 1–15.

Brock, William A., 'Contestable Markets and the Theory of Industry Structure: A Review Article', *Journal of Political Economy* (December 1983), pp. 1055–1066.

Brozen, Yale, 'Concentration and Structural and Market Disequilibria', *Antitrust Bulletin* (Summer 1971), pp. 241–248.

Caves, Richard E., Fortunato, M., and Ghemawat, P., 'The Decline of Dominant Firms, 1905–1929', *Quarterly Journal of Economics* (August 1984), pp. 523–546.

Clarke, Roger and Davies, Stephen, 'Market Structure and Price-Cost Margins', *Economica* (August 1982) pp. 277–287.

Dasgupta, Partha and Stiglitz, Joseph, 'Industrial Structure and the Nature of Innovative Activity', *Economic Journal* (June 1980), pp. 266–293.

Demsetz, Harold, 'Industry Structure, Market Rivalry, and Public Policy', *Journal of Law and Economics* (April 1973), pp. 1–10.

Fisher, Franklin and McGowan, John, 'On the Misuse of Accounting Rates of Return To Infer Monopoly Profits', *American Economic Review* (March 1983), pp. 82–97.

Gale, Bradley, 'Market Share and Rate of Return', *Review of Economics and Statistics* (November 1972), pp. 412–425.

Geroski, Paul and Jacquemin, Alexis, 'Dominant Firms and Their Alleged Decline', *International Journal of Industrial Organization*, Vol. 2, No. 1 (1984), pp. 1–27.

Jensen, Michael and Ruback, Richard, 'The Market for Corporate Control', *Journal of Financial Economics*, Vol. 11 (1983), pp. 5–50.

Kwoka, John and Ravenscraft, David, 'Collusion vs. Rivalry: Price-Cost Margins by Line of Business', working paper (1984).

Levin, Richard, Cohen, W. M. and Mowery, D. C., 'R & D Appropriability, Opportunity, and Market Structure', *American Economic Review* (May 1985), pp. 20–24.

Long, William F. and Ravenscraft, David, 'The Misuse of Accounting Rates of Return: Comment', *American Economic Review* (June 1984), pp. 494–500.

Loury, Glenn, 'Market Structure and Innovation', *Quarterly Journal of Economics* (August 1979), pp. 395–410.

Mancke, Richard B., 'Causes of Interfirm Profitability Differences', *Quarterly Journal of Economics* (May 1974), pp. 181–193.

Masson, Robert T. and Shaanan, Joseph, 'Stochastic-Dynamic Limiting Pricing: An Empirical Test', *Review of Economics and Statistics* (August 1982), pp. 413–422.

Mueller, Dennis, *The Determinants of Persistent Profits*, report to the Federal Trade Commission, Washington, D.C. (June 1983).

Ravenscraft, David, 'Structure–Profit Relationships at the Line of Business and Industry Level', *Review of Economics and Statistics* (February 1983), pp. 22–31.

Ravenscraft, David, 'Collusion vs. Superiority: A Monte Carlo Analysis', *International Journal of Industrial Organization*, Vol. 2, No. 4 (1984), pp. 385–402.

Schelling, Thomas C., *The Strategy of Conflict*, Cambridge, MA: Harvard University Press (1960).

Scherer, F. M., 'Research and Development Resource Allocation under Rivalry', *Quarterly Journal of Economics* (August 1967), pp. 359–394.
Scherer, F. M., *Industrial Market Structure and Economic Performance*, Second edition: Boston, MA: Houghton-Mifflin (1980).
Scherer, F. M., 'Inter-Industry Technology Flows and Productivity Growth', *Review of Economics and Statistics* (November 1982), pp. 627–634.
Scherer, F. M., 'The World Productivity Growth Slump', keynote address, EARIE meetings (August 1984).
Scherer, F. M., 'Mergers, Sell-offs, and Managerial Behavior', EARIE Proceedings (August 1984), Volume III, pp. 306–334.
Schumpeter, Joseph A., *Theorie der wirtschaftlichen Entwicklung*, Leipzig (1912).
Schumpeter, Joseph A., *Capitalism, Socialism, and Democracy*, New York: Harper (1942).
Shepherd, William G., 'The Elements of Market Structure', *Review of Economics and Statistics* (February 1972), pp. 25–37.
Shepherd, William G., '"Contestability" vs. Competition', *American Economic Review* (September 1984), pp. 572–587.
Solow, Robert A., 'Technical Change and the Aggregate Production Function', *Review of Economics and Statistics* (August 1957), pp. 312–320.
Spence, Michael, 'Contestable Markets and the Theory of Industry Structure: A Review Article', *Journal of Economic Literature* (September 1983), pp. 981–990.
Sultan, Ralph G. M., *Pricing in the Electrical Oligopoly*, Vol. II; Boston, MA: Harvard Business School Division of Research (1975).
Tandon, Pankaj, 'Rivalry and the Excessive Allocation of Resources to Research', *Bell Journal of Economics* (Spring 1983), pp. 152–165.
Yamawaki, Hideki, 'Dominant Firm Pricing and Fringe Expansion: The Case of the U.S. Iron and Steel Industry, 1907–1930', International Institute of Management preprint, Berlin (November 1982).

2. ON THE CORE CONCEPTS OF INDUSTRIAL ECONOMICS

W. G. Shepherd*

Industrial economics is the study of competitive and monopoly conditions as they may affect market outcomes. An assessment of the field now is timely. For a century, it has been developing a variety of concepts, research methods, and estimates of functional relationships. Recently 'new' models of increasing rigor have been offered. The field continues to be rich in alternative concepts and methods.

I will try to identify the basic methods and concepts which comprise the field's mainstreams. This core has often been obscured in the process of debate.

The mainstream approach focuses on the ways in which morphology can disturb competitive outcomes. A market's structure influences in some degree its behaviour and performance. Conversely, each firm's performance can influence in some degree its future market position. Scale economies can justify monopoly, in some degree.

Competition is a complex process of mutual pressure. If the pressure is sharply uneven among rivals, then competition is usually not effective. Cause and effect in this field are soft, not rigid, and normative evaluations need to include not only allocative efficiency but also X-efficiency, innovation and equity.

These fundamentals can be tested by logic, econometrics, case studies and the general observation of business. The ideas derive from Marshall, Schumpeter, Mason, Bain, Caves and others, with their varied perspectives and methods.[1] Their shared focus is on the real but usually imprecise patterns of real markets.

This mainstream has been challenged since 1970 from two directions. One is from neo-conservatives, suggesting that (1) market power is actually only rare and weak, (2) collusion is the only form of market power and (3) market dominance only reflects a firm's superior efficiency, not its market power. The other challenge is from pure theorists, who

de Jong, H. W., Shepherd, W. G. (eds) Mainstreams in Industrial Organization
 ISBN 978-94-017-0495-3

have offered certain usually short-run determinate models of duopoly and/or entry as the 'new' analysis.[2] Both of these new lines could enrich the field, by enlarging the stock of valid ideas. But both of them have sometimes run to extreme assertions and assumptions, seeking to displace the mainstream altogether.

That danger gives this book a special importance, as an effort to identify the scientific core of the field. The matter is complex, requiring discussions of methodology, concepts and measurement.

The paper is divided into six sections. The first section sets the framework and explores the value of quasi-static, soft analysis as an alternative to static determinate models. Section II considers structure; what it is and what it shows. Section III reviews concepts of the determinants of structure, especially the economies of scale. Then certain concepts of behavior (especially price discrimination) are assessed in Section IV, and performance in Section V. There are conclusions in Section VI.

I. BASIC ISSUES

1. Causation

The basic logic of the structure-behavior-performance 'triad' continues to be the intellectual framework of the field. That structure influences behavior and performance in some degree is undeniable. The causation may be soft or even reversed in some cases, but the three triad elements (structure, behavior and performance) are the essential building blocks. Even in pure theory, whenever a market setting is posited and its outcomes are explored, the triad underlies the analysis.

Some have declared the triad outmoded, because causation can be reversed: a firm's superior performance can raise its market share. That is obviously possible, though once high market share is obtained, it can still be applied to gain advantage of market power. The question is empirical: which direction of causation usually prevails in real cases? Empirical research so far has not established reverse causation as the norm. The evidence linking structure with probable effects on prices, profits efficiency, and innovation is much stronger and more general.

Pending new and different findings, the triad is still the basic intellectual framework of the field. The triad also organizes concepts in the context of the *market*, as the arena of action. That is essential, because competition among firms in markets is the core of the process. The triad permits static, quasi-static, and dynamic analysis of competition. It can show the effects of given structures and/or behavior patterns, and it also can trace feed-back effects and processes of competitive interactions.

It also permits a focus on the individual *firm*, as the true actor. Markets, or groups of firms, are no more than the summed outcomes of the single firms' choices.

2. *Market categories*

It is customary to fit the main concepts within six market types; pure monopoly, dominant firm, tight oligopoly, loose oligopoly, monopolistic competition, and pure competition. The last three cases are effectively competitive, on the whole. The first three cases cover the pathology of industrial economics, where the results are usually socially costful in some degree. Recent work has focused on the dominant-firm and tight-oligopoly cases. Dominant firms – that is, those with market shares above 40 percent and no close rival – were usually cast as passive in the few theoretical articles about them in the 1950s and 1960s (e.g., Worcester, 1957). Recently their ability to suppress rivals and control market results has been recognized more fully (e.g., Geroski, 1985). Dominance remains a leading research frontier. Tight oligopoly (especially the duopoly special case) has drawn extensive modeling since 1975.

The importance of the first three categories has shrunk sharply in the U.S. economy since 1960, and perhaps in other countries, too.[3] Yet they still pose important technical and normative issues. They are the main focus for the conceptual debate between static, determinate models and the full, complex competitive process.

3. *Competition as process and/or model*

Competition is pervasive, perhaps the dominant social process of our time. It permeates not only the whole of the industrial activity but also the political process, international relations, personal efforts and, of course, all manner of sporting competition. Yet there has never been a full analysis of its elements and varieties. For example, the structure of market shares among a group of rivals can be infinitely varied, and the scale of profit rewards to 'winners' and 'losers' can also assume sharply varying gradients. Which of these is optimal, for efficient pricing, innovation, or other goals? The answers are still largely unknown.

Economists have instead taken competition largely for granted, as embodied in the firm's static demand and cost conditions. One searches vainly in the classics, such as Marshall (1920), Chamberlin (1933), Mason (1957), Fellner (1949), and Bain (1956, 1968) for a discussion of competition's fundamental nature and varieties.

The past treatments fit broadly in two traditions, both derived from neo-classical roots. The first approach is theoretical, using static, pure logic. The market is a simple, clear zone of choice, with one good and one equilibrium price. The price-output results are determinate under pure competition and monopoly. Degrees of monopoly may alter the efficient competitive outcomes if one firm dominates or several oligopolists collude, thereby reducing consumer surplus. The oligopoly range is commonly reduced to two-firm games, with nash assumptions so as to attain determinate results at any cost.

In the second concept, competition is an ongoing process, rather than a sequence which reaches a terminus. Interactions occur in a variety of structures and reward patterns, which can change. Because technology and demand are not rigid, they too can change as events progress. In judging welfare effects, allocative efficiency is often a minor element compared to X-efficiency and technological change. Partly Schumpeterian, this concept begins with real processes and rivalries, and it tries to define general relationships that hold across the range of real industries.

Both concepts have value and relevance. Theory can cut cleanly and show essentials, while the analysis of real processes can clarify social effects more fully.

4. Quasi-statics and soft analysis

Methodology is also at stake. The main debate is between precise, deterministic models and the looser exploration of complex processes and actual patterns: between pure 'modeling' on one hand, and 'quasi-statics' or 'soft analysis', as I will call them, on the other.

The key issue is *determinacy*. Can one deduce precise, complete results, which are also significant? The question arises most clearly in oligopoly, where modelers recently have renewed the earlier search for determinate outcomes. Some analysts now argue that one needs only to specify the nature of responses and between two or more rivals; that is, are they fixed-price, fixed-quantity, etc.? With the *response* functions chosen, the results then follow for a wide variety of questions.

Yet the problem is much more difficult. Determinacy also requires that precise *cost* and *demand* functions exist, as embodied in bright-line curves and exact equations. For many decades, the field has taken this precision for granted. In defining costs, technology is assumed to be rigidly defined for each peroid, and for all firms in the industry. As for demand, consumer choices are assumed to be specified and fixed for each period.

Only if all three sets of conditions (cost, demand and responses) are rigid and known, can one derive unique results. Otherwise determinacy is lost.

In actuality, the conditions are never known precisely or, in many cases, even approximately. Many functions exist as regions or zones, not as bright lines. In response to that problem, analysts have assumed that the functions exist precisely but are merely hard to measure. If that is true, then enough research effort would eventually discover and formulate them.

Instead, a more useful concept may be that nature itself is *soft* rather than sharp-edged. Even if the three sets of functions could be perfectly known, they will often be blurred zones, rather than sharp lines. The blurring would reflect the true complexities and indeterminacy of the underlying real conditions.

The blurred regions on zones are not merely ranges next to the exact border of best results, such as the border on a set. The blurred zone *is* the border. It is blurred because the outcomes reflect many complex factors, too numerous and inter-related to specify.[4] For example (as Michael Porter (1985) and the organization literature), firms may consider over 30 different significant factors in deciding their production techniques, product strategies, personnel, marketing, quality changes, financing, and other real choices. Each set of decisions may yield a different cost-output result in the short and/or long run, but the whole result may not be accurately predictable. Also, workers' effort can be crucial to the level of cost (as I discuss in Section III below), but that effort may not be precisely controllable or predictable by the firm's managers. Therefore both average and marginal costs are commonly soft. That is further confirmed by the frequent abilities of firms to cut costs deeply during recessions and then resume output at costs 30 percent or more lower than before.

For demand, similarly, many factors are involved. Products are partly differentiable: selling efforts of many kinds (advertising, discount promotion, sales network, etc.) can affect demand, but imprecisely; rivals' actions are neither known nor rigidly patterned; price can often be differentiated; and so on.

In fact, nearly all conditions and functions in this field are soft *ex ante* (that is, not validly represented by sharp lines or precise mathematical forms). We can gain scientific validity by recognizing that *much industrial economics is not determinate*. For example, the causation in the triad is soft.[5] Market definition usually involves shaded edges, and therefore market shares can only be approximated. Demand elasticities and cross-electicities are soft. The market types themselves shade into each other. And oligopoly's entire role can be seen as softening (or spreading out) the effects of firms' market shares upon their profit results (as I will illustrate in Figure 3).

But first, Figure 1 illustrates such soft cost and demand patterns, in familiar general shapes.[6] Such soft functions are analogous to the 'new' atomic physics of the 1920s, which replaced precise functions with probabilistic ones. Recent advances in scientific logic have also included various kinds of soft analysis. In our field, soft functions can still be analyzed in any degree of abstraction, to yield meaningful but *approximate* results, in terms of ranges rather than unique values. The assumptions, methods and results would simply avoid the hyper-determinacy and specious precision that occur when reality is soft but is treated as if it were sharp-edged. Such a new soft analysis would modify the post-1970 trend toward determinate static modeling, but there is no inherent conflict. Soft analysis recognizes that reality itself reaches solutions that are only approximately predictable, and so the analysis itself reflects that indeterminacy. Soft analysis focuses on core ideas that are valid and testable, rather than beginning with bizarre assumptions because determinacy requires them. It tends to consolidate the core concepts and effects.

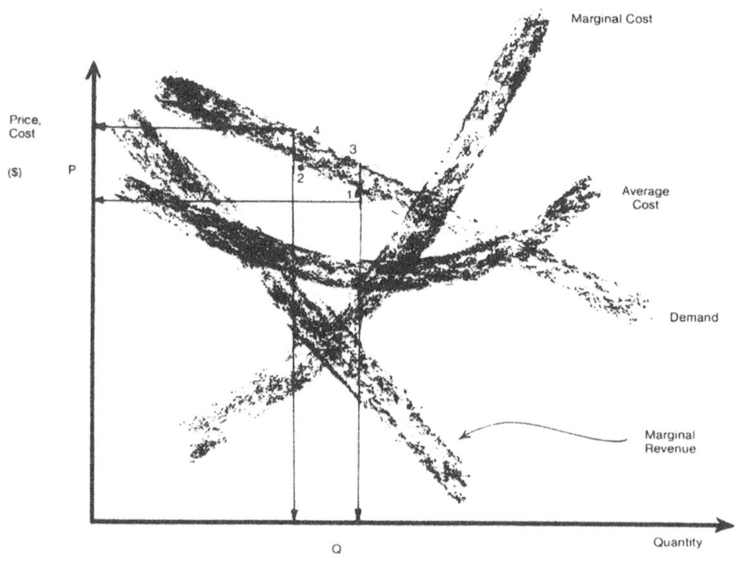

Fig. 1. A soft, quasi-static monopoly outcome.

The approach is also *quasi-static*, because it allows for further adjustments within the indicated zone of outcomes. A first-period result might be point 1 in Figure 1, which illustrates the outcomes for a firm holding some market power. The firm may then adjust its strategies and cost-affecting choices, yielding point 2 in the next period. Subsequent points 3, 4, . . . etc., are also within the *ex ante* zone of outcomes. Rather than attempt to pre-determine which of points 1, 2, . . . , *n* is 'the' outcome, quasi-static analysis merely defines the zone within which the outcomes will fail.

Figure 1 shows, of course, conditions similar to neo-classical static analysis. But the softness and room for further adjustment are now explicit. The notation *P*, *AC*, *MC*, etc., indicates *ex ante* ranges of price, average costs and marginal costs, rather than specific *ex post* values.

The competitive and monopoly outcomes can be compared, as before, but now only approximately. All of the usual effects are definite, but they now lie within ranges. The basic *logic* of causation still holds, but the degrees of effect can only be specified as ranges.

The effect of a rival's action is no longer a matter only of price. This variety also faithfully reflects corporate reality. Faced with a rival's new action, for example, this firm can devote some or all of its response to reducing costs, so as to extract (or impose) greater effort from its employees. That moves this firm's actual results down to a lower-cost point within the blurred cost zone. That in turn generates larger profits, and/or more opportunity to cut prices, if this firm wishes to do so. The result of the episode may also change the output level. Alternatively (or in addition), the firm's response may be to take action toward raising its demand opportunities, via costly selling efforts. That too could open up larger profits, as well as changing the chosen output level. But the raising of demand is not a determinate shift; its amount depends on multiple factors, which are not possible to specify precisely.

In short, managerial responses can go – and they do in reality go – toward any combination of adjustments within the cost and demand zones. The outcomes are predictable, but only as ranges of values.

For another illustration, Figure 2 shows the effect of a possible incursion by a rival or entrant. That shifts down the demand zone above the price range *P*. The demand zone now has a soft kink reflecting true indeterminacy of the possible effects on demand. At *P*, the range of possible *Q* values is now wide. That wide range validly reflects reality. Under bright-line curves and precise (often implausible) assumptions about responses, an exact *Q* would be specified for this limit-pricing firm. But given the true indeterminacy of the conditions, such a bright-line model, with its unique solution is spurious.

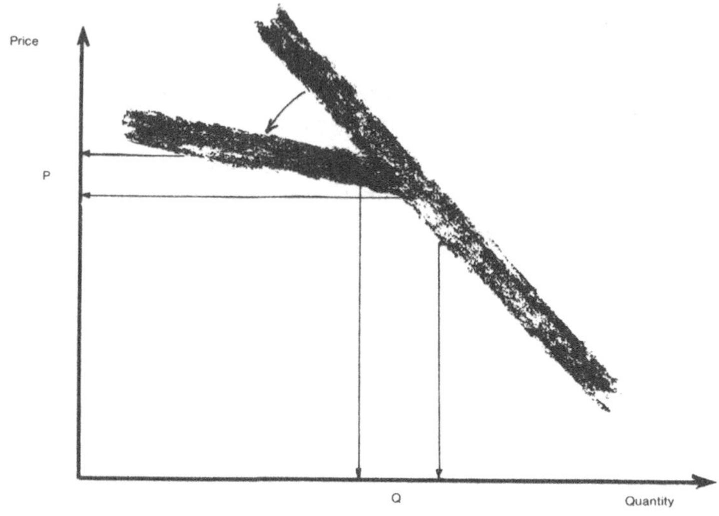

Fig. 2. A soft kink.

Substituting zones for functions still permits casting the issues in concise logical models. Rather than rejecting deductive models, it merely limits them to valid *degrees* of precision. But soft quasi-static models pose at least three new methodological issues:

1. They will not give unique, determinate results. Solutions will usually lie in middle ranges of values, rather than in extreme cases, binary yes–no outcomes, or one-step results.
2. The assumptions need greater care, to avoid absurd or extreme premises.
3. The elements of the model will usually be *fewer*, as one focuses on the most important factors rather than trying to include all possible or 'interesting' ones.

A 'loss' of unique determinacy may seem hard to accept, because neo-classical theory has promised determinacy for so long. Indeed, a renuciation denies a popular aim of many theorists in the last 15 years. It may also seem to admit defeat in making the analysis 'scientific'. Yet the opposite is true. The hyper-precision has always been artificial; it can be more scientific to fit the models to a soft reality rather than to impose determinacy based on vacuous assumptions. The analysis of ultra-free entry and inert monopolists (Baumol, Panzar and Willig, 1982) can be seen as perhaps the final crest of this wave (see Section III). It denied both the softness of reality and the variety of firms' actual choices.

5. Brief History

These issues can be seen more clearly in light of the field's development through several methodological stages.[7] The early developments by 1925, or even 1910, were surprisingly complete and important, despite their neglect by many current analysts.[8] Concepts of monopoly power, economies of scale, predatory actions, collusion, potential entry, profitability and risk, overhead costs, competitive rates of return, and efficiency were discussed extensively and with some sophistication. Moreover, there was detailed empirical research into the main problem industries (oil, steel, railroads, electricity, cigarettes, farm equipment, etc.), as part of the early antitrust and regulatory efforts during 1895–1920. Students are invariably surprised at the content offered, for instance, by Bullock (1901) (economies of scale), Knight (1922) (profits and risk), J. M. Clark (1922) (overhead costs), the Industrial Commission (many industry studies), and even John Moody (1904) (mergers), all before 1925.

The 'new' wave starting in the 1930s made further advances in both theory and evidence (Chamberlin, 1933; Robinson, 1933; Neumann and Morgenstern, 1944). It devoted most of its attention to deriving determinate results out of the fog of oligopoly complexity. It also focussed on price discrimination, in Robinson's work, but this direction was unfortunately soon dropped. The oligopoly interest peaked in the 1950s, and then it faded with the recognition that the results were almost all merely heuristic, useful for little more than illustrating possibilities.

Econometric work developed in the 1960s, as computers made it possible to do large-scale mutli-variate regressions of the 450 Census industries.[9] The focus of this work on concentration ratios was partly artificial, reflecting the sheer abundant availability of those ratios. Some analysts have tended to use the official concentration data incautiously, without screening or adjusting them for major errors. Crude proxies were widely used for a number of factors, and linear functions often were assumed despite the likelihood of curved relationships.

The concentration results were bound to display low correlation; the official Census concentration ratios, and the profits and price-cost data, are error-ridden. Most important, oligopoly is so varied that any concentration ratios must always be inherently weakly related to pricing. Valid models can give significant results even with r^2 values as low as 0.10. Yet neo-liberal colleagues have often cited these low correlations to 'prove' that market power has no impacts. That inference is not tenable; affirmative proof from other directions is needed.

At the other extreme, a few complex models were developed in an effort to embody simultaneity, to test the importance of economies of scale, etc. But their complexities and refinements were ill-suited to the use of data concentration data riddled with errors. Testing 10-variable models on error-permeated data is dubious science, in this field as well as in others. The neo-liberals' 'proofs' that market power either (1) does not matter and/or (2) merely achieves efficiencies, largely suffer from these two technical problems: defective data, and/or mis-specified models.

Yet much econometric work has been valuable. The dimensions and main effects of monopoly power have emerged with some clarity (Scherer, 1980; Shepherd (1975 and 1985a). The evidence indicates soft functions, within the structure-behavior-performance framework. The econometric wing of the field continues vigorously.

Faced with growing mainstream evidence, neo-liberals have sought ways to deny it. One is to try turning the tables, declaring that performance really causes structure. In the current conservative climate, those assertations have gained some acceptance. Indeed, much of such 'new' analysis can be seen as a diversion from the core concepts of the field into refinements, models and implausible alternatives.

The influx of theorists since 1970 has seemed to offer a new and more incisive, compact analysis of the core issues. Theorists have scored some successes, especially in defining efficient prices and certain components of entry barriers (such as excess capacity). But the weaknesses of the 'new' line of study have been several, as I have noted. The achievements so far are real, but they are modest, not yet amounting to a major change in the field. The main streams of the field have been little altered.

6. Theory and substance

Intuition plus formalism?

Theory is of course absolutely essential, but it has limits. Its strength is in seeing new reality, beyond the limits of current facts. It can give powerful, concise results, cutting through masses of mixed conditions in order to reach fundamental truths. Theory also has limits. It can be irrelevant and vacuous. And it needs testing of its assumptions, relationships and true contribution. One would never oppose implausible assumptions *per se*; they may lead to important insights. But they may instead lead to mere formalistic exercises focused on trivial elements.

The risk in the latest 'new' applied theory is twofold. First, the assumptions come from *intuitions*, often of theorists who are inexperienced in the mainstream research on real markets. Intuition in making assumptions is no more reliable than using intuition in evaluating evidence. It can even be riskier, because intuition's role is hidden in the assumptions and it leads to seemingly powerful conclusions, which are often quite wrong.

Little of the 'new' theory has been tested against reality. Indeed, there are signs that a new Mandarin language is emerging, merely telling 'stories'. There are exceptions, with important results; the task is to sift them out from the rest.

Removing substance

There is also a more general tendency to define away the substance of the field, by sanitizing the specific words and concepts being adopted.[10] In these changes, the real-world problems of monopoly power become mere abstractions, by definition. The changes may seem to improve objectivity. Objectivity is important, but a main result instead has been to lose touch with objective reality. Concepts that deal with secondary elements, that are obscurely labeled, and which are not measurable may divert the field rather than improve it.

There is no simple way to screen the newer technical work. But the basic questions to ask of any research remain valid. Is the insight new and important, or just reworking? Does it clarify real markets? What does it really add to understanding?

II. STRUCTURE AND COMPETITION

In judging the core concepts of the field, a guiding scientific objective is simplicity. There are many competing concepts, which cannot all be equally valid. Applying Ockham's Razor, we seek the most elegant basis, combining the fewest important concepts in a unified, comprehensive system. A scale of priority needs to be established among the main possible elements. If this task is not addressed explicitly, then priority will be assigned implicitly and unsystematically (*e.g.*) that all concepts are of precise equal weight.

1. The market and structure

The setting includes a market, defined as precisely as possible.[11] Reality is soft. Most markets have shaded edges. There may be variations among products (and competitors) inside 'the' market. Markets may have segments and gradients within them. But the basic concept of competition occurring within a zone of consumer choice is central.[12] In antitrust cases, the courts have sought to define 'the' market in question, often drawing severe criticism. Yet market power does exist, even if it can be estimated only roughly. The search for precise measures of markets and market power may be misguided, but so is a general denial of the whole exercise.[13]

Structure

The degree of competition can be predicted at least approximately by knowing the structure within the market. The fundamental condition is each firm's elasticity of demand; that defines the degree of competition (that is, of substitutability by other products and/or firms) which the firm faces. Pure competition is a simple, unique case; all other degrees of monopoly are less determinate, for demand elasticity can vary widely. *Inelasticity is the most general measure of market power*, for it expresses the degree of control over price. It need not vary closely with market shares across markets, because markets vary in their internal degrees of substitution, in inter-market substitution, and in ease of entry.

Market share

Within each market, each firm's degree of market power will usually vary directly with its market share.[14] High market shares cover a variety of customers, giving opportunities for price discrimination. High market shares often reflect higher consumer loyalty and lags in changes. There are also pecuniary economies, especially from access to cheaper capital because dominance gives the firm lower risks. High shares also give the firm a broad scope for strategic actions to restrain small rivals and possible new competitors. As has been long familiar in real markets, market shares are the single most important element defining each firm's scope for influence over the market outcome.

These conditions provide many ways in which market shares can yield monopoly pricing. The theory of these impacts is familiar and sufficient. The actions are unilateral; no collusion is necessary. Indeed, colluson is only an imperfect exertion of combined market share. Market shares provide *direct* market power; collusion is *indirect* market power.

Some neo-liberal analysts assert that the market-share focus 'lacks theory', but that claim is mistaken. It reflects a naive, pure hypothesis that each market contains only one good, with one price. If that were so, then profit differences could indeed only reflect scale economies, and market power could only be exercised uniformly throughout the market, via collusion. This has come to be called the 'revisionist' view.

But real markets are much less pure. High market shares are often gained by taking advantage of lags, consumer loyalites, changes for price discrimination, signaling, and other strategic actions. Market dominance is sought by every firm in real markets, precisely because it involves these imperfections and can yield high profitability. If there is a 'lack of theory', it lies in over-simple textbook models which ignore real markets.

Within any given market, there is a (blurred) positive function relating market share to rates of return. The slope and shape of the function can vary among industries, because given market shares may have different marginal profitability yields in different markets. But all functions will normally have a positive slope, as suggested by both logic and evidence. If higher market shares did not yield higher profitability, they would not be sought as relentlessly as they are. Indeed, firms would voluntarily sub-divide to give lower market shares, which they virtually never do in fact.

The widespread cross-section regressions showing a correlation between market shares and profit rates therefore reflect only the average slope, not necessarily any individual markets' function. The estimated general relationship also is disturbed by errors in measuring both profits and shares. Despite these factors, the actual correlations have been close (Shepherd, 1972, 1975, 1979; Gale and Branch, 1982; Martin, 1983), and so their significance is all the greater.

Low market shares commonly coexist with high ones in the same market. *The small share gives the firm a highly elastic demand*, regardless of the structure of the rest of the market. The same market may contain high monopoly power and profits in a dominant firm, while small rivals are under severe competitive pressure. The whole 'market outcome' is only an average of all of the firms' individual results. And those individual outcomes are strictly what motivates the firms. While firms may occasionally act in some degree of coordination, that too only reflects each one's pursuing the balance of its individual gains. Market share is the first fact to learn, as a predictor of market outcomes. It is not, of course, the only element of structure.

Concentration

The degree of concentration in several firms may also influence some outcomes, especially a tendency to collusion. But the prediction can only be vague, because there may be great variation among the group's members.[15] Here is softness, indeed. *Oligopoly concentration merely causes a degree of variation around the central market share-profit rate function*, as illustrated in Figure 3. Oligopoly is mainly a secondary element in structure.

Concentration is merely incomplete market share. A group with concentration of X percent may occasionally approach the influence of a single firm holding X percent, but usually the several firms' concentration will have much lighter effects. Conversely, if several firms can gain market power by cooperating, then a single dominant firm can achieve that impact even more fully. This gap will vary with the group's structure; moreover, the outcomes will fluctuate as the oligopolists' coordination veers between cohesion and collapse.

The claim that collusion is the only source of market power is obviously untenable. Direct market power can exist and will usually be stronger than indirect market power. That the naive focus only on collusion could gain any acceptance is a strange lapse in the field.

At any rate, both market share and concentration are *internal* elements of structure. Theory, econometric results and wide business experience all show strongly that they are central to the main lines of market outcomes.

2. External conditions: possible entry

Nonetheless, external conditions may have some influence, as has been noted for a century or more.[16] Since 1956, 'potential entry' has drawn rising attention, reaching its extreme in the Baumol-group view that entry (and exit) supersede internal conditions.

New entry should in fact be subsumed under actual competition, because *new entry only affects existing firms by taking away their market share*. Indeed, entry is most correctly defined as the loss of market share by existing firms. But such losses occur most commonly and directly from actions by other already existing rivals; that is, from competitive actions *within* the market. Therefore entry is only a secondary, indirect source of the common internal form of actual competition. Rather than replace market share as the focus, *entry is itself defined by market shares of existing firms.*

Moreover, barriers' role is ambiguous. Barriers are at the edge of the market, and their effect requires the existence of outsiders who would indeed supply powerful new competition if they chose to enter.[17] If not, then barriers are irrelevant. Also, barriers can arise from many sources, including discretionary actions taken by the firms inside the market, as they choose to repel or threaten the newcomers.[18] Therefore, despite Bain's early hope in the 1950s (echoed by Modigliani (1958)), barriers are not clearly a basic element of structure. Rather, they are a vauge mix of conditions which may affect a secondary condition (potential rather than actual competition).

These general properties have been borne out by repeated econometric testing, case studies, and the mainstream of business activity in actual markets. A recent typical set of results is given in Table 1, covering large U.S. firms during 1960–1969.[19] Market share is clearly the main factor; concentration and barriers are significant but secondary. For more discussion of these patterns, see Scherer's chapter in this volume, and Shepherd (1975, 1979, and 1985c).[20]

Figure 3 illustrates the relative roles of the main structural elements. The share-profit function reflects market share's central role. Oligopoly conditions can cause specific firms to deviate from this basic function, as illustrated by Firm A and B. Entry barrier's can also cause deviations, as illustrated by Firms C and D. The soft zone of variation around the market share relationship defines the basic role of oligopoly and barrier.

If oligopoly were central, then the concentration-profile function would supersede the market share-profits function. Instead, the measured role of concentration is much weaker. If entry barriers were central, then no share-profits function would exist at all, and barriers would show strong effects on profit rates. Instead the reverse is true: the market share-profits relation is strong, and barriers' effects appear to be modest.

Note that markets share's central role exists, with its resulting monopoly harms, *regardless* whether market power or scale economies are the main underlying cause of higher profit rates.

These lessons help in judging the recent trends in research. Models of oligopolies (usually of pure duopolies) deal with a secondary phenomenon. The recent 'revisionist' claim that collusion is the only source of market power is, evidently groundless. In any event, few

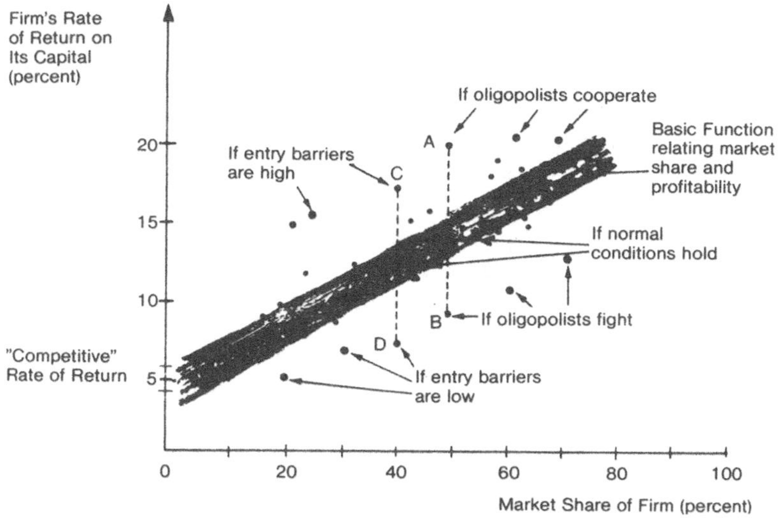

Fig. 3. The role of market share and related elements of structure.

Table 1. Regression analysis of profitability and *q*, 117 large U.S. industrial corporations, 1960–69.

Regression number	Dependent variable	Constant term	Independent variables								Corrected R^2 (F value)
			Market share M	Concentration C	Group (C–M)	Log of asset size	Advertising sales ratio	Medium barriers	High barriers	Growth	
1	Profit rate (*p*)	+7.69	+0.24		+0.04	−0.56	+0.26			+0.51	0.573
		(3.21)	(8.42)		(1.55)	(1.79)	(3.98)			(2.09)	(32.18)
1q	*q* ratio	+1.09	+0.06		+0.01	−0.19	+0.09			+0.27	0.558
		(1.42)	(7.05)		(0.79)	(1.94)	(4.09)			(3.48)	(30.28)
2	*p*	+7.69	+0.20	+0.04		−0.56	+0.26			+0.51	0.573
		(3.21)	(6.27)	(1.55)		(1.79)	(3.98)			(2.09)	(32.18)
2q	*q*	+1.09	+0.06	+0.01		−0.19	+0.09			+0.27	0.558
		(1.42)	(5.64)	(0.79)		(1.94)	(4.09)			(3.48)	(30.28)
3	*p*	+3.77	+0.23	+0.02				+1.76	+2.99	+0.51	0.516
		(2.38)	(6.71)	(0.74)				(1.88)	(2.32)	(1.95)	(25.70)
3q	*q*	−0.21	+0.07	+0.004				+0.26	+0.59	+0.27	0.475
		(0.41)	(5.96)	(0. 41)				(0.86)	(1.40)	(3.21)	(21.96)

t-ratios are in parentheses.

genuine duopolies exist and fewer still have been fitted to the new models. Much the same lessons apply to barriers; they actually have only a limited impact, as shown by research, and there are few well-estimated case studies of them. The recent vogue for oligopoly and barriers therefore has exaggerated their true importance.

Market share unifies the normative analysis

Market share's central role unifies the normative appraisal of disparate industry conditions. In general, market share is the key criterion in judging whether an action is pro-competitive, neutral, or anti-competitive. Commonly, actions are pro-competitive when done by firms with market shares under 10 percent; anti-competitive when done by leading firms with market shares over 50 percent; and subject to a specific appraisal in the middle range.

Recognition of this has been gradually rising, but there is resistance. Concentration ratios have often been used instead, but they are a particularly soft and secondary indicator of true market power. Indeed, neo-liberals reject any structural indicator at all as a basis. And some barriers enthusiasts claim that only barriers matter, not market shares.

That emphasis on barriers is triply disintegrative. First, it divides attention between at least two elements, so that the evaluations are indecisive. Second, barriers are literally a peripheral matter compared to market shares; to focus on them is to abandon the more important element. And third, barriers are virtually impossible to define clearly and measure well, and so their 'height' is endlessly debatable.

Capital markets

A great hidden issue of the field is whether capital markets are perfect, or nearly so. If they were, then various neo-liberal lessons would hold, because monopoly could not last unless it had superior efficiency. If not, then market power could be large, lasting and harmful. The actual conditions in real financial markets are controversial. U.S. capital markets have become distinctly more competitive since 1960, probably encouraging the general rise of competition. But they still contain imperfections, so that current market values often deviate from long-run values. This is a research frontier.

3. Ultra-free entry into inert markets

Recently the barriers emphasis has been carried to its extreme, with Baumol, Panzar and Willig (1982) claiming to provide a 'new' analysis which displaces the mainstream concepts of the field. The results are stated in categorical terms, and Baumol *et al.* have immediately applied them to important cases in regulation an antitrust. Yet the enthusiasm appears limited to the Baumol group and to graduate students interested in pure modeling. Most economists have already set it aside as a mere oddity. Yet the Baumol group continues to promote it as a momentous new system, and many young careers are being committed to it.

It deserves special attention, as an example of 'new industrial organization' gone awry and the antithesis of soft analysis. I have noted its main defects elsewhere (Shepherd, 1984), and so I will merely summarize those points and add a few others. The idea has little weight, and it has been causing confusion, by diverting attention from mainstream concepts.

A misnomer

Ultra-free entry yields distinctive results only in the extreme case, when entry is utterly free, incumbents are totally inert, and sunk cost is strictly zero. The term 'contestability' misleads, by suggesting degrees of entry. Any such deviation from purity puts the matter back into the long-familiar Bain–Caves analysis of entry conditions.

Contradictory assumptions

Baumol *et al.* assume entry to be (1) *total*, and yet also (2) *trivial* (on the Bertrand-Nash assumption that incumbents don't bother to react). The contradiction here is readily apparent, and the flaw is a fatal one. Such illogical theory cannot offer insights, much less a powerful new approach.

Pure statics

The Baumol theory is static, confined to consumer surplus. It ignores innovation and other values given by the full process of competition.

Evidence and cases

Mainstream evidence is overwhelmingly against any general role for ultra-free entry. Internal structure is central. A few cases in the transport sector with mobile equipment (especially airlines and trucking) might exemplify ultra-free entry. But they depart from the model, and so they offer little support.[21] Baumol *et al.* have erected a fairy castle without foundation, declaring it to be respreme before doing any empirical research to support it.

Foreign competition

For the U.S., trade involvement has risen sharply since 1965, causing much of the recent rise of competition (Shepherd, 1982a). Caves (1985) and Nakao (in this volume (provide excellent reviews of their role in industrial organization. Imports now pose hard questions of market definition and competitive pressure in some major industries. Foreign competitors may be more potent than local rivals, because they have different values and collude less easily. Imports may also provide an interesting hybrid form of new entry, which may provide barriers analysis an important application. Yet imports (that is, inward shipments of products) differ from true entry in major respects. The topic is an important but controversial research frontier. Some cases of it may give some use to the theory of ultra-free entry.

III. DETERMINANTS OF STRUCTURE

1. The economies of scale

Progress has been substantial in defining and measuring the technical economies of scale. They may explain market power and justify it normatively in some degree. The empirical task is to estimate minimum efficient scale (MES) and compare it with actual market dominance, so as to find the extent of *excess market share* (the actual share, minus MES).[22] The cost gradients (the degree of steepness of the economies and diseconomies) are also important. The crucial task is to separate *technical* from *pecuniary* grains. Survivor tests, actual cost patterns, actual size distributions, and profitability measures fail this task. The literature now offers a consensus that the issue can best be tackled directly, by questioning officials who may know the technological choices.

That is what Bain (1956), Scherer *et al.* (1975), Weiss (in Masson and Qualls, 1976), and others have done, in estimating MES and cost gradients for *plants* in about 40 significant industries, especially in the U.S. and Britain. Scherer (1980) has further estimated *company-wide* MES levels and cost gradients for some 12 industries in the U.S. Moreover, various case studies and antitrust cases have provided extensive evidence about cost conditions in some other industries.

This body of evidence has limits. Many major industries have escaped coverage, and the gradients aren't precisely measured in many cases. More seriously, the *diseconomies* of scale have been ignored, even though they are likely to be substantial in a number of markets. The common belief that cost curves are L-shaped may merely reflect the widespread omission of estimates of cost curves above MES levels.

Even so, the results have clarified the role of economies. They show that excess market share is large in many major markets. MES values are in the range of 1 to 10 percent shares of most lead US national markets, and probably declining. Also, the cost gradients below the MES are small in most cases.[23]

These results, plus the strong recent trend toward decentralization in actual firms, have shifted confidence away from size as a source of efficiency. The old cult of bigness is largely dead. Yet in academic life there still are neo-liberals, or 'revisionists', who embrance all concentration as representing efficiency *ex definitio* (e.g., Peltzman, 1977). They advance an 'efficient structure' hypothesis: that structure inherently reflects efficiency. But the research offered to support the hypothesis has been indirect and shaky.[24] Indeed, it relies mainly on assertions, not evidence. Only the direct study of scale economies can be accepted as reliable.

Why so much excess market share persists is therefore a key topic. There is a general process of erosion of dominant market shares, at about one point of market share per year.[25] Some important dominant firms (IBM, Eastman Kodak, Campbell Soup) have escaped this erosion, staying at 70 percent or above for decades. Recent study has focused on 'first-mover' and 'pioneer' advantages to explain this persistence (Robinson and Fornell, 1984). Once it is established, a dominant firm has many ways to retain its market share, even while obtaining a high degree of profitability.[26]

Market share is therefore partly a matter of long-run choice, by the firm, in which MES and cost gradients may be only minor factors. Gaskins (1971), Encaoua, Geroski and Jacquemin (1983), and Geroski and Jacquemin (1984) are among the leading discussions, showing how growth and other factors may shape the series of choices. The Baumol *et al.* effort to make structure 'endogeneous' is only short run, and so it does not give basic results.

2. Indeterminacy of cost

There are also signs (noted earlier) that costs are not determinate, so that scale economies cannot really be as precisely defined and measured. Harvey Leibenstein's (1976) analysis of X-efficiency reflects the fact that work effort by employees is highly variable and hard to predict. As effort levels vary, costs will vary, perhaps over a wide range. Therefore the standard average cost curve is really a blurred shape, as illustrated in Figure 1, rather than a clear single line.

Michael Porter's work also suggests that costs are not determinate. His two recent books (1980, 1985) show in detail the many specific factors that influence business actions and costs.[27] Each firm's unique set of such factors will give it unique cost opportunities, even if all workers' efforts are somehow uniformly maximized. Therefore, cost curves for real markets will be blurred for that reason.

This is a major topic for future research, involving both worker (and manager) effort and multiple cost factors. The task is to reduce the substantial range of cost indeterminacy, which now conflicts with conventional cost curves and with the seeming accuracy of the measures of scale economies. The MES and gradient estimates can still emerge from research on soft cost functions. But their reliability would be improved if the elements causing the blurring could be specified and estimated.

3. Learning, search and transactions costs

The cost of learning new production methods, searching for alternatives, and arranging transactions have drawn interesting discussion. These costs can be large, causing significant departures from the results under costless, instant equilibrium adjustments. Yet instead, normally the costs may be small, so that they raise only marginal issues. Each cost has had its proponents, urging the need for a new branch of theory and study for it. The question is whether these are differences of *kind*, needing a redirection of analysis, or merely small differences of *amount*.

Learning curves have perhaps the best claim for distinctive importance. As developed after World War II, they relate average costs to total cumulated past output rather than to the single-period planned output of conventional cost curves. The concept has been stressed since 1970 as a possible source of 'first mover' or 'pioneer'' advantages, explaining why dominant firms may emerge and persist even when they are not justified by economies of scale (see also Spence, 1981). Some recent testing has been done to assess the learning gradients, but the concept itself has stayed largely unchanged for 30 years.

Search and information costs were emphasized by George Stigler (1964) as a 'new' basis for oligopoly theory in 1963–64. Full, instant knowledge of rivals' actions will enable faster reactions which nullify the gains from price cutting. Therefore oligopolies are more competitive when they can hide their moves. Fewness prevents that, by making rivals more quickly aware of competitive actions. Actually the theory largely recognizes the obvious, as discussed by Chamberlin (1983), Fellner (1948), and others. Stigler offered insight into the role of information, but information itself has gotten only modest testing and it offers no major new result.

Transactions costs have been stressed by Oliver Williamson. He sees them as influencing the ability of firms to make agreements or impose 'credible threats'. Transactions costs can indeed limit the possibilities and affect the specific nature of the outcome. Moreover, some cases of sizable transactions costs can be found. But the matter appears still to involve marginal adjustments rather than need a shift to a 'new' theory. The 'transactional analysis' has focused heavily on duopolies or (which is much the same) incumbent-entrant situations. Therefore the theory is largely confined to special cases and is largely untested as a factual matter. It may yet attain general importance, but that seems to await a broader set of analyses and empirical tests.

4. Mergers

Mergers can raise market shares even if efficiencies are absent. But some mergers may achieve technical economies of scale and (by take-overs) remove inferior management. The leading study, edited by Dennis Mueller (1980), provides careful tests across seven industrial countries during 1955–75, and it suggests several conclusions (see also Mueller, 1985).

Mergers are not motivated by the hope to achieve scale economies, on the whole. They do achieve some gains in profits, but the acquiring companies tend to suffer declining profitability. Mergers do not generally promote growth, as would happen if the mergers achieved efficiencies: 'The conclusion that mergers increase economic efficiency, as evidenced by profit *and* growth inceases, was rejected in every one of our seven countries'.

These patterns support the market power and random explanations of mergers, rather than the hypotheses that asset markets invariably remove mismanagement and achieve scale economies.

IV. CERTAIN TOPICS IN BEHAVIOR

As a matter of volume, two topics of behavior have engrossed recent attention: oligopoly modelling, and 'predatory' pricing. Since oligopoly appears to be a secondary phenomenon, as I noted in Section II, I will not attempt here to review the recent theoretical modelling of it.[28] As for predatory pricing, it can best be discussed after dealing with the more general topic of price discrimination. Then comes advertising, a popular topic during 1965–75.

1. Price discrimination

In 1933 Joan Robinson placed price discrimination at the center of the new study of imperfect competition. The field promptly chose instead to focus on oligopoly interactions, as posed by Edward Chamberlin, also in 1933. Forty years later, price discrimination is emerging from this eclipse to be recognized as a crucial feature of market dominance. While Baumol *et al.* (1982) emphasized its possible efficiency role in Ramsey prices, that analysis holds only for strict 'natural monopoly' firms with, marginal costs below average costs. For other cases, price discrimination can have strategic anti-competitive effects, as I will note shortly.

As a profit source

First, note that price discrimination is important. It alone could be a sufficient condition to explain virtually all of the observed excess profit in large U.S. firms with high market shares.[29] It is known to have been sharp in a variety of domiant firms. Price discrimination is the missing link between the firm's market share and its monopoly profit. Even if simple price-raising effects and pecuniary gains were absent, discrimination could cause most or all of the observed profits.

Effects on competition

Price discrimination can promote or reduce competion, depending on the situation.[30] The two critical features are: (1) the market position of the firm doing the discrimination, and (2) how systematic and complete the discrimination is. The higher the firm's market share is, the more likely it is that competition will be reduced. Small-share firm's can rarely know or divide their customers effectively by differences in elasticity, as do high-share firms. Systematic discrimination tends to raise the degree of market control and excess profits.

These two criteria are applied in Figure 4. Price discrimination can occur in any combination of those conditions. But it is clearly pro-competitive in zone A: sporadic discrimination by firms with small market shares. But in zone B, when it is done forcefully and systematically by dominant firms, price discrimination is usually anti-competitive. By contrast, effective competition attacks the most lucrative markets, forces lower price–cost ratios, spreads to all submarkets, and drives prices down toward costs evenly throughout the whole market. Systematic discrimination (which prevents that process) is a prime indicator of market power.

In the middle range (zone C), the effects are mixed. One must assess each case carefully, looking at the setting and the pricing actions.

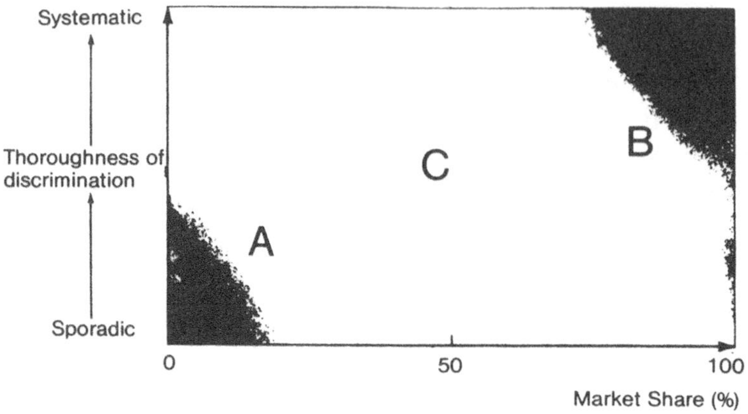

Fig. 4. Price discrimination can be procompetitive or anticompetitive.

The analysis is soft; zones A, B and C have shaded edges which cannot be rigidly specific. Yet the basic concept distinguishing the zones is valid and important.

2. *'Predatory' pricing*

Economists have long endeavored to distinguish 'fair' (pro-competitive or neutral) actions from 'unfair' (anti-competitive) actions (e.g., Dirlam and Kahn, 1954, Scherer, 1980). No simple rule suffices, but the issue is important wherever dominant firms face small rivals. The correct analysis is soft and quasi-static rather than precise and static, as I now explain.[31]

In the 1970s, the debate became narrowed down to defining 'predatory' actions, especially in Areeda and Turner (1975). The issue blended price theory with strong commercial interests of antitrust defendants (particularly IBM and AT&T, who were each defending over 20 sizable antitrust cases). Areeda-Turner offered only a cost criterion; if price wasn't cut below cost by the aggressor firm, then no irrational sacrifice had occurred in order to victimize unfairly an efficient rival. Since the aggressor hadn't gone 'too far', no predation had occurred. Others noted that cost was often vague and unworkable as a benchmark, and that firms often gained from hurting one victim as an effective 'signal', or threat, to other rivals.

Though the term 'predatory' has little economic content, the issue focuses on selective, discriminatory actions. Such actions can hurt or promote competition, depending on the setting in which they occur.

Each firm can use many specific devices (or weapons) to compete. Some of these devices are selective; others are applied uniformly. Selective actions include price discounts to specific buyers or groups, product changes aimed at specific rivals, or promotional campaigns fitted precisely against one or several competitors in an area (Yamey). Uniform actions include such examples as across-the-board price cuts and broad-scale advertising campaigns. Selectivity is a matter of degree, but it is a condition that can be evaluated. All selective actions can be pro-competitive; only in certain settings do they reduce competition.

All firms, all of the time, use any or all of these weapons (selective and/or uniform) in their efforts to defeat competitors and to gain market control. Full competion itself is comprised of the totality of such actions, in the ongoing give and take of the struggle. When competition is effective and sustained, the competing firms have access to the same weapons, and their use of these devices is mutually constraining among all participants.

Yet some firms, in some situations, are able to harm competition by going 'too far'. Dominant firms dealing with much smaller competitors are usually in this category. They can damage or eliminate efficient small competitors if they choose to do so, because they have sufficiently larger financial and other resorces.

Such firms will often go 'too far', for two reasons. First, the firm may have a larger strategy in which this first (money-losing) action is only one step toward a larger total profit. Second, the action may be a signal to other firms for the future. By treating one competitor severely, a firm may deter others from entering or intimidate other small rivals into passive behavior. The sacrific therefore has a multiple payoff.

Therefore, actions that harm the competitive process are *not* self-averting. Dominant firms have inducements to intimidate or eliminate smaller competitors. They will presumably do so by using the least costly method. That method involves selective actions, which aim precisely to compel the lesser firm's surrender (that is, closure or merger into the larger firm at the least price) with the least cost to the larger firm. Selective actions are the dominant firm's ideal device for adding market share profitably.

Selective actions are not equally available to the smaller firms. Their attempts at selective actions have only minor effects, because the competitive pressures on the firm are so pervasive and restrictive. The result gives to dominant firms a category of effective weapons unavailable to lesser competitors.

In short, *selective actions are anti-competitive when they are taken by a firm whose market share is high and (much) higher than the share of the target firm.* Only the specific category of selective tactics done by dominant firms is anticompetitive. Restraining those actions will equalize competition, giving all firms access to comparable effective competitive tactics.[32]

The correct economic criterion is therefore relatively simple. It proscribes substantial selective actions by dominant firms. There need be no price-cost tests, no measures of effects or intent, and no evaluations of relative efficiency. Though there are some complexities, they are small compared to those of the other tests.

The debate is still proceeding, but two points seem clear now. First, the price-cost analysts wrongly narrowed the issue to just one element, belittled the factual problems, and sought an impossible yes-no lawyer's answer. Second, this encouraged a flood of over-technicalized papers, lacking touch with real conditions. The effort has been susbstantial, with results that *neglected* some basic elements. When technical analysis was used without a sufficient research basis in real conditions, it gave empty results.

3. Advertising

Advertising involves behavior, not structure. It reflects key strategic choices by rivals.

Around 1970–74, advertising was the focus of an intense debate, and perhaps scores of dissertations were written about it (see Comanor and Wilson, 1979). It might raise entry barriers; indeed, advertising has emerged as probably the one most important possible cause of entry barriers. Comanor and Wilson (1974) led this research line, showing that advertising intensity was correlated with profit rates during 1955–57 in U.S. industries. Moreover, others had long noted that much advertising is waste, with oligopolists locked in a costly process of neutralizing each others' selling efforts.

Yet, on the other side, advertising can also be a pro-competitive weapon for small or new firms to blitz their way to higher market shares. Also advertising is partly an investment in consumer loyalty. The excess profits found by Comanor-Wilson may just be normal profits on past advertising investments. Moreover, there may be large economies of scale in advertising, so that dominant firms prevent advertising wastes.

The econometric debates were lengthy, often rude, and largely effective in settling the soft lines of the main issues. Advertising (and other selling activities) does tend to fortify dominant firms against small rivals and new entrants. This effect occurs above and beyond any investment role that advertising may have.[33] Yet there are two valid neo-liberal points: advertising can be subject to scale economies, and that it can promote competition in specific cases.

The advertising issue actually applies to only about ten consumer goods markets. The vogue for studying it can now be seen as an interesting episode, but not a general one.

V. PERFORMANCE

The final major topic is performance, with its elements of profitability, allocative efficiency, technological progress, and equity.

1. Analyzing profitability

Two issues have been important recently: the role of risk, and the measurement of profitability by profit rates or a *q* ratio.

Risk and return

A long-standing research frontier is the role of risk in profitability. Frank Knight's early discussion (1921) noted that risk could affect profitability, but little concrete research followed. Then the Tobin-Markowitz analysis of the 1950s encouraged the estimation of risk by past yearly variation in returns. Research in the 1960s attempted to relate such risk-adjusted profit rates to market structure, but with little clear results. Then came the flood of business-finance work on beta, as a measure of portfolio risk. Further testing in our field has been moderate, but it is easy to use beta and related estimators to test how 'risk-adjusted returns' may be related to market power.

The main question is whether such a risk measure is useful. Risk is the likelihood of substantial losses in the future. It arises from basic changes in demand, technology, and competitors. These basic risks have little, if any, relation to yearly fluctuations in the past. The best hope is probably to develop estimators of this basic risk. They will inevitably be soft and approximate, at best. Short run variability may be easy to measure 'precisely', but it appears to be largely irrelevant to the basic phenomenon in this research topic (see Shepherd, 1975, Scherer 1980).

Rates of return and q ratios

Rates of return have always presented accounting problems and variety. Random error may occur, so that correlation analysis understates the true closeness of fit. Bias may also occur. As part of the defense of IBM in antitrust matters, Franklin Fisher (1983) and others have recently claimed that profit rates are nearly useless in measuring true profitability. This has encouraged the use of a '*q*' ratio instead. Indeed, the results in Table 1 include *q* ratios, for comparison.

Are *q* ratios preferable? They offer certain conceptual advantages, but they contain two main categories of defects.[34,34a] In any event, *q* ratios are highly correlated with profit rates. And Table 1's testing of structural models, the profit rates and *q* show similar patterns. In large part, profit rates and *q* are merely alternative measures of the same phenomenon. At best, the *q* ratio may usefully supplement the cautious use of profit rates.

2. Allocative efficiency

The welfare triangle has been estimated repeatedly since 1953 (see Scherer). The methods have not changed radically. Given assumed values for cost curves and demand elasticities, and assigning some proportion of accounting profits to monopoly, the estimated areas then emerge both for the whole economy and for specific industries. Yet the estimates vary sharply, from 0.08 percent to 0.13 percent of national income.[35] The estimates are inevitably soft, because the conditions are soft.

Two interpretive points can be made here. First, research findings on this topic have reflected ideological inclinations, even more than is usual in this field. The softness of the data, and the mix of technical elements in the procedures, permits a wide range of estimates. This debate has no easy resolution; no single approach is clearly superior.

Second, this form of inefficiency is only one among several real costs of monopoly; scale diseconomies, X-inefficiency, and retarded innovation are also involved. The others are less easily modelled, but they are probably a good deal larger in actuality. Here the temptation to focus just on static allocation especially needs to be resisted.

As in other issues, the main problem is conceptual, not empirical.

3. X-Efficiency

X-efficiency has largely escaped accurate measurement. It can be defined loosely, but its concepts are not precise. It is pre-eminently a soft, quasi-static phenomenon. Though it lies squarely in business-school research areas, X-inefficiency has not gotten systematic study there. It can be posed in two alternative ways. First is the increment that 'slack' or 'fat' adds to costs, above barebones cost levels. Electric utilities have been analyzed, using regression models to explain costs (Iulo, 1957). The residual unexplained differences in costs give a first approximation of differences in X-efficiency. This method has not worked for normal industries, where outputs are heterogeneous and changing.

A second appproach focuses on the reduction which X-efficiency causes in profits, below the levels that otherwise would be reached. That can be estimated by the models of structure explaining the rates of return. If the model is complete, then each firm's residual between its actual and predicted profit rates is an accurate measure of management's success in obtaining X-efficiency. The residual might also reflect limit pricing, but that should already be filtered out adequately by the variables for entry barriers. This method was applied to large U.S. firms, showing about 15 firms with large negative residuals in the 1960s.[36] Each of these firms suffered severe difficulties after 1970, including take-overs or bankruptcy in some cases. The measure of X-inefficiency may therefore have been accurate.

4. Equity

Despite neo-liberal claims to the contrary, distribution is an important economic impact of monopoly, and economists can clarify it. Wealth is affected most immediately, but opportunity is also influenced. The past research has two features, which reflect the soft nature of the conditions.

First, the research effort has been slight, for such an important topic. Monopoly has created many of the leading family fortunes, and it may sharpen discrimination. Yet beyond Comanor and Smiley's major paper (1975) on wealth, and several others on monopoly and job discrimination, there is little systematic research. Compared to the flood of papers since 1960 on advertising, predatory pricing and duopoly models, the studies of distribution are remarkably few.

Second, the Comanor–Smiley paper exemplifies good research technique. It derives its predictive model from a firm sense of reality about the main elements. Complicated relationships are combined artfully to reach a testable form. Then data are used to reach a range of alternative predictions, which the reader can compare and choose among. Finally, the results are interpreted carefully.

Rarely do pioneering papers combine deduction and empirical work so creatively. Yet the topic is still a research frontier.

5. *Technological change*

Another strong research area has been technological change. The main conceptual lines laid down by 1965 reflected the soft, quasi-static nature of the process. There have been substantial additions to concepts and evidence since then (see especially Scherer, 1980; Mansfield *et al.*, 1971; and Kamien and Schwartz, 1975, 1984).

The main question is monopoly's impact on invention and innovation; there the broad lessons have held steady. A small degree of monopoly may encourage both invention (the ideas) and innovation (the first production), but more substantial degrees of monopoly tend to retard both activities. Rivalry stirs innovation; perfect competition may discourage it. Loose oligopoly is approximately the optimal structure for promoting innovation. Only very large scale economies in innovation (i.e., gigantic improvements, requiring massed armies of R&D people) may offset the retarding effects of dominance. Yet effective capital markets should fund all worthwhile projects, no matter how large. Therefore the case that monopoly promotes innovation is inconsistent with neo-classical premises of perfect capital markets.

The main lasting concepts include technological opportunity, the Schumpeterian process, and the time-cost trade-off. All of them reflect soft, quasi-static reality.

Technological opportunity (see Scherer, 1980) is basic to any normative analysis, which compares actual invention and innovation levels with the levels that might have happened in any event. Opportunity differs widely, from rich possibilities for many easy advances (e.g., recent electronics) to barren industries with little chance for any gains. Moreover, the question of opportunity focuses attention correctly on the true source of the gains. That source is often outside the industry, in inventions that are *autonomous*. For instance, many computer-industry advances have been handed to it by the progress in the speed and miniaturization of silicon chips and other components. Also, many inventions occur autonomously rather than being induced by the hope of riches. For example, computers were bound to evolve once electronics, metallurgy, silicon chip and other technologies had developed by 1960.

Though opportunity is hard to measure, it is a fundamental element in the topic; it can be conceptualized and analyzed abstractly and rough estimates could be made (at least as accurately as the estimates of entry barriers, for example).

The Schumpeterian process has never been thoroughly defined, but its general nature is known and important. It contrasts with neo-classical competition on most key points, and it correctly stresses that cumulative gains from innovation may easily exceed the allocational niceties of pure competition. A Schumpeterian process may actually occur only in a minority of industries, but it may operate implicitly even where dominant firms stay in place perpetually. In those cases, innovation may be forced by fear, even though rivals never manage actually to dislodge the leader.

Yet the process remains vague. It deserves much more work, on its nature and actual role. Its relation to potential-entry concepts needs especially to be clarified. After nearly 40 years, the Schumpeterian process is a research frontier.

More recently *the time-cost trade-off* for innovations (Scherer, 1967) has emerged as a valuable framework. It captures the basic elements in firms' choices of when to innovate. It permits comparisons between firms of varying market positions, and even potential entrants. It yields interesting and plausible predictions, though not definitive ones. And it can be used as a basis for further conceptual and empirical research.

VI. CONCLUSIONS

There are several significant lessons. The structure-behavior-performance format is still the field's main framework, as used with sophistication. Soft, quasi-static analysis may be a more fruitful and general direction than determinate, short-run modelling. Internal structure and especially market share, is the central influence.

Dominance (above 40 percent of the market) is an important problem, usually causing social costs. Market share is the unifying basis for evaluating market power, pricing behavior and restrictive actions. Market structure is not closely determined by costs; substantial excess market share exists. Reducing the issue to (1) collusion versus (2) an efficient-structure hypothesis is wrong and misleading. Competition's effects on innovation probably outstrip the static allocative impacts.

The field has always blended theory with testing and cases. In suggesting the quasi-static approach, I wish to develop theory rather than inhibit it. In a field as rich as this, there can continue to be a variety of approaches.

But the field is vulnerable to outside pressures. I will conclude with several points about policy and the hazards of interest groups.

1. Policy choices

The quasi-static, soft-function approach gives important lessons for policy. Actions should not be based on pure models or extreme assumptions, nor should it seek pure goals. Because only large gaps can be identified with confidence, policies should seek only to make shifts in the intermediate degrees of competition rather than move to border solutions. Pure competition is not to be sought. In dealing with the several elements of structure and strategy, policies should be fitted to a scale of priority about the main elements. Complex, soft reality must be respected; pure models can give empty or deceptive lessons. Officials usually need to proceed by steps, testing the marginal effects. Reality also evolves, and so policies usually need adjusting.

2. *The link of research to policy*

Research lessons have recently come to be applied swiftly in policies. Research has always had some influence on policies in the U.S. Henry C. Adams and Richard T. Ely influenced regulation's early content. J. B. Clark, Charles J. Bullock and Frank Taussig had some effect on the first wave of antitrust decisions. Berle and Mean's (1932) and Chamberlin's work helped encourage the second antitrust wave (1937–52); the 1930s concept of 'tacit collusion' was applied in the 1946 tobacco case, for example. Corwin Edward's (1955) alarms about conglomerate mergers stirred concern in the 1960s; but Donald Turner and various Chicagoans cooled the fever for action, and (perhaps wisely) little has been done.

More recently, the pace has quickened. On predatory pricing, the 1975 Areeda–Turner cost criterion swept into ten court decisions within two years. Since 1980, the Chicago-school preoccupation with collusion has been applied in a drastic cut-back of antitrust by Reagan officials, leading in turn to the fourth and biggest merger wave in U.S. industrial history. The Baumol group is urging their 1982 'contestability' ideas in large, current antitrust and regulatory cases.

New ideas now can have immediate impacts. In fact, the ideas often originate in work done by the economists as advisers on cases! Their professional publication comes after the testimony – often given in emphatic tones – which shapes the case.

These instant impacts can be a hazardous development. The process short-circuits the orderly sifting and testing of ideas by scholars, via the journal process, in which (one hopes) only the best ones get adopted. It tends to glorify the latest idea over the stock of all other concepts, including established ones. It can give a spurious legitimacy to shallow new ideas, when they are established in case precedents even before the professional testing of them has begun. And it causes rapid switches and confusion, as ideological and electoral events change, and new political appointees rush to use ideas that suit their immediate purposes.

The cure for this problem is not obvious. The danger arises partly from the rising involvement of our field with consulting, testimony and partisan lobbying (see below). That could not easily be curtailed, nor perhaps should it be. Probably the matter hinges on the judgement of the scholars themselves, in avoiding the rush to claim relevance and permanence for their new ideas. A decent reticence in claiming scientific proof and policy value is crucial to the validity of the field.

3. Corporate sponsoring

A firm facing an antitrust or regulatory action has incentives to spend on its defensive activities any amount of money to the level of the profits which are at stake. In large cases, these stakes can involve many billions of dollars. Economic studies and expert testimony are just one among many corporate tools to deploy in its strategies.

In the U.S., the field has experienced a rising tide of such money for the last two decades, most of it from large firms interested in promoting conservative doctrine. The flow goes to campuses, departments and research institutes, as well as to individuals. For example, AT&T in the 1960s created its own economic analysis department, started and paid for the *Bell Journal*, and sponsored scores of seminars on regulatory issues.[37] Large corporations have sponsored an ongoing program, now at Emory University, which has provided neo-classical economic training to over half of all the 750 U.S. federal judges. NERA, Lexecon, Mathematica, and other consulting groups provide any package of support which a client firm may need: large-scale supportive research and/or favorable expert witnesses, either from their own staff or by engaging university professors. Large firms sponsor extensive research and seminar programs at leading universities, mingling objective research with results and testimony which support the sponsor. Even the antitrust agencies' economic staffs have been converted under the Reagan Administration since 1980 into enclaves of conservative analysis.

These resources dwarf the relative handful of leading independent scholars. The wonder is that the field is able to do as much objective research as it does. There are three important hazards, which are probably more serious than in earlier decades.

First, talent is diverted to other activities, and so the volume of basic research is reduced. Second, the field is subjected to bias in some degree. Sponsored activities create or reinforce an interest in ideas which suit the sponsors.[38] Doubtful ideas are advanced more enthusiastically. Careers are linked to ideas which arise in research for clients. Therefore some fraction of actual published research is altered in nature. Third, the field generally is more entwined with, and hyper-sensitive to, vested industrial interests.

These problems may have reached their peak with AT&T and IBM's involvements in the 1970's, and now be receding. But many young careers and expectations are now dependent on further growth of this field as a profitable industry of its own. Some involvement in real markets is healthy, of course. But there are danger signs, which a volume such as this needs to recognize.

4. Methodology

Despite these outside pressures, the field evolves largely by voluntary choices by scholars as they consider alternative problems and techniques. The danger of empty theorizing can be met by a skeptical insistence on reasonable assumptions, translation into meaningful prose, and thorough empirical testing. Modelling does *not* offer definitive lessons. The field's mainstreams require careful, sophisticated research. In retrospect, the recent wave of applied theory may be seen as another useful addition, if we treat it skeptically.

NOTES

* I am grateful to William J. Adams, Mark Bagnoli, Joe S. Bain, William J. Baumol, Donald J. Dewey, John Heywood, Henry de Jong, Bart Lipman, and Takeo Nakao for discussions of the various ideas in this paper. I am also indebted to seminar participants at the Universities of Massachusetts, Montreal and Michigan, Michigan State University, Doshisha University and the University of Chicago.

1. See Bain (1968), Schumpeter (1942), Caves (1985), Caves and Porter (1976, 1977), Scherer (1980), Shepherd (1985a), and Williamson (1975).
2. Good examples of the genre include Baumol, Panzar and Willig (1982), von Weizsacker (1980), Encaoua and Jacquemin (1980), Shubik (1980), Milgrom and Roberts (1982), and various papers in Salop (1981).
3. I show in Shepherd (1982a) that the summed share of pure-monopoly, dominant-firm, and tight-oligopoly industries has declined from 44 to 24 percent of GNP during 1960–1980. The tight oligopoly share alone has shrunk from 36 to 18 percent.
4. For example (as Michael Porter (1985) and the organization literature note), firms may consider over 30 difficult significant factors in deciding their production techniques, product strategies, personnel, marketing, quality changes, financing, and other real choices. Each set of decisions may yield a different cost-output result in

the short and/or long run, but the whole result may not be accurately predictable. Also, workers' effort can be crucial to the level of cost (as I discuss in Section III below), but that effort may not be precisely controllable or predictable by the firm's managers. Therefore both average and marginal costs are commonly soft. That is further confirmed by the frequent abilities of firms to cut costs deeply during recessions and then resume output at costs 30 percent or more lower than before.

5. Scherer (1980) occasionally speaks of a 'soft determinism' in the field. I am suggesting that this be incorporated as a central assumption.
6. The blurred functions might be regarded as the standard errors of the estimates, located in parallel to the true curves which presumably are lying in the middle between them. Or instead, the probabilities of specific values may be equal throughout the zone.
7. Useful histories of the field are given by Phillips and Stevenson (1974) and Shepherd (1985a).
8. This can be seen from Bullock (1901), J. B. Clark (1887), and J. M. Clark (1922), Knight (1921), Letwin (1967), Moody (1904), and Williams (1985).
9. Examples include Nelson (1959), Shepherd (1964, 1972), Scherer (1965), and many studies by Leonard Weiss.
10. For example, excess profits are now termed 'rent'; firms now 'seek quasi-rents' rather than obtain monopoly profits. The monopoly problem itself, rising from the market power of individual firms, is being abandoned in a preoccupation with oligopoly models and new entry from outside the market. 'Contestability' is offered to replace competition; but contestability is a meaningless term with no neoclassical roots, and it is largely unmeasurable (as I discuss in Section II). Price discrimination is restated as a matter of 'Ramsey prices'; the name and connection to competitive impacts are obscure, and the connotations of static efficiency are favorable. Direct measures of structure (such as market shares and concentration) are replaced by the HHI (see Section II). The HHI is a pure number, with no intrinsic content or real values; and even its name has been replaced by an obscure acronym. A q ratio is presented to replace imperfect profit rates in assessing monopoly impacts. Yet q is also difficult to measure, and it is subject to biases (see Section V). In framing models, virtually any assumption is permitted, no matter how bizarre, if it gives 'insights'.
11. Among leading discussions are Marshall (1920), Steiner (1968), and Sherer (1980). They and many others are included in Elzinga and Rogowsky (1984).
12. *Demand* conditions define the market. Supply conditions (especially where non producers can easily convert to produce the good in question) have been urged as co-equal with demand conditions. But that is confusing, because it mixes the possibility of entry with the definition of the market. It also serves the interests of antitrust dependants, whose experts have been most vigorous in claiming supply conditions as relevant (so as to define as large a market as possible). The more correct approach is to define the market by demand conditions and then consider supply conditions as a source of entry.
13. One of the 'new' techniques claims to define markets more scientifically (U.S. Antitrust Division, 1982). One begins with the narrowest plausible market. Then one hypothesizes a 'significant' price rise (5 percent) and tests whether within a 'reasonable' period (1 year) a 'significant' shift (10 percent) to substitute goods occurs. If so, the market is redefined to include the substitutes. The analysis is repeated, step by step, until the further substitution is not significant and the market's edge is reached. The method has been officially adopted by the Antitrust Division since 1982.

Unfortunately, it is probably worse than the conventional approach, which relies on rough judgments. All three of its benchmarks (for price changes, time period, and quantity shifts) are arbitrary and highly debatable. Most important, the exercise is strictly hypothetical guesswork. No actual tests can be done, and so the theoretical underpinnings have little practical use. Again a 'new', supposedly 'scientific' method turns out to be merely intuition clothed in formalism.

14. This is attested by logic and many empirical studies, including Shepherd, 1972, 1975, 1979, and 1985c, (see other studies listed in 1979), and Martin (1983).
15. Recently the Hirschman-Herfindahl index (or HHI) has drawn renewed attention, as a comprehensive index of monopoly power in a market. Its comprehensiveness is welcome, and the simple three or four firm concentration ratio ignores fringe firms which might be significant.

Yet the HHI has serious defects. It is arbitrary. Squaring the market shares has no inherent superiority over raising them a power of 1.5, 1.8, 2.5, or any other number. Each number implies a distinctive weighting among large and small market shares. To pick a single power (2.0) without serious evaluation is bad scientific method; yet that is what has happened.

The HHI is as sensitive to market definition as any other index. And it requires more important (*all* significant market shares) than conventional concentration ratios. If all individuals market shares are known and available, they then are the critical information. To merge them into a single number is a detour.

The ratio is a pure number, with no intrinsic meaning. This is a serious flaw. 'Critical' values (of 2000 + for 'significant' market power and 1000 or less for effective competition) have no basis in content. The HHI enthusiasts have invariably used *real* concentration ratios to explain and justify them!

Most discussion so far has focused on its use in measuring oligopoly conditions, especially in the range of HHI values from 1000 to 2000 (which are very roughly similar to 4-firm concentration ratios of 50 to 80 percent): see Table Al. Meanwhile, its relation to the market power of the *individual* firm, particularly a dominant firm, has largely been ignored.

Yet the HHI may reflect individual firm's market power with particular validity and accuracy. The levels of the HHI vary geometrically with market share, as shown in Table A1. This curvature corresponds to the shape of the profits volume curve, which reflects the extra profits associated with higher market share. In fact, the HHI and profit volumes are linear transformation of each other, varying in direct proportion. Therefore, the HHI is an index of the excess profits caused by market power, and so it can be adopted as an estimator of the market power held by individual firms at varying market shares.

Consider those HHI values specifically, as in Table A1. The HHI values rise sharply in the 40–70 percent range of market shares (from 1600 to 4900), compared to the small rises in the market-share range of 1–30 percent (from 1 to 900). That difference in HHI values accurately reflects the larger monopoly gains achieved as the firm attains dominance over the market. Even the high HHI values in the 80–100 percent ranges of market shares may measure market power correctly, because complete monopoly permits a complete use of opportunities for price increase and price discrimination.

This is intuitively confirmed in Table A1 by comparing single-firm values with multiple-firm oligopoly values. For example, a single firm with a 50 percent market share would indeed have market power (an HHI of 2500) comparable to that of

Table A1. Values of HHI for varying market shares.

Market shares (%)	
For single firms	HHI values
1	1
10	100
20	400
30	900
40	1600
50	2500
60	3600
70	4900
80	6400
90	8100
100	10000
For oligopolies	HHI values
10 firms, 10 percent each	1000
8 firms, 12.5 percent each	1250
6 firms, 16.7 percent each	1667
5 firms, 20 percent each	2000
4 firms, 25 percent each	2500
3 firms, 33.3 percent each	3333
2 firms, 50 percent each	5000

oligopoly with four firms, each holding a 25 percent market share. At the maximum the four firms might achieve total collusion and reach pure monopoly results (with an HHI equal to 10,000), but that would be infrequent, perhaps one-fourth of the time. Conversely, they might usually lapse into intense competition the rest of the time. That would give a weighted average HHI of 2500, which corresponds well with the market power exercised steadily by a single firm with 50 percent of the market.

Similarly, two duopolists each with 50 percent of the market would be expected, *on average*, to exert about as much market control as a single firm with 70 percent; and the HHIs for those cases are indeed about equal at approximately 4900–5000.

The HHI values represent the *average* expected levels of the firm's market power. For each such market share, the remaining rival firms may have a variety of market shares, ranging from source of tiny firms to just one other firm.

In short, whatever its other defects may be, the HHI has validity as an index of market power over the full range of market shares.

16. Both Henry Carter Adams and John B. Clark discussed potential entry as a limit on monopolist's power.
17. Caves and Porter (1977) have also proposed 'mobility barriers' which limit competition within the market. Much of their role could, instead, be explained by lags and dominant-firm advantages, as have long been recognized in the literature.
18. Spence (1977) and others have added excess capacity as another strategic action to discourage entry. While logical, this factor may be of little real importance in significant markets. It has attracted extensive modelling with virtually no testing of its actual role.
19. Both profit rates and q ratios are used; the q results are assessed in Section V.

20. Schmalenshee (1985) offers contrasting conclusions, based on FTC 1975 line of business data. But the paper contains several methodological flaws. The use of dummy variables suppresses the role of market shares. The hypotheses are reduced to only two: that only collusion matters (not market dominance), and that any market-share-profitability correlation reflects only efficiency. Also the data are suspect. Therefore the lessons are highly debatable.
21. There are no recognized actual cases of entry-dominated monopolists; that is, markets where incumbents hold large market shares but could be easily replaced, and where the firms do not respond quickly to competitive challenges. At first, the Baumol group presented the U.S. *airlines* sector (after deregulation) as their leading case. Airline capital appears to be mobile and entry could be rapid. Yet the evidence shows that monopoly power is still exerted in the standard patterns: airlines with high market shares tend to set significantly higher price-cost ratios. Airlines are mainly concerned with their *actual* rivals, as well as the possibility of new ones. They respond swiftly and sharply to price actions, in many cases within hours. They strongly defend their market positions, and nothing close to instant replacement of dominant positions has occurred.

    Therefore the contestability assumptions do not hold. The industry closely fits the established analysis of market structure. The Baumol group itself has recently noted that U.S. airlines do not illustrate ultra-free entry (Bailey and Baumol, 1984).

    Other examples might include *long-distance telephone service* in the U.S. But entrants there were unable to gain more than 10 percent of that market during the five years, 1979–84, even though AT&T was prevented from matching their prices. And AT&T is now taking strong price actions. The newcomers, in any event, have had no conceivable chance to replace AT&T completely (in line with the first assumption), either instantly or in a matter of years.

    Railroads are another of the few cases offered by the Baumol group. But they too are unsatisfactory. First, inter-model competition does exist in varying degree, but *that is not ultra-free entry*. It is simply a degree of interaction between trains, trucks, barges, and other forms of transport. The task then is to define the markets carefully to include true overlaps and then consider the market shares of each of the carriers. The share held by a railroad firm in a given market will suggest if it has market power. The assumptions of ultra-free entry are not met in this sector. In some geographic areas and some classes of goods, trucks could not replace railroads, because railway costs are lower. Railroads are not strictly passive to truckers' tactics; they now respond vigorously in a variety of competitive settings. Nor are sunk costs really zero. Yet Baumol has asserted that ultra-free entry prevents all monopoly power, even in railroad monopolies. He attempts to convert trucking and barges (which surely can have some effect on many classes of freight) into a limitless force of ultra-free entry.
22. Actually, the socially optimal market share may be lower than MES, depending on the balance between the cost gradient and the degree of monopoly effects at market shares below MES. (Shepherd, 1982b).
23. Commonly (Scherer, 1980), the cost penalty is only 1 to 5 percent at outputs one-half of MES. My study of 85 large U.S. corporations (Shepherd, 1982b) found that in the 1960s only 5-15 percent of their supra-normal profits were attributable to scale economies. Of course in many smaller markets, scale economies may set important lower bounds on market shares. But these are not the main problem cases for competitive policies.

24. Smirlock *et al.* are a recent case (1984). But their methods are flawed and their interpretation is incorrect (see Shepherd, 1985c). See also note 20 above.
25. The measures are not exact, because data are scarce; see Shepherd (1975) and Weiss and Pascoe (1982).
26. These advantages were noted earlier under market share, in the structure discussion.
27. The whole business strategy literature teaches the same lessons of complexity and indeterminacy; as also does the literature examining organizational factors, e.g., Williamson (1970, 1975).
28. I recognize that this is a major topic, but its importance (and the value of the mass of short-run Nash-based models) is debatable. At any rate, others can provide a full evaluation of this flood of writings, with more space than I have here.
29. Consider the demand elasticities that would be required for firms to reach high rates of return, even though they can set high price-cost margins on only a small part of their output. I focus on net profit, above the cost of capital. In large U.S. firms, sales revenue has been about 2.75 times the volume of equity capital, on average, while taxes have run about 42 percent of gross profit. Therefore, a 10 percent net return on equity (after taxes) translates to a price-cost margin of 5.1 percent. One uses the familiar elasticity formula (where elasticity = P/P − MC). To a first approximation, average cost is a reasonable estimate of marginal cost where constant costs prevail (as is common).

    On this basis, the table (from Shepherd, 1982b) presents the elasticities that would be required for monopoly rates of return on the entire firm's equity (that is, the margin above the cost of capital) or between 5 and 15 percent, for varying portions of the firm's sales. The extra profit is assumed to be gained only on 20 or 50 percent of sales: the rest of the firm's sales are conservatively assumed to be made at zero extra profit (above the cost of capital).

Price discrimination as a source of monopoly profit.

Company-wide rates of return on equity (above the cost of equity)	Percentage of company sales from which monopoly profit is extracted:		
(percent)	100%	50%	20%
	Required demand elasticity on that portion of sales		
(1)	(2)	(3)	(4)
5 percent	40.0	19.6	7.8
10 percent	19.6	9.8	3.9
15 percent	13.3	6.7	2.7

The lesson of the table is clear: the price discrimination can be a powerful source of extra profits. The elasticities in the table are equal or above those observed in the common run of firms with high market shares. Elasticities of two to five would be the usual range for the entire output of such firms. Evidently, price discrimination alone can generate substantial rates of true profit, even if the monopolized scales are below 50 percent of the firm's sales and the elasticities on those sales are at four and above. For example, the 3.9 in line 2, column 4 shows that a 10 percent extra rate of return for the *entire* firm would result even if demand elasticity is as high as 3.9 on only one-fifth of the firm's output (and infinite on the other 80 percent).

High elasticities reflect strong actual or potential competition. The elasticities noted here – infinite on at least half of sales and at three or more on the rest – embody rather small degrees of monopoly.

30. This discussion draws on Shepherd (1985a).
31. Fuller analysis can be found in Shepherd (1986).
32. The three alternative criteria for 'predation' are less valid or workable. The Areeda-Turner *price-cost test* ignores the many other competitive devices available to firms, and it faces large complexities in measuring costs and in setting the correct limits on prices in actual cases. Its seemingly objective price-costs tests are in fact mostly unworkable as a practical matter (as Areeda-Turner and many other writers recognize). In short, Areeda-Turner ignore many of the relevant anticompetitive devices; their tests often founder on unclear measures of costs; and they ignore the crucial competitive setting of the actions.

    Second, the *effects* of the larger firm's actions might be used as the tests. But that approach will face impossible difficulties. As noted, *all* successful competitive actions by all firms will inherently harm their rivals in some degree. Trying to measure those effects and to separate the 'excessive' ones from (1) the endless variety of impacts from 'fair' competition and (2) differences in the firm's efficiency is virtually a hopeless task. Also futile would be an effort to set threshold levels for the severity of the permitted effects. For example, if the smaller firm is only crippled but not killed, would the action not be rated as excessive.?

    Third, policies might be based on judgments about the firm's *intent*. But that approach is neither logical nor feasible. All firms naturally intend to defeat their competitors, and their resulting actions are usually part of healthy competition. What matters is the setting of the action and the weapons used by the rivals. If they are equivalent, then intent is irrelevant. If the setting and weapons are imbalanced, intent is also irrelevant. In any event, intent is usually a complex mixture of attitudes that are virtually impossible to discover and to measure against an objective scale.
33. Dixit and Norman (1978) also show a tendency for advertising to exceed the socially optimum levels.
34. The following points are drawn from Shepherd, 1985. First, q ratios are conceptually debatable. They are a phenomenon of capital markets, not of the firm itself. The ratio's numeratory (the firm's current market value) depends on the balance among various investors' expectations about the firm's stream of future profits. This market value is fundamentally indirect and subjective, based on speculation about future possibilities. The value is also unstable, subject to swings fed by changing moods, rumors, herd movements and extraneous factors. The q ratio's validity depends on there being perfectly efficient stock markets, a condition disproved by much research.

    Second, the seemingly simple q ratio turns out to be a very complicated thing to measure, as a recent study shows (Smirlock *et al.*, 1984). Combining mixed and debatable parts, the estimated q ratios cannot be taken as obviously superior to profit rates, and they may be inferior.

34a. In a recent major attempt to use q ratios, Smirlock *et al.* (1984) were forced to adopt 'intricate' methods, which included arbitrary and debatable steps. In the numerator, debt and other categories had to be estimated by arbitrary methods.

    The denominator was even more complex and debatable. Replacement cost was sought, despite decades of literature showing the near-impossibility of defining it clearly or estimating its reliability. There were technical problems with the rate of depreciation, and the inflation adjustment, and inventory valuation. The resulting denominator is a hybrid book-and-replacement value figure that contains unknown degrees of error and possible bias.

35. A recent summary of all estimates is given in Shepherd (1985a); see also Sherer (1980).
36. The estimates are drawn from a larger study in Shepherd (1974).
37. The 'contestability' and 'sustainability' ideas of William Baumol and his team were developed on the Bell payroll. AT&T's defense team of economists for antitrust cases after 1974 was said to include 27 professors from five leading departments, supervised by Paul MacAvoy, then of Yale. IBM used many well-known economists, in addition to Franklin Fisher, in its successful antitrust defenses during 1969–82, either in actual testimony or in 'preparing advice' by writing papers or doing background research.
38. This has been admitted as a problem by Fisher, whose book denouncing the U.S. antitrust case against IBM reflects his decade of deep involvement as an advisor and witness defending IBM.

REFERENCES

Adams, Henry C., *Relation of the State to Industrial Action and the Economics of Jurisprudence*, ed., Jospeh Dorfman, New York: Columbia University Press (1954).

Areeda, Phillip and Turner, Donald F., 'Predatory Pricing and Related Practices Under Section 2 of the Sherman Act', *Harvard Law Review*, 88 (February 1975), pp. 697–733.

Bailey, Elizabeth E. and Baumol, William J., 'Deregulation and the Theory of Contestable Markets', *Yale Journal on Regulation* (Spring 1984), pp. 111–137.

Bain, Joe S., *Barriers to New Competition*, Cambridge, Mass.: Harvard University Press (1956).

Bain Joe S., *Industrial Organization*, rev. ed., New York: Wiley (1968).

Baumol, William J., 'Contestable Markets: An Uprising in the Theory of Industry Structure', *American Economic Review*, 72 (March 1982), pp. 1–15.

Baumol, William J., Panzar, John, and Willig, Robert D., *Contestable Markets and the Theory of Industry Structure*, New York: Harcourt, Brace Jovanovich (1982).

Berle, Adolf A. and Means, Gardner C., *The Modern Corporation and Private Property*, New York: Harper & Row (1932).

Brock, William A., 'Contestable Markets and Theory of Industry Structure: A Review Article', *Journal of Political Economy*, 91 (December 1983), pp. 1055–1066.

Bullock, Charles J., 'Trust Literature: A Survey and Criticism', *Quarterly Journal of Economics*, 15 (February 1901), pp. 167–217.

Caves, Richard E., 'International Trade and Industrial Organization: Problems, Solved and Unsolved', *Discussion Paper 1131*, Cambridge, Mass.: Harvard Institute of Economic Research (January 1985).

Caves, Richard E. and Porter, Michael E., 'Barriers to Exit', chapters in R. T. Masson and P. D. Qualls, eds., *Essays on Industrial Organization in Honor of Joe S. Bain*, Cambridge, Mass.: Ballinger (1976).

Caves, Richard E. and Porter, Michael E., 'From Entry Barriers to Mobility Barriers: Conjectural Decisions and Contrived Deterrence to New Competition', *Quarterly Journal of Economics*, 91 (1977) pp. 241–261.

Caves, Richard E., Fortunato, Michael, and Ghemawat, Pankaj, 'The Decline of Dominant Firms, 1905–1929*', *The Quarterly Journal of Economics*, 99 (August 1984), pp. 523–46.

Chamberlin, Edward H., *The Theory of Monopolistic Competition*, 8th ed., Cambridge, Mass.: Harvard University Press (1962).
Clark, John B., 'The Limits of Competition', *Political Science Quarterly*, 2 (March 1887), pp. 42–53.
Clark, John M., *Studies in the Economics of Overhead Costs*, New York: Macmillan (1922).
Comanor, William S. and Smiley, Robert H., 'Monopoly and the Distribution of Wealth', *Quarterly Journal of Economics*, 89 (May 1975), pp. 177–194.
Comanor, William S. and Wilson, Thomas, *Advertising and Market Power*, Cambridge: Harvard University Press (1974).
Comanor, William S. and Wilson, Thomas, 'The Effect of Advertising on Competition: A Survey', *Journal of Economic Literature*, XVII (June 1979), pp. 453–476.
Dirlam, Joel B. and Kahn, Alfred E., *Fair Competition*, Ithaca: Cornell University Press (1954).
Dixit, Avinash, 'The Role of Investment in Entry-Deterrence', *Economic Journal*, 90 (March 1980), pp. 95–106.
Dixit, Avinash, 'Recent Developments in Oligopoly Theory' *American Economic Review*, 72 (May 1982), pp. 12–17.
Dixit, Avaniash and Norman, Victor, 'Advertising and Welfare', *Bell Journal*, 9 (Spring 1978), pp. 1–17.
Elzinga, Kenneth G. and Rogowsky, Robert A., *Relevant Markets in Antitrust*, Vol. 19, No. 2 of *The Journal of Reprints for Antitrust Law and Economics*, New York (1984).
Encaoua, David, Geroski, Paul, and Jacquemin, Alexis, 'Strategic Competition and the Persistence of Dominant Firms: A Survey', in F. Matthewson and J. Stiglitz, eds., *New Developments in the Analysis of Market Structure*, Boston: MIT Press (1983).
Fellner, William J., *Competition Among the Few*, New York: Knopf (1949).
Fisher, Franklin M., 'On the Misuse of Accounting Rates of Return to Infer Monopoly Profits', *American Economic Review*, 73 (March 1983), pp. 82–92.
Fisher, Franklin M., McGowan, John J., and Greenwood, Joen E., *Folded, Spindled, and Mutilated: Economic Analysis and U.S. vs. IBM*, Cambridge, Mass.: MIT Press (1983).
Gale, Bradley T. and Branch, Ben S., 'Concentration and Market Share: Which Determines Market Share and Why Does it Matter?', *Antitrust Bulletin*, 27 (Spring 1982), pp. 83–106.
Gaskins, Darius, 'Dynamic Limit Pricing: Optimal Pricing Under Threat of Entry', *Journal of Economic Theory*, 3 (September 1971), pp. 306–322.
Geroski, Paul, 'Do Dominant Firms Decline?' *Discussion Paper 8509*, University of Southampton (August 1985).
Geroski, Paul and Jacquemin, Alexis, 'Dominant Firms and Their Alleged Decline', *International Journal of Industrial Organization*, 2 (1984), pp. 1–27.
Iulo, William, *Electic Utilities – Cost and Performance*, Pullman, Washington: Washington State University Press (1961).
Kanien, Morton I. and Schwartz, Nancy L., 'Market Structure and Innovation: A Survey', *Journal of Economic Literature*, 13 (March 1975), pp. 1–38.
Kanien, Morton I. and Schwartz, Nancy L., *Market Structure and Innovation*, New York: Cambridge University Press (1982).
Knight, Frank H., *Risk Uncertainty and Profit*, New York: Harper & Row, (1921).
Leibenstein, Harvey J., *Beyond Economic Man*, (Cambridge, Mass.: Harvard University Press (1966).

Letwin, William, *Law and Economic Policy in America*, New York: Random House (1967).

Lewis, W. Arthur, *Overhead Costs*, London: Allen & Unwin (1948).

Mann, H. Michael, 'Seller Concentration, Barriers to Entry, and Rates of Return in 30 Industries, 1950–1960', *Review of Economics and Statistics*, 48 (August 1966), pp. 296–307.

Mansfield, Edwin *et al.*, *Research and Innovation in the Modern Corporation*, New York: Norton (1971).

Marshall, Alfred, *Principles of Economics*, 8th ed., London: Macmillan, (1920).

Martin, Steven, *Market, Firm and Economic Performance*, Monograph Series in Economics and Finance, New York University (1983).

Mason, Edward S., *Economic Concentration and the Monopoly Problem*, Cambridge, Mass.: Harvard University Press (1957).

Masson, Robert T. and Qualls, P. David, eds., *Essays on Industrial Organization in Honor of Joe S. Bain*, Cambridge, Mass.: Ballinger (1976).

Milgram, Paul and Roberts, John, 'Predation, Reputation and Entry Deterrence', *Journal of Economic Theory* (1982).

Modigliani, Franco, 'New Developments on the Oligopoly Front', *Journal of Political Economy*, 66 (June 1958), pp. 215–32.

Moody, John, *The Truth About the Trusts*, Chicago: Moody Publishing (1904).

Mueller, Dennis C., ed., *The Determinants and Effects of Mergers: An International Comparison*, Cambridge, Mass.: Oelgeschlager, Gunn and Hain (1980).

Mueller, Dennis C., *The Determinants of Persistent Profits*, Washington, D.C.: Federal Trade Commission (1983).

Mueller, Dennis C., 'Mergers and Market Share', *Review of Economics and Statistics*, 67 (May 1985), pp. 259–267.

Neumann, John von and Morgenstern, Oskar, *Theory of Games and Economic Behavior*, Princeton, N.J.: Princeton University Press (1944).

Peltzman, Sam, 'The Gains and Losses from Industrial Concentration', *Journal of Law and Economics*, 20 (October 1977), pp. 229–263.

Philips, Almarin and Stevenson, Rodney E., 'The Historical Development of Industrial Organization', *History of Political Economy*, 6 (Fall 1974), pp. 324–342.

Porter, Michael E., *Competitive Strategy: Techniques for Analyzing Industries and Competitors*, New York: Free Press (1980).

Porter, Michael E., *Competitive Advantage: Creating and Sustaining Superior Performance*, New York: Free Press (1985).

Rhoades, Stephen A., 'Market Share as a Source of Market Power: Implications and Some Evidence', *Journal of Economics and Business* (forthcoming, 1985).

Robinson, Joan, *The Economics of Imperfect Competition*, London: Macmillan (1933).

Salop, Steven, ed., *Strategy, Predation and Antitrust Analysis*, (Washington, D.C.: Federal Trade Commission, 1981).

Salop, Steven, 'Practices That (Credibly) Facilitate Oligopoly Coordination', Federal Trade Commission Working Paper No. 73, August 1982, pp. 1–40.

Scherer, F. M., 'Firm Size, Market Structure, Opportunity and the Output of Patented Investigations', *American Economic Review*, 55 (December 1955), pp. 1104–1125.

Scherer, F. M., 'Research and Development Allocation Under Rivalry', *Quarterly Journal of Economics*, 71 (August 1967), pp. 359–394.

Scherer, F. M., *Industrial Market Structure and Economic Performance*, 2nd ed., Boston: Houghton Mifflin (1980).

Scherer, F. M., Beckenstein, Alan, Kaufer, Erich, and Murphy, R. Dennis, *The Economics of Multiplant Operations: An International Comparisons Study*, Cambridge, Mass.: Harvard University Press (1975).

Schmalensee, Richard, *The Economics of Advertising*, Amsterdam: North Holland (1972).

Schmalensee, Richard, 'Economics of Scale and Barriers to Entry', *Journal of Political Economy*, 89 (1981) pp. 1228–1238.

Schmalensee, Richard, 'Do Markets Differ Much?' *American Economic Review*, 75 (June 1985), pp. 341–51.

Schwartz, Marius and Reynolds, Robert J., 'On the Limited Relevance of Contestability Theory', *Antitrust Division, Discussion Paper, EPO 84-10*, Washington, D.C. (1984).

Schumpeter, Joseph A., *Capitalism, Socialism and Democracy*, New York: Harper (1942).

Shepherd, William G., 'Change in Concentration of U.S. Manufacturing Industries, 1947–58', *Review of Economics and Statistics.*

Shepherd, William G., 'The Elements of Market Structure', *Review of Economics and Statistics*, 54 (February 1972), pp. 25–35.

Shepherd, William G., 'The Yields from Abating Market Power', *Industrial Organization Review*, 1 (1973), pp. 47–55.

Shepherd, William G., *The Treatment of Market Power*, New York: Columbia University Press (1975).

Shepherd, William G., *The Economics of Industrial Organization*, Englewood Cliffs, N.J.: Prentice-Hall (1979).

Shepherd, William G., 'Causes of Increased Competition in the U.S. Economy, 1939–1980', *Review of Economics and Statistics*, 64 (November 1982), pp. 614–620.

Shepherd, William G., 'Monopoly Profits and Economies of Scale', chapters in John V. Graven, ed., *Industrial Organization, Antitrust and Public Policy*, Boston.: Kluwer Nijhoff (1982, 1982b).

Shepherd, William G., '"Contestability" versus Competition', *American Economic Review*, 74 (September 1984), pp. 572–587.

Shepherd, William G., *The Economics of Industrial Organization*, rev. ed., Englewood Cliffs, N.J.: Prentice-Hall (1985, 1985a).

Shepherd, William G., 'Tobin's *q* and the Structure-Performance Relationship: A Comment', Working Paper, University of Massachusetts, May 1985 (1985b).

Shepherd, William G., 'Assessing Predatory Actions by Market Shares and Selectivity', *Antitrust Bulletin* (1986) (in press).

Shubik, Martin and Levitan, R., *Market Structure and Behavior*, Cambridge, Mass.: Harvard University Press (1980).

Smirlock, Michael *et al.*, 'Tobin's *q* and the Structure-Performance Relationship', *American Economic Review*, 74 (December 1984), pp. 1051–1060.

Spence, A. Michael, 'Entry, Investment and Oligopolostic Pricing', *Bell Journal of Economics*, 8 (Autumn 1977), pp. 534–544.

Spence, A. Michael, 'The Learning Curve and Competition', *Bell Journal of Economics*, 12 (1981), pp. 49–70.

Steiner, Peter O., 'Markets and Industries', *International Encyclopedia of the Social Sciences*, New York: Crowell, Collier and Macmillan (1968), pp. 575–581.

Steiner, Peter O., *Mergers: Motives, Effects, Policies*, Ann Arbor: University of Michigan Press (1975).

Stigler, George J., 'The Theory of Oligopoly', *Journal of Political Economy*, 72 (February 1964), pp. 44–61.

Tesler, Lester G., 'Advertising and Competition', *Journal of Political Economy*, 72 (December 1964), pp. 537–62.

Thorelli, Hans B., *The Federal Antitrust Policy*, Stockholm: Stockholms Hogskola (1954).

U.S. Antitrust Division, *Merger Guidelines*, Washington D.C.: Department of Justice (1982, amended 1984).

Weiss, Leonard W. and Pascoe, George, 'The Extent and Permanence of Market Dominance', manuscript, University of Wisconsin (1982).

von Weizsacker, Christian C., *Barriers to Entry: A Theoretical Treatment*, Berlin: Springer Verlag (1980).

Williams, Phillip L., 'The Influence of the Economics Profession on the Sherman Act', manuscript, University of Melbourne (1985).

Williamson, Oliver E., *Corporate Control and Business Behavior*, Englewood Cliffs, N.J.: Prentice-Hall (1970).

Williamson, Oliver E., *Markets and Hierarchies: Analysis and Antitrust Implications*, New York: Free Press (1975).

Worcester, Dean A., 'Why "Dominant Firms" Decline', *Journal of Political Economy*, 65 (August 1957), pp. 338–347.

Yamey Basil S., 'Predatory Price Cutting: Notes and Comments', *Journal of Law and Economics*, 15 (April 1972), pp. 137–147.

3. EUROPEAN INDUSTRIAL ORGANIZATION: ENTREPRENEURIAL ECONOMICS IN AN ORGANIZATIONAL SETTING

H. W. de Jong

INTRODUCTION

This paper presents a survey of continental European thinking on the ways firms organize market transactions. This, as far as I know, has not been undertaken before, which should make one doubly cautious. On the one hand, there is no precedent, which could guide us to explore lines of development, and so there is the danger that one may attribute undue importance to particular problems, theories or writers. On the other hand, one could only see trees and miss the wood.

The second rock can only be avoided by taking a long-term perspective, looking for recurring common themes and connecting threads in the writings of those who have dealt with the subject of enquiry. Obviously, this need not exclude attention for the enfolding of concepts, theories and methods.

The first problem is a matter of debate. In order to facilitate this, the substance of the paper discusses the contributions made in the main language areas of continental Europe, viz. the German, Dutch, French and Italian.

Notwithstanding the differences in thinking between those areas, I have found as a common thread the paradigma of dynamic market development. Behind the given market structures, European economists have, throughout this century and before, detected the entrepreneur, as the moving force, who creates, reforms and destructs the organizational market forms. Such a way of viewing the field, while distinguishing it from other lines of thinking, has implications for the types of analysis. It stresses the importance of some topics and methods, while neglecting others. In presenting these European ideas as unmixed as possible (and may be even somewhat stylized), I hope that the comparison with Anglo-Saxon thinking can be promoted and, in this way,

de Jong, H. W., Shepherd, W. G. (eds) Mainstreams in Industrial Organization progress towards a future unified, industrial organization theory will be made.

Necessarily, I had to confine myself to a choice of the materials, for the subject would merit a whole book.*

I. TOWARDS A EUROPEAN MARKET THEORY; DEVELOPMENTS BETWEEN 1900 AND 1960

Industrial organization passes under various names in Europe. I will confine my remarks to continental European countries for two reasons: (1) the common language in the Anglo-Saxon countries makes reference to British developments mostly unnecessary and (2) there are, as we will see, common strands in continental thinking, which distinguish it from Anglo-Saxon.

Frequent usage is made of labels like market theory, competitive theory, external organization of the firm or the organization of the market economy and even meso-economics, as the field of studies which deals with branches of industry or the interrelationships between firms on markets. Industrial economics is a less frequently heard name, which, at least in most European languages, confines the subject, mistakenly, to the problems of manufacturing industry.

It is more important, however, that most writers, both in the past and at present, treat the same core of problems, and are moved by a basically similar way of approaching them.

These problems refer to the questions of competition and monopoly (or dominant firms or concentration) as they manifest themselves in the real world. Obviously, some abstractions are necessarily made, but they do not go so far as is usual in neo-classical micro-economic theory, where the thinking eliminates both time and space and therefore carries on the discussions on a highly abstracted plane. (H. Arndt, 1984).

In the context of this real world approach, industrial organization or market theory, has a very long history in Europe. It dates back to the Middle Ages and to the seventeenth and eighteenth centuries when the problems of competition and monopoly were intensively debated by writers in Italy, France, Germany and the Low countries. The topics discussed were the just price, the combinations of firms and their monopoly positions, the influence of the guilds, the development of industries, patents, and the Governmental regulation of markets and

*The author is grateful for discussions with and comments by H. Arndt, H. O. Lenel, P. Mariti and W. J. Vogel.

prices, to mention some of the more important.[1] Cantillon, the Physiocrats (including Turgot), J. B. Say and Adam Smith imparted a great push to the study of markets, though Smith's influence was on the continent of Europe never of such importance as in the United Kingdom or in the United States.

The same holds true for Marshall's great works. By the time Marshall dominated Anglo-Saxon economic thinking, other schools had captured the European field, namely Walrasian general equilibrium theory, the Austrian subjective value theory and the historical school. I will neglect the latter, because it hardly inspired authors to develop theories, though its adherents assembled and published wealth of empirical and historical studies. In Germany, the historical school remained dominant until the early twenties, under the influence of Sombart, Bücher, Kleinwächter, a.o. For the development of European industrial organization theory, the Austrian school has been the more important; it gave continental writers a theoretical background, which is recognizable till today.

The European approach to the study of markets is characterized by five traits:

1. *Competition* between firms in markets is seen as the central organizing principle, from which associations among firms and concentration by firms are clearly distinguished, but not as aberrations or deviations. Associations or concentration are considered to be organization principles in their own right, having their specific merits. Only, they are regulated by the all pervasive competitive principle, inherent in any market economy.

2. This was considered to be the case, because markets and their structures are not conceived statistically, but *dynamically*, that is incorporating the time element. In other words, one could not speak of a market, save in an evolutionary way, in which the roles of demand and of the entrepreneur receive a more prominent position than in the Anglo-Saxon tradition.

3. Industrial organization problems have to be treated by taking into account the *international dimension*. The background of this approach is the existence of the numerous national markets in Europe, many of which were traditionally of a small scale.

4. Partly because of the foregoing, but also because Europe for a long time lacked an adequate supply of statistics, most writers in the industrial organization field have confined themselves to *case studies* of firms and industries, many of which were made already in pre-war times. Also, the Austrian conviction that one could come far by means of deductive reasoning and 'common observation' has made its influence felt.

5. Finally, the idea that governments are involved in the market process, not as an exogeneous, correcting influence, but as one amongst the various participants – be it with its distinguishing traits – has been prominent. In this sense, European industrial organization economics has always been *policy-oriented* and remains so today with the discussions about how to promote innovation, and how to use industrial, commercial and similar policies besides competition policy. Government has often been seen as an actor, which could help steering the market process to desirable wider goals. However, since World War II, government is also seen as the authority to make the market work better, e.g., by freeing it from monopolistic constraints. This is a legacy of the Eucken school in W. Germany.

I will discuss some of these points, and show how they came about from a unified body of theory – the older Austrian school of economists – before dealing with modern developments. Modern tendencies in thinking no doubt reflect many influences from the current Anglo-Saxon approach, yet, these are grafted upon a canvas of thinking, summarized in the above mentioned points.

Competition as the central concept of market theory, was seen as the rivalry for scarce resources and for scarce customers among suppliers/ producers, and the rivalry for scarce supplies among consumers in order to improve their private positions. When writers used the term competition, they did not have in mind a state of equilibrium with many individual small suppliers but a process evolving in time, in which firms or organizations battled with each other.[2] When, in the final quarter of the nineteenth century the cartel and trust-problem made its appearance, these market organizations again were not discussed as stable market configurations, but as the processual behaviour of firms, dialectically linked with the competitive rivalrous moves.

The widely read German economist Robert Liefmann, for example, distinguishing between the absolute monopoly of a single seller (mostly based on legal privileges) and the relative monopoly (a dominant firm with a few, mostly smaller suppliers having some disadvantages) remarks that latent competition is always in the background and will be activated by price increases.[3] In reverse, competition, which in the modern economy is fiercely stimulated by the progress of technology, by the extension of communications and the reduction of transport costs and by the growth of capital, so that new firms are founded, may become so intense, that monopolistic combinations like cartels and trusts, arise. Economic reality is therefore pictured as a dialectical process of competition moving towards loose and tight combinations of firms (including monopolies) and vice versa.[4] The background of this process is the power of the other side of the market: the choosing consumer. The possibility of creating cartels and monopolies *that work*, depends on the relationships prevailing on the demand side; for, says Liefmann: not production costs determine prices, but prices determine the upper level of costs. And he goes on to list the alternatives which consumers can command. (Liefmann, 1930, pp. 133–136) The picture drawn up is far removed from the static, neo-classical market forms. It explains rising concentration (in the sense of larger firms) as the result of market extension, and the accompanying mass production and mass distribution.[5]

Austrian theory has inspired continental economists with the idea that markets evolve in time, and develop, as Carl Menger maintained, from 'bilateral monopoly' to trade between more parties and ultimately to large-scale competitive markets. Monopoly comes first when a new market arises, and, only with time does the growth of markets make competition possible (C. Menger, 1981, p. 191–225). All markets start with monopoly and move toward becoming more and more competitive. If markets grow larger, monopoly is reduced and competition is broadened. Varying Adam Smith's famous dictum, one could say that competition is limited by the extent of the market. The 'economic progress of civilization' leads to competition (Menger, 1981, pp. 224–225), for market forces break down monopoly. If the monopolist behaves in the traditional way, by under-supplying the total market, potential buyers are not satisfied when demand increases and the market grows, and the monopolist will bring about his own demise. This is not because competition reverts to a state of perfectedness, which does not exist. Menger denies that a good in a state of competition has a unique price; instead, prices are varied and dispersed (Menger 1981, pp. 191–193 and pp. 236–285). Van Wieser extended this analysis to what he called the 'monopoloïd constructions', such as public and private groupings like cartels and trusts, in which 'monopoly and competition do meet not only externally, but one and the same construction unites both, so that theory is posed with a new problem'. Here again, it is the consideration of time which colours the analysis and thereby supports the previous point, viz. that the market organization forms stand to each other in a dynamic, even dialectical relationship (Von Wieser, 1927, pp. 158–162).

Levy rounded off this analysis by arguing that the Mengerian view of declining prices in case the number of competitors increases, implies that both the level of the extra profit rate and the duration of that rate diminish with market growth. Monopoly can only persist in exceptional circumstances, for monopoly is at once being the first and the unique seller. The idea, entertained by Marx, Marshall and later on Sraffa and

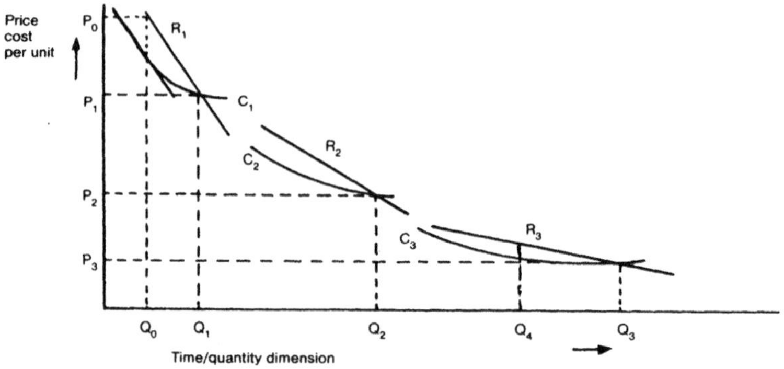

Fig. 1. The Mengerian process.

J. Robinson that monopolists exist because of a continuously declining long run average cost curve is not accepted by Austrian theory.

When demand extends, new product varieties and new processes can be introduced in accordance with the Smithian principle, and the changes that a monopolist will be able to realize these better than competitors are extremely small. Figure 1 demonstrates the sequence.

Revenue curves R_1, R_2 and R_3, both shift to the right and become more elastic. Cost curves C_1, C_2 and C_3 (representing improved and more varied products as well as lower cost processes) are pushed downward and the profit rate declines continually.

It is here that Schumpeter moved in. Well versed in older Austrian theory he had to solve the basic question implied in Figure 1: why do entrepreneurs come forward, either as initiating monopolists or as imitating competitors?

In the second edition of his Theory of Economic Development he clarified the points made by Menger and Von Weiser by defining the entrepreneur as the economic agent who exerts leadership through setting different goals and behaving differently from the common run of economic decisionmakers. Such entrepreneurs are generated by an ethnically homogeneous population according to a frequency curve: entrepreneurial capacities are distributed like the capacities for singing, playing chequers, tennis, etc. This position explains at once:

1. why numbers of competitors cannot explain competition
2. why a developed society generates a continuous stream of entrepreneurs
3. why there are small and big entrepreneurs
4. why entrepreneurs are always a minority of the population
5. why entrepreneurs are different from 'normal' businessmen ('Wirte schlechtweg und Unternehmer').

To do different things in a different way runs, however into three obstacles: it is objectively difficult, it requires subjective capacities for initiating change and it runs into social resistance. Economic leadership ('innovation') overcomes these obstacles, because it is motivated by the '*plus ultra*': to found an empire, to battle and succeed and to create something new (Schumpter, 1926, pp. 122–139). This view of the entrepreneur – perhaps somewhat exalted – is not debased when one includes material motives.

Levy* – while being fundamentally in agreement with the above – carried the pre-war analysis an important step further by discussing concentration taking the form both of trusts and cartels. In Figure 1, the initial monopolist would like to restrict supply to q_0 and fetch the high price p_0. He cannot. Competition will force the price down to p_1, where no profit is left. New product varieties and processes come forward (C_2) and, again, after an interval, competition reduces the price to p_2. The process is repeated until p_3 is reached. No profits (apart from 'normal' profits required to attract able managers and risk capital) are made by the numerous competitiors in the larger sized market.

This situation, according to Levy, may persist. But if some enabling conditions prevail, it may be changed towards concentration and even monopoly. In that case, output would have to be diminished to q_4 (Figure 1) and that could be achieved by a cartel, buying out some competitors, or a trust rationalizing production and/or sales.

Here, it is not simply a matter of reducing the number of competitors. For the suppression of competition depends not, as classical economists maintained, on the number of competitors, but on the relationship between number of suppliers and 'the anticipated monopoly advantages accruing from combination' (Levy, 1911, pp. 291–292). The greater the number of competitors is, the higher must be the anticipated increase in extra-profits (π) and the longer their prospective duration (t) in order to make effective combination (cartel or trust) worthwhile. A combination among a small number of competitors can already be achieved if the rewards are modest and/or limited in time whereas high extra-profits on a long-term basis are required to unite numerous competitors.

The curve in Figure 2 is representative for this trade-off between numbers of competitors and the expected advantages from combination.

*Levy, not an author with a wide influence (may be due to his not presenting an explicit, formal model), was to my mind, a very perceptive economist, who anticipated several points others later came to develop, e.g., the lesser importance of numbers of competitors in comparison with their behavioural dynamics, the difference between technical and economic concentration, entry barriers, product differentiation, etc.

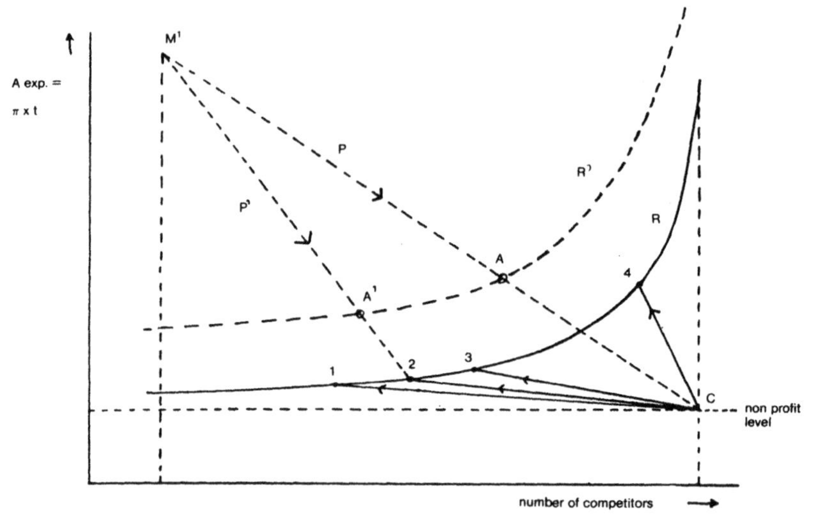

Fig. 2. Levy's model.

It shows the required levels of profits to effectuate combinations of firms with a monopoly advantage.

The line from the innovatory monopolist's position (M_i) to the state of fierce competition (C) reflects the Mengerian process depicted in Figure 1. But this state will probably not last. Some entrepreneurial organizer may perceive the opportiunities for profit inherent in the possible movement from C to points 1, . . . , 4, on the R-curve – that is, cartellization, or the formation of a holding company uniting the separate firms or of a dominant firm through concentration of output or supply.

What point can be reached on the R-curve by means of concentration, depends, according to Levy, on five enabling conditions, and their degree of fulfilment:

1. Whether the national market is protected by import duties or not. Pre-1914, C was more applicable to many industries under British free-trade conditions than to U.S. or German markets which were protected, for example at the level of point 4; similar considerations apply to other protective institutional arrangements.

2. Whether the scale of optimal plant or firm in relation to market demand is large or small. The higher the relative scale, the better a point like 1 on the R-curve can be achieved, because the risk of excess capacity for an intruder is enhanced. Even with a higher anticipated profit level, he will not enter.

3. Inelastic supply of (essential) inputs is again a factor moving a rewarding combination towards a point on the *R*-curve, for example point 2.

4. So does vertical integration which can be achieved with reductions of average cost p.u. (point 3).

5. 'Finally, the reputation of an established firm, with its own accustomed markets or regular clientele, or the inherited skill of a special class of operatives, form in certain circumstances, an element in a monopoly which must not be undervalued' (Levy, 1911, pp. 303–304) (e.g., one of the points on the *R*-curve).

It should be noted that combinations, taking up a position above the *R*-curve, like A cannot be maintained: 'If a relatively small concern is economically profitable, so that a slight increase in demand or price gives a new competitor a fair chance of existence, existing makers cannot maintain a monopoly even if they can obtain it'. It follows too that positions below *R* represent unexploited opportunities, which would remain unused if there are no enabling conditions or if entrepreneurs do not perceive the advantages inherent in the situation.

Let me add that the position of the *R*-curve within the quadrant is determined by the long-term relationship between supply and demand for the good(s) in question; in other words, excess demand shifts the curve higher, excess supply lower, so that A might be a tenable profit level for a combination facing relative excess demand in the market (on R').

If a market is created (at M_i the innovating monopolist), price is high, the number of competitors small and they face an untapped demand. However, because of this situation, competitors will come forward and shift the *R*-curve to the right, the more the potential demand is satisfied. Profits decline according to the *P*-curve as the number of competitors increases, until *C* is reached. If at the same time potential demand is exhausted, *C* will be an equilibrium point, because*R* passes through *C*. This is the limiting case of perfect competition, the only case in which it is sensible to speak of equilibrium. In points above, and to the left of *C* there is only an 'equation' of demand and supply in a temporary situation. And whereas equilibrium is hardly a reality, equation is a recurring phenomenon, be it temporary.

If *R* remains above the horizontal non-profit line because Levy's enabling conditions apply, some entrepreneur may seize the opportunity to effect a combination. For example, he might move his branch association to propose the government to introduce an important tariff. If so, point 4 on the *R*-curve, would be reached, with all firms achieving extra profits. But this is *not* an equilibrium point, it only equates demand and supply in the protected market. If a foreign firm enters and starts competition, point 4 will move downwards and to the right. The entrepreneur would then be forced to propose a new combination (e.g., a branch sales syndicate) thereby moving point 4 to the left and upwards. The entrepreneur might rationalize production within the syndicate (increasing economies of scale) or use the syndicate to control some inelastic input, and the new point 4 might become a tenable position. It follows that entrepreneurial activity is crucial in the whole process of market development between M_i and C. At first, the Mengerian competitive process exerts a pressure towards (but probably never arriving at) the state of equilibrium at C, both by increasing the number of competitors and by shifting R to the right. But, because both factors interact, entrepreneurs can hardly determine at what location they are. Only if demand growth stabilizes, and the growth rate becomes predictable an entrepreneur can spot an opportunity for combination, and see what form this combination should have.

All this means that entrepreneurial action (the process) determines the market structure, and, in reverse, given structures may (provided the enabling factors prevail) prompt entrepreneurs to start a process of combination. Process and structure are seen as interdependent.

Up till now, it was assumed that the P-curve (profit decline as the market grows and competitors increase) follows a straight line from M_i to C. But suppose the rivalry is exceptionally fierce, based, e.g., on successive innovations or the presence of some very efficient firms. Then the P-curve may decline faster (P') and, even with the same number of competitors, the profit level will be lower.

Given R, a profit position of A^1 of the combination would not be tenable, but a position in 2 might well be, for example, based on reputation.

If, however the R'-curve applies (temporary excess demand, or an untapped long-term demand) A' might well be a tenable position. A further inference is that fierce competition exerts a tendency towards the formation of high concentration whereas less intense competition (e.g., P'' above P) exerts a tendency towards the making of cartels or loose collusions.

Thus, in Levy's model – which I have diagrammatically presented – the question of the formation of a combination and its possible and tenable profitability depends on:

– the supply-demand relationships during market development
– the intensity of competition, only partially given by numbers of competitors and

– a set of objective, enabling factors, partly of technical and partly of an institutional/political nature.

However, the moving agent of the process is always an entrepreneur, spotting the opportunities inherent in the situation.

The culmination of research into the concentration problem found its expression in the publication of the two volumes on Economic Concentration in 1960 (second edition 1970), edited by H. Arndt. Arndt said in the introduction that concentration had become an all embracing phenomenon in modern society, with far reaching implications for various domains. It needed a broad approach, taking into account not only the economic, but the many non-economic aspects (legal, fiscal, etc.) as well. At the same time he noted a trend in thinking towards theoretical explanations away from the prevailing empiricism which had been current before the war. No doubt, the many contributions by international authors to the volumes were partly responsible for this, as well as the attractions the new field offered to theoretically minded economists. More important, the concept of dynamic competition started to make headway, as we will see in the next sections.

As regards the policy inferences to be drawn from the growth of trusts and combinations, economists parted company. Some, like Levy argued that planning by the state comes near to compulsory cartellization and should be avoided because it would (1) expose the state to many risks and responsibilities it could not bear, and (2) might lead up to over-concentration, 'which might have just as fatal results as has had the rationalization craze' (Levy, 1936, p. 265) because the natural tendencies towards concentration are not present, everywhere and at all times and 'sometimes not at all' (Levy, 1936, p. 257). Others, like F. de Vries and J. Marchal, insisted that the structure of the economy which had been determined by individualistic principles was being fundamentally transformed under the influence of associationist movements and that both theory and policy had to be radically tranformed.[7]

In the immediate postwar period a very influential line of thinking came forward with the writings of the so-called Eucken school. It added another dimension to the problem. One of the central points – Eucken maintained – is the possible divergence in market economies between private and social interests. The treatment of monopoly power requires competition and other policies on behalf of the state which has the obligation to maintain a competitive order. Eucken was less fortunate in posing as a norm for such a policy the concept of 'full competition', by which he understood, not a market structure but the behaviour of firms – even of oligopolists – who accept the market price as given. The criticisms in following decades by 'neo-Austrians' on this concept, in which they rightly pointed out that firms in dynamic competition also set prices in the game, nevertheless erred in simultaneously equating private and social interests, as long as those dynamic firms are free to act as they please. That means, as Lenel pointed out, a retrogression from Smith to Quexnay, with his dubious philosophical concept of a 'natural order'. (Lenel, 1957). There is no doubt that the views, expressed by the Eucken school contributed to the inauguration of competition policies in W. Germany as well as in the European Community, a historical breakthrough on the continent.

II. THE FLOWERING OF DYNAMIC MARKET THEORY IN GERMANY AND HOLLAND SINCE 1960

Levy's was not a bad piece of analysis, formulated already in 1911, even in comparison with Schumpeter's which appeared in 1912. It might be argued that the model is not specific enough; though this is true, it has to be balanced against other advantages. If one opts for a dynamic analysis, the gains in realism carry the price of some indeterminism. Also, dynamic analysis can provide for a theoretical framework, encompassing the market process, which is lacking from static analysis. Into such a dynamic framework, static market situation models can be inserted and given their place.

This is what European economists have done in the postwar period and what differentiates them from the Anglo-Saxon approach using the structure-conduct-performance paradigm. Indeed, many continental Europeans have followed the market growth-decline paradigm, distinguishing between phases of development and the market situations prevailing during those phases.[8] The plausibility of this was strongly underlined by the course of many European industries, which started their growth curves in the post-war years, adopting new products and new technological and organizational processes often originating in the United States. After fast expansion in the fifties and sixties, maturity was reached in the seventies and decline followed in the early eighties. Naturally, the expansion paths differed in the timing between the sectors. In general, the approach led to the idea that the market development phases show different forms and intensities of competition, as firms use alternative competitive parameters (price, advertising, product innovation and variation, take-overs, diversification, etc.) suited to differing conditions of demand growth and demand elasticities. Processes of concentration had to be explained by falling back '. . . on the specific development conditions of an industry or market sector, because a durable growth advantage of large units in all sectors cannot be proved historically. Concentration processes thus have to be seen as industry specific' (K. Brandt, 1971, p. 280).

These basic ideas were worked on in Germany and the Netherlands starting from the Schumpeterian innovator, and in this way a truly entrepreneurial economics arose. The Schumpeterian view had the great advantage that it freed economic theory from the homo economicus, who was central in neo-classical theory. In one stroke, the shackles of the mechanistic view of economic life were broken. But, as Heuss (1965, pp. 9–16) noted, the Schumpeterian entrepreneur has two important limitations:

– first that he acts only within the context of the economy as a whole, giving rise to innovations and clusters of these, investment waves and various types of cycles, relevant to the total economy;
– second, that the Schumpeterian entrepreneur was contrasted only with the traditional type of businessman – the non-pioneer.

In addition to this, my main point was, that, whatever Schumpeterian theory said about motives and types, the continuity and the directions of entrepreneurial moves are left in the dark, whereas this is of fundamental importance for the problems of industrial organization. This naturally leads to the research into horizontal, vertical and diversification strategies of firms.

So two routes were chosen.

Heuss, in West Germany, developed a typology of entrepreneurs, dividing them into four types:

1. the innovator-pioneer;
2. the imitative entrepreneur, showing initiatives like the first type but not in a pathbreaking way;
3. the conservative entrepreneur adapting to the changing market circumstances, initiated by others; and
4. the immobile businessman not even adapting, but simply doing the usual things until he is ousted from the field.

These four types were not meant to be a general typology, reflecting innate human characteristics, but conceptional, analytical instruments, used for explaining the stages of market development. For, as Heuss underlined, entrepreneurial acts are 'mirrored' in the making and unmaking of markets. Production, costs, demand, etc. are not simply given, as is maintained in traditional theory, but are the parameters of action, through which market types arise. In one and the same person, therefore, different conceptional types may occur at different times, as for example, with Schumacher (in the U.S. cereals industry) or Henry Ford and Heinz Nordhoff in motor-cars who were one-time pioneers, but thereafter remained dedicated to old-fashioned products or methods. Now, two general propositions follow:

1. The entrepreneurial type changes with market development phases, and
2. The relationships between these entrepreneurial types shift with either complementary and reinforcing effects or with substitutive consequences.

The first proposition is supported by a probability analysis, in which the supposition is made that among 10 entrepreneurs, one will be of the initiating type and 9 will be of the conservative type. Depending on whether the entrance of new firms to the industry is supposed to occur (and this is linked to the development phase) and the likelihood that initiating entrepreneurs will shift to successive stages, it follows that sooner or later, the conservative type will come to prevail, and market behaviour will show different characteristics in the course of time. With respect to the second proposition, Heuss' analysis of a number of combinations of similar and different entrepreneural types shows that, depending on the stage of market development, entrepreneurs may stimulate or block each other's actions. I cannot follow the intricate analysis here in all its complexity, but one example may suffice: the action of imitative entrepreneurs during the expansion stage will reinforce the pioneer's behaviour, extending the market, bringing prices and costs downwards, etc., whereas the same type will block innovative behaviour during the maturity phase.[9]

There is not enough 'market room' during maturity to accommodate imitation. If, in contrast, the pioneer rivals with conservative and *a forteriori*, immobile types of businessmen, he may continue introducing innovations because these types afford him 'competitive room'.

The picture which emerges from this analysis is that a complementary relationship will prevail if there is sufficient 'room', whereas a substitutive relationship between firms occurs if that is not the case. The 'room' provided depends on market and competitive factors, and both are linked to the development stages of a market. If firms have a tendency to block each other, cartels, mergers and other combinatory moves will follow. But suppose the types diverge very much (for example one pioneer among many conservative firms), the expansion phase will be held back in its development, whereas the declining phase will be speeded up. This analysis, based on types of entrepreneurs is preceded by a penetrating research of each development stage and rounded off by bringing into the game the demand and cost factors in one- and multi-product firms (Heurs, 1965, Chapter 5).

One important objection against the Heussian type of analysis may be that it easily gets too complicated, not resulting in testable hypotheses. In fact, the analysis is rich in deductive, probabilistic and mathematically orientated derivations, but short of empirical contents. This objection was met by later researches, analysing sectors and firm cases (H. Schlögl, 1972; Kanfer, 1980; I. Oberender, 1984) from the point of view of a simpler model of market development.

Another objection might be that it leaves the development directions of firms in the dark. The Dutch analysis was oriented towards the directions entrepreneurial moves take, may be inspired by the growth of large firms like Shell, Unilever, Philips, Sté Générale, and the like.[10]

The basic fact about a market economy is that firms do have relationships with each other, because they cannot avoid each others actions. Entrepreneurial acts determine the timing and direction of these relationships in order to combine resources with a view to future production and sales. If markets develop according to growthcycles, entrepreneurial acts of a greater or lesser importance are required in every stage of development and not only when founding a new firm or plant as Schumpeter said. With such acts, responding to new oppportunities, entrepreneurs stamp both the market process and the required structures. The 'right' moves generate profits, the 'wrong' ones losses: both are residuals, arising out of performances, windfalls and power positions. Market structures are composed out of the working of three basic principles of coordinative behaviour between firms, namely those of (1) a rivalrous, competitive nature, or cooperatively and collusively oriented, or of a dominating nature (de Jong, 1982, Chapter 1). These principles of coordinative behaviour operate along horizontal, vertical and diagonal lines as entrepreneurs direct their creative and imitative activities towards the improvement of their firm's market position. However, entrepreneurs' freedom of action and their choices of directive strategy are limited by the stages of market development and the related characteristics. This means, for example, that competitive, horizontal rivalry increases during the expansion phase, but subsides and/or changes substantially during the maturity phase of a market, whereas a market in decline normally shows so-called ruinous competition (which should be taken literally, not morally: capacities have to be reduced to a lower level, or scrapped). Similarly, vertical integration and disintegration are often linked to expanding and contractive tendencies,* while diversification is pursued when the firms reach maturity in their previous activities and are sufficiently profitable to finance take-overs. In expansion there is no need to diversify, in decline there are usually no resources available. It is worthwhile to underline a few qualifying comments:

1. The theory only predicts tendencies, because individual firms may either do nothing, or make the wrong decisions, or be late in adapting themselves. Being a 'thruster' or a 'sleeper' also affects performance.

2. Major innovations may distort the sequence of market phases. For example, an important innovation may mean renewed growth for an industry after maturity, or may prolong the expansion phase.

3. The use of action parameters (pricing, advertising, merger activity, location, etc.) will shift during market phases, and will be chosen by entrepreneurs in accordance with the prevailing type of market organization.

4. Policy measures as well as general cyclical movements are influential in retarding or accelerating the tendencies and may occasionally shift the direction of market development.

5. Welfare considerations can be applied to this version of the growth-cycle theory. Two examples may illustrate this:

(a) Dynamic market theory implies that governmental policies which sustain mature and/or declining industries by means of protection, subsidies or the permitted formation of structural cartels are seriously mistaken, because they bring about wastages of scare resources and lead to industrial senility. Dutch economists of the growth cycle orientation have fiercely opposed such 'aid'. Support for innovative industries can, on the contrary and under certain conditions, be defended as more sensible (G. J. Wyers, 1981. For contrary news see Hindley, 1983).

(b) Kaufer has argued that mergers in the introductory and expansion phases practically always are – per se – opposed against the achievement of a net welfare benefit, whereas mergers in the late maturity phase and, in particular, during stagnation, may well achieve these. He bases this conclusion on the possiblility that the latter type of mergers can reduce costs through rationalization and the closing of suboptimal plants (Kaufer 1980, pp. 305–310). This is what Levi maintained in the twenties. In Figure 3 average costs per unit are reduced from AC_1 to AC_2. If the merged firm gets a monopoly or a dominant position, it will be able to raise the price from p_0 to p_1, reducing output to q_1. A net welfare benefit will follow if: $W_2 > W_1 + W_3$ (the analysis is a bit more complicated

*Research in this field, which is meagre, suggests the links are tenuous and apply may be more to individual firms.

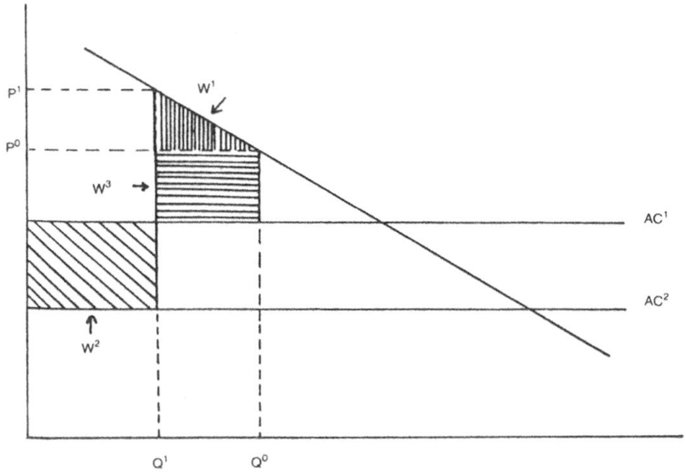

Fig. 3. A cost reducing merger in the maturity phase.

than can be reproduced here, taking into account suppositions are demand elasticity, m.o.s. in relation to current scale, degree of market power before merger, etc.). The main considerations are that introductory phase mergers *between market participants* (diversification mergers is another matter) do not achieve scale advantages faster than internal growth, whereas the interdependency between the investment decision of oligopolists in maturity/stagnation, which threatens/deadlock, can be avoided by merger. On the basis of reasonable assumptions, the maturity mergers bringing small savings in costs would be a net benefit, even if the monopolistic price increases were substantial[11] (Kaufer, 1980, pp. 305–310).

Analytically, dynamic market theory is an extension of the previously described Mengerian process and of the Levi model. From an innovatory monopoly, the market expands towards fierce competition, ending in the reorganization of the industry by entrepreneurs, who devise combinations (cartels, syndicates, dominating firms through take-overs and mergers) during maturity. When market decline enters, the dialectical pendulum gets reversed: from concentration to ruinous competition, with reorganizations, and, sometimes, splitting-up of firms and de-mergers. Basic innovations are necessary to start the wheel turning again. Mostly, these will imply new growthcycles, either in the same or in different industries.

What is the truth value of the theory ('truth' is meant here to express correspondence to reality, not internal consistency or coherence to use Blanshard's term)? Numerous sector studies have found that industries, products or brands, go through growthcycles, though the number and lengths of stages, as well as the periodicity and amplitude of cycles vary. And, application of the theory to a particular episode – e.g. overcapacity problems during stagnation in the synthetic fibres market (Fehland Oberender, 1984) – may also be enlightening. But cross-sectional researches have been scarce and suffer from the difficulty to adequately measure the real degree of concentration. One such study for Dutch industry as a whole as well as for manufacturing industry in particular (89, three digit product classes) during the period 1952–1983, confirmed the theory in a general sense: 'One could describe the development of the Dutch economy with the aid of the growth-cycle. Analysis of the postwar period shows that manufacturing industry in the fifties and sixties went through strong expansion, but meanwhile has reached the maturity or stagnation phase. In contrast, commercial services are clearly in a more favourable position; notwithstanding the stagnating economy reasonable growth figures are reached. This sector is in a previous phase of the growthcycle than manufacturing industry' (Webbink, 1984, p. 20). For the Dutch building and construction industry, a former colleague (Hendriks, 1984), traced a cycle throughout the twentieth century and predicted in the late sixties a structural turnaround in the seventies and eighties, because capacity had outrun demand on a long-term basis, and the composition of demand was changing. Up till now this prognosis has been perfectly right, though policymakers and employers did not accept the advice to low down building activity. Let me add that this industry became heavily concentrated during the stagnationary period (a five firm oligopoly) and diversified abroad. Still, the failure rate, also among the big five, has been severe when ruinous competition followed in the late seventies.

However, growthcycle theory is not a perfect description of economic reality. No theory can achieve that. Its main advantage is that it teaches economists that markets are dynamic and that process, structure and performance are interrelated, because of entrepreneurial action.

III. OPTIMAL COMPETITION DEBATED

Another dynamic theory which has found adherence among European economists is the theory of workable competition, of which the most prominent representation is due to Erhard Kantzenbach.[12] (Kantzenbach, 1966). Fierce discussions have followed the introduction of the concept of workable competition in Europe, following the trial set by J. M. Clark in the United States. Rejecting static equilibrium theory, Kantzenbach described competition as an evolutionary and disequilibrium process, in which rivalry prevails. The rivalrous competition is only an instrument to achieve social welfare goals, of which three are outstanding: the growth of the social product, the optimal distribution and composition of the social product and the promotion of a flexible adaptation of the economy to changing circumstances.

These goals are not served equally by the two main functions (technical progress, flexible adaption) which require substantial degrees of monopoly and market imperfection. Consequently, optimal competition is a compromise between the two extremes, and, though difficult to quantify or to measure, is to be found when loose oligopolistic market structures with some degree of product differentiation and market intransparency prevail.

For Kantzenbach, the distinction between potential and effective intensity of competition is decisive. Oligopoly is not general interdependency of sellers, but the dependency of a particular seller on the behaviour of an individual competitor, who may threaten his existence. This creates a high degree of insecurity, which is at a maximum in a homogeneous duopoly situation and very low in polypolistic markets.

The insecurity depends on the divergence of cost functions, relative liquidity reserves as between companies and the short term demand shifts in the market, which are all difficult to know. Both owner controlled and management controlled firms strive for long term security (be it for different reasons), however, so that potential and effective competitive intensity diverge the more strongly the less the number of competing oligopolists and the more homogeneous the products sold become.

Stated simply: potential competition intensity rises when less and less sellers of homogeneous goods threaten to wipe out one of them by means of unforeseen actions. The same facts induce restraints on competition though, because nobody wants to be wiped out. Figure 4 gives a simple presentation, in which Kantzenbach's three dimensional scheme (cf. p. 93 of his book) has been reduced to two dimensions. A duopoly will have unlimited potential competition, but the effective degree will be very low. Between 6 and 12 competitors, there will be workable competition, and the optimal degree will be at 9 competitors.

The six competitors who have effective competition amongst themselves (because the curve bends backwards from this point, the area of workable competition is reached), have a much higher degree of potential competition, so that they will have either some product differentiation or will practise some restraints of competition, which are tolerable. Beyond 12 competitors, the degree of effective competition sinks below the tolerable, and gradually mergers or other restraints of competition would become desirable (obviously, the chosen numbers are artificial).

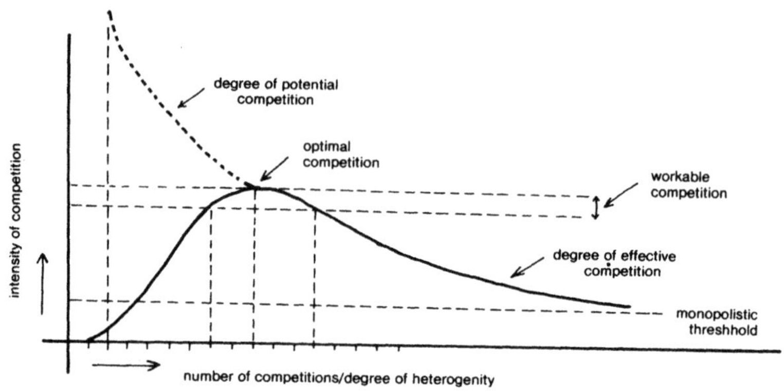

Fig. 4.

Oligopolistic interdependency is not restricted to horizontal relations between firms, but also relate to vertical liaisons. Schematising the intensity and the direction of controls between firms, one arrives at the following presentation of competitive restraints (Kantzenbach, p. 101), which are further discussed by the author.

It follows that real markets may have either over or under optimal degrees of competition. Competition policy's task is therefore to counter both situations and tendencies in which the intensity of competition potentially is suboptimal (e.g., promotion of concentration, the raising of scale of operations and an increase in product differentiation or particular cartel types) or overoptimal (some splitting up of trusts, the prevention of some mergers, or the prevention of oligopolistic pricewars in order to avoid the formation of uncontrolled monopolies). Essentially, polypolistic competition lacks dynamic progress, while tight oligopoly

Table 1. Organizational forms of competitive restraints

Intensity	Direction	
	Horizontal	Vertical
Coordinated behaviour	Groupdiscipline, concerted action	Traditional business relationships
Agreements	Cartels, agreed business conditions	Long term delivery agreements
Interlocking relationships	Capital participations, syndicates, interlocking directorates	Capital participations, interlocking directorates, co-direction
Mergers, takeovers	Trusts, concerns	Vertical concerns

carries the dangers of non-functional power battles and/or collusion. Typically, ruinous competition occurs in polypolistic situations, according to the workability theory, because firms are too small, do not have financial means to undertake innovations and behave only traditionally (recall that in the growthcycle theory, ruinous competition occurs in recessionary stages between large firms).

As stated before, the workability theory was criticized from various sides.

1. One criticism of the workability concept (by Hoppmann and others) has pointed out that the inherent antithesis between perfect competition (polipoly), in which there is no progress and monopoly/tight oligopoly in which there is no optimal allocation or distribution, is wrong. There is a dilemma in the goals competition has to serve only if competition is seen as an instrument to serve general economic goals. If, in contrast, competition is conceived of as a discovery process, the freedom (equated to an atomistic market structure) to compete and the achievement of desirable results are identical: there will be no dilemma. Exceptionally, Hoppmann says, some natural barriers (economies of scale, exit barriers, etc.) may prevent competition altogether. However, this objection assumes an identity of private freedom of action and the resulting advantages with social advantages. Such an assumption is difficult to sustain; by means of competition firms may discover worthwhile economic advantages as well as ways to reduce or eliminate competition itself.

2. The Dutch Competition Law of 1956 was also based on the theory of workable competition. Reviewing the achievements of 25 years of Dutch competition policy, the president of the competition commission remarked that the concept is rather vague: if the intensity of competition is judged by the fastness with which a seller's advantage is spoiled, the reactionary move may not be too fast, otherwise the creation of the advantage will not be undertaken, nor too slow, so that monopoly will last longer than necessary. But what is 'too' in both cases? In addition, the judgement can only be made ex-post, which is too late for policy actions. And, finally, what is wanted in present times is the stimulation of price competition, and this is not served by meticulous considerations of 'optimality' (Van der Weijden, 1981). While it is true that in inflationary times more emphasis could be given to price competition in competition policy, the objection with respect to vagueness would not seem to dismantle the structural version of the workability theory. For the theory maintains that in the 'right' structural composition of a market – that is loose oligopolies – advantages will be created and competed away. As long as both types of actions occur, the system does work, may be not

in an absolutely optimal sense, but at least relatively as compared to atomistic and monopolistic market structures.

3. Let me discuss another point. It is by no means clear that monopolies and tight oligopolies do promote innovations best, as is assumed in the workability theory. My former colleague Hennipman (1954) reviewed the deductive arguments pro and con already in the fifties and came to the conclusion that no clear verdict can be given. Recently published industry studies sustain that position.

On the basis of two books, assembling European industry studies (Shepherd *et al.*, 1983; Oberender (ed., 1984) two tables were constructed comprising resp. 32 European and 14 West German industries. In these tables (Tables 2 and 3) degrees of concentration and of innovativeness,

Table 2. Concentration and innovativeness in four European countries and the EEC

Industries	W. Germany		France		Italy		U.K.		E.C.	
	Conc.	Inn.	Conc.	Inn.	Conc.	Inn.	Conc.	Inn.	Conc.	Inn.
Textiles	C	M	W	L	C	H	T	L	C	L/M
Steel	T	H	T	L	M	M	M	L	W	M
Ship-building	W	H	T	L	M	L	T → M	L	W	M
Motorcars	T	H	T	M/H	M	M/H	T	L	W	M/H
Elec. power plant	T	H	T	M/H	M	L	T	M	T	M
Process plant contracting*	W	H	T	L	T	L	T	M	W	H
Machine tools	C	H	C	L	C	M	C	L	C	M
Semiconductors	W	M	W	M	W	M	W	M	W	M

*Means technology autonomously generated (Germany), or by plant manufacturers or institutes, as in France, the U.K., and Italy.

Matrix

		Degree of innovativeness			
		Low	Medium	High	
Levels of concentration	C	2	2	2	6
	W	1	3	3	7
	T	6	3	4	13
	M	4	2	–	6
Total industries		13	10	9	32

Note: Based on the industry studies made in G. Shepherd, F. Duchêne and C. Saunders (ed. 5), Europe's industries, Public and private strategies for change, London 1983.
Legend: C = competition: W = wide oligopoly; T = tight oligopoly; M = monopoly or dominant firm.

Table 3. Concentration and innovativeness in West German industries.

Industry	Degree of concentration	Innovativeness
Breweries	Wide oligopoly	No innovations
Pharmaceuticals	Tight oligopolies in therapeutic markets	High, but decreasing rate of innovativeness
Synthetic fibres	High concentration	Many innovations
Spirits	Protected monopoly with many firms	Exceptional innovations
Tourism	Dominant, tight oligopoly	Few innovations, recently
Press, magazines	High concentration	Many innovations
Banking	Wide oligopoly	Important innovations
Insurance	Low concentration	Very few innovations
Transport (counted as 2 sectors)	Very high to very low	No innovations
Cigarettes	Tight oligopoly, with initially dominant firm	Continuous stream of small innovations
Motorcars	Tight oligopolies in mass cars and expensive cars	Stream of small innovations, with a few more important
Mineral oil industry	Tight oligopoly	Not much in the past but some important ones underway
Electricity generation	Long standing, high concentration with interrelationships between firms and public regulation	Mixed record in the past; not generally impressive

Matrix

		Degree of innovativeness			
		Low	Medium	High	Total
Levels of concentration	C	2	–	–	2
	W	1	–	1	2
	T	2	2	4	8
	M	2	–	–	2
Total industries		7	2	5	14

Note: Based on industry studies made in P. Oberender (ed.), Marktstruktur und Wettbewerb in der Bundesrepublik Deutschland, München 1983 (Market structure and competition in the Federal Republic of Germany).

Legend: C = competition or low concentration; W = wide oligopoly; T = tight oligopoly; M = monopoly or dominant firm.

as reported by the economists who made these studies, were linked to each other for the four major European countries, and seperately for West Germany. They reflect concentration and innovativeness as it was during the seventies. Concentration is divided into low (competition), medium (wide oligopoly), high (tight oligopoly) and very high (monopoly or a dominant supplier). Innovativeness is compared internationally within the branch, not between branches, and is divided into three categories.

In the *first table*, some industries have also been given a European rating, as their sales are to a large extent internationally oriented. The matrix, linking concentration and innovativeness gives a dispersed outcome. Competitive industries, with a low degree of concentration, are in all three categories of innovativeness, as is the case with wide oligopolies, which score much better in the medium and highly innovative categories, though. There is a tendency for tight oligopolies and monopolies to be more represented in the category of low innovativeness. The best one could say on the basis of this matrix, is that monopolies and dominant positions (the fourth entry), do not seem to be linked with innovative progressiveness.

In the second table, the two tendencies seem to be that monopolistic, competitive and widely oligopolistic industries, product little or no innovations, whereas some six tightly organized sectors generated medium to high amounts of innovativeness. This picture does not square completely with the one following from the German record in the first table, where a number of competitively structured sectors like textiles and machine-tools, scored relatively well, as did a few wide oligopolies (shipbuilding, process plant contracting and semiconductors). The two tables, in so far as they report on West Germany, do overlap only in motorcars, so the choice of sectors seems important. In the second table, there is a high proportion of non-manufacturing sectors. (Two sectors in the German book were not reported: the agricultural industry and residential building. Both are too regulated to be instructive.)

IV. FRANCE/BELGIUM: THE FIRM'S MARKET STRATEGY

The concept of the growth cycle has not been absent in French language publications on market theory in the post-war period, but was joined by two other types of theory starting resp. from the firm's strategy and the Marxist accumulation principle. In common with the European tradition, these alternative theoretical orientations were dynamic but the distinguishing characteristic is the emphasis on the behavior of individual firms.

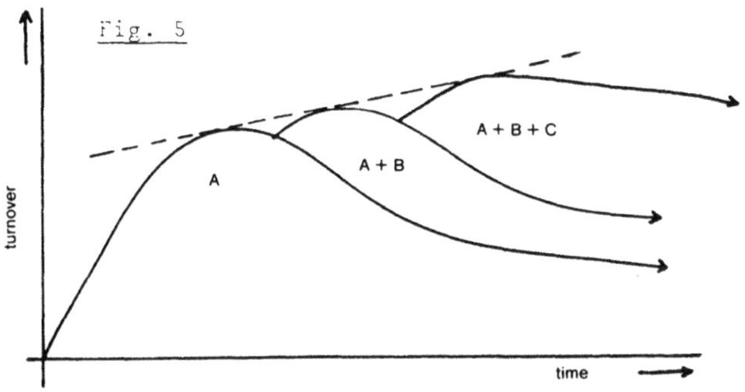

Fig. 5.

Teissier du Cros described the life of an enterprise as 'a sequence of projects'.[13] Such projects take first an increasing share of the firm's turnover, then decrease and are followed by successive projects. When the cumulative revenue of these projects ensures a rising envelope curve, the firm's growth is assured be it with ups and downs. It may benefit from an ample supply of production factors, like specialized labour, capital or credits and use the institutional power, linked with its name (Figure 5). This picture is fairly representative of the growth of large European firms, especially in complex sectors like electrotechnical industry (Philips, Siemens), chemical industry (the big three in Germany or AKZO and DSM in Holland) or foods (Unilever, Nestlé).

Moreover, this way of looking at the firm provides a link with those theorists who may be reluctant to accept the industry life cycle idea schema but put an emphasis on the firm's strategic long term policies and its use of market and extra market power. The desire for power is directly linked with that for profits, says Jacquemin (1967, 1975), for power is to be defined as the capacity to change the environment including the market structure by the firm's conduct. Like Teissier du Cros, he underlined the possibility that such firms, by means of their entrepreneurial dynamism and power, may convert barriers of entry into stimuli, or to put it otherwise, to turn the tables on their competitors. This type of analysis may also be linked to internal synergy or economies of scope and to the Penrosian economies of growth.

Still one step further, firms may develop endogeneous competition, which can be defined as the use of stimulating competitive impulses in specific markets between economic resources which are generated and controlled by a unique and joint power centre (Linda, 1980 and 1984). Various forms may be distinguished (see Table 4). Endogenous competition can take place at the level of firms and of products. In the first case, the competition may assume both a simple and a complex character.

Table 4. Forms of endogenous competition.

		Level of firms → *Simple*	*Complex*
Level of products	*Global*	Tuborg-Carlsberg } compete Heineken-Amstel } in beers but belong to same group	Zanussi machines sold by AEG, Hoover, etc. Different firms
	Partial	Volkswagen components supplied to Volkswagen cars and Audi cars, belonging to same group	Thomson Brand motors and compressors incorporated in own products as well as in competitors'.

If two companies within the same firm compete with similar products, the endogenous competition is said to be simple (one firm) and global (the whole product), for example Tuborg and Carlsberg beers, or Heineken and Amstel beers. It is said to be complex and global if the firm sells its product itself, as well as through its competitors, who stamp it with their own brands (Zanussi electrical white goods, sold by AEG, Bosch and Hoover and by Zanussi).

In contrast, endogenous competition may also develop in a complex-partial way, if a firm delivers parts of products to itself and to competitors, e.g., Thomson Brand selling motors, pumps and compressors for incorporation into competitors' washing machines and refrigerators as well as into its own products. And endogenous competition may be simple and partial, when parts are used in products of subsidiaries which compete directly with each other: a case would be Volkswagen's components used in both Volkswagen-cars and Audi-cars. In the partial variant, vertical relationships always prevail, in contrast to the global variant.

Endogenous competition may be promoted by high overhead costs, because the lure to take additional orders on the basis of low marginal costs is great; by a possible realization of important economies of scale, while the decentralization of decisionmaking within a group is an essential prerequisite. It may achieve non-negligible advantages, such as the recognition of the entrepreneurial factor and flexibility.* Endogenous competition can easily degenerate, however. In the global variant that might bring over-intensive competition, as occurred between the divisions

*Especially within diversified forms with many subsidiaries in Europe one will nowadays encounter many large firms of which the top management cultivates endogenous competition.

of Apple computers, or between the subsidiaries of a Dutch transport group who fought each other until no profits were left. In the partial variant, squeezing and discriminating pricing strategies always lurk in the background. Moreover, here as in other cases of very intensive competition, the way out is often a policy of centralization, that is horizontal and vertical concentration of decisionmaking. The unsolved problem of endogenous competition is therefore: how to make the group's decisionmaking organization as 'flat' as possible (currently much in fashion in Europe), without spoiling the necessary minimum amount of coordinated behaviour. What is saved in costs may be easily lost at the competitive front.

The French/Belgium approach was initially strongly influenced by Jacques Houssiaux, who stimulated the study of industrial organization in France in the fifties and sixties (Houssiaux, 1958, 1960).

1. In the sixties and early seventies, the study of concentration, optimal firm size and economic power dominated the scenery. A. Bienaymé (1969) and J. Parent (1970) for example, started from the big firm; Parent said that 'the enlargement of markets and technical progress are the two most powerful dynamic forces behind the processes of growth and concentration of enterprises' (Parent, 1970, p. 51). For a given technique, there is a minimum of production costs. An increase of output would necessitate a second, third or fourth unit within the same firm or more firms of the same nature, having an optimum production rate. No particular incitation to increase concentration is involved in this state of affairs. But a new technique would do so, becoming more efficient if market size permits. It will only be introduced if the maket is enlarged, bringing concentration in its train. So for each size of market, there is a necessary and optimum degree of concentration, which is only broken if market growth occurs. The competition will bring down profit rates, speed up the introduction of new techniques and declench further concentration. In this way, Parent, like Levy, explained the irregular phenomenon of concentration, or alternatively stated, the dialectics of competition and combination between firms. Several factors, however, spoil this simple model. According to Parent:

(a) different branches have different rates of market-growth, and undergo different technical developments, leading up to varying optimal sizes.

(b) the concentration movement might be retarded or speeded up, depending upon whether new techniques are ready and have only to be applied, or still have to be developed, often in successive steps.

(c) again, firms may well react with different speeds, and, also, fast market expansion generates investment euphories, which lead up to 'overcapitalization' (over-investment) when market growth declines, and stagnation occurs. 'The concentration which is linked to economic growth will therefore come when growth becomes less vivid' (Parent, 1970, p. 59).

Big firms have a number of advantages over small firms, and by means of their internal dynamics (innovation, merger, vertical integration, etc.) assure their vitality, because growth is not so much – as in the small firm – an act of will; growth of the large firm is based on an institutionalized organization, is promoted by the lure of monopoly or dominancy and by lesser vulnerability to incidental developments (Parent, 1970, pp. 86–88). Between big firms an uneasy relationship comes to prevail: monopolies though not absent, are rare, so oligopoly situations (tight oligopoly, mostly with a fringe) are common and pose two main problems: price fixing and the sharing of profits, as well as the stability problem, the latter derived from the former. The relationships between large firms oscillate between two poles: rivalry, coupled with, often secretive pricing policies, and cooperation or collusion in combinations, though the result is the same; the rivalry 'with drawn knives' or the cartellization/merger activities ensure that 'oligopoly is only a transitory form' (Parent, 1970, p. 180). Cartels and other combinations, far from being stable structures, are transitory and play havoc with concentration, with the long term goal to dominate the sector market. Parent arrives at the same conclusion as Levy six decades earlier: the fiercer the rivalry among oligopolists, the earlier they will settle for an embracing concentration even with relatively low profit margins, the more so as the merged group may well be able to rationalize on cost and inefficient structures. Less intensive competition may lead up to cartellization, which, to maintain intact, needs higher profit margins (Parent, 1980, pp. 186–7).

However, there are restraints and stimuli. These are dependent on entry by new producers, or lateral entry, and on market growth, on the one hand; on scale economies in relation to market size, vertical integration advantages, the command of scarce resources and the creation of loyalties on the other hand. The outcome is uneasy balance, in which two factors will be decisive: public policy and internationalization. Public policy often promotes concentration of firms in large enterprises, many times in the form of public companies. And these large groupings issue in multinationalization, which is the irreversible modern phenomenon. The more firms are able to handle both dimensions, the better will they be able to survive in the battle field.

2. A second approach, clearly visible in the French language area, is to start from the theory of the firm. This is a method oriented towards a micro-economic analysis which puts great emphasis on the decision

making system, on growth objectives and on the resulting performance. Market structure is made dependent on firm strategy, as in the first approach, but the striving for maximum profits is replaced by the maximalization of a utility function specific to a firm or on 'satisfactory profits'. In a dynamic approach, made obligatory, because the firm, with its long term strategy, uses the market structures as variables, performance has only a faint relationship with the outcomes of static competition, monopoly or oligopoly models; instead, the innovation dimension often assumes primary importance. 'The entrepreneur is not the slave of his environment, . . . but . . . acts on the development of markets (Jacquemin, 1975, p. 7). This point of departure has inspired numerous European authors to publish general works on possible strategies, in which statistical and econometrical analyses do not figure: a failure to measure phenomena either because data were not available or because of the supposed qualitative nature of events. Jacquemin's work was the first in the French language to try to remedy this and he used many data and previous findings to test partial theories or relationships in the European context. This was an ingenious work, though the findings mainly confirmed previous views. For example, on the relationship between size and profitability, growth and R&D, the findings were (Jacquemin, 1975, Chapter 44):

– As to the relationship between size and profitability, the conclusion is only negative: European statistics reject a positive connection, though there is a significant and negative relationship between size and profit variability (recall that Levy in 1911 and Parent in 1970 had derived these results theoretically).

– As to the relationship between size and growth, the conclusion was again negative, in accordance with Gibrat's law, though important derivations were noted from an implication of the same law, viz. that size and growth variability are independent. Thus, explanations could be diverse. Again, this conclusion had been anticipated by several authors simply because size of firms varies between different branches in various stages of development.

– On the relationship between size and R&D, the finding was that though firms of larger size have more R&D inputs, the achievement of innovations (R&D outputs) has probably less to do with market structures than with the use of R&D activities within the policy of the firm (i.e. the entrepreneurial acumen).

The general conclusion in a positive sense is therefore that the large firm shows a lesser performance variability: being large is less risky. This conclusion is concomitant with another one, recently put forward by the same author: that dominant firms do persist through time, or dominancy '. . . is more assured the more exogenous and slow moving is the process generating entrants' (Jacquemin and Geroski, 1984). One could state that these confirmations of previous theories are important: 'theory without measurement' is now placed on a more secure basis. On the other hand, the investigative results show declining marginal results, and one may well ask whether new topics, relatively unresearched, do not promise more. One such field is the complex of cooperation networks between firms, of which agreements, joint ventures, consortia and the like are examples (see Section 5). A third consideration is that such results, achieved by industrial organization economists guard against so-called 'new views', inspired by neo-Austrian views that power does not matter.

The second novelty which Jacquemin's book brought in France was the introduction of Anglo-Saxon welfare appreciations in industrial organization though with a characteristic slant. He went back to a time-honoured European tradition, according to which competition is only one means among others. 'In all times, the virtues of competition have been considered with relativism in European countries'. Citing the first Report on competition policies of the EEC, he stressed that government intervention is necessary to orient business decisions towards an economic and social optimum. That might mean both competition promoting or competition restraining interventions, in the sense Kantzenbach maintained in West Germany.

A policy variant, entertained by authors of a leftist persuasion, mainly in France and Italy, sustains the view that Governments can use public enterprises to promote policies which hold in check and guide private power positions, or alternatively to promote new (small) enterprise for innovatory purposes. These views influenced Italian policy, though to a lesser extent Mitterand's large-scale nationalizations in France of industrial and banking firms. In the northern EEC countries (Germany, Denmark, Holland) a relatively strong persuasion is that the government should be allowed to intervene in the market process but only in a 'market conforming way'. The prevention of outright monopolies, liberalization of markets from obstacles, the creation of sufficient infra-structures figure large in this view, which only introduces the welfare aspect in a very broad and indirect way.

In general one could say, that analyses of welfare losses due to concentrated market structures (how great are the quantitative losses deriving from concentrated industry structures?) have not been pertinent in

Europe.[14] One reason follows from the diversity of viewpoints among European economists and, above all, from the emphasis on dynamic developments in markets; another reason is that European policies, as practised by states, entertain a much broader gamma of arguments than monopoly considerations: national prestige, key industries, employment, environmental aspects. Also, one hardly finds statistical estimates of welfare losses due to monopoly because of a paucity of data.

3. A third approach is constituted by Marxist economists. Though not numerous, there are a few centres, such as Grenoble in France, where they study industrial organization problems with the aid of a coherent, global analysis.

Those economists start from the concentration of capital, in the hands of oligarchic groups and deny the managerial thesis about the separation of ownership and control of large firms. Control depends on the performance of the firm, which in turn determines the conduct of shareholder groups who do not control the firm. Thus, Chevalier (1977) distinguishes between, (1) a controlgroup, (2) a group composed of financial investors, (3) a group of dispersed shareholders and, possibly (4) a group hostile to the controlgroup (e.g., a firm intent on takeover). The controlgroup can influence the other parties' behaviour through the dissemination and withholding of information and the choice of the lines of business in which to invest. After having acquired control it wants to maintain it. A controlling threshold – as is used in managerial theories – is difficult to define: it may be between 1 and 51%, depending on the structure of the division of shareholder capital and the behaviour of groups, i.e., the degree of loyalty to the controlling group. This concept of 'dynamic control' explains the mobility of capital, the link with the banks and the goals of the firm. The stronger the control group, the more profit maximizing behaviour the firm's policy will show (Chevalier, 1977, p. 92).

One weak spot in the theory is the admittance of battles between oligarchistic fractions: if that is the case one may as well call this entrepreneurial action which intends to set the firm on another track. But the security of control in the hands of a group type one, assured of the loyalty of groups two and three, will contribute to the unequal growth of firms, which in general can be inscribed in the product life cycle scheme (Chevalier, 1977, Chapter 5).

The dynamic control concept is, to my mind, and improvement upon the dichotomy of owner or managerial control, especially in Europe, where a strong variety of forms exists, as a number of firm and country studies shows (Jacquemin and de Jong, 1977, p. 160 *et seq*, and E. Kaufer, 1980, p. 414 *er seq.*).[15] Yet, the question is open whether the whole problem should not be discarded as Kaufer maintains. After a penetrating analysis of the literature and a survey of the four main behaviouristic models (Fisher, Baumol, Marris and Williamson) he finds that the managerial theory offers few possibilities for empirical testing, because, when the management's time horizon is not short and its discount rate not high, the differences between the models, with respect to the qualitative characteristics of comparative – static reactions, are slight.

In addition, managerial models work with the assumption of a continuous and equilibrium rate of growth of the firm, which goes on indefinitely. The value of such a firm is the discounted value of its dividend payments.

Dropping this general assumption and recognizing instead that firms do have periods of expansion and relative stagnation leads on to the conclusion that, though the apparent behaviour is different, the fundamental is not.

For, a firm in expansion will reinvest as much as possible of its profits in order to finance a high rate of growth. It should maximize its opportunities in a growth market, while retaining control. Its shares will rise spectacularly, because future dividends are anticipated. In contrast, a firm in a stagnating or declining stage of market development will distribute a higher share of profits, because the need to reinvest is lower, and shareholders have to be satisfied currently. Replacement and rationalisation investments are substituted for expansion investment. The first type of firm resembles the Baumol or Marris firm; the second resembles the Fisher type of firm. In both cases, though the apparent behaviour is different (growth maximization versus profit maximization), the real conduct is similar: firms strive for a maximization of their market value. A firm's market value depends not only on a maximization of the future rate of profit, but also on the degree of risk, connected with investments. And the latter shifts with market development stages. Whereas a firm in an expansionary stage can to some extent control the risks, firms in a stagnationary or declining phase have less possibilities. So, if the firms differ only in the intensity of behaviour, due to shifts in risks the empirical testing of alternative theories becomes very difficult, if not impossible.

V. ITALIAN INDUSTRIAL ORGANIZATION: THE TOPICAL APPROACH

Italian economics has traditionally been less closed to foreign influences than French or German. There has been a mixture of works, translated from foreign writers or inspired by them, with original contributions by Italians.[16] Industrial economics forms no exception. On the occasion of the introduction of a Government Bill to protect competition in 1959 in Parliament (the Bill never became law) two volumes were published on competition and monopoly in the series *Problemi economici d'oggi* (F. Vita, 1961). The volumes combined Italian and foreign views, which is also the case in the Rivista di Economia e Politica Industriale, the main industrial organization journal and in Momigliano's handbook, a tome of over 1000 pages(!), widely used in the seventies at Italian universities. This handbook devoted much attention to Anglo-Saxon writings, yet it also had many chapters in which topics figured not usually discussed in standard texts on industrial organization: e.g., location theory, multinational enterprise and the methods of prognosis of demand for sectors and for individual firms. In the early eighties it was replaced in the leading universities by a translated text.[17]

This mixture of authors and problems may well have been due to the late arrival of industrial organization problems on Italian soil, in its turn linked with retarded industrialization and the formation of larger combiners. Apart from a number of books and articles on cartels and coalitions which appeared in the late twenties and early thirties,[18] (F. Vita, p. 59) not much was published in our field until the fifties and sixties, when the questions of large scale firms, concentration, restructuring and mergers made themselves felt. Since then, however, Italian economists have published a spate of books and articles devoted in the main to four topics.

1. First, studies of the concentration problem, in which the measurement of concentration and its development in time was prominent. The books of Boni and Gros-Piëtro, Battara and the writings of R. Linda exemplify this.[19] Starting from the writings of Italian statisticians like Gini, de Vergottini and Mortara, Battara distinguished between concentration and inequality, and maintained, that if the number of firms had changed in an industry (which usually was the case) one had to make use of dynamic concentration measures.

Battara used the formula

$$C_d = m.G_1 + (1 - m), \quad \text{in which } m = \frac{n_1 - 1}{n_1 + v - 1}$$

G_1 is the Gini-coefficient of n_1 elements who share the characteristic at time t, and C_d is the dynamic concentration index for all elements, inclusive those with the intensity zero for the characteristics (v). Except when $v = 0$, C_d will always be larger than G_1 and if m diminishes (a reduction in the number of firms), C_d rises above G_1. If G_0 is the Gini coefficient at time t_0 of n_0 elements, there will be dynamic concentration if $C_d > G_0$, even if $G_1 < G_0$, because the reduction in the number of firms from n_0 to n_1 may overcompensate the lesser inequality at t_1.

De Vergottini had a somewhat simpler dynamic concentration index:

$$C_d = \frac{G_1 p_1 - G_0 p_0}{p_d}$$

in which p_0 and p_1 are the absolute values of the variables and $p_d = p_1 - p_0$.

For example, if at t_0 there are 3 firms with resp. 7, 5 and 3 thousand employees and at t_1, 5 firms with 12, 8, 5, 2 and 1 thousand employees, the concentration index will be (taking into account two firms at t_0 with zero employees):

$$C_d = \frac{\frac{112}{280} \times 28{,}000 - \frac{76}{150} \times 15{,}000}{13{,}000} = 0.28$$

As G_0 was 0.18, concentration has increased to $C_d = 0.28$. Not taking into account the entrance and exit of two firms, the Gini-coefficient for t_1 would have been $G_1 = 0.40$, which would overestimate the degree of concentration.

In this way, Battara calculated dynamic concentration ratios on the levels of establishment, firm and group (if possible) between 1937 and 1960. There was a slight overall tendency towards deconcentration, linked with consistent growth in many branches, but most remarkable were the diverse tendencies in branches.[20] Boni and Gros-Pietro, who studied the period 1951–1961, for 41 sectors, found a general tendency towards deconcentration, but again varying sector experiences. Fast growth was linked with rising numbers of firms and deconcentration; slow growth or stagnation in a sector went hand in hand with stable or rising concentration.

Linda, as is well known, developed his L-index, to measure the 'dynamic oligopolistic equilibrium'. This index has been used extensively in a great number of studies made on behalf of the EEC Commission (see R. Linda's contribution in the second volume of this book). Essentially, the L-index measures the deviation between the existing oligopolistic market situation and a perfectly equilibrated situation, in which all oligopolistic firms have equal market shares: $1/n$.

For any individual firm in an oligopolistic situation one can measure an M-value, which takes into account the number of relationships it has with other firms ($(n - i)/i$), its relative market share ($A_i/(A_n - A_i)$), and the total number of firms (n):

$$M = \frac{\frac{n-i}{i} \, \frac{A_i}{A_n - A_i}}{n}.$$

From this results a maximum value of M, and the position of the firm with which this maximum value is correlated. This position and this value designate 'maximum oligopolistic disequilibrium'. The value of the L-index follows from $L = \Sigma M/n - 1$. L and M (and other indices such as $L - PL$ and $M - L$) are meant to have a diagnostic value, that is the higher they are, the more the suspicion will be that market power disequilibrium exists. The big problem here (as with other indices) is to determine the relevant market, in which the firms have their market shares. Assuming that this problem can be adequately solved, its diagnostic value, both for a given situation and for comparing development situations over time, can be appreciated, in the sense that the indices signal where further investigations are necessary. Though the method obviously does not give a solution to the determination of an individual market power problem (which is what is required under art. 86 of the EEC treaty, and which no index can achieve), it provides for a useful signalling system with the aid of which Antitrust authorities can supervise the concentration process.

By far the most numerous studies carried out within the European community were industry or sector studies, which combined quantitative approaches. During the seventies and early eighties, many reports were published, covering the period 1962–1982, in which tendencies of competition and concentration were discussed. The main findings were initially:

(a) a long-term growth of concentration in the various markets; the number of firms showed a steady and striking decline;

(b) a continuous growth, in both absolute and relative terms, in the size of industrial production units, and even more so in the size of trading units;

(c) the development of new forms of oligopolistic specialization and cooperation, with a tendency away from single-firm dominance towards duo-polistic and trio-polistic dominance, and

(d) increasingly, there arrived new products and new manufacturers on markets, which, together with changes in market shares helped to produce changes in market patterns and a fall in 'relative prices' in a large number of markets.

Thus, the Commission concluded: 'Keener competition within the Community is not in itself incompatible with a high degree of concentration and a strong trend towards oligopoly.[21]

2. A great number of industry studies were also undertaken in Italy: shoes, aluminium, food, paper and paper products, pharmaceuticals,

cement, etc. Besides, monographs were written on varying topics, such as the diffusion of innovations, industrial restructuring and price control.[22] The general characteristics of most of these studies are, I think, typical of the European approach.

– They are empirically oriented, without using econometrics.
– They are integrative, that is they consider and discuss wider aspects such as demand and supply factors, as well as technological features, the composition of firm sizes, localization, the several product markets, industry structure as well as financial problems and the behaviour of firms and groups.
– They take into account the time dimension both in a historical and in a prospective sense.
– They are policy oriented.

To achieve all that within the frame of a single book, these applied studies are, often, less specific and more general than comparable Anglo-Saxon works. It depends on what is preferred: a more analytic, microscopic view as well as functional view of the working of sectors, or a more balanced, overall, and genetic approach, which has a lesser intention to 'prove' than to illuminate.

3. Italian economists have subscribed to the idea that competition in markets is dynamic, and in a number of cases they referred to the market stages scheme, linked to entrepreneurial activities. Prodi (1968) worked this out towards the behaviour of oligopolistic firms, underlining that these firms oftem practise price competition, in contrast to what static oligopoly theory maintains, and towards the diffusion of innovations, in which no systematic links between diffusion and size of firm, or first adopting country were found; instead, the obstacles of insufficient organization and lacking financial means for investment leaps in the diffusion process were underlined. R. Linda (1969), distinguishing between oligopolistic groups and small and medium-sized firms, maintained that the first strive for decentralization of decisions, in order to grow towards optimum dimension in sectors and diversification through sectors. The group commands a leaway which small firms do not have: the latter must maximize profits in order to survive. From this point of view, Linda questioned the applicability of the limit-pricing model, for prices are essentially a function of the elasticity of demand, and serve the transfer of resources from old sectors towards new markets. Moreoever, the model implies 'two absurdities': instant entry and absolute price rigidity. Instead, oligopolistic groups try to maintain high prices *and* surplus capacity,

together constituting a barrier to entry, in stagnant markets. The internationalization of markets is another factor, promoting competition among the dynamic oligopoly groups.

A. Aquino wrote a book on the relationship between the spreading of technological knowledge within single industries and mutations in the structure of international specialization. This he called 'the technological elasticity' of the sector and he showed that, for the period 1951–1974 in 15 industrial advanced countries, the product cycle concept was applicable to most of the 21 sectors surveyed: 'in many industries for which the technological elasticity was positive, with a high level of statistical significance, at the beginning of the sixties, it declined gradually in value and in significance',[23] and drew the policy conclusion that financial support for old sectors was wasted and could be better directed at the promotion of new sectors. A similar analysis and conclusion was arrived at in Holland, when the massive study of the scientific council was published.[24]

P. Mariti, finally, stressed the importance of looking towards the changing structure of an industry, determined both by competitive and complementary relationships between firms, as a result of evolving firm activities; the attention had been too one-sidedly directed towards the economies of scale of single plants and firms, he said, determining optimum size, whereas 'the problem probably more important from the point of view of the organization of the industry as a whole, which is that of the optimum distribution of functions, or activities of firms' has been lost out of sight (Mariti, 1977, 1983). Joining Salvati (1974), he maintained that the theory of the firm, as it has been developed is largely irrelevant. It impedes the proper study of industrial organization problems, because it focusses on the behaviour of the individual firm, instead of paying attention to the relationships between firms. The division of labour is not exclusively determined by technological (scale) factors, but also by factors internal to the firm and by social (institutional) forces such as the growth of demand. This is called 'restructuring', to which is opposed the 'reconversion' of a firm's products and production methods, based on economic calculations, given the state of technology and demand tendencies.

Applying this line of thought to a most typical Italian industry: marble excavation and processing, Mariti shows how the industry broke into two sectors under the influence of diamond cutting, a new technique introduced in the sixties. Only two stages – sawing and some types of processing – felt the influence and the astonishing variety of types and sizes of firms was only partly modified. The greater availability of techniques to firms created flexibility margins on the commercial level and could counterbalance the relative shift in labour costs due to the introduction of economies of speed, which diamond cutting brought in the sawing stage. Thus, restructuring and reconversion occurred simultaneously, giving rise to a different emphasis on intrasectoral quality competition, by some firms, as well as intersectoral price competition by others. In Europe, Mariti says, industrial rationalization often follows the growth and organization of demand; industry structure adapts to such a development in the market process.

These observations apply to many industries: watches, woollens and textiles, instruments, pharmaceuticals, bread baking,[25] etc. For industrial organization theory, this approach opens a wide, mostly unexplored field. It requires a look into the industries, researching what types of reorganizations both horizontally and vertically occur under the influence of various forces. Also, links could be made to another area, also relatively unexplored: The formation of industrial networks as is exemplified by the operation of joint ventures, consortia and agreements between firms relating to exports, research, representation, etc. For example, are the aims and policies of joint ventures a mixture of competitive restraints and of savings, as Lenel maintains, or are they better regarded as forms of 'organized entrepreneurship' (Lenel 1978, Hockman, 1984), used to cope with changing and complex developments?* And what about the often 'symbiotic' relationships between large companies and their numerous suppliers (of parts, components, specialties, etc.) or processors (as in the plastics or metal trades). What determines these relationships, how are they changing, what types of entrepreneurial initiatives are taken and who makes the innovative moves? What role does power play and is it true that all-round specialization (in markets, products and clients/suppliers) endangers the existence of small firms, or, on the contrary, puts it into a long-term viable position, as business economists have said?

If the giant firm of today resembles the sun in the midst of a planetary system, as Carlo Ruffolo (1967) said long ago, it would seem that such types of networks deserve more attention from industrial organization economists. In these researches the questions of efficiency, competition and economic power would remain as important as in the more traditional enquiries.

4. Finally, many articles were written on the very small and very large firms – like IRD, ENI and other public enterprises – that are so typical of the Italian economic scenery. The first ones carry much weight in the Italian industrial structure, both in an absolute sense and relatively as compared with other countries, in terms of number of firms, employees

*This is also discussed in the EEC's memorandum: Towards positive guidelines on joint ventures, Brussels 7.11.1985.

and value added. They were mainly published in the second journal devoted to industrial organization studies, viz. Economia e Politica Industriale – Rassegna Trimestriale.

VI. CONCLUSION

European economists have devoted only scant attention to some of the problems which were so intensively discussed in the Anglo-Saxon countries. For example, the time-honoured debate whether there exists a positive relationship between the concentration ratio and profitability, has found a weak echo: only one or two economists in each European country discussed this. Not only have the drawbacks and artificialities of the methods used been pointed out by writers,[26] but also conclusions were drawn which seemed to go against the grain of the theme. When, in the seventies and early eighties, investment stagnated at a low level with direct consequences for expansion and employment, and this was attributed to low enterprise profitability, a Dutch economist proposed that the government pursue a concentration raising policy in sectors. His research for the Netherlands had sustained the link between concentration and profitability, so that the inference was that increased concentration would promote investment, expansion and employment.[27]

I think the inference is perfectly logical – within the reference system of a static economy. Once you ask what types of entrepreneurs (if any) do command those low profit enterprises, and what they will do with the possibly earned extra profits – viz. serve their own utility functions, or distribute them, or invest the profits abroad, etc. – the dynamic dimension of the market economy comes into sight. Then, the inference might as well put the cart before the horse. In view of such problems with static models it seems to me that European economists are well advised to retain their time-honoured paradigma. It is a dubious gain to acquire greater scientific precision at the cost of relevancy.

NOTES

1. There is obviously an extensive literature in various languages, which I abstain from mentioning here. As one exception, let me mention the writings of the late Belgian economic historian Raymond de Roover, who discussed all the topics mentioned in the text, and others, such as the structure and behaviour of large business firms as well.
2. Earlier writers were quick to recognize the fast changing economic organization, viz. from individual competition to organizational competition, often accompanied by

fierce battles. Von Wieser said the shift was connected with the uprise of strong leadership figures, who commanded large and varied resources, above all capital. Yet '. . . competition remains a force of so extraordinary power, that it will have to be rated, also under present conditions, as a general economic power of primary importance'. (Fr. von Wieser, 1927, pp. 148–151). Liefmann, more enlightening, made the distinction between 'freie Konkurrenz' (by which he understood classical, individualistic competition) and 'Wettbewerb' (rivalrous competition) and maintained that whereas the former was reduced or even eliminated in modern society, the latter 'continued to exist as the organization principle, as long as there are more sellers'. (R. Liefmann, 1930, pp. 54–61).

3. 'With cartels, in contradistinction to legal monopolies like patents, the rise of new competition by means of the founding of new firms, is never excluded, but always in the background. And it is the more the prospect, that this latent competition, this possibility to compete, becomes a fact, the more the cartel exploits its monopoly position by means of high prices and through higher profits gives a special stimulus to the foundation of new firms' (p. 10). Before the war (World War I) he says (Liefmann, 1930), one could observe that even a small rise in profits led to the formation of new competitive firms. But this could not last either, because the more efficient cartel members, willing to remain fully occupied, extended their output, at the cost of weaker rivals . . . All longer existing cartels have called forth a very important increase in output and supply' (pp. 131–132).
4. 'In fact both extremes of exchange, monopoly and competition (freie Konkurrenz) were never achieved, but both, carried to an extreme, turn into its contrary'. '. . . Competition carried to its extreme leads up to the monopoly of the remaining strongest. But the same applies in reverse to monopoly, in so far as it is not legally secured: when monopoly positions are exploited and lead to monopoly effects, they call new competition in the field'. One cannot say that the one organizational form is better than the other nor that economic life has ever been carried on by the one or the other principle exclusively; there was always a combination of both. (R. Liefmann, 1930, p. 59). The same idea pervades the works of another economist, H. Levy, who was a professor at Heidelberg, and wrote extensively about English and German industrial organization in the period 1900–1940. Examples: Monopoly and competition. A study in English industrial organization, 1911 (translated from the German edition of 1909); Industrial Germany, Cambridge 1935; and: The new industrial system. A study of the origins, forms, finance and prospects of concentration in industry, London 1936. Levy's approach reflected a combination of theoretical, statistical and historical (case study) elements.
5. H. Levy, 1930, p. 208 *et. seq.*: '. . . that an increasing demand is satisfied by a continually decreasing number of firms, the greater productive power of the single unit reducing from decade to decade the aggregate number of firms'. The same arguments, but more broadly worked out, are advanced in the new industrial system, Part III, in which Levy also takes to task several other economists, for providing 'partial' and 'eclectic' explanations; he distinguishes between technical concentration and economic concentration as a result of horizontal and vertical integration. Only the latter may have something to do with monopoly, he says (p. 127) while maintaining that the striving for monopoly gains may be difficult to separate from the achievement of technical and organizational economies (p. 107). Technical concentration is seen as dependent upon technique of production and size of the market, determining optimal size of the industrial unit (p. 91). Both vary with

countries and sectors, so that generalizations are wrong, even though a similar tendency exists (p. 105).

6. Both Schumpeter and Kirzner have discussed many aspects of the entrepreneurial role in an illuminating way. Apart from pointing to an absence of recognition of the entrepreneur's role in classical and neo-classical economics, and pursuing the line of thinking of French and German economists in this respect (Schumpeter, 1954), Kirzner discussed the entrepreneurial role in Menger's system. He disagrees with Streissler and Jaffé, who saw Menger as underlining entrepreneurial activity. Instead he points to the 'entrepreneurial gap' in Menger's principal work. But I fail to see the point, for (Kirzner, 1979, pp. 69–70) as he argues it is Menger's position that men, by converting goods from a lower order into those of a higher order, create additional value. The first man to do so is, obviously, an entrepreneurial monopolist, expanding the value of goods and their variety. Increasing competition reduces the monopolist's profits in the course of time, until 'Menger's law' (that the value of ends comes to be attached to the means) applies again. This is what Kirzner himself argues in Chapter 10 (esp. pp. 162–168). The picture of a market developing from monopoly, via imperfect competition to a state of no profitability, is entirely Mengerian.
7. In the Netherlands, the most prominent economist in the period 1920–1950, F. de Vries shifted during the depression from 'freedom of enterprise' towards 'ordening' (i.e., private and public regulation of business). And in France, J. Marchal called for a fundamental revision of theory. See M. H. J. Dullaart, Regulation or freedom. Dutch economic thinking in the interwar period. Diss. Rotterdam 1984. J. Marchal, La crise contemporaine de la science économique, in: Annales d'économie politique (1950–1951).
8. A great number of publications has followed this line of thinking, e.g., *in Germany*: H. Arndt, Schöpferischer Wettbewerb und Klassenlose Gesellschaft, Berlin 1952; E. Heuss, Allgemeine Markttheorie, Tübingen, Zürich 1965; K. Brandt, Concentration and economic growth, in: H. Arndt (ed.). Die Konzentration in der Wirtschaft, Schriften des Vereins für Sozialpolitik, Neue Folge Band 20, Berlin 1960/61,[1] and 1971,[2] pp. 280–288; H. G. Krüsselberg, Marktwirtschaft und Ökonomische Theorie, Freiburg im Breisgau, 1969; H. Schlögl, Mehrproduktunternehmung, Marktentwicklung und Wettbewerb, Frankfurt/M, 1972; E. Kaufer, Industrieökonomik, München 1980; I. Schmidt, Wettbewerbstheorie und – politik, Stuttgart 1981.
   In the Netherlands:
   H. W. de Jong, Marktanalyse en markttheorie, Leiden, 1971. H. W. de Jong, Dynamische markttheorie, Leiden, 1972,[1] 1981,[2] 1985;[3] G. J. Wijers, Industriepolitiek, Leiden, 1981; J. J. van Duijn, De lange golf in de economie, Leiden, 1979; I. Webbink, Innovatie en het midden- en kleinbedrijf, Zoetermeer, 1984.
   In France and Belgium:
   A. Piatier, Paper presented at the Colloque des Economistes de Langue Française, 1950; A. Teissier du Cros, La recherche d'activités et de produits nouveaux, Paris 1976; A de Bethune et H. Heyvaert, L'innovation dans la politique industrielle, Anales des Sciences Economiques, Louvain 1976; J. M. Chevalier, L'économie industrielle en question, Paris 1977; A Piatier, Barriers to innovation, London 1984.
   In Italy:
   R. Prodi, La diffusione delle innovazione dell'industria italiana, Bologna 1971; A. Aquino, in: Rivista di economia e politica industriale, nr. 3, 1977.
9. See the analysis of a homogenous, duopolistic market with a pioneering and an imitating firm, resp. a conservative type of firm on pp. 115–117 of Heuss' book.

10. See my Ondernemingsconcentratie, Leiden, 1971, chapter on concentration developments in Benelux for an empirical analysis of these firms. This idea was worked out theoretically in: Dynamische concentratietheorie, Leiden 1972,[1] 1981,[2] 1985.[3] I first encountered the growthcycle concept in the late fifties, when working for a multinational container-firm, which experienced maturity in the U.S. market, but not in Europe.
11. An important question is whether mergers do indeed lead up to rationalization and cost reductions, and if so, do so faster than international growth. On the basis of Dutch evidence, assembled by the Central Statistical Bureau, I previously doubted this and found, on the contrary, that the overwhelming majority of mergers are initiated for market strategic reasons. See: Theory and evidence concerning mergers: an international comparison, in: A. P. Jacquemin and H. W. de Jong (eds.) (1976). An empirical W. German research among 100 firms, taking over other companies during the seventies, came to similar conclusions: merger intensity rises with the size of firm; the majority (71 to 75% depending on size of firm class) are of a horizontal nature; successes and partial successes of the mergers are severely limited and depend on the type; and the author says 'Concluding, the result following from the intensive Dutch research can be confirmed. Mergers are mainly undertaken because of market oriented motives. Aims which have been discussed extensively in the literature, e.g., joint research, better utilization of knowledge, cost reduction, etc. play only a subordinate role'. (W. P. Möller, 1983, p. 170). On the other hand, the EC Commission in a recent report on competition policy suggests that an important minority (some 25%) of mergers and takeovers, undertaken by large European firms are motivated by rationalization reasons. See 14th report on competition policy (1984).
12. Among the numerous writings by Kantzenbach and others only three may be mentioned here, because the first two references contain an extensive literature, in particular with respect to the debates between Kantzenbach and E. Hoppman, a.o., who defend in Germany the sort of neo-classical, freedom of competition approach, reminiscent of the Chicago school in the U.S. (1) E. Kantzenbach/H. Kallfass, Das Konzept des funktionsfähigen Wettbewerbs – workable competition, in: H. Cox, U. Jens, K. Markert (eds.), 1981. (2) R. Clapham, Das Wettbewerbspolitische Konzept der Wettbewerbsfreiheit, in Cox, Jens, Markert, Handbuch des Wettbewerbs, o.c. (3) In the Netherlands the competition law of 1956 took up, as Van der Weyden (president of the Dutch competition commission) underlined a similar position. See his Toestaan of verbieden: een beschouwing rond de wet economische mededinging, in: Econ. Stat. Berichten 23/30, 12, 1981. A good survey of the German discussions is also provided by I. Schmidt, Wettbewerbstheorie und politik, o.c. part. 1. The concept of ruinous competition was extensively discussed by Tolksdorf, both for concentrated and unconcentrated markets. (M. Tolksdorf, 1971).
13. A. Teissier du Cros, 1976. Here an old idea returns: the 'projector' of eighteenth century British economists (Defoe, Postlethwayt and A. Smith), a term, used to distinguish the inventor and creative entrepreneur from the capitalist 'undertaker', who was simply an ordinary businessman.
14. Among the thirteen studies, based on branch researches, cited by Böbel (1984, pp. 192–201) only one applies to a European country. For W. Germany, Böbel found an efficiency loss of only 1.28 (1.89)% for the period 1965–1973, depending on whether sales or added values were used, occasioned mainly by five leading branches (70%) or ten corporations (66%).

15. Four in-depth studies of Dutch industrial firms show indeed appreciable shifts in control within the period of a decade: Haank and De Lange on the Nederhorst group, where control shifted to the banks and the Government, Wassenbergh on the RSV shipbuilding firm, where first a competing firm and later on the Government exercised control, and the two studies by Vleesenbeek and Van Schelven of two large textile firms, where family ownership shifted to managerial control in the first case and, in the second case, though remaining intact, changed from personal management to collegiate leadership.
   – D. Haank and R. de Lange, *De uitvaart van Nederhorst*, Gorcum 1979.
   – A. Wassenbergh, *Dossier RSV*. Leiden 1984.
   – H. Vleesenbeek, *De eerste grote industriële fusie in Nederland na de Tweede Wereldoorlog*. Het ontstaan van Nijverdal-Ten Cate, een bedrijfshistorische analyse, Rotterdam 1981.
   – A. L. van Schelven – *Onderneming en familisme* (v Heek & Co), Leiden 1984.
16. In the eighteenth century, for example, Beccaria was heavily inspired by Cantillon, and in the nineteenth century Pantaleoni by Menger's Principles. See K. Pribram, *A History of Economic Reasoning*, Baltimore and London 1983, pp. 86–88 and 362.
17. F. Momigliano, *Economia industriale e teoria dell' imprese*. Bologna, 1975. A. P. Jacquemin and H. W. de Jong, *Economia e politica industriale in Europe*, H. Mulino, Bologna 1979. (Translated from the English edition, with a preface by R. Prodi).
18. These writings had much to do with the granting of fiscal privileges accorded to mergers and cartels by the Italian Government in 1927 and with the law of 1932 which made cartellization obligatory under certain conditions.
19. P. Battara, *La concentrazione industriale*, Atti della commissione parlementare. Camera dei deputati, Doc. XVIII – no 1. Rome 1965. M. Boni e G. M. Gros-Pietro, *La concentrazione industriale in Italia*, Torino 1967. R. Linda, Le système des indices d'équilibre et son application concrète á la sidérurgie des Etats-Unis, *Rivista di Politica Economica*, anno LVIII, mag. 1968.
20 Let us recall that H. O. Lenel in Germany also proposed a dynamic index to measure the concentration process, combining firm share, average share and number of firms. Such dynamic measurements illuminate the tendencies within sectors, but, because they require more detailed knowledge, are less easy to operate throughout sectors, in comparison with concentration indices or summary indices. cf. H. O. Lenel, *Ursachen der Konzentration*, 1962,[1] 1968.[2] pp. 1–9.
21. E.E.C. Commission, *Reports on competition policy*, numbers 8, 9 and 10 (Section 2).
22. R. Frigeni & W. Tousyn, *L'industria della calzatura in Italia*, Bologna 1976; M. Balconi, *La strategia di expansione dei mercati: il caso dell' aluminio*, Bologna 1977. L. Sicca, *L'industria alimentare in Italia*, Bologna, 1977; F. Gobo, *L'industria italiana della carte: un oligopoli imperfetto*, Bologna 1974. P. Bianchi, *Politiche pubbliche e strategie della impresa nell' industria europea del cimento*, Bologna, 1980; G. Querini (ed.), *La concentrazione industriale*. Problemi teorici e consideriazioni empiriche con particolare riferimento all' industria farmaceutica. Milano, 1979; Soris e R. Linda, *I processi di concentrazione industriale: metodologico e applicazione all' industria alimentare italiana*, Milano, 1976; R. Prodi, *La diffusione delle innovazione nell' industria italiana*, Bologna, 1971; E. Pontarollo, *Il salvataggio industriale nell' Europa della crisi*, Bologna, 1976; F. Gobbo, *Il controllo dei prezzi industriale in Italia*, Bologna, 1982.
23. A. Aquino, Innovazione technologica, spezzializzazione internationale e politica industriale, in: *Rivista di economia e politica industriale*, anno III, no 3, 1977, pp. 417–453.

24. See: W.R.R., *Plaats en toekomst van de Nederlandse industrie*, The Hague 1980.
25. The Dutch bread baking industry likewise 'broke' into two sectors under the influence of technical and demand factors during the seventies, see H. W. de Jong *et al.* *Concentration and competition in the Dutch food industry*, part 4, E.E.C. Commission series no 43, 1982.
26. See for example Böbel's book. Böbel was a student of M. Neumann at Nürnburg, the only other economist in West Germany who published about the relationship. I. Böbel, *Wettbewerb und Industriestruktur*, Heidelberg, 1984, pp. 140–177. In France, A. P. Weber and F. Jenny published in their book: *Concentration et politique des structures industrielles*, Paris 1974, (pp. 117–140) results which confirmed the relationship; concentration made itself the more felt, the more economies of scale and absolute capital entry costs are of importance.
27. P. de Wolff, De relatie tussen concentratiegraad en winstgevendheid in Nederlandse bedrijfsklassen, *Econ. Stat. Berichten*, 26.5.1982; De Wolff's article is the only one in Dutch literature to discuss the issue.

4. MAINSTREAMS IN INDUSTRIAL ORGANIZATION: CHALLENGES AND TASKS

C. Green

If I correctly comprehend the term, 'mainstream industrial organization' has primarily been concerned with *domestic* markets, characterized by the size distribution of sellers of products, the nature of the product, and entry conditions. With the help of some basic micro theory, weak theoretical ties between structural conditions and firm behavior and performance are postulated. The resultant hypotheses are empirically tested using cross section data and econometric techniques to tease out some statistically significant relationships. Flesh is added to the bones in the form of industry studies, case studies of firm behavior, and analysis of public policies toward business, particularly antitrust policy.

During the past decade, *mainstream* industrial organization has been challenged in at least three different ways. First, the basic structure-conduct-performance paradigm was attacked by a Chicago–UCLA school of industrial organization economists who argued that the line of causation runs from conduct to performance and structure. Managerial or technical superiority, reflected in lower costs or the creation of better products (including services), generates higher profits *and* larger market shares. Thus the observed relationship between market structure (or share) and leading-firm profitability, far from representing a causal relationship between the two, is said to be attributable to the joint dependence of both on some form of 'superiority': on efficiency rather than market power. In my view, the heart of the difference between the two paradigms, the mainstream one and the UCLA-Chicago alternative, is the relative importance of scale and non-scale difference in costs, with the mainstream model emphasizing the former and the alternative model the latter.

The second challenge to *mainstream* industrial organization is increasing theoretical rigour. In the 1970's one began to hear references to

de Jong, H. W., Shepherd, W. G. (eds) Mainstreams in Industrial Organization
 ISBN 978-94-017-0495-3

'theoretical industrial organization', a phrase which at the time seemed to me to be a contradiction of terms, given the field's empirically-oriented foundations and inductive methodology. Nevertheless, many microeconomic theorists looking for new territory on which to apply their increasingly high powered technology, invaded the field of industrial organization and have left their mark. Barriers to entry, product differentiation, vertical restrictions, invention and innovation, oligopolistic interdependence, and natural monopoly, have each been subjected to the analytical skills of the new wave of industrial organization theorists. The result is precision and insight on the one hand and a plethora of models constrained in their general applicability by strong assumptions on the other.

The third challenge to mainstream industrial organization is from adherents of 'contestability'. 'Contestability' challenges the importance of mainstream industrial organization's most prominent structural variables: the size of distribution of firms and barriers to entry and the role of economies of scale in generating both concentration and entry barriers. Essentially, contestability rests on a strong and empirically testable assumption: the relative unimportance in many industries or settings of sunk (as distinct from fixed) costs. If sunk costs are nonexistent or negligible and there are no artificial (government-created) restrictions on entry, then, according to adherents of contestability, access to and exit from an industry is essentially costless. In the absence of barriers to entry and exit so defined, the size distribution of incumbent firms exercises no effective impact on prices, output and welfare. In these circumstances external competition is as effective as internal competition would be in assuring good performance. The problem is to find those cases where fixed costs associated with entry do not entail sunk costs – i.e., those cases where the entry process is reversible without cost.

In my view, the field of industrial organization has profited from all three challenges, but the gains are at the margin. None of the challenges replaces the essential task of industrial organization of explaining the structure, behaviour, and performance of real industries and firms and explicitly recognizing and comprehending observed international differences. Optimization models are no substitute for description and testing of hypotheses whose plausibility is embedded in observed market structure and firm behaviour. The recognition of *nonscale* cost differences, although it has had the healthy effect of reintroducing the entrepreneur, giving greater attention to the theory of the firm and the performance of its managers, and has opened up a whole new literature on incentives in the form of agency theory, does not diminish the importance of scale economies, now abetted by economies of scope. Finally, while contestability is no doubt an 'uprising' of a sort, the significance of which I shall have more to say below, its impact on the framework of industrial organization is not likely to be significantly greater, in relative terms, than that of the Peasants' Revolt of 1381 on the structure of English society.

Having briefly described the main challenges to mainstream industrial organization during the past decade, I would like to comment on what might be included in the agenda for the next decade. There seem to me to be at least four areas in which industrial organization can (and in some cases present developments suggest will) be enriched. Let me list them and briefly elaborate on each.

1. THE ROLE OF INTERNATIONAL COMPETITION AND BARRIERS TO THAT COMPETITION

Textbook treatments of industrial organization typically give no *systematic* account of the role of international competition whether via trade or international corporations, and the impact of tariffs and non-tariff barriers on market structure is almost wholly ignored.[1] Two decades ago, one might have attributed these gaps (in the U.S. literature, at least) to the huge size of the U.S. economy ((absolutely and relatively), the relative unimportance of trade, and rarity of multinational corporations. The tremendous growth in trade and challenges to U.S. economic might from several quarters make the failure to formally introduce the international economy into the most widely available industrial organization literature, a major shortcoming of mainline industrial organization – at least as it has developed in the U.S.

While textbook treatments of industrial organization have generally failed to systematically introduce international and multi-national firm competition, there is abundant research on the multinational firm (see especially R. Caves, 1982) and a growing literature relating trade and industrial organization, in particular the increasingly important phenomenon of intra-industry trade. The importance of scale economies in a product differentiated world, particularly those related to length of production run are widely recognized. That they have important implications for industrial structure, behaviour and performance and for trade-related policies needs to be emphasized in the years to come, if for no other reason than as an antidote to growing protectionist pressures.

2. THE IMPACT OF LABOUR UNIONS ON INDUSTRIAL STRUCTURE AND BEHAVIOUR

It is somewhat surprising that institutions as powerful, widespread, and important to the (industrial) production process as are labour unions should be given so little attention in the study of industrial organization. (Again, one may attribute this to the relative unimportance of trade unions in the U.S. where mainline industrial organization received its main development.) True, the impact of trade unions has been introduced into a number of market structure-performance studies as a means of more precisely indicating the independent impact of such structural variables as concentration, market share and entry barriers on profitability. In fact, two recent studies (Salinger, 1984; Clark, 1984) clearly indicate that unions extract a substantial share of the rents in concentrated industries. But with the notable exception of Williamson (1968) there has been almost no attempt to examine the impact of unions on market structure and/or behaviour. Perhaps unions do not have any identifiable impact on market structure or firm size and behaviour, but the matter is worth investigating – at least outside of the U.S. in countries where unions are both more widespread and militant.

What I have in mind is the possibility that trade unions may affect the size distribution of firms and act as a barrier to entry to (typically smaller) firms whose best techniques are relatively labour intensive. Surely, the optimal scale(s) or size(s) of plant or firm depends on (relative) factor prices as well as technology. If these prices are influenced by trade unions then this fact needs to be recognized and registered in studies of industrial organization.

Trade unions may also play a role in molding a nation's industrial policies. Unions are an institution of 'voice' (Hirschman, 1970), and many union members may gave good reason to prefer 'voice' to 'exist' in the face of economic change. Much of the wealth of industrial workers takes forms which are nonportable and/or nontransferable – or very imperfectly so.[2] Examples of assets with what I have termed the 'fixities' characteristics of nonportability or nontransferability (Green, 1984) include owned homes in single industry communities, location specific rights to subsidized housing (e.g., Council housing in Britain), nonportable employer pension plans, seniority or tenure, industry or job specific skills protected by union rules, spouses' jobs, and local amenities and reputation. Unexpected economic change which places some industries, firms, or locations in decline can result in a substantial erosion in the wealth of many workers. In these circumstances, one would expect that those persons heavily endowed with nonportable and nontransferable wealth would rather 'fight than switch'. Many such workers are likely to be unionized. This may explain why unions appear to have become powerful voices favoring interventionist and protectionist industrial policies. These policies, of course, may have an impact on industry structure, behaviour, or performance.

3. THE USE OF GAME THEORY IN THE STUDY OF INDUSTRIAL ORGANIZATION

Twenty years ago, there was a widespread feeling that despite the elegance and brilliance of the contributions of Von Neumann and Morgernstern (1944), the applicability of game theory to economic analysis, including oligopoly theory, was limited. In recent years, however, the application of game theory in economics, *particularly* industrial economics, has shown signs of becoming a growth industry. The reversal so far as industrial organization is concerned is attributable, in my view, to two developments.

(i) The 'rational expectations' revolution has made more plausible the idea that independent oligopolists can arrive at a Cournot equilibrium *without* actually going through the iterative process that is usually associated with a description of the workings of Cournot's model. Rather, Nash's game theoretic approach is grafted on to the Cournot model in such a way that rational oligopolists who understand each potential play of the game will each independently choose, from the very beginning, the (equilibrium) output (and price) – i.e., the output and price a deviation from which will reduce profits, assuming all rivals make the same choice.

(ii) Increasing recognition of the usefulness of the insights of Schelling (1960), Rapaport (1965) and others who focus on variable sum games and, in particular, the famous Prisoner's Dilemma. A particularly useful application of game theory is in the barriers to entry literature where Schelling's distinction between threat and commitment had already taken hold (Spense, 1977). Salop (1979) and Dixit (1982) make very good use of game theory to depict the choices open to incumbents and potential entrants.

As the high technology of microtheory infiltrates the field of industrial organization, I find it somewhat reassuring that game theoretic techniques which recognize large discrete elements in decision making may be given greater attention than the calculus with its attendant emphasis on optimization and marginalism. Even in the rarified atmosphere of oligopoly theory, game theoretic techniques provide grounds for optimism. For example, there is the possibility of unifying noncooperative and cooperative behaviour via game theoretic analysis. Why may independent, non-cooperative (in the sense of J. W. Friedman, 1977) oligopolists act in a way which the observer may term cooperative? Axelrod's (1984) experimental study of behaviour in prisoner's dilemma situations may provide an answer. A 'Tit for Tat' strategy tended to dominate all others: it calls for cooperation on the first move followed by a strategy of doing whatever one's rival has done on the previous move.

4. THE APPLICABILITY OF THE CONTESTABILITY ANALYSIS

While Baumol *et al* (1982) have tended to oversell contestability, particularly its applicability in single output, homogeneous product markets, there is an arena in which I believe it has a considerable degree of explanatory power – or at least potentially so. It is somewhat surprising that Baumol, Panzar and Willig, who made seminal contributions to the understanding of the concept of natural monopoly in the multiproduct case, should fail to see that the multiproduct case provides the most important argument for contestability. Why? The multiproduct example suggests that large scale entry or the threat of such entry into a market is likely to come from established firms – from firms incumbent to other, probably related, markets. For a number of reasons firms in existence in market B are better placed to engage in 'hit and run' entry and exit in Market A. They already have (sunk) plant in place, which may with relative ease be adaptable to other lines of production. They may already have built up a brand or trade name, a sales staff and R & D facilities. Moreover, their existing human and nonhuman capital may be expandable or underutilized. There may be what a colleague terms 'latent capacity'. This latent capacity has some similarities with, but is nonetheless distinct from, the traditional concept of 'excess capacity'. The latter term is easiest to comprehend in single product terms, while 'latent capacity' is more closely aligned with the common costs in multiproduct analysis (Weldon, 1948).

In my view, study of the behaviour of multiproduct firms, already stimulated by the interest in economies of *scope*, may provide important insights into the entry-exit problem and the nature of industrial competition. In the established, multi-product firm context, sunk costs in basic capacity, brand name, etc., rather than being a deterrent to entry, may provide the basis for incumbent firms in industry A engaging in 'hit and run' entry and exit in industry B. Thus in a manner analogous to commitments of incumbent firms in standard entry analysis sunk costs of established firms give them an advantage over *de novo* firms where entry into another industry or product line is concerned. Thus contestability might be viewed as an analytic extension of work done a decade or two ago on diversification and entry (see, for example, Berry, 1974). Large established firms can vary the number and type of product lines in a manner that is typically impossible for a new firm. It is the 'portfolio' choice among product lines by existing firms which may make markets 'contestable' and force incumbent firms, in any given industry or product line, to keep $p = AC \geqslant MC$, the basic welfare maximization result touted by proponents of contestability analysis. It is along these lines that 'contestability' may have its most important impact in remolding mainline industrial organization.

In conclude that while there is much new work to be done in industrial economics, the field of industrial organization is in a reasonably healthy state. The field has attracted many bright minds, without destroying its main foundations. Synthesis rather than warfare between competing paradigms and approaches should mark the next decade of development in the field. Also, there should be an effort to be more 'dynamic', in the historical or evolutionary sense of the term. This has characterized the 'European' approach to industrial organization, which is nicely described in the paper by de Jong. The evolution of markets from monopoloid toward competitive and then 'cooperative' is a major insight of the European tradition. The process-oriented and evolutionary approach is too often ignored on the American side of the Atlantic. Among other things, this omission unnecessarily exacerbates the conflict between competing paradigms and the policies (particularly antitrust) that are presumed to flow from them.

NOTES

1. An exception is found in the Canadian literature where the Eastman-Stykolt (1967) analysis plays and important role. See Harris (1984) and Green (1985).
2. Some may prefer the terms 'location specific' or 'individual specific'.

REFERENCES

Axelrod, Robert, *The Evolution of Cooperation*, New York: Basic Books (1984).

Baumol, W. J., Panzar, J. C., and Willig, R. D., *Contestable Markets and the Theory of Industry Structure*, Harcourt Brace Jovanovich (1984).

Berry, C. H., 'Corporate Diversification and Market Structure', *Bell Journal of Economics and Management Science* (Spring, 1974), pp. 196–204.

Caves, Richard E., *Multinational Enterprise and Economic Analysis*, Cambridge: Cambridge University Press (1982).

Clark, Kim B., 'Unionization and Firm Performance: The Impact on Profits, Growth, and Productivity', *American Economic Review*, (December, 1984), pp. 893–919.

Dixit, A., 'Recent Developments in Oligopoly Theory', *American Economic Review* (May 1982), pp. 12–17.

Eastman, H. C. and Stykolt, S., *The Tariff and Competition in Canada*, Toronto: Macmillan of Canada (1967).

Friedman, James W., *Oligopoly and the Theory of Games*, Amsterdam: North Holland (1977).

Green, C., *Industrial Policy: The Fixities Hypothesis*. Toronto: Ontario Economic Council (1984).

Green, C., *Canadian Industrial Organization and Policy*, Toronto: McGraw-Hill Ryerson (1985).

Harris, R., 'Applied General Equilibrium Analysis of Small Open Economies with Scale Economies and Imperfect Competition', *American Economic Review* (December 1984), pp. 1016–1032.

Hirschman, A. O., *Exit Voice and Loyalty*, Cambridge, Mass., Harvard University Press (1970).

Rapoport, A. and Chammah, A., *Prisoners' Dilemma: A Study in Conflict and Cooperation*, Ann Arbor: The University of Michigan Press (1965).

Salinger, M. A., 'Tobin's q, Unionization and the Concentration-Profits Relationship', *Rand Journal of Economics* (Summer 1984), pp. 159–170.

Schelling, T. C., *The Strategy of Conflict*, Cambridge: Harvard University Press (1960).

Salop, S. C., 'Strategic Entry Deterrence', *American Economic Review* (May 1979), pp. 335–338.

Spence, Michael, 'Entry, Capacity, Investment and Oligopolistic Pricing', *Bell Journal of Economics* (Autumn 1977), pp. 534–544.

Von Neumann, John and Morgenstern, Oskar, *Theory of Games and Economic Behaviour*, Princeton: Princeton University Press (1944).

Weldon, J. C., 'The Multi-Product Firm', *Canadian Journal of Economics and Political Science*, (1948), pp. 176–190.

Williamson, O. E., 'Wage Rates as a Barrier to Entry: The Pennington Case in Perspective' *Quarterly Journal of Economics* (February, 1968), pp. 85–116.

5. ON THE CURRENTS IN MAINSTREAM INDUSTRIAL ORGANIZATION

A. M. Hendricks*

Several themes flowing through the study of industry structure are particularly apparent in the papers of Professors de Jong, Scherer, and Shepherd. These are: the relationships between theoretical and empirical work, between basic research and policy analysis, and the use of static and dynamic models. All three themes are important in shaping industrial organization economics and Scherer has identified two as contributing to an intellectual crisis in the field. The response of the mainstream to date cannot resolve the crisis because it has not addressed the root of the problem. However, the above papers show that at least one opposing paradigm, contestable markets, cannot satisfy the criticisms either. Indeed, until there is a true Kuhnian revolution, the mainstream is preferable to the alternatives currently offered.

THEORY VS. EMPIRICISM

Mainstream industrial organization has generally emphasized empiricism over the development of new theory. The research agenda has been set, in the United States at least, by neoclassical theory. This paradigm has often been challenged by behavior revealed in industry studies. Empirical work shows a rich diversity of behavior not addressed by the theory. *Ad hoc* models can be used to explain behavior in specific oligopolistic industries, but the lack of a unified theory is pointed to as a major weakness.[1] Whether the anomalies suggest a Kuhnian revolution or not, the crisis identified by Scherer is driven by failures of theory to explain existing empirical observations.

One cross-current in this flow of ideas is supplied by W. J. Baumol's candidate for a replacement theory – contestable markets. This approach would dismiss mainstream concerns with anti-competitive behavior and market concentration. In doing so, it also dismisses the traditional empirical agenda of the field.

The mainstream defense against this thrust is well articulated by Scherer and Shepherd. In particular, both point out the inconsistencies between contestability and existing evidence concerning entry and exit conditions for a broad range of industries. Both also examine the theoretical inconsistencies inherent in this proffered replacement candidate and reject it as a mere formalism, rearranging old ideas in new circles.

Scherer and Shepherd also reassert the mainstream concern with empirical work. While expanded research is a noble goal for the field, it fails to address the other cross-currents: that much empirical work is not well-founded in theory or that the theory is too limited. This view is put forward by Bothwell, Cooley and Hall, who point out that the relationship of oligopoly to market outcomes has remained relatively unsusceptible to theoretical analysis.[2] They also strongly suggest that the problems with empirical studies is not the lack of data but rather the lack of the theory to distinguish the flow of causality in correlations that have been uncovered.

To borrow Scherer's analogy, these critics are calling for Copernicus before they are willing to journey to Prague to amass more precise observations. New theory preceded empiricism in Kepler's work. To resort to a purely empirical approach leaves the field of industrial organization open to the fate of the German Historical School.

Further, Kuhn has pointed out that empiricism is shaped by the theoretical paradigm: '. . . the decision to employ a particular piece of apparatus and to use it in a particular way carries an assumption that only certain sorts of circumstances will arise'.[3] The crisis stemming from indeterminate theoretical outcomes will not be resolved by more detailed data, the collection of which presumes what circumstances would arise.

Shepherd's paper recognizes that these criticisms will not be resolved empirically. For example, he points out that part of the current debate is over the nature of competition itself. If managerial responses to rivalry 'can go toward any combination of adjustment within the cost and demand zones. The outcomes are predictable, but only as ranges of values'.[4] More data will primarily document the wide range of the combinations; this documentation alone will not help us to understand them better.

However, the suggestion to embrace indeterminacy through 'soft' analysis, while appealing, does not satisfy the needs of basic economic understanding. Rather, it underscores the opposing needs of policy analysis and basic research.

BASIC RESEARCH VS. POLICY ANALYSIS

Antitrust and regulatory policy is set for political or ethical reasons that are broader than the normative outcomes of economic theory. Industrial organization economists are turned to after the fact to provide the specific parameters for policy: What constitutes monopoly? When is monopoly reasonable? How can one infer from price data whether a conspiracy may have existed?

In this arena, determinacy is impossible. A case must be decided or a policy set without knowledge of the true parameters. Policymakers must be satisfied with knowing middle ranges or tendencies of conduct. *They* are also concerned with avoiding extreme assumptions, even if absurd puzzles may open new avenues of intellectual discovery. Kuhn points out that in a *science* these indeterminacies are precisely the puzzles to be resolved. They will not be tolerated: 'Normal science consists . . . [of] . . . increasing the extent of the match between these facts and the paradigm's predictions, and by further articulation of the paradigm itself'.[5] A renunciation of precise determinacy cannot be accepted for basic science even though indeterminancy itself can be lived with, especially in policy applications.

STATIC VS. DYNAMIC MODELS

The conflict over the use of static and dynamic industry models also relates to the relationship of mainstream industrial organization to policy. For almost one hundred years there has been a need for normative work in the field due to the nature of antitrust and regulatory policy in the United States. Antitrust cases require judgments about what exists in a given instance. Similarly, regulatory policy requires knowledge that will permit the setting of 'fair' or efficient prices and guidelines for behavior. The nature of these policy prescriptions requires static analysis. An appeal to some future good brought on by the evolution of the industry cannot legally justify an action in the present. The research agenda based on static, indeterminate models must proceed until there has been a major change in the basis for industrial policy.

This leads me to comment on Professor de Jong's very interesting summary of the economic field of European industrial organization. In those countries where antitrust policy is moving toward the American experience, I predict the industry analysis will move toward a greater use of the static neoclassical paradigm. This will occur because of the need of policymakers to reach justifiable decisions in antitrust or regulatory matters.

On the other hand, where policymakers question the role of an industry's organization in innovation and growth, the use of new dynamic models can be fostered. While I do not see a Schumpeterian analysis as the most productive direction,[6] there are many other currents in the field that could carve out a new approach.

The papers presented in this session focus attention on the major areas of debate within the field of industrial organization economics. While they are not aimed at many of the counterarguments, they reassert the norms by which a new paradigm or approach must be judged. No current candidate can meet that challenge of straddling so many different conflicting currents.

NOTES

* Assistant Professor of Economics, Tufts University.

1. Baumol, W. J., Panzar, J. C., and Willig, R. D., *Contestable Markets and The Theory of Industry Structure*, New York: Harcourt Brace Jovanovich, Inc. (1982), '. . . we hope to provide a unifying framework for a pure theory of industrial organization where none was available before'. p. 3. See also, Baumol, W. J., 'Contestable Markets: An Uprising in the Theory of Industry Structure', *American Economic Review*, 72 (March 1982), pp. 1–15.
2. Bothwell, J. L., Cooley, T. F., and Hall, T. E., 'A New View of the Market Structure-Performance Debate', *The Journal of Industrial Economics*, XXXII (4) (June 1984), pp. 413 and 397, respectively.
3. Kuhn, T. S., *The Structure of Scientific Revolutions*, International Encyclopedia of Unified Science, Vol. 2, Number 2, Chicago: University of Chicago Press (1970), p. 59.
4. Shepherd, this conference, pp. 9–10.
5. Kuhn, *op. cit.*, p. 24.
6. Helwege, A. and Hendricks, A., 'Contestability and Creative Destruction: Two Approaches to Monopoly', unpublished paper (September 1985).

PART II. INTERNATIONAL ASPECTS

6. INTERNATIONAL COMPETITION, PRODUCTIVITY CHANGE AND THE ORGANIZATION OF PRODUCTION

Gunnar Eliasson

1. THE PROBLEM[1]

The international opportunity set

Extensive foreign trade in manufacturing products is characteristic of the European industrial nations. One consequence of a foreign industrial sector that grows faster than the national economy is that the national economies become more firmly knitted together, not only through trade flows but also through a production and distribution organization, and in finance. From an analytical point of view the national boundaries soon cease to be of interest, except as a statistical observation post and a source of trouble. It is global firm and market behavior that matters. However, the set of nationally unrestricted international firms have a wider business opportunity set than the domestic firms and their resource dispositions tend to frustrate national authorities in their effort to control the domestic economy through policies.

This last observation is no minor thing. In some of the more advanced, small European countries the foreign part of industrial firms employ more than a quarter of the industrial labor force. The 10 largest Swedish forms that directly and indirectly employ some 30 percent of the domestic manufacturing labor force employ even more people abroad and dominate Swedish exports.

When an undisciplined, post oil-crisis economic policy in Sweden released extreme wage overshooting in Swedish manufacturing industries in the mid-70s a worried discussion followed about losses of market shares and the nose dive in machinery and equipment spending that occurred. It is interesting to observe how the picture changes with the definition of market shares. According to Jagrén (1985) the international Swedish firms as a group did not lose market shares. In both measures

de Jong, H. W., Shepherd, W. G. (eds) Mainstreams in Industrial Organization
© 1986 Martinus Nijhoff Publishers, Dordrecht. ISBN 978-94-017-0495-3

OECD production plus net imports minus net exports by sectors are used as denominator. Deliveries from Sweden slowed relative to foreign market growth, but actual global sales of the multinationals outside Sweden kept up with market growth. While hardware investment may have dropped, R & D investment and investment in marketing – mostly abroad – increased. It appears as if Swedish multinationals kept up their foreign market shares by adding value through more service production abroad than through production for direct exports out of Sweden.

We also know that Swedish multinationals concentrated production significantly in response to the domestic, so-called cost crisis, abandoning loss or low profit activities. This often meant a lower growth in the total volume of output and exports. Using the definitions of markets that firms themselves use to assess their market power, this meant gains of market shares in their main markets, but often losses of shares if we use the broader market definitions used to assess the international market position of an exporting country. Whatever definition is used expansion of exports from factories at home as well as expansion of deliveries from foreign subsidiaries were made possible by a parallel expansion of foreign establishments (Eliasson–Bergholm–Jagrén–Horwitz, 1985).

At least 75% of all foreign employees in Swedish multinationals are engaged in operating the global market network of the business organization and close to the market, customized production. This activity appears to be critical for the profitability of domestic activies, especially factory production.

For most of Europe, hence, we have to make a distinction between the firm, the manufacturing sector and the nation when discussing competitiveness.

As a consequence, endogenous organizational change among the institutions called firms (entry, reconfiguration and exit) and endogenous change of the rules of the market game become a part of industrial economies – and a necessary part if one wants to understand the macroeconomic growth process that underlies the national competitive problem. The Swedish micro-to-macro model partially responds to Arrow's (1959) quest about the need for a theory of general monopolistic competition. It is still, however, very crude in its representation of how temporary knowledge-based rents are generated, and how institutions use information in the market process. The economic systems' properties (market process and interdependency) are, however, there. When discussing the firm as the institution that generates productivity change in a 'technical' sense, as distinct from the market process, the only major thing that we miss completely appears to be endogenous institutional change occurring in response to the market process.

Differing objectives matter

The special feature of European firms in the context of the market allocation process is that many of them, and the large ones in particular, operate across national boundaries in the trade, production and/or finance dimensions. The objectives of firms and of nations differ. Business firms are solely concerned with their long-term profit objectives, even though their policy manuals may suggest otherwise. The objectives of Government and Nations are oriented towards the welfare of their citizens and towards the pursuit of a domestic and international power game. It has been a well-nursed notion in economics since Adam Smith that all these ambitions fit together nicely within a well-organized market economy. How that is accomplished, or not accomplished, is part of the dynamic market story. But it is obvious that the ambitions of governments to pursue welfare ambitions through extensive interference in the market process explain the various degrees of success in economic performance between the industrial nations (Eliasson, 1984b). It also helps to explain the fact that national economies can be in bad shape, while the industry sector at large carries on well in an international comparison.

A particular instance of the conflict between the micro objectives of agents in the market, and the macro objectives of governments are the difficulties of democratically organized nations to pursue a consistent long-term policy in times of distress. The *discount rate* in policy making at various levels of aggregation figures importantly in any understanding of dynamic markets, and the economic competitiveness of nations. With the business unit defined as a financial decision unit the trade-off between the long term and the short term occurs in the capital market. In the capital market process any conflict in that respect between micro agents and policy bodies is sorted out. The new feature of international trade, investment and finance is that the discount rate in domestic (investment) decisions in European countries in particular nowadays is largely determined in the international markets for finance.

The origin of productivity growth and comparative advantages

In the modern, market based firm productivity growth occurs through institutional reconfiguration rather than through the transmission of technical innovations in the production process. Economies of scale appear to be increasing in the development and global marketing of specialized products, while they are decreasing in the production of standard products. Institutional change is the vehicle for exploiting such new technologies associated with the organization of overall production, marketing and distribution of constantly changing specialized products. The result appears as productivity increases at the level of the firm as a financial organization.

The emergence of the 'modern', international firms, the competitive edge of which is generated through an ongoing investment process in learning and knowledge accumulation, is making the comparative advantages of a nation indeterminate and blurring the economist standard notion of 'a market'. It is argued in this paper that the modern firm, its development into a major service producer, its foreign dimension and its competitiveness cannot be understood if not framed in a theory of profit oriented firm decision making and behavior, with the firm being seen as an autonomous, financial decision unit, and operating in an explicit dynamic market process. The knowledge to manage large business organizations efficiently, and large international groups in particular, may, in fact, constitute the main competitive advantage of the advanced industrial nations. Hence, to understand the policy problems of industrial economies, and the small open economies in particular, we need a theory that explains *how* institutions change and *how* macro economies behave in terms of that process.

Such a theory will certainly modify, or change a number of standard conclusions from the theory of competition and trade. This paper will present evidence supporting the need for such a revision of theory, or indicate some approaches to take.

The need for a general theory of dynamic markets and their institutions

The Swedish Schumpeterian economist Johan Åkerman once (1950) observed that a theory pretending to capture the dynamics of a market economy 'has to incorporate the four fundamental ideas of interdependency, value, process and institutions'.

I am following Åkerman in spirit in organizing this paper. The special role of (foreign) competition, whether viewed from the point of view of a firm or a nation, has to do with how it affects the dynamics of resource use, within the administrative system of a business organization (*institutions*), or between business entities in the market. We are not only concerned with how it affects competition through the market *process* – the traditional concern of industrial organization. The supply process, or a dynamic theory of the firm in a broad sense has to be integrated into a general analysis of the interaction of institutions in all markets (*interdependency*). One particular aspect of this is the internationalization of firms and how it affects market behavior. Without a 'notion' of general dynamic market interaction it is not possible to understand the 'cost crisis' of, for instance, the Swedish economy during the 1970s that brought industrial production to a complete stand still for almost 10 years.

In doing so I may be broadening the content of my paper beyond what was originally intended by the organizers of this conference. For small, advanced industrialized countries like the Netherlands, Switzerland or Sweden, this in my view is, however, the natural approach. Foreign competition exercises a discipline on the policy makers and hence on the macroeconomy. Foreign markets widen the opportunity set of business firms. This is true also for larger industrial countries, but to a smaller extent.

To understand the 'unusual' economic events among the industrial countries in the past decade the foreign dimension has to be brought into the analysis both from the point of view of the firm and the macro economy.

During the last decade the industrial world has witnessed a diverse restructuring of the production system of various countries. While admiration has been expressed for the vitality of the US economy, the Japanese industrial restaging still escapes understanding if looked at through western glasses. European industries, on the other hand, have been regarded with concern.

Part of, or most of, our lack of understanding of the new macroeconomic phenomena in the industrial world has to do with our lack of (quantitative) understanding of the dynamics of the market allocation process, and our limitation to data generated by a national statistical system. (In fact, none of the phenomena discussed are new to economics. They are simply forgotten by economists.)

Preoccupation with the static theory of economic interdependency has prevented the development of the dynamic theory of interacting markets that I am asking for to carry my analysis to the aggregate level of the national economy (*welfare*). Our lack of empirical understanding of what goes on within the paramount institution of the western economy – the firm – has led us to view the firm as a hardware processing unit. With a given number of production functions being ex ante price takers in markets and no explicit representation of the price and quantity realization process we miss the point that a market economy is best represented as an ongoing process *of general, monopolistic competition* (my interpretation of Arrow 1959) between a varying number of actors, competition being based on knowledge rents acquired through experimentation and learning in the markets. Since we are carrying on extensive research in both areas at my institute I take this broader approach and discuss firm behavior and reorganization, with special attention to its foreign dimension in the context of a micro-to-macro (M–M) analysis.

The main content of this paper will be to present evidence of the changing nature of the business organization and its growing dependence on a unique knowledge base. I will then discuss what this implies for the theory of the firm and market behavior in both cases with particular emphasis on the international dimension. I will also sketch my ideas about what this means for the development of a dynamic market based macro theory, which is lacking in economics (Pelikan, 1985).

I want to present my story about the international organization of production at three levels of aggregation:

1. the interior life of the business unit defined as a financial entity (next section on institutions and the determination of productivity change);
2. the interaction of such business units in markets, defining as clearly as possible what a dynamic market is (Section 3);
3. the welfare aspect of foreign competition; nationally and globally (Section 4).

The third level of aggregation makes up, of course, the micro–macro consequences of the other two, and integrates the four fundamentals of Åkerman (1950).

2. THE MULTIDIVISION FIRM AS A MULTINATIONAL CORPORATION

What does a firm do?

This section introduces the business organization and its interior life. We will do this broadly to pave the way for the next two sections on the market and on the micro–macro–aggregation problem. The market process can be no more than the combined action of all its institutions. The institutions that we discuss are the suppliers and traders of goods and services. Their market engagement tends to be very fragmented and technological change is constantly reshaping, more than ever before, the content of its activities.

We begin by introducing a listing of the normal activity set of a manufacturing firm to hammer home three main points, namely *that* every business firm to some extent internalizes activities that are normally part of the market process, as distinct from factory production, *that* the extent of these activities within a manufacturing firm varies and depends on technological and market circumstances, and *that* the major source

Table 1. Major tasks in a business organization.

1.	Organizational change
2.	Innovative activities, organizational change
3.	Product development
4.	Portfolio management
5.	Banking
6.	Insurance and risk reduction
7.	Factory production
8.	Marketing and sales
9.	Education
10.	Welfare tasks

of productivity advance has been internal reorganizations in the activity set. During the last decade these recombinations have occurred primarily *between* the activities in the list above. (An especially important organizational change is the extension of a foreign marketing arm.)

Productivity advance within the firm to a large extent appears to be associated with these recombinations of activities. A special feature is the expansion of marketing (item 8) in the international dimension and of product development (item 3), together shifting the firm onto a product technology base. In addition, the growing financial and portfolio management activities of firms (also in an international direction, items 4, 5 and 6) emphasize the diffuse borderlines between the market and the administrative system called a firm. In order not to look ridiculous, the theory of the firm and of the market economy soon has to come up with an explicit representation of these other dominant non-factory-process activities that essentially deal with the firm as an *information processor*, as a *trader* in the market, and as an administrative user of information to dynamically coordinate interior production activities.

Knowledge matters for international competitiveness

Successful business organizations in small, but advanced industrial nations soon outgrew their national boundaries. One reason for that is that advanced industrial production is always based somehow on specialization. To grow big, therefore, requires extensive trade across national boundaries.

Second, the knowledge to operate large business organizations is a prerequisite for an advanced industrial nation. Many production activities can be rub on a small scale. But some require a large scope of operations. In this respect I think economics has been much too preoccupied with the

Table 2. The share in domestic manufacturing employment of the largest manufacturing firms – global firm employment in percent of domestic manufacturing employment 1983.

	Sweden	U.S.*	U.K.†	Switzerland	Japan	West Germany	Canada	France
5 largest	26.1	7.9	10.6	53.7	3.4	10.8	11.8	11.5
10 largest	36.2	11.2	16.8	73.2	5.2	16.5	16.7	17.1
20 largest	46.4	15.3	25.5		7.2	21.6		
40 largest	57.0	21.4						

*1984. The numbers for the U.S. may appear large. The reasons are that the largest U.S. manufacturing firms – as in Sweden and Switzerland – are very internationalized and that U.S. manufacturing employment in percent of total employment is relatively low.
†Excluding Shell and Unilever.
Source: Jagrén (1986), Fortune, Annual Reports, Common Market Official Statistics.

Table 3. Global value added of firms in percent of domestic manufacturing value added – Nordic countries 1982 and in brackets 1976.

	Sweden	Denmark	Finland	Norway
5 largest	22.0 (13.6)	10.9 (8.2)	16.3 (13.6)	16.7 (12.8)
10 largest	32.9 (21.7)	13.9 (11.5)	23.3 (19.7)	21.8 (16.1)

Note: Comparison between 1976 and 1982 has a selection bias, since the firms included are those that were the largest in 1982.
Source: Oxelheim (1984).

scale of hardware processing. While plant size seems to be on the decline as an indicator of competitiveness, financial scale, the capacity to embark on 'large' projects, to commit funds long term, and to absorb risks appear to be growing in importance (Eliasson–Fries–Jagrén–Oxelheim, 1984). The knowledge to run large organizations efficiently was recognized already by Marshall (1919) as the third production factor, but has not been much elaborated in production theory. I have, in fact, stumbled on an old Swedish economics text from 1768[2] which is much more elaborate in this respect than any modern text I have seen. It compares Swedish industry with British and Dutch industries and takes extensive note of the deficient knowledge base of Swedish firms, and of shipyards in particular. (The industrial knowledge base upon which nations like Sweden, Switzerland, and the Netherlands base their economic welfare today is virtually impossible to accumulate without the parallel development of a large foreign business sector. To me this is a much more useful way of looking at the determinants of national welfare than to begin at the trade end.)

Hence, a small, advanced industrial nation also has to develop the knowledge to operate firms across national boundaries through trade, international production and finance. (The more dominant a few firms in the national economy (see Tables 2 and 3), the more internationalized are firms.)

The knowledge to operate across national boundaries has been typical of European firms in all of recorded history because of the national fragmentation of Europe. The 'international side' of that knowledge has not been developed until recently in U.S. firms, probably because of the size of domestic U.S. markets. Somehow, Japanese producers have been able to reap the returns from international trade in the classical way through direct goods exports from a domestic production base. (This makes it interesting to see what distinguishes Japanese firms from European firms, and – in addition – what distinguishes European firms with extensive international production from those who export from a production base at home, like the Japanese firms.)

The concentration of financial control

What I just said suggests first that the smaller the successful industrial nation, the larger the proportion of the industrial labor force concentrated in a small group of large companies that critically affect macroeconomic behavior of the nation. This can be observed in Table 2 (compare the U.S., Japan, West Germany, Switzerland and Sweden). The unexpected observation is probably that Japan has such a low concentration ratio while the U.S. concentration ratio is so large. Second, the smaller the national economy, the larger the fraction of total value added generated outside the domestic economy. Third, we should also expect that – given the size of the country – concentration will increase with *quality of industrial* performance. This requires impressionistic reading to see in Table 2. The proposition is however confirmed in Table 3 of the Nordic countries, of comparable size, but with different qualities of the industrial sectors. For the Nordic countries, we have had access to value added data for the individual firms which gives more appropriate concentration ratios.

The table also exhibits a growth in concentration ratios of all the four Nordic countries. This may reflect the combined specialization of production that we know has continued. But the table also shows a different tendency that has been at work simultaneously. The data cover the firms defined as financial units, not as production establishments. Hence, they exhibit the concentration of financial control rather than production. For instance, the group of ten for Sweden include the three firms Electrolux, ASEA and Ericsson. This group carries on production that corresponds roughly to what Siemens in West Germany, Philips in the Netherlands and General Electric in the U.S. do. The three Swedish companies together employed (globally) more than 223 thousand people in 1984, Siemens 319 thousand, Philips 344 thousand and General Electric 340 thousand people. With the same financial organization of 'the four', concentration would be much higher in Sweden.

The difficulties of designing meaningful size and concentration measures are nicely illustrated by Pratten's (1976) observations from comparing 'matched' Swedish and U.K. firms. The Swedish firms were much smaller as financial units than their U.K. counterparts, but they, nevertheless, operated larger, or much larger production plants. Hence, the productivity performance and output growth rates of Swedish firms were much higher

Table 4. Average size of the five largest firms in 1984.

	Number of employees of corporate group (thousands)						
	The Netherlands	Sweden	US	UK*	West Germany	Japan	Switzerland
1972	121	51	451	219	195	–	70
1983/84	100	67	444	167	223	134	85

*Excluding Unilever and Shell.

than those of U.K. firms. However, the U.K. firms recorded a higher rate of return to capital on the average.

It is interesting in this context to ask whether the decentralized organization of Swedish electrical and electronics production reflects the size of the nation, or a different industrial finance and banking tradition. The latter seems to be the case. But we also note that the last decade has witnessed an intense merger activity across the industrial nations combined with an intense shedding of unprofitable lines of business. The result of this 'recombinatorial activity' appears to be (see Table 4) that the very large business organizations in the U.K. have shrunk while they have increased somewhat in Sweden. This may reflect different responses to profitability problems in the 70s, that have been solved in Sweden through increased technological specialization, combined with increased global scale of operations, but also a shift in the direction where economies of scale matter, namely in finance and risk reduction.

From cost efficient factory production towards a product technology base

The most obvious structural change of the past decades has been the emergence of fast growing engineering, fine chemicals and pharmaceutical firms among manufacturing industries. These are firms having their unique knowledge base in a product technology, rather than in the efficient factory processing of simple products for staple goods markets, where the competition parameter is 'price'. Some firms have managed to change their internal structure from a basic industry towards a product innovator orientation. (The Swedish company Sandvik is one example.) Such a transformation as a rule is a very long winding affair, stretching over several decades, and is not normally successful. The general picture is that 'product based' firms have grown faster than 'process based' firms. However, also companies already based on product technologies have experienced great difficulties evolving into what I call the modern

Table 5A. Investments* in the 5 and the 37 largest Swedish manufacturing groups, 1978.

	Firms have been ranked by foreign employment Percent			
	The 5 largest groups		The 37 largest groups	
	All group	Foreign subsidiaries only	All group	Foreign subsidiaries only
R & D	25	10	21	6
Machinery and buildings	45	41	52	42
Marketing	30	49	27	52
Total	100	100	100	100

*Investments in Marketing and R & D have been estimated from cost data.

industrial firm. A particular endowment of prior industrial knowledge, often infused through a change of top management, appears to be an important prerequisite. The main qualification for success appears to be the ability to engage in continued successful product innovations, and to develop the marketing network necessary to establish the right customer relationships for highly specialized products. This requires changing the knowledge base of the entire organization, which is difficult, and the investment of huge financial resources in 'soft' capital, which, as a consequence, is highly risky. Nevertheless, Swedish engineering firms at large have been successful in managing this transformation. We currently have a research project at IUI devoted to investigating what prior knowledge and what management methods were needed to do exactly that. The data in Tables 5A and 5B give an idea of the content of activities of the largest Swedish firms. If we had picked the most successful firms, the concentration of invested resources to products developed through R & D spending and marketing, mostly abroad would have been even more pronounced than the 50 percent for the 37 largest firms in 1978.

If economies of scale are diminishing in importance in hardware production, while they are on the increase in R & D spending on product development and global marketing – as seems to be the case – an extremely dynamic and aggressive international market economy is developing. R & D spending for product development and global marketing are reinforcing each other, generating new institutional combinations and overall productivity change. But shifting into specialized product markets competing with rapid product quality change appears to be a highly risky commercial strategy. This is something firms

Table 5B. Wage and salary costs in different spending categories in the 5 and the 20 Swedish groups, 1978.

	Percent			
	The 5 largest groups		The 20 largest groups	
	All group	Foreign subsidiaries only	All group	Foreign subsidiaries only
R & D	7	3	7	2
Processing and other	63	52	70	58
Marketing and distribution	30	45	23	40
Total	100	100	100	100

Note. That we have been unable to separate out administrative costs etc. from production process cost data and that wages and salaries in marketing and distribution probably are underestimated. The 'other' item should be in the neighborhood of 15 percent of total costs according to preliminary data from an ongoing IUI study.

Source: Eliasson, G., *De utlandsetablerade företagen och den svenska ekonomin*, IUI Research Report No. 26, Stockholm 1984.

in most markets for engineering products have experienced during the 70s and 80s, but notably firms in electronic industries.

Increased uncertainty breeds growth in financial organizations

Increased market uncertainty has to be coped with, and firms tend to do that through diversifying and increasing their size as financial units. This, however, tends to have adverse effects on productivity through increasing bureaucratization of firms and diminishing internal flexibility.

A commercial bank is the typical exploiter of economies of scale. A manufacturing firm carries on a multitude of financing functions internally. Technically the banking activities of firms can be expanded. Incentives to do so have existed during the entire post-war period. Credit markets of European countries have been controlled or regulated, providing – together with corporate taxation systems – an incentive to keep internal financial resources within the organization. This may have pushed rate of return requirements down (see Södersten–Lindberg, 1983). In addition, manufacturing business has become more risky, emphasizing the need for internal risk reduction. The shift towards a product based technology places new demands on financing and makes access to traditional, 'conservative' banking finance more difficult. Product development takes longer, and finance requirements grow, but once in the market, product life has been consistently shortened. New capital structures require various forms of internal, or equity finance rather than conventional loan finance. One response has been the development of larger, financially defined manufacturing firms, that incorporate some major functions of a bank, an investment company, and an insurance company in order to internalize the markets for money and risk (see Table 1).

While economies of scale appear to be diminishing in factory production[3] they have been on the increase in marketing, finance and risk management. This has also led to the creation of larger business organizations. This development clearly requires a parallel development of management technology to successfully coordinate the diverse activities of a large manufacturing firm listed in Table 1. One could also say – and this takes us over to the next section on the market – that the larger firms grow as financial organizations, the more of the market coordination functions in finance, production, distribution etc. are internalized as administrative coordination, and the less of total resources devoted to factory production (item 7 in Table 1). Non-factory production also requires a relatively larger input of knowledge, or human capital, than factory production. Hence, I venture to propose that the more advanced the industrial nation, the less of total resources within manufacturing that are devoted to factory production. The non-processing part of resource use is altogether devoted to various forms of information processing. Part of the human capital formation is learning through constant trial-and-error experimentation in the market. Firms that succeed develop a competitive base in knowledge, the value of which depends on how fast and for how long they can update and maintain their 'knowledge edge' in international markets. This change is not only messing up our statistical nomenclatures. It will also force a change in our notions of a comparative advantage, the competitive situation of a national economy and a market.

3. THE INTERNATIONAL MARKET PROCESS

We begin this section with a few words on the standard notion of a market theory and observe that the profession has had great difficulties in breaking loose from static general equilibrium theory. But even a dynamic general theory of monopolistic competition called for by Arrow (1959) is not enough. One also has to allow for a varying number of players in the market. This is how Åkerman's fourth factor 'institutions' – enters the picture. But it is not enough to allow for free pricing and free entry and exit to ensure a viable market process. The major vehicle for productivity change is *institutional reorganization within existing units* and – even though we know little about this phenomenon – institutional fragmentation, recombination and merger activities. This section particularly emphasizes international markets and the factors that make business organizations transcend national boundaries. Once you have a theory for institutional change you also have a theory for technological change. Since technological change in a broad sense is the base from which competitive entry and aggressive pricing behavior is exercised, a theory of dynamic markets has to be explicit – not necessarily formal – about the ways institutional change is engineered. We discuss this on the basis of some fragmentary evidence from Swedish firm data, and then go on in the next section to Åkerman's second factor, welfare, but in a new, dynamic setting. The reason for taking this view is that the internationalization of firms plays a major role both in defining performance of the market process and (in the last section) in disciplining and restricting the scope of action of Governments.

What is a market?

The economist's standard notion of a market theory – general equilibrium theory – lacks the essential features of a dynamic market process. It is static, while all market activities take place in time. The concept of equilibrium does not signify the end point of a market process. Hence, it is difficult to envision the Walras–Arrow–Debreu–Hahn model as a formalization of the real 'invisible hand' Adam Smith thought of. All information needed to find 'the equilibrium' is assumed to be available, and can be gathered and interpreted immediately and at no, or at a known, cost. This is a theory of central planning, not of a market economy, according to Pelikan (1985) in his reinterpretation of the discussion from Lange (1936) to Malinvaud (1967).

When the auctioneer is removed and agents are allowed to be price setters general monopolistic competition with a variable number of players becomes the market game. Furthermore, the competitive process becomes part of the information gathering process. If information gathering and use is a major cost item in total production it will also be a major determinant of whatever equilibrium properties the macroeconomic process possesses. Also a major part of the competitive process is to make information processing more efficient. This – as we have just observed – occurs mainly through institutional reorganization. As a consequence, full information is not theoretically possible and the meaningfulness of standard notions of equilibrium become doubtful (see Eliasson 1985a, Chapter VII). Since such a notion of equilibrium is the base of standard welfare analysis, and of related normative analysis of trade and market organization there may be a great principal problem lurking behind the small and reasonable improvements in theory suggested by Åkerman (1950).

This is also the 'model' of the micro–macro market process that is needed to understand the dynamics of resource allocation or aggregation in the next section. The preceding account of the modern firm emphasized how the firm devoted the bulk of its resources to doing exactly what the auctioneer in the Walrasian general equilibrium system does at no charge.

There is a large literature in which information costs are brought into the Walrasian framework. Search theory, notably labor market approaches (Diamond, 1984) is perhaps the most well-known approach. Matching theory, principal agent theory, the theory of teams, etc. and Williamson's (1975) theory on the hierarchical structure of business organizations are other approaches. Clower–Friedman (1985) introduce traders in information explicitly, and they come closest to what I have in mind, namely that 'information processing' is a natural part of the production process that can be handled by producers of goods, or special agents that they hire. It all depends. Clower–Friedman's agents are price-setters in a very restricted sense, i.e., no more than allowed for the existence of a static equilibrium. The actors also make up a fixed set. I believe empirical evidence is such that both of these simplifying notions will have to go, and that causes problems for the analysis of the next section.

The business unit; a producer, an information processor or a market intermediator

Table 5 gives data on the allocation of internal investment activities in the largest Swedish firms. They tell that service production is significant, or even dominant in manufacturing, and that it is oriented towards improving the quality of the product as it eventually reaches the final user. In a broad sense R & D activities – mostly oriented towards product improvement – and marketing should be classified as information gathering and use.

The importance of information and knowledge becomes even more important if we take a close look at each activity. A significant part of costs – not explicit in the table – is devoted to the (management) task of holding the entire business entity together (budgeting, profit control, reporting etc.), making the firm entity transparent as to where profits and losses occur, and taking action upon this information. (Eliasson, 1976; Eliasson–Fries–Jagrén–Oxelheim, 1984).

We have learned from other IUI studies that each production task resulting in a given product can be organized in a variety of ways and that studies of firms reveal all that variation. Some solutions are motivated by relative factor costs. But many solutions that are superior in all respects clearly depend on a superior product, productivity and market knowledge and know-how to combine it. If the right person, or group of persons, enters a firm, an upgrading can often be achieved at an insignificant investment. I have had the opportunity to see how that was done when a Swedish company bought a British company and introduced the Swedish organization and management of production.

Institutional fragmentation and recombination

In many firms information processing, transacting and trading draw more resources than factory production. While economies of scale appear to be of declining importance in factory production, they gain in importance in marketing, finance and 'insurance' in a broad sense. To some extent this must be the consequence of more efficient administrative management techniques and hence an internalization of market processes. But it is also – as we observed in the previous section – a result of a changing market environment (more uncertainty, etc) and technological change, especially in terms of bringing the right type of product to the right customer. Production and product development to an increasing extent require highly specialized inputs. In some areas not even the world's largest companies can afford to, have the time to or can develop and keep all these specialities inhouse.

The increasing multiplicity and service orientation of total manufacturing production is setting the stage for institutional, or organizational fragmentation. Sometimes service production is located inside the firms, sometimes the same services are hired. It all depends and this clearly blurs the concept of a firm and of manufacturing industry. 'Deindustrialization' has been a key note for political concern in the industrial world meaning a diminishing share of employment. In fact, the sector 'business services' has been the fastest growing employer in most industrial countries. If employment in business services is added to manufacturing employment, the decline in the use of man-hours in manufacturing and business services together in percent of total employment in the U.S. or in Sweden is not pronounced and the downward trend has been present for more than 20 years (see Figure 1). In fact, the *level* of employment in the U.S. increases strongly. If employment in foreign manufacturing establishments of U.S. and Swedish firms and in domestic wholesale and retail sale associated with manufacturing is also added manufacturing and related activities together appear to be expanding rather than declining activities in relation to the rest of the economy. The bulk of these external service activities are substitutes for internal transactions costs for similar service activities (see Lindberg–Pousette, 1985). They are either internally operated as part of the administrative system called a firm, or the corresponding services are externally hired in the market. We have found in several IUI studies that the way service production is organized and integrated with goods production is highly important for overall business performance.

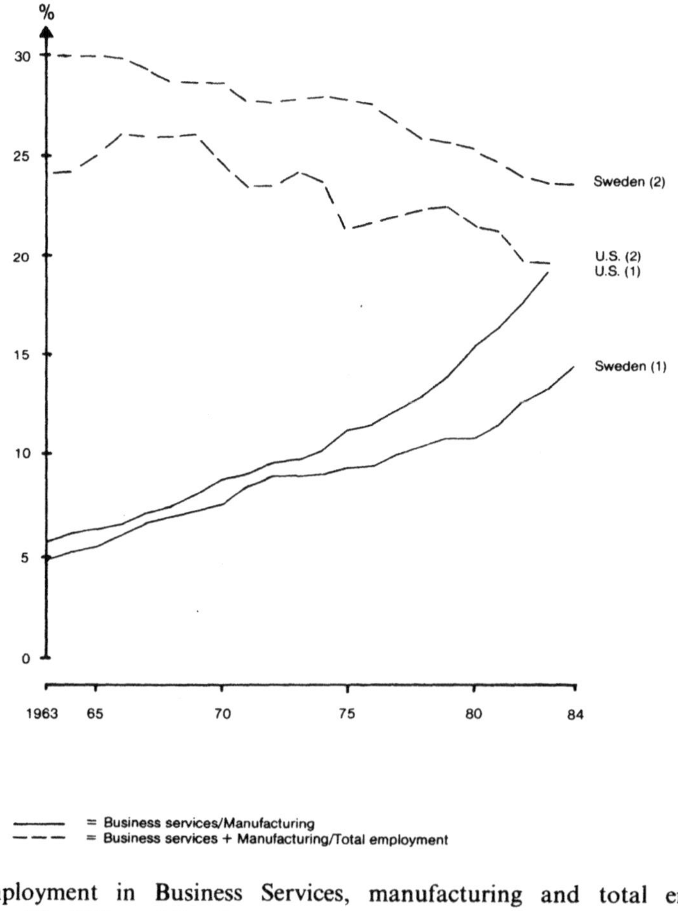

Fig. 1. Employment in Business Services, manufacturing and total employment 1963–1984 – The U.S. and Sweden.

Customer markets

The bulk of manufacturing service production concerns product development or marketing, sales and distribution. The more complex the product, the more customized service customers require. If factory production is a small fraction of value added, while value added more than doubles after having left the factory gate and is boosted by service, maintenance guarantees etc., it is obvious that price in the simple meaning of production theory ceases to be the dominant market parameter.

The bulk of foreign activity of Swedish firms, and probably of other European firms as well, is devoted to marketing activities of various kinds, boosting the value of the product and bringing the producer into the customer's shop. With a specialized machine installation you don't shift suppliers easily, as in staple goods markets. Okun (1981) has coined the term 'customer markets' for this kind of supplier-customer relationship. And the relationships can take on a multitude of 'institutional forms'.

What do we mean by a free market that contributes to efficient resource allocation?

Looked at from this end the concept of 'a free market' that we use to derive welfare conclusions in trade theory and general equilibrium theory takes on several new dimensions. First of all the bulk of cost applications has to do with the processing of information to design the product to suit the customer and move the products to the right customer. Costs associated with running the auctioneer activity, or rather the invisible hand, are more important for determining the welfare optimum, than national factor endowments and comparative advantages associated with factory production of goods and the trading of goods per se. As McKenzie observed already in 1954, if exports from one country depends on imports of raw materials, parts or components from another country, 'comparative advantages' begin to be unstable. When the comparative advantage in one particular area of production depends on the local ability to exploit an internationally available pool of technical and commercial information, for one thing comparative advantages become very shifty since any competitor any time can come up with a better idea. Furthermore, they become critically dependent upon the local efficiency in learning and keeping up with competitors. If a marketing organization in addition transcends national borderlines and is the prime profit determinant of the exporting firm comparative advantages become indeterminate. This conclusion is further reinforced in a situation when a country's exports originate from a combination of domestic product design and development knowledge and final assembly know-how from imported parts and components, that are marketed through an international network of subsidiaries. This is more or less true for between 25 and 50 percent of industrial production in countries like the Netherlands, Sweden and Switzerland.

The importance of free competitive entry

The free movement of goods is one criterion for a free market, but free access to, and use of information may be as important. With information costs in the forefront, free pricing by suppliers and free competitive entry of new competitors and new products and services become critical welfare determinants. However, if the knowledge to use information in efficient and innovative ways can be accumulated as part of the ongoing production process, you would still expect to find monopolies – or firms – even in very open economies and in extremely competitive market environments (cf. the query in Caves–Parker–Spence–Scott, 1980). At least ongoing IUI studies are accumulating an overwhelming evidence that it is the knowledge to run and innovate complex manufacturing organizations that explains the development of the modern firm, based on a temporary Schumpeterian knowledge rent, as presented in the previous section. The foreign establishment of subsidiary activities may in some cases be motivated by factory production cost considerations. In the bulk of cases, however, it is either a profitable marketing investment or – which is the same thing – a profitable way of climbing trade barriers establishing a form of competitive entry in protected markets (Eliasson–Bergholm–Horwitz–Jagrén, 1985; Swedenborg, 1979).

4. MACROECONOMIC PERFORMANCE, POLICY AND WELFARE

When reading this section on macro economic performance keep the data in Table 6 in mind.

The picture conveyed is that of a group of large, international marketing organizations that develop and assemble goods from imported parts and components. These firms dominate outgoing foreign trade of the entire country, and partly also import trade, and hence economic performance of the macro economy. In addition, a large part of product value in the hands of the final customer, often more than half, has been added

Table 6. The 10 largest Swedish manufacturing corporations.

- account directly and indirectly in Sweden for 30 percent of the domestic manufacturing labor force, and
- in addition employ more people abroad, mostly in activities associated with marketing.
- account for 30 percent of total Swedish exports, most of it being delivered to controlled foreign subsidiaries
- account for more than 70 percent of total Swedish foreign employment
- account for almost half of total R & D spending in Swedish manufacturing
- are world product leaders in at least one set of products.

in marketing and distributive networks outside the producing country. Sometimes autonomous traders produce the extra value added, but to an increasing extent marketing, distribution and customer service is run within the producing organization.

The firms base their dominant market position on a unique product and market know-how that has to be updated and renewed at a faster rate than that with which competitors learn about it. Their market monopoly lasts as long as they are able to stay ahead in that race. The temporary monopoly rent is a means of investing in knowledge to stay ahead. On the surface this situation appears to support Schumpeter's gloomy prediction of the automatization of development, increasing concentration and the merging of the industrial and the political systems. On the whole, the large, international Swedish firms have been successful in adjusting their structures to the new, market situations of the 80s. And the Government has indeed, on and off, been attempting to run industrial policies through the large firms (Eliasson–Ysander, 1983; Eliasson, 1984b). However, these policy attempts have generally been failures, prolonging the adjustment process, saving some capital for the owners and leaving the responsibility to switch off final terminal support to dead industrial capital to the politicians, who are the least suited to perform that task. Even though the large firms are old and dominant, there has been some significant turnover through relative growth, with a gradual phase down of the dominant basic industries of the 60s. Moreover, a significant innovative activity has occurred among the small firms (Granstrand, 1985).

With some exceptions, the large firms of the small European countries are not large compared with the large firms of large countries. In addition, few firms are large when placed in a global market setting. Success in global markets has made it possible for some firms in small countries to grow very large compared to the national economy where they happen to reside. They are still small in an international setting and as long as competition in international markets remains intense, the concentration problem should not be a problem. From this, however, does not follow that we can return to traditional, general equilibrium analysis to evaluate the welfare consequences of foreign trade.

A welfare analysis of trade, and of foreign trade in particular, has to recognize (1) the market process as being that of general monopolistic competition and, hence, the existence and constant turnover of temporary rents. While Schumpeter (1934) saw innovating entrepreneurs as disturbers of the Walrasian equilibrium, and the engines of the growth process, Kirzner (1973) rather viewed entrepreneurs as an equilibrating force that responded to potential temporary rents with innovative behavior. Together these principles capture the dynamics of product competition among firms, which is something fundamentally different from the notion of competition implicit in general equilibrium theory. In addition, it appears as if the sustenance of diversity of structures through a steady, innovative, rent creating process is a necessary condition for stable, macroeconomic growth (Eliasson, 1984c). If this is accepted free competitive entry in the production process, and the acceptance of free, competitive exit will be the prime welfare enhancing attributes to watch for. In a global setting, Japanese competition is probably a far better anti-trust policy than any anti-trust law, and all labor and parliamentary noise bears witness to that. This is why we now return to the diversity of objectives among firms and politicians.

Dynamic market competition as we have presented it generates benefits in the long-term in the form of growth in output at the expense of a rapid and, to a disquieting microeconomic adjustment process. Nations badly organized to accommodate this adjustment tend to lose in long-term economic welfare, i.e., nations badly organized to impose a long-term view on its inhabitants, or a low political discount rate. This problem is largely political and pedagogical.

To understand and support this competition process through policies it becomes necessary to understand how temporary rents are generated, which means being knowledgeable about the ways firms take their long-term profit oriented decisions. Foreign trade will be one of many macroeconomic consequences of these decisions. Unfortunately, the economics profession is *not* very knowledgeable about the *dynamics of market competition* (Day–Eliasson, 1986). The development of relevant theory and solid empirical research in this area should hence be the mainline of industrial economics.

Dynamic market allocation and macro economic performance – suggestions towards a theory of industrial economics

The disorderly economies of the 70s have produced statistical records that puzzle observers trained on data from the previous decade. Denmark, for instance, has experienced an extremely high, real interest rate for more than 10 years. It has recorded significant drops in manufacturing investment spending and employment, but, nevertheless, output during the same period has grown at a rate on par with OECD Europe. The opposite patterns prevail for Sweden and Norway.

The high real interest rates in the U.S. have not prevented manufacturing investment there from growing steadily for several years. At the same time, European politicians, observing stagnating investments and output and mounting unemployment problems (see Figures 2A–C) because of high interest rates, complain to president Reagan about the tight U.S. monetary policies that drive up world interest rates. European politicians will have even more reason to grumble when U.S. interest rates come down together with the dollar and European firms have to face structurally updated U.S. firms in competitive world markets.

Such diverging macroeconomic developments, that were not predictable from the theoretical repertoire, and statistical data of the 60s call

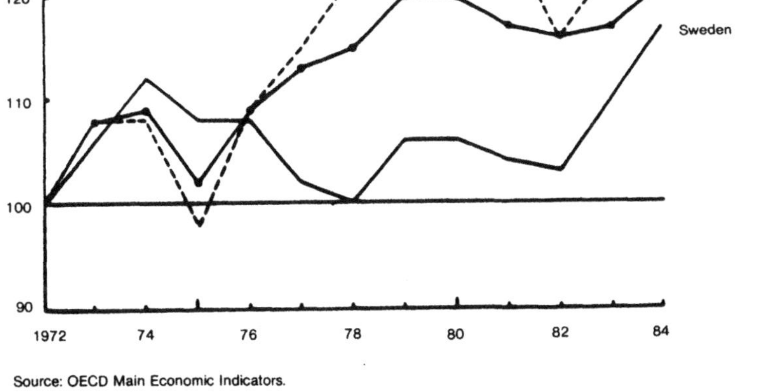

Fig. 2A. Investment, employment and output of manufacturing industry in some OECD countries. Manufacturing output.

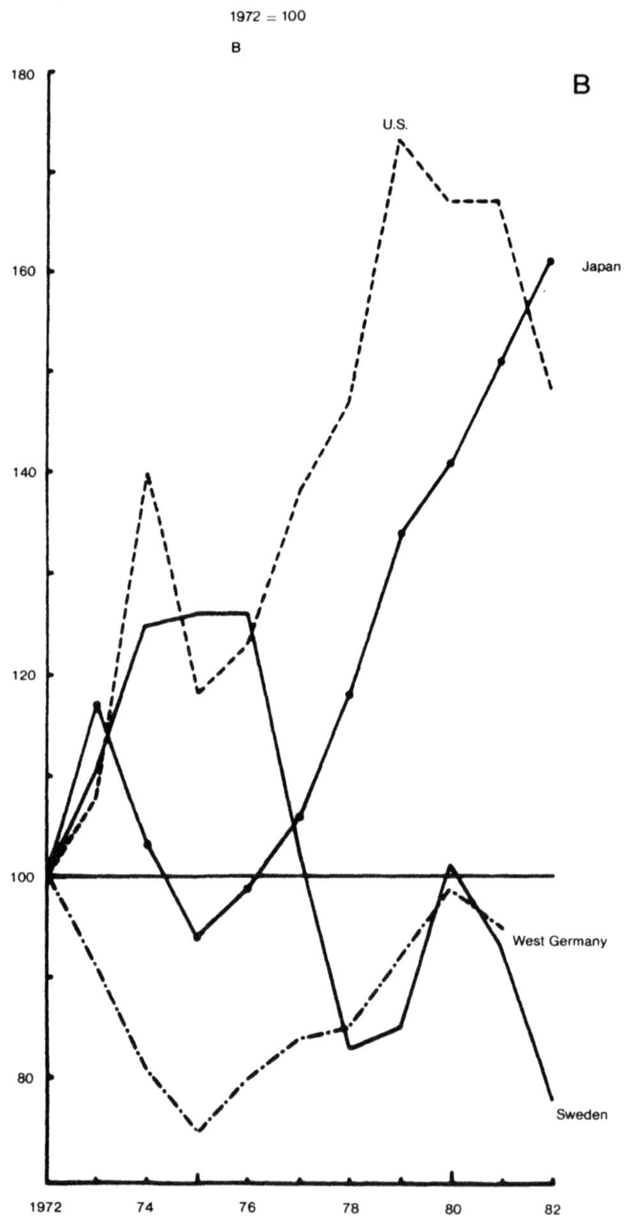

Fig. 2B. Investment, employment and output of manufacturing industry in some OECD countries. Manufacturing investment spending.

attention to the competitive situation of firms and the dynamic efficiency of capital and labor markets in the various countries. In particular, it suggests that the competitive situation of a national economy requires a dynamic micro-to-macro analysis to be understood. The firms – we have

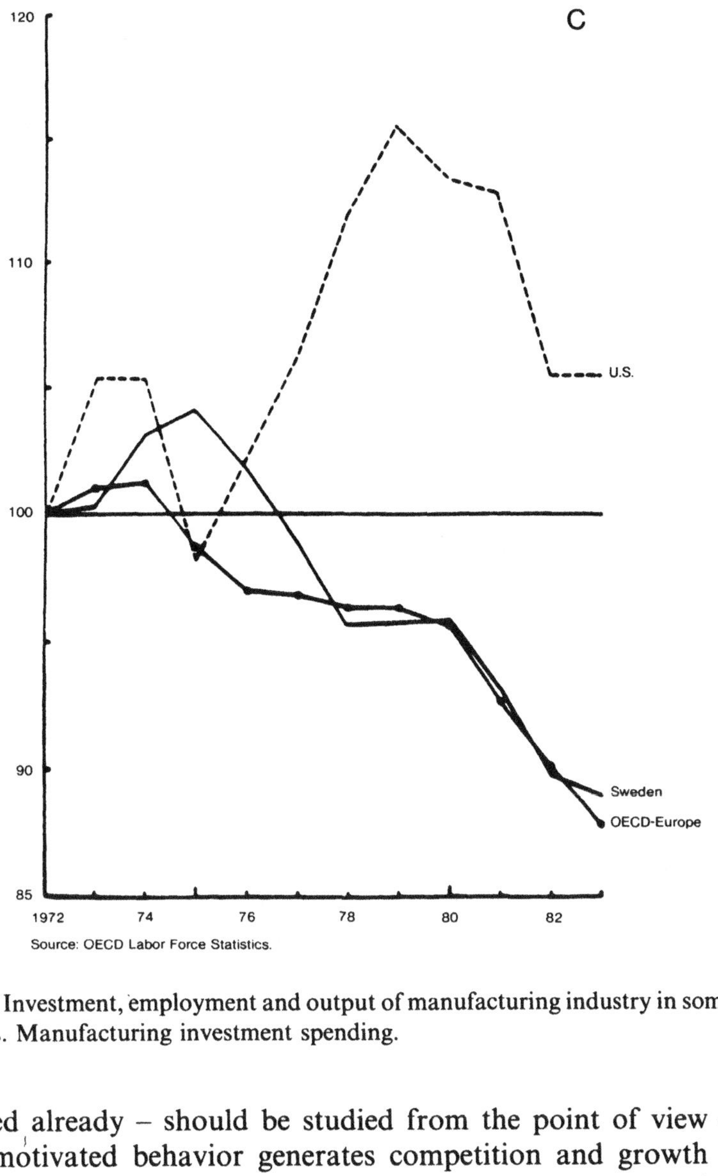

Fig. 2C. Investment, employment and output of manufacturing industry in some OECD countries. Manufacturing investment spending.

observed already – should be studied from the point of view of how profit motivated behavior generates competition and growth in output. If the macroeconomic consequence – the policy problem – is a long-term, balanced growth in output that is faster than in other countries, we can talk about a competitive nation (Eliasson, 1972). As a rule, increased trade with other countries contributes to such growth through facilitating specialization, etc. But there is no unique way of predicting the trade patterns that follow from the exploitation of quasi monopoly, knowledge rents that accumulate within the modern firms as they participate in, and learn from the ongoing market process.

The problem is that the formulation of a micro–macro theory that incorporates all features we have claimed to be necessary, becomes an intellectually overwhelming task.

If free entry and free price setting by individual agents is allowed in all markets, you remove standard equilibrium properties from theory, *and* lose the possibility to pass clear and simple normative statements on welfare. If the only way to reach clear welfare conclusions is to fall back on static equilibrium theory, or a theory of central planning, in which economic growth cannot occur, as an endogenous consequence of the way the economic system is organized and operates, one might as well pass.[4]

The main 'policy problem' that confronts us when we introduce 'institutional dynamics' into the analysis of trade is that we lose intellectual control of the distributional consequences of the growth process, both as regards the distribution of faster growth over nations, and the micro distributions of welfare within the nations.

To begin with, we need a new analytical tool for the analysis of economic growth, efficiency and distribution. This will eventually have to be a *general theory of monopolistic competition* called for already – as I interpret him – by Arrow (1959). A general theory of monopolistic competition will have to be explicit about the creation of knowledge and rents in institutions, and the use of information of institutions in the market process.

In the modern, market based firm productivity growth occurs through institutional reconfiguration rather than through the transmission of technical innovations in the production process. Economies of scale appear to be increasing in the development and global marketing of specialized products, while they are decreasing in the production of standard products. Institutional change is the vehicle for exploiting such new technologies associated with the organization of overall production, marketing and distribution of constantly changing specialized products. The result appears as productivity increases at the level of the firm as a financial organization.

We need a micro-macro theory of dynamic aggregation. Here is a suggestion how to begin.

A micro-macro-(M–M) theory of dynamic aggregation

We have developed a simplified version of dynamic M–M aggregation model at IUI. It includes profit motivated entry of new firms and free exit of entire firms.

It is not explicit about the multifaced set of internal production activities that I have declared very important on the previous pages, but it is capable of quantifying the dynamics of allocation under the assumption of exogenous institutional change. But what we have is enough to endogenize structural change and the efficiency of the economic growth process – factors that make it possible for some national economies to advance faster than other national economies for decades.

The critical analytical problem is how to handle 'technological change' or productivity change at the firm level. Technological change, as we measure it at any level of aggregation is partly the result of pure technical improvements, but mostly the result of institutional adjustment factors that are not explained in the model. The higher the level of aggregation, the more of economies and allocation that enters into measured total factor productivity change. In the M–M model we simply do as Schumpeter suggested and make productivity change exogenous at the level of new investments of individual firms. This amounts to an assumption that new technologies are internationally available. The firm problem is to what extent specific firm knowledge exists to exploit the internationally available knowledge. Hence, new technologies are introduced into the production structure of the individual firm through the endogenous investment process.

The main point, however, is that even with larger and larger flows of new technologies associated with new investment the economics of the investment decision and of labor and product markets largely determine the local economic outcome. Technological knowledge available may set the upper bound for output, but the economics of the allocation process determines how far below this potential the economy will operate, and what relative product and factor prices will be.

The differences in productivity and production growth that can be generated on the basis of the Swedish micro-to-macro model on a given set of technological data, assuming different market processes exceed those observed between countries in Figure 2. In fact, by simply varying the parameters, determining the speeds of price and quantity adjustments in factor markets, holding everything else the same, we have been able to generate macro output growth trajectories over 50 year time spans that differ by as much as one to two percent per annum (Eliasson, 1983; Eliasson–Hanson, 1986).

As we have defined it, reorganization of firm structures in the direction of relatively more resources devoted to product development and marketing is a form of technological change in the sense that more profits and perhaps more output are obtained from the same inputs. The extension of marketing abroad promotes volume expansion in the form of foreign trade that promotes – in the Micro-to-Macro model – significant domestic production growth from the same resource base. The ways the market regime is organized, means more for industrial output than technical change at the macro level (Eliasson, 1985b). The market regime determines the dynamics of market competition in the M–M-model, or the ways temporary rents are created and competed away. For small economies foreign competition may mean more in this respect than domestic competition.

How the old Swedish policy model promoted welfare through promoting dynamic market competition

To open up an economy to unrestricted foreign competition requires a viable, differentiated and innovative industry (Eliasson, 1984c, 1985d). Opening up a protected industry with inferior producers, and a sticky factor price structure will invariably cause a socially unacceptable adjustment process; (This is probably the main explanation behind the bad economic performance of the British economy, and the large adjustment problems when the protection diminished.) The 'old Swedish policy model' was a way of preserving a viable, innovative industry and combining it with a fast, competitive market regime. This was 'policy engineered' in the following ways. *First*, (the welfare function) welfare was associated with *macroeconomic growth* in output, and with relative stability of growth, i.e., it was considered important to keep cyclical variations within a reasonable range. Distributional ambitions were – to begin with – very cautiously – introduced through a redistribution system via progressive taxation, Government transfers and the expansion of public sector production. *Second*, all aspects of factor mobility were officially removed from the national welfare function. *Third*, as an explicit agreement between employers, the unions and the ruling Government, free *competitive entry* was organized through keeping the economy open to foreign competition and through the understanding between Government, employers and Unions that new technical solutions to production would be freely introduced in the most efficient ways, i.e., as the employers saw it. This free entry policy was coupled with a *full employment* commitment by the Government. In fact, the Government even generated a faster adjustment process in the labor market through the *solidaric wage policies* and part of the full employment understanding was that labor should accept to move and adjust in pace with the market. Besides these three policy principles the Government maintained a *hands off* policy vis-à-vis the production and investment process. One could say that the political system supported a very competitive market game in both product and labor markets, making it possible for firms to stay competitive through technical and organizational innovations, including free exit.

The reader should observe that the first departure from the free competitive entry and exit principles was not the extreme industrial subsidy program of the 70s (Carlsson, 1983); it was the excessive growth of monopolized, price-controlled public sector protected from competitive entry and exit.

Hence, the old Swedish policy model, engineered by the ruling social-democratic party was in relevant respects a free market model, coupled with a *political indoctrination system* designed to impose the social discipline necessary for the acceptance of the market adjustment process. The latter, indoctrination aspect of the Swedish policy model may in fact be its most important feature. This 'device' solved the dilemma of conflicting policy objectives between the long term and the short term. The policy model, however, was gradually abandoned from the late 60s and onwards. The macroeconomic 'development' since then has been disastrous. The interesting question is to what extent the new, less market oriented policies caused economic stagnation, or whether the old model simply would not have been workable today. The latter is the common conclusion (see, e.g., Lundberg, 1985). My conclusion is the opposite.

NOTES

1. I am grateful for a number of constructive suggestions for improvement and critical comments from Magnus Blomström, Lars Jagrén, Ken Hanson and Thomas Lindberg.
2. Westerman, J., 1768, *Om svenska näringarnes undervigt emot de utländske förmedelst en trögare arbetsdrift*, (About the inferiority of Swedish business activities compared to foreign business, because of a slow work process), Stockholm.
3. See, e.g., Albrecht (1986).
4. I do not think replacing deterministic models – suggested during the discussion – with stochastic models will help. Complex deterministic models always generate behavior that resembles a stochastic process in some dimensions. The scientific problem is to determine when behavior departs from the stochastic mode and for what kind of problem this matters. Thus, for instance, the outcome of high risk R & D projects in industry may occasionally appear random. But more resources spent, the ways R & D work is organized, the choice between imitating and developing the knowledge yourself, the way new ideas are picked up in the operating divisions of firms, etc., must matter.

REFERENCES

Åkerman, J. 'Institutionalisering', *Ekonomisk Tidskrift* (1950).

Albrecht, J., *A Description and Analysis of the IUI and Federation of Industries Planning Survey Data.* IUI Working Paper (forthcoming) (1986).

Arrow, K., 'Towards a Theory of Price Adjustment', in M. Abramowitz (ed.), *The Allocation of Economics Resources*, Stanford, Ca.: Standford University Press, (1959, 1937).

Bergholm, F., *Svenska företags investeringar i maskiner och byggnader i utlandet 1974-1978*, IUI Research Report No. 19, Stockholm (1983).

Bergholm, F., *De utlandsetablerade företagens multiplikatoreffekter på svensk ekonomi – några simuleringar* (Multiplier Effects of Swedish Multinationals – some simulation experiments) in Eliasson (1984).

Carlsson, B., 'Industrial Subsidies in Sweden; Macro-Economic Effects and An International Comparison', *The Journal of Industrial Economics*, Vol. XXXII. (Sept. 1983).

Caves, R. E., Porter, M. E., Spencer, M. A., and Scott, J. T., *Competition in the Open Economy*, Cambridge and London (1980).

Clower, R. and Friedman, D., *Trade Specialists and Money in an Ongoing Exchange Economy.* IUI Working Paper No. 141 (1985).

Coase, R. N., 'The Nature of the Firm', *Economica*, New Series IV, Nos. 13–16 (1937).

Day, R. and Eliasson, G. (eds.) *The Dynamics of Market Behavior*, forthcoming IUI and North-Holland (1986).

Diamond, P., *A Search Equilibrium Approach to the Micro Foundations of Macroeconomics*, Cambridge and London: The MIT Press (1984).

Eliasson, G., *International Competitiveness – An Empirical Analysis of Swedish Manufacturing*, No. 3 Research Series B, Stockholm: Federations of Swedish Industries (1972).

Eliasson, G., *Business Economic Planning*, London: John Wiley & Sons (1976).

Eliasson, G., (ed.) *A Micro-to-Macro Model of the Swedish Economy*, IUI Conference Reports 1978:1, Stockholm (1978).

Eliasson, G., 'On the Optimal Rate of Structural Adjustment', in Eliasson–Scharefkin–Ysander (eds.) *Policy Making in a Disorderly World Economy*, IUI Conference Reports 1983:1, Stockholm (1983).

Eliasson, G., *De utlandsetalerade företagen och den svenska ekonomin* (International Corporate Operations and the Swedish Economy), IUI Research Report No. 26, Stockholm (1984a).

Eliasson, G., The Micro Foundations of Industrial Policy in Jacquemin (ed.) *European Industry: Public Policy and Corporate Strategy*, Oxford: Oxford University Press (1984b).

Eliasson, G., Micro Heterogeneity of Firms and the Stability of Industrial Growth, *Journal of Economic Behavior and Organizations*, Vol. 5, Nos. 3–4 (1984c).

Eliasson, G., *The Firm and Financial Markets in the Swedish Micro-to-Macro Model*, IUI, Stockholm (1985a).

Eliasson, G., *Skattekilar, inflation och fördelning* (Tax Wedges, Inflation and Distributions) in Eliasson–Björklund–Pousette *et al.* (1985b).

Eliasson, G., *Information Technology, Capital Structure and the Nature of Technical Change*, IUI Working Paper No. 138 (1985c).

Eliasson, G., *Dynamic Micro-Macro Market Coordination and Technical Change*, IUI Working Paper No. 139 (1985d).

Eliasson, G., *The Stability of Economic Organizational Forms and the Importance of Human Capital*, IUI Working Paper No. 143 (1985e).

Eliasson, G., Fries, H., Jagrén, L., and Oxelheim, L., *Hur styrs storföretag?*, ('How Are Large Companies Run?'), IUI, Stockholm (1984).

Eliasson, G., Bergholm, F., Jagrén, L., and Horwitz, E. C., *De svenska storföretagen*, ('The Large Swedish Companies'), IUI Stockholm (1985).

Eliasson, G., Björklund, A., and Pousette, T., *Att rätt värdera 90-talet* (Evaluating the 90s), IUI, Stockholm (1985).

Eliasson, G., and Hanson, K., *Pricing and Markets in the Swedish Micro Simulation Model*, forthcoming IUI Working Paper (1986).

Eliasson, G., and Ysander, B. -C., 'Sweden: Problems of Maintaining Efficiency under Political Pressure', in Hindley (ed.), *State Investment Companies in Western Europe*, London (1983).

Granstrand, O., *Measuring and Modelling Innovative New Entry in Swedish Industry*, IUI Working Paper No. 140 (1985); to be published in Day–Eliasson (1986).

Jagrén, L., 'Svenska utlandsetablerade företags marknadsandelar' (Market Shares of Swedish Multinationals) (1985); in Eliasson–Bergholm–Horwitz (1985), IUI, Stockholm.

Jagrén, L., 'Svenska utlandsetablerade företags marknadsandelar' in *De svenska storföretagen*. IUI, Stockholm (1985).

Jagrén, L., *Företagens tillväxt i ett historiskt perspektiv*, Forthcoming IUI Working Paper (1986).

King, M. and Fullerton, D., *The Taxation of Income from Capital – A Comparative Study of the United States, The United Kingdom, Sweden, West Germany*, (NBER, IFO, IUI), Chicago University Press (1984).

Kirzner, I., *Competition and Entrepreneurship*, Chicago: University of Chicago Press (1973).

Lange, O., *On the Economic Theory of Socialism Review of Economic Studies* (1936–37).

Lundberg, E., The Rise and Fall of the Swedish Model, in *JEL*, Vol. XXIII, No. 1 (March 1985).

Malinvaud, E., Decentralized Procedures for Planning, in Malinvaud–Bacharach (eds.) (1967).

Marshall, A., *Industry and Trade*, London (1919).

McKenzie, L. N., 'Specialization and Efficiency in World Production', *Review of Economic Studies*, 21 (1954), pp. 165–180.

Okun, A. M., *Prices and Quantities in Macroeconomic Analysis*, London: The Brookings Institutions (1981).

Oxelheim, L., 'The Largest Nordic Manufacturing Companies', Special Study in *Economic Growth in a Nordic Perspective*, ETLA-IFF-IUI-IØI (1984).

Pelikan, P., *Private Enterprise vs. Government Control: An Organizationally Dynamic Comparison*. IUI Working Paper No. 137 (1985).

Pousette, T. and Lindberg, T., *Services in Production and Production of Services in Swedish Manufacturing*, IUI Working Paper No. 148 (1985).

Pratten, C., *A Comparison of the Performance of Swedish and U.K. Companies*, Cambridge University Press (1976).

Schumpeter, J., *The Theory of Economic Development*, Cambridge (1934).

Schumpeter, J., *Capitalism, Socialism and Economic Democracy*, New York (1942).

Södersten, J. and Lindberg, T., *Skatt på bolagskapital*, Sverige i jämförelse med Storbrittannien, USA och Västtyskland, IUI Research Report No. 20 (1983).

Swedenborg, B., *The Multinational Operations of Swedish Firms An Analysis of Determinants and Effects*. IUI Stockholm (1979).
Westerman, J., *Om svenska näringarnes undervigt emot de utländske förmedelst en trögare arbetsdrift*, Stockholm (1768).
Williamson, O., *Markets and Hierarchies. Analysis and Anti-Trust Implications*, London (1975).

7. INDUSTRIAL ORGANIZATION IN AN INTERNATIONAL FRAMEWORK

Takeo Nakao

INTRODUCTION

In recent years the importance of foreign competition as a cause of increased competition has been rising substantially (Shepherd, 1982), and it may be high time to give a systematic treatment of industrial organization within an international framework. The study of foreign competition combines the theories of industrial organization and international trade, and in doing so there are two approaches. One focuses on how the theory of international trade has to be changed if one of the industries in the world is monopolized. The other approach considers how the problems in industrial organization have to be changed if international trade is taken into consideration.

Traditionally it is the market structure-conduct-performance paradigm that provides an overall approach to industrial organization analysis. In this study I intend to extend the structure-conduct-performance paradigm to the problems in industrial organization in international settings, since the structure-conduct-performance approach seems to provide the easiest way to get an overall picture of industrial organization under international framework. We seek to identify sets of attributes of both home and world markets that affect social welfare through their influences on the behavior of home firms, and to build theories detailing the properties of the relationships between those attributes, conduct, and social welfare. Thus my purpose in this paper is to construct the systematic theory of industrial organization within an international framework.[1]

I. STRUCTURE AND TECHNOLOGY IN NATIONAL AND WORLD MARKETS – THE ELEMENTS OF INTERNATIONAL MARKET STRUCTURE

In this section I discuss the elements of market structure that should be regarded as important in the international settings. In the traditional

de Jong, H. W., Shepherd, W. G. (eds) Mainstreams in Industrial Organization
 ISBN 978-94-017-0495-3

theory of industrial organization, the important elements of market structure are three: (1) concentration, (2) product differentiation, and (3) entry barriers. But if we wish to analyze the performance-structure relationship or the effects of market power on the welfare of the world as well as home country in the international framework, we need to introduce some other structural or technological elements that affect the behavior of the home firms. Also, we need to examine how important each structural or technological element is in the international framework. Thus, in the following we shall enumerate the important elements of structural and technological conditions and examine their relevance to the behavior of the firms in the international settings and the welfares of the home and world.

A. Various structural and technological settings in national and world markets – partial analysis

Structure of home and world markets – concentration

In studying the complete problem, we have to pay attention to all the important elements of market structure of not only the home economy but also the world economy. As emphasized by Caves (1980), because if this home-world economy relationship the theory of industrial organization in the international framework becomes more complicated than the traditional theory of industrial organization that has concentrated essentially upon the autarkic economy.

In the theory of industrial organization, the analysis of the behavior of the firm could begin with a simple monopoly and then be extended to some kind of oligopoly. But in the international framework a simple starting model would be one in which there is monopoly in the home economy and competition in the world economy or monopoly in the foreign economy. A more realistic model might be oligopoly in the home market and oligopoly or competition in the world market. *Theoretically*, the analysis of the behavior and the welfare impact of the firms possessing some kind of monopoly power in the international framework may have to cover all the cases shown in Table 1.

The concept of an oligopolistic world market may seem unrealistic, but when the large country has an oligopolistic market structure, we would have to regard the world market in question as oligopolistic. The existence of oligopolistic interdependence makes the behavior of oligopolists very complex. But in the international framework the home-world economy relationship makes the analysis of the behavior of oligopolists even much more complicated. Due mainly to this difficulty, the analyses

Table 1. Structure of home and world markets.

Number of firms in home markets	Number of firms in world or foreign markets		
	One	Few	Many
One	Monopoly–monopoly	Monopoly–oligopoly	Monopoly–competitive
Few	Oligopoly–Monopoly	Oligopoly–Oligopoly	Oligopoly–competitive
Many	Competitive–monopoly	Competitive–oligopoly	–

of the behavior and of the welfare impact of the more realistic cases such as an oligopoly–oligopoly model or oligopoly–competitive model have almost been neglected until recently (Jacquemin (1982) and Dixit (1984) studied the oligopoly model assuming Cournot-type reactions by both the home and foreign firms).

Competitive fringe

In many oligopolistic markets, the existence of a competitive fringe has important effects on social welfare through its influence upon the behavior of dominant firms or collusive oligopoly in the industry (Gaskins, 1971). Hence the fringe may occupy an important part even in the international settings. Imports usually do not dominate domestic markets. Their shares in the domestic markets are relatively small, and so they often constitute the competitive fringes of the domestic markets. But we can expect significant differences in the impacts of competitive fringes consisting of domestic small firms and of foreign firms. If those foreign firms are already well established large firms in their home markets, they will be able to compete on equal terms in many respects with domestic leading firms, and hence the behavior of the domestic leading firms could be constrained by a great deal.[2] This is especially true when the foreign competitors produce high quality goods with low costs, and there are prospects of a large increase in the share of imports in the long run. Moreover, domestically – small firms often adopt aggressive behavior in foreign markets so as to exploit scale economies, and this could help make the world market more competitive.[3]

The size of a home firm in the world market

Even if the home-world market structure is the same, the behavior of oligopolists in the home market would be critically different depending upon the size of the home firms relative to the world market. Caves (1974) has analyzed the monopoly–competitive market structure assuming that home country is small in the world and concluded that under free trade the welfare losses due to monopoly disappear. But if the size of the home market is relatively large in the world market, the impacts of foreign competition on the domestic collusive oligopoly could be in many respects the same as those of competitive fringe in the home market. In this case, the collusive oligopoly in the domestic industry could cause welfare losses not only in the home country, but also in the world by making use of its monopoly power in the world market (Stegemann, 1984). Thus, the relative size of the home country's market in the world can be a decisive factor in determining the structure-behavior-performance relationship.

Barriers to trade and entry in national and world markets

Stykolt and Eastman (1960) suggested that a domestic monopolist or collusive oligopoly would set price taking into accounts the threat of potential competition from imports as well as from new entrants. Esposito and Esposito (1971) and Gorecki (1976) pointed out that barriers to entry referred to in most industrial organization textbooks do not often become important barriers to trade or entry for foreign established firms. Foreign established firms would suffer no cost disadvantages, could have been taking advantage of scale economies thoroughly in their home markets, and have the ability to differentiate their products successfully or the experience of establishing the goodwill among consumers. Hence the barriers to entry for domestic potential firms might not be effective to deter imports by the formidable foreign firms. However, foreign established firms have their own disadvantages; international trade barriers such as tariffs, transport costs, non-tariff trade barriers, and risk involved in international trade.

If the barriers to international trade in the home market is nonexistent, even a monopolist or collusive oligopolists in the home market will not be able to secure above normal profits without incurring a flood of imports. However, if the barriers to entry for domestic potential firms are lower than the barriers to international trade in the home market, foreign competition might not produce any substantial differences in the home market, since the behavior of the domestic monopolist or collusive oligopolists will be mainly influenced by the possibility of entry by domestic potential firms. Note that the barriers to trade in the world market also affect the competitiveness of the home market since the existence of the small domestic firms depends upon how much they can exploit scale economies by exporting their products to the world market.[4]

Product differentiation

If the product of a firm is not differentiated and the size of the firm is small relative to the world market, the firm would be unable to raise the price of its product above the competitive world price even if it is a monopolist in the home market. On the contrary, if its product is differentiated, even a small firm would obtain power to raise its price so as to maximize profits in the home market as well as in the world market. The small firms specializing in production of the differentiated goods with high quality often set exceedingly high prices in the world market. Thus, whether a good is differentiated or homogeneous would call forth considerable differences in the behavior of a firm and economic performance. For firms producing differentiated goods international trade would mean the increase in the number of the markets with different demand elasticities. Market power created by product differentiation does not seem to be alleviated by international trade.

Demand and cost conditions

The behavior of a monopolist or collusive oligopolists in the home market will be strongly influenced by the cost conditions of firms and the demand conditions in the national and world markets, and hence the effects of the existence of monopolistic power in the home and/or world markets on the home and world welfares are often crucially dependent upon the relative values of demand elasticities in the home and world markets. Whether marginal costs are increasing, constant, or decreasing, and the importance of the economies of scale (the importance of these conditions can be seen in Auquier and Caves (1979)).

Product cycles

Vernon (1966) and Grossman (1982) have argued that the stages of production of a good in the home and world markets play an important role in the determination of international trade flows. But the behaviour of firms as well as market structure is also closely related to the stages of production of the good (see Norman and Nichols (1982) and Shepherd (1979), for example).[5] In the early stages of production of the good, the rates of demand growth are very high and the opportunities to decrease production costs by introducing new technology are abundant, and these dynamic circumstances affect the behavior of established firms and the decisions to enter the market by potential firms, often entailing dynamic changes in market structure. Thus, if the production of the good in the home market is at the mature stage in which the stable market conditions often enable oligopolistic firms to behave collusively, and that in the foreign market is at early stages, international trade would drastically increase the competitiveness of the home market by introducing the aggressive young firms in the foreign markets into the domestic market. Due to differences in the levels of economic development among countries, there would, almost always, be aggressive young firms in the world that come from the countries in which the good is at the early stages of production.

Riskiness of national and world markets

As Turnovsky (1974) remarks, 'international trade is one of the riskiest economic activities', and hence we can not disregard the effects of uncertainty on the behaviors of firms in an open economy. For example, the risk involved in a market or a country (which is often created by the lack of information) would constitute a barrier to international trade, and hence weaken the effects of foreign competition. Using the partial equilibrium approach the effects of uncertainty on the output decisions of a risk-neutral monopolist are analyzed by White (1974) and those of a risk-averse monopolist by Donnenfeld and Strebel (1983) and Hu (1975). But most of the theoretical analyses of industrial organization in the international framework overlook the problems involved in uncertainty. For example, such an important problem as the effect of monopoly on the home and world welfares in an open economy under uncertainty remains to be seen.

B. Structure and technology of the rest of the industries in national and world markets – general equilibrium analysis

The theory of industrial organization has customarily used partial equilibrium analysis while the theory of international trade has mostly relied upon general equilibrium approach. Even though the partial equilibrium approach is simple and often gives important insights, the conclusions derived from it do not necessarily hold in the general equilibrium framework. It would be preferable that we use the general equilibrium framework to analyze the effects of monopoly power on welfare in an open economy: the existence of, at least, two goods is a prerequisite for the analysis of the welfare-increasing effects of international trade, and the effects of the changes in relative prices due to trade or industrial policy on the demand and cost conditions are interrelated between the competitive and monopolistic sectors. The partial equilibrium analysis often cannot take these aspects into consideration.

If we use the general equilibrium framework to delve into the probelms of industrial organization in the international settings, we have to pay attention, not only to the characteristics of market structure of the industry in question, but also to those of the rest of the industries. Our model will become, for example, monopoly in one of the home markets, competition in the corresponding world market, and competition in the rest of the industries in the home and world (which could be called the 'monopoly–competition = competition–competition' model). Not only the firm-size-and-distribution structure of market but also the other elements of international market structure such as entry barriers, the economies of scale, product differentiation, riskiness of the industry, barriers to trade, the stages of productions of the good and so forth have to be specified for both home and world markets in the general equilibrium model. An example is shown in Table 2 by using one of the basic models used in Harris (1984).

The general equilibrium model with so many endogenous variables is too complicated to conduct a theoretical analysis. In order to construct a tractable model one has to forgo many of the conditions described in Table 2. But any changes in one or some of these conditions would produce qualitatively or quantitatively different results. Depending upon a set of conditions one selects any conclusions might be possible to draw.[6] Thus, it seems imperative not only to model the essential characteristics of imperfect market structure in the international settings, but also to recognize what assumptions concerning these elements of international market structure are used in the model. Otherwise, one would

Table 2. Structural and technological settings in Harris's model.

An industry's structure and technology		
Size of home market: small		Product: homogeneous
Marginal costs: constant		Economies of scale: existent
Entry barriers: fixed cost barrier		
	Home market	Foreign market
Market structure:	oligopoly	competition
Riskiness:	nonexistent	nonexistent
Trade barriers:	existent	existent
Product cycles:	static	static
The other industry's structure and technology		
Size of home market: small		Product: homogeneous
Marginal costs: constant		Economies of scale: nonexistent
Entry barriers: nonexistent		
	Home market	Foreign market
Market structure:	competition	competition
Riskiness:	nonexistent	nonexistent
Trade barriers:	existent	existent
Product cycle:	static	static

probably make an inconsistent analysis. For example, suppose that in presenting the theoretical hypothesis the following conditions are used: (1) the country is small, (2) the firm is a dominant firm, and (3) the product is homogeneous. But if these assumptions are not recognized one may gather data that include the differentiated goods produced by non-top firms in the large country. To avoid this kind of inconsistency in analyzing such complicated problems of industrial organization in international settings, one has to be aware of the implicit as well as explicit assumptions on the elements of international market structure.

II. THE EFFECTS OF INTERNATIONAL TRADE ON MARKET STRUCTURE AND FIRM BEHAVIOR

A. Structural conditions affected by free trade

Concentration

In the case where economies of scale are important, specifically the minimum efficient scale is large relative to the home market, the sellers' concentration in the domestic market will become high if it is an autarky economy. But in an open economy both export and import have the possibility to decrease sellers' concentration.

If domestically small firms could export a large amount of their outputs and make use of scale economies, they could overcome cost disadvantages and get a fair chance to compete equally with larger firms in the domestic market. Thus, export could cause a decrease in the domestic producers' concentration in the domestic market where scale economies are important.

Import could provide the home market with foreign producers whose market shares may not be large but could compete without any cost disadvantages. Then, import could raise their shares over time and lower domestic sellers' concentration. Also, as pointed out by Caves and Porter (1978) international trade will probably increase the instability of market shares of the domestic leading firms.[7]

Instead of interpreting foreign competition as a factor that decreases domestic sellers' concentration, there may be the cases in which international trade creates worldwide free markets by integrating the small national markets of different countries whose markets are open to the world. In these cases the concept of the domestic sellers' concentration ratio would lose its significance, and the concept of the sellers' concentration in the world markets would become the dominant factor in determining the behavior of the firms in the world. In this context the empirical findings by Leitzinger and Tamor (1983) that world market concentration ratios better explain the levels of profitability in US manufacturing industries than the concentration ratios in the US markets seem to suggest that the 'almost' worldwide free markets exist in reality in some cases. In general, the concept of the worldwide free markets becomes the key to the problems related to domestic monopolies only when the barriers to trade in many countries are entirely removed.

Barriers to entry

In entering foreign markets firms have two possibilities, exports and direct investment. If it is profitable, they will enter the foreign markets by selecting one of these methods. But due probably to the existence of high risk involved in investment in the foreign countries, they will usually start with exporting which is less risky.[8] Then, the barriers to international trade (rather than to entry) could play a crucial role in the determination of the level of limit price in the domestic market (see Section 1.A).

Product differentiation

Product differentiation has been paid much attention in recent years in relation to intra-industry trade among the developed countries (Helpman, 1981; Krugman, 1979, 1980; Lancaster, 1980). But, as suggested in Section I.A, for firms producing differentiated goods international trade would mean the increase in the number of the markets with different demand elasticities, and market power created by product differentiation does not seem to be alleviated by international trade.

The increase in the variety of products without causing increases in production costs could be one of the major changes due to international trade that take place in a market with differentiated products. If product differentiation is achieved mainly through the intrinsic heterogeneity of the product, the increases in the variety of product available to consumers could imply an increase in national welfare (see Brander (1981) and Gabszewicz *et al.* (1981)).

B. The behaviors of the firm affected by free trade

Price-output decisions – imports and exports

In examining the price-output decisions of a monopolist or oligopolists in an open economy and the effects of international trade on quantities imported and/or exported, one has to model various structural and technological factors, and hence the conclusions derived depend upon what kind of structural and technological settings one assumes. For example, White (1974) in deriving the conclusion that the existence of monopoly increases imports used the following model: (1) the firm-size-and-distribution structures of markets are monopoly in the home and competition in the world, (2) the product is not differentiated, (3) barriers to entry are prohibitively high in the home market but do not exist in the world market (an implicit assumption), (4) marginal costs are increasing in the relevant region, and the economies of scale are negligible (implicit assumptions), (5) the size of the home market is small, (6) the demand and cost conditions are stable (or static), (7) the barriers to international trade do not exist in the home market but prohibitively high in the foreign market, (8) there is uncertainty in the foreign or domestic market, and (9) the existence of the rest of the industries is neglected (partial analysis). But Caves (1974) derived the conclusion that international trade deprives market power of a domestic monopolist and the equilibrium point is the same in an open economy between competition and monopoly. His basic model could be characterized by: (1)–(6) stated in White's model hold, also, in this model, (7) there are no barriers to international trade in the home and world markets, (8) there is no uncertainty in the foreign as well as in the domestic market, and (9) the markets for the rest of the goods in the home and world are competitive and satisfy the analogous structural and technological conditions. (2)–(8), stated above.

The analysis of the effects of international trade on the output decisions of a monopolist or oligopolists and on quantities exported or imported are important, since they are closely related to the welfare losses caused by monopoly power in the home and world markets. But the results depend crucially upon what kind of structural and technological conditions we assume. Thus, it seems imperative to recognize the limitations in application of the conclusions derived from theoretical models by making certain of both the explicit and the implicit assumptions regarding the structural and technological settings of the models.

Collusive actions – conjectural variations

There seems to be no doubt about the effects of international trade to discourage collusive actions among sellers in domestic markets. As pointed out before, it would lower sellers' concentration in the domestic markets and foreign producers could be formidable competitors even if their market shares are not large in comparison with those of domestic leading firms. Moreover, the foreign competitors often do not take part in the tacit collusive actions that might have been established by the domestic leading firms, since they lack the common knowledge and experience or they behave aggressively to capture certain market shares in the foreign markets. Hence, the theoretical models that assume the Cournot-type reactions not only by domestic firms but also by foreign firms do not seem to grasp one of the essential characteristics of foreign competition.

Product quality and advertising decisions

By strengthening product-quality competition foreign competition could raise the levels in qualities of the goods produced by leading domestic firms. Since a firm producing the product with higher quality would get a larger share of the market, international competition could enforce the domestic firms to improve the quality of their products to keep their market shares, provided that the qualities of the foreign competitors' products are not much lower than those of the domestic firms' products. But if product differentiation is not related to the intrinsic heterogeneity of a good and achieved mainly through persuasive advertising, foreign competition might call forth increased advertising expenditures by domestic firms to cope with the advertising campaign by the foreign firms.

R&D activity and investment behavior

Foreign competition could affect the investment behavior of the domestic firms with considerable market power. Monopolistic firms have no strong incentive to spend vast money in R&D activities and they are slow in introducing new technologies, since they have already been earning large excess profits thanks to their monopoly power. This kind of behavior could be altered dramatically by foreign competition if there are competitive firms in the world market that are eager to introduce new technologies. If such firms behave actively in international markets, monopolistic firms in the other countries could be obliged to invest in new-technology-equipped production facilities and also to start making serious efforts in R&D activities.[9]

C. A model of collusive oligopoly with competitive fringe consisting of foreign competitors

In the real world the shares of imports are often not allowed to grow freely in the domestic markets. The policies that protect domestic firms from foreign competition would succeed in keeping the shares of imports to the levels at which foreign competitors constitute only the competitive fringe of the domestic markets, even if they could produce high-quality goods with low costs. Thus, the models of collusive oligopoly with competitive fringe of the domestic market consisting of foreign competitors describe best the conditions of the many markets in the real world. In spite of its importance such models have virtually been neglected in the literature of industrial organization under international framework.

In the following to help close the gap I shall examine the effects of foreign competitors being confined to the competitive fringe of a domestic market on the behavior of the collusive oligopolists producing differenciated goods.

Following Nakao (1982, 1983), I shall make use of the concept of the stock of technology denoted by T_i, which represents the relative superiority of the i-th firm's product quality. Letting X_i be the R&D inputs of the i-th firm, if we assume the relation $dT_i/dt = X_i - vT_i$, where v is the depreciation rate of stock of technology, at the long-run equlilibrium we obtain the relation $T_i = X_i/v$.

Assuming that foreign competitors constitute the competitive fringe of the industry, the present value, $v(u)$, of a foreign competitor's expected profits obtained from export started at time u will depend on its initial investment required for exporting, k_0, the time path of the price of its product, p, and its stock of technology (both in product quality and production), F, the expected time path of the domestic oligopolists' prices, P_i, and stocks of technology, T_i, the height of the international trade barriers, B, and the quantity supplied by all the foreign competitors, S, who have already been exporting to the market (see Nakao (1980)). Letting $P = (P_1, \ldots, P_N)$ and $T = (T_1, \ldots, T_N)$, where N is the number of the domestic oligopolists in the industry considered, we obtain

$$v = v(p, k_0, P, T, S, F, B).$$

Since the foreign competitor is small in the domestic market, it would behave as if it expected the policies of its rival firms to be unchanged during its planning horizon, t_0. Then, the foreign competitor's profitability function will be defined by

$$v^*[P(u), T(u), S(u), F, B]$$

$$= \max_{\substack{p(t),\, u \leqslant t \leqslant u + t_0 \\ k_0}} \{v[p, k_0; P(u), T(u), S(u), F, B] - k_0\},$$

where, in order to make F a parameter, we assumed that the foreign competitor determines the level of its stock of technology so as to maximize its profit in the home market (which should constitute the main part of its entire profits). Note that the profitability of import will be increased by the increases in the foreign competitor's stock of technology and the oligopolists' price and by the decreases in the oligopolists' stocks of technology, the quantity supplied by the other competitors, and the international trade barriers. From the relation $v^*(P, T, S, F, B) = 0$ we may obtain the foreign competitors' supply function $S = S(P, T, F, B)$, which satisfies the following properties:

$$\begin{aligned} &S_P > 0, \quad S_T < 0, \quad S_F > 0, \quad S_B < 0, \\ &S_{TF} > 0, \quad S_{PF} < 0, \quad S_{PB} > 0, \quad S_{TB} < 0. \end{aligned} \tag{1}$$

where $S_{TF} > 0$ and $S_{TB} < 0$ ($S_{PB} > 0$ and $S_{PF} < 0$) means that the negative effects of the oligopolists' stock of technology (the positive effects of the oligopolists' product prices) on the foreign competitors' total supply in the domestic market are weakened (strengthened) if the foreign competitors' stocks of technology are raised or the international trade barriers are lowered.

The total demand for the oligopolists' products, Q, will be obtained by subtracting the foreign competitors' total supply from the market demand,

$$Q = Q(P, T, F, B) = D(P, T) - S(P, T, F, B),$$

where the function D is the market demand function. Since the foreign competitors' prices are functions of P, T, F, and B, we will not treat them as independent arguments in the market demand function.

To study the effect of foreign competition on collusive oligopoly we assume that the oligopolists' prices and stocks of technology are determined so as to maximize the joint profits of the oligopolists in the industry. But due to the complicated property and heterogeneity of R&D activity, the joint profit-maximization by the oligopolists will be imperfect in the sense that the R&D activity is carried out independently (without helping each other) by each oligopolist.

Let C be the average costs of the oligopolists, r be the discount rate and P^T be the price of R&D inputs. Under the symmetric equilibrium we can omit the subscript i, and at the long-run equilibrium (P^*, T^*), the following conditions will be satisfied (see Nakao (1982)):

$$R_P(P^*, T^*, F, B) = 0, \tag{2}$$

$$R_T(P^*, T^*, F, B)/N - (r + v)P^T = 0, \tag{3}$$

where

$$R(P^*, T^*, F, B) = (P^* - C)Q(P^*, T^*, F, B).$$

If we assume that the gross marginal profitability of R&D outlays with and without optimal price policy decreases as the stock of technology increases (i.e., the strict concavity of R), we obtain

$$A = R_{PP}R_{TT} - (R_{PT})^2 > 0, \quad R_{PP} < 0, \quad R_{TT} < 0. \tag{4}$$

Differentiation of (2) and (3) with respect to F yields (we omit the asterisk when doing so causes no confusion),

$$\mathrm{d}T/\mathrm{d}F = (P - C)(S_{TF}R_{PP} - S_{PF}R_{PT})/A,$$

and

$$\mathrm{d}P/\mathrm{d}F = (P - C)(S_{PF}R_{TT} - S_{TF}R_{PT})/A.$$

Therefore, we obtain $\mathrm{d}T/\mathrm{d}F < 0$ and $\mathrm{d}P/\mathrm{d}F \geqslant 0$, if $R_{PT} \leqslant 0$, which is satisfied if the demand function for the oligopolists' products is a Cobb–Douglas form (in which case we get $R_{PT} = 0$). *The increase in the stock of technology of the foreign competitors would result in the decrease in the profitability of R&D activity for the collusive oligopoly which, in turn, lowers oligopolists' stock of technology, and to compensate the decrease in their market shares the oligopolists raise their product prices by using monopoly power in the domestic market.*

Also, under the same conditions we obtain $\mathrm{d}T/\mathrm{d}B > 0$ and $\mathrm{dP}/\mathrm{d}B < 0$; the increases in the international trade barriers (such as tariffs) would promote the R&D activity of the domestic oligopolists and lower the prices of their products.

The crucial assumption in the above analysis is that the shares of foreign competitors in the market are small in the long run and so foreign competition does not alter the joint-profit-maximizing behavior of the domestic oligopolists. If the foreign competitors capture substantial share in the domestic market, the collusive behavior will become difficult to maintain effectively unless the foreign competitors also take part in the collusive actions. But, since monopolistic firms are politically influential, they usually succeed in putting some kind of policy into effect which protects them from foreign competition (see Adams (1977) and Saunders (1980), for example). Hence, it may be unlikely that foreign competitors' shares in the domestic markets are allowed to grow to the extent that they threaten the existence of collusive oligopoly.

III. WELFARE ANALYSIS – PERFORMANCES

III.1. National welfare

A. Static or short-run analysis

The effect of intentional trade on consumption

International trade could increase the welfare of every nation in the world if all the markets are perfectly competitive. But Melvin and Warne (1973), Rieber (1982), Singh (1977) and Sweeney (1974) have shown that international trade is not necessarily beneficial to all of the countries in the world if firms with monopolistic power exist in one or some of the markets in the world. This is so because monopolistic firms in large countries are able to influence price levels of their products sold in the world market.

Welfare loss to monopoly – hypotheses on profitability

We have elucidated that the effects of monopoly on the home welfare can be altered by international trade in various ways: through changes in market structure into more competitive directions, and through its effects on the decisions by the domestic monopolists on such important behaviors as collusive actions, product policy, R&D activity, etc. by supplying the formidable, and often aggressive, foreign competitors. But with respect to empirical studies on the effects of international trade, (due to the tradition in industrial organization) attention of the economists in the field seems to have mostly attracted to the relationship between structure and performance (usually represented by profitability) in the international settings which provides a hypothesis appropriate for the study of the effect of international trade on collusive oligopoly in the home market.

The analysis of the structure-conduct-performance paradigm extended to the international framework can provide sets of hypothetical relationships between profitability and the elements of international market structure, and we shall show some of these important relationships below:

1. Concentration ratios not only in the home market but also in the world market would affect economic performance in the home market. Irrespective of the degree of concentration in the home market, the higher concentration ratios in the world market could produce the higher profitability in the home industry by raising the world price, and hence the home price, of the good.
2. The well-established foreign firms might have the considerable effect to constrain the behavior of the domestic leading firms even if their shares in the domestic market are not large, provided that the foreign competitors are allowed to grow in the domestic market and there is a possibility that they could threaten the existence of collusive oligopoly in the long run.
3. The impact of foreign competition on the domestic collusive oligopoly could be almost the same as that of competitive fringe in the home market if the size of the home market is relatively large in the world market. But for a small country foreign competition could have devastating effects on the profitability of the industry should the barriers to international trade be nonexistent. The effect of international trade on profitability would be the greater, the larger the relative size of the home market in the world.
4. Foreign competition could play the major role in determining the long-run level of profitability in the home industry if the barriers to international trade is lower than the barriers to entry.

5. Successful product differentiation by the home firms would weaken the impact of foreign competition by raising the barrier to international trade.

6. In the industry where the economies of scale are important the increase in the amounts of exports by the domestic firms would lower their production costs, and hence raise the profitability of the industry. But the foreign competitors that exploit scale economies fully in their home markets could have destructive effects on the profitability of the industry where the minimum efficient scale-home market size ratio is substantially large.

7. If some of foreign competitors' home markets are at the early stage of production of the good where innovative new technologies are introduced almost incessantly, the effect of foreign competition could become overwhelmingly important.

8. The least risky market would require the lowest risk premium and might suffer most from foreign competition.

Welfare loss to monopoly – empirical studies on profitability

By now there are a number of empirical studies that have examined the effects of international trade on profitability. Table A1 in the Appendix summarizes some of these studies. Most of them have used the shares of imports in the domestic scale (or the analogous variables) and/or the effective or nominal rates of tariffs as the key variables that are supposed to represent the strength of foreign competition. Many of these empirical studies have found that profitability is related negatively to imports or tariff (especially in the concentrated industries), and also positively to exports. In the interpretation of these relationships one is inclined to extrapolate from the well-known profitability-structure relationship. The negative relationship between profitability and import could be considered to have the same implication as the profitability-concentration relationship, and so it now seems fairly well-established that imports increase competitiveness of the industry and raise social welfare by lowering welfare losses due to monopoly.

But we have to be very careful in interpreting the relationship between profitability and imports, since their relationship may not be as simple as that between profitability and concentration, especially in relation to social welfare. As White (1974) pointed out, the large share of imports may be caused by monopoly in a domestic market, and if marginal cost of domestic production is smaller than import price (it could happen if the supply of imports is imperfectly elastic or the product is differentiated), an increase in imports caused by the domestic monopoly means a decrease in social welfare (Stegemann, 1983, 1984). Thus, the large share of imports in a concentrated industry may decrease monopoly profits but may not increase national welfare.

Moreover, the negative relationship between profitability and imports does not necessarily imply the increase in competitiveness of the industry. For example, in the case of a small country the large share of imports may enforce domestic monopolists to produce at suboptimal scales, and by increasing production costs deprive domestic firms of excessive profits. Even in the case of a large country profitability in the industries with large minimum efficient scales in comparison with the sizes of the home markets could be lowered by imports for the same reason as stated in the small country case. Since large minimum efficient scales often take place in the concentrated industries, it is conceivable that the negative relationship between profitability and imports found in the concentrated industries are caused by suboptimal scale productions.

In the case of a differentiated product the large share of imports may be the result of heavy advertising expenditures by the foreign firms and it could become the cause of excessive advertising expenditures by domestic firms causing the decreases in the level of profits of the domestic firms by squeezing profit margins.

The relation between the shares of imports and the level of the domestic firms' profits can be examined more rigorously with the aid of the theoretical model of collusive oligopoly under threat of foreign competition introduced in Section II. To do so, define the total profits of the domestic oligopolists at the long-run equilibrium, R^*, as

$$R^* = R(P^*, T^*, F, B) - vP^T T^* N,$$

and the share of imports, MS, as $MS = S/D$. Differentiation of R^* and MS with respect to B yields

$$\mathrm{d}R^*/\mathrm{d}B = rNP^T(\mathrm{d}T/\mathrm{d}B) - (P - C)S_B,$$

and

$$\mathrm{d}MS/\mathrm{d}B = [S_B + S_P(\mathrm{d}P/\mathrm{d}B) + S_T(\mathrm{d}T/\mathrm{d}B)]/D,$$

from which we obtain $\mathrm{d}R^*/\mathrm{d}B > 0$ and $\mathrm{d}MS/\mathrm{d}B < 0$, if $R_{PT} \leqslant 0$. The international trade barriers are related positively with the total profits of the domestic oligopolists and negatively with the shares of imports; the reductions in the international trade barriers decrease the total profits of collusive oligopoly in the domestic market, and increase the shares of imports.

Thus, our analysis predicts the existence of the negative correlation between profitability and the shares of imports. But this negative correlation does not stand for the causal relation between them and hence it does not imply the increase in the competitiveness of a market which leads to the increase in the welfare of a society (because, as shown in Section II.B, the reductions in the international trade barriers lower the R&D activities of collusive oligopolists but raises the prices of their products). It is just the result of the simultaneous effects of changes in the height of the international trade barriers. Thus, parts of the negative correlation between profitability and the share of imports found in many empirical studies that use cross section data could have been caused by differences among industries in the height of the international trade barriers and in the technologies of foreign competitors.

Also, Katrak (1980) have shown that the larger share of exports could be caused by a domestic monopoly and mean the larger losses in the home welfare due to monopoly. Thus, the analysis of the effect of monopoly in the international framework has to take into accounts the possibility of welfare losses related to monopoly-induced changes in both export and import.[10]

Technological efficiency – suboptimal scale productions

If the economies of scale are important there will be the tradeoff relationship between resource allocation and technological efficiency, i.e. in order to make full use of scale economies the existence of large monopolistic firms would become inevitable. In some cases this difficulty could be resolved by international trade, since minimum efficient scale should be relatively small in the world market.[11]

If the economies of scale are *very* large in relation to the domestic market, free trade would eliminate inefficient firms in the home market. In the cases where the world market is competitive this could call forth the improvement in national welfare (see Basevi (1970) and Corden (1967)). If some firms in the world market posses market power and the domestic demand for the good in question is inelastic, national welfare may be decreased since the foreign firm might set a monopoly price after eliminating domestic firms.

The other objectives[12]

Technological changes in foreign countries could produce an effect of increasing *unemployment of labor and capital* through international trade. It could be considered as the short-run phenomenon provided that all the markets in the home economy are competitive. If some of the domestic markets are monopolized, however, such increases in unemployment of labor and capital caused by foreign competition could exist for a long period of time.

Firms with monopoly power may not wish to engage in international trade since they have already been getting excessive profits. Rather they might prefer to be protected from foreign competition. This will cause reductions in *the extent of an industry's participation in international trade*.

B. Dynamic or long-run analysis of the effects of international trade on national welfare

Technological progress, growth of capital and inflation

So far the analysis of the effects of international trade on social welfare have been confined to the static one. The effects of monopoly in an open economy on economic growth, technological progress and inflation have not fully been analyzed. But, international trade could promote technological progress by increasing technological competition in the world markets. Also, it could decrease the rate of inflation related to market power of domestic firms by creating the circumstances difficult even for the monopolistic firms to raise prices (see DeRosa and Goldstein (1981)).

The effects of international trade on capital growth should not be disregarded. As Nakao (1981) and Laitner (1982) have shown, the change in relative price caused by monopoly affects the long-run stock of capital even in a closed economy. In an open economy the prices of domestic monopolist's products are influenced by international trade and the changes in relative price could call forth changes in the domestic aggregate stock of capital in the long-run. This is especially so if international capital investment is not severely restricted. If foreign competition decreases monopoly profits of domestic firms, they might choose closing some of their domestic plants and invest in more profitable foreign countries, or conversely, they might invest in new plants with technologically improved equipments to counter foreign competition. In the former case the domestic aggregate stock of capital could be lowered in the long-run, while in the latter case it could induce economic growth by increasing the aggregate stock of capital in the home economy.

III.2. World welfare

In the previous sections we emphasized the effects of international trade under imperfect structure on the national welfare. But the existence of market power in the world market such as concentrated industries in the large countries and product differentiation would affect the welfare of the rest of the world by changing per capita consumption, monopoly welfare losses, technological efficiency, unemployment of labor and capital, product quality, economic growth, inflation and so on. Unfortunately in many cases where some markets in the world are imperfect there would be severe conflict between national and international welfares. How to reconcile this conflict is a very difficult problem.

IV. INTERNATIONAL TRADE POLICY IN IMPERFECT MARKET SETTINGS

A. National welfare maximization with and without constraints

In the literature it seems usual to assume that the country's objective is maximization of national welfare without any constraints. Some authors (Berkowitz and Kotowitz (1983), for example) justify this behavior by asserting that in the case of a small country such a behavior will not cause any retaliatory reactions by the rest of the world. But it is easy to see that if all the small countries in the world behave that way, even large countries would have to take retaliatory measures. Thus, the rational behavior of, even, small countries seems to be maximization of national welfare with constraints, some of which might be explicitly reflected in various international trade agreement and treaties. In spite of this fact, the effects of various kinds of constraints on the welfares of the home and world with imperfect market structure have not been examined in details.

B. World welfare maximization with side payments

In order to enjoy fully the welfare-increasing effects of international trade under imperfect market structure, the policy to maximize the world welfare with side payments would be better than the national welfare maximization with some constraints, since maximization of individual welfares with constraints in many parts of the world does not generally coincide with maximization of its total welfare. In spite of its importance the concept of world welfare maximization with side payments does not seem to be paid due attention in the analysis of imperfect market structure in the international framework.

V. CONCLUDING REMARKS

There is no doubt about the possibility that the international trade reduces or sometimes eliminates welfare losses caused by monopolies in the home markets. But it seems extremely difficult to construct simple theoretical models by combining and capturing the essential features of both industrial organization and international trade. Besides, the effects of both monopoly in an open economy and of international trade with imperfect market structure seem to differ in various ways among countries depending upon the country's and/or the industry's structural and technological conditions. Hence in applying the theoretical models to the phenomena in reality one has to ascertain the structural and technological conditions used in the models and their accordance with the real world in which the phenomena in question are taking place: otherwise the interpretation of the phenomena in the real world could become misleading.

ACKNOWLEDGEMENT

I am indebted to Professors W. G. Shepherd and H. Odagiri for their comments on the earlier version of the paper. Also, participants in the conference on 'Main Stream in Industrial Organization' provided useful comments in deriving the final version of the paper.

APPENDIX

Table A1. Empirical studies on effect of international trade on profitability.

Name(s) of authors	Countries	Import	Export	Home CR	Other trade variables	No. of sample	Major control variables
Adams (1976)	Transnational	?	?	?		331	
Baba *et al.* (1977)	Japan	+	?	–	Growth of import share ?	81	
Caves and Uekusa (1976)	Japan		?	+		35	GR A/S
Caves and Khalilzadeh	UK	?	+	+		60	MES GR
Caves *et al.* (1980)	Canada	?	–	+		123	A/S
This study applies a comprehensive simultaneous-equation model of structure and performance to Canadian manufacturing industries							
DOI (1979)	Japan		+	?		224	GR
Esposito *et al.* (1971)	USA	–		+		76 IRS	A/S GR
Geroski (1982)	UK	–	+	?		52	A/S GR
Hart (1977)	UK	?		+		113	A/S
Hitiris (1978)	UK			+	Tariff effect +	40–80	A/S GR
House (1973)	Kenya		?	Import adjusted +		31	
Hutchinson (1981)	Ireland	–	+	?	Tariff Effect Nominal ? ?	24	

Table A1. (continued)

Jacquemin *et al.* (1980)	Belgium	–	?	?			32	GR DIV
This study estimates a system of two equations where profitability and concentration are endogeneous, and concentration is related negatively with the export variable								
Jenny *et al.* (1976)	France		–	+			44	PD
Jones *et al.* (1973)	Canada	+		+			30	PD
Khalilzadeh (1974)	UK	–	+	+			61	GR PD MES
					CR in the world market			
Leitzinger *et al.* (1983)	USA				+		45(IRS)	A/S
Marvel (1980)	USA	–	?	+			38	A/S Size CONS
This study presents estimates of the determinants of profitability and commodity composition of trade flows, and found that the increase in concentration increases import								
					Tariff effect			
McFetridge (1973)	Canada			+	?		43	A/S
Neumann (1979)	West Germany	–	–	+			334	Size risk GR
Pagoulatos *et al.* (1976a)	Belgium	–	?	?	?		38	CONS GR
Ditto	France	–	–	+	–		38	GR
Ditto	Netherlands	–	?	?	–		38	CONS
Ditto	Italy	?	–	?	?		38	CONS
Ditto	Germany	–	?	+	?		38	GR
					Multinational activity	NTB		
Pagoulatos *et al.* (1976b)	USA	–	?	+	+	+	88	CONS
Pugel (1980)	USA	–	+	+				GR A/S
Main analysis of this study lies in the estimation of interactive specification, the results of which are not reported here								

Table A1. (continued)

Name(s) of authors	Countries	Import	Export	Home CR	Other trade variables	No. of samples	Major control variables
Turner (1980)	UK	–		–	Growth of import share –	32	A/S

*Bloch (1974) found that prices were high when both tariffs and concentration were high by comparing differences of the mean in his profit index of the Canadian manufacturing industries.

The plus (minus) symbol means that the estimated coefficient is statistically significant, at least, at 10% level and coefficient is plus (minus), and the question mark means that the estimated coefficient is not statistically significant.

The variables listed in the major-control-variables column are all statistically significant, at least, at 5% level.

Notations for trade variables
Import, the ratio of import to industry output or the analogous variables; Export, the ratio of import to industry output or the analogous variables; CR, concentration; Tariff effect, effective rates of tariff; NTB, non-tariff trade barriers;

Notations for control variables
A/S, advertising sales ratio or the analogous variables; CONS, consumer goods variables; DIV, diversification variables; GR, the growth of demand variables; MES, minimum efficient variables; PD, product differentiation variables; Size, firm size variables; Risk, risk variables;

NOTES

1. An interesting survey on the recent developments in this field is given by Caves (1985).
2. The domestic sellers' concentration ratios obtained by, say, subtracting exports from and adding imports to domestic production do not take into accounts the differences in the effects of small domestic firms and imports on the behavior of the domestic leading firms. See Cannon (1978) and Shepherd (1972).
3. For few countries the relation between the sizes of firms and their export activities are examined. See, for example Auquier (1980) and Glejser *et al.* (1980).
4. Even though we have not considered the possibility of exports by entrants, Brander and Spencer (1981) emphasized the importance of its effects on the level of profits of the established firms.
5. Especially the rate of demand growth causes important changes in the behavior of firms and market structure (see Nakao 1979, 1980).
6. An example is given in the first part of Section II.2.
7. Using Japanese data Baba (1974) examined the effects of multinational firms on concentration, and found no relationship between them.
8. Foreign direct investment may take place later depending upon transport costs and tariffs as emphasized by Horst (1972) and Norman and Nichols (1982) or upon the scarcity of managerial resource among countries as emphasized by Komiya (1975).
9. For example, facing with the import pressure of the 1960's US steelmakers forged major technological innovations such as oxygen converters, vacuum degassing and continuous casting.
10. The estimation of welfare costs due to monopoly in an open economy by Wahlroos (1982) has failed to take into accounts the possibility of wasteful imports and exports caused by monopoly.
11. A literature survey on the relationship between international trade, scale and efficiency is given in Caves (1979).
12. Some people seem to consider the reduction in the country's trade deficit as one of the objectives of trade policy, and often urge one or some of the countries that are responsible for parts of the country's trade deficit to eliminate international trade barriers. But as long as there are economic circumstances in the country that induce foreign capital inflows, in order to clear the market the value of country's currency must be kept at the high level which produces trade deficits. Elimination of international trade barriers in one or some of countries with trade surpluses will end in the hike of the value of the country's currency and in the enlargement of the trade surplus by the rest of the countries.

REFERENCES

Adams, William J., 'International Differences in Corporate Profitability', *Economica* 43, (November 1976), pp. 367–379.

Adams, Walter and Dirlum, Joel B., 'Import Quotas and Industrial Performance', in *Welfare Aspects of Industrial Markets*, eds. A. P. Jacquemin and H. de Jong, Leiden: Martinus Nijhoff Social Science Division (1977), pp. 153–181.

Auquier, A. A. and Caves, R. E., 'Monopolistic Export Industries, Trade Taxes, and Optimal Competition Policy', *Economic Journal*, 89, (September, 1979), pp. 559–581.

Auquier, A. A., 'Sizes of Firms, Exporting Behavior and the Structure of French Industry', *Journal of Industrial Economics*, 29(2), (December 1980), pp. 203–217.

Basevi, Giorgio, 'Domestic Demand and Ability to Export', *Journal of Political Economy*, 78(2), (May/April 1970), pp. 330–337.

Berkowitz, M. K. and Kotowitz, Y., 'Patent Policy in an Open Economy', *Canadian Journal of Economics*, 15(1), (February 1982), pp. 1–17.

Bloch, H., 'Prices, Costs, and Profits in Canadian Manufacturing: The Influence of Tariffs and concentration', *Canadian Journal of Economics*, 7(4), (November, 1974), pp. 594–610.

Brander, James A., 'Intra-Industry Trade in Identical Commodities', *Journal of International Economics*, 11, (February 1981), pp. 1–14.

Brander, James A. and Spencer, Barbara J., 'Tariffs and the Extraction of Foreign Monopoly Rents under Potential Entry', *Canadian Journal of Economics*, 14(3), (August 1981), pp. 371–389.

Cannon, C. M., 'International Trade, concentration and Competition in U.K. Consumer Goods Markets', *Oxford Economic Papers*, 30(1), (March 1978), pp. 130–137.

Caves, R. E., 'International Trade, International Investment, and Imperfect Markets', *Special Papers in International Economics*, No. 10, Princeton: International Finance Section, Department of Economics, Princeton University (November 1974).

Caves, R. E., 'International Cartels and Monopolies in International Trade', in *International Economic Policy: Theory and Evidence*, eds. R. Dornbusch and J. A. Frenkel, Baltimore: Johns Hopkins University Press (1979), pp. 39–73.

Caves, R. E., 'International Trade and Industrial Organization: Introduction', *Journal of Industrial Economics*, 29(2), (December 1980), pp. 113–117.

Caves, R. E., 'International Trade and Industrial Organization: Problems, Solved and Unsolved', Harvard Institute of Economic research Discussion Paper No. 1131 (January 1985).

Caves, R. E. and Khalilzadeh-Shirazi, J., 'International Trade and Industrial Organization: Some Statistical Evidence', in *Welfare Aspects of Industrial Markets*, eds. A. P. Jacquemin and H. de Jong, Leiden: Martinus Nijhoff Social Science Division (1977), pp. 111–127.

Caves, R. E. and Porter, M. E., 'Market Structure, Oligopoly and Stability of Market Shares', *Journal of Industrial Economics*, 26(4), (June 1978), pp. 289–313.

Caves, R. E., Spence, A. Michael, and Scott, John T., *Competition in the Open Economy: A Model Applied to Canada*, Cambridge, Mass.: Harvard University Press (1980).

Caves, R. E. and Uekusa, Masu. *Industrial Organization in Japan*, Washington D.C.: The Brookings Institute (1976).

Corden, W. M., 'Monopoly, Tariffs and Subsidies', *Economica*, 34, (February 1967), pp. 50–58.

Derosa Dean A. and Goldstein, Morris, 'Import Discipline in the U.S. Manufacturing Sector', *IMF Staff Papers*; 28(3), (September 1981), pp. 600–634.

Dixit, Avinash, 'International Trade Policy for Oligopolistic Industries', *Economic Journal*, Supplement, 94, (1984), pp. 1–16.

Donnenfeld, Shabtai and Strebel, Paul, 'Industry Structure and Trade Policy under Fluctuating Import Prices', *European Economic Review*, 23, (1983), pp. 203–215.

Esposito, Louis and Esposito, Frances Ferguson, 'Foreign Competition and Domestic Industry Profitability', *Review of Economics and Statistics*, 53(4), (November 1971), pp. 343–353.

Gabszewicz, J. J., Shaked, A., Sutton, J., and Thisse, J. F., 'International Trade in

Differentiated Products', *International Economic Review*, 22(3), (October 1981), pp. 527–534.

Gaskins, Darius, W. Jr., 'Dynamic Limit Pricing: Optimal Pricing under Threat of Entry', *Journal of Economic Theory*, 3, (1971), pp. 306–322.

Geroski, P. A., 'Simultaneous Equations Models of the Structure-Performance Paradigm', *European Economic Review*, 19, (1982), pp. 145–158.

Glejser, Herbert, Jacquemin, Alexis, and Petit, Jean, 'Exports in an Imperfect Competition Framework: An Analysis of 1,446 Exporters', *Quarterly Journal of Economics*, 94, (May 1980), pp. 507–524.

Gorecki, Paul K., 'The Determinants of Entry by Domestic and Foreign Enterprises in Canadian Manufacturing Industries: Some Comments and Empirical Results', *Review of Economics and Statistics*, 58(4), (November, 1976), pp. 485–488.

Grossman, Gene M., 'Import Competition from Developed and Developing Countries', *Review of Economics and Statistics*, 64(2), (May 1982), pp. 271–281.

Harris, Richard, 'Applied General equilibrium Analysis of Small Open Economies with Scale Economies and Imperfect Competition', *American Economic Review*, 74(5), (December 1984), pp. 1016–1032.

Hart, P. E. and Morgan, Eleanor, 'Market Structure and Economic Performance in the United Kingdom', *Journal of Industrial Economics*, 25(3), (March 1977), pp. 177–193.

Helpman, Elhanan, 'International Trade in the Presence of Product Differentiation, Economies of Scale and Monopolistic Competition', *Journal of International Economics*, 11, (August 1981), pp. 305–340.

Hitiris, Theodore, 'Effective Protection and Economic Performance in UK Manufacturing Industry, 1963 and 1968', *Economic Journal*, 88, (March 1978), 107–120.

Horst, Thomas, 'The Industrial Composition of U.S. Exports and Subsidiary Sales to the Canadian Market', *American Economic Review*, 62(1), (March 1972), pp. 37–45.

House, William J., 'Market Structure and Industry Performance: The Case of Kenya', *Oxford Economic Papers*, 25(3), (November 1973), pp. 405–419.

Hu, Sheng Cheng, 'Uncertainty, Domestic Demand, and Exports', *Canadian Journal of Economics*, 8(2), (May 1975), pp. 258–268.

Hutchinson, R. W., 'Price-Cost Margins and Manufacturing Industry Structure', *European Economic Review*, 16, (1981), pp. 247–267.

Jacquemin, Alexis, De Ghellinck, Elizabeth, and Huveneers, Christian, 'Concentration and Profitability in a Small Open Economy', *Journal of Industrial Economics*, 29(2), (December 1980), pp. 131–143.

Jacquemin, Alexis, 'Imperfect Market Structure and International Trade-Some Recent Research', *Kyklos*, 35(1), (1982), pp. 75–93.

Jenny, Frederick and Weber, Andre Paul, 'Profit Rates and Structural Variables in French Manufacturing Industries', *European Economic Review*, 7, (1976), pp. 187–206.

Jones, J. C. H., Laudadio, L., and Percy, M., 'Market Structure and Profitability in Canadian Manufacturing Industry: Some Cross-Section Results', *Canadian Journal of Economics*, 6(3), (August 1973), pp. 356–368.

Katrak, Homi, 'Multi-National Monopolies and Monopoly Regulation', *Oxford Economic Papers*, 32(3), (November 1980), pp. 453–466.

Khalilzadeh-Shirazi, Javad, 'Market Structure and Price-Cost Margins in United Kingdom Manufacturing Industries', *Review of Economics and Statistics*, 56(1), (February 1974), pp. 67–76.

Krugman, Paul R., 'Increasing Returns, Monopolistic Competition, and International Trade', *Journal of International Economics*, 9, (1979), pp. 469–479.

Krugman, Paul R., 'Scale Economies, Product Differentiation, and the Pattern of Trade', *American Economic Review*, 70(5), (December 1980), pp. 950–959.

Lancaster, Kelvin, 'Intra-Industry Trade under Perfect Monopolistic Competition', *Journal of International Economics*, 10, (May 1980), pp. 151–175.

Laitner, John, 'Monopoly and Long-Run Capital Accumulation', *Bell Journal of Economic*, 13, (1982), pp. 143–157.

Leitzinger, Jeffrey J. and Tamor, Kenneth L., 'Foreign Competition in Antitrust Law', *Journal of Law and Economics*, 26, (April 1983), pp. 87–102.

Marvel, Howard P., 'Foreign Trade and Domestic Competition', *Economic Inquiry*, 18, (January 1980), pp. 103–122.

McFetridge, Donald G., 'Market Structure and Price-Cost Margins: An Analysis of the Canadian Manufacturing Sector', *Canadian Journal of Economics*, 6(3), (August 1973), pp. 344–355.

Melvin, James R. and Warne, Robert D., 'Monopoly and the Theory of International Trade', *Journal of International Economics*, 3, (1973), pp. 117–134.

Nakao, Takeo, 'Profit Rates and Market Shares of Leading Industrial Firms in Japan', *Journal of Industrial Economics*, 27(4), (June 1979), pp. 371–383.

Nakao, Takeo, 'Demand Growth, Profitability, and Entry', *Quarterly Journal of Economics*, 94, (February 1980), pp. 397–411.

Nakao, Takeo, 'The Effects of Demonopolization on the Aggregate Stock of Capital and the Welfare of a Society', *Southern Economic Journal*, 48, (1981), pp. 358–364.

Nakao, Takeo, 'Product Quality and Market Structure', *Bell Journal of Economics*, 13, (1982), pp. 133–142.

Nakao, Takeo, 'Profitability, Market Shares, Product Quality, and Advertising in Oligopoly', *Journal of Economic Dynamics and Control*, 6, (1983), pp. 153–171.

Neumann, Manfred, Bobel, Ingo, and Haid, Alfred, 'Profitability, Risk and Market Structure in West German Industries', *Journal of Industrial Economics*, 27(3), (March 1979), pp. 227–242.

Norman, George and Nichols, Nancy K., 'Dynamic Market Strategy under Threat of Competitive Entry: An Analysis of the Pricing and Production Policies Open to the Multinational Company', *Journal of Industrial Economics*, 31(1/2), (September/December 1982), pp. 153–174.

Pagoulatos, Emilio and Sorensen, Robert, 'Foreign Trade, Concentration and Profitability in Open Economies', *European Economic Review*, 8, (1976), pp. 255–267.

Pagoulatos, Emilio and Sorensen, Robert, 'International Trade, International Investment and Industrial Profitability of U.S. Manufacturing', *Southern Economic Journal*, 42(3), (January 1976), pp. 425–434.

Pugel, Thomas A., 'Foreign Trade and US Market Performance', *Journal of Industrial Economics*, 29(2), (December 1980), pp. 119–129.

Rieber, William J., 'Discriminating Monopoly and International Trade', *Economic Journal*, 92, (June 1982), pp. 365–376.

Saunders, Ronald, 'The Political Economy of Effective Tariff Protection in Canada's Manufacturing Sector', *Canadian Journal of Economics*, 13(2), (May 1980), pp. 340–348.

Shepherd, William G., 'Structure and Behaviour in British Industries, with U.S. Comparisons', *Journal of Industrial Economics*, November 21(1), (1972), pp. 35–54.

Shepherd, William G., *The Economics of Industrial Organization*, Englewood Cliffs, N.J.: Prentice-Hall (1979).

Shepherd, William G., 'Causes of Increased Competition in the U.S. Economy, 1919–1980', *Review of Economics and Statistics*, 64(4), (November 1982), pp. 613–626.

Sigh, Ajit, 'UK Industry and the World Economy: A Case of De-Industrialization', in *Welfare Aspects of Industrial Markets*, eds. A. P. Jacquemin and H. de Jong, Leiden: Martinus Nijhoff Social Science Division (1977), pp. 183–124.

Stegemann, Klaus, 'Wasteful Import Due to Domestic Monopoly in a Spatially Differentiated Market', *Southern Economic Journal*, 49(3), (January 1983), pp. 734–742.

Stegemann, Klaus, 'The Social Costs of Monopoly in an Open Economy', *Canadian Journal of Economics*, 17(4), (November 1984), pp. 718–730.

Stykolt, Stefan and Eastman, Harry C., 'A Model for the Study of Protected Oligopolies', *Economic Journal*, 70, (June 1960), pp. 336–347.

Sweeney, Richard James, 'Monopoly, the Law of Comparative Advantage, and Commodity Price Agreements: A Simple General Eqilibrium Analysis', *Weltwirtschaftliches Archiv*, 110, (1974), pp. 259–287.

Turner, Philip P., 'Import Competition and the Profitability of United Kingdom Manufacturing Industry', *Journal of Industrial Economics*, 29(2), (December 1980), pp. 155–166.

Turnovsky, Stephen J., 'Technological and Price Uncertainty in a Ricardian Model of International Trade', *Review of Economic Studies*, 41, (April 1974), pp. 201–217.

Vernon, Raymond, 'International Investment and International Trade in the Product Cycle', *Quarterly Journal of Economics*, 80(2), (May 1966), pp. 190–207.

Wahlroos, Bjorn, 'The Welfare Cost of Imperfect Industrial Competition in an Open Economy With an Application to Finland', *Scandinabian Journal of Economy*, 84(3), (1982), pp. 457–470.

White, Lawrence J., 'Industrial Organization and International Trade: Some Theoretical Considerations', *American Economic Review*, 64, (December 1974), pp. 1013–1020.

JAPANESE REFERENCES

Baba, Masao, *Han-Dokusen no Keizaigaku*, Tokyo, Japan: Chikumashobo (1974).

Baba, Masao, *et al.*, 'Kaitekozo to Shijoseika', *Keizai Bunseki*, 64, (February 1977), pp. 121–143.

Doi, Noriyuki, 'Kigyo no Kibokozo to Rijunritsu', *Kansai Gakuin Daigaku Keizaigaku Ronkyu*, 32(4), (April 1979), pp. 57–99.

Komiya, Ryutaro, *Kokusai KeizaiGaku Kenkyu*, Tokyo, Japan: University of Tokyo Press (1975).

8. EXPORTING BEHAVIOR AND MARKET STRUCTURE: EVIDENCE FROM THE UNITED STATES

Richard E. Caves

One clouded area in our understanding of the relation between international trade and industrial organization is the mutual influences among the exporting activities of an industry's producers, the market structures surrounding them, and the industry's performance. On the existing evidence, national manufacturing industries that export heavily seem to function not purely as small segments of worldwide competitive industries. Rather, their export patterns and their market structures and performance levels exhibit complex associations that are not consistent with pure competition. We certainly need to invoke product differentiation and heterogeneity in order to explain the patterns that have been observed empirically, and oligopolistic behavior may also play a role.

One complex but useful point of entry to the relations between exporting activity and market structure is through the variation among production units in the fractions of their output exported. In a purely competitive industry that exports part of its output, we expect the allocation of each seller's output between exports and domestic sales to be indeterminate and random. That is, at the market-clearing price n identical pure competitors each place equal amounts of output on the market, and which units are taken by foreign and which by domestic buyers is entirely random with respect to the originating producers. Yet existing empirical studies seem to identify patterns that are behaviorally more complex than these, and that call for taking into account locational factors, product differentiation, and oligopolistic behavior (along with the structural factors that underlie the fewness of the sellers).

The main purpose of this paper is to analyze data newly available for the United States on the variability among producers of the proportions of their output exported. Subject to serious limitations that are explained below, the data set permits us to test for the United States patterns that have been observed in several other industrial countries. Before

de Jong, H. W., Shepherd, W. G. (eds) Mainstreams in Industrial Organization
 ISBN 978-94-017-0495-3

turning to those tests, we review the relevant theory and existing evidence.

I. THEORETICAL BASES AND EXISTING EVIDENCE

The evidence available to us, as to previous investigators, bears on two aspects of the exporting behavior of plants or firms: whether larger units export bigger fractions of their outputs; and how much the ratios of exports to shipments vary among units. We first identify the theoretical bases that might explain these patterns of exporting behavior.

Theoretical considerations

Scale economies provide a basis for associating exporting patterns with firm size. Assume that an industry's production function is subject to significant economies of scale that are realized in varying degrees by existing producers. This assumption immediately raises the question why different-size units varying in scale efficiency should be viable in a long-run market equilibrium; we simply assume that some unexplained factor makes it feasible for sellers of diverse sizes to obtain revenues that cover their costs on some domestic sales.

In order to link the existence of scale economies to exporting behavior, we must specify the form of the cost function. Scale economies due solely to fixed costs are consistent with all sellers having identical marginal costs, which would leave us with no basis for differentiating their exporting behavior. However, scale economies may be due to increasing returns in the production function, for example, if the elasticity of scale (ratio of average to marginal cost) is constant and greater than one. Alternatively, each unit's total cost may consist of fixed costs plus variable costs that are proportional to output, but random factors cause some producers to enjoy lower unit variable costs than others. If such producers exhibit Cournot conjectures in setting their outputs, then the larger outputs will emanate from the more efficient producers who, again, will experience lower marginal costs (Clarke and Davies, 1982).

Suppose now that demand in export markets is highly elastic at a price (and thus marginal revenue) less than what some small-scale sellers can command on the domestic market. Then, if producers who attain greater economies of scale also have lower marginal costs, large units' marginal costs are more likely to lie below the levels of marginal revenue attainable from foreign sales. Larger producers are therefore more likely to export some of their output. We cannot, however, establish that the proportion of output exported increases with total output, among those units that sell some exports, without additional assumptions.

Product differentiation clearly suffices to predict that firms of diverse sizes make some sales abroad, regardless of the degree to which they attain scales that minimize long-run average costs. Assume that preferences of buyers are heterogeneous with respect to the characteristics embodied in different brands of a product, and that scale economies limit the number of producers (and brand configurations) relative to the possible range of "custom made" varieties. Suppose further that buyers' tastes are correlated imperfectly (if at all) with their geographic residence.[1] These assumptions suffice to predict that more firms will export some of their output in an industry supplying a differentiated product than one with identical costs and conditions of total demand but no differentiation. We may conjecture that (with cost conditions given) as the attribute complexity of a product increases, the proportion of producers making some export sales increases.

To say more than that, we must specify more about the conditions of product differentiation. Suppose (again) that differentiation rests upon attribute bundles, and that attribute complexity and cost conditions together dictate that any given variety will be supplied by at most a few producers in the world (for example, Lancaster, 1980). Following Auquier (1980), we assume that the small producers present in a national market supply varieties subject to thin densities of demand, whereas large producers supply more commonly demanded varieties, and that these patterns of demand density apply to the world and not just the national market. Then small producers are not only likely to export, but to export larger proportions of their output. Large suppliers, conversely, offer varieties in dense demand that may also be produced in other locations and hence find the bulk of their customers in the domestic market. Other sets of assumptions about differentiation will predict quite different exporting patterns, but this one serves to illustrate the possibilities.

Differential transaction costs of exporting may take either variable or fixed form. Higher transportation charges and tariffs inflate the variable costs of export sales, while higher information costs of foreign marketing or costs of revising specifications, adapting attributes, and translating instructions are largely fixed with respect to the volume exported. Differential fixed costs imply that exports are more likely to emanate from large producers *ex post*,[2] and that firms exporting at all are likely to export large fractions of their output. Extra variable costs of exporting do not affect the interfirm distribution of exports but rather reduce both the probability that any given unit can export profitably and the mean rate of exporting overall.

Transportation costs that are substantial but not biased against exports also hold a distinctive implication for the pattern of exporting. Consider a product (fresh bread) sold in localized markets considerably smaller than the nation. Assume that buyers are evenly distributed over a homogeneous space, that transport costs for the output are proportional to distance, and that inputs have no effect on producers' locational choices. Then cost conditions and the density of demand jointly determine the number of producers and the sizes of local markets, which take the familiar form of Losch's hexagons.

Now allow soldiers and statesmen to draw political boundaries across this terrain that in general do not coincide with economic market boundaries. Then the national boundaries will cut across some local market areas and give rise to "border trade'. Producers in such transborder markets may export substantial shares of their output while other (inland) producers export none (Auquier, 1980).

Competitive conditions may influence patterns of exporting behavior in various ways, although no single, compelling model suggests itself. Price discrimination, conditional upon sufficiently high concentration of domestic producers, is expected to imply dumping in foreign markets and thus an increased proportion of the industry's physical output (although not necessarily value of shipments) sold abroad.[3] However, the interfirm variance of exports/shipments is not affected unless a leader-follower distinction confines the dumping to the market leaders. Much empirical evidence suggests that industries are concentrated because one activity subject to scale economies (whether production or something else) both limits the number of rivals and makes them relatively homogeneous; if so, highly concentrated producers should exhibit similar exporting behavior, because high concentration implies homogeneity of their assets and strategies generally. Alternatively, imitative behavior in moderately concentrated oligopolies may give rise to parallel exporting behavior, in the way that it has been found to promote parallel foreign-investment behavior (Knickerbocker, 1973) and other forms of nonprice rivalry.[4] In short, we lack a strong theory to connect producer concentration to patterns of behavior and thereby exporting patterns, but a connection may emerge through several channels.

Empirical evidence

Empirical evidence on a few countries permits a preliminary screening of these hypotheses. The studies known to me are confined to analyses of data on exports/shipments ratios aggregated across companies or plants in individual industries for Japan (Rapp, 1976), France (Loup, 1969; Auquier, 1980), and Austria (Stankovsky, 1982), plus a study based on individual exporting firms in Belgium (Glejser, Jacquemin, and Petit, 1980). The former studies all agree on the prevalence of two patterns in the data: (1) the proportion of firms in each size-class that export increases with firm size; (2) of those firms that do some exporting, smaller ones export larger proportions of their output. To explain the first pattern, one needs to invoke either scale economies in production or fixed costs associated with exporting. The second can be explained by the configuration of product differentiation proposed by Auquier (1980) and probably by other configurations coupled with firm-specific fixed costs of exporting.

Auquier concluded that scale economies (or fixed costs) exist in exporting that are independent of scale economies in production. He also found specific evidence that product differentiation (measured, however, only in a rough way) is associated with a narrowed gap between the proportions of output exported by large and small firms, although with more specialization in exporting activities for firms of any given size. He also concluded that tariff protection surrounding the national market increases the prevalence of small firms specialized in serving only the domestic market.

The study of Belgian exporters (Glejser, Jacquemin, and Petit, 1980) found that firms' ratios of exports do domestic sales decrease with the concentration of domestic sales (Herfindahl index) but increase with that concentration measure interacted with product differentiation (inferred simply from consumer-good status). They found significant influences of locational factors and firms' access to information on foreign markets as well as a complementarity between firms' multinational status and their exporting activity (we discuss this further below). These data also agree with the patterns noted above: for firms that export, the mean exports/shipments ratio declines with firm size within industries, but the variability of this ratio is also greater for small firms.

II. DATA ON EXPORTING PATTERNS OF U.S. MANUFACTURING PLANTS

These questions can be pursued for United States manufacturing industries with the aid of a data set secured from the U.S. Bureau of the Census incidental to an investigation of technical efficiency.[5] These data, pertaining to the year 1977, comprise the mean and standard deviation of exports/shipments ratios reported in value terms for plants classified to each four-digit manufacturing industry.

Properties and limitations of data

In analyzing these data, we must work within a number of limitations and special properties. First, they pertain to plants, not enterprises, as units of observations. A multiplant firm is likely to allocate its production for exports among its facilities differently from a group of single-plant firms managing identical facilities, and that fact both requires recognition in the statistical analysis that follows and limits the comparability of the results to those of other investigators. This property also qualifies the use of the data to test hypotheses about exporting activity and firm size. Fortunately, a good deal of evidence (notably Lyons, 1980) supports the hypothesis that large multiplant firms tend to possess large plants. Thus, the rank correlations within industries between the sizes of firms and the sizes of the plants that they operate must be extremely high, even if the slope coefficient of exporting on plant size might differ quantitatively from one fitted to firm size.

A second limitation of the data lies in the coverage of plants. The information pertains not the whole population identified in the quinquennial Census of Manufactures, only the panel of plants that provide data each year for the Annual Survey of Manufactures. This panel consists of all plants employing 250 or more persons plus a sample of smaller plants, the sampling frequency increasing with plant size. The proportion of total employment covered by plants in the Survey panel is fairly high in most industries, but the proportion of plants covered is not. Because we do not know how the proportion covered varies from industry to industry, the resulting data diverge substantially from parallel random samples of plants, and we cannot preclude the possibility that coverage differences are correlated with other interindustry differences that enter into the following analysis.

A third limitation, which affects all studies of this type, is that export sales to foreign purchasers by manufacturers do not exhaust all export transactions, which include those made by brokers, trading companies, and other such intermediaries. For some countries, such as Japan and West Germany, the roles of such intermediaries may be quite important. Although little evidence exists on the point, our impression is that such intermediaries are relatively unimportant for U.S. manufactured exports. Also, it should be noted, some of our hypotheses apply to producers' export sales rather than to physical export shipments.

A final limitation is that the data for industry means and standard deviations of plants' exports/shipments ratios came to us rounded to integer percentages. Because the means and standard deviations are quite small for many industries, considerable information was lost in the rounding. Indeed, for no less than 75 of the 344 industries for which data could be secured, the mean exports/shipments ratio rounds to zero.[6]

These two statistics, the mean and standard deviation of plants' exports/shipments ratios for each industry, were used to generate two other statistics that in turn served as the dependent variables in our cross-section analysis. One of these is simply the coefficient of variation (*CV*), the ratio of the standard deviation to the mean. The other measure was designed to indicate the concentration of exporting activities in the larger plants. Data are published on total exports and total shipments for these industries, and an industry's aggregate exports/shipments ratio calculated from them can be regarded as a shipments-weighted average of the exports/shipments ratios of its individual plants. The mean ratio for our Annual Survey panel is unweighted, and so the difference between the weighted and unweighted means can be taken to indicate the concentration of exports in an industry's larger plants. We denote this indicator as *DIF*.

Some further peculiarities of the data affect the accuracy of *DIF*. Exports are matched to output by the U.S. Bureau of the Census through an elaborate concordance that relates the commodity-based classification of exports of the industry-based classification of activity for the measurement of production. This concordance is not perfect or complete, so that some industries elude matching entirely and others are subject to some discrepancies in coverage. We employed our own judgement in accepting certain matches on the basis, say, of matched statistics reported in U.S. Bureau of the Census (1981) for most but not all of the 5-digit product groups classified to a 4-digit industry. Although it was necessary to perform this matching manually for 1977, we did have access to industry-wide exports-shipments ratios assembled with some care at the U.S. Department of Commerce and averaged over 1972–76. Although that period is a temporal mismatch for 1977, the year of observation for our unweighted means and standard deviations, we did use it as an alternative estimate of each industry's shipments-weighted ratio of its plants' exports/shipments ratios. Thus, the variable *DIF* is designated *DIF1* when it represents the shipments-weighted 1977 mean exports/shipments ratio minus the unweighted 1977 mean ratio, *DIF2* when it represents the shipments-weighted exports/shipments ratio averaged for the years 1972–76 minus the unweighted 1977 mean. Besides the advantage of putatively greater accuracy, *DIF2* may offer a significant advantage for evening out year-specific random fluctuations.[7]

Table 1. Means and standard deviations of variables describing intraindustry patterns of plants' exports/shipments ratios (expressed as percentages).

Variable	Industries with positive values of XS (269)		All industries (including XS rounded to zero) (344)	
	Mean	Standard deviation	Mean	Standard deviation
CV	2.36%	1.43%	n.a.	n.a.
DIF1	5.41	8.25	4.58	7.52
DIF2	3.66	6.97	3.16	6.37
XS	4.45	4.54	3.48	4.42
WXS77	9.85	10.96	8.05	10.31
WXS726	8.11	9.54	6.64	89.7

Descriptive statistics

In Table 1, we present some descriptive statistics for these variables, covering *CV*, *DIF1*, and *DIF2* already defined, plus the unweighted mean exports/shipments ratios (*XS*) and their aggregate or shipments-weighted counterparts for 1977 and 1972–76 (*WXS77* and *WXS726*, respectively). The interindustry mean and standard deviation of each variable is given both for the 269 industries reporting unweighted intraindustry mean exports/shipments ratios rounding to a figure greater than zero and the larger sample (344) that includes the observations rounded to zero. *CV* is of course calculated only for the former group of industries.

For both samples the weighted means are roughly double the unweighted mean, and accordingly the mean values of *DIF1* and *DIF2* are positive. (They do not exceed their standard deviations, but that fact probably testifies mainly to the extent of data errors that inflate the standard deviations.) The preponderance of positive values for *DIF* confirms the pattern noted in the preceding section: the typical large plant in the U.S. manufacturing sector exports a larger proportion of its output than does the typical small plant. The mean value of *CV*, 2.4, is quite large; it reflects some very high values for the standard deviations of industries' exports/shipments ratios that may involve data errors.

We calculated correlations among industries for several of these variables. The correlations between *XS* and both *WXS77* and *WXS726* are 0.73, high enough to give comfort in light of the possible errors in data and concordance. The correlation between *WXS* for 1977 and for 1972–76 is 0.81. *DIF1* and *DIF2* exhibit substantial positive correlations with *XS*, 0.42 and 0.34 respectively, indicating that *DIF* and *XS* vary together despite the entry of *XS* with a minus sign into *DIF*'s definition.

Specifically, these correlations suggest that *DIF* normalized by either *XS* or *WXS* would not exhibit much variation among industries: the 'excess' exporting of the larger plants increases more or less proportionally to the industry's overall level of exporting activity. Finally, *CV* is negatively correlated with *WXS*, −0.31 for 1977, −0.35 for 1972–76. In the sense measured by the coefficient of variation, participation in exporting tends to be more even in industries that export more heavily overall.[8]

III. DETERMINANTS OF EXPORTS CONCENTRATION IN LARGE UNITS

To get beyond these general correspondences between the U.S. data and the hypotheses that have been tested on other countries, we undertake a regression analysis of the interindustry variation in *DIF* and *CV*. These two variables together provide reasonably satisfactory vehicles for testing most of the hypotheses that have been put forth concerning the differences in exporting behavior among an industry's production units.

Hypotheses about statistical determinants of DIF

We first set forth the variables employed to test hypotheses about what determines differences among industries in the predominance of large plants as suppliers of exports (*DIF1* and *DIF2*). Scale economies are represented by a statistical proxy that, while open to criticism, has given plausible results in many statistical applications and is correlated with engineering estimates of scale economies in those sectors for which the latter are available. The proxy involves two elements. The first is an estimate of minimum efficient scale (*MES*) at the plant level. It is taken to be either the size of the plant that accounts for the 50th percentile of the industry's output when plants are ranked from the largest to the smallest (*MES1*) or the average size of all plants larger than this 50th-percentile plant (*MES2*). The other element is the cost disadvantage ratio (*CDR*), value added per employee in plants smaller than the 50th percentile divided by value added per employee in larger plants. We constructed:

$$MES1CD = MES1/CDR \quad \text{and} \quad MES2CD = MES2/CDR.$$

Either variable should be positively related to *DIF*.

With scale economies controlled, *DIF* should be negatively related to the extent of structural differentiation of an industry's products. This hypothesis has been recognized in previous research, but the statistical embodiments of differentiation have taken only the roughest forms. We employ a strategy, explained in full elsewhere (Caves and Williamson, 1985), of applying factor analysis to various indirect indicators of the structural differentiation of an industry's products in order to expose the underlying theoretical bases for differentiation. The underlying variables utilized include the industry's ratio of media advertising to sales, its ratio of other selling expenses to sales, its ratio of company-financed research and development to sales, the proportion of its production made to order rather than to stock, the degree to which its marketing is directed to trade channels or advisors rather than the ultimate buyer, the importance of auxiliary services supplied along with the goods, the frequency with which purchases are made by final buyers, and the degree to which the good represents a minor purchase for the final buyer. Factors were estimated using a maximum likelihood technique and subjected to a varimax rotation. Theoretical priors about the underlying bases for differentiation were then used to attach refutable hypotheses to the influences of these factors. We assigned them these interpretations on the basis of the factor loadings on the underlying variables:

FAC1 indicates the extent to which the good is standardized and a minor purchase for the buyer promoted mainly by media advertising;

FAC2 indicates the extent to which varieties of the good have complex and diverse attribute structures and are subject to intensive research;

FAC3 indicates the extent to which the good is subject to low density of demand as reflected by infrequent purchase.

How firmly these factors can be signed as determinants of *DIF* depends on how constraining a hypothesis is attached to the character of product differentiation. On Auquier's (1980) argument, summarized in Section I, the coefficients of *FAC2* and *FAC3* should be negative: smaller producers offer varieties subject to thin densities of demand and complex attribute structures. However, the plausibility of that pattern depends on the overall structure of the nation's competitive advantage in international trade as well as the attribute structures of individual industries' products. *FAC1* is difficult to sign on any basis; evidence on multinational companies (discussed below) indicates that the aspects of product differentiation flagged by *FAC1* promote foreign direct investment as a substitute for merchandise trade but do not provide an apparent basis for predicting the distribution among producers of what exports are observed. In summary, we expect *FAC2* and *FAC3* to influence *DIF*, but impose no prior as to sign; *FAC1* is probably destined for nonsignificance on the basis of prior evidence.

Foreign investment, as just mentioned, bears a potential relationship to the intraindustry pattern of exports because a multinational enterprise

(MNE) is expected to determine its international trade and investment transactions jointly. The traditional hypothesis holds that exports and foreign investment are substitutes, in that the MNE serves overseas markets either by exporting or local production in a subsidiary. However, recent empirical evidence and consideration of the growth process of MNEs have cast some doubt on the issue. The MNE maximizing its global profits uses each national unit to best advantage as both a production and marketing agent. The addition of a new overseas subsidiary therefore may either displace exports from MNE affiliates or create opportunities for the profitable exporting of components or product-line complements. At least in this partial-equilibrium and evolutionary sense, complementarity is both theoretically plausible and empirically supported.[9]

Whichever relation – substitution or complementarity – prevails between exports and overseas investments for MNEs, it has clear implications for *DIF*. That is because evidence indicates that the MNEs among an industry's firms tend strongly to be the largest ones. If we base a prior on a the recent evidence that MNE status increases the exports from a firm's plants, *DIF* should be positively related to:

FAS = foreign assets expressed as a percentage of total assets, companies classified to the industry.[10]

We mentioned above that competitive conditions might affect the distribution of exporting activities among producers in a variety of ways. With no single convincing model in hand, we approached this issue inductively by employing as regressors the conventional four-firm concentration ratio (*C4*) and also dummy variables that could serve to segment it into ranges in which oligopolistic coordination might be respectively absent, incomplete, and extensive. Another variable employed in the same spirit addresses the fact that our data pertain to plants whereas the hypotheses apply to firms as decision units. The slippage results from multiplant operations, typically extensive only among the leading firms. We employed the variable *MP*, the proportion of sales by the industry emanating from enterprises that operate more than one plant within the industry.[11] *MP* can be employed either as an additive regressor or as a check for heteroskedasticity in the residuals from the regression.

The last exogeneous variable embodies the hypothesis that the concentration of exporting activities in the largest units depends on the industry's overall comparative-advantage position. This hypothesis is congenial to the model set forth above based on scale economies. It rests on the proposition that in an industry with a strong comparative advantage, units that can obtain scale economies that place their marginal costs below the marginal revenues from export sales may find large expansions of exports (and production) profitable. Symmetrically, with imports low (especially due to tariff protection), a large proportion of an industry's smaller units may serve solely the domestic market. A useful variable to indicate an industry's competitive advantage position is:

NEXP = difference between industry exports and imports divided by sum of exports and imports.

Normalizing the variable by total trade abstracts from differences in the cost of transporting the product. We expect a positive coefficient for *NEXP*.

Statistical results

Table 2 shows the results of estimating this model, with *DIF1* serving as dependent variable in the first pair of equations, *DIF2* in the second pair. Although the explanatory power of both is low, the model fits better for *DIF2* than for *DIF1*. This is partly because of the larger error component in *WXS77*, we expect, but also because *NEXP* (which has a strong influence on *DIF2*) contains *WXS726* in its definition.

Of the exogenous variables, *MES2CD* (which proves slightly more significant than its alternate, *MES1CD*) takes the expected positive coefficient and is statistically significant. It is substantially more significant for both variables if *FAC2* is omitted; they are subject to some multicollinearity. Of the measures of product differentiation, *FAC1* has no influence (as expected), but both *FAC2* and *FAC3* take significant positive coefficients. That is, for U.S. manufacturing industries, both complex and innovative products and those subject to thin densities of demand find their exports concentrated in the industry's larger plants. This finding differs from Auquier's (1980) for France and can be rationalized with respect to the structural bases for differentiation if small-scale production is undifferentiated or provides varieties with excellent home-market substitutes, while large-scale units serve differentiated international markets.

Foreign investment activity (*FAS*) promotes the concentration of exports in the larger establishments, as expected on the assumption that the relation among companies between exporting and foreign investment is on balance complementary. The extent of multiplant operation (*MP*) is insignificant and erratic as to sign. It and *FAC1* are accordingly omitted from the second and fourth equations in the table as inappropriate to the model.

Table 2. Determinants of concentration of exports in industries' larger plants (*DIF*).

Independent variable	Dependent variable			
	DIF1	DIF1	DIF2	DIF2
Constant	2.849 (3.34)	2.788 (3.50)	0.404 (0.63)	0.751 (1.24)
MES2CD	30.188^{b} (1.94)	30.563^{b} (1.98)	20.554^{b} (1.75)	19.294^{c} (1.65)
FAC1	0.068 (0.15)	–	0.111 (0.32)	–
FAC2	1.946^{aa} (3.75)	1.938^{aa} (3.81)	1.580^{aa} (4.03)	1.515^{aa} (3.92)
FAC3	0.873^{bb} (2.01)	0.893^{bb} (2.14)	1.058^{aa} (3.23)	0.921^{aa} (2.91)
FAS	8.017^{c} (1.56)	7.961^{c} (1.59)	9.014^{b} (2.32)	10.628^{a} (2.71)
MP	−0.540 (0.14)	–	4.615 (1.62)	–
C4DH	−3.324 (1.64)	−3.379^{cc} (1.69)	−2.760^{cc} (1.81)	−2.385 (1.58)
C4DM	−0.223 (0.22)	−0.248 (0.26)	(0.480) (0.64)	0.745 (1.01)
NEXP	0.941^{c} (1.47)	0.925^{c} (1.46)	1.855^{a} (3.82)	1.854^{a} (3.85)
$\bar{R}^2$	0.090	0.096	0.183	0.181
F	4.35^{a}	5.62^{a}	8.57^{a}	10.62^{a}

Note: Levels of statistical significance: where one-tail tests are appropriate, a = 1%, b = 5%, c = 10%; where two-tail tests are appropriate, aa = 1%, bb = 5%, cc = 10%.

Diverse and somewhat conflicting hypotheses link *DIF* to competitive conditions in the industry, and so we attempted several specifications of *C4* that might be appropriate. A linear form proved quite insignificant, but somewhat interesting results did emerge from dividing industries into groups that could be characterized as highly concentrated, loose-knit oligopolies, and unconcentrated, my means of:

$C4DH = 1$ when $C4 \geqslant 70$ percent, 0 otherwise;

$C4DM = 1$ when 40 percent $\leqslant C4 < 70$ percent, 0 otherwise.[12]

With a two-tail test applied, *C4DH* takes a negative coefficient that is significant around the 10 percent level. Parallel exporting behavior in highly concentrated markets is a hypothesis consistent with these coefficients.

Finally, the industry's comparative-advantage position as measured by *NEXP* wields the expected positive influence on the concentration of exports in the larger plants.

We mentioned one concern with the dependent variable used in Table 2 – that the difference between shipments-weighted and unweighted export intensities is significantly correlated with an industry's export-intensity overall. Because several regressors in Table 2 should also influence an industry's overall participation in international markets, we were concerned to determine whether any rejections of null hypotheses in Table 2 could be due to collinearity with industrywide exports/shipments. We therefore expressed *DIF1* and *DIF2* as proportional variables, dividing each by the average of *XS* and *WXS77* (or *WXS726*). This change did knock out the significance of two regressors – *FAC2* and *MES2CD*. Because both are indeed theoretically substantial influences on industrywide exports/shipments, we have to leave unsettled the question of whether they influence the concentration of exports in large plants directly or indirectly through their effect on in the industry's comparative-advantage position. At the same time *FAC1*, which indicates simple goods differentiated through media advertising, becomes a significant positive influence on the transformed dependent variable. This result itself is plausible enough, because scale economies in sales promotion (including fixed costs of establishing a brand in overseas markets) could well be expected to have a strong positive influence on concentration of exports in large plants, even though they are negatively related to an industry's overall participation in exporting.

Overall, although the model's explanatory power is low, and some tests are compromised by problems with the data, the results generally tell a fairly rich story that is consistent with the preceding hypotheses.

IV. DETERMINANTS OF DISPERSION OF EXPORTING ACTIVITIES

The other dependent variable, *CV*, is a coefficient of variation that measures the dispersion of plants' exporting activities. It is an unconditional measure of dispersion, while *DIF* is a measure conditional on differences in plant size. If each plant in an industry exports the same proportion of its output (and no measurement errors intrude), both *DIF* and *CV* will equal zero. Accordingly, we expect some overlap in the variables that determine them. However, if plants' exports/shipments ratios do in fact vary, *CV* can be high while *DIF* is zero or even negative. In our sample *DIF1* and *DIF2* are both negatively correlated with *CV*, so there must be ample variance in plants' exports/shipments ratios that is not associated with their sizes.

Hypotheses about determinants of CV

We start with two hypotheses that apply to *CV* but not *DIF*. The first, outlined in Section I, concerns the effect of localized markets, which may restrict international trade to transborder flows within local market areas on the nation's frontiers. *CV* should increase with market localization, which we measure *inversely*:

DIST = distance from U.S. plant locations within which 80 percent of outbound shipments move.

A low value indicates predominantly short-distance shipments within local market areas, and so the coefficient of *DIST* should be negative.

The other hypothesis is that exporting activity varies because levels of technical efficiency differ among plants in an industry. As output of another project, we have available one of several possible measures of technical inefficiency generated from the estimation of stochastic frontier production functions (Forsund, Lovell, and Schmidt, 1980). In brief, this methodology partitions the variance in the residuals around an ordinary fitted production function into two components. One is the conventional random noise, assumed as usual to be normally distributed. The other is a one-sided distribution (the half-normal was used, in this case) that can be though of as indicating the dispersion of plants' efficiency levels below the best-practice frontier. The resulting estimate of an industry's average technical efficiency can be expressed in various ways. The one available at this stage in the project is the ratio of the variance of the residuals due to technical inefficiency to those due to random noise.[13] Notice that inefficiency is inferred from the variance of productivity among actual production units: all members of an industry could be inefficient, yet leave no trace on this measure. That property is congenial to testing the hypothesis that the dispersion of an industry's plant exports/shipments ratios increases with the dispersion of its plants' levels of technical efficiency.

This measure of technical inefficiency cannot, however, be used directly in our analysis without some thought to its own determinants. That is because it reflects not only 'outright' inefficiency but also the effect of product differentiation, spatial fragmentation, scale economies, and other factors that may cause variations in plants' productivity levels that suffer no normative taint. Of more immediate concern, those factors have already entered into our model as determinants of exporting patterns. Pending a fuller simultaneous analysis of these variables, we took the short-run procedure of regressing our technical-inefficiency measure on *C4*, *FAC1*, and *MES1CD* and taking residuals. These residuals, denoted *INEFR*, then are entered as an independent variable to test the hypothesis that *CV* increases with the extent of apparent technical inefficiency *not* explained by these factors. As a check, we also include the variable in its original form (*INEF*).

We can now turn to other hypotheses that utilize variables already defined as determinants of *DIF*. We expected (and found) scale economies in production to favor large plants as originators of exports. It is not clear that they should increase the coefficient of variation, however, because of the drop-off in sampling frequencies in our data set for plants with fewer than 250 employees. Roughly speaking, *CV* is measured over most plants larger than the statistically estimated MES plus a varying but small proportion of those smaller than MES. Therefore, while the variability of exports/shipments ratios over an industry's whole population of plants should increase with scale economies, it may decline with our statistical measure of scale economies for the sample actually covered. We impose no prior on the sign of *MES1CD* or *MES2CD*.

The three factors indicating product differentiation are also included in the model. As with *DIF*, signs cannot confidently be predicted for each factor without imposing restrictive assumptions about the character of product differentiation. However, *FAC2* and *FAC3* do indicate differentiation based on specialized attribute combinations, and (with scale economies controlled) these should reduce the variance of producers' exports/shipments ratios. Therefore, we do predict negative signs for *FAC2* and *FAC3*, although no expectation is offered for *FAC1*.

Descriptive evidence summarized in Section I suggested that *CV* may decline with the industry's overall participation in exporting. The theoretical basis for this, given the variables already specified, is not entirely clear, but the following is plausible. In an industry lacking a comparative advantage, most producers will not export; however, a few – probably offering specialized or dissimilar goods – may have substantial exports. If the industry's comparative advantage is substantial, however, many producers find it profitable to make some export sales, and *CV* is reduced. What remains troubling about this otherwise reasonable suggestion is that variables such as *MES1CD*, *DIST*, and the measures of product differentiation should already control for these things. Nonetheless, we employ the industry's proportional net exports, *NEXP*, as an indicator of comparative advantage, expecting a negative coefficient. Because what may matter is not net comparative advantage but simply gross participation in export markets, we use the alternative:

EXP = average share of the industry's output exported, 1972–76.

Finally, we tested the influence of concentration (*C4*). The hypothesis that loose-knit collusion may tend to homogenize exporting behavior calls for the dummy variables *C4DM* and *C4DH*, defined above. The hypothesis of loose-knit interdependence implies a negative coefficient for *C4DM*, possibly also for *C4DH*.

Statistical results

Table 3 present three versions of out model of the determinants of *CV*, all showing quite reasonable explanatory power in light of the large number of observations (191, after losses of some industries due to missing exogenous variables). The significant negative coefficient of *DIST* supports the hypothesis based on border trade. *MES1CD* takes a negative coefficient (highly significant when concentration is not included) indicating that (at least among the larger plants) scale economies tend to homogenize exporting activities. Put another way (Glejser, Jacquemin, and Petit, 1980), for some industries exporting may play a significant role in achieving economies of scale. *FAC2* takes a highly significant negative coefficient, indicating that in an industry offering complex and innovative differentiated goods the bulk of the producers get drawn into exporting status. That finding has implications for *FAC2*'s uncertain influence on *DIF*, strengthening our suspicion that its effect operates via industrywide exports/shipments. *FAC1* and *FAC3* are always entirely insignificant, and their omission has no effect on the other results (equations 1, 3).

The results for technical inefficiency turn out contrary to expectation. When the variable is purged of its obvious structural influences (*INEFR*, equations 2 and 3), it takes an insignificant negative coefficient instead of the positive one expected. When entered in its original form (*INEF*, equation 1) it takes a wrong-signed coefficient that approaches significance. Our best explanation is that the causation may run in the opposite direction from the one we expected, with some producers enjoying otherwise unexplained bases for profitable export sales that increase the variance of plant's productivity levels in their industry. Because *INEF* is not the ideal measure of technical inefficiency, we do not pursue the matter further at this time. Dropping the variable from the model affects the results only by increasing the significance level of *NEXP* to 1 percent and lowering that of *MES1CD* to 10 percent.

Table 3. Determinants of coefficient of variation of plants' exports/shipments ratios (*CV*).

Equation no.	Exogenous variables							R^{-2}
	DIST	MES1CD	FAC1	FAC2	FAC3	Constant	Other	
1.	−0.595[a] (3.18)	−2.564 (1.37)	–	−0.327[aa] (2.97)	–	3.643[aa] (18.62)	−0.330 INEFR (1.15) − 0.0.48[a] EXP (4.41)	
							0.515[a] C4DM (2.67) − 0.995[a] C4DH (2.31)	0.306
2.	−0.526[a] (2.78)	−4.842[aa] (2.78)	–	−0.359[aa] (3.22)	–	3.421[aa] (18.47)	−0.380 INEFR (1.31) − 0.0.49[a] EXP (4.41)	0.276
3.	−0.608[a] (3.04)	−5.476[aa] (3.01)	−0.011 (0.10)	−0.512[aa] (4.63)	−0.023 (0.24)	3.741[aa] (11.67)	−0.581[bb] INEF (1.93) − 0.322[b] NEXP (1.95)	0.213

Note: See note to Table 2.

With these factors controlled, *CV* does decrease significantly with the industry's export orientation, and this influence is substantially more significant when measured by the overall share of output exported (*EXP*) rather than by net comparative advantage (*NEXP*).

Finally, the data do offer support for the hypothesis that competitive conditions influence exporting patterns. Equation 3 indicates increasingly negative coefficients for moderately and highly concentrated industries (*C4* entered as a linear variable gives a similar result). One is always concerned that concentration is merely proxying its own many influences, but controls in the model for scale economies and product differentiation make that seem unlikely. The stronger influence in the most concentrated industries runs somewhat counter to the maintained hypothesis; it is not implausible, but the exact behavioral basis for this influence remains in doubt.

V. CONCLUSIONS

This paper has explored a new set of data on the distribution of exports-shipments ratio among plants for U.S. manufacturing industries. The same general patterns found in several other countries seem to hold for the United States, and the factors previously identified as wielding theoretical influences operate in American markets. We confirm, for example, influences of scale economies, local markets, and foreign investment that have appeared in studies based on other countries. However, some aspects of the U.S. patterns seem novel. Using what we hope are sophisticated measures of product differentiation, we find a pattern suggesting that structural differentiation (complex and innovative goods) homogenizes units' participation in overseas markets (when plant size is not controlled) and concentrates exporting in the larger units.

These findings have implications for the analysis of industrial competition. Producer concentration does seem to have a homogenizing influence on exporting activity that may reflect parallel behavior among close oligopolistic rivals. This is consistent with the evidence on the general prevalence of dumping. Also, it underlines the importance of recent findings (Yamawaki, 1984) that the competitiveness of an exporting industry depends not only on its market structure but also on its rivalry with foreign producers in their home markets. As on previous occasions, incorporating international influences into industrial organization does not simplify the analysis (by demoting national producers to an anonymous subsegment of a world industry) but rather enriches it by identifying many complex influences on competitive conditions of both export opportunities and import competition.

ACKNOWLEDGEMENT

I am grateful to David R. Barton for assistance in securing data, to Michael Hemesath for assistance with the computations, and to the General Electric foundation for research support.

NOTES

1. So that not all Belgians want the same variety, and some non-Belgian buyers do prefer Beglian-made varieties.
2. Strictly speaking, firms that can expect to spread the fixed cost over a large volume of exports. Notice the ambiguity (emphasized by Glejser, Jacquemin, and Petit, 1980) of characterizing firm size by output *including* exports.
3. A good deal of casual evidence and some systematic data (e.g., Gribbin, 1971) affirm the widespread occurrence of dumping. Auquier (1980) argued that, with or without dumping, exports/shipments ratios are likely to vary among competing sellers in ways that affect their differential incentives not to 'spoil' the domestic market.
4. The model behind this result assumes that cost and demand conditions do not closely determine rival producers' optimizing choices of nonprice market variables. An incomplete oligopolistic agreement limits price competition with some effectiveness but is less complete for averting nonprice rivalry. Nonprice competitive variables hence are both inflated and homogenized. The inflation represents the incompleteness of the consensus, the homogenization the joint appreciation that highly deviant strategies may destabilize it.
5. This investigation, supported by the U.S. Department of Commerce, involves the calculation of stochastic frontier production functions and the measurement and explanation of technical inefficiency levels for about 340 manufacturing industries in 1977.
6. The data set covered only 344 of the 451 four-digit manufacturing industries defined in the Standard Industrial Classification for reasons associated with the larger project. Chief among these is the presence of only a small number of plants in the Annual Survey panel. Thus, the sample is biased against highly concentrated industries served only by a few plants. Considering the size of most markets for manufactures in the United States, the effect of this bias is not so much to cut out highly concentrated industries as to delete very small ones.
7. It is thought that export values are recorded subject to considerable error. For dutiable imports, the importer and the customs inspector have conflicting interests in the stated value, such that their mutual surveillance may result in something reasonably accurate. No party has an interest in the accurate valuation of exports. Furthermore, significant time may elapse between when goods are recorded as shipped from the plant and when they are exported, so that timing discrepancies in the annual figures may be substantial for some industries. Our unweighted means

and standard deviations, in contrast, are reported at the plant level and are not subject to this discrepancy (whatever other limitations may affect their accuracy).

8. The correlations quoted in this paragraph are for the sample of 269 industries with nonzero mean exports; where applicable, correlations calculated for the larger sample are almost identical.
9. See Caves (1982, pp. 141–7) and references cited therein.
10. For evidence on the correlation between firm size and multinational status see Horst (1972). The data for *FAS* are taken the Enterprise Statistics of the 1972 Census of Manufactures; no equally comprehensive data on industries' foreign investment is available for a later year.
11. *MP*, like *FAS*, was taken from the 1972 Enterprise Statistics. Industries in the classification of the Enterprise Statistics are somewhat more aggregated than at the four-digit level of the Standard Industrial Classification, a source of error.
12. We did not 'fish' for these class boundaries. Rather, they judgmentally reflect the results of a number of statistical studies that have tested and confirmed hypotheses about behavior patterns associated with loose-knit oligopoly in U.S. manufacturing.
13. This variable is denoted lambda in the notation that has become customary in the literature on technical inefficiency.

REFERENCES

Auquier, Antoine A., 'Sizes of Firms, Exporting Behavior, and the Structure of French Industry', *Journal of Industrial Economics*, 29 (December 1980), pp. 203–218.

Caves, Richard E., *Multinational Enterprise and Economic Analysis*, Cambridge: Cambridge University Press (1982).

Caves, Richard E. and Williamson, Peter J., 'What Is Product Differentiation, *Really*?', *Journal of Industrial Economics*, 34 (December 1985).

Clarke, R. and Davies, S. W., 'Market Structure and Price-Cost Margins', *Economica*, 49 (August 1982), pp. 277–288.

Forsund, Finn R., Knox Lovell, C. A., and Schmidt, Peter, 'A Survey of Frontier Production Functions and of Their Relationship to Efficiency Measurement', *Journal of Econometrics*, 13 (May 1980), pp. 5–25.

Glejser, Herbert, Jacquemin, Alexis, and Petit, Jean, 'Exports in an Imperfect Competition Framework: An Analysis of 1,446 Exporters', *Quarterly Journal of Economics*, 94 (May 1980), pp. 507–524.

Gribbin, J. Denys, *The Profitability of UK Exports*, HM Treasury, Government Economic Service Occasional Papers, No. 1, London: Her Majesty's Stationary Office (1971).

Horst, Thomas, 'Firm and Industry Determinants of the Decision to Invest Abroad: An Empirical Study', *Review of Economics and Statistics*, 54 (August 1972), pp. 258–266.

Knickerbocker, Frederick T., *Oligopolistic Reaction and Multinational Enterprise*, Boston: Division of Research, Harvard Business School (1973).

Lancaster, Kelvin, 'Intra-industry Trade under Perfect Monopolistic Competition', *Journal of International Economics*, 10 (May 1980), pp. 151–176.

Loup, J., 'La Concentration dans l'Industrie Francaise d'apres le Recensement Industriel de 1963', *Etudes et Conjonctures*, 2 (1969).

Lyons, Bruce, 'A New Measure of Minimum Efficient Plant Size in UK Manufacturing Industry', *Economica*, 47 (February 1980), pp. 19–34.

Rapp, William V., 'Firm Size and Japan's Export Structure: A Microview of Japan's Changing Export Competitiveness since Meiji', *Japanese Industrialization and its Social Consequences*, ed. Hugh Patrick, Berkeley: University of California Press (1976), pp. 201–248.

Stankovsky, Jan., 'Erweiterte Exportkennzahlen der osterreichischen Wirtschaft', *Monatsberichte des osterreichischen Instituts fur Wirtschaftsforschung*, No. 4 (1982), pp. 245–258.

U.S. Bureau of the Census. *Commodity Exports and Imports as Related to Production, 1977*, Washington: Government Printing Office (1981).

Yamawaki, Hideki, 'Exporting, Foreign Market Structure, and Profitability: Some Evidence from Japanese and U.S. Manufacturing Industries', Discussion Paper No. IIM/IP 84-33, International Institute of Management, Berlin (1984).

Mainstreams in Industrial Organization

Book II. Policies: Antitrust, Deregulation and Industrial

edited
by

H.W. de Jong

University of Amsterdam, The Netherlands

W.G. Shepherd

University of Michigan at Ann Arbor, U.S.A.

SPRINGER-SCIENCE+BUSINESS MEDIA, B.V.
1986

Library of Congress Cataloging in Publication Data

Mainstreams in industrial organization.

(Studies in industrial organization ; 6)

1. Industrial organization--Congresses.
2. Managerial economics--Congresses. 3. Trade regulation--Congresses. 4. Industry and state--Congresses. I. Jong, H. W. de. II. Shepherd, William G. III. Series.
HD29.M25 1986 338.6 86-12345

ISBN 978-94-017-0495-3 ISBN 978-94-017-0493-9 (eBook)
DOI 10.1007/978-94-017-0493-9

PREFACE

The present two volumes contain the essays and part of the discussions as presented at the conference on Mainstreams in Industrial Organization, held at the University of Amsterdam, 21–23 August 1985. The thema was chosen because the field of studies commonly designated "industrial organization" in the Anglo-Saxon countries, or "market theory" in Continental Europe, has experienced important alterations during the past decade.

Partly this reflects changing theoretical views inside the field, in which shifts in the core concepts have occurred and different emphasis is laid on time-honoured views and results. Partly, critical views have been voiced from outside the field. As in all open scientific debate, they have to be weighed and, if necessary, taken into account. Partly also, divergent developments in thinking between the Anglo-Saxon, European and Japanese areas need to be considered, because both the problems and the ways of approaching them still differ.

The variety of views, theories and results is testimony to the vitality of this field of economics; variety is generated by the creative endeavours, from which the chaff is being beaten out by critical discussions. That is especially true for the concept of competition itself, which industrial organization economists are debating intensively.

But it should not be thought that the participants lack a common understanding. As this conference brought forward again, the economists assembled here share the view that the study of the market economy needs a measure of realism in order to be worthwhile. Realism involves taking note of market situations as well as market processes, of recognizing entrepreneurial actions as well as power games, of modelling behaviour as well as investigating empirical evidence, of looking for shifts in explanations of what occurs as well as for policies that need to be widened or trimmed. Negatively, such realism rejects "l'art pour l'art" theorizing as well as pure empiricism or description.

Such a program is strewn with difficulties, as a reading of the two volumes brings out. No useful purpose is served by denying that industrial organization means to study very complex phenomena. It should nevertheless encourage industrial organization economists to persevere in their efforts, for amidst useless shells many valuable pearls can be found.

The editors are grateful, both to the organizing institutions – the University of Amsterdam and the Universities of Michigan and Massachusetts – for their support and to the economists who presented papers and who took part in the lively discussions. They also invite readers from a wider audience to join in the experience, which shows that industrial organization economists do not represent a single orthodoxy or "school". For a school of thinking has some resemblance to a cartel: it easily degenerates into predictable behaviour and the blocking of new initiatives.

The pairing of views on five different themes, contained in these volumes, should therefore be a challenge to readers to contribute themselves the innovations required in this fascinating field in the coming decades. If that occurs the highest hopes of the conference's organizers will be fulfilled.

W. G. SHEPHERD
University of Michigan

H. W. DE JONG
University of Amsterdam

CONTENTS

BOOK II. Policies: Antitrust, Deregulation and Industrial

Part III. Antitrust Policy

Part IV. Deregulation

Part V. Industrial Policy

LIST OF CONTRIBUTORS

Walter Adams, Associate Professor of Economics and Law, The University of Michigan, Ann Arbor, Michigan, U.S.A.

Kenneth D. Boyer, Professor of Economics, Michigan State University, East Lansing, U.S.A.

Richard E. Caves, Professor of Economics, Harvard University, Cambridge (Mass), U.S.A.

Gunnar Eliasson, President, The Industrial Institute for Economic and Social Research (IKI), Stockholm, Sweden.

Eleanor M. Fox, Professor of Law, New York University, New York, U.S.A.

Chris Green, Professor of Economics, McGill University, Ottawa, Canada.

Ann M. Hendriks, Assistant Professor of Economics, Tufts University.

Dennis C. Gribbin, Economist, The Monopolies Commission, London, U.K.

Henk W. de Jong, Professor of Economics, University of Amsterdam, The Netherlands.

Eberhard Kantzenbach, Professor of Economics, University of Hamburg, President of Monopol Kommission, West Germany.

William Kingston, John Good Senior Lecturer (Innovation), Trinity College, Dublin, Ireland.

Remo Linda, Economist, Commission of the European Communities, Brussels, Belgium.

Stephen Martin, Assistant Professor of Economics, Michigan, Maryland, U.S.A.

Dennis C. Mueller, Professor of Economics, University of Maryland, Maryland, U.S.A.

Takao Nakao, Professor of Economic, Doshisha University, Kyoto, Japan.

H. Odagiri, Professor of Economics, University of Trukuba, Sakura, Japan.
Jacques Pelkmans, Professor of Economics, European Institute of Public Administration, Maastricht, The Netherlands.
Frederic M. Scherer, Joseph Wharton Professor of Political Economics, Swarthmore College, U.S.A.
William G. Shepherd, Professor of Economics, University of Michigan, Ann Arbor, U.S.A.
Mike A. Utton, Professor of Economics, University of Reading, U.K.

BOOK II

POLICIES: ANTITRUST, DEREGULATION AND INDUSTRIAL

PART III. ANTITRUST POLICY

9. UNITED STATES' ANTITRUST: AT THE CROSSROADS

Dennis C. Mueller

The enforcement and interpretation of the United States' antitrust laws have gone through several phases of stringent and lax enforcement over the nearly 100 years since the Sherman Act's passage. It is tempting to interpret the recent permissive posture of the courts and the antitrust enforcement agencies as yet another phase that will pass with a new restructuring of the Supreme Court and the lower courts, and a new antitrust philosophy at the Justice Department and the Federal Trade Commission. Such an intepretation would be misleading, however, in two respects. First, it would fail to recognize the important and I think permanent shift in judicial opinion as to the proper role of economic analysis in antitrust proceedings. Second, it would ignore the shift in thinking within the economics' profession regarding the weight of evidence in support of the various provisions of the antitrust laws.

A more accurate characterization of recent U.S. antitrust experience is to say that it has started down a new path, which, if followed much further, is certain to produce a radical revision of antitrust enforcement, a *de facto* repeal of several sections of the antitrust laws.

In this context, the title of this paper is a bit of a misnomer. We passed over the crossroads in the United States at least as early as January, 1981, and had pointed ourselves toward the new path well before that. But we are not so far down the new road that we cannot pause and take stock of where we are and where we are going, and if we choose, retrace our steps, or set out in a new direction. In this paper, I sketch in broad outline some of the changes in antitrust enforcement that have taken place in the United States (Section I), and then examine the economic evidence in support of these changes (Section II). I then offer my own interpretation of recent empirical results in economics (Section III), and some suggestions for how the antitrust laws might be strengthened in the light of these results.

de Jong, H. W., Shepherd, W. G. (eds) Mainstreams in Industrial Organization
 ISBN 978-94-017-0495-3

I. ECONOMICS IN ANTITRUST PROCEEDINGS

The explicit objectives of the antitrust laws, to prevent attempts to monopolize and conspiracies to monopolize, can be easily defended using standard economic welfare analysis. Preserving competition provides society with the added consumers' surplus of the welfare triangle, which is lost when the monopoly price is charged. But, while the antitrust laws can be rationalized using economic welfare analysis, their purpose has not, until very recently, been defined solely in terms of economic welfare criteria. Thus, Judge Learned Hand could write in 1945 in *United States v. Aluminium Company of America*

> True, it might have been thought adequate to condemn only those monopolies which could not show that they had exercised the highest possible ingenuity, had adopted every possible economy, had anticipated every conceivable improvement, stimulated every possible demand. No doubt, that would be one way of dealing with the matter, although it would imply constant scrutiny and constant supervision, such as courts are unable to provide. Be that as it may, that was not the way that Congress chose; it did not condone 'good trusts' and condem 'bad' ones; it forbade all. Moreover, in so doing it was not neccessarily actuated by economic motives alone. It is possible, because of its indirect social or moral effect, to prefer a system of small producers, each dependent for his success upon his own skill and character, to one in which the great mass of those engaged must accept the direction of a few. These considerations, which we have suggested only as possible purposes of the Act, we think the decisions prove to have been in fact its purposes.

Chief Justice Warren expressed a similar sentiment for a united Court in the *Brown Shoe* decision in 1962,

> '. . . we cannot fail to recognize Congress' desire to promote competition through the protection of viable, small, locally owned businesses. Congress appreciated that occasional higher costs and prices might result from the maintenance of fragmented industries and markets. It resolved these competing considerations in favor of decentralization. We must give effect to that decision'. Again in 1966 in *Von's Grocery*, Justice Hugo Black would write, for the majority of a now divided court, 'To arrest this 'rising tide' toward concentration into too few hands and to halt the gradual demise of the small businessman, Congress decided to clamp down with vigor on mergers . . .'

But in the seventies and eighties, first the courts and later the antitrust authorities themselves backed away from this extra-economic interpretation of the antitrust laws' objectives to a more narrow, economic interpretation. This shift was forsaged in the dissenting opinions of Justices Stewart and Harlan in the sixties. Stewart's dissent in *Von's Grocery* (with which Harlan joined) characterized Black's opinion as 'little more than a requiem for the so-called Mom and Pop grocery stores', and goes on to demand that the Court confine its analysis to the probable effect of the merger on competition in the relevant market. The dissenting opinions of Stewart and Harlan in the sixties were to become the majority opinions of the court in the seventies. Moreover, the antitrust authorities have themselves decided not to attempt to hold back the 'rising tide' of economic concentration, even within well-defined markets.[1] Under the Justice Department's 1982 and 1984 Merger Guidelines, neither the *Brown Shoe* nor *Von's Grocery* cases would have even been initiated.

In addition to the increased weight given to economic evidence in recent years, there has been a shift of emphasis away from concern over the possible anticompetitive effects of business actions to their possible pro-efficiency effects. This shift is perhaps most apparent in Section 2 monopoly cases, and in the courts' interpretations of what constitutes predatory behavior. In 1945, Judge Hand feld justified in condemning *ALCOA*'s actions in preserving its monopoly position because 'Alcoa effectively anticipated and forestalled all competition' by such practices as anticipating increases in the demand for ingot and supplying them. In 1953, United Shoe lost a famous monopoly case despite having compiled an impressive research and development record, and despite 'United's power not rest[ing] on predatory practices'. So stringent had been the enforcement of Section 2 of the Sherman Act that the statement by that perceptive foreign student of U.S. antitrust Alfred Neale regarding the law with respect to 'bottleneck' cases might have been applied to all Section 2 Sherman Act cases as recently as 1966 (U.S. v. Grinnell). Neale stated 'that if you have dominant power in the market, no matter how innocently and inescapably you come by it, you are obliged under antitrust to take the greatest care not to "throw it about"' (1980, p. 132). The IBM and Berkey Photo-Kodak cases in the 1970s make clear that this statement does not apply to Section 2 cases today. Few objective observers would argue that IBM and Kodak had not 'thrown their market power about' in their struggle to retain their market positions, whatever their views as to the ultimate merits of the charges brought about these two, progressive giants.

The recent IBM and Kodak cases are also illuminating with respect to the criteria used to judge predatory behavior. Ever since the 1911 *Standard Oil* and *American Tobacco* decisions, the establishment of predatory intent on the part of a dominant firm has been sufficient to ensure conviction under Section 2. Even the hint of predatory behavior has often proved damaging in other types of cases. Thus, in *Utah Pie v. Continental Baking* in 1967 the Court gave heavy weight to the possibility that *Pet's* charging of lower prices in the Salt Lake City area than in other areas was possible predatorially motivated. The Court specifically noted that Continental's price was less than 'its direct cost *plus an allocation for overhead*' (emphasis added). In finding against the defendants, the Court obviously was concerned with the possibility that the large, geographically diversified companies (*Continental, Carnation*, and *Pet*) had the power to undercut *Utah Pie's* prices in the Salt Lake City area, and drive the regionally based firm out of existence, despite Utah Pie's dominant position in its market, and despite its having been the initiator of many of the price cuts.

The term 'predatory behavior' conjures up an image of an intertemporal sequence of acts. A point in time must exist in which the predator and its target both exist. If the predator is successful, some subsequent point in time must occur at which the target no longer exists. For the action to be rational, the predator must have the power and intent to raise its price in this subsequent post-predation period. The economic welfare losses from predation occur from these post-predation higher prices.

It is difficult to see why one would condemn prices that eliminate rivals or how one would differentiate them from normal competitive behavior, if some sort of sequence like the above were not anticipated. Yet the salient feature of Areeda and Turner's (1975) proposed criterion for judging predatory pricing is that it rules out consideration of the alleged predator's conduct before or after the time period in which the alleged predatory behavior takes place. The only issue to consider is whether price during the period in question is less than *short run* marginal costs, or, if these are unmeasurable, *short run* average costs. Any consideration of the prices the predator will charge in the future, once the target of its action is gone, is ruled out on the grounds that these 'long run possibilities must be disregarded because they are intrinsically speculative and indeterminate' (Areeda and Turner, 1976, p. 897). But, if today's price is less than *long run* average cost, as is allowed under the Areeda–Turner rule, tomorrow's price *must be* higher than todays'. No speculation is required to reach this conclusion. A price less than long run average costs is unsustainable. It is for this reason, presumably, that the courts typically compared price to long run average cost estimates (e.g., direct costs plus overhead as in *Utah Pies* cited above), or at least did so prior to 1975.

Areeda and Turner's paper on predatory pricing was published in that year and had an almost immediate impact on judicial thinking re-predatory behavior. It played a key role in several of the private antitrust suits against IBM (e.g., *Cal Comp*, 1979). Seldom has academic research moved so quickly from journal page into judicial decision, and seldom has an economic doctrine's effect upon the outcome of a case been so consistent. Since Areeda and Turner's rule on predatory pricing was first proposed, defendants in predation cases have been successful 90 percent of the time (Hurwitz *et al.*, 1981, pp. 143–53). The quick and unequivocal acceptance of Areeda–Turner is indicative of the recent trends in U.S. antitrust for the criterion is purely economic (Is the price of alleged predator below its short run marginal cost?) and places short run economic efficiency gains above all other objectives. The major advantage of Areeda and Turner's proposal over all others is that it allows the dominant firm maximum discretion in choosing prices at all points in time. So long as the criterion is met, i.e., price exceeds marginal cost, no short run gains to consumers from dominant firm-small firm rivalry are lost. That consumers might be worse off over the long run, because of the demise of the smaller firms, or because they choose never to enter knowing that they must cover long run costs while the dominant, incumbent can legally price so as to cover only short run costs, is regarded as of less consequence than the danger in other rules of inhibiting competition in the short run.[2]

Yet another area in which the shift to greater emphasis on economic efficiency is apparent is U.S. antimerger policy. The economic approach to evaluating a merger is conceptually simple. If a merger increases efficiency and does not increase monopoly power, it obviously should be allowed. If it increases both efficiency and market power, it should be allowed if the social gains from the increase in efficiency outweigh the monopoly welfare loss, as Williamson's (1968) classic article argued almost twenty years ago.

The law on mergers is also simple. It makes no provision for a monopoly loss-efficiency gain trade-off. It prohibits all acquisitions 'where . . . the effect of such acquisition may be substantially to lessen competition, or to tend to create a monopoly', regardless of the magnitude of any efficiency change the acquisition might cause. And the courts have consistently refused to consider efficiency increases as an offset to a potential lessening of competition. In *Brown Shoe* the Court noted that 'occasional higher costs and prices might result' from preserving competitive market structures. In *Procter & Gamble* (1967), Douglas went even further, arguing that the savings in advertising costs the merger with Clorox would produce would have the anticompetitive consequence of raising entry barriers. His statement on the place of evidence on efficiencies in a merger case was unequivocal. 'Possible economies cannot be used as a defense to illegality. Congress was aware that some mergers which lessen competition may also result in economies but it struck the balance in favor of protecting competition . . .'.

If Congress disagreed with the Court's interpretation of Section 7 in *Brown Shoe* and *Proctor & Gamble*, it has had ample opportunity in the intervening years to revise the law and introduce a Williamson-like efficiency defence. Its failure to do so can only be interpreted as tacit acceptance of the interpretation of the law offered by Black and Douglas.

In June of 1982, the Justice Department chose to enact as administrative policy what Congress has refused to enact as law. The 1982 Justice Department guidelines state that efficiencies can be a defense in 'extraordinary cases' that are 'otherwise close'. The 1984 revisions to the guidelines drop the qualifications of the use of efficiencies evidence. Efficiencies are listed as one of several relevant factors, presumably to be given equal weight with all others. Under the 1982–84 guidelines mergers, which might substantially lessen competition, would presumably be allowed were the Justice Department convinced by the merging firms that the promised efficiency gains would be even more substantial. Thus, mergers that are illegal under Section 7, and would be found so in court will never go to trial, if the Justice Department estimates that the mergers potentially will bring about a sufficient increase in efficiency.

As further evidence of the change in attitude toward mergers by the antitrust authorities one can cite the many mergers within the petroleum and steel industries which have taken place in recent years. In the fifties and sixties, it was commonplace to block a merger by showing that it would raise concentration substantially in some specific submarkets. Thus, in 1962 in *Brown Shoe*, evidence that a merger between the two large, national producers and distributors of shoes would increase concentration at the retail level in markets like Topeka and Dodge City helped to block the merger. Today, when a proposed merger would lead to an increase in concentration above the guidelines in some submarket, the firms are allowed to spin off some of their assets in the relevant submarket so that the merger can go ahead (e.g., Texaco's acquisition of Getty in 1984). The FTC and Justice Department's willingness to accommodate firms wishing to merge stems presumably from an underlying belief that the mergers have a largely beneficial effect on economic efficiency.

What accounts for this increasing emphasis on economic evidence of efficiency? Undoubtedly, a variety of social and political developments do. But, certainly one of the contributing factors is the change in thinking within the economics profession as to the potential dangers from monopoly power and the potential gains from increased competition.

II. THE NEW LEARNINGS RE EFFICIENCY AND MONOPOLY

The above-described change in the weight given to economic evidence of efficiency would not have resulted in such a major shift in the boundaries of antitrust enforcement had it not been accompanied by an even more dramatic shift in opinion within the economics profession regarding the relative sizes of monopoly welfare losses and efficiency gains accompanying various business practices and market structures. These developments are typified by the growing acceptance of the 'new learning' as to why concentration and profitability have usually been found to be positively correlated. But this is only one example of several parallel shifts in thinking that all lead in the same direction: a more lax enforcement of existing antitrust laws in unregulating markets; thus, the reference to new learnings in the heading to this section.

Let us begin with the original new learning hypothesis itself. Papers by Brozen (1971a, b) and Demsetz (1973, 1974) in the early seventies argued that more efficient firms grew more rapidly than their rivals, and thus that a correlation between concentration and profitability might simply be reflecting the greater efficiency of the largest firms. At its heart, this new learning reverses the causal chain between size and efficiency. The conventional view among industrial organization economists at least since Joe Bain's (1954, 1956) original contributions has been that firms within an industry all have access to a common technology and thus, effectively, pick points along a common average cost schedule. In the presence of scale economies, a firm would be more efficient (have lower average costs) if it were bigger. Thus, size caused efficiency (lower costs). Bain's findings that concentration levels generally exceeded those necessary to realize scale economies led to the abandonment of the size-causes-efficiency hypothesis, and the substitution of a size (concentration) facilitates collusion explanation.

But the new learning, in effect, reverses the causal chain. Firms may be of different degrees of efficiency, and greater efficiency can lead to more rapid growth and eventually greater size.[3] Efficiency causes size. A variety of empirical evidence has been interpreted as supporting this hypothesis (Demsetz, 1973; Carter, 1978; Peltzman, 1977), but perhaps none seems so clearly consistent as that indicating that firm market shares and profit rates are more strongly correlated than profit rates and concentration (Shepherd, 1972, 1975; Gale and Branch, 1982; Ravenscraft, 1983; Smirlock *et al.*, 1984).

The second major development in economics that has inadvertently led to a weakening of the stringency of the antitrust laws has been the rise of the 'transaction costs approach'. This line of reasoning studies the development of economic institutions as means for saving on transactions costs (see, Williamson, 1975, 1979; Klein, Crawford, and Alchian, 1978; De Alessi, 1983). An important strand of this research has emphasized the possible savings from vertical contractual linkages ranging from outright vertical integration to the kinds of vertical contractual ties (e.g., exclusive dealing and requirements contracts) that have traditionally been found illegal under Section 3 of the Clayton Act (Klein, Crawford, and Alchian, 1978; Carlton, 1979; Klein, 1980; Marvel, 1982; Monteverde and Teece, 1982; Williamson, 1983). While perceptive contributors to this literature, like Oliver Williamson (1975, Ch. 6, 1983), have recognized that vertical contractual ties can have monopolistic intent and effect, the thrust of the literature is on the transaction costs savings vertical agreements create. Thus, the impact of this literature on antitrust enforcement has been entirely one-sided: to strengthen the arguments in favor of vertical integration and vertically restrictive contracts on efficiency grounds.

Empirical support for the 'transaction costs approach' at least insofar as it impinges upon antitrust issues is far more fragmentary and equivocal than for the 'new learning' re-profits and concentration. Indeed, the approach's growing popularity in the profession rests largely on its ability to rationalize on efficiency grounds institutions, which are widely observed, and for which an explanation based on monopoly power gains is considered implausible.

Related in spirit and often employing similar logic have been explanations of the existence of tying arrangements, resale price maintenance, and delivered price systems (Klein and Saft, 1985; Telser, 1960; Marvel and McCafferty, 1984, 1985; Carlton, 1983). Together these lines of research have served to provide a long list of possible efficiency gains from practices traditionally proscribed by the courts.

The traditional posture of economists toward mergers has been to view their possible efficiency effects with considerable caution. Thus, George Stigler (1950) in his review of early merger history viewed the likely efficiency gains from these mergers to create monopolies and oligopolies with skepticism. Employing 'survivor technique' logic, he argued that these mergers could not have been motivated to achieve efficiency gains from scale economies, since many small firms survived in the same industries in which the mergers occurred. Jesse Markham (1955) listed economies as only one of many possible explanations for the early merger waves, and noted that a preponderance of these mergers did not succeed in creating a stable dominant firm, and thus, by implication, could not have created a significantly more efficient one (pp. 158–65).

Prior to 1950, the typical merger had involved significant horizontal or vertical aspects, and even during the first few years after 1950 horizontal and vertical mergers continued to be dominant as major consolidations of industry structures took place in the dairies, textiles, paper, beer and other industries. But decisions like *Brown Shoe* and *Reynolds Metal Co. v. FTC* (1960) made it clear that the courts and the antitrust authorities indended to place severe limits on the ability of companies to expand by horizontal and vertical integration. Thus, to expand by acquisition companies needed to acquire firms in industries less directly related to their own operations.

While the potential market power and cost economies from a horizontal or a vertical acquisition are easy to envisage, they are less readily apparent in diversifying merger. As these conglomerate mergers grew in number and scale during the fifties and sixties, the economics' profession was presented with the challenge of explaining these mergers. It responded by inventing a plethora of hypotheses.[4] Many of these were drawn directly from the pages of the financial press, e.g., P/E magic. The word 'synergy' was added to the economist's lexicon. While some of the explanations for the popularity of this 'new' form of merger involved potential gains from anticompetitive behavior, as in reciprocal dealing relationships, the preponderance of the new hypothesese explained mergers by some synergistic cost reduction or efficiency gain.

Coincidental to the conglomerate merger wave of the sixties, the capital asset pricing model (CAPM) was developed in the finance literature. This model explained individual investor behavior in terms of the risks and returns on diversified portfolios. Since diversification was the most conspicuous attribute of many of the mergers of the sixties, the analysis of this new form of merger with this new analytic tool seemed a natural development. During the seventies, a large number of studies appeared, which analyzed the causes and effects of mergers using the CAPM. Numerous individual studies and several surveys of this literature have reached the conclusion that the mergers of the post-World War II time period have generated additional stockholder wealth and thus must result in greater profits.[5] Since evidence that they have had significant anticompetitive effects is lacking (Goldberg, 1973; Ellert, 1976; Eckbo, 1983), the conclusion follows that these mergers must have increased economic efficiency. This interpretation of the empirical evidence on the effects of mergers is not shared by all observers (e.g., Mueller, 1977; Scherer, 1980, pp. 138–41; Steiner, 1975, Ch. 8). But it is the one the Reagan administration has accepted (Council of Economic Advisors, 1985, Ch. 6), and it guides antitrust policy in the United States today.

Thus, the new posture of the courts and the antitrust enforcement agencies is consistent with the new learnings among a substantial number of economists about the effects of high concentration, mergers, and various contractual ties among businesses. A famous statement in Justice McKenna's opinion in *United States Steel* repeated over and over again in probably every monopoly case since, was that 'the law does not make mere size an offense or the existence of unexerted power an offense'. But the new learning pushes McKenna's position a giant step forward. Not only is size not an offense, under economics' new learning it becomes a virtue. If a company enjoys a dominant market position, it must be because its products are superior, or its prices are lower. If it wishes to make a large acquisition, then it must expect an increase in profits and efficiency to follow from the merger. The courts' positions in the recent *IBM* and *Kodak* cases are consistent with the new learning view. IBM and Kodak were presumed to have achieved their dominant positions from greater efficiency and innovativeness,[6] and they were to be left free to exert their market power in any way they chose, except by doing something obviously inconsistent with the achievement of economic efficiency like setting price below marginal cost in the short run. Similarly, the Justice Department and FTC's accommodating policies towards mergers is consistent with a view that they by and large led to greater economic efficiency.

III. THE NEW EVIDENCE ON THE NEW LEARNINGS: AN ALTERNATIVE VIEW

Although the new economic learnings described above are consistent with one another in that they lay stress on the possibilities of greater economic efficiency, and downplay the importance of anticompetitive effects, it must be kept in mind that there are three separate sets of arguments involved here, and three separate empirical bases for these arguments. I take issue with two.

I do not address the transactions cost motivated arguments in favor of vertical restraints, tying agreements, resale price maintenance and the like. I refrain, not so much because I accept the arguments of those advocating a relaxation of the antitrust laws in these areas, but because both the nature of the *a priori* arguments and the empirical evidence offered in their support are such that it is more difficult to form a judgment as to the general merits of the changes in policy recommended. The theoretical basis for the arguments consists of defining a monitoring cost or agency cost or, more generally, a transactions cost that could be reduced by the practice in question. Empirically, the literature consists of examples of firms and industries, which appear to fit the hypothetical situations as defined. Acceptance of the argument rests on a judgment of whether the facts in the examples presented seem more consistent with the proposed transactions cost explanation than others, e.g., an anti-competitive explanation. While in many instances, the transactions-cost-saving explanation does appear to offer a more plausible explanation for

STUDIES IN INDUSTRIAL ORGANIZATION

Volume 6

MAINSTREAMS IN INDUSTRIAL ORGANIZATION

the existence of the practice discussed, the situation and examples selected obviously do not in any way constitute a random sample. Thus, the issue of what fraction of all tying arrangements, resale price agreements, etc., improve efficiency is left unanswered. Moreover, it is an issue which is inherently unanswerable given the nature of the hypotheses and 'data' employed in this literature to data (see, Marvel and McCafferty, 1985, pp. 378–79).

Such is not the case with regard to the other two new learnings. The hypotheses with respect to market share or concentration and efficiency, and with respect to the efficiency effects of mergers are testable using large, random samples of data and standard econometric techniques. It is these two bodies of evidence which I wish to discuss. Let us begin with the literature on profitability and market share.

Every study which I have seen has found a strong, positive relationship between market share and profitability, however the latter is measured (profits-to-sales, profits-to-assets, Tobin's *q*).[7] Moreover, when concentration is also included in the study it has either a weaker positive relationship with profitability (often statistically insignificant), or a negative relationship (often significant).

The inclusion of both market share and concentration in a profits equation can be rationalized in a model in which firms are assumed to differ with respect to both the level of their costs and the quality of their products, and the degree of cooperation in an industry is a function of the level of concentration (Mueller, 1985a, Ch. 4). In such a model, profitability is predicted to be a positive function of the product of market share and the degree of product differentiation. Estimates of this model using long-run projected profits for a sample of 551 companies yielded a highly significant positive relationship between profitability and the market share-product differentiation interaction terms, when product differentiation was measured by industry advertising- and patents-to-sales ratios. Similar results were reported by Ravenscraft (1983). Although these results regarding profitability and market share are consistent with the emphasis of the new learning on firm characteristics, they cast the new learning hypothesis in a somewhat different light than is commonly assumed. It is the combination of selling a differentiated product *and* having a high market share that generates greater profitability. Firms with large market shares in differentiated product industries are more profitable presumably because they have higher quality products or products which are perceived to be of higher quality. If one wants to describe the most profitable firms as being more efficient, they appear to be more efficient at differentiating their products through advertising or patentable product improvements.[8]

Usually when one speaks of firm *A* as being more efficient than firm *B*, one thinks of *A* having lower costs of production. If *A* is bigger than *B* one presumes that that is because *A* charges a lower price than *B* and thereby captures a larger market share. But an examination of the list of persistently most profitable firms suggests that this image of efficiency does not characterize these firms. Coca Cola, General Motors, Gerber, Gillette, Hershey, IBM, Kodak, Maytag, Polaroid, Xerox, and Wrigley are all industry leaders that have persistently been among the most profitable firms in the United States. They have maintained their profitability and their market positions not by charging lower prices than their competition, but by being able to charge higher prices, because their products are of higher quality or are perceived to be so. The most profitable companies out-compete their rivals in the nonprice modes of competition. This fact is of utmost importance in appraising the new posture of the courts and the antitrust authorities to large size. We return to this issue in the following section.

The literature on the effects of mergers is a vast and somewhat contradictory set of findings. There is no way within the appropriate confines of this paper to review this literature thoroughly. Thus, I shall simply sketch out in broad outline the nature of the evidence in support of the hypothesis that mergers have tended to increase efficiency, and the basis upon which I have reached a different conclusion. The reader wishing to delve deeper must turn to the more detailed surveys of this literature by myself and others, or plunge directly into the literature itself.

The argument that mergers increase economic efficiency runs as follows: Managers seek to maximize the wealth of their shareholders, indeed they are constrained to do so by the fear of being taken over themselves. They undertake mergers promising a synergistic interaction between their company and the acquired firm, or acquire companies whose current market value is less than its potential market value either because the market mistakenly undervalues the target firm today, or because its assets are worth less in the hands of the current management than they will be in the acquiring firm's management's hands, i.e., the target firm is at present badly managed.

The empirical evidence in support of this position is entirely of a single kind: the returns on common shares of the merging companies around the time of the acquisition. The universal finding is that the shareholders of the acquired companies make substantial percentage gains from being acquired. The median gain for 21 studies which I recently reviewed was 18.7 percent (Mueller, 1986).[9]

Once a bidding firm announces its intention to acquire a given company, the price of the target's shares must rise. Some current shareholders place a higher value on the shares than their preannouncement price; many shareholders will hold out for a higher price knowing that someone is intent on buying them. The gains to the acquired firm's shareholders are largely a reflection of the premium paid to bring the acquisition about. The evidence that the acquired firm's shareholders benefitted from being taken over tells us little more than that the acquiring firm's management was willing to pay the price needed to bring the merger about.

The important question in judging the efficiency effects of mergers is how they have affected the acquiring company's shareholders. Here the evidence is more equivocal. Several studies have observed a reduction in the wealth of the acquiring firm's shareholders, and the gains when they are positive are quite modest and often statistically insignificant. The median increase in the returns to acquiring company shareholders *around the time of the merger* is only 1.6 percent.

While small in comparison with the gains to acquired company shareholders, this median return to acquiring firm shareholders is positive. Thus, one could argue that both acquiring and acquired company shareholders benefit from mergers, or more conservatively (since this median return to the acquiring firm's shareholders is not statistically different from zero), that acquired company shareholders gain while acquiring shareholders do not lose. Wealth appears to have been created, and this newly created wealth is attributed to the efficiency gains, the synergy, inherent in the merger.

Such is the nature of both the logic and the empirical evidence in favor of the propositions that mergers increase efficiency. The argument rests on several, crucial assumptions: (1) that managers maximize shareholder wealth, (2) that the stock market is efficient in the sense that market values immediately reflect new information that will effect future profit streams, like a merger announcement, and (3) that shareholders have rational expectations, i.e., the market acts both immediately and on average accurately to any new information affecting future profitability.

There is reason to question all three assumptions. The bulk if not all of the wealth gains from mergers accrue to the shareholders of the acquired companies. The explanation for this phenomenon typically offered is that the 'market for corporate control' is a competitive market, and the gains from a merger are tied entirely to the assets of the acquired firm, i.e., it is badly managed or for some reason undervalued. An implicit bidding for the acquired company occurs in the typical merger in which there is but one announced buyer, or an explicit bidding when two or more firms seek to acquire the same firm, and this bidding drives up the price of the target to a level which reflects all or nearly all of the gains from the merger. While this explanation can account for the lopsided distribution of the gains from mergers, it cannot explain why the managers of the acquiring firms persist in participating in a market in which the mean returns are negligible, and their variance is known to be substantial, if their only goal is to enhance the wealth of their shareholders.

Shiller (1981, 1984) has recently argued that movements in stock market prices cannot be explained as a rational reaction to future changes in dividends that are on average correctly perceived. Swings in stock market values are far too large, and seem to reflect bandwagon behavior on the part of shareholders. This interpretation is particularly relevant to the issue of acquiring firm share performance, because merger waves have tended to coincide with stock market booms and thus may reflect the same underlying psychological mood.[10]

During the mid- and late-sixties, conglomerate mergers were in vogue in the United States and the conglomerate firms' share prices did rise substantially as they made their acquisitions. In the early seventies, conglomerate firm shares went out of vogue and their share prices plummeted.[11] Since 18 of the 21 studies of merger effects on share prices, i.e., virtually all of the studies published to date, employ samples heavily weighted by the mergers of the sixties, it is important to examine how the acquiring companies' shares performed after the mergers were completed. Eighteen of the 21 studies report the returns to acquiring firm shareholders for at least one year after the announcements. Thirteen of the eighteen report declines in returns. The median post-merger return to acquiring firm shareholders is −2.0 percent.

Interesting also are the figures on the returns to acquiring firm shareholders in the period prior to a merger's announcement. Since the prevailing view among those who believe mergers are efficiency enhancing is that the gains in efficiency are tied to the acquired firm's assets, the premerger return performance of acquiring firm shares is often not reported, and is not commented upon when it is reported. Yet, 10 of the 11 studies that do report acquiring firm share performance for at least 2 years prior to the merger's announcement record positive gains. The median premerger gain to acquiring firm shareholders is 11.7 percent, a figure that dwarfs the gain at the time of announcement.

The large, average gains to acquiring firm shareholders prior to the mergers casts doubt on the mergers-cause-efficiency thesis in two respects. First, the finding suggests an alternative motivation to the mergers that shareholder wealth maximization. Acquiring firm managers may be spurned to make acquisitions not by the expected gains from synergy or the improved performance of the target firms following the merger, but by the above normal performance of their own company's shares prior to the merger. A period in which a firm's profits and share price are unusually high is an attractive time to announce a merger, especially if one anticipates that the merger may not be a success.

Second, the substantial increase in shareholder returns prior to the merger's announcement, in some cases beginning as much as six years prior to announcement, suggests that the increased returns observed around the announcement may not be a result of the merger announcement, but may simply be a continuation of the existing trend. Every study to date has ignored the premerger upward trend in acquiring firm returns and measured the 'gains' at announcement as if they were caused by the announcement, and would have been zero in its absence. At a minimum, the changes in returns at announcement should be measured relative to the prior trend line, and even then one cannot say whether the 'gains' thus observed were 'caused' by the announcement, or whether the announcement and the gains are both reflections of the company's abnormally good performance.

When one combines the pre- and post-announcement results with those at the time of announcement, the following picture of acquiring firm share performance emerges, at least for those studies with substantial representation of mergers in the sixties.[12] Acquiring firm share prices enjoy a substantial and sustained rise prior to a merger's announcement. This gain levels off sometime between the announcement of the acquisition and its consummation. Then a long, steady decline in returns commences. The return to acquiring firm shareholders over the combined announcement and post-announcement period is negative. The median for the 16 studies reporting more than a couple of months after announcement was −2.5 percent for the combined announcement and post-announcement period, measured against a zero trend line rather than the positive, premerger trend. While this number is small in comparison with the 18.7 percent gain to acquired firm shareholders, it must be recalled that acquiring firms are many times larger than the firms they acquire, in my study of 282 U.S. mergers they were 10 times larger, thus a 2.5 percent loss to acquiring firm shareholders may more than outweigh the 18.7 percent gain to their merger partners.

Evidence of the absence of efficiency gains from mergers can also be found in the studies of merger effects on profitability, growth, and market shares. In the seven country, cross-national comparison of merger effects on profitability, a roughly even split was found between countries reporting slight increases in profit rates, and countries reporting slight declines (Mueller, 1980). Meek's (1977) exhaustive study of more than 1,000 mergers in the United Kingdom reported a decline in profitability following mergers.

In none of the seven countries did we observe an increase in relative growth rates for merging firms following their acquisitions, as might be expected if the mergers improved efficiency. In two countries, Holland and the United States, we observed declines (Mueller, 1980). Similar declines in post-merger growth rates have been recorded by Hogarty (1970) and Lev and Mandelker (1972).

Finally, no study of the effects of mergers on market shares has observed an improvement in market shares, following a merger. Goldberg (1973) reported no change in market share for a sample of 44 firms. I estimated a significant decline in the market shares of the acquired firms for a sample of 210 acquisitions (Mueller, 1985a). Outside of the evidence of gains to acquired firm shareholders, the empirical support for the hypothesis that mergers improve efficiency simply does not exist.

IV. IMPLICATIONS FOR A NEW APPROACH TO ANTITRUST

The economic premises underlying the U.S. antitrust laws are remarkably simple. Competition produces desirable outcomes, Pareto optimality if you will. Competition can be maintained, if dominant firms do not drive their smaller rivals from the market by predatory behavior, if rivals do not collude, if vertically linked firms do not contract to foreclose a market to competitors, if those mergers which would lessen competition are prevented. Central but implicit in the U.S. antitrust philosophy is the assumption that all competition is price competition. Absent from the antitrust laws is any suggestion that some forms of competition may be socially unbeneficial, yet nonpredatory. Thus, no section of the antitrust laws could be used to prevent excessive nonprice competition, rent-seeking or the like. The antitrust laws are similarly indifferent to any efficiency- or welfare-reducing consequences of mergers, so long as they do not arise form a potential lessening of competition.

With one exception the new antitrust movement in the United States with its new learning underpinning rests upon an equally simplistic view of the competitive process. The exception is the many transaction costs-agency costs-free-rider costs arguments defending tying and vertical contracts. Here the conventional wisdom has often been simplistic – 'tying agreements serve hardly any purpose beyond the suppression of competition' (S. O. Calif. v. United States, 1949) – and the new learning has developed a catalogue of arguments for why this or that practice might under certain circumstances increase efficiency and market performance. But, the possibility that each of the respective business practices would lessen competition remains. Thus, the new learning with respect to the practices governed by Section 3 of the Clayton Act is at its core an argument for a rule of reason approach to all of these practices rather than the *per se* or nearly *per se* approach that existed. But the question of whether a *per se* approach should be abandoned in favor of a rule-of-reason approach rests largely on a comparison of the additional transactions costs inherent in the application of a rule of reason with the costs of preventing the employment of practices in some instances in which they would improve efficiency. The resolution of this issue depends, however, in turn on the frequency with which the latter occur, an empirical issue, which the existing literature with its argument-by-example approach cannot resolve. Thus, whether and to what extent Section 3 Clayton Act cases should be governed by a rule-of-reason approach remains an open question. The new learnings in this area demand an increase in the complexity of the antitrust policy, the substitution of a rule-of-reason for a *per se* rule. Although some would favor the repeal of Section 3 (Posner, 1976; Bork, 1978), which certainly would simplify the administrative process, to interpret the new learnings on the efficiency properties of these practices as justifying such a move would be a gross exaggeration of the weight of 'empirical' evidence in this area.

The economic logic underlying the new learning with respect to profitability and market share is simple in the extreme. A process of Darwinian competition is presumed in which the survivors are by definition the most efficient. First-mover advantages of the kind Schmalensee (1982) has examined, rent-seeking losses from creating and maintaining large market shares, and the social costs of a Darwinian process of nonprice competition are all ignored. The biggest have been revealed to be the best and society must be better off with production concentrated in these firms. Given this view of the world, the Areeda–Turner rule on predatory pricing is easy to defend. The dominant firms have been revealed to be more efficient by the competitive process, and thus should be free to compete in any manner they choose other than to adopt practices that clearly produce inefficient outcomes, like charging prices below marginal costs.

Equally simple is the logic underlying a hands-off policy with respect to mergers. First, it is assumed that mergers are governed by market forces. Second, it is assumed that this market for corporate control is like any other market (Louis Lowenstein, 1985, quotes two 'Chicago economists' as comparing the market for corporate control to the market for apples). Third, the conclusion is drawn that corporate assets will be optimally allocated, just as apples are optimally allocated, when the government refrains from interference with the normal working of the market. The invisible hand theorem applies to the market for corporate control without qualification.

For the reasons stated above, I do not agree with this simple view of how the market mechanism guides modern corporate capitalism. Any normative evaluation of this system must explicitly take into account the nonprice nature of much of competition, the existence of rent-seeking investment, and the complex and diverse motivations that govern activity in the market for corporate control. I do not propose to offer such an evaluation in the closing pages of this essay. Nor do I propose to set out specific antitrust and other policy reforms that I believe ought or certainly could be adopted in the near future. Rather, I wish to suggest the kinds of legislation one should contemplate, given the evidence outlined above, and the broader issues this evidence raises. The discussion is speculative. I wish only to indicate that more options exist than merely those from which we are moving and those to which we seem headed.

Numerous companies with large market shares are observed to earn persistently above normal profits. These might arise from continued greater efficiency, superior product quality, or from first-mover advantages unrelated to quality and efficiency. When attributable to the latter, the perpetual dominance of a market by a single firm or small group of firms can lower social welfare by preventing newcomers with equally good or superior products from earning sufficient profits to survive. Moreover, the dominant firm, which owes its continued success to buyer inertia and risk aversion typically cannot be challenged under behavioral rules, like even a resusticated rule on predation, since its dominance stems as much from what its competitors and customers are not doing, as it does from overtly anticompetitive behavior by the dominant firm. To correct the inefficiencies generated in these situations, market dominance must be attacked directly.

Some time ago, Oliver Williamson (1972) suggested that when a market was dominanted for a prolonged period by one firm, a presumption should be made that the dominant firm be broken up, a presumption that could be rebutted by a demonstration that the firm owes its long run position of dominance to greater efficiency or superior product quality.

Although not without administrative complications, the Williamson proposal is noteworthy because it addresses an important class of potential monopoly welfare problems. While some firms may experience substantial monopoly rents for short periods due to a variety of reasons, persistent profits and dominant market positions can arise from only one of two classes of reasons. Either the dominant firm has a superior price-quality combination, or firms with equally attractive price-quality characteristics are prevented from establishing themselves due to the first-mover advantages of the dominant firm. If the former cannot be proved the latter can be presumed and the dominant firm's position removed.

Williamson's proposal is a zero-one proposal. Some market share is chosen above which dominance might be presumed. Below this market share no action is taken. William G. Shepherd (1975, pp. 196–201) proposed a more continuous attack on market dominance in the form of a tax on profits graduated according to market share. This policy would tend to erode market share by giving firms an incentive to reduce market share, where it is not generating sufficient extra profits to cover the tax. In particular, it might encourage firms which maintain high market shares through advertising and R and D to reduce some of these outlays and allow their market shares to decline.

The wastes from nonprice competition and rent-seeking activities are difficult to address. But they are not impossible. In the late 1970s, the FTC attempted to come to grips with the issues raised by nonprice competition in one particular market characterized by heavy advertising expenditures, stable and large market shares, and high profits – the ready-to-eat cereals industry. Building on current developments in the product differentiation literature, the FTC sought to put together a case that hinged on the incumbent cereals firms blocking entry through their strategic coverage of the product-characteristics space (Schmalensee, 1978; Scherer, 1979b). Whatever the overall merits of the FTC's case, it was based on a correct perception of the salient characteristics of the industry: an absence of price competition, heavy advertising, a range of product characteristics and consumer perceptions of product quality. Shortly after Reagan's appointees took control of the FTC, the case was abandoned. The issue of whether the courts would entertain more sophisticated theories of how monopoly power is created and preserved remains unresolved.

The importance of nonprice competition in creating and maintaining market positions is particularly relevant to the issue of predatory behavior. In markets in which nonprice modes of competition are significant, the preferred predatory strategy need not involve price at all. Much of the alleged predatory conduct of IBM, for example, involved its frequent modifications of mainframe-peripheral hook-ups, which made it difficult for the small peripheral manufacturers to maintain plug-compatibility with IBM mainframes. Moreover, investments in nonprice competitive strategies are more in the nature of fixed or sunk costs. Thus, a rule like Areeda–Turner, which allows firms to choose any price above short run average costs, allows dominant firms with heavy nonprice investments to set price below the level necessary to maintain their nonprice capital in the long run, should they choose to use price as a strategy to eliminate their smaller rivals.

It should be stressed that were one to come to grips directly with the welfare issues raised by nonprice competition and rent-seeking, it is not obvious that antitrust-type polices offer the most effective remedy. Suppose, for example, one were able to show that advertising levels in a given industry, or in toto, were excessive. Currently, we effectively subsidize advertising by allowing companies to expense what is an investment. Forcing firms to treat advertising as an investment with some given depreciation schedule would reduce its attractiveness slightly. A larger curtailment of advertising expenditures could be achieved by disallowing a certain fraction of advertising expenditure deductions. This fraction could, in turn, be made to vary with the level of the firm's advertising, its industry's advertising, and so on. Similar policies could be implemented for other marketing expenditures, and other rent-seeking outlays like R and D, and antitrust outlays.

When one recognizes that the motives for mergers are many, one realizes that many mergers probably neither increase efficiency nor lessen competition, but rather allow management to achieve some other goal. In many cases mergers appear to have actually reduced the efficiency of one or both of the merging firms. The significant losses in market shares I recorded represent the shrinkage and in some cases outright disappearance of many firms which were, prior to their acquisition, viable, healthy competitors. The prevailing policy on mergers presumes that the disappearance of these firms was in the interest of enhancing economic efficiency. But if other interests were enhanced, then the American economy has witnessed a drastic reduction in the number of potential price cutters, and potential innovators over the last quarter of a century. If, for whatever reason, one does prefer a system of small producers, each dependent for his success upon his own skill and character, to one in which the great mass of those engaged must accept the directions of a few (*ALCOA*), then mergers are without question the most immediate and persistent force destroying that system.

A policy for preserving this system without sacrificing economic efficiency would be a flat ban on mergers subject to an efficiencies defense. To ease the administrative burden and maintain the overall objective of such legislation the ban could exempt all mergers for which *both* partners were less than a given size (e.g., smaller than the 500th largest, or 1,000th largest).[13] Included among the efficiency defenses would be a failing firm defense, so that the smooth transference of assets in the obviously necessary cases would transpire. While efficiency defenses have traditionally been feared as posing a great administrative burden on the courts, the courts could take a fairly liberal attitude toward the evidence presented the first time a firm proposed a merger, and could place heavy weight on a firm's experience with previous acquisitions. If my reading of the literature is correct, many mergers could not pass an efficiencies' defense *ex post*, and would probably not even be proposed on the basis of the highly speculative *ex ante* evidence upon which the mergers must take place.

As in the area of nonprice competition, revisions in the antitrust laws are not the only reforms to consider to deal with the issues raised by the vast transfer of assets through mergers that occurs today. A comprehensive ban on mergers would remove some of the constraint on managers to maximize shareholder wealth. Thus, it should be complemented by reforms that enhance stockholder control: elimination of laws which protect management from being removed by shareholders, and forcing a more detailed reporting of profits and other information to facilitate shareholder monitoring of managers, to name but two.

The presumptions underlying the U.S. antitrust laws and their current enforcement are that managers maximize profits, that competition insures the survival of the most efficient, and that all competition increases social welfare like price competition does. In this imaginary world, all actions by business that do not clearly suppress competition are presumed to be efficiency enhancing. The proper role of antitrust is to prevent those few actions that suppress competition and stand aside and allow business a free hand in all other matters.

The view presented here is of a more permissive economic environment. Large firms survive although their products may be dearer and inferior; some forms of competition flourish although they lower social welfare; managers have discretion to persue goals that are neutral or debilitating to efficiency. In this world government, perhaps acting through antitrust policy, can play a more active role promoting efficiency in the business sector.

Government is itself a wieldy and inefficient agent, however, and care must be taken in giving it any regulatory role that it not worsen the situation. I have thus proposed but two areas, in which the potential for inefficiency is large, where the presumption regarding efficiency might be reversed. Firms which have dominated a given market for a sustained period might be dismembered, and large firms might be prevented from merging unless it could be shown that the preservation of the dominant firm and consummation of the merger served the interests of promoting efficiency. It must be stressed that such changes, although a dramatic break with the prevailing antitrust philosophy, would affect only two conspicuous aspects of the market environment. Most firms would not be affected by the dominant firm rule, and no firms would be affected by the merger rule, whose managers were simply maximizing shareholder welfare by seeking to improve corporate efficiency. Beyond these antitrust policy reforms, I have suggested consideration of policies that would recognize the existence of inefficient modes of competition.

These policies, when developed and refined, could constitute an important component of an enlightened industrial policy. The term 'industrial policy' induces negative responses in most economists and many other supporters of a market-controlled economy. The reason for this is, I presume, because what is envisaged is another program assigned to an agency in which some bureaucrat decides what level of investment, or imports in a given industry, is best for the economy. Of this form of industrial policy I am also skeptical. If, however, by 'industrial policy' is meant a government's policy toward industry, then all countries must and do have at least one form of industrial policy in defining and enforcing the 'rules of the game' in which industry competes. Antitrust is one important component to this latter form of industrial policy. The tax laws as they affect the taxation of profits, and the returns on different types of expenditures are another. Laws regulating the issuance of securities, tariffs and other trade regulations are additional examples. An enlightened industrial policy would consider the optimal set of 'rules of the game' to enact across all of these policy dimensions to induce desirable outcomes from the industrial sectors of the economy. It is toward shaping this type of industrial policy that the analysis of this chapter has been directed.

ACKNOWLEDGEMENT

This paper was drafted in part while I was a fellow at the International Institute of Management, Science Center, Berlin, during the summer of 1985. My thanks go to the Science Center for its support, and to Hiroyuki Odagiri and William G. Shepherd for helpful comments on an earlier draft.

NOTES

1. Richard Nixon's first appointee as Assistant Attorney General in charge of antitrust, Richard McLaren, tried to use Section 7 'to arrest' the rising tide in aggregate concentration by attacking purely conglomerate mergers. He failed. The effort was squashed in one of its first attempts, *ITT*'s acquisition of *Grinnel*. Chief Judge Timbers of the District Court of Connecticut would write in 1970 that 'the legislative history . . . indicates that Section 7 as amended was not intended to proscribe all mergers which result in economic concentration', but only those increasing concentration 'in any line of commerce'.

2. For criticism of the Areeda–Turner proposal and alternative proposals, see Scherer (1976), Williamson (1979), Baumol (1979), and Joskow and Klevorick (1979).
3. See, in particular, Peltzman (1977).
4. See the articles in the *St. John's Law Review*, special edition, Spring, 1970; and Steiner, 1975, Chs. 2–5.
5. Surveys reaching this conclusion include (Benston, 1980; Brozen, 1982; Halpern, 1983; and Jensen and Ruback, 1983). The individual studies are referenced in the surveys.
6. The only dominant firm that has had trouble with the antitrust authorities in recent years has been *AT&T*. It is certainly the exception that proves the rule. Its claim that it owed its dominant position to greater efficiency was severely undermined by its long time protection from competition because of regulation.
7. Shepherd (1972, 1975), Gale and Branch (1982), Ravenscraft (1983), Smirlock *et al.* (1984), and Schmalensee (1985).
8. A similar interpretation of Sam Peltzman's new learning results is offered by F. M. Scherer (1979a), who observed that the most rapid increases in concentration since World War II occurred in advertising intensive-differentiated product industries.
9. See, Mueller (1977, 1980, 1985c) and Scherer (1980, pp. 138–41). The pro-efficiency effects interpretation of the evidence is offered by Benston (1980), Brozen (1982), Halpern (1983) and Jensen and Ruback (1983).
10. See, Nelson (1959, 1966); Melicher, *et al.* (1983), Geroski (1984), and Shughart, III, and Tollison (1984). Geroski offers the interpretation to his findings that stock market and merger behavior are jointly caused by the same underlying changes in the market (psychological) environment.
11. Both Reid (1971) and Melicher and Rush (1974) document the early phases of the dramatic decline in the conglomerates' share and bond prices in the early seventies.
12. Only three published studies are based on samples drawn entirely from the post-1968 stock market boom period (Dodd, 1980; Firth, 1980; Malatesta, 1983). They are consistent with the efficient capital market hypothesis in that the stock market's reaction appears to be complete within anywhere from a year to a matter of days. All three studies find substantial losses to acquiring firm shareholders. These declines definitely are so large as to outweigh the gains to acquired firm shareholders in two studies, and probably do so in the third. Given enough experience, perhaps the stock market can evaluate the effects of mergers accurately.
13. In 1979, Senator Kennedy and four other Senators introduced legislation, which would have banned mergers when the *target* firm was beneath a given size. If managers undertake mergers simply to expand the size of their company, such a partial ban would have simply diverted avid acquirers from the larger firms in the economy to the smaller ones, thereby excellerating the disappearance of small producers. In light of this likelihood, it is ironic that the legislation was named the 'Small and Independent Business Protection Act of 1979'.

References

Areeda, Philip, and Turner, Donald F., 'Predatory Pricing and Related Practices Under Section 2 of the Sherman Act', *Harvard Law Review*, 88 (1975), pp. 697–733.

Areeda, Philip, and Turner, Donald F., 'Scherer on Predatory Pricing: Reply', *Harvard Law Review*, 89, (1976), pp. 891–900.

Bain, Joe S., 'Economies of Scale, Concentration, and the Condition of Entry in Twelve Manufacturing Industries', *American Economic Review*, 44 (March 1954), pp. 15–39.

Bain, Joe S., *Barriers to New Competition*, Cambridge: Harvard University Press (1956).

Baumol, William J., 'Quasi-Permanence of Price Reductions: A Policy for Prevention of Predatory Pricing', *Yale Law Journal*, 89 (November 1979), pp. 1–26.

Benston, George J., *Conglomerate Mergers*, Washington, D.C.: American Enterprise Insitute (1980).

Bork, Robert H., *The Antitrust Paradox*, New York: Basic Books (1978).

Brozen, Yale, 'Bain's Concentration and Rates of Return Revisited', *Journal of Law and Economics*, 14 (October 1971a), pp. 351–369.

Brozen, Yale, 'Concentration and Structural and Market Disequilibria', *Antitrust Bulletin*, 16 (1971b) pp. 241–248.

Brozen, Yale, '*Concentration, Mergers, and Public Policy*, New York: MacMillan (1982).

Carlton, Dennis W., 'Vertical Integration in Competitive Markets Under Uncertainty', *Journal of Industrial Economics*, 27 (March 1979), pp. 189–209.

Carlton, Dennis W., 'A Reexamination of Delivered Pricing Systems', *Journal of Law and Economics*, 26 (April 1983), pp. 51–70.

Carter, J. R., 'Collusion, Efficiency and Antitrust', *Journal of Law and Economics*, 21 (October 1978), pp. 435–444.

Council of Economic Advisors, *Economic Report of the President*, Washinton: Government Printing Office (1985).

De Alessi, Louis, 'Property Rights, Transaction Costs, and X-efficiency: An Essay in Economic Theory', *American Economic Review*, 73 (March 1983), pp. 64–81.

Demsetz, Harold, 'Industry Structure, Market Rivalry, and Public Policy', *Journal of Law and Economics*, 16 (April 1973), pp. 1–9.

Demsetz, Harold, 'Two Systems of Belief about Monopoly', in Harvey J. Goldschmid, H. M. Mann and J. F. Weston, eds., *Industrial Concentration: The New Learning*, Boston: Little, Brown & Co. (1974), pp. 164–184.

Dodd, Peter, 'Merger Proposals, Management Discretion and Stockholder Wealth', *Journal of Financial Economics*, 8 (June 1980), pp. 105–137.

Eckbo, B. Espen, 'Horizontal Mergers, Collusion, and Stockholder Wealth', *Journal of Financial Economics*, 11 (April 1983). pp. 241–273.

Ellert, J. C., 'Mergers, Antitrust Law Enforcement and Stockholder Returns', *Journal of Finance*, 31 (May 1976), 715–732.

Firth, Michael, 'Takeovers, Shareholder Returns, and the Theory of the Firm', *Quarterly Journal of Economics*, 94 (March 1980), pp. 315–347.

Gale, Bradley J. and Branch, Ben S., 'Concentration versus Market Share: Which Determines Performance and Why Does it Matter?', *Antitrust Bulletin*, 27 (Spring 1982), pp. 83–106.

Goldberg, Lawrence G., 'The Effect of Conglomerate Mergers on Competition', *Journal of Law and Economics*, 16 (April 1973), pp. 137–158.

Geroski, P. A., 'On the Relationship Between Aggregate Merger Activity and the Stock Market', *European Economic Review*, 25 (1984) pp. 223–233.

Halpern, Paul, 'Corporate Acquisitions: A Theory of Special Cases?' mimeo, University of Toronto (1982).

Halpern, Paul, 'Corporate Acquisitions: A Theory of Special Cases? A Review of Event Studies Applied to Acquisitions', *Journal of Finance*, 38 (May 1983), pp. 297–317.

Hogarty, T. F., 'The Profitability of Corporate Mergers', *Journal of Business*, 43 (July 1970), pp. 317–327.

Hurwitz, James D., Kovacic, William E., Sheehan III, Thomas A., and Lande, Robert, H., 'Current Legal Standards of Predation', in Steven C. Salop, ed. *Strategy, Predation, and Antitrust Analysis*, Washington: Federal Trade Commission (1981), pp. 101–153.

Joskow, Paul L. and Klevorick, Alvin K., 'A Framework for Analyzing Predatory Pricing Policy', *Yale Law Journal*, 89 (December 1979), pp. 213–270.

Jensen, M. C. and Ruback, R. S., 'The Market for Coroportate Control', *Journal of Financial Economics*, 11 (April 1983), pp. 5–50.

Klein, Benjamin, 'Transaction Cost Determinants of "Unfair" Contractual Arrangements", *American Economic Review*, 70 (May 1980), pp. 356–362.

Klein, Benjamin, Crawford, R. C. an Alchian, A. A., 'Vertical Integration, Appropriable Rents and the Competitive Contracting Process', *Journal of Law and Economics*, 21 (October 1978), pp. 297–326.

Klein, Benjamin and Saft, Lester, F., 'The Law and Economics of Franchise Tying Contracts', *Journal of Law and Economics*, 28 (May 1985), pp. 345–361.

Lev, B. and Mandelker, G., 'The Microeconomic Consequences of Corporate Mergers', *Journal of Business*, 45 (January 1972), pp. 85–104.

Lowenstein, Louis, Statement before the Subcommittee on Securities, Senate Committee on Banking, Housing and Urban Affairs, Washington, D.C. (April 3, 1985).

Malatesta, Paul H., 'The Wealth Effect of Merger Activity and the Objective Functions of Merging Firms', *Journal of Financial Economics*, 11 (April 1983), pp. 155–181.

Markham, Jesse W., 'Survey of the Evidence and Findings on Mergers, Business Concentration and Price Policy', New York: National Bureau of Economic Research (1955), pp. 141–182.

Marvel, Howard P., 'Exclusive Dealing', *Journal of Law and Economics*, 25 (April 1982), pp. 1–25.

Marvel, Howard P. and McCafferty, Stephen, 'Resale Price Maintenance and Quality Certification', *Rand Journal of Economics*, 15 (Autumn 1984), pp. 346–359.

Marvel, Howard P., 'The Welfare Effects of Resale Price Maintenance', *Journal of Law and Economics*, 28 (May 1985), pp. 363–379.

Meeks, Geoffrey, *Disappointing Marriage: A Study of the Gains from Merger*, Cambridge, England: Cambridge University Press, (1977).

Melicher, Ronald W., Ledolter, Johannes, and D'Antonio, Louis J., 'A Time Series Analysis of Aggregate Merger Activity', *Review of Economics & Statistics*, 65 (August 1983), pp. 423–430.

Melicher, R. M. and Rush, D. F., 'Evidence on the Acquisition-Related Performance of Conglomerate Firms', *Journal of Finance*, 29 (March 1974), pp. 141–149.

Monteverde, Kirk and Teece, David J., 'Appropriable Rents and Quasi-Vertical Integration', *Journal of Law and Economics*, 25 (October 1982), pp. 321–328.

Mueller, Dennis C., 'The Effects of Conglomerate Mergers: A Survey of the Empirical Evidence', *Journal of Banking and Finance*, 1 (December 1977), pp. 315–347.

Mueller, Dennis C., ed., *The Determinants and Effects of Mergers: An International Comparison*, Cambridge: Oelgeschlager, Gunn, and Hain (1980).

Mueller, Dennis C., 'Mergers and Market Shares', *Review of Economics and Statistics*, 67 (May 1985a), pp. 259–267.

Mueller, Dennis C., 'The Corporation: Growth, Diversification, and Mergers', mimeo, University of Maryland (1985b).

Mueller, Dennis C., *Profits in the Long Run*, Cambridge: Cambridge University Press (1986).

Neale, A. D. and Goyder, D. G., *The Antitrust Laws of the USA*, 3rd ed., Cambridge: Cambridge University Press (1980).

Nelson, Ralph L., 'Merger Movements in American Industry, 1985–1956', Princeton: Princeton University Press (1959).

Nelson, Ralph L., 'Business Cycle Factors in the Choice Between Internal and External Growth', in W. Alberts and J. Segall, eds., *The Corporate Merger*, Chicago: University of Chicago Press (1966).

Peltzman, S., 'The Gains and Losses from Industrial Concentration', *Journal of Law and Economics*, 20 (October 1977) pp. 229–263.

Posner, Richard A., *Antitrust Law*, Chicago: University of Chicago Press (1976).

Ravenscraft, David J., 'Structure-Profit Relationships at the Line of Business and Industry Level', *Review of Economics and Statistics*, 65 (February 1983), pp. 22–31.

Reid, S. R., 'A Reply to the Weston/Mansinghka Criticisms Dealing with Conglomerate Mergers', *Journal of Finance*, 26 (September 1971), pp. 937–946.

Scherer, F. M., 'Predatory Pricing and the Sherman Act: A Comment', *Harvard Law Review*, 89 (1976) pp. 869–890.

Scherer, F. M., 'The Causes and Consequences of Rising Industrial Concentration: A Comment', *Journal of Law and Economics*, 22 (April 1979a), pp. 191–208.

Scherer, F. M., 'The Welfare Economics of Product Variety: An Application to the Ready-to-Eat Cereals Industry', *Journal of Industrial Economics*, 28 (December 1979b), pp. 113–134.

Scherer, F. M., *Industrial Market Structure and Economic Performance*, Chicago: Rand McNally (1971); second edition (1980).

Schmalensee, Richard, 'Entry Deferrence in the Ready-to-Eat-Breakfast Cereal Industry', *Bell Journal of Economics*, 9 (Autumn 1978), pp. 305–327.

Schmalensee, Richard, 'Product Differentiation Advantages of Pioneering Brands', *American Economic Review*, 72 (June 1982), pp. 349–366.

Schmalensee, Richard, 'Do Markets Differ Much?', *American Economic Review*, 75 (June 1985) pp. 341–351.

Shepherd, William G., 'The Elements of Market Structure', *Review of Economics and Statistics*, 54 (February 1972), pp. 25–37.

Shepherd, William, G., *The Treatment of Market Power*, New York: Columbia University Press (1975).

Shiller, Robert J., 'Do Stock Prices Move Too Much to be Justified by Subsequent Changes in Dividends?', *American Economic Review*, 71 (June 1981), pp. 421–436.

Shiller, Robert J., 'Stock Prices and Social Dynamics', *Brookings Papers on Economic Activity* (1984), No. 2, pp. 457–498.

Shughart III, William F., and Tollison, Robert D., 'The Random Character of Merger Activity', *Rand Journal of Economics*, 15 (Winter 1984), pp. 500–509.

Smirlock, Michael, Gilligan, Thomas and Marshall, William, 'Tobin's q and the Structure-Performance Relationship', *American Economic review*, 74 (December 1984), pp. 1051–1060.

Steiner, Peter O., *Mergers: Motives, Effects, Policies*, Ann Arbor: University of Michigan Press (1975).

Stigler, G. J., 'Monopoly and Oligopoly by Merger', *American Economic Review*, 40 (May 1950), pp. 23–34.

Telser, Lester G., 'Why Should Manufacturers Want Fair Trade?', *Journal of Law and Economics*, 3 (October 1960), pp. 86–105.

Williamson, Oliver E., 'Economies as an Anti-Trust Defense: The Welfare Trade-offs', *American Economic Review*, 58 (March 1968), pp. 18–36.
Williamson, Oliver E., 'Dominant Firms and the Monopoly Problem: Market Failure Considerations', *Harvard Law Review*, 85 (1972), pp. 1512–1531.
Williamson, Oliver E., *Markets and Hierarchies: Analysis and Antitrust Implications*, New York: Free Press (1975).
Williamson, Oliver E., 'Predatory Pricing: A Strategic and Welfare Analysis', *Yale Law Journal*, 87 (Decemeber 1977), pp. 284–340.
Williamson, Oliver E., 'Transaction Cost Economics: The Governance of Contractual Relations', *Journal of Law and Economics*, 22 (October 1979), pp. 233–262.
Williamson, Oliver E., 'Credible Commitments: Using Hostages to Support Exchange', *American Economic Review*, 73 (September 1983), pp. 519–540.

10. THE TREATMENT OF DOMINANT FIRMS IN THE UK COMPETITION LEGISLATION

J. D. Gribbin and M. A. Utton

The first competition legislation, introduced in 1948, was predominantly concerned with cartels which were then the main form of industrial structure. A Monopolies and Restrictive Practices Commission was established as an independent investigatory body which conducted enquiries directed to it by the Board of Trade. 'Monopoly' was defined as a single firm, or group of firms acting together to restrict competition, and which controlled at least one third share of the market. There was presumption that monopoly as defined was per se detrimental. This was partly a consequence of earlier government encouragement to, and use made of cartels. There was a contrary belief that as much of industry was dominated by small and high cost firms, the efficiency of large scale firms would more than offset any adverse effects of single firm dominance. An economic definition of the public interest was laid down, and if monopoly of either kind met the performance tests which derived from the definition it was allowed to continue.

Between 1948 and 1956 the Commission investigated 20 industries, of which 18 were cartelised, and the remaining 2 were controlled by dominant firms. These investigations gave a substantial insight into the nature and extent of the restrictions on competition, and the consequences of the cartels in terms of the retention of high cost capacity. In 1956 the accumulated evidence led to the Restrictive Trade Practices Act, which effectively abolished cartels. Of over 3000 which were registered in the late 1950's and early 1960's, only 1, the Cement Makers Agreement, remains effective in manufacturing. Thus, the 1956 Act swept away a major impediment to structural change, and encouraged those economic forces which were leading to increasing concentration.

The present UK competition legislation has a wide and flexible application to the supply of goods and services, whether by privately or publicly owned firms, and there are strictly limited exceptions to its

de Jong, H. W., Shepherd, W. G. (eds) Mainstreams in Industrial Organization
 ISBN 978-94-017-0495-3

jurisdiction. The main provisions are now contained in two principal statutes; the Fair Trading Act 1973, and the Competition Act 1980. The Fair Trading Act consolidates earlier Acts, and defines the legislative and institutional framework, as well as the remedial powers. It is applicable to monopoly, mergers, anticompetitive practices, and a control over mergers involving newspapers.

The starting point is the definition of 'monopoly', now established as being 25 per cent of the market held by one firm, or two or more who act together to prevent, restrict, or distort competition, but have no agreements or arrangements between them which would bring them within the cartel legislation. Thus, single, or multiple firm dominance is within the scope of the law. The creation of a single firm 'monopoly', i.e., 25 percent share through merger also brings that process within the scope. 'Merger' is flexibly defined as any kind of arrangement whereby material influence or control can be exercised over another firm. There is also a size criteria if the market share criteria does not apply. Any proposed merger is within the scope of the control where the gross value of the assets to be acquired exceed £30m. Merger control began in 1965.

There are three institutions involved in the implementation of the law. The first is the Office of Fair Trading, headed by its Director General who has an independent power to refer 'monopolies' to the second body, the Monopolies and Mergers Commission. The Director General is also the principal adviser to the third, the Secretary of State for Trade, on whether the Commission should be asked to investigate a proposed merger. Only the Secretary of State may make merger referrals.

The procedures established by the laws are administrative. The investigatory body is the Commission whose function in monopoly and merger enquiries is to examine the structure, conduct, and performance of the firms, or industries, and apply the 'public interest' test to determine whether the monopoly, or aspects of it, or a proposed merger operates, or would operate against the public interest.

The 'public interest' test is set out in a broad form in the legislation, and is essentially economic, but not necessarily or exclusively so. The Commission may take any relevant matters into account, but it must consider the promotion and maintenance of effective competition, the promotion of the interests of consumers, users and producers through competition, and if relevant, the effects in economic regions of the UK, or on its foreign trade.

After it has conducted its enquiry and reached conclusions on the public interest, the Commission must make a report to the Secretary of State which he in turn must publish. When the Commission has concluded that there are adverse effects on the public interest there is a wide range of powers which may be used to implement remedies proposed by the Commission. These include the power to stop a proposed merger, or to compel a reduction in ownership, and there is a similar power to divest which might be a remedy in a monopoly situation. Normally, the Director General of Fair Trading is given the task of implementing the Commission's recommendations following monopoly enquiries, and also where necessary after merger enquiries.

Two major innovations were introduced in the Competition Act 1980. The first was to make the Commission responsible for investigations into the efficiency, costs, quality of service, and possible abuses of monopoly by the publicly owned enterprises. The second introduced a formal process for dealing with an anti-competitive practice by a single firm even where it held less than 25 per cent of the market.

THE WORK OF THE COMMISSION

Table 1 shows the Commissions workload since it ceased to be concerned with cartels. Over 75 per cent of the reports have been on monopoly or mergers. Of the 24 monopoly investigations in services, 9 concerned restrictions on advertising imposed in the legal professions in England and Scotland, and by stockbrokers, veterinary practicioners, and accountants, while 2 were into the charging of recommended scale fees by surveyors and architects.

Monopoly investigations

Investigations into monopolies usually take up to 2 years, and follow a standard pattern, unless the terms of the reference limit their scope. The investigation first describes the markets or submarkets, and definitively

Table 1. Investigations of the Monopolies and Mergers Commission 1958–May 1985.

Type	Number
Monopoly in goods	45
Monopoly in services	24
Mergers	57
Newspaper mergers	15
Publicly owned industry	15
General references	6
Anticompetitive practices	4
	166

establishes whether one or more suppliers meet the statutory definition of monopoly. Then, a substantial amount of information is collected from the 'monopoly suppliers' on their conduct and performance, for example, pricing behaviour, competitive strategies, relationships with other suppliers including those abroad, costs, prices, profits, technical developments, and investment strategies. Information of a similar nature is collected from other suppliers, and also as appropriate from purchasers, users and customers.

The purpose of the data collection is to determine how competition operates in the markets, how the 'monopolists' have acquired their market shares, the nature and extent of entry barriers, whether conduct limits or restricts competition, and the links between structure, conduct, and performance. Performance is assessed in a number of aspects; for example prices, costs, profits, the provision of capcity, efficiency, innovation, export performance, and any contribution to regional policies for industry.

The conclusions in monopoly enquiries

In reaching its conclusions in an enquiry which is not limited to one or more aspects of conduct the Commission begins with performance. Most frequently, this centres on costs, prices and profits. If the conclusion is that one or more aspects of performance raise public interest issues, then the same question is posed about stucture and conduct. Where performance is judged to be seriously adverse to the public interest, a similar judgement might be made about conduct and structure. Thus, the monopoly itself could be found to be against the public interest. There have, however, only been 4 such findings; more frequently, performance and aspects of conduct are judged to be adverse. In 7 industries the Commission made no adverse findings after it had fully investigated the markets.

Table 2 contains the conduct and performance found to be against the public interest in the 45 reports on the supply of goods. The findings are put in two groups. In the second, the Commission has usually found the conduct to be adverse wherever it occurred, whereas in the first there were more instances where it was not condemned, i.e., vertical integration. Boardly, the dividing line has been the effect on competition in the market.

This table illustrates the wide range of behaviour which has been found to have adverse consequences. The most frequently condemned has been the imposition of restrictions on the sales of competitors goods.

Table 2. Practices found to be against the public interest in investigation into the supply of goods 1969–April 1985 (45 reports).

Practice	No. of reports
Group 1	
Monopoly pricing/monopoly profit	12
Discriminatory pricing	9
Vertical integration	3
Acquisition of competitors	2
Recommended or imposed resale prices	6
Patent licensing policy	1
Delivered pricing system	2
Financial interest in competitors	1
Failure to disclose ownership of subsidiary	1
Group 2	
Restrictions on supply to certain outlets	3
Restrictions on sales of competitors goods	15
Restrictions on supply of inputs to competitors	1
Full line forcing	2
Rental only contracts	1
Tie in sales	4

Source: Table 1. Review of Monopolies and Mergers Policy 1978 CMND 7198, updated.

Price discrimination has also been relatively frequent, and this is followed by imposing or recommending resale prices. However, largely because of the growing power of retailers, recommending prices has diminished in importance in the 1970's and 1980's, and imposing resale prices has been illegal since 1964.

Monopoly pricing and/or monopoly profits have been found to be adverse in just over one quarter of the investigations. The Commission pays particular attention to profitability as it often summarises the effects of the more important aspects of stucture, conduct, and performance. There are no absolute standards by which it is assessed. Against the industry background of structure and conduct, profitability is assessed over time, usually a minimum of 5 years, compared with an average and dispersion for manufacturing industry, and where possible for comparable industry groupings. Five factors appear to influence judgements; first, the industry comparisons, which might give a preliminary indication of the ability to earn monopoly profits, second, whether profits are rising or falling, third, the conditions of entry, particularly whether there has been recent successful new entrants, fourth, the efficiency of the firm, and finally the degree of risk in the market.

Most of the investigations into services have been limited to one practice which has been imposed as a condition of membership of a closed profession or occupation which is exempted from the cartel legislation. Even where the cartel exemption is not applicable, the investigations of services have tended to be into group behaviour, as in the wholesale supply of newspapers, or roadside advertising where a joint selling organisation acted as the monopoly seller for all the suppliers of sites.

Merger investigations

Policy towards mergers has reflected the consensus thinking about structural change in the UK economy. The power to intervene in proposed mergers was not taken until 1965 when merger activity was in the later stages of its long postwar boom. The view then was that the power to hold up mergers by investigation, and perhaps then prohibit them on public interest grounds would only be used in a minority of cases as many mergers were positively in the public interest. This view was repeated in later ministerial statements, even though concern was expressed in 1973 about mergers and the growth of industrial concentration. The July 1984 statement of policy does not depart from the long held general belief about mergers, and it could even be interpreted as a loosening of the control because it seems that conglomerate mergers are less likely to be sent for investigation.[1]

A brief summary of the main trends in mergers and referrals to the Commission is given in Table 3.

A peak of merger activity was reached in the early 1970's. In the following decade the number of mergers had halved, although their average size has increased partly as a consequence of inflation. The percentage of mergers referred has remained quite low, but the annual

Table 3. Merger activity, and referrals 1965–1984.

Period	Within legislation	Referred to		All known mergers
		Commission	Percent	
1965–69	466	10	2.1	4423
1970–74	579	19	3.3	4595
1975–79	903	19	2.1	2250
1980–84	987	31	3.1	2338

Note: the criteria of minimum assets to be acquired was raised from £5m to £15m in April 1980, and to £30m in July 1984.
Source: Annual Reports of Board of Trade and Director General of Fair Trading.

average number has increased from 2.0 in the first 5 year period, to 3.8 in the decade of the 1970's, and then to just over 6 in the 1980's.

The main form of structural change involved in the potentially referable mergers has been horizontal; these have averaged 73 percent over the whole period when measured by the value of the assets to be acquired. Conglomerate mergers have varied in popularity over the two decades, they averaged 7 percent in the first five years, 31 percent in the second, and fell slightly to 27 percent in the decade 1974–84. An analysis of proposed horizontal mergers between 1965 and 1977 showed that 43 percent would have created or increased market shares of over 50 percent.[2]

The history of mergers referred to the Commission is contained in Table 4.

Use of the power to refer led to the abandonment of 57 percent of the proposed mergers; thirty percent before investigations began, and the remainder as a consequence of the public interest decision.

The Commission has evolved a framework for investigating a proposed merger. To make its judgement about the balance of the public interest, it has to predict the likely outcome of the merger, and compare this with what might result if the merger did not take place. Four public interest issues arise most frequently, they are the consequences for competition, the efficiency of the companies, employment, and the balance of payments. These are not exclusive, and they may not be relevant in every inquiry. In keeping with the view that only a small proportion of mergers should be prevented, to do so the Commission has to find that the public interest detriments exceed the benefits. The parties do not have to demonstrate the reverse. A circumscribed framework has been put on this test. It was explained in the report on the proposed merger between S & W Beresford and the British Sugar Corporation[3] where the Commission stated that the expectation must be greater than a mere possibility of detriment, as this latter could arise in any merger. Its view was, 'the required conclusion is not', 'This may happen', but 'We expect that this will happen'.

Table 4. Mergers referred to Monopolies and Mergers Commission 1965–1984.

Structural charge	Referred	Abandoned	Public interest conclusion	
			Against	Not against
horizontal	48	10	17	21
vertical	6	1	1	4
conglomerate	25	11	5	9
	79	22	23	34

Source: Review of Monopolies and Mergers Policy 1978, CMND 7198 updated.

The power to investigate single practices by individual firms, even if they do not hold a monopoly position was an innovation of the Competition Act 1980. Its purpose is to provide a quick acting remedy where the concern is over conduct rather than structure. The process begins with an investigation by the Office of Fair Trading to indentify an 'anticompetitive practice', and if it does so it will try to obtain an undertaking that the conduct ceases or is modified. If the Office cannot obtain a suitable undertaking it may refer the issue to the Commission. The Commission must then reach a conclusion about the balance of the public interest arising from the practice and if it considers that it is adverse it may make remedial recommendations.

There have not been sufficient investigations so far to provide a basis for forming conclusions about the effectiveness of this new remedy. The topics have varied over a restricted distribution system adopted by the major UK bicycle manufacturer, the discounting practices of local newspaper which affected competition from free newspapers, cross-subsidisation of the showrooms of the London Electricity Board which allegedly induced unfair competition in the sale of electrical appliances, and the refusal of the Ford Motor Co. to grant licenses under their copyright to make replacement body parts.

PROFITS AND MARKET SHARE IN OLIGOPOLY

This Section draws on the results of a forthcoming monograph on *Profits and Stability of Monopoly* (C.U.P. for the National Institute of Economic and Social Research), the study was supported by a grant from the Office of Fair Trading.

An important by-product of the deliberations of the Commission and one of which industrial organisation economists have made insufficient use is the publication of data on such variables as market shares and profitability in a form superior to most other sources. The hypothesis of a positive association between these variables (ceteris paribus) has been extensively discussed and tested in the U.S. especially by Shepherd. He has argued that in a particular market firms with larger shares will not only have the benefit of technical economies but also pecuniary factors may help, up to a point, to reduce their costs. In addition larger market shares may contribute to the discipline required for price coordination. Consequently we may expect a positive (although not necessarily linear) relationship between profitability and market shares. Others have emphasised that any observed relationship rests essentially on efficiency and progressiveness rather than collusion, largely on the premise that competition will erode any significant market share that does not rest on low cost.[4,5]

In these studies while market share was estimated at approximately the correct level of aggregation profitability has generally been available only for the enterprise as a whole. For the largest enterprises profits will be generated for a diverse range of markets and the measured relationship between total profitability and a weighted average of market shares may therefore tend to obscure the fundamental association between individual market shares and profits. The central advantage, therefore, of using data from the Commission's reports is that these refer to markets narrowly defined. The main source was these reports but in a number of cases similar information from reports of the Price Commission was used. The market share data probably comes as close as is feasible in practice to the theoretical concept of a market. Similarly in many reports rates of return on capital are published which relate as strictly as possible to that part of the enterprise's activities under review. Even though the firm with the leading share may be part of a much larger organisation, the profit figures will relate only to the market concerned. For example, Unilever ranked ninth overall amongst U.K. quoted enterprises in the middle of the 1970s has leading shares in three of the markets in the sample – ice cream, detergents and frozen food – but market share and rate of return on capital figures are given individually for each case.

In both respects, therefore, profits and market share, the data are superior to those which have to be taken from the whole enterprise. There are also, however, a number of drawbacks. First, the markets investigated are a non-random sample where there is some ground for expecting possible abuses of market power, although the Commission itself must treat each reference to it in a neutral fashion. There is no presumption on its part that the firm or firms concerned are acting against the public interest. Nevertheless it remains true that, say, the degree of concentration in the markets referred is considerably higher than for industry generally. Secondly, and more serious, only relatively few reports are published each year. Consequently, although a substantial number of cases is available, the data relate to different years because of the timing of publication. In most of the analysis that follows, therefore, profitability is taken relative to that for manufacturing industry as a whole (the details are set out more fully below).

A third limitation follows directly from the second point. Many other factors, in addition to market share, may affect profitability. Much empirical research has been undertaken, for example, to explore the relationship between profitability and market concentration, product differentiation, productivity and trade levels (see in particular Notes 6 and 7). For the most part this work has been carried out at a level of aggregation (the three digit industry) which allows the simultaneous observation of a multivariate relationship, but which because of the breadth of most of the industries included, strays somewhat from the individual market. On the other hand, while the data on market shares and profitability from the Commission come close to what is ideally required, data on other variables which may affect the relationship are generally not available on a comparable basis. For this reason most of the subsequent analysis is bivariate rather than multivariate.

A fourth objection that may be raised against using the data to examine the question in hand is that since they come from an 'antitrust' source they are likely to be biased downwards. Firms in a prominent position in a particular market anticipating the close attention of the Office of Fair Trading can, on this view, take steps to disguise the true position by recording lower profits than actually earned in the hope that this will forestall an expensive inquiry. Although this possibility should be recognised, its practical impact is likely to be slight. The enterprises referred do not learn much in advance that they are being considered or which particular market of theirs may be involved. Also once an inquiry has commenced the financial analysis is carried out by the Commission's own accountants. It is reasonably well established that large, diversified firms have detailed and decentralised monitoring systems for their own internal purposes and much of the data published in the Commission's reports is probably derived from these records. The quality of the information is therefore likely to be as good as can be obtained both for market share and profitability.

Inclusion in the sample clearly required that sufficient information on market shares and profitability was published in the relevant report. Also we used the cut-off points of 1960–61 and 1980–81, so reports published in the early 1960s but referring to the late 1950s were not included. On this basis we were able to assemble data on 52 different products which for present purposes are treated as separate 'markets' although we are aware that in some instances the product is too narrowly defined and in others too widely defined to match the theoretical ideal. The three categories into which they were initially grouped were as follows: dominant firm, concentrated oligopoly and loose oligopoly. A complete list of the three groups is given in Profits and Stability of Monopoly. In the first category the leading firm had a market share of 50 percent or more and the second ranked firm had to have a share of less than half that of the market leader. This group, therefore, should conform fairly closely to the dominant firm model of economic theory where the market leader has considerable discretion in its pricing policies, although it may have to take due account of the likely outputs offered by fringe suppliers at various prices. The factors mentioned by Shepherd, especially the influence of market power should be at the strongest for members of this group. In the second category we have tried to include markets shared between two large firms so that opportunities for co-operation rather than conflict are most likely to produce high rates of return. The two leading firms had to share 50 percent or more of the market to qualify for this group. It also included cases where the market leader had more than half the market but where the second-ranked firm had a share more than half as great as the first. The market was thus much more akin to duopoly than the dominant firm case. Finally in group three we included the remaining cases where the two leading firms shared less than half the market and where frequently there was little difference between the market share of the leading 4 or 5 firms.

It is clear from the description of the three groups that our sample is taken from the more concentrated half of markets in manufacturing industry. There is no representation of markets where the largest 4 or 5 firms account for as little as one quarter or a third of the total. The bias stems from the source of most of the data. Nevertheless there is still sufficient differentiation in basic market structure for the relationship between profitability and market share to show up in the sample if it actually holds in practice. As Stigler remarks 'Almost every economist believes that an industry with 2 (and certainly with 5) firms behaves differently from a monopoly' (p. 217).[8]

To determine whether the firms in the three groups behave differently enough to produce distinct rates of profit we have had to relate the rates of return on capital (usually taken over five years) to a suitable base since, as we mentioned above, the profit figures refer to different periods depending on when the reports were published. The average rates of return earned by the leading firms in the three groups were expressed as a proportion of the average for quoted companies in manufacturing industry for the relevant period. We are thus implicitly assuming that whatever their market share, leading firms can respond equally to cyclical influences on general profitability.

To test the reliability of this procedure the following analysis was carried out. For the period 1972–1974 data were available for 42 firms compared with the 97 firms included in the full sample and covering the period 1960–1980. The former were treated as a control group. The simple regression of profitability on market share was then carried out for both groups. If there was little difference between the results for the two samples this would support the use of profit relatives as the dependent variable. On the other hand if the results were quite different this would suggest the profit relative was unreliable. In fact there was little difference in the results for both samples: the regression coefficients were of similar size, positive and significant at the 1 percent level. For more details see Profits and Stability of Monopoly.

Returning, therefore, to the market leaders in the three groups, their relative profits are set out in Table 5. We consider below the related question of whether there is the difference between profit rates for market leaders and market followers within each group.

The share of the market leaders in the first group was on average more than three quarters as high as those of the leaders in the second group, while the average market share of leaders in the third group was about two-thirds of those in the second group. The relative profitability figures in the third column of the table suggest that market leaders in the dominant firm group were able to earn, on average, profits about twice the level for quoted companies in manufacturing industry, while firms in the concentrated oligopoly group managed profits about one and a half times the industry average. Where oligopolistic interdependence may have been much less, in the third group, profits were only 16 percent above the manufacturing industry average. Using a standard analysis of variance test for differences between the mean profit relatives suggests that the differences were significant at the five percent level. The calculated value of F was [4.00] and the critical value of F with 2 and 46 degree of freedom is 3.20 at the 5 percent level. As noted in the table,

Table 5. Relative profitability of leading firms in three types of oligopoly.

Group	Number of markets	Average market share of leader (%)	Average profit[1] relative
Dominant firm	19[2]	72.9	2.03 (0.95)
Concentrated oligopoly	21	39.6	1.53 (0.68)
Loose oligopoly	9	26.1	1.16 (0.76)
Total	49	50.1	1.66 (0.86)

Notes: [1] Standard deviations in brackets
[2] Three extreme observations omitted from the table. The conclusion is confirmed if they are included.
Source: Profits and Stability of Monopoly, C.U.P. (forthcoming).

3 extreme observations were omitted from this calculation. However, if all three cases are included in the analysis of variance the result is an estimated F value of 4.81 with a critical value of F = 3.19 at the 5 percent level. The values given in the Table, however, seem to reflect more accurately the differences between the groups.

There is thus some support for the view that profitability and market share are directly related, at least as far as the market leaders are concerned, and if the more general characteristics of the oligopolistic market structure are taken into account. It suggests that a very large market share not only confers on the leader substantial economies of scale but also allows discretion over price. Where the market is shared more or less equally between two or three firms, as in group two, incomplete co-ordination of policies and intermittent intense rivalry may restrain profit levels, although these are still on average 50 percent or so above the 'normal' level. In the 'loose oligopoly' category for which we only have 9 cases, competition may be sufficiently acute to keep average profits closer to the normal level, although it should be remembered that members of this group are still firmly in the oligopoly class.

A related question and one which has recently been at the centre of a considerable amount of controversy, is whether the relatively high profits earned by leaders in concentrated markets also apply to firms with smaller market shares. In particular Demsetz[5] has argued that if collusion in oligopoly is really the explanation of observed correlations between profitability and concentration then firms with small market shares should also earn high profits, as their reward for tacit participation in co-operation policies that avoid competition. On the other hand, if the higher profits for the market leaders are due to their efficiency in production and ability in meeting consumer demands then smaller firms in the markets concerned should earn lower profits, because they are likely to be less efficient. Demsetz then presents some evidence from U.S. manufacturing industry which supports his contention and he added that his results also helped to explain the frequency observed positive association between profits or price cost margins and concentration in multivariate cross-section studies. In concentrated industries most of the profits earned will be by the larger firms. Consequently it is these profits that contribute to the positive association, but if they are really attributable to efficiency rather than collusion, the policy implications are quite different from those usually drawn. In particular any attempt at deconcentration (or possibly merger prevention) may sacrifice efficiency.

The influence of these conclusions on policy thinking, both in the U.S. and the U.K. has been considerable, despite the controversy they aroused. First, it was argued that his bivariate results must be set beside the considerably body of multivariate analysis for a number of countries which has been interpreted as giving support to the collusive hypothesis. Secondly, and more directly relevant to the present study Porter[9] has offered an alternative interpretation in terms of 'strategic group' within industries which may explain the observed differences between profit rates for different groups of firms of the same industry.

Unfortunately, the notion of a 'strategic group' within an industry seems very much to depend on how the industry is defined. The three digit industry level used by Porter in his analysis may be much too broad for our purposes with its focus on distinct, narrowly defined markets. One point that Porter makes, however, is relevant. He observes that 'my results show that in many industries the leading firms are not the most profitable at all' (p. 227) and that this is inconsistent with Demsetz's hypothesis.

The same point can be made about the UK data. In 21 of the markets in the sample, market share and profit data are given not only for the leaders but also for at least one other firm with a smaller share. In no less than 14 cases the profit relative of the market leader was below that of the smaller firm. The details of these cases are set out in Table 6.

In eight cases in the lower part of the table the firm with the highest profitability was ranked third or fourth according to market share. These cases, therefore, tend to go against the Demsetz view that high profits (in concentrated markets) are a reflection of efficiency due in part to scale economies, although in some cases like detergents, winding wires and rolls for rolling mills the market share the second ranked firm was so large (one third or more) that it is consistent with his view.

The hypothesis can be considered further by comparing the profit relatives of the market leaders with all firms in each oligopolistic group for which information is available. Although it can only be a partial test because of the composition of the sample, we should still expect a noticeable difference between the relative profitability of the market leaders and that of other firms, and some of which will have considerably smaller market shares, if Demsetz is correct. On the other hand, if some degree of collusion exists between firms in oligopoly, all firms should benefit and no difference in relative profitability should be observed between the market leaders and others.

The results of this comparison are set out in Table 7.

We have to confine the comparison to the second and third oligopoly groups only, since profit and market share data for firms other than the market leader are only available for two markets in the first group. Although the average market shares of non-market leaders in both

Table 6. Highest profit relatives in 21 markets.

Market	Firm	Market share (%)	Profit relative
A. Markets where the market leader had the highest profits			
Ice cream	Unilever	47.5	1.93
Cat and dog food	Pedigree Petfoods	50.3	3.11
Domestic gas appliances	Thorn	34.7	1.51
Bread	Rank, Hovis, McDougall	24.2	0.32
Frozen food	Unilever	33.5	1.22
Beer	Bass	20.0	1.01
Savoury snack foods	United Biscuits	30.0	1.58
B. Markets where a market 'follower' had the highest profits			
Flour	ABF	19.4 (3)[1]	2.95
Detergents	Proctor and Gamble	42.2 (2)	4.21
Meters	GEC	20.5 (4)	2.33
Winding wires	AEI	32.0 (2)	0.83
Electric lamps	GEC	20.5 (3)	1.65
Ceramic sanitary ware	Ideal Standard	18.5 (3)	1.74
Concrete roofing tiles	Sandtoft Tileries	8.1 (3)	3.72
Glass bottles	Redfearn National Glass	16.5 (3)	1.32
Rolls for rolling mills	Davy International	33.6 (3)	1.39
Cement	Rugby Portland	15.0 (3)	1.73
Industrial gases	Air Products	20.0 (2)	1.60
General wiring cable	AEI	6.6 (4)	1.65
Ready mixed concrete	Pioneer Concrete	9.7 (3)	2.92
Petrol distribution	Esso	19.0 (2)	0.73

[1] The figures in brackets give the market share rank of the company cited, according to the Commission's reports.
Source: As Table 5.

groups were much smaller than those of the market leaders, there was very little difference between their relative profitabilities. For the 13 market leaders in the concentrated oligopoly group the average profit relative was 1.55 compared with 1.36 for the 26 non-market leaders. In the loose oligopoly group the market leaders average profit relative was 1.07 compared with 0.94 for other firms in the group. The difference in both cases was about 14 percent and is in the direction that Demstz predicts: market leaders earn more, on average, than smaller firms operating in the same market. Neither of the differences is, however, statistically significant.

On the other hand, supporters of the conventional view that all firms in oligopoly enjoy higher prices because of collusion could argue that the differences observed in Table 7 are so slight as to support their contention. If leading firms owe their higher profits mainly to efficiency

Table 7. Relative profitability of leading firms and other firms in two types of oligopoly.

Group	Number of firms	Average market share (%)	Average profit relative
Concentrated			
Oligopoly: market leader	13	38.1	1.55 (0.79)[1]
Others	26	21.1	1.36 (1.00)
Loose			
Oligopoly: market leader	6	27.3	1.07 (0.85)
Others	14[2]	11.7	0.94 (0.96)

[1] Standard deviations in brackets
[2] Three firms with market shares of under 4 percent in the ready mixed concrete market were not included. The conclusion is reinforced if they are.
Source: As Table 5.

compared with smaller firms in their markets then there should be no difference between the relative profitability of the non-market leaders in both groups, yet non-leaders in the concentrated oligopoly group earned relative profits 45 percent higher than non-leaders in the loose oligopoly group. (1.36 against 0.94). Furthermore, since the average market share of non-leaders in the concentrated oligopoly group is not much less than that of the leaders in the loose oligopoly group they might be expected to earn similar profits. In fact, however, as Table 7 shows, relative profits for the former group are 27 percent higher (i.e., 1.36 compared with 1.07) than the latter group, although the difference is not significant.

The analysis of the market share and profitability data suggests, therefore, that oligopoly type has a positive effect on relative profits, at least for the market leaders. Very often, however, firms ranked second or third by market share earn higher returns than the market leader. This point, together with some evidence (in Table 7) that there are comparatively slight profitability differences between market leaders and others within oligopolistic groups, tends to work against the Demsetz view.

PROFITABILITY, BARRIERS TO ENTRY AND PRICING BEHAVIOUR

In this section of the paper we present our analysis of the Commission's reports to test two hypotheses about dominant firms. The first links back to the data presented above, and examines whether the differences in the number and nature of entry barriers provide an explanation of the differences in market structure and profitability in the three groups. Then, the Commission's descriptions of pricing behaviour are used to see to what extent collusion was present in each type of structure, and whether this explains differences in relative profitability. Before setting out the findings three points should be made about the quality of the information. First, although the structure of the investigations is determined by the legislation, each is independent as the Commission is not bound by precedent. The members are required to base their judgements on what they find in each market, hence it is reasonable to suggest that there is no major serial correlation in the conclusions. Second, the accuracy of the information is not in doubt. When the Commission has prepared its first draft of the descriptive material this is sent to those who provide information to verify its accuracy. Also, the report is published, and there have been no subsequent claims that facts on which conclusions were based were wrong.

Finally, although the objectivity of the enquiry process and quality of the data cannot be challenged, a valid point is that the reports do not publish all the information collected and this may make subsequent interpretation difficult. This has to be accepted. While the Commission's reports are designed to contain sufficient material to support its conclusions, the extent to which they do varies. To use them later, and for another purpose inevitably means that interpretations contain elements of personal judgement. This caveat applies to what follows.

Barriers to entry

For this analysis we defined 5 types of barriers. They were technical, legal, price, distribution, and 'other'. 'Technical' comprised substantial economies of scale, production based vertical integration, and large capital requirements by then current standards. An example occurs in the production of zinc carbon batteries where the Tanfield Lea plant owned by Ever Ready was large enough to supply the whole of the UK market as well as support a substantial export trade.[10] Legal barriers were either patents, high effective tariffs, or an enforceable contract which prevented entry, for example collulosic fibres where there was a high effective tariff.[11] Pricing barriers covered a range of behaviour, and included 'loyalty' discounts, 'special' prices to very large customers, for example the Rank Xerox sale of plain paper copiers to the government owned Stationery Office[12] or the free supply of the tranquilisers Librium and Valium by Hoffman La Roche to National Health Service hospitals.[13]

Distribution barriers were of two main forms. There were requirements imposed by the manufacturer or suppliers to restrict access to the distribution chain; for example wholesalers of replacement clutch mechanisms for motor vehicles could not stock supplies from other than the dominant firm, Automotive Products.[14] The second barrier was advertising, it being generally difficult for new entrants to heavily advertised consumer goods markets to get entry to the distribution system unless their products were also advertised, as in the household detergents market.[15] The 'other' category embraced barriers not included above. An example was 'rental only' contracts, with the user not having an option to purchase, as in the supply of shoe making machinery.[16] Tying arrangements were included in 'other', for example Rank Xerox tying the supply of 'toner' to machines and paper.

After barriers were classified by type, they were then assessed according to their deterrent effect into 'high', 'medium' or 'low'. The basis for this was the weight which they appeared to have in the Commission's conclusions on the public interest. Necessarily, this classification exercise involved some judgement on our part, as frequently the Commission did not attempt to assess the relative deterrent effect of the barriers which it identified. To avoid influencing each other we made separate assessments, and then compared our views. There was substantial agreement between us on the subjective measurement of the deterrent effect of the barriers. The results of the classification of barriers appears in Table 8. This analysis suggests that there are differences in the barriers which might partially explain the variations in structure and relative profitability.

Table 8. Entry barriers and market structure.

Barrier	Dominant firms				Concentrated oligopoly				Loose oligopoly				Grand total
	Hi	Me	Lo	To	Hi	Me	Lo	To	Hi	Me	Lo	To	
Technical	7	2	1	10	1	5	1	7	0	3	0	3	20
Legal	5	2	2	9	0	2	0	2	2	0	1	3	14
Price	7	6	1	14	3	5	0	8	1	2	0	3	25
Distribution	4	3	0	7	4	3	1	8	3	3	0	6	21
Other	7	6	1	14	6	6	1	13	0	1	1	0	28
Total	30	19	5	54	14	20	3	37	6	9	1	16	108
Number of markets		20				21						9	50

Note: The match market and rolls for roll making are not included in the dominant firm group as the reports on the proposed mergers did not provide information on barriers.
Source: Monopolies Commission and Price Commission Reports

In the dominant firm group there were, on average, more barriers in each market, 2.7 compared with 1.8 for each of the other two. The barriers in the dominant firm group were also different in two ways. There was a greater proportion, 56 percent, classified as high, compared with 38 percent for the concentrated and loose oligopoly groups. The proportion classified as technical and legal was 35 percent, compared with 24 percent for the concentrated oligopoly group, and 38 percent for the loose oligopoly group. This latter may be higher because of the small sample.

Table 9 lists the markets in the dominant firm group with high barriers. Apart from flat glass, all the markets had at least one other barrier classified as high. Industrial gases had most; in addition to the economies of scale there were high import duties on gas producing plant, the British Oxygen Company had been able to control the supply of plant to potential competitors, and had concealed its ownership of a 'fighting company' used to make selective price reductions for gas against competitors. The data suggests that firms may not find it sufficient to rely on technical and legal barriers to preserve market power. In themselves, these may not be powerful enough to exclude determined entrants. Thus, even if the technical barriers indicate a dimension of efficiency, other barriers may be needed before it can be exploited.

The date of Table 8 also suggests a conclusion of relevance to a criticism often made about UK competition policy; that the remedies have concentrated on altering behaviour rather than seeking structural change. The fact was that two thirds of the barriers were behavioural. In respect of these the differences between the groups were not so marked. There was an average of 1.8 behavioural barriers in the dominant firm group, compared with 1.4 and 1.1 for the oligopoly groups, and the proportions of these classified as high were 51, 45 and 40 percent respectively.

Given that 'structural' solutions would have involved the sacrifice of economies of scale, selective changes in trade policy, and interference with intellectual property rights, antitrust remedies in these directions would have been much more difficult to achieve even had the Commission been prepared to recommend them. The fact that it did not suggests that it was thought the 'trade off' might represent too great a loss of economic efficiency. The major problem was behavioural, and the legislation has been effective enough to bring important modifications in this respect.

Price behaviour

An analysis of price behaviour is a central feature of the Commission's investigations, as it can be an important indicator of the nature and

Table 9. Dominant firm group: markets with high barriers.

Technical	Legal	Price	Distribution	Other
Zinc carbon batteries	Cellulosic fibres	Plain paper copiers	Contraceptive sheaths	Zinc carbon batteries
Cement	Industrial gases	Plasterboard	Zinc carbon batteries	Plasterboard
Flat glass	Plain paper copiers (Rank Xerox)	Contraceptive sheaths	Clutch mechanisms	Colour film
Contraceptive sheaths	Librium and Valium	Colour film	Colour film	Librium and Valium
Clutch mechanisms	Cigarette filter rods	Librium and Valium		Cellulosic fibres
Cellulosic fibres		Industrial gases		Industrial gases
Industrial gases		Cement		Breakfast cereals

Source: Monopolies Commission and Price Commission Reports.

intensity of competition, often through the structure of prices, and particularly in the resulting levels of profits. Our primary objective in analysing the examinations of price behaviour was to determine the extent to which collusion, open or hidden, had been present in the three types of market structure, and might be a contributory explanation of the associated relative profitability.

Defining and detecting collusion presents considerable difficulties. Frequently, when complaints are investigated the most likely explanation turns out to be parallel behaviour based on a desire not to compete. The incidence of firms getting together to successfully co-ordinate positive actions to achieve a given end such as establishing a level of prices or eliminating a competitor is relatively rare. Experience suggests that many attempts to collude fail as soon as the agreement is tested because of a divergence of interest.

For our purposes we defined collusion as behaviour which would be caught by the cartel legislation, and although this does not eliminate all the uncertainties there is a well established framework which can be used. The legislation is contained in the Restrictive Trade Practices Act 1976 which requires, subject to specified exceptions, that all written or oral agreements or arrangements, whether enforceable or not, under which two or more parties accept restrictions on their freedom to compete, be registered with the Office of Fair Trading. The most frequent types of behaviour which were caught by this legislation were price fixing, market sharing, collusive tendering, control of entry, and the collective enforcement of agreements. Such agreements or arrangements are presumed to be against the public interest, but the parties may rebut the presumption by pleading specified defences. Few have succeeded in doing so.

Establishing hidden collusion is universally one of the greatest anti-trust obstacles. However, in a monopoly enquiry neither the procedures or the vigour with which the issue is pursued are deficient, and it is reasonable to believe that collusive behaviour which results from registerable agreements and understandings between suppliers is revealed.

As it was known that the incidence of such collusion shown in the reports was not high, the secondary objective was to see whether there were any particular types of behaviour which might be associated with the different market structures. Given the recent history of the abolition of cartels which covered about 50 percent of manufacturing industry, a long merger boom, and an unprecedented growth in industrial concentration two other types of non competitive behaviour suggest themselves as being likely to occur. They are price leadership, and oligopolistic interdependence.

These two categories were used in the analysis which follows. Classification was based on the Commission's description of price behaviour, and generally this was quite clear; where it thought there was price leadership it said so, as for example in the breakfast cereals, wire ropes, and zinc carbon battery markets.

Price leadership is usually taken to mean that one firm is accepted by the remainder of the industry as being the best judge of, for example, the need for and timing of price increases. However, in a number of the markets in the dominant firm group this concept lost some clarity where the 'monopolist' was overwhelmingly dominant, and other suppliers might be regarded as residual, as in the cellulosic fibre market (Courtauld), and plasterboard (British Plasterboard Ltd.) Where this was so we defined the pricing behaviour as monopoly supply. Where dominance in that sense did not exist, the behaviour was classified as either dominant price leadership, where because of the market structure the supplier was able to dictate terms and conditions, or simply as price leadership where the reactions of competitors had to be taken more into account. We have used the term 'oligopolistic interdependence' to cover the more fluid type of behaviour where the leading suppliers were more equally matched and no clear leadership pattern had been established, yet the firms were acutely conscious of the effects of their pricing decisions on other suppliers. The household detergent market was an example, in describing behaviour the Commission said the companies wanted 'to avoid the appearance of price competition'.

Pricing behaviour in the dominant firm group

The price behaviour in this group of markets has been classified as shown in Table 10.

The two markets where collusion took place were cement, and diazo copying materials. In the former there is a cartel which has obtained clearance under the legislation; in the second the Commission's investigation

Table 10. Dominant firm pricing.

Type	Number of markets
Collusion	2
Monopoly supplier (greater than 90%)	3
Dominant price leadership	11
Competitive	4
	20

Source: Monopolies and Price Commission reports 1960–1981.

revealed hidden agreements on prices and discounts. In the flat glass industry there was minor collusion between the dominant firm and other European suppliers on discounts in a sector of the market, but this was not classified as collusion as the predominant behaviour was that of monopoly supplier. There was also an intermittent exchange on discounts in the wire rope market, but the main form of behaviour was price leadership. Hence, with these exceptions, the incidence of collusion which might influence price and profit levels was low.

The three markets classified as monopoly supply were cellulosic fibres, plasterboard, and contraceptive sheaths. In the latter the Commission found the monopoly, the level of prices, and the level of profits to be against the public interest, as were a number of practices, such as price discrimination, but did not make an adverse finding on price or profit levels. The adverse findings in plasterboard concerned aspects of the distribution system, and the uniform delivered prices.

The most common form of behaviour in this group was dominant price leadership. Table 11 sets out the 11 markets in which it occurred, and the Commission's public interest findings on the levels of prices and/or profits.

In none of these was the practice of price leadership found to be against the public interest, but in 4 there were adverse findings on these two aspects of performance, and in breakfast cereals the Commission thought that it was possible that profits could become excessive in the future. There were also other adverse findings on conduct, but these are not reported here.

The existence of 4 markets where price behaviour was competitive suggests that it would be wrong always to equate concentrated markets

Table 11. Markets with dominant price leadership, and the Commission's findings on price and profit levels.

Market	Public interest findings on
Plain paper copier	Not against public interest
Breakfast cereals	Might be against in future
Zinc carbon batteries	Not against
Mercury batteries	Against
Wire ropes	Not against
Flat glass	Not against
Clutch mechanisms	Against
Industrial gases	Not against
Colour film	Against
Librium and Valium	Against
Wallpaper (limited to specified distribution practices)	

with an absence of competition. Notwithstanding the presence of high entry barriers there is sometimes countervailing power, in some markets the monopoly supplier may fail to keep up with the dynamic aspects of demand, or the profit potential may be sufficient to attract a powerful new entrant.

In the general line and open top metal can markets foreign direct investment resulted in the emergence of competition; in the safety glass market own manufacture and countervailing power restrained prices to competitive levels, and in cigarette filter rods imports from an international market strengthened the buying power of the tobacco companies so that UK prices were considered to be competitively determined.

This classification of structure and price behaviour provides an insight into one aspect of the virtual abolition of cartels. In 9 of the 20 markets there were cartels in existence when the 1956 Restrictive Trade Practices Act became operative. In cement the manufacturers were able to persuade the Restrictive Practices Court that the cartel should continue, and in the diazo market the manufacturers continued to secretly collude, but in the narrower area of discounts. Of the remaining 7, cellulosic fibres was classified as a monopoly supplier, in 5 markets dominant price leadership was established after agreements were abandoned, and in safety glass prices were determined by competition.

Pricing behaviour in the concentrated oligopoly group

Table 12 contains the classification of pricing behaviour in this group.

There was a higher incidence of collusion compared with the dominant firm group, and there had also been a higher incidence of cartels before 1956, 12 in the 21 markets. The 4 markets where collusion was discovered illustrate a spectrum of motives for doing so. In the first two the collusion was on the determination of price levels. In the flour for breadmaking market the operation of government imposed price control made it virtually impossible for the suppliers to avoid agreeing the timing and

Table 12. Concentrated oligopoly group pricing.

Type	Number
Collusion	4
Price leadership	8
Oligopolistic interdependence	6
Competitive	3
	21

Source: Monopolies Commission and Price Commission reports 1960–1981.

amounts of price increases. In the telephone cable market the investigation resulted in the disclosure of a secret collusive tendering arrangement for supply to the Post Office. The four suppliers agreed prices so that contracts were rotated. The Post Office subsequently obtained repayment of £9m to compensate for excessive prices.

Collusion amongst suppliers when faced with a powerful buyer also occurred in the domestic gas appliance market. The publicly owned British Gas Corporation was almost the sole retailer, and as a response to its use of that power the manufacturers colluded in a number of ways, principally to limit the level of discounts. (The monopoly was declared to be against the public interest).

Cartels had characterised much of the earlier history of the electric lamp industry, but the post 1956 arrangements were not as wide ranging or as formal. There was no agreement on prices, the suppliers exchanged information on customer purchases, discounts, and the timing and amount of price changes. These were probably intended to remove some of the uncertainties which developed after formal collusion was no longer possible.

Again, in contrast to the dominant firm group, there were fewer adverse findings on prices and profit levels, in only 2 markets out of 11.

Table 13. Markets with price leadership and oligopolistic interdependence with the Commission's findings on price and profit levels.

Price leadership	Public interest findings on price and profit levels
Electric supply meters	Not against
Glucose	Not against
Winding wires	Not against
Building bricks	Not against
Cat and dog food	Not against
Supertension cable	Not against
Fibre cordage	Not against
Biscuits (merger not against public interest)	
Oligopolistic interdependence	
Ice cream	Not against
Household detergents	Against
Ceramic sanitaryware	Not against
Concrete roofing tiles	Against
Glass bottles (Price Commission, and MMC merger investigation)	
Rolls for rolling mills (MMC merger investigation)	

Source: Monopolies Commission and Price Commission reports 1960–1981. Again, in contrast to the dominant firm group, there were fewer adverse findings on prices and profit levels, in only 2 markets out of 11.

The 3 markets in which the Commission thought prices were competitively determined were footwear machinery, asbestos goods, and savoury snack foods. In footwear machinery it was accepted that the industry was competitive. The asbestos market was different in that competition came from the other suppliers while the major supplier was steadily losing market share. The savoury snack food market, although concentrated, was growing rapidly and the existing suppliers were attempting to increase their shares by price and product competition.

In 12 of the 21 markets there were cartels before 1956. Their history is that in 3 some forms of collusion persisted, there were flour, electric lamps and telephone cables, in 5 price leadership emerged, i.e., electric supply meters, winding wires, fibre cordage, biscuits and supertension cable; in 3 there was oligopolistic interdependence, these were ceramic sanitaryware, glass bottles, and rolls for rolling mills. The market which became competitive was asbestos.

Pricing behaviour in loose oligopoly markets

In this group of markets the price behaviour was:

Table 14.

Behaviour	Number
Collusion	1
Dominant firm pricing	1
Price leadership	3
Competitive	4
	9

Source: Monopolies Commission and Price Commission reports 1960–1981.

In only one of these nine markets did enquiry reveal collusion, that was in the bread market. This was not surprising, as the main suppliers were vertically integrated from the flour milling to bread baking, and price control, to be effective, had also to encompass flour prices. In return for low prices and profits on bread the suppliers were allowed to take high profits on flour.

While there was only one market where the price behaviour was collusive, the reference to the Commission of ready mixed concrete arose because some years prior to it an extensive series of local secret collusive tendering arrangements had been uncovered. These had included the major suppliers. Discovery led to the abandonment of the practice, and at the time of the Commission's investigation the pricing was considered to be competitive.

The market with dominant firm pricing was high quality china where the major supplier, Royal Doulton, through product differentiation had been able to price independently of competitors. Price leadership had emerged in two markets with cartels before 1956, general winding cables, and main cables, the price leader being the same supplier, British Insulated Callender Cables. The other case of price leadership was in frozen foods, but as a relatively new and high growth industry, there were no known cartels in the immediate postwar period. The same was broadly true of ready mixed concrete. In addition to ready mixed concrete, the price competitive markets were beer, petrol wholesaling, and starch.

Although other aspects of conduct were found to be against the public interest in these 9 markets such as the discount structure of the principal frozen food supplier, there were no adverse findings on price and profit levels.

Conclusions on price behaviour

The analyses of price behaviour were done to test the hypothesis that concentrated market structures facilitate collusion on prices, and the reward for this is high relative profitability. To bring out the conclusions more clearly the classification of the price behaviour is summarised as follows;

Table 15. Pricing behaviour and profitability in alternate market structure.

Behaviour	Market structure				
	Dominant firm	Concentrated oligopoly	Loose oligopoly	Average relative profit	Number
Collusion	2	4	1	1.35	7
Dominant firm/ price leadership	14	8	4	2.09	26
Oligopolistic interdependence	–	6	–	1.57	6
Competitive	4	3	4	1.76	11
Number	20	21	9	1.85	50
With cartels at 1956	9	12	4	–	25

It seems reasonably clear from this table that collusion cannot be a major explanation of high relative profits in these 50 markets. Although there were half with formal cartels with more or less established patterns of industry co-operation at 1956, apart from cement, in only 6 markets had concealed collusion survived, or been revived, and in only 2 of these was there well established arrangements on prices, (diazo copying materials, and telephone cables).

There were some results from collusion, an average elevation of profits by 35% compared with the average for manufacturing industry. However, on the basis of the data any of the other 3 strategies would have been more rewarding, but a qualification must be made. The high average relative profits in the markets classified as price competitive are affected by 3 very high returns; on safety glass, cigarettes filter rods, and ready mixed concrete. Even if the competitive returns are ignored, the data strongly suggest that dominant firm pricing, and price leadership, the behaviour characteristic of concentrated market structures, bring greater rewards in terms of profitability.

CONCLUSION

It has been the dual purpose of this paper to give first, an up-to-date account of how UK competition policy has evolved in response to changes in industrial structure, and secondly to use the considerable body of data assembled by the Commission in an analysis of oligopolistic price behaviour and profit performance, and the underlying entry barriers.

The Commission, with 28 years experience of investigating competition questions has evolved a comprehensive economic framework which puts flesh on the 'public interest' guidelines by which the structure, conduct and performance of markets shaped by dominant firms is judged. Major restrictions on competition especially barriers to entry are likely to be judged adverse, but a flexible view is taken of high profits with due allowance being made for efficiency and risk.

Partly in recognition of the intractable nature of structural remedies imposed on dominant firms and the inefficiencies and losses of scale economies that might result, UK merger policy has developed in such a way that it must now be very doubtful whether any substantial horizontal merger which would create a new position of dominance would be allowed. In contrast, conglomerate mergers are unlikely to encounter much official resistance.

An important conclusion from the empirical analysis, however, is that conduct remedies which are much more accessible to competition policy may be more effective than is often suggested. The study of the sample of oligopolistic markets certainly indicated that leading firms with a dominant market share could earn profits substantially above the manufacturing industry average. Part of the explanation for this was the extent and variety of entry barriers that such firms could erect. But when these entry barriers were more closely analysed it was evident that they depended in relatively few cases on technical economies of scale. In most instances they were derived from a combination of legal, pricing or distributional factors. Furthermore, effective collusion between firms in most markets had not proved possible, even though about half of the sample was taken from a section of industry most prone to collusion and where it had been common prior to the 1956 Restrictive Practices Act. Taken together, therefore, these points suggest that the kinds of market conduct remedies recommended in Commission reports and usually taken up subsequently by the Office of Fair Trading, are likely to have a considerable impact. Although it is probable that firms will seek the same result by a different form of restriction, presumably these will be less effective and weaker than their predecessors. Their impact on market performance is thus likely to be less and less detrimental as the policy matures.

NOTES

1. A Review of Monopolies and Mergers – A Consultative Document. Cmnd 7198 HMSO, London 1978, and Press Statement, 5 July 1984, Department of Trade and Industry.
2. Cmnd 7198 Appendix Table 6.
3. S & W Beresford and the British Sugar Corporation, HC 241, 1980–81. HMSO, London.
4. Brozen, Y., *Concentration, Mergers and Public Policy*, Macmillan Publishing, New York (1982).
5. Demsetz, H., 'Industry Structure, Market Rivalry and Public Policy', *Journal of Law and Economics* (1973).
6. Comonor, W. S. and Wilson, T. A., *Advertising and Market Power*, Harvard University Press (1974).
7. Hart, P. E. and Clarke, R., *Concentration in British Industry 1935–75*, Cambridge University Press (1980).
8. Stigler, G. J., *The Theory of Price*, Collier-Macmillan (1966).
9. Porter, M. E., 'The Structure within Industries and Companies Performance', *Review of Economics and Statistics* (1979).
10. The Supply of Primary Batteries, HCl, 1974–75, HMSO, London.
11. The Supply of Man-Made Cellulosic Fibres, HC 263, 1967–68, HMSO, London.
12. The Supply of Indirect Electrostatic Reprographic Equipment, HC 47, 1976–77, HMSO, London.

13. The Supply of Chlordiazepoxide and Diazepam, HC 197, 1972–73, HMSO, London.
14. The Supply of Clutch Mechanisma for Road Vehicles, HC 32, 1968–69, HMSO, London.
15. The Supply of Household Detergents; HC 105, 1966–67, HMSO, London.
16. The Supply and Export of Machinery for the Manufacture of Footwear, HC 215, 1972–73, HMSO, London.

11. THE TREATMENT OF DOMINANCE IN GERMAN ANTITRUST POLICY

Erhard Kantzenbach

In their invitation to this conference, Professor de Jong and Professor Shepherd have emphasized, that 'the field of industrial organization has undergone large changes in recent years, with new concepts and research methods and with major changes in policies toward business occurring in many countries'. Indeed, if we look to the United States we notice fundamental changes in the theory of industrial economics as well as in the practical antitrust policy. Chicago microeconomists have caused a revolution, which is comparable with that one of their macroeconomic colleagues and it seems to be worth while to see, what influences this revolution had on the theory and policy in Europe and Japan.

According to the schedule of our hosts it is my task, to talk about the developments in antitrust policies, including the treatment of dominance. And, as three distinguished colleagues from Italy, the UK and the US will share this task with me, I can concentrate my attention on the development in my home country, West Germany.

Let me begin with a general statement. It seems to me, that, although the changes in the American industrial organization theory and antitrust policy have raised much attention under German academic lawyers and economists, its influence on practical competition policy until now has been very small. The development of the German competition law by the legislature and by the courts followed its own patterns. And as a result of the fact, that the American policy changed during recent years from rather rigorous law enforcement to a more laissez-faire-approach, the German policy seemed to be much more tolerant before this change and now it seems to be much more rigorous than the American one.

In the following I shall try to illustrate the German competition policy and its recent development by discussing some of its aspects, which seem to me are most important for its undestanding. As most participants of this conference are probably quite familiar with the basic concept and the

de Jong, H. W., Shepherd, W. G. (eds) Mainstreams in Industrial Organization
 ISBN 978-94-017-0495-3

development of the American antitrust policy, I shall use these as a yardstick.

First I shall give a short outline of the German law against restraints of competition and the experiences which led to the major amendment in 1974.

Secondly I shall describe the German merger control, which was enacted in that amendment and I shall draw some comparisons to the American merger control.

Thirdly I shall make some remarks about the main critics of the German competition policy, which are put forward by members of the so called Neo-Austrian School.

As you will notice, this is a rather comprehensive program. I, therefore, have to restrict myself to few main remarks at each point. I shall be glad to elaborate some of these ideas in the following discussion, if you ask me to do so.

I. THE BASIC CONCEPT OF THE GERMAN COMPETITION POLICY UNTIL 1974

(1) At the beginning I should like to call your attention to a fundamental difference in the basic philosophy of the American antitrust law on one side and the British and French competition law on the other side.

The *American law* is based on the general assumption, that *free competition is in the public interest*. Therefore the general purpose of the antitrust laws is to inhibit any kind of restraints of competition. This may be done by per se prohibition of certain market behaviour. With respect to other kinds of behaviour the rule of reason may be applied. But even in the latter cases there is no room for balancing the goal of free competition against possibly conflicting policy goals as the promotion of exports or employment for example. The rule of reason is only applied to the question, whether or not a certain market behavior has under the given circumstances restrictive effects.

I understand, that the basic assumptions, on which *the British and the French competition laws* are based, are fundamentally different. According to them *competition is basically neutral*. It may be in the public interest or it may be against it, due to the special circumstances. Therefore cartels, mergers or other types of restraints of competition are judged with respect to their expected economic effect, whether they are expected to promote employment, innovations or international competitiveness or to have negative effects on the supply situation of the consumer.

With respect to this basic question *the German law follows the American pattern.*[1] This is already expressed in its name: 'Act against Restraints of Competition'. Under this law, the Federal Cartel Office has the only authority to inhibit different types of restraints of competition, which are enumerated in the law. It does not have the power to balance these against competing economic or social goals. Only two exemptions of this principle exist in Section 8 and Section 24. Under certain circumstances it is possible to permit, because of public interest, cartels and mergers, which are forbidden under other provisions of the law. But the power to these exceptional permissions is given to the Minister of Economic Affairs (Sect. 8 and 24 III) as the political institution, not to the Federal Cartel Office with its semijudicial functions.

(2) The German Act against Restraints of Competition was passed in 1957 after several years of rigorous political discussions. Its main provisions were:

– a general prohibition of cartel agreements in Section 1 and
– a prohibition of abusive practices by market dominating enterprises in Section 22.

The general prohibition of *cartel agreements* is similar to Section 1 Sherman Act. But, contrary to the American law, several types of minor cartel agreements are enumerated in the law, which may be permitted under special conditions. Those are especially agreements concerning general terms of business, rebates and standards (Sect. 2, 3 and 5). Only under very restrictive conditions, if substantial competition continues to exist, agreements concerning prices and supply restrictions may be permitted (Sect. 4, 5, 5a and 5e). These exemptions from the general prohibition of cartels have been criticized by some lawyers and economists. My personal opinion of this matter is, that these loose agreements do not have much influence on the overall economic performance.

With respect to *market dominating enterprises* the Cartel Office was only given the authority to control their market behaviour and prohibit any kind of abusive practices. Under the second amendment of the law in 1974 there existed no merger control in the German law and until now it is not possible to dissolve market dominating firms.

The Federal Cartel Office used its power to control the market behaviour of dominant firms mainly in two ways:

– On one hand, it intervened against the horizontal abuse of market power against competitors.

– On the other hand it inhibited, that firms abuse their market power vertically against their customers by raising prices above the competitive level.[2]

If we compare it with the formal system of the American law, we find two very different approaches in this one provision. The first one can be compared with the prohibition of monopolizing in Section 2 Sherman Act, although the possible interventions are much more limited. The second kind implies a control of market performance, which is not at all known in the American antitrust law. It can be compared only with the price regulation of American public utilities. But there is the main difference, that the price control of dominant firms in Germany is limited to cases in which the cartel authority presumes abusive practices.

During the last ten years we have had some cases of both types, which were brought to the Federal Court of Appeal (Bundesgerichtshof). The experience was, that while the cases of horizontal abuse of market power could be solved rather satisfactorily, the vertical cases raised many problems. It appeared to be extremely difficult to determine a price level, which would have been the result of competition without market domination and which therefore was not abusive.[3]

(3) One main experience with this law was, that the provisions against cartels and those against dominating firms seemed not to be well balanced There was a contradiction in the fact, that the rather loose organizational form of restraining competition – the cartel agreement – was hit by an outright prohibition, while the much more stable form – the dominant single firm – was only subject to a behavioral control. Probably it was this unequal treatment of alternative ways to restrain competition, which contributed much to the strong concentration process during the sixties.

In 1974 the second and most important *amendment of the law* was put into effect. It tried to reduce the unbalance, which I mentioned, by two provisions:

– First it *expanded the possibilities for cartel agreements* between small and medium size firms, in order to give them better chances for competing big firms (Sect. 5b).

– And secondly it *established a merger control*, in which all mergers are prohibited, which are expected to create or strengthen market dominating positions (Sect. 24).

The model for this merger control was Section 7 Clayton Act, although the criteria for intervention are slightly different. Today one may say, that the merger control has become the most important provision of the law and it employs a large share of the Cartel Offices' resources.

II. MARKET DOMINATION AS INTERVENTION CRITERION OF THE MERGER CONTROL

(4) Together with the introduction of the merger control in 1974 the *legal criteria for a market dominating position* were newly defined. The new criterion now has a double function. It served as the intervention threshold for the already existing control of market behaviour and it became the intervention threshold for the newly introduced merger control.

Since 1974 dominant firms according to Section 22 were not only those which have 'no competitors' or were 'not exposed to any substantial competition'. In addition those firms were included, which had 'a paramount market position in relation to their competitors'. In addition the law enumerates some structural criteria, by which a paramount market position can be identified. Those are 'its share of the markets, its financial strength, its access to the supply or sales markets for goods and services, its links with other firms and the legal or actual barriers to the market entry'.

Furthermore the law provides legal presumptions for market domination of a single firm, if its market share exceeds one third and for oligopolies, if the market share of the biggest three or five exceeds one half or two thirds respectively. These presumptions should make it easier for the Cartel Office to submit the proper evidence to the Courts.

(a) Horizontal mergers

(5) If we compare the German merger control with the American one according to Section 7 Clayton Act we find, that *at the time of its introduction it was probably less severe.* This is certainly true, if we restrict the comparison to horizontal mergers and if we accept the merger guidelines of the US-Department of Justice of 1968 as a yardstick. In these guidelines the critical market share for merging firms were between 8 and 12%. The corresponding German criteria were much higher.

But the 1968 merger guidelines have never been fully accepted by the courts and meanwhile they have been replaced by the new guidelines of 1982 and 1984. As you will know, the new guidelines replaced the concentration ratios by Herfindahl indices and placed the critical values between 1000 and 1800. A simple conversion of Herfindahl indices into concentration ratios of course is impossible. Yet a rough comparison is possible and it was done by Schmidt and Ries.[4] These calculations show, that the critical indices of the new merger guidelines are under realistic assumptions in the neighbourhood of the German critical concentration ratios.

(6) But another aspect has to be taken into account until we can draw any conclusions from this comparisons. It is obvious, that concentration measures can only be compared *if the product markets are equally defined.* We can assume, that this has been the case before the new merger guidelines were issued. American and German authorities defined the product markets rather narrowly and included only such competitors, who actually supplied the product.

This method had been changed in the new merger guidelines. Now potential competitors are also included in the market. The relevant criterion is the expectation, that the potential competitor would enter the relevant product market if the price level would rise by 5%. It is obvious, that this kind of measurement will lead to much lower concentration figures, no matter what indices are used. If we take this fact into account, we come to the conclusion, that today the German merger control with respect to horizontal mergers is much more rigorous than the present American one.

What strikes Continental Europeans, who are used to a different legal system, most, is the fact, that this fundamental change of the American antitrust policy took place without any action of the American legislative bodies and without any change of the law. This would be absolutely impossible under our system of law.

(7) Generally I have much sympathy for the new approach of the US-Justice Department in defining the relevant market. The traditional way very easily leads one to overlook important competitive forces. Recent developments in economic theory as well as the investigation of antitrust cases lead to the conclusion, that potential competition may have stronger influences on the market performance than the concentration of actual competitors of that single product market. To some extent these influences are more easily taken into consideration, if the relevant market by definition includes potential competitors.

But on the other hand, I have some doubts, whether this new concept will always lead to satisfactory results:

– At first, it seems rather difficult to me to estimate, which firms would enter a relevant market, if the price level of that market would rise by a certain percentage. This is especially so, in the most common cases, where the potential competitor has to undertake irreversible investments when he enters the market and at the same time does not know, what kind of price strategy the incumbent firm will undertake as reaction. So the new critical concentration indices rest on less solid ground, than the old ones.

– Secondly, actual and potential competitors are evaluated equally. In extreme cases the new procedure may lead to the result, that the critical Herfindahl index is not reached, although there is no actual competition in the product market at all. I have doubts, whether potential competition can substitute actual competition with respect to all performance criteria.

– Thirdly, even if we ignore these two arguments, I still have doubts, whether the two concentration thresholds of HHI 1000 and HHI 1800 are low enought with respect to the broad market definition. They are certainly much higher, than the German legal presumptions with respect to the traditional narrow market definition and until now I did not have feeling that these were much below the threshold, where one had to expect some kind of collusive behaviour.

(8) *The considerations of the German Monopolies Commission* went into a slightly different direction. We too think, that structural criteria of the traditionally defined product market cannot explain the competitive environment of firms completely. We, therefore, propose in addition, to include in the analysis firms which supply substitution goods or which, because of similar production techniques might easily enter the relevant market. The Federal Court of Appeal used in its landmark decision about the merger of Guest, Keen and Nettlefolds (GKN) and Sachs[5] the expression, that these firms operate in the 'neighbourhood of the relevant market' and the Monopolies Commission has elaborated this concept in particular in its last main report of summer 1984.[6]

The commission proposes an analysis of a competitive situation in two steps:

– First the actual, short run competition on the relevant product market should be analysed in the traditional manner. On this step the market concentration and the product heterogeneity are the most important criteria.

– In a second step the competitive influences, which operate in the long run from the 'neighbourhood of the market' should be taken into consideration. These are especially the elasticity of substitution on the demand side and the flexibility of production on the supply side.

Although the competitive pressures on the behaviour of the firms are strongest under conditions of almost homogeneous market competition, for the overall performance of the economy the competitive forces from neighbouring markets and industries are at least as important. The Monopolies Commission therefore has always emphasized, that in cases of market domination competition policy should at least guarantee, that suppliers of substitutional products and potential competitors in the neighbourhood of the market stay independent of the dominating firm. With great suspicion do we watch for example the emergence of energy conglomerates and media conglomerates.[7]

(b) Non horizontal mergers

(9) The differences between the German and American merger control are even greater with respect to non-horizontal mergers, especially towards pure conglomerates.[8] As I understand the American development today there exists practically no barrier at all any more for conglomerate mergers. And even more surprising, with this respect the new policy seems to find approval by many lawyers and economists, who usually are ideologically not located at the Lake Michigan.

My personal opinion in this matter could not be more different. The German Monopolies Commission, which also was established in 1974, evaluated the German merger control from its beginning. Already in its first main report it pointed out, that the Cartel Office should not concentrate its attention on horizontal mergers only, but also *investigate carefully the anti-competitive effects of conglomerate mergers.*[9] These may be expected from the combination of financial resources of the merging firms or from the combination of high market shares with financial strength. On the basis of a proposal of the Monopolies Commission another amendment of the law was passed in 1980 in which corresponding legal presumptions were established (Sect. 23a).

I think it is justified, to call special attention to one of these provisions. According to Section 23a it is presumed, that a market domination will arise, if two or more firms, with total sales of 12 billion DM or more, merge. This provision violates an important principle of the American antitrust jurisdiction namely that 'mere size is no offence'. Of course, it does not make mere size an offence. But it acknowledges, that mere size, and especially the financial strength, which goes together with size, might endanger competition. It might alter the character of the competitive process and discourage smaller firms to compete rigorously against the growing giant.

(10) This consideration of financial strength in the determination of market domination is *not based on non-economic, political goals.* In its motivation it, therefore, differs very much from the bills of the Senators Hart and Kennedy and the FTC in the sixties and early seventies, which also had the purpose, to inhibit the formation of giant firms by merger. We do not follow the common American view, that limitations to firm size can only be justified by non-economic goals, especially by the ideal of a Jeffersonian middle class democracy.

We believe, there are also *good economic reasons against a paramount concentration of financial resources.* These have the property, that they can easily be transferred from one branch of the enterprise to another and, therefore, can be used as a strategic instrument in any market, in which the enterprise is engaged. They can be used for the development and introduction of new products, for advertising and subsidizing of certain products, for deterrence of new entry and so on.

Of course this is the old-fashioned '*deep pocket doctrine*'[10] and I know, there have been published many statements against it in recent years. Especially there have been found only very few cases, in which conglomerate enterprises have been convicted for predatory action.[11]

But on the other hand we know the *strategic model of product portfolios*, which were first developed by the Boston Consulting Group. Within these models it appears to be the most natural business strategy of conglomerate firms to drag money out of old products with strong market position (to milk the cash cows), and to use it for the development and marketing of new products (to feed the wild cats). I do not argue, that these are abusive practices per se. But is seems to be obvious, that in this respect a conglomerate multiproduct firm has competitive advantages over single product firms with much smaller financial resources. These advantages have nothing to do with the production costs or the quality of one product and therefore with the allocative, technical or qualitative efficiency of the relevant market. They may be used to drive smaller competitors out of the market, although that does not seem to be the rule. But the existence of paramount financial strength as such implies a threat to the competitors which induces them to behave well, to accept a price leadership for example. Therefore, it seems to be justified, to acknowledge the overall size of an enterprise and the financial strength which goes with it, as a possible independent cause for market domination.

The Federal Court of Appeal adapted this view with some limitations in the merger case GKN/Sachs. According to this decision the financial resources of one merging firm will strengthen the market dominating position of the other merging firm, if the first firm operates in the 'neighbourhood of the market' of the other firm. With other words, the courts expects, that the profits of one product may be used on another product market, if there are some 'commonalities' between these two products. The decision could be interpreted as the acceptance of the deep pocket doctrine in *product extension* merger cases.

A few weeks ago, in the case Württembergische Metallwarenfabrik (WMF) and Rheinmetall[12] the court seemed to have dropped the limitations of the former case. It pointed out, that the financial resources of one merging firm must generally be expected to be at the disposal for competitive action on the markets of the other merging firm. So it seems, that the court adopted the deep pocket doctrine also for *pure conglomerate* mergers.

III. MAIN CRITICS OF THE GERMAN COMPETITION POLICY

(11) Until now I have tried to show, that the German competition policy comes to quite different conclusions than the present American antitrust policy, although it rests on the same basic philosophy. I want to close with a few remarks about the criticisms, which are brought forward against this policy.

The present German competition policy has more similarities with the American policy of the sixties than with the present one. One would expect, that in such a situation many authors would accept the theory, which led to the fundamental change in the American policy. One would expect, that such authors would propose a similar change in the German competition policy. Surprisingly, this is the case only to a very limited extent. As far as I can see, only the German Association of Manufacturers (Bundesverband der Deutschen Industrie) adopted the theory and the reasoning of the Chicago school without substantial changes.

In academic discussions and professional journals another kind of critique gained some attention. Some authors, especially Erich Hoppmann[13] and Dieter Schmidtchen,[14] are holding the view, that competition policy, because of its very nature, can only pursue one goal, namely freedom of competition. The only criterion to evaluate a competitive process, according to them, is the individual market behaviour, whether it unpaires the competitive freedom of other firms in the market or not. The authors in particular reject the use of market structure and market performance criteria to evaluate competitive processes. Market structures in their view are rather results than causes of market processes. Neither the outcoming market structure nor the common performance criteria justify any conclusion, whether the underlying market process had been competitive or not. From this point of view many antitrust actions are criticized as interventionistic and directed against the free economic order.

These authors are deeply influenced by the thinking of Friedrich von Hayek. Sometimes they call themselves the *Neo Austrian School.* One outstanding American author of that school is Israel Kirzner.[15]

Although with respect to competitive policy these authors reach quite similar final conclusions, the Neo Austrian School may not be confused with the Chicago School, with Richard Posner, Harold Demsetz, Yale Brozen and others. Their starting points are quite different. For Chicago people – and for the present American govenment policy – economic efficiency is the only goal of antitrust. For the Neo Austrians efficiency is a collectivistic (holistic) fiction with no expressive power at all. What should be taken into account are only individual goals and individual freedom is the only possible criterion for a free economic order.

(12) So, from our comparison of American and German competition theory and policy we reach a rather strange and confusing conclusion. In America we observe a very passive, almost laissez faire antitrust policy, which is justified by its supporters with purely economic reasoning. The critics of this policy are asking for more rigorous antitrust action on general political in particular Jeffersonian arguments.

In Germany the situation seems to be quite contrary. Present competition policy is rather active with growing perfection. Its orientation is mainly, although not exclusively, economic. The theoretically most influential critics of this policy recommend less policy intervention into the market process and they justify their recommendations on non economic socio-philosophical grounds.

I admit, things are rather confusing today. Perhaps the discussion can help us out of this maze.

NOTES

1. For a comparison in detail about the German and the American law see: Schmidt, Ingo (1973, 1983), Edwards, Carvin D. (1978), Mestmäcker, Ernst-Joachim (1983).
2. Monopolkommission (1975). Since the fourth amendment of the law in 1980 three kinds of abusive practices are explicitly enumerated in sect. 22.

   'An abuse within the meaning of sentence 1 is present, in particular, it a market dominating enterprise as a supplier or buyer of commercial services.

   1. impairs the competitive possibilities of other enterprises in a manner relevant to competition on the market in the absence of facts justifying such behaviour,
   2. demands considerations or other business terms which deviate from those which would result in all probability if the effective competition existed; in this context in particular the

practises of enterprises on comparable markets characterise by effective competition have to be taken into account,

3. demands less favourable considerations or other business terms than are demanded from similar buyers on comparable markets by the market dominating enterprise, unless there is a factual justification for such differentiation'.

3. Monopolkommision (1975).
4. Schmidt and Ries (1983).
5. GKN/Sachs, *Wirtschaft und Wettbewerb*, Entscheidungsammlung BGH 1051.
6. Monopolkommission (1984) Chapter VII.
7. With respect to energy see: Monopolkommission (1976), Chapter IV. With respect to media see: Monopolkommission (1981). See also Kantzenbach (1984).
8. Monopolkommission (1984) Chapter VIII.
9. Monopolkommission (1976) Chapter V.
10. Edwards (1955), Narver (1967).
11. Markham (1973).
12.
13. Hoppmann (1967a, 1967b, 1968).
14. Schmidtchen (1978).
15. Kirzner (1973). For a discussion of the different positions in particular see: Gotthold (1981, 1982), Möschel (1981).

REFERENCES

Edwards Corvin, D., 'Conglomerate Bigness as a Source of Power', in: *Business Concentration and Price Policy*, NBER, New York/Princeton (1955).

Edwards Corvin, D., 'American and German Policy towards Conduct by Powerful Enterprises: A Comparison', *Antitrust Bulletin*, Vol. 23 (1978), p. 83 ff.

Gotthold, Jürgen, 'Neuere Entwicklungen in der Wettbewerbstheorie', *Zeitschrift für das gesamte Handelsrecht und Wirtschaftsrecht* (*ZHR*) Band 145 (1981).

Gotthold, Jürgen, 'Nochmals: Kritische Bemerkungen zur neo-neoliberalen Theorie der Wettbewerbspolitik, *ZHR* Band 146 (1982).

Hoppmann, Erich, 'Wettbewerb als Norm der Wettbewerbspolitik, *Ordo* 18 (1967).

Hoppmann, Erich, 'Workable Competition als wettbewerbspolitisches Konzept', in: *Theoretische und institutionelle Grundlagen der Wirtschaftspolitik*, Festschrift für Theodor Wessels, Berlin (1967).

Hoppman, Erich, 'Zum Problem einer wirtschaftspolitisch praktikablen Definition des Wettbewerbs', in: Schneider, H. -K. (ed.), *Grundlagen der Wettbewerbspolitik*, Schriften des Vereins für Socialpolitik, N.F. 48, Berlin (1968).

Kantzenbach, Erhard, '10 Jahre Monopolkommission', *Wirtschaft und Wettbewerb* Vol. 34 (1984), Nr. 1.

Kirzner, Israel M., *Competition and Entrepreneurship*, Chicago (1973), in German: *Wettbewerb und Unternehmertum*, Freiburg (1978).

Markham, Jesse, *Conglomerate Enterprise and Public Policy*, Boston (1973).

Mestmäcker, Ernst-Joachim and Richter, Rudolf (eds.), 'Competition Policy: German and American Experience, A Symposium', *Zeitschrift für die gesamte Staatswissenschaft*, Band 136, Heft 3 (1980).

Monopolkommission, 'Anwendung und Möglichkeiten der Mißbrauchsaufsicht über marktbeherrschende Unternehmen seit Inkrafttreten der Kartellgesetznovelle', *Sondergutachten 1*, Baden-Baden (1975).

Monopolkommission, 'Mehr Wettbewerb ist möglich', *Hauptgutachten I*, 1973/75, Baden-Baden (1976).

Monopolkommission, 'Wettbewerbsprobleme bei der Einführung von privatem Hörfunk und Fernsehen', *Sondergutachten 11*, Baden-Baden (1981).

Monopolkommission, 'Ökonomische Kriterien für die Rechtsanwendung', *Hauptgutachten V*, 1982/83, Baden-Baden (1984).

Möschel, Wernhardt, 'Kritische Bemerkungen zu kritischen Bemerkungen', *ZHR*, Band 145 (1981).

Narver, John, C., *Conglomerate Mergers and Market Competition*, Berkeley (1967).

Schmidt, Ingo, *US-amerikanische und deutsche Wettbewerbspolitik gegenüber Marktmacht*, Berlin (1973).

Schmidt, Ingo, 'Different Approaches and Problems in Dealing with Control of Market Power: a Comparison of German, European and US. Policy Towards Market-dominating Enterprises', *Antitrust-Bulletin* Vol. 28 (1983), p. 417 ff.

Schmidt, Ingo and Ries, Wolfgang, 'Der Hirschmann-Herfindahl-Index (HHI) als wettbewerbspolitisches Instrument in den neuen US-Fusionsrichtlinien 1982', *Wirtschaft und Wettbewerb*, Vol. 33 (1983), p. 178.

Schmidtchen, Dieter, *Wettbewerbspolitik als Aufgabe: Methodologische und systemtheoretische Grundlagen für eine Neuorientierung*, Baden-Baden (1978).

12. COMPETITION POLICIES AND MEASURES OF DOMINANT POWER

Remo Linda

1. ANTITRUST POLICY AND THE MARKET

Government planning and intervention are recognized as being a potential source of inertia, abuse and waste and, in the final analysis, a threat to economic freedom. On the other hand, it is realized that individual economic freedom can also be threatened by excessive concentrations of economic power in private hands, and that in our modern post-industrial countries there is therefore a need for governments to pursue an antitrust policy. However, as the Chicago School has often pointed out, it is exceedingly difficult to pursue an antitrust policy without disturbing the very competitive mechanisms the policy seeks to protect and promote.[1]

To minimize this damage it is necessary to set strict, objective limits to the intervention and coercion which are a natural part of this or any other government policy.

One way of imposing such objective limits is for the antitrust authorities to lay down general quantitative criteria by which they will voluntarily abide in their administration of antitrust law. This will give firms and businessmen greater confidence ('legal certainty') in their behaviour knowing that they have a certain leeway within which they are safe from government intervention. The increased visibility of the criteria underlying a more systematic and better understood antitrust policy will thus enhance economic freedom.

2. THE NEW MERGER GUIDELINES OF THE US ANTITRUST AUTHORITIES

In 1982 the US Justice Department issued new merger guidelines to spell out the circumstances in which the Department would approve or

de Jong, H. W., Shepherd, W. G. (eds) Mainstreams in Industrial Organization
 ISBN 978-94-017-0495-3

disapprove of a proposed merger under the antitrust rules. The new Guidelines were an historic departure in that for the first time in the history of US antitrust enforcement the Department was to employ econometric methods and criteria derived from theoretical economics to solve practical problems arising in the enforcement of business, and in particular antitrust, law.[2]

3. THE HERFINDAHL (OR HERFINDAHL–HIRSCHMANN) INDEX (HHI)

The Herfindahl (Herfindahl–Hirschmann) Index is calculated from the market shares of all the independent firms competing on a particular market. Since the 1982 Merger Guidelines it has been an integral part of the assumptions underlying US merger policy. It serves as a basis for a preliminary broad classification of mergers into three 'regions':

- Where the post-merger HHI in a market is less than 1000, the market is assumed to be unconcentrated and a merger would not normally be challenged.
- Where the post-merger HHI is between 1000 and 1800, the market is considered to be moderately concentrated, but a post-merger HHI of 1400 or over would set off alarm bells in the Justice Department.
- A merger which increased the HHI by over 100 points and left it over 1800 would be challenged by the Justice Department.

Examples of the HHI values for various US industries are 1400 for synthetic rubber, 1600 for copper, approximately 1500 for beer, 2760 for ready-to-eat cereals, 3650 for portable typewriters and almost 5000 for office typewriters (dominant firm: IBM), 2036 for electric light bulbs and 5026 for telephone equipment (dominant firm: American Telephone and Telegraph).

Thus, in spite of almost a century of antitrust enforcement in the US, certain of its industrial sectors and markets are highly concentrated. The chief merit of the HHI measure of concentration is its extreme ease of calculation. The squares of the percentage market shares of the firms considered are simply added. The market shares of minor firms can safely be ignored if they are unavailable. For example, if four firms each hold 25% of the market, the HHI is four times 25^2, i.e., $4 \times 625 = 2500$. If one firm controls 45% of the market and the next three largest 10% each, the HHI will be 2325.

These two questions immediately prompt two questions.

First, do the results obtained by the HHI index agree with those obtained by use of the four-firm concentration ratio (CR4)?

Second, is it certain that the HHI index is able effectively to reflect changes in market power?

As we shall now show, the answer to both questions is No.

4. COMPARISON OF CR4 AND HHI – A FEW DISTURBING EXAMPLES

It is worth looking more closely at the two examples given below.

Example	No.	Market shares		CR4	HHI
		Leading firm	Other firms		
I	4	25%	25% × 3	100%	2.500
II	9	45%	(10% × 3) + (5% × 5)	75%	2.450

Therefore, if the leading firm controls 45% of the market, the next three firms 10% each and another five firms 5% each, the HHI will be 2.450.

A comparison of the first and second examples shows that, although the market power of the leading firm has increased, both the CR4 concentration ratio and the Herfindahl Index have decreased. In other cases, CR4 and HHI move in different directions. This is so in the following three examples:

Examples	No.	Market shares		CR4	HHI
		Leading firm	Other firms		
III	9	20%	(20% × 3) + (4% × 5)	80%	1.680
IV	34	40%	(10% × 3) + (1% × 30)	70%	1.930
V	12	50%	(6% × 3%) + (4% × 8)	68%	2.736

These examples represent three very different structures involving a progressive increase in imbalance and market power (in III four firms have 20% each and the next five 4% each, in IV the leading firm has 40%, the next three 10% each and another thirty firms 1% each, and in V the leading firm has 50%, the next three 6% each and another eight firms 4% each).

The conclusion must be:

- CR4 is obviously a very poor measure of market power since in these examples the ratio falls as market power increases.[3]
- HHI is apparently sometimes a good measure of this power and at other times an inadequate and deceptive measure. How is it possible that when the leading firm doubles its market share (from 20% in example III to 40% in example IV) the HHI rises by only 250 points (1680 to 1930), whereas when the leading firm increases its market share by only 10 points (from 40% in example IV to 50% in example V) the HHI shoots up by 806 points, from 1930 to 2736? Even more misleading is the fall in the HHI from 2.500 to 2.450 from example I to example II when the market share of the leading firm is spectacularly increased from 20% to 45%.

A comparative analysis of these five examples shows that the HHI measure is an inconsistent measure of market power, being more or less reliable in some cases but decidedly misleading in others.

5. MEASURES OF CONCENTRATION AND THE AIMS OF ANTITRUST POLICY

The US Merger Guidelines spell out objectively for firms and groups operating on the American market the legal limits beyond which they may not go in corporate mergers.

The limits are clearly intended to discourage the trend towards economic and financial gigantism.

Yet, in our opinion the main aim of any antitrust policy in this area is simply to maintain and promote competition.

This principle is visible in the Guidelines when they state that vertical or conglomerate mergers are only considered to harm competition where they have horizontal effects, i.e., where they help increase to an excessive degree the merged firm's power on the relevant market.

In view of this, it appears inconsistent that the antitrust authorities are continuing to use the HHI measure of concentration, which, as we have seen, does not reliably measure market power.

6. THE DIFFERENCE BETWEEN CONCENTRATION AND MARKET POWER

This inconsistency stems quite simply from an unfortunate confusion between

- measures of concentration and
- measures of market power.

Since the two concepts – and phenomena – of concentration and market power are not the same, it is wrong to use a measure of one phenomenon as the basis for conclusions to be applied to the other phenomenon.

We do not dispute that the Herfindahl Index can be a good measure of concentration. In the close on 150 studies published by the EC Commission in its 'Trends of Concentration and Competition' series between 1970 and 1981, we have calculated the Herfindahl–Hirschmann Index as well as the Gini, Linda and Entropie indices.[4]

Our objection is to the way the U.S. antitrust authorities propose to use the Herfindahl–Hirschmann Index. In certain circumstances use of the Index can have effects which harm competition, by causing the antitrust authorities to exercise their powers to challenge mergers which actually promote competition, and, in the process, to protect and reinforce existing dominant and even monopoly positions.

In our opinion, to assess how a change in a given market structure will affect competition, it is necessary to look not only at the degree of concentration but also at the balance of the market.

In an oligopolistic market, a balanced distribution of market power between the various competing producers does not inhibit competition but is one of the essential conditions for it.

7. THE INAPPLICABILITY OF THE HERFINDAHL INDEX IN THE EEC

We believe that in the EEC use of the Herfindahl Index would very often lead to a bolstering of existing dominant or even monopoly positions. We therefore support the Commission's reserved and circumspect attitude in not adopting the Herfindahl Index criteria in its competition policy enforcement under Article 86 of the EEC Treaty.

In the EEC competition policy is faced with a different set of problems than in the US because the common market is not a single economic area but a series of national markets with different structures and conditions, although these national markets are

- interdependent and
- gradually becoming economically integrated.

Promoting competition in the common market as a whole, that is, throughout the Community of ten countries, involves weakening certain dominant national positions. However, such a positive development may sometimes go hand in hand with a strengthening of some dominant national positions, which would not be such a positive development from the point of view of national competition policy.

8. CONCENTRATION THRESHOLDS AND U.S. MERGER DECISIONS: THE BEER CASE

As noted above, the use of concentration thresholds based on the Herfindahl Index can lead to a bolstering of existing monopolies, an effect which would be particularly undesirable in the EEC.

The inconsistency of using quantitative thresholds based on the Herfindahl Index in antitrust enforcement can be seen from the example of recent decisions on two proposed brewery mergers in the US involving G. Heileman Brewing Co, of La Crosse, Wis., the sixth largest US brewer, and other, larger breweries. Heileman was successively refused permission to acquire Joseph Schlitz Brewing Co. (the fourth largest producer) and Pabst Brewing, of Milwaukee (the third largest).

We will not go into the regional factors which may well have carried considerable weight in the antitrust authorities' decision to challenge the two mergers. Our remark would be that if the challenge was based on a rigid application of the 'concentration thresholds' then it was ill-conceived, for in that case there was confusion between concentration and market power.

In our opinion, one of the two mergers – it is immaterial which, since the market shares of Pabst (8.6%) and Schlitz (8.5%) are almost the same – could have been allowed without the slightest damage to competition, at least not when the U.S. market is taken as a whole.

9. USE OF A MEASURE OF MARKET POWER: INs

We will attempt to demonstrate this using our composite index (indicateur de synthèse'), INs, which was specially designed to measure market power as a quantitative influence on the working of competition.[5] The key to the meaning of the INs index numbers is as follows:

Maximum: INs = 4: monopoly situation or situation in which competition is seriously threatened;

INs $\geqslant$ 3.5: major structural imbalance and threat to competition;

Table 1. Comparison of the values and interpretations of the INs and HHI indices for market structures composed of firms of equal size.

n	Market share in %	HHI	INs	Interpretation	
				HHI	INs
1	100	10 000	4	Very serious danger for competition	
2	50	5 000	2.75	Very serious danger	Potential danger*
3	33	3 000	2.50	Very serious danger	Potential danger*
4	25	2 500	2.25	Very serious danger	Danger unlikely
5	20	2 000	2	Serious danger	Danger unlikely
6	17	1 734	1.50	Serious danger	Danger remote
7	14	1 372	1.25	Danger	No danger
8	12	1 152	1.25	Danger	No danger
9	11	1 089	1.25	Danger	No danger
10	10	1 000	1.25	Danger unlikely	No danger
11	9	891	1	No danger for competition	
12	8	768	1	No danger for competition	
> 12	< 8	< 768	1	No danger for competition	
50	2	200	1	No danger for competition	
100	1	100	1	No danger for competition	

*To be watched.

Note: It may be seen that the two indices diverge sharply especially for balanced structures consisting of four to seven firms (oligopolistic competition), the types of structure that are most prevalent in modern markets for manufactured products.

3.5 > INs ⩾ 2.5: structural imbalance and relatively disturbing situation for competition which should be watched;
2.5 > INs ⩾ 1.5: relatively balanced situation compatible with the working of market mechanisms
INs < 1.5: situation not giving ground for concern as far as competition is concerned;
Minimum: INs = 1: competitive model – either very broad and balanced oligopoly or atomistic structure.

Table 1 underlines fundamental differences between INs and HHI indices for 'Oligopolistic Equilibrium' hypotheses, i.e., for market structures composed of firms of equal size.

10. THE ANALYSIS OF MARKET STRUCTURE IN ITS COMPONENT PARTS AND THE CLASSIFICATION OF THE INTENSITY OF EACH COMPONENT

The basis of the INs index is an analysis of market structures in four components, viz.:

I. MON: The intensity of the power held by the market leader relative to all other firms in the market and particularly to the relative strength of the second largest firm.

II. DUO: The cumulative market share and relative strengths of the two largest firms in the market relative to all the other firms and particularly to the third largest firm.

III. OLI: The cumulative market shares of the three and four largest firms relative to those of smaller firms.

IV. IMB: (for 'imbalance') the degree of imbalance between the sizes and hence strengths of the leading firms in the market.

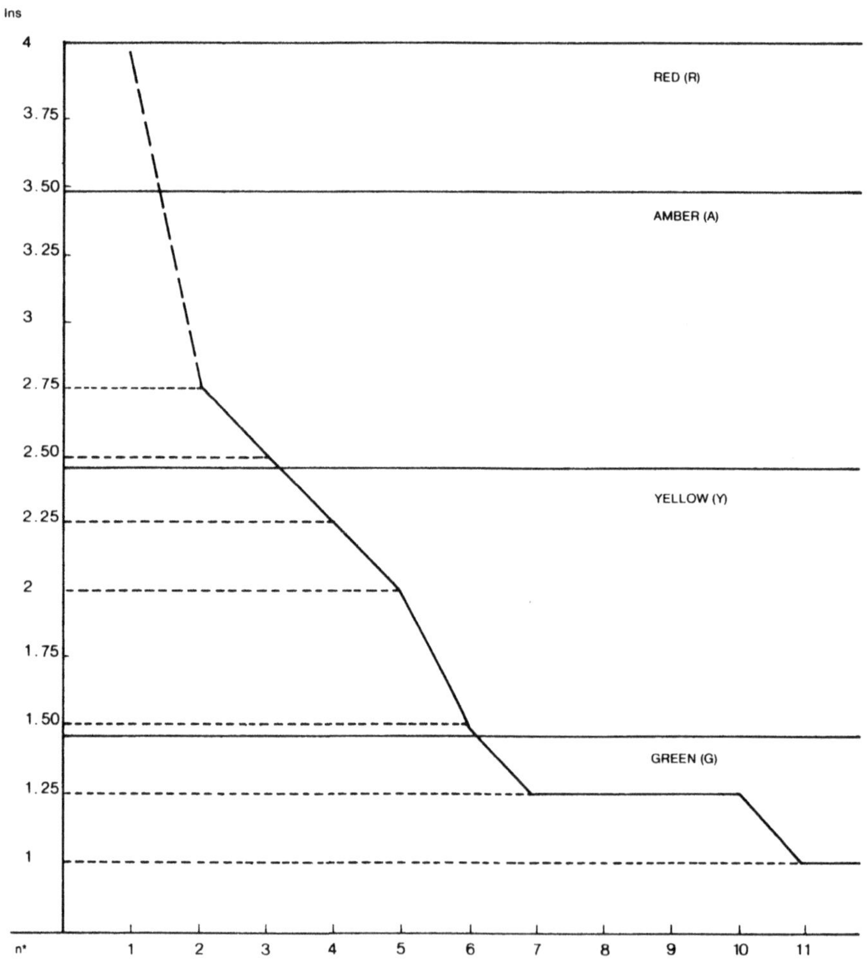

Fig. 1.

The intensity of each component (monopoly power, oligopolistic dominance, imbalance, etc.) in a given market structure is placed in one of four numbered categories, which are also designated by colours. In descending order of intensity the numbers and colours are 4: red (the maximum), 3: amber, 2: yellow and 1: green (the minimum). Exactly how the intensity of each structural component is calculated will be shown later (Fig. 1).

The INs composite index is the average of the four components. It can range from a maximum of 4 (red zone – monopoly or a very imbalanced structure in which the market leader has virtual monopoly power), through 3 (amber) and 2 (yellow) to a minimum of 1 (green – competitive structure, as represented by a very balanced oligopoly or an atomistic market in which no firm really has any market power).

11. PROPENSITY TO EXERCISE MARKET POWER AND PROPENSITY TO COMPLETE

The composite index INs has the advantage of reflecting the structural coordinates of each market and not just a global indicator. Table 2 shows, for market structures involving an increasing number of firms again of equal size, the intensity values (here as colours) that would be given to each of the four components and also the operational demarcation line or watershed in the final INs index between market structures having a propensity towards market power and those having a propensity towards competition. In the former, indicating also in the final composite index by the colours red or amber, competition will tend to be stifled; in the latter, indicated by yellow or green, it will tend to flourish because of a balance of power between the firms in the market and the absence of any dominant firm.

Let us look at the values assigned to the various components in the market structures shown in Table 2. In the monopoly case ($n = 1$) all four components and their composite predictably have the value 4 (red). This would also be the case for a near-monopoly situation of several firms one of which absolutely dominated the market.

For duopoly, the INs falls sharply to 2.75. The reason is that the previous monopolist now sees its market power offset by a second firm with which it shares the entire market. Here the values for the four components are:

Table 2. Values of the four structural components of the INs index and value of the final index for market structures composed of firms of equal size.

n*	Market share in %	MON	DUO	OLI	IMB	COMP[a]	INs[a]
1	100	R	R	R	R	R	4
2	50	Y	R	R	G	A	2.75
3	33	Y	A	R	G	A	2.50
4	25	G	A	R	G	Y	2.25
5	20	G	Y	R	G	Y	2
6	17	G	G	A	G	Y	1.50
7	14	G	G	Y	G	G	1.25
8	12	G	G	Y	G	G	1.25
9	11	G	G	Y	G	G	1.25
10	10	G	G	Y	G	G	1.25
11	9	G	G	G	G	G	1
12	8	G	G	G	G	G	1
+12	−8	G	G	G	G	G	1

Key: n* = number of firms
MON = monopoly power (I)
DUO = duopolistic dominance (II)
OLI = tightness/looseness of oligopoly (III)
IMB = imbalance (IV)
COMP = composite of I–IV.
Propensity to market power: R = RED, A = AMBER (INs $\geqslant$ 2.50).
Propensity to competition: Y = YELLOW, G = GREEN (INs < 2.50).
[a] See Figure 1.

I: 2 (yellow) : no monopoly power;
II: 4 (red) : maximum duopolistic power because the two firms control the entire market;
III: 4 (red) : maximum oligopolistic power also because a duopoly is an extreme form of oligopoly;
IV: 1 (green) : balance is optimal by definition (firms of equal size).

Moving on to the three-firm market, the INs is 2.50 (also amber). This results from the four component values I: 2 (yellow), II: 3 (amber), III: 4 (red) and IV: 1 (green), thus:

$$\frac{2 + 3 + 4 + 1}{4} = \frac{10}{4} = 2.5.$$

The first component here is 2 (yellow) because the power of the potential market leader is counterbalanced by the equal power of the second and third firms. Thus no firm has monopoly power. The value of the second component (DUO) is no longer 4 (red) as in the duopoly case but 3 (amber) because here there is a third firm of equal size to the first two which reduces their cumulative power.

12. THE VALUE OF COMPONENT III (OLI) IN TIGHT OLIGOPOLIES

A value of 4 (red) is assigned to OLI in any market structure involving between two and five firms, which represent tight, and in this case pure, oligopolies since the firms concerned share the entire market.

From markets of six firms or over, however, the oligopoly is no longer tight but becomes more and more loose. This is reflected in the changing value for OLI from 3 (amber) for $n = 6$ to 2 (yellow) for $n = 7$ to $n = 10$ and 1 (green) for loose oligopolies of $n > 10$.

13. COMPONENT IV (IMB) IN BALANCED STRUCTURES

In Table 2, component IV (degree of imbalance) is always at the minimum value of 1 (green) for any market structure between $n = 2$ and $n = 12$ because all the markets in question are assumed to be composed of firms of exactly equal size and hence perfectly balanced. The obvious exception is monopoly, where the market contains only one firm and so is completely unbalanced.

The minimum reading of component IV (IMB) in the balanced oligopolies shown in the Table has a strong influence on the falling values of the final index as the oligopoly becomes looser, since the minimum value of IMB cancels out the maximum value of component III (OLI). Thus, four equal-sized firms the INs is 2.25:

$$\frac{1 + 3 + 4 + 1}{4} = 2.25,$$

and for five it is 2:

$$\frac{1 + 2 + 4 + 1}{4} = 2.$$

14. CALCULATION OF THE INTENSITIES OF THE FOUR STRUCTURAL COMPONENTS

We have seen how the four components of market structure are weighted in the composite index INs and how the resulting index appears to reflect well the extent of the market power capable of being wielded by firms and the consequent danger for competition in different types of markets. Let us now look in detail at how the values for the four structural components are arrived at.

Altogether, seven variables are used for the four structural components, a different set for each component. To arrive at the value of each component, the readings of the relevant variables are matched against a key (see Tables 3, 4 and 5). Depending on the component, the variables must either be taken together (MON, DUO) or compared and only the maximum or minimum value taken (OLI, IMB). For consistency all the variables are expressed as percentages.

The seven variables are:

(1) the concentration ratios CR1, CR2, CR3 and CR4, whose maximum reading is 100%;
(2) the relative firm size ratios (Linda indices) 2L, 3L and 4L, whose minimum reading is 100%.

The concentration ratios CR1, CR2, CR3 and CR4 are simply the percentage market shares held by the largest firm and the combined shares of the largest and the second, third and fourth largest firms respectively.

The Linda (relative firm size) indices are calculated as follows:[6]

(a) 2*L* (in %) is equal to the ratio between the sizes of the largest and the second largest firm. For example, if the largest firm has 50% of the market and the second largest 25%, 2L is 200% ($\frac{50}{25} \times 100$).
(b) 3*L* (in %) is equal to the arithmetic mean of the following two ratios:
   (i) the ratio between the size of the largest firm and the arithmetic mean of the sizes of the second and third largest;
   (ii) the ratio between the arithmetic mean of the sizes of the two largest firms and the size of the third largest.
(c) 4*L* (in %) is equal to the arithmetic mean of the following three ratios:
   (i) the ratio between the size of the largest firm and the arithmetic mean of the sizes of the three next largest firms;
   (ii) the ratio between the arithmetic mean of the sizes of the two largest firms and the arithmetic mean of the sizes of the next two (third and fourth) largest;
   (iii) the ratio between the arithmetic mean of the sizes of the three largest firms and the size of the fourth largest.

Table 3. Operational criteria for value of structural component I (monopoly power).

Red		Amber		Yellow		Green	
CR1	2*L*	CR1	2*L*	CR1	2*L*	CR1	2*L*
> 60%	–*	> 50–60%	⩽ 150%	> 40–50%	< 150%	> 20–25%	< 200%
> 50–60%	> 150%	> 40–50%	150–500%	> 30–40%	< 200%	> 15–20%	< 300%
> 40–50%	> 500%	> 30–40%	200–1000%	> 25–30%	< 300%	10–15%	< 500%
> 30–40%	> 1000%	> 25–30%	⩾ 300%	> 20–25%	200–1000%	< 10%	< 1000%
		20–25%	> 1000%	> 15–20%	300–1000%		
				10–15%	500–1000%		
				< 10%	> 1000%		

*A CR1 of this size is sufficient for the classification red.

Table 4. Operational criteria for value of structural component II (duopolistic dominance).

Red		Amber		Yellow		Green	
CR2	3*L*	CR2	3*L*	CR2	3*L*	CR2	3*L*
⩾ 60%	> 175%	⩾ 60%	⩽ 175%	40 > 50%	< 325%	20 > 40%	< 200%
50 > 60%	⩾ 325%	50 > 60%	< 325%	30 > 40%	200 < 325%	10 > 20%	< 400%
		30 > 50%	⩾ 325%	20 > 30%	⩾ 200%	< 10%	–*
				10 > 20%	⩾ 400%		

*A CR2 of this size is sufficient for the classification green.

Table 5. Summary of operational criteria for values of structural components I–IV.

Zones	I. MON (monopoly power)		II. DUO (duopolistic dominance)		III. OLI (tightness/looseness of oligopoly)			IV. IMB (imbalance of oligopoly		
					Concentration ratios*			Firm size ratios		
	CR1	2*L*	CR2	3*L*	CR2	CR3	CR4	2*L*	3*L*	4*L*
1	2	3	4	5	6	7	8	9	10	11
R = RED	See Tables 3 and 4				$\geqslant$60%	$\geqslant$70%	$\geqslant$80%		$\geqslant$400%	
A = AMBER					$\geqslant$40%	$\geqslant$50%	$\geqslant$60%		$\geqslant$240%	
Y = YELLOW					$\geqslant$20%	$\geqslant$30%	$\geqslant$40%		$\geqslant$150%	
G = GREEN					< 20%	< 30%	< 40%		< 150%	

*In practice, only CR3 and CR4 are taken into consideration if they are available.

The variables taken into account in arriving at the values of the four components are:

I. MON (monopoly power): 1 : CR1
2 : 2L

The two variables are taken together and matched against the key to determine the classification (Table 3).

II. DUO (duopolistic dominance): 1 : CR2
2 : 3L.

Here too, the variables are taken together to determine the classification (Table 4).

III. OLI (tightness/looseness of oligopoly): 1 : CR3
2 : CR4

or, in their absence, as for example in a highly concentrated market or for lack of data on CR3 and CR4, 3 : CR2.[7]

Here, the variables are matched singly against the key (Table 5) and,if they show different intensities of the component, that showing the greatest intensity is taken, for example red in preference to amber, amber in preference to yellow, to determine the final classification.

E.g., if CR3 = 72% (red) and
CR4 = 79% (amber)

the value taken is red.

IV. IMB (imbalance of oligopoly): 1 : 2*L*
2 : 3*L*
3 : 4*L*

Here too, the three ratios are matched singly against the key (Table 5) but in this case that showing the weakest intensity is taken, e.g., amber in preference to red, yellow in preference to amber.

15. IN_s AS MEASURE OF MARKET POWER APPLIED TO THE BEER CASE

Before commenting further on the IN_s Index, let us go back to the beer case (Section 8). Table 6 shows three scenarios of the structure of the US beer market:[8]

A: present situation;
B: situation which would have resulted from a merger between Heileman and Schlitz if this had been allowed;

Table 6. Three scenarios of the US beer market: the values of CR4, HHI and INs.

Scenario A			Scenario B			Scenario C		
No.	Firm	% Market share	No.	Firm	% Market share	No.	Firm	% Market share
I	Anheuser-Busch	28	I	Anheuser-Busch	28	I	Anheuser-Busch	28
II	Miller	21	II	Miller	21	II	Heileman-Schlitz	24.6
III	Pabst	8.6	III	Heileman Schlitz	16	III	Miller	21
IV	Schlitz	8.5	IV	Pabst	8.6	IV	Coors	7.8
V	Coors	7.8	V	Coors	7.8			
VI	Heileman	7.5						
	CR4	66.1		CR4	73.6		CR4	81.4
	HHI	1400		HHI	1600		HHI	2000
	INs	2		INs	2		INs	2.5

C: situation which would have resulted from the merger of Heileman and Schlitz followed by a further merger with Pabst, if they had been allowed.

Only scenario C can really be said to point to a possible, but still quite slight, deterioration in the competitive situation owing to the tightening of the oligopoly following two successive mergers by Heileman.

How does the INs Index reflect this situation?

The INs remains unchanged at level 2 between scenarios A and B. This structure is one which, at Federal level, and in quantitative terms, is compatible with the operation of market mechanisms.

Market power has not increased between scenarios A and B because:

- although the merger between Heileman and Pabst or Schlitz may weaken the competitiveness of the other smaller breweries,
- on the other hand, the new group, now in third place nationally with a market share of 16%, necessarily weakens the market power of the market leader (Anheuser-Busch: 28%), and to some extent also that of the second largest firm (Miller: 21%), both of which now face a formidable new rival which with 16% of the market has the financial, technological, commercial and marketing capacity which a competitor with only 8.6% of the market previously did not have.

This would have a very positive effect on competition outweighing the adverse effect of the increased concentration on smaller firms.

Our composite index is based on assumptions which any competition economist should have no trouble accepting.

I. Market power influences competition.
II. This influence is generally speaking in descending order of size of firm, from the leading firm down to the smaller firms.
III. The maximum intensity of market power, that is, the maximum influence on competition, is to be found in the leading firm.

Given these assumptions, the question which arises is:

Will the market power of the leading firm be greater or less if the size of the next largest firms is fairly close to its own (balance principle) or far inferior ('cumulative concentration' or 'imbalance' principle)?

On the answer to this question depends the economic philosophy of the econometric system that is chosen to measure market power.

In the econometric approach of the INs it is the balance principle that predominates though with some, but much less, account being taken of the role of the barriers to entry that may be thrown up against firms excluded from the oligopolistic 'inner circle' as the oligopoly is tightened by mergers.

16. THE HERFINDAHL INDEX AND THE DEFENCE OF EXISTING DOMINANT POSITIONS

The simplicity and formal elegance of the Herfindahl Index disguises an irredeemable inconsistency in the method from the point of view and for the purposes of antitrust policy, which in extreme cases could lead to a bolstering of existing dominant positions instead of an intensification of competition.

This can be demonstrated with a theoretical example.

Example	No.	Market shares		CR4	HHI	IN_s
		Leading firm	Other firms			
VI.	62	37%	(3% × 1) + (1% × 60)	42%	1.438	2.75
VII.	6	20%	(20% × 4) + (11% × 1) + (9% × 1)	80%	1.802	2

In Example VI the leading firm has 37% of the market, the second largest 3% and all the others 1% or less. The market power of the leading firm is beyond all doubt.

Now let us suppose the industry is hit by a severe crisis and it is decided to break up the leading firm and restructure the entire industry.

The result might be an oligopolistic 'inner circle' of four firms (each with a market share of 20%).

It would seem to us at first sight, and in the absence of collusive agreements or other illicit practices, that the competitive situation in Example VII is far better than that in Example VI which obtained before.

No firm would be in a dominant position as the leading firm used to be with 37% of the market. The four new firms of similar size would each be driven to compete fiercely to carve out a bigger market share. The change is favourably recorded by the INs Index, which falls from 2.75 in Example VI to 2 in Example VII.

The Herfindahl Index, on the other hand, would rise from 1438 to 1802 which is fairly over the critical threshold of acceptability, thus bringing down the wrath of the antitrust authorities on the scheme.

To keep faith with the published guidelines and the quantitative HHI thresholds, would not the antitrust authorities in this case have to come down on the side of dominant positions and thus against the mergers (or restructuring) which would tend to promote competition?

This question deserves an answer.

17. THE REVISED MERGER GUIDELINES (1984)

On 14 June 1984 the US Justice Department issued new guidelines on the application of the antitrust rules to corporate mergers.

The new Guidelines broadly confirm several key points of the 1982 Guidelines, including the use of the Herfindahl Index.[9]

However, with the new Guidelines the Justice Department wishes to 'correct any misperceptions that the Guidelines are a set of rigid mathematical formulas that ignore market realities'.

It lays stress on the principle, which deserves wholehearted support, that the analysis of each merger much take account of its likely competitive impact within markets that could be subject to the exercise of market power.[10]

Thus, the concept of market power, and not concentration, has become the key to assessing the competitive situation in the new Guidelines.

This basic stance is confirmed by the announcement of an additional criterion under which the Justice Department will challenge any merger by the market leader with a smaller firm (holding 1% or more of the market) where the leader already has at least 35%.

The Justice Department is evidently now aware of the shortcomings and inconsistencies of the Herfindahl Index in antitrust enforcement. We believe that the Merger Guidelines have thus moved closer to the operational philosophy behind our own composite index INs based on the 'colour zone' approach, and consider this to be a very positive step.

Yet the Justice Department has not taken the further logical and desirable step of abandoning the Herfindahl Index, which will go on being a source of rigidity, confusion and controversy.[11]

The theoretical inconsistency of the Herfindahl Index is shown up beyond redemption by the need for an additional criterion of absolute size – the 35% market share threshold announced by the Department of Justice. This ad hoc principle arbitrarily and irrevocably overrides the rigid criteria (division into three regions: HHI 1000, HHI between 1000 and 1800, and HHI 1800) based on the Herfindahl Index, which is a completely inadequate measure of market power. The addition of the 35% criterion makes it clear that the Herfindahl Index fails to measure what is most important for competition policy, the area of the market subject to the market power of the leading firm, which is the area most important for competition.

What is the point of working out a complex index as the basis for rigid, selective and complicated criteria if it is necessary also to have an ad hoc rule quite separate from the index to deal with the potential impact on the market of market power exercised by the leading firm? The question answers itself.

In our opinion, the simple replacement of the Herfindahl Index by the composite index INs and the colour zone approach would have made the new US merger guidelines much more incisive, consistent and clear in favouring mergers likely to increase balance in oligopolistic competition.

NOTES

1. See Henry Lepage, *Marchés et Monopoles: des vérités pas si évidentes* in: 'Analyses de la SEDEIS', Paris, No 40, July 1984. See also, from Lepage's bibliography: Yale Bronzen, *Concentration, Mergers and Public Policy*, MacMillan Publishing Co, 1982; Harold Demsetz, *The Market Concentration Doctrine*, American Enterprise Institute, 1973; idem, *Two Systems of Belief about Monopoly*, in: Goldschmid, Mann and Weston, *Industrial Concentration: The New Learning*, 1974; P. Asch and J. J. Seneca, *Is Collusion Profitable?*, in: Review of Econometrics and Statistics, February 1976.

   It may be helpful to remind 'For . . . competition to be effective, the crucial thing seems to be that prices be independently made under conditions that give some competitors an incentive to aggressive action that others will have to meet . . . (J. M. Clark, *Competition As a Dynamic Process*, Washington: Brookings Institution, 1961, p. 18).

2. The new Guidelines announced by the Attorney General, William French Smith, and the Assistant Attorney General in charge of the Justice Department's Antitrust Division, William Baxter, were widely reported in the business press (see, for example, 'Time' of 28 June 1982, p. 45, 'The Economist' of 19 June 1982, p. 25, 'Business Week' of 17 May 1982, pp. 82–83). Of especial interest is the article by David S. Weinstock, *Using the Herfindahl Index to measure concentration*, in: Antitrust Bulletin, Summer 1982, p. 285 et seq. In June 1984 the Justice Department issued revised Guidelines which clarify and refine the 1982 version (Department of Justice, June 1984, AT 202-633-2016); see Section 17.
3. David S. Weinstock, op. cit., notes '. . . a market in which each of the four largest firms has 20% of the market will show the same degree of concentration as another market in which the top four firms have shares of 55%, 20%, 4% and 1% respectively. In each case, the ratio will be 80%. But four equal-size firms may compete with each other differently than four firms of disparate size'. Weinstock's remarks in 1982 link up directly with what the author of this paper himself wrote in 1976: 'Take a given industry or market A, in which the first four firms control 75% of the total (the first firm holding 72% and the other three only 1% each) and an industry or market B in which the first four firms control 80% of the total, all the same size (20% each). The reading of the C_4 (or A_4) by itself suggests that the industry or market A is less concentrated than B, while the opposite is in fact the case'. (R. Linda, *Methodology of Concentration Analysis Applied to the Study of Industries and Markets*. Commission of the European Communities, 1976, Brussels, p. 14.

   As regards the concepts of market structure, see: William G. Shepherd, *The elements and evolution of market structure* in A. P. Jacquemin–H. W. de Jong (editors), *Markets, corporate behaviour and the state: international aspects of industrial organization*, Martinus Nijhoff, The Hague, 1976, pages 169–212. See also: H. W. de Jong, *Theory and evidence concerning mergers: an international comparison*, ibidem, pages 95–123.
4. See R. Linda, *op. cit*, p. 15 *et seq*. The titles of the studies in the series are given in the Commission's annual *Report on Competition Policy*, published each April–May. See, in particular, Part III of the Reports for 1977 to 1982. The credit for inventing the Herfindahl Index may have to be shared between Herfindahl and Profs Corrado Gini and Albert O Hirschmann; see the latter's article, *The Paternity of an Index*, in: American Economic Review, September 1964.
5. An extensive application of the methodology to the whole of industry in the EEC is to be found in the Eleventh Report on Competition Policy, published by the EC Commission, Brussels, in 1982 (Part III, Section 2, Market structure, paras 262–265 and Table 4).
6. The formulae for the calculation of $2L$, $3L$ and $4L$ are as follows:

$$2L = \frac{x_1}{x_2} \times 100$$

$$3L = \frac{\dfrac{x_1}{\dfrac{x_2 + x_3}{2}} + \dfrac{\dfrac{x_1 + x_2}{2}}{x_3}}{2} \times 100$$

$$4L = \frac{\dfrac{x_1}{\dfrac{x_2 + x_3 + x_4}{3}} + \dfrac{\dfrac{x_1 + x_2}{2}}{\dfrac{x_3 + x_4}{2}} + \dfrac{\dfrac{x_1 + x_2 + x_3}{3}}{x_4}}{3} \times 100$$

7. The earliest versions of our method also used CR8 until it was found that the inclusion of this ratio did not add to the rigour of the approach.
8. The crude data for the industry are taken from Weinstock's article, *op. cit.*, pp. 295–296, and the other sources given in note (2) (*Time, The Economist, Business Week*).
9. 'Although the revisions make some important refinements and clarifications, the Department believes that the 1982 Merger Guidelines provide a sound framework for applying the antitrust laws to mergers and do not require extensive modification' (Statement by the Justice Department accompanying the new Guidelines).
10. The exact wording of this important statement of principle is as follows (Justice Department's underlining): '*The standards in the Guidelines are designed to ensure that the Department analyses the likely competitive impact of a merger within economically meaningful markets – i.e., markets that could be subject to the exercise of market power. Accordingly, for each product of each merging firm, the Department seeks to define a market in which firms could effectively exercise market power if they were able to coordinate their actions*'.
11. The Department is obviously somewhat embarrassed at the implicit indictment of the logic of the econometric system underlying the Herfindahl Index which the addition of the further criterion involves: '*Notwithstanding those standards* (author's underlining), the Department is likely to challenge the merger of any firm with a market share of at least one per cent with the leading firm in the market, provided the leading firm has a market share that is at least 35 per cent'.

13. LESSONS OF ECONOMICS FOR ANTITRUST; PROBLEMS OF ANTITRUST FOR ECONOMISTS

Eleanor M. Fox

There is an imperfect fit but symbiotic relation between United States antitrust law and industry organization economics. The United States antitrust laws were adopted to control discretionary power and coercive combinations, to give opportunity to entrepreneurs, to preserve a politically decentralized society, and to provide a fair system of governance over the marketplace.[1] Professor Walter Adams has eloquently framed the questions for antitrust as follows:

> Who shall make what decisions on whose behalf at what cost and for whose benefit? To whom shall the decision makers be accountable, and what safeguards shall be built into the system to guard against abuse?[2]

Professors Paul Geroski and Alexis Jacquemin, while writing generally of antitrust policy, have captured the essence of American antitrust:

> It is hard to accept conventional Pareto welfare analyses as forming the sole basis for antitrust intervention. It is well known that achievement of efficiency is neither necessary nor sufficient as a criterion of ideal policy. For example, it could be argued that the question of the means by which the social outcomes are achieved is more important than the social allocation outcome itself: for many, an allocation that is inefficient but arrived at in a spirit of voluntary cooperation under law is far better than an ideal allocation established by dictatorial decree.[3]

At least from the 1950s until the mid-1970s the United States courts interpreted the antitrust laws in the above spirit. That period was, coincidentally, one of general economic advance for U.S. business. Since the mid-1970s, however, the bloom has been off the economic rose. United States' trading partners have become more powerful and progressive and have made stark inroads into U.S. markets. The country has become more concerned with scarcity, on the one hand, and with the

de Jong, H. W., Shepherd, W. G. (eds) Mainstreams in Industrial Organization
© 1986 Martinus Nijhoff Publishers, Dordrecht. ISBN 978-94-017-0495-3

eroding leadership of U.S. firms in international markets, on the other hand. Particularly since the Supreme Court of the 1960s had continually expanded the realm of antitrust to foster the growth and independence of small entrepreneurial firms, the stage was set for claims that antitrust was impairing efficiency and that it should be all but abolished.[4]

The assault on antitrust has come in two forms. First it has been argued and sometimes demonstrated, in law reviews, economics journals and in court, that particular principles of law threatened net harms to consumers and should therefore be overturned. The law, it was urged, should not promote inefficiency. In response several principles of law have been changed,[5] and, I believe, appropriately so.

The second assault, however, is a much more powerful form of engagement. The attack is on roots, not branches. Proponents assert that antitrust protects competition only as a means to achieve efficient outcomes and therefore that no antitrust enforcment is merited unless the challenged act can be shown to be inefficient. In turn, inefficiency is defined as a reduction in the sum of producer profits and consumer surplus. Artificial output restriction is treated as a necessary but not sufficient attribute of an inefficient (and thus anticompetitive) transaction.[6]

Much of the economic analysis in support of this latter world-view is static only. Some, however, purports to be dynamic in the following sense. The analysts treat static (welfare) loss as the only possible *loss* that can result from the error of not banning anticompetitive transitions, but they presume that much larger dynamic losses occur from erroneously blocking efficient transactions. Erroneous interventions, it is said, result in total bans against 'beneficial' ways of producing or getting to market, and thus they deprive firms of the freedom they need to engage in creative responses to consumer wants. On the other hand erroneous non-interventions are said to be harmless on grounds that the market will discipline the offending firm and will do so faster than courts.[7]

This conception – often attributed to the Chicago School – is the springboard for proposed constructions of existing law that would virtually abolish antitrust. Indeed it is self-evident that if the only reason for antitrust law were to produce efficient outcomes and if the market virtually always works better than government intervention in doing so, antitrust law woud be superfluous.

The Chicago approach is, however, seductive. It is appealing to jurists, who may hestitate to 'stand in the way' of 'national progress' or 'technological advance' by leading American firms.

Despite claims of victory,[8] however, and despite current government enforcement policies[9] and many successes in appellate courts,[10] the Chicago School has not won. In case after case, although sometimes by close margins, the Supreme Court of the United States has rejected the invitation to eviscerate antitrust. In Hyde v. Jefferson Parish Hospital District No. 2,[11] the Supreme Court (4 to 3) declined to accept the Chicago view that tie-ins should be presumed legal on the grounds that they 'merely' facilitate price discrimination or allow the seller to offer a more attractive package. In Monsanto Company v. Spray-Rite Service Corporation,[12] the Court sidestepped the invitation to abolish the per se rule against agreements that fix resale prices, despite the Chicago argument that when manufacturers terminate discounting distributors in order to maintain resale prices the termination almost surely reflects the discounter's failure to provide important services and its destructive free ride on service-providing distributors. In Arizona v. Maricopa County Medical Society (4–3),[13] the Court declined the invitation to abolish the per se rule against maximum price-fixing and rejected the Chicago argument that if the Maricopa doctors agreed on maximum prices they must have done so to provide a better insurance package to insureds. In National Collegiate Athletic Association v. Board of Regents of the University of Oklahoma,[14] the Supreme Court found illegal the agreement among college football teams to sell television rights to their games only through the NCAA. It rejected the Chicago argument that football was a small part of the true market and that, since the restraint could not have been imposed to exercise nonexistent power, it must have been necessary to provide the public good of amateurism. Finally, last June, the Supreme Court decided its first monopoly case in 19 years and upheld, 8 to 0, a treble damage judgment for a competitor plaintiff.[15] It rejected the argument that Aspen Skiing Company (owner of three of the four mountains in Aspen) could not have been using predatory strategies when it refused to cooperate with Aspen Highlands in issuing a four-mountain pass. The argument was based on the Chicago supposition that, if Aspen Skiing had tried to use market power, the skiers would have gone elsewhere. The Court also implicitly rejected the Chicago assumption that when a competitor sues it wants protection against competition and that a judgment for a plaintiff competitor is therefore protectionist and anticompetitive.

The battle, however, is not over. Much of the law hangs in balance. The Chicago School's postulates that private transactions are efficient and that duties on dominant firms will hold back progress are powerful and appealing, may tip the balance, and may have a profound influence on the structure of American industry. It is therefore critical that jurists and legislators[16] understand whether these assumptions are merited or not. The papers of Professors Shepherd, Scherer and Mueller make important advances in testing Chicago's crucial assumptions.[17]

NOTES

1. See Fox, The Modernization of Antitrust: A New Equilibrium, 66 Cornell L. Rev. 1140 (1981) (hereafter 'Modernization'); Spivak, The Chicago School Approach to Single Firm Exercises of Market Power: A Response, in Fox and Halverson, eds., Antitrust Policy in Transition: The Convergence of Law and Economics 83 (1984).
2. Adams, Antitrust and a Free Economy, in Fox and Halverson, eds., Industrial Concentration and the Market System 33 (1979).
3. Geroski and Jacquemin, Dominant Firms and Their Alleged Decline, 2 International J. of Indus. Org. 1, 21–22 (1984). The authors continue:

> It is also the case that the Schumpeterian competition arguments which are a familiar part of antitrust defenses sit very uneasily with Pareto-type welfare calculations. These two points together suggest that distribution and equity ought to loom large in policy decisions: do would-be entrepreneurs have equal or 'fair' access to the means necessary to attempt a creative breakthrough? Do successful competitors in innovative processes have a 'fair' return for their efforts, or access to a 'fair' mechanism for determining rewards? Reinforcing this, it is the case that distribution and equity issues dominate the evaluation of the consequences of whatever competitive process is under consideration both because market power affects the distribution of economic rewards . . . and because market power affects the decision of what to produce, which must be evaluated vis-a-vis consumer tastes . . . . All of these would be important considerations even if creatively destructive competition involved a regular turnover of winners; when, however, small asymmetries can be solidified into dominant positions that persist, then the inequities they create become institutionalised, creating long-term problems in the performance of the economic system which cry out for policy attention.

   Id. at 22.
4. See Modernization.
5. See, e.g., Continental T.V., Inc. v. GTE Sylvania, Inc., 443 S. Ct. 36 (1977).
6. See, e.g., R. Bork, Thc Antitrust Paradox (1978); R. Posner, Antitrust Law – An Economic Perspective (1976); Easterbrook, The Limits of Antitrust, 63 Texas L. Rev. 1 (1984).
7. See Easterbrook, *supra*.
8. See Posner, The Chicago School of Antitrust Analysis, 127 U. Pa. L. Rev. 925 (1979).
9. See, e.g., U.S. Department of Justice Vertical Restraints Guidelines (Jan. 23, 1985), printed in 48 BNA Antitrust & Trade Reg. Rep., Special Supp., Jan. 24, 1985; U.S. Department of Justice Merger Guidelines (June 14, 1984), printed in 46 BNA Antitrust & Trade Reg. Rep., Special Supp., June 14, 1984.
10. See, e.g., Brunswick Corp. v. Riegel Textile Corp., 752 F. 2d 261 (7th Cir.), cert. denied, – U.S. – (1985); California Computer Products, Inc. v. International Business Machines Corp., 613 F. 2d 727 (9th Cir. 1979).
11. 104 S. Ct. 1551 (1984).
12. 104 St. Ct. 1464 (1984).
13. 457 U.S. 332 (1982).
14. 104 S. Ct. 2948 (1984).
15. Aspen Skiing Co. v. Aspen Highlands Skiing Corp., 1985–2 CCH Trade Cas. ¶66, 653 (1985).

16. U.S. Secretary of Commerce Malcolm Baldrige has proposed adoption of legislation that would repeal Section 7 of the Clayton Act (the statute that prohibits mergers that threaten to lessen competition), give a five-year exemption from the Sherman Act for mergers in depressed industries, and partially eliminate the treble damage remedy. The theory of the proposal is that the U.S. antitrust laws restrain efficient transactions and thereby handicap U.S. firms, especially in world markets. President Reagan is sympathetic to this proposal. See 'Reagan May Seek Trust Law Easing', N.Y. Times, Sept. 19, 1985, D 21, c.l.
17. In American antitrust jurisprudence, the critical question of the moment is whether private transactions (e.g., mergers, even big mergers) and single firm acts (e.g., dominant firm product-change and pricing strategies) are entitled to the presumption of efficiency. It is this presumption that tips the legal scales and has caused the dramatic shift in the law over the past five to ten years. Even when courts recognize that the focus of the law is the maintenance of competitive markets, not the crystallization of the last drop of efficiency, they do not want to hurt consumers.

    In this context, attempts to prove that big mergers are preponderantly inefficient (either power-producing or doomed to failure), that monopoly-sized firms are economically less desirable than alternative break-ups, and that therefore Congress should enact more regulatory laws, are more ambitious than the immediate task at hand. Also, they reflect a more difficult undertaking and an undertaking that is more likely to fail – either because the data may be ambiguous or because the conclusions may involve normative elements.

PART IV. DEREGULATION

14. WHAT DO WE UNDERSTAND ABOUT THE ECONOMICS OF REGULATION: THE EFFECTS OF U.S. TRANSPORT DEREGULATION

Kenneth D. Boyer

In a 1981 overview of the theory and practice of economic regulation [47], Joskow and Noll list the following as the core elements of current approaches to understanding the nature and behavior of traditional regulated industries:

1. The regulation of industries with competitive structure causes inefficiencies associated with excessive service quality. In this theory, regulated firms can not enjoy the profits resulting from high rates, but dissipate the profits by directing rivalry towards service quality rather than price.
2. Optimal prices for regulated natural monopolies may be unsustainable. Regulation of such industries may thus require artificial entry restrictions. In some other cases, natural monopoly pricing may be adequately constrained simply by the threat of entry, thus making regulation unnecessary. (This approach has become known as the 'theory of contestable markets' [12].)
3. Peak-load-pricing and related models are useful for understanding a wide variety of practices of regulated industries.
4. The regulation of industries with monopoly structure may cause Averch–Johnson type of incentives toward excessive capital intensity.

While not holding Joskow and Noll responsible for the theories they describe, I believe that their list conveniently and accurately represents the state of the 'theory of economic regulation' before our experience with deregulation.

During the last decade, American transportation industries have been deregulated. This provides a convenient laboratory in which to test the usefulness of these theories of regulatory behavior. In this paper, I offer a survey of all studies published to date which claim to have analyzed

de Jong, H. W., Shepherd, W. G. (eds) Mainstreams in Industrial Organization before-and-after effects of deregulation in U.S. transportation industries. I have attempted to summarize all results of deregulation that academic observers found sufficiently interesting to comment on – I have thus not limited myself to the variables considered to be *ex ante* interesting by Joskow and Noll.

Industries other than transportation have been deregulated within the last ten years. Stock brokerage and banking are examples [22]. While the theories of regulatory behavior might be applicable in these other sectors, the traditional regulated sector offers a more direct evaluation of the usefulness of those theories. The experience of the transportation sector is not a complete test of the theories, but it is the best that we have at this point. Within several years, the deregulated telecommunications sector can also be used to test the usefulness of theories of regulatory behavior, but as yet there has been too little experience with the effects of telephone deregulation to be conclusive.

This paper begins with a description of transport deregulation since 1976. Sections 2 through 5 describe the effects of deregulation in the main industries – trucking, railroads, airlines, and busses. I have tried to maintain a parellelism where possible between the modes. Section 6 summarizes the effects of deregulation across the transportation industries.

In Section 7, I compare the predictions of each of the theories listed above to what occurred in each of the industries. The paper concludes (in Section 8) with some comments on useful directions for further research in the economics of regulation.

1. THE NATURE OF AMERICAN TRANSPORTATION DEREGULATION

Most studies of the effects of deregulation have a difficult time placing a starting date on deregulation. There is no confusion on dates of the Acts: 1978 for airlines; 1980 for (separately) railroads and motor carriers; and 1982 for busses. But in each case, the Act of Congress deregulating the industry was preceded by a period of administrative deregulation. This period began around 1976 when the composition of the regulatory agencies changed radically to include a majority of members favoring deregulation.

On the other hand, when should the transition period from regulated to unregulated behavior be presumed to have begun, and how do we recognize that the transition to an unregulated equilibrium is complete? There are no obviously correct answers to these questions. Unfortunately, this is important for evaluating the theories of regulatory behavior. To some extent, we are still in a period of transition to a new equilibrium. Those who wish to deny the usefulness of observing behavior for determining policy, argue that the intermediate stages through which an industry passes on its way from a regulated equilibrium to an unregulated long run equilibrium need bear no resemblance to the latter. I believe that this approach invites ignorant analyses of the effects of deregulation. While conceding that the transportation industries have not yet achieved long run equilibria, in this paper I assume that the direction of movement since deregulation has been in the direction of the unregulated equilibrium

The transportation industries in the United States are not completely deregulated. An editorial in the conservation *Regulation* magazine notes that,

> 'In the maritime area, decontrol is nowhere in sight: in fact, Congress is debating whether to extend the scope of cargo preference laws. In air transport, federal intervention is likely to continue indefinitely on international routes, and even on domestic routes, the 1978 Airline Deregulation Act guarantees 'essential' air service to small communities through 1988, a provision that Congress could easily extend. In surface transport, the law continues to prescribe safety and insurance rules for truckers and rate ceilings for 'captive' shippers, however those may be defined'. [74]

The fact is, however, that these regulations are of vanishingly small importance compared to those in place before 1976.

- For all practical purposes, entry into any of the transportation industries is unrestricted by law. There are minor exit restrictions for railroads and busses only, and in practice, these restrictions have not been enforced.
- Except for parts of the railroad business, pricing of services should be considered free of government intervention.
- For all practical purposes, common carrier obligations have disappeared for all modes.
- No mode of transportation is subject to quality of service restrictions.

In short, with the partial exception of railroads, all modes of transportation have been deregulated at the federal level [56] – busses for somewhere between two and nine years, motor carriers and railroads for between four and nine years, and airlines for between seven and nine years, depending on how one dates the start of deregulation. The next sections describe what has happened to each of these modes over that period.

2. TRUCKING DEREGULATION

Effect on total tonnage in the trucking industry

The Motor Carrier Act of 1980 has had no observable effect on the total output of the trucking industry. There was a decline in the tonnage of the industry as a whole following the passage of the MCA, but this decline is easily explained by the recession of 1981–1982 [42]. Traffic levels in 1984 had recovered to the same level as in 1980 [85, p. 7].

There has similarly been no discernible change in the modal splits between motor carriers and their competitors. Motor carriers hauled 38% of total inter-city tons in 1975, before the ICC began administrative deregulation, and hauled the same percentage in 1984, four years after legislative deregulation. Measured in terms of ton-miles, the motor carrier share has fluctuated around 23% for the past ten years. The most recent truck share is 24% [85, p. 6].

Effect of deregulation on price levels

There is some anecdotal evidence that deregulation has depressed rates for motor carrier services [56], but there have been no academic studies that have attempted to confirm the relationship. Between 1973 and 1981, the Rate Index of General Freight Common Carriers rose 105%., the same amount as the CPI, but less than the 117% rise in the Producer Price Index [72, p. 274]. The real average revenue per ton mile for General Freight Motor carriers declined from 7.11 (1967) cents/ton mile in 1975 reaching a low of 6.87 cents just prior to deregulation in 1980, and then has risen to stand at 7.61 cents/ton mile in the most recent reporting period. General Freight Carriers are predominantly LTL truckers. Real price movements for specialized (predominantly TL carriers) declined somewhat immediately following the passage of the Motor Carrier Act of 1980, but have risen over the last year [85, p. 11]. Economists have yet to determine how much of these changes is explainable by deregulation, and how much by other factors. It is possible, that traffic composition effects have determined most or all of the apparent movement in average rates.

The only attempts to date to measure rate level effects of deregulation that do not depend on observing average revenue per ton mile have been through shipper surveys. Typically, researchers ask shippers whether their average rates are greater or less than rates at some previous time [13, 14, 38, 43]. The answers vary depending on the time of the before and after comparison. Surveys that compare rates in 1980 with rates in 1981 or 1982 are more likely to show that rates have decreased than are surveys comparing rate levels in 1976 and after 1980.

Effect on the rate structure

The effect of deregulation on rate structures has taken the form of discounts from listed prices rather than changes in the posted prices themselves. Estimates from 1984 suggest that between 40% and 80% of truck traffic is being moved under some form of discount instituted independently by carriers. These discounts vary among shippers and may account for more than 20% of the total shipping charges [65]. All studies of trucking deregulation have discovered that the presence of such 'flexible pricing' or discounts from posted prices. The quantity-tied discounts tend to be targeted at particular shippers in a manner that would have been illegal under old interpretations of the Interstate Commerce Act [43]. Discounting is so widespread that published tariffs are no longer a reliable guide to the actual prices being paid [68].

Some shipper surveys find that urban shippers are more likely than rural shippers to receive discounts [38]. The main predictive characteristic of shippers that determines the likelihood of being offered a discount is the quantity of freight offered by the shipper [38, 13]. However, the rate discounts explainable by the size of the shipper does not appear to be sufficiently large as to cause complaints among small shippers [13, 14, 38, 43].

Effect on the availability of service to rural areas

None of the studies of deregulation has been able to discover rural areas that have completely lost trucking service because of deregulation. The current consensus is that the structure of regulation before 1977 theoretically could not have induced carriers to provide service to small communities if it were unprofitable to do so [23, 37, 72].

Effect on service quality

There is no evidence that service quality has dropped following deregulation. Two surveys, one in 1974 and a second in 1982, asked shippers to describe characteristics of the carriers they dealt with. There was no statistically significant difference in the characteristics of the services offered in the two years [60].

Surveys of shippers following deregulation suggest that buyers of transport services do not see a significant difference in the quality of trucking service. Somewhat more shippers believe that there has been an improvement in on-time performance or in equipment availability following deregulation than believe that service quality has dropped. [13, 38, 43].

Effect on service innovations

Following deregulation, one of the most noticeable changes was an increase in the service options available to shippers [13, 14, 38, 43, 60]. For example, carriers now offer guaranteed delivery times and will pick up and deliver at night and on weekends. They offer computerized record keeping and shipment tracking. These new options are often part of a price-discount package. Examples include discounts for pickup of multiple shipments and discounts for giving a carrier a certain volume of freight per month. Many of these service options were forbidden under regulation as part of policy of guaranteeing equal treatment for all shippers.

Effect on the structure of the industry

Different segments of the motor carrier industry have been differently affected by deregulation. The traditional distinction between specialized carriers and carriers of general freight is disappearing. The expected bifurcation of the industry into a small number of large national Less-Than-Truckload (LTL) carriers and a large number of small Truckload carriers has not occurred [18]. The LTL carriers have tried to expand their territories by the addition of new operating rights rather than by mergers, leading to an effective increase in the number of large carriers offering service to shippers at any locality. If deregulation eventually leads to increased concentration in the less-than-truckload freight segment, this movement has not yet appeared [42, 43]. The LTL segment currently has excess capacity, however, and some form of shakeout through mergers or additional bankruptcies is likely [83].

The number of common carriers in the industry increased by more than one half between 1980 and 1984 to 25 000 [42]. Most of the new applicants were owner operators. The new applicants are heavily concentrated in the truckload segment of the market. This increase in the number of new firms occurred at the same time that some of the most famous trucking firms were being forced into bankruptcy. Between 1979 and 1984, carriers representing more than 16% of the general commodity common carrier revenues had gone out of business [42]. There is disagreement among analysts on what benchmarks to use to determine whether this bankruptcy rate is unusually high [42, 62, 63]. The truckload sector of the market, where the entry pressures have been most severe, has not had an unusually high bankruptcy rate.

A goal of the Motor Carrier Act of 1980 was to improve the financial position of owner-operators. Although some owner-operators have applied for and received operating certificates, most such carriers have been unaffected by deregulation [29]. The use of truckers who trip-lease or permanently lease their services to other firms has stayed constant.

Effect on financial condition of motor carriers

Immediately following passage of the Motor Carrier Act of 1980, trucking companies reported large losses. This was due partly to writing off the value of the certificates of convenience and necessity (made worthless by the policy of free entry into the industry), and partly due to the severe recession of 1981 and 1982. As noted above, some carriers with familiar names were forced into bankruptcy and were liquidated.

There is, however, surprisingly mixed opinion on the effect that deregulation has had on the financial condition of carriers. The rates of return on equity of publicly traded companies has dropped from the early 1970's, and changes in the security values of motor carriers indicate that investors expected deregulation to lower the stream of future earnings [77]. However, the average reported return on equity is still above that for other transport modes [83]. The financial press believes that the current profitability of the LTL segment is below equilibrium levels; the expected capacity shrinkage should increase margins, though not to pre-deregulation levels [56, 83].

Some observers argue that deregulation, by encouraging more efficient use of labor and equipment and more flexible pricing, will improve motor carrier profitability in the long run. These observers note that the stocks of motor carriers, which under-performed the market before the passage of the Motor Carrier Act of 1980, out-performed the market following 1980. Measures of systematic risk in rates of return fell following the passage of the MCA, especially for specialized carriers [25, 52]. Using market data, it appears that the large carriers and carriers of specialized commodities were expected to benefit most from deregulation [62, 63].

Effects on labor

All studies of the effects of deregulation agree that the group that has unambiguously lost from deregulation is the membership of the Teamsters Union. The pressure on the Union to offer carriers lower wage rates and more flexible working conditions comes from the expansion of non-union carriers, especially in the truckload market. The entry of non-union carriers has not affected carriers equally [77]. Those most affected are regional truckers. They have recently broken off from the main employer group in the hope of reaching a wage settlement more favorable than the National Master Freight Agreement.

Union labor costs are about \$20/hr compared to \$13/hr for non-union carriers. Since labor costs are about 63 cents of every cost dollar, this difference allows non-union carriers to undercut prices of unionized carriers by 10% and still make a profit [65]. Competition from non-union carriers, allowed entry into the market because of deregulation, has led to the layoff of as much as one third of the teamsters union membership. It has also prompted existing trucking companies to set up parallel non-union carriers to compete for traffic with themselves. Deregulation has reduced wages and time paid for but not worked, and has forced more flexible work rules. Teamsters' drivers have also lost loads to the newly deregulated railroad piggyback services [17].

3. RAILROAD DEREGULATION

Effect on rail traffic

The Staggers Act of 1980 appears to have had no effect on the aggregate level of rail traffic. While there are not many years of data available since the passage of the Act, the trends in tonnage statistics do not seem to have reversed or slowed during the deregulation episode somewhere between 1976 and 1980. The data continue to show that rail traffic generally rises and falls with the level of output in the manufacturing sector. Rail ton-miles, which had dropped from 932 billion ton miles in 1980 to 810 billion in 1982, rose to a new high of 935 billion ton-miles in 1984 [85, p. 6]. The rail share of inter-city ton miles has fluctuated between 35% and 38% since 1973 [1], and does not seem to have moved in reponse to deregulation [87].

There are some exceptions. Wide publicity has been given to the effects of deregulation of piggyback traffic (in 1981), and of fresh fruits and vegetables traffic (1979) [61]. A study in 1984 estimated that, adjusting for all other factors that determine the level of piggyback traffic, deregulation accounts for 12% of the first year increase in such traffic [8]. After the Staggers Act, piggyback traffic has continued its rapid growth and there are now some documentable instances of traffic which has been diverted from motor carriers [66]; the extent to which increases in piggyback traffic represents new business as opposed to traffic formerly handled without intermodal equipment remains speculative. The increases in piggyback traffic have been erratic, and the most recent trend is down [2].

The increases in fruit and vegetable traffic carried by railroads have been spectacular. Rail traffic in these commodities had dwindled before deregulation, so large percentage increases were easy to come by. Following deregulation, all of the major western railroads have shown increases ranging in several hundred percent which can not be otherwise explained by such factors as levels of agricultural production [39]. The success of fruit and vegetable deregulation is attributed to the rails' ability to react quickly and flexibly to take advantage of market opportunities, without long rate hearings or ICC car-service orders. The rail share of fresh fruit and vegetable traffic has nonetheless remained a small fraction of the total. At most, deregulation can be credited with reducing the motor carrier share of the traffic from 90% to 87% of the total [89].

Despite the existence of instances where deregulation has had a noticeable affect on rail traffic, most commodities show no such shifts. For example, following deregulation, lumber traffic has continued to move from rail to truck, with little expectation that deregulation will have major effects [45]. It is hard to argue with the assessment that 'The notion that trucks are a suitable competitive alternative for rail shippers in any market is baseless [83]'. Deregulation did not and will not shift substantial amounts of traffic between modes [21]. The current differential between average rail rates of 3.12 cents per ton mile and average truck rates of 21.4 cents per ton mile [87] is not a reflection of service quality differences in overlapping markets, but of the existence of generally non-competing markets for freight transportation.

Effect on price levels

Real rail rates continued their slight downward trend following deregulation, with real rates (in 1967 dollars) falling from 1.25 cents/ton-mile in 1975 to 1.15 cents/ton-mile in 1980 to 1.06 cents/ton-mile in 1984 [85, p. 11]. The drop in rates has been erratic, however. Compared to motor carrier and air traffic, there is a wider variation between the lowest and highest rail rates. Railroad average revenue per ton mile is thus more easily affected by traffic composition. It is possible, then, that the actual charges for a typical shipment has risen, while the average revenue per ton mile has fallen. The most reasonable guess, however, is that deregulation has not significantly affected real rate levels either up or down.

Effect on rate structures

The rate level was never of as much interest to regulators, carriers, or shippers, as was the rate structure [19]. Deregulation has undoubtedly had a profound effect on rate structures, although the effect is in general invisible to outsiders. Although posted rates do not seem to have changed significantly after passage of the Staggers Act (at least for lumber shipments) [88], the most significant change of the Staggers Act was the encouragement of contracts between shippers and carriers [5].

Since the terms of the contracts are secret, and since their use has become widespread within the last several years, it is impossible to describe the nature of the post-deregulation rate structure. Some of the larger railroads now move 50% of their traffic under long-term contracts; for smaller railroads, the amount of contract traffic is as high as 95% [83]. Contracts enable railroads to require a shipper to move pre-specified amounts of traffic to get a volume discount and prevent competitors from knowing what price they need to beat. Shippers are able to specify service conditions in return for volume commitments. Contracts need not be offered to all shippers, and railroads presumably bargain knowledgeably to maximize the profitability of serving each shipper. All of these – targeted price reductions, volume discounts, and specification of service quality – would have been illegal under the old regulatory regime.

Several shipper groups have been reluctant to sign service contracts. Notable in this group is coal shippers, some of whom have reported rises in rates of 20% or more within one year [44]. Coal rates are the most sensitive of all rail charges. The industry has been at pains to argue that, at least in the period between 1983 and 1985, rail rate increases have lagged behind cost increases [3].

Grain shippers have similarly been uneasy with the removal of rate protections under the Staggers Act. Studies disagree about what has happened to grain rates since 1980 – one done for the Association of American Railways [4] reports a drop in grain rates of 18.4% in the first four years after passage of the Staggers Rail Act (the sampling technique for this study weights heavily the rates of the largest shippers – rates which have presumably shown the largest decreases.) Another report, done by the Bureau of Labor Statistics reports that railroad grain rates have increased [71].

Another group that is not fully satisfied with the terms of the Staggers Act is chemical shippers. Led by coal and utility interests, these groups have been pressing for scaling back of the rate freedoms given to railroads in the Staggers Act.

Effects on costs and service quality

Following deregulation, railroads have become more sensitive to shippers' requests for specialized services [79]. All railroads have reorganized to give more emphasis to marketing departments. There are no figures on service attributes that demonstrate improved service quality, and only limited shipper surveys that suggest better service [41], but it is assumed that the use of service quality clauses in contracts has served to tailor services more according to the wishes of shippers. At least one railroad has been able to redesign services to allow for just-in-time shipping of parts and products [69].

Deregulation has encouraged measures which both improve service quality and cut costs – notably the greater use of unit trains and intermodal services. In addition abandonment procedures have been streamlined, although the effect of the Staggers Act on line rationalization is not pronounced [50], and many of the abandoned lines have remained in operation under state and local subsidy [32]. Lastly, some of the more burdensome rules covering equipment and traffic interchange have been altered since 1980 – rules that formerly sacrificed efficiency for the sake of equity [75].

Effect on the structure of the industry

The Staggers Act has had the effect of improving the position of long railroads relative to short ones. This, together with explicit encouragement of mergers contained in the Staggers Act, has set off a merger wave of unprecedented proportions. There are currently six major railroad systems in the nation – three on either side of the Mississippi River. More mergers are inevitable as the industry retreats to a two-or-three system structure.

Effect on financial condition of railroads

The Staggers Act has unquestionably been successful in its stated goal of improving the financial condition of the railroad industry [35]. Reported net income in 1984 was $2.66 billion, an all-time high [70].

Whether railroads are considered to be 'revenue adequate' is important for determining residual oversight of the ICC. The question thus has been disputed between the industry and shipper groups. Railroads appear currently profitable or unprofitable depending on the standard that one uses. The reported rate of return on net investment for 1984 was 5.58% – well below the average return on all manufacturing, but at historic highs for the industry as a whole.

Railroad accounting, however, is an historical curiosity. Some part of the improved prosperity since 1980 is simply the result of a change to more standard depreciation procedures [16]. Moreover, the asset base used to determine the level of investment includes some assets that have been on railroad books undepreciated for more than 100 years. Railroads are currently flush with cash and have been making investments outside the industry. Recent reports of cash flow as a percent of equity show the industry to be equally as profitable as the rest of American industry [83]. This is in marked contrast to the financial condition of the industry before deregulation.

Effects on labor relations

It is striking how little railroad labor has been affected by deregulation. Unlike the motor carrier and air transport industries where labor costs are at the center of competitive maneuvering, rail labor has been insulated by the absence of a non-union sector which can effectively take away markets from individual carriers [49]. Railroads have tried to aggressively address work rules in labor negotiations, but have been able to get only limited concessions on long-standing issues. There have been no revolutionary changes in labor relations remotely like those in the other transportation industries. The changes that have occurred in rail labor relations are claimed to result not from deregulation but from reductions in other Federal programs targeted at the transport sector – from job preservation clauses in mergers, to subsidies for failing carriers [55].

Owing to the variety of long-standing work rules and pay agreements, railroad workers are now the highest paid of all transport labor. In 1983, total earnings and fringe benefits for railroad employees averaged $41,310, compared to $38,951 for air transport, the mode that traditionally has had the highest labor costs [85, p. 20].

4. AIR TRANSPORT DEREGULATION

Much more has been written on Airline deregulation than deregulation in any other mode of transportation. Readers should be aware, however, that many of the post-deregulation evaluations have been done by economists who played an advocacy role in promoting deregulation. While these analyses are generally of scholarly quality, they can not be considered to be disinterested.

Effect on air traffic

Airline traffic, which had consistent year-to-year increases in passenger loads through late 1970's, experienced their first decline in passenger loads in the period following deregulation, when there was a drop in domestic passengers from 295 million in 1979 to 275 million in 1980 and 267 million in 1981. By 1983, passengers levels had returned to 1979 levels and 1984 again showed an increase in industry output, to 317 million. Demand in 1985 is running 11% ahead of levels in 1984 [85, p. 9]. Air passenger miles as a percent of all passenger miles increased from 10% immediately before deregulation to 13.4% in 1979, after which it fell somewhat; in 1984 air travel as a percentage of all travel was again on the rise, reaching 14%.

The role that deregulation has played in the leveling-off of airline demand between 1979 and 1983 and its subsequent increase is unclear. [82, 91]. The period beginning in 1976 has seen structural changes in the costs of flying due to fuel price fluctuations and an artificial restriction in output resulting from the air traffic controllers' strike.

Effect on fare levels

The general expectation preceding the 1978 Act was that fare levels would drop to reflect the cost savings of lower service quality expected to accompany deregulation [51]. In fact, nominal average revenue per passenger mile did drop between 1978 and 1979, but then rose strongly between 1979 and 1981 as fuel prices increased [11]. Nominal fare levels slid from 1981 to 1983, then rose during a period of tacit collusion through 1984. They have been falling since that time [82].

Since 1977, fare level increases have in general been less than increases in costs per passenger mile [11]. In real terms, average revenue per passenger mile is currently about 4.0 (1967) cents compared to approximately 4.7 cents prior to deregulation [85, p. 11] – approximately a 14% drop in real average fare levels over the ten year period. This figure is sensitive to changes traffic composition and may not reflect actual changes in typical fares.

Changes in fare structure

The fluctuations in fare levels noted above have not been the result of rises or falls in the standard fares. Rather, the changes have been brought about by changing the structure of fares, and particularly by varying the availability of discounts [59]. The drop in average revenue per passenger mile between 1980 and 1983 is a reflection of the increase in the percentage of passengers flying on discounted tickets from 45% to 87% between those two years [82]. The increase in yields between 1983 and 1984 resulted from the institution of a mileage-based pricing formula as a coordination tool and the restricted use of discounts.

There have been three main changes in the fare structure: first, a movement away from the old linear distance-based fare scheme toward one that also reflects the importance of traffic density. Fare structures now contain what would have been considered long-haul–short-haul discrimination and discrimination against small communities [24]. To the extent that there is a public demand for re-regulation, it derives from the imbalance in fare changes for different communities. The new fare structure undoubtedly better reflects the costs of serving different airports [11]. Several studies have demonstrated, however, that the concentration of sales in individual inter-city pairs also affects the fares on those routes [40, 80, 84].

The second main change in rate structures is the increasing use of discounts. To some extent, the discounts can be explained by peak load pricing. It is difficult to reconcile such capacity motivations with typical restrictions on discount tickets. The restrictions appear to be designed to insure that businesses pay more than leisure travelers. The post-deregulation fare structure thus contains both cost-determined as well as demand-determined elements.

The third main change in the fare structure is the proliferation of frequent-flier programs. These programs are costly for the airlines [54], but presumably increase the ability to discriminate by decreasing the firm-specific demand elasticity for certain classes of airline travel.

Economic analysis had not anticipated that the main effect of deregulation would be seen in changes in fare structure rather than fare levels [11, 53]. Deregulation has apparently increased rather than decreased the importance of systematic price discrimination and product differentiating in the industry, even as it has moved rates closer to costs. Confirming the increasing importance of product differentiation is the movement in the advertising-sales ratio – it stood at 1.7% in 1978, but had increased to 2.2% in 1984 [54].

Effect on costs

A striking effect of deregulation has been the restructuring of airline networks as hubs and spokes [48]. Combined with an adaptation of the aircraft stock to service such a system, this change should have the effect of increasing load factors, thereby increasing productivity and lowering costs [58]. This adaptation of the aircraft stock to the new route structure is still going on. The full effect of route restructuring on productivity has yet to be felt [64].

Since the birth of the industry, changes in productivity have been associated with changes in the size and utilization of aircraft. One of the most important effects on productivity claimed for regulation is that it induced buying aircraft that were larger than appropriate for the routes served [11]. Such a policy should have led to lower load factors and reduced productivity. Immediately after deregulation, the increase in fuel prices made some of the older, larger jets obsolete. The increase in load factor associated with grounding these jets increased measured productivity immediately after deregulation [76]. Since 1978, load factor has fluctuated with the fare yield and the level of GNP, but has generally been above pre-deregulation levels [82, 91].

A paper by Caves, Christiensen and Tretheway claims that deregulation improved total factor productivity in the industry [27]. This result is sensitive to the timing of the presumed effects of regulation, and virtually all of the measured improvements in productivity associated with deregulation are explainable by improvements in load factor [51]. As airlines have changed their network structure, some increases in productivity have resulted from increases in aircraft utilization and longer stage lengths [11]. Until recently, however, there were no effects on productivity associated with changed work rules or decreased manning requirements on aircraft [11]. Because of the upheaval in labor relations in the last several years, increases in productivity resulting from better labor utilization can be expected in the coming years.

Effects on service quality

Product quality is notoriously difficult to measure, and thus has been ignored in most standard economic analyses. In the airline industry, however, the analysis of service quality played a central role in the deregulation effort, where excessive service quality was offered as an explanation for why airline profits were not excessive before deregulation [31]. Quality attributes have variously been identified as load factor, size of aircraft, food preparation, baggage handling, and flight frequency [7, 84, 86].

Whether service quality dropped after deregulation depends on which aspect one considers. Flight frequency generally did not fall following deregulation [15]. Load factors, as noted above, generally have risen though they have fluctuated considerably. There has been an increasing use of smaller aircraft – a factor that has been demonstrated to be perceived as less desirable service [30]. Some studies suggest that non-capacity aspects of air service (amenities, comfort, on-time service) have declined in quality following 1978 [15, 76].

Any movements in the average level of service quality are overwhelmed by changes in the structure of service quality between city pairs. There has been a marked increase in flight frequency between large hubs and a decrease in frequency to smaller airports [11, 64]. Some smaller cities have lost air service completely, and those that retain it are served by companies using smaller aircraft [46]. It is reasonable to expect that fare schemes motivated by peak load pricing may have decreased the likelihood of being denied seats on crowded flights; there is no confirmatory evidence on this point, however.

Structure of the industry

Deregulation has not caused the decline of any of the three sectors of the air transport industry – the majors, nationals, and regionals (which tend to be affiliated with larger airlines). The last of these (also known as commuters) has been the fastest growing of the three sectors. The majors have had static passenger counts for the last 7 years [82]. Although the names of the companies have not changed since deregulation, the service territories and network configuration of each of the airlines has changed radically. All airlines have abandoned some services, added others, and moved to a hub-and-spoke network configuration [33]. All airlines have engaged in experimentation on routes and fares that would have been illegal under the previous regulatory regime.

The best publicized change in the industry has been the rise of new, generally non-union airlines [58]. These airlines have lower costs and fares as a result of higher load factors, less restrictive work rules, and lower wage rates. These airlines have had a far larger effect on old airline management than their passenger levels appear to indicate.

An equally important change has been the national and international spread of airline networks. The demand advantages of a large network are forcing all companies to expand into each other's territories. The net effect has been to lower the average concentration of sales in individual inter-city pairs [53]. Some observers believe that the current industry structure is inherently unstable and that the smaller majors may be forced to merge or exit from the market [24]. Bankruptcies and mergers among the majors and the regionals is reducing the number of carriers [90]. Within a decade we may see an industry structure that looks much more like the intercity bus industry with one or two large companies competing against the number of smaller regional airlines [26].

Financial effects of deregulation

In 1982, the rate of return on investment hit a seven-year low [91]. In 1984, the 11 major airlines registered their first collective net profit in 5 years [82]. Nonetheless, the airlines are unanimous in believing themselves to be better off under deregulation than they would have been under regulation [28]. The financial distress of airlines has not been evenly distributed. Several carriers have been bankrupted, but some others have fared well. This was predicted by Spiller [81], who noted that the differences across markets served by different airlines should lead to differential effects of deregulation. Managements believe that deregulation has given the airline companies the ability to respond flexibly to a changed environment. The airlines that were bankrupted were in general predictable on the basis of financial weakness and other indicators of poor management [6].

Effect on labor

Economists failed to anticipate the pressure that airline deregulation would place on organized labor [53]. Deregulation permitted non-union carriers to enter markets traditionally flown only by unionized airlines. Non-union airlines have eliminated craft distinctions and enjoy wage rates that are 25–30% below union pay scales. This combination has allowed them to charge lower prices. Although they have not yet diverted substantial amounts of traffic from the major carriers, the new airlines are the major cause of the concession bargaining in the industry [55].

The new union contracts increase pilot hours per month, permit employees to cross craft lines, allow limited use of part-time workers, and reduce cockpit crew requirements. The contracts also contain lower wage increases than were traditional, and permit a two-tier wage structure with much lower wage-tenure profiles for new workers. The two tier contracts give an incentive to existing airlines to expand more rapidly as a means of increasing the percentage of low-cost workers [26], thus exacerbating the possibly destructive nature of airline competition [24].

5. SOME EARLY EFFECTS OF BUS DEREGULATION

The bus industry is the most recently deregulated transportation industry. Since the Bus Regulatory Reform Act was passed only in 1982, the effects of deregulation described in this section are preliminary and incomplete.

The 1982 Act was patterned on the Motor Carrier Act of 1980. The Bus law also contains two features that were not contained in truck deregulation: first, after a phase-in period, the ICC is to lose all authority over interstate rate making; second, the ICC gained the power to review and overturn decisions by state commissions on intrastate service by interstate carriers [36], Preemption of state regulation was especially important to the bus industry since state regulators were far more restrictive about rates and service requirements than was the ICC.

Following the pattern of the motor carrier and air transport industries, deregulation has led to an increase in industry members (the new carriers are almost solely charter carriers, however) and to a restructuring of routes, with existing carriers simultaneously abandoning certain routes and applying to serve others [92].

The industry as a whole has long been unprofitable. It has lost its market primarily to private automobiles, but also to rail and air carriers as bus fares rose more rapidly than rail or air fares before deregulation [9]. Real bus rates continued to rise after deregulation at about the same rate as they had before [67]. Some observers believe that following the scheduled lapsing of the antitrust exemption for ratemaking in 1986, general rate increases may be more difficult to institute [73]. However, the industry is still organized as a duopoly with a competitive fringe.

Deregulation apparently has been ineffective at reducing general concentration levels in the industry. These are conditions in which traditional analysis would expect to find continued price coordination.

Greyhound, the dominant carrier, enthusiastically supports complete deregulation of the industry [34]. Smaller carriers have a more ambiguous attitude toward deregulation. The main benefit to the industry has been the preemption of state regulation. The appeal provisions of the 1982 Act, which allowing the industry to argue before the ICC that state regulators were unduly strict in preventing abandonments or setting rates too low, have been used often. As of 1984, the industry had yet to have an appeal denied by the ICC [67]. Nonetheless, the appeal process is costly in time and money [34]; the bus industry would prefer a less cumbersome means of circumventing state regulations.

The main opposition to complete deregulation comes from state regulatory commissions who are concerned about loss of service to small communities [34]. A recent report says these concerns are exaggerated since the current minimal level of service to rural areas is only lightly used [73].

As in the motor carrier and air transport industries, organized labor has been asked to accept lower wages following deregulation. Unlike the other industries, however, Greyhound was not obviously losing significant amounts of traffic to non-union carriers when it took the strike to enforce its lower wage offer.

6. SUMMARIZING THE EFFECTS OF DEREGULATION

In the air travel, motor freight and bus industries, deregulation seems to have had similar effects. Deregulation has affected railroads somewhat differently.

1. The most pronounced effect on the non-rail industries has been a change in labor relations to concessionary bargaining. This has been associated with threatened and actual loss of traffic to non-union carriers. (Of course, industries other than in the former regulated transport sector have been able to gain concessions from labor; deregulation may not be solely responsible.) To the extent that there have been noticeable changes in production costs in the transport industries, one of the major sources of cost savings has been in wages. Railroads, however, despite drastic deregulation, have not had major changes in labor relations.

2. Deregulation has allowed carriers to tailor price and service offerings to different markets. This change has been seen in all modes of transportation, and especially among railroads. Apparently, the effect of deregulation has been to de-homogenize service and price offerings within and across markets. Deregulation has freed carriers to offer different services in different markets; to move prices closer to the true costs of serving a market, rather than such rough indicators of costs as distance; to provide innovative service offerings where customers are willing to pay for them; and to abandon unprofitable service. In the rail mode, deregulation also has allowed rates to move in the direction of what the market will bear. Regulation appears to have had a chilling effect on innovation and a leveling effect on services and prices, an effect that is reversed by deregulation.
3. Deregulation has changed the structure of the industries. All carriers have been moving to restructure their networks. Railroads have been doing this primarily by mergers and abandonments, while trucking and airline companies have been invading the territories of competing carriers. Airlines have increased the use of hub and spoke systems. All modes of transport apparently believe in the advantages of large networks, although the advantage enters primarily on the demand rather than the cost side. It is still too early to determine whether these demand advantages will lead to destructive competition.

It is also important to emphasize those aspects of business that deregulation has apparently left unaffected.

1. Fare levels have not changed markedly in any of the modes. The largest movement has been a 14% drop in average real air rates between 1975 and 1984. Alterations in average rail, truck, and bus prices are ambiguous and difficult to observe. Movements in average fare levels in all transportation industries are dominated by and determined by changes in the fare structure.
2. There has not been a major change in the average quality of service in any of the modes following deregulation. As with the fare level, however, this constancy of service quality is the result of wide changes in the quality of service offered to different users. Large shippers and large localities are more likely to have seen improvements in the quality of service. Perhaps more importantly, however, a wider menu of price/service offerings are available in each of the modes. This may have improved the effective utility of service to the average user, even as the average characteristics of the services have shown no change.

3. There has been no perceptible effect on the overall growth of demand or on the modal split of traffic between modes of transport. This may be the result of either the lack of movement in the average price level of each industry, or of modal demands that are price and quality inelastic.
4. There have been modest effects of deregulation on costs and productivity. It is reasonable to anticipate larger gains in the future from better adaptation of equipment to individual markets and restructuring of the transport networks to achieve higher equipment utilization. These results are already beginning to be visible in the airline industry. Lower labor costs resulting from union concessions and the entrance of non-union carries will also lower production expenditures in the future, although most cost savings from this source should be treated as income transfers rather than savings in real resources.
5. Some carriers have fared well financially and some poorly following deregulation. In the motor and air carrier industries there have been some bankruptcies as well as some success stories. As a group, airlines believe themselves better off under deregulation than they would have been under regulation. Railroads agree, as do the largest bus companies and some trucking firms. Railroad profitability has improved markedly under deregulation, while trucking companies' income has tended to declined.

As a general rule, deregulation has had a far greater effect on the structure of variables like fares, profitability, service levels, and quality than it has had on the levels of those variables. Regulation's main effects were to homogenize and level prices and service offerings and to deaden incentives for innovation and experimentation; as an unintentional side effect, regulation also conferred bargaining power on transport labor. Deregulation reverses all of these effects.

7. EVALUATION THEORIES OF REGULATORY BEHAVIOR

A successful theory of regulatory behavior would have predicted the changes brought about by deregulation. In the succeeding pages, each of the theories listed at the beginning of this paper will evaluate according to how well it predicted the results of deregulation.

Endogenous quality

The central prediction of the endogenous-quality theory of behavior in regulated markets with competitive structure is that both fare levels and average quality would drop with deregulation, but carrier profits would stay the same [93].

Airline profits in fact have not shown much movement following deregulation, but the predictions of markedly lower average fares and lower average quality are not borne out by observation. In the airline industry, there is some tentative evidence of lowered levels of service attributes, but not in the core characteristic of flight frequency. In the motor carrier and bus industries there is absolutely no evidence of declining service quality under deregulation.

One reason that endogenous quality models failed to predict the effects of deregulation was the neglect of labor and other costs as an alternate sink for excess profitability [77]. Another reason was the ignoring the interesting questions of the structure of prices and service quality among the multiple markets served by every transportation company. Regulation has as its primary rationale the control of the structure of prices and service offerings. It is not surprising, then, that theories like endogenous quality models that assume that transportation companies operate in single markets – thus merging the questions of rates structures and rate levels – fail to predict the consequences of deregulation.

Sustainability and contestability

It is difficult to make a fair test of the predictive power of the theory of contestability since it is not clear exactly what the theory is. One aspect is a generalization to multiple markets of Demsetz' prediction that an unregulated monopolist with no sunk costs would price at minimum average total cost. Another aspect is the refutable proposition that entry barriers (defined as sunk costs) are more important than market structure in determining the behavior of firms in the industry. A third aspect is a restatement of J. M. Clark's belief that we not strive for the ideal of perfect competition, but should settle for workably competitive markets.

The creators of the theory concede that no market is perfectly contestable, but Alfred Kahn's image of airplanes as marginal costs with wings portrays transportation markets as ideally suited to the application of the 'hit-and-run' entry and exit that has been associated with the contestable markets paradigm. But an attempt to apply the theory stumbles at the first step: how to define the transportation market into which entry and exit is frictionless. It clearly can not be defined at the level of an inter-city pair since this does not correspond to any definition of markets or industries available in the current literature [20, 78].

To determine collusive behavior of an industry, one must include as members sellers of both demand as well as supply substitutes. Carriers not currently serving an inter-city pair are producers of supply substitutes because they have the capital and technology to undercut a collusive agreement by existing suppliers. Even if they do not currently serve the inter-city pair, they must be counted as market participants. Who should be included in the market for motor carrier services between Springfield, Massachusetts and Springfield, Illinois? All motor carriers who would be necessary to complete a collusive agreement covering service between those two points, regardless of the number of carriers currently providing service.

Once transport markets are properly defined, it becomes clear that entry involves larger sunk costs than appears at first. For example, if one focuses on air service from New York to Chicago, it is possible that the market will be defined to include all owners of commercial passenger aircraft in the United States appropriate for this length of run. To enter this market, then, requires an investment in aircraft as well as personnel and stations. Entry into the market cannot be considered to be subject to 'hit-and-run-entry'. Any market in which such entry appears possible is not properly defined.

Some writers have produced clear evidence that concentration of airline sales in inter-city pairs ('micro-markets' below) can predict deviations of fare levels from costs [84]. This is advanced as evidence of the inapplicability of contestable markets theory to transportation markets. Additional evidence comes from observing the relative behaviors of the motor carrier and airline sectors following deregulation. There is no evidence that truck pricing has been affected by collusive agreements, but all observers agree that the increasing fare yields in 1983 and 1984 resulted from a tacitly collusive agreement to set fares by a mileage formula. Current airline pricing is unquestionably strategically motivated [10, 26].

The difference in behavior between the two industries is easily explainable by the difference in the structures of the industries – the airline industry has a sufficiently small number of members that strategic behavior and tacit collusion are possible. The motor carrier industry is not so structured. A naive application of contestable markets theory to individual micro-markets would predict the absence of collusive behavior since in both cases, entry into micro-markets is apparently easy.

Baumol and Bailey correctly recognize that current price wars in the airlines industries are made possible by the disequilibrium stock of aircraft in the country as a whole [10]. Motor carrier earnings are also currently depressed by excess capacity [83]. But contestable markets theory is a statement that prices and market structure are simultaneously determined by the position of the long-run cost curve. To assert that prices are also determined by the relationship between vehicle demand and supply in all micro-markets (which is undoubtedly true) is to retreat from contestable markets theory. One could alter contestable markets theory in transportation markets to assert that price will be equal to short run average total cost, but pricing will then be determined primarily by supply and demand in a nation-wide market for vehicles, where competitive markets theory is more useful than contestable markets theory. Also lost is the simultaneous determination of industry structure and prices. In any case, the influence of vehicle stocks on pricing levels in the transportation industries create problems for the application of contestable markets theory.

Since contestable markets theory is ill-defined, it cannot be disproven. If it means setting a standard of workable instead of perfect competition, the evidence in this paper neither supports nor contradicts the theory. If it means that prices in unregulated transportation mico-markets will be set non-strategically at minimum long run average total cost, the evidence decisively contradicts the theory. If it means that entry barriers are more important than industry structure, in determining pricing behavior, limited evidence contradicts the hypothesis [84].

To be fair, it should be noted that contestable markets theory predicts behavior in unregulated markets. Thus it cannot be blamed for failing to anticipate the major changes that deregulation brought about in the transportation markets. Still, it is difficult to see how our predictions would have been improved if we used a 'contestable' standard rather than a competitive standard for post-deregulation behavior.

Peak load pricing

Peak load pricing and related variants, the third of the core elements of the analysis of economic regulation outlined at the beginning of this paper, continued to be useful in explaining unregulated pricing. Deregulation has freed carriers to engage in lower prices for backhauls; the new discount fare structures used by airlines are partially explainable by the standard micro-economics of joint and common costs (or economies of scope as the analysis is sometimes called).

Averch–Johnson effects

Averch–Johnson effects predict excessive capital/labor ratios when, in monopoly markets, allowed rates of return under regulation are above market levels. Only the motor carrier industry could be considered to be characterized by such rates of return under regulation, and it is not structured as a monopoly. There is no evidence that the industry has lowered its capital/labor ratio following deregulation.

8. CONCLUSION: THE NEED FOR APPROPRIATE MODELS

Of the models identified as core to the analysis of regulation, only one-peak load pricing and its variants – is useful for analyzing the movement from a regulated to unregulated transportation sector. Contestable markets theory does not add to our understanding of the behavior of deregulated transportation industries, endogenous quality models are contradicted by the evidence, and Averch–Johnson effects cannot be observed.

Moreover, the results of deregulation contradict political or capture theories of regulatory origin. All major carriers, except a few trucking companies, are happy to be deregulated. The only public demands to re-institute transport regulation come from transport labor, some state regulatory commissions, and some rail shippers. Contrary to currently popular interpretations of the effects of regulation [57], there is little evidence that deregulation caused a significant shift in rents away from carriers to their customers.

Deregulation has had its major effects on price structures (but not price levels) and on the structure (but not level) of service quality offerings. Why is it that regulation has had the effect of homogenization of service offerings and price leveling? We do not yet have any economic models that can explain the phenomenon. One reason is that we do not use economic models in which there is a clear distinction between price structures and price levels. Such models will have to be able to describe market linkages on both the cost and demand sides: a demand side analysis is necessary since the main changes in the structure of transport networks are motivated by the demand-advantages of service to more points. Theories of regulatory behavior must explain the source of these demand advantages of network extent.

My guess is that the recent restatement of the economics of joint and common costs as 'economies of scope' will not produce useful results in this area. The phrase is an attempt to unify and simplify the analysis of cross-market cost interactions, when what is needed is greater precision and specificity. In the five years since the concept of 'economies of scope' has been available, the profession has not made use of the definition to explain observable behavior.

I believe that a more fruitful line of research will be the economics of shared facilities associated with the mathematics of network theory. To this point, network theory is concerned with minimum cost network configurations, and has not yet dealt with the demand-side effects that appear to be driving the restructuring of the transportation industries. Nonetheless, I believe that a demand side can be integrated with the theory. Network theory is, at a minimum, capable of distinguishing between price levels and structures. Since the effect of regulation is to affect the structures of variables more than levels of variables, it is worth investigating.

REFERENCES

1. *Railroad Ten Year Trends*, Economics and Finance Department, Association of American Railroads (1984).
2. Association of American Railroads, Revenue Freight Loaded and Received from Connections by Commodities, Statement C5-54A, Association of American Railroads, Washington, D.C. (1985).
3. *Railroad Coal Rates in the Competitive Marketplace*, Economics and Finance Department, Association of American Railroads, (March, 1985).
4. *Railroad Grain Rates in the Competitive Marketplace*, Economics and Finance Department, Association of American Railroads (April, 1985).
6. Allen, Benjamin, J., 'Nature and Implications of the 'Partial Deregulation' of the Railroad Industry in the United States', *Revista Internationale di Economia dei Transporti*, Vol. X, No. 1–2 (April–August, 1983), pp. 373–384.
6. Altman, Edward I. and Gritta, Richard D., 'Airline Bankruptcy Propensities: a ZETA Analysis', *Transportation Research Forum: Proceedings of the Twenty-Fifth Annual Meeting*, Vol. XXV, No. 1 (1984), pp. 150–154.
7. Anderson, James E. and Kraus, Marvin, 'Quality of Service and the Demand for Air Travel', *The Review of Economics and Statistics*, Vol. LXIII, No. 4 (November, 1981), 533–540.
8. Babcock, Michael W. and German Wade H., 'The Impact of Deregulation on Rail TOFC Carloadings', *Logistics and Transportation Review*, Vol. 20, No. 3, (1984) pp. 205–212.
9. Babcock, Michael W. and German Wade H., 'A Model of the Demand for Intercity Bus Travel', *Transportation Research Forum: Proceedings of the Twenty-Second Annual Meeting*, Vol. XXII, No. 1 (1981), pp. 187–193.
10. Bailey, Elizabeth E. and Baumol William J., 'Deregulation and the Theory of Contestable Markets', *Yale Journal on Regulation*, Vol. 1, No. 2 (1984), pp. 111–137.
11. Bailey, E. E., Graham, David R., and Kaplan, Daniel P., *Deregulating the Airlines*, Cambridge: MIT Press (1985).
12. Baumol, William J., Panzar, John C., and Willig, Robert D., *Contestable Markets and the Theory of Industry Structure*, New York: Harcourt Brace Jovanovich (1982).
13. Beilock, Richard and Freeman, James, 'Carrier and Shipper Perceptions of Motor Carrier Deregulation in Florida', *Proceedings of the 23rd Annual Meeting of the Transportation Research Forum*, Vol. XII, No. 1 (1982), pp. 250–237.

14. Beilock, Richard and Freeman, James, *Initial Impact of Motor Carrier Deregulation in Arizona*, Arizona Department of Transportation (January, 1983).
15. Bennet, Randall, 'Quality of Service in Non-monopoly Air Travel Markets: an Empirical Investigation of Alternative Measures of Quality', unpublished Ph. D. Dissertation at Michigan State University (1984).
16. Boburg, Kevin, 'Track Structure Accounting and Reported Earnings of U.S. Railroads', *The Transportation Journal*, Vol. 24, No. 3 (Spring, 1985), pp. 18–28.
17. Bohlander, George W. and Farris, Martin T., 'Collective Bargaining in Trucking – The Effects of Deregulation', *Logistics and Transportation Review*, Vol. 20, No. 3. (1984), pp. 223–238.
18. Boisjoly, Russell P. and Corsi, Thomas M., 'The Aftermath of the Motor Carrier Act of 1980: Entry, Exit and Merger', *Proceedings of the 23rd Annual Meeting of the Transportation Research Forum*, Vol. XII, No. 1 (1982), pp. 258–264.
19. Boyer, Kenneth D., 'Equalizing Discrimination and Cartel Pricing in Transport Rate Regulation', *Journal of Policial Economy*, Vol. 89 (April, 1981), pp. 270–86.
20. Boyer, Kenneth D., 'Is there a Principle for Defining Industries?', *Southern Economic Journal* (January, 1984), pp. 761–70.
21. Boyer, Kenneth D., 'The Costs of Freight Transportation in Retrospect', Unpublished paper at Michigan State University (September, 1985).
22. Boyer, Kenneth D., 'Deregulation and Technical Change: Which Way is the Causality?', Paper prepared for November, 1985 meeting of Inter-University Committee for Public Utility Economics, Ann Arbor, Michigan.
23. Breen, Dennis, 'Antitrust and Price Competition in the Trucking Industry', *The Antitrust Bulletin*, Vol. XXVII, No. 1 (Spring, 1983), pp. 201–225.
24. Brenner, Melvin A., 'Air Deregulation: Price, Service, and Financial Disparities', *Transportation Quarterly*, Vol. 39, No. 2 (April, 1982), 175–178.
25. Bruning, Edward R. and Morash, Edward A., 'Deregulation and the Cost of Equity Capital: The Case of Publicly Held Motor Carriers', *The Transportation Journal* (Winter, 1983), Vol. 23, No. 2, pp. 72–81.
26. Carley, William M., 'Major Airlines Step Up Battle for Key Markets, Endanger Weak Lines', *Wall Street Journal*, Vol. LXV, No. 172 (June 18, 1985), p. 1.
27. Caves, D. W., Christiensen, L. R., and Tretheway, M. W., 'Productivity Performance of U.S. Trunk and Local Service Airlines in the Era of Deregulation', *Economic Inquiry* (July, 1983), 21(3), pp. 312–24.
28. Chapman, R. Stanley, 'Once Divided Airlines United in Supporting Deregulation Law', *Traffic World*, (May 30, 1983), pp. 12–14.
29. Corsi, Thomas M., Truck, J. Michael, and Gardner, Leland L., 'Owner-Operators and the Motor Carrier Act of 1980', *The Logistics and Transportation Review*, Vol. 18, No. 3, pp. 255–276.
30. Davis, Grant M. and Dillard, John E. Jr., 'The Professional Traveler and the Airline Deregulation Act of 1978: An Appraisal', *Transportation Research Forum: Proceedings of the Twenty-Third Annual Meeting*, Vol. XXIII, No. 1, (1982), pp. 419–426.
31. Douglas, George W. and Miller, James C., III, *Economic Regulation of Domestic Air Transport: Theory and Policy*, Washington, D.C.: The Brookings Institution (1974).
32. Due, John F., 'New Railroad Companies Formed to Take Over Abandoned or Spun-off Lines', *The Transportation Journal*, Vol. 24, No. 1 (Fall, 1984), pp. 30–40.
33. Ellison, Anthony P., 'The Structural Change of the Airline Industry Following Deregulation', *Transportation Journal* (Spring, 1982), pp. 58–69.

34. 'Report of Joint Conference Eno Foundation Board of Directors and Board of Consultants, October 17 and 18, 1985: Transportation in an Era of Deregulation', *Transportation Quarterly*, Vol. 39, No. 2 (April, 1985), pp. 171–206.
35. Farris, Martin T., 'Evolution of the Transportation Regulatory Structure of the U.S.', *Revista Internationale di Economia dei Transporti*, Vol. X, No. 1–2 (April–August, 1983), pp. 173–193.
36. Farris, Martin T. and Daniel, Norman E., 'Bus Regulatory Reform Act of 1982', *Transportation Journal* (Fall, 1983), pp. 4–15.
37. Flexner, Donald L., 'The Effects of Deregulation in the Motor Carrier Industry', *The Antitrust Bulletin*, Vol. XXVII, No. 1 (Spring, 1983), pp. 185–200.
38. Frey, N. Gail, Krolick, Rueben H., Nidiffer, Leone, and Tontz, Jay L., 'Effects of Deregulation of the California Intrastate Trucking Industry', *Transportation Journal*, Vol. 24, No. 3, (Spring, 1985), pp. 4–17.
39. German, H. Wade, and Babcock, Michael W., 'The Impact of Rail Deregulation on the Movement of Fresh Fruit and Vegetables', *Logistics and Transportation Review*, Vol. 18, No. 4 (December, 1982), pp. 373–384.
40. Graham, D. R., Kaplan, D. P., and Sibley, D. S., 'Efficiency and Competition in the Airline Industry', *The Bell Journal of Economics*, Vol. 14, No. 1, (Spring, 1983), pp. 118–138.
41. Harbridge House, *Report on Harbridge House Survey of the Impact of Transportation Deregulation on Major U.S. Manufacturing Firms*, Boston: Harbridge House (June, 1981), 26 pages.
42. Harmatuck, Donald J., 'The Effects of Economic Conditions and Regulatory Changes upon Motor Carrier Tonnage and Revenues', *Transportation Journal*, Vol. 24, No. 2 (Winter, 1984), pp. 31–39.
43. Harper, Donald V., 'Consequences of Reform of Federal Regulation of the Motor Trucking Industry', *Transportation Journal* (Summer, 1982), pp. 35–58.
44. Hilton, George W., 'American Railroad Deregulation of 1980', *Revista Internationale di Economia dei Transporti*, Vol. X, No. 1–2, April–August, 1983, pp. 357–371.
45. Horn, Kevin and Tyworth, John E., 'The Impact of Railroad Boxcar Deregulation: A Case Study of Transcontinental Lumber', *Transportation Research Forum: Proceedings of the Twenty-fifth Annual Meeting*, Vol. XXV, No. 1 (1984), pp. 280–289.
46. Jones, J. Richard and Cocke, Sheila I., 'Commuter Airline Service to Non-Hub Airports', *Transportation Research Forum: Proceedings of the Twenty-fourth Annual Meeting*, Vol. XXIV, No. 1 (1983), pp. 692–699.
47. Joskow, Paul L. and Noll, Roger G. Noll, 'Regulation in Theory and Practice: An Overview', in Gary Fromm (ed.), *Studies in Public Regulation*, Cambridge: The MIT Press (1981), pp. 1–65.
48. Keeler, Theodore and Abrahams, M., 'Market Structure, Pricing, and Service Quality in the Airline Industry under Deregulation', in W. Sichel and T. Gies, (eds.), *Applications of Economic Principles in Public Utilities Industries*, Ann Arbor: Graduate School of Business Administration (1981).
49. Keeler, Theodore E., *Railroads, Freight, and Public Policy*, Washington, D.C.: The Brookings Institution (1983).
50. Kindworth, Keith A., 'Impact of Staggers Rail Act on Branchline Abandonment Process', *Transportation Research Forum: Proceedings of the Twenty-fourth Annual Meeting*, Vol. XXIV, No. 1 (1983), pp. 453–460.
51. Koran, D. W., 'The Welfare Effects of Airline Fare Deregulation in the United States', *Journal of Transport Economics and Policy* (May, 1983), Vol. 17, No. 2, pp. 177–189.

52. Kretovich, Duncan, 'The Effect of the Motor Carrier Act of 1980 on the Risks of Motor Carrier Securities', Unpublished Ph.D. Dissertation at Michigan State University (1985).
53. Kyle III, Rueben, and Philips, Laurence T., 'Deregulation: Did Economists Promise too Much or too Little?' *Logistics and Transportation Review*, Vol. 21, No. 1 (1985), pp. 3–25.
54. Leet, James O., 'Air Deregulation Changes in Marketing Strategies', *Transportation Quarterly*, Vol. 39, No. 2 (April, 1982), pp. 179–182.
55. Lieb, Robert C., 'The Changing Nature of Labor/Management Relations in Transportation', *The Transportation Journal* (Spring, 1984), pp. 4–14.
56. Machelaba, Daniel, 'Shippers' Market: Moore Companies Push Freight Haulers to Get Better Rates, Service', *Wall Street Journal*, Vol. LXVI, No. 47 (December 18, 1985), p. 1.
57. McCormick, Robert E., Schugart, William F., and Tollison, Robert D., 'The Disinterest in Deregulation', *American Economic Review*, Vol. 74, No. 5, (December, 1984), pp. 1075–1079.
58. Meyer, John R. and Oster, Clinton Jr., *Deregulation and the New Airline Entrepreneurs*, Cambridge: MIT Press (1984).
59. Meyer, John R. and Oster, Clinton, (eds.), *Airline Deregulation: The Early Experience*, Boston: Auburn House (1981).
60. Miklius, Walter, 'Effect of Regulatory Reform on Motor Carrier Quality of Service', *Revista Internationale di Economia dei Transporti*, Vol. X, No. 1–2, (April–August, 1983), pp. 311–325.
61. Moore, Thomas Gale, 'Rail and Truck Reform – The Record so Far', *Regulation* (November/December, 1983), pp. 33–41.
62. Morash, Edward A. and Enis Charles, 'The Effects of Motor Carrier Deregulation: A Stock Market Perspective', *Proceedings of the 23rd Annual Meeting of the Transportation Research Forum*, Vol. XII, No. 1 (1982), pp. 265–271.
63. Morash, Edward A. and Enis, Charles R., 'Investor Perceptions of the Impact of Deregulation on Motor Carrier Earnings', *The Logistics and Transportation Review*, Vol. 19, No. 4, pp. 309–323.
64. Morrison, Steven A. and Winston, Clifford, 'Intercity Transportation Route Structures under Deregulation: Some Assessments Motivated by the Airline Experience', *American Economic Review, Papers and Proceedings*, Vol. 75, No. 2, (May, 1985), pp. 57–61.
65. Murphey, Stephen P., 'Current Concerns of Deregulated Motor Carriers', *Transportation Quarterly*, Vol. 39, No. 2 (April, 1985), pp. 191–194.
66. James, C. Nelson, 'The Emerging Effects of Deregulation of Surface Freight Transport in the United States', *Revista Internationale di Economia dei Transporti*, Vol. X, No. 1–2 (April–August, 1983), pp. 219–236.
67. Pinkston, Elizabeth A., 'The Rise and Fall of Bus Regulation', *Regulation*, (Sept/Dec, 1984) pp. 45–52.
68. Pustay, Michael, 'regulatory Reform of Motor Freight Carriage in the United States', *Revista Internationale di Economia dei Transporti*, Vol. X, No. 1–2, (April–August, 1983), pp. 259–280.
69. 'Grand Trunk in Michigan: Just-in-Time Railroading', *Railway Age* (January, 1985), Vol. 816, No. 1, p. 36.
70. *Railway Age* (June, 1985), Vol. 816, No. 6, p. 13.
71. *Railway Age* (May, 1985), Vol. 816, No. 5, p. 15.

72. Motor Carrier Ratemaking Study Commission, 'Collective Ratemaking in the Trucking Industry: A Report to the President and the Congress of the United States', Washington, D.C. (June, 1983).
73. Motor Carrier Ratemaking Study Commission, 'Collective Ratemaking in the Intercity Bus Industry', report submitted to the President and the Congress of the United States, Washington, D.C. (May 15, 1984).
74. Unsigned Editorial, *Regulation* (May/June, 1983), p. 11.
75. Unsigned Editorial, 'Boxcar Decontrol: No Empty Gesture', *Regulation* (Sept/Oct. 1983), pp. 8–11.
76. Rose, Warren, 'Three Years After Airline Passenger Deregulation in the United States: A Report Card on Trunkline Carriers', *Transportation Journal* (Winter, 1981), pp. 51–58.
77. Rose, Nancy, 'The Incidence of Rents in the Motor Carrier Industry', *The Rand Journal of Economics*, Vol. 16, No. 3 (Autumn, 1985), pp. 299–318.
78. Sheffman, David T. and Spiller, Pablo T., 'Geographic Market Definition under the DOJ Guidelinges', Working Paper No. 129, Bureau of Economics, Federal Trade Commission, Washington, D.C. (August, 1985).
79. Sines, Guerdon S., 'Railroad Deregulation', *Transportation Quarterly*, Vol. 39, No. 2 (April, 1985), pp. 195–197.
80. Smith, Jon L., 'Market Performance in Domestic Airline Markets', *Transportation Journal*, Vol. 24, No. 1, (Fall, 1984), pp. 51–57.
81. Spiller, Pablo, 'The Differential Impact of Airline Regulation on Individual Firms and Markets: an Empirical Analysis', *Journal of Law and Economics*, Vol. XXVI (October, 1983), pp. 655–689.
82. 'Aerospace and Air Transport', *Stand and Poor's Industry Surveys*, (December 6, 1984).
83. 'Railroads and Trucking', *Standard and Poor's Industry Surveys* (December 20, 1984).
84. Strassmann, D. L., 'Contestible Markets and Dynamic Limit Pricing in the Deregulated Airline Industry: An Empirical Test', Unpublished paper at Rice University (1985).
85. Transportation Policy Associates, *Transportation in America, Third Edition*, Transportation Policy Associates, Washington D.C. (1985).
86. Trapani, John M. and Olson, C. Vincent, 'An Analysis of the Impact of Open Entry on Prices and the Quality of Service in the Airline Industry', *The Review of Economics and Statistics*, Vol. LXIV, No. 1 (February, 1982), pp. 67–76.
87. 'Nation's 83–84 Freight Bill Indicates Modal Shares Steady, Revenues Down', *Traffic World* (April 22, 1985), pp. 17–18.
88. Tyworth, John E., 'Regulatory Reform and Railroad Freight Rate Structures for Lumber', *Transportation Research Forum: Proceedings of the Twenty-fourth Annual Meeting*, Vol. XXIV, No. 1, (1983), pp. 659–666.
89. U.S. Department of Agriculture, *Fresh Fruit and Vegetable Market News*, AMS, U.S. Department of Agriculture, Washington (1985).
90. Bradley, Kathleen, *National Transportation Statistics: Annual Report, 1985*, Cambridge: US Department of Transportation, Transportation Systems Center, Research and Special Programs Administration (June, 1985).
91. U.S. General Accounting Office, *The Changing Airline Industry: A Status Report Through 1982*, Washington, D.C. (July 6, 1983).
92. U.S. Interstate Commerce Commission, *The Intercity Bus Industry*, Washington, D.C. (January, 1984).
93. White, Lawrence J., 'Quality Variation when Prices are Regulated', *The Bell Journal of Economics*, Vol. 3, No. 2 (Autumn, 1972), pp. 425–436.

15. DEREGULATION OF EUROPEAN AIR TRANSPORT

Jacques Pelkmans

The title of the paper – though convenient for comparison with the US deregulation – is not meant to raise false expectations. The purpose is and must be modest because actual deregulation is scarce and scant in Europe and the state of empirical economic analysis about the topic is bafflingly weak, if indeed data are available at all. Available literature comprises only a few attempts to apply the case for deregulation to European air transport (e.g., Sichelschmidt, 1984) and some contributions to the intricate political economy of European air transport (de-)regulation (e.g., Kappetijn (ed.), 1983; Michaud and Thoenig, 1982).

The objective is to present the reduction of restrictive regulation at the EC and the bilateral European Countries level and attempt to identify attributable effects in the industry and the market for air travel in the Community. The discussion will be preceded by a sketchy comparison between the European and the US air travelmarket and by brief sections on the impact of US deregulation on the (North) Atlantic air transport market as well as on European reactions at the regulatory and the market level. A few conjectures about the future of European Community air transport regulation close the paper.

I. EUROPEAN AND US AIR TRANSPORT COMPARED

In many respects, the temptation to compare the European Community with the United States is understandable and justifiable. Dependent on the subject matter and on the continental origin of the observers, fascination about the other side of the Atlantic translates either in an urge for imitation, or an appeal to emphasize distinction. It is obvious, however, that, where too many differences will be found, the comparison will tend to become less and less instructive analytically. Rather, the merits of the

de Jong, H. W., Shepherd, W. G. (eds) Mainstreams in Industrial Organization
 ISBN 978-94-017-0495-3

comparison will consist in those of a juxtaposition of broader societal or political value systems, partly based on a set of objectively different circumstances and partly on disparate preferences, fed by tradition and vested interests.

A comparison of the EC and the US air transport shows fundamental differences both in the market and in the regulatory regime. Some of the differences in the market relate to the specific characteristics of the industry, others to the economic climate in which the industry operates.

Key market differences include the following:

I.1. Size

In market terms, it is artificial to compare the European Community (since 1 January 1986 including Spain and Portugal as well) with the US; in fact one should include the EFTA countries (Norway, Sweden, Finland, Switzerland, and Austria) and perhaps even Yugoslavia. These countries are organized in the ECAC (European Civil Aviation Conference) at the government level. Comparing intra-ECAC *cross border* passenger air traffic with the US *domestic* one, the relation is one to four (76 billion passenger-kilometers in ECAC; 330 billion in the US).[1] Not surprisingly, this translates in size differentials of firms and of aircraft. Concentrating on the mere comparison of intra-ECAC and intra-US air traffic (hence, ignoring intercontinental air transport, where similarities between the US and the EC are greater), the average volume of traffic carried by US airlines inside the US is eight (!) times the intra-European traffic flown by their European counterparts. The three biggest airlines in Europe (British Airways, Air France and Lufthansa) would need their entire intercontinental output to remain in the first-10-league of US airlines: in 1982, British Airways would be on par with no. 3 in the US (Eastern), counting the latter's domestic output only. Another striking example is that People Express achieved the same (domestic) output in 1982 – the second year of its operations – as the *European* output of KLM. Since People Express is a new entrant and since its market share in the US is very small, this example is particularly telling. Another interesting comparison concerns the large (relative) size of regional-hub airlines: British Airways has fewer departures to *European* destinations (including domestic) from Heathrow (the biggest European airport) than US Air (formerly Allegheny) has from its hub Pittsburgh.[2]

I.2. Competition among transport models

For short and medium hauls in Europe, it is easy to substitute rail or car transport for scheduled air transport, whereas, in the US, it is frequently difficult, cumbersome or (for rail) impossible, although bus services may cause some competition (unlike in Europe). Passenger air traffic in Europe is never cheaper and usually (much) more expensive than rail transport, even for first class rail; medium haul international rail transport offers overnight sleepers at lower prices than competing trunk route economy air fares – for travellers that discount the night, no time is lost. Moreoever, the train network in Europe is extremely dense and connections are easy so rail competition is particularly strong on 'thinner' routes to smaller airports.[3] Also passenger car transport strongly competes with air transport, especially if

- routes are shorter than 400–500 km
- two, three or four persons have to travel together (even on longer hauls).

In general, one might say that only very brief 'hops' over medium hauls (as well as longer hauls) have little substitution possibilities. Typically, fares are high for these products, given the demand from the time-sensitive business men or civil servants. Much lower fares exist for short/medium hauls with one or more nights stay in response to heavy competition from alternative modes of transport. Add other differences between the US and the EC, such as higher speed limits on the European roads and a smaller, more densily populated continent, and the (*ceteris paribus*) much smaller size and different structure of the air transport industry in Europe can be partly attributed to the differently structured competition in the transport sector as a whole.

The arguments are even more important in cargo and parcel mail. In freight road haulage is overwhelming and intra-European freight traffic by air amounts to a trickle: it is nearly only express parcels for 24 hour delivery. In parcel mail, rail transport is equally overwhelming, although there is an incipient express air parcel market. The growth of the European cargo/mail market is to be attributed almost entirely to intercontinental air freight, where competition by sea transport satisfies a different price/time combination. Competition by road haulage and rail is further increased by significant improvements in customs facilities and reduction in formalities, following the establishment of the EC customs union, the harmonisation of indirect taxes into the VAT system and the recent series of measures to further reduce frontier nuisance to the very minimum.[4] The advantages of road haulage are so great that many airlines transport air cargo within the ECAC area *by truck*, while retaining a flight number. Only the new specialized fast-delivery-air-cargo-firms have been able to find a niche in the market at airports with 24-hour customs service by vertical integration of all middle-men functions at the spot.

I.3. Production costs

There has been some controversy about the possible degree of cost cutting in Europe. It arose from the vivid public debate in Europe about allegedly too high fares for *scheduled* intra-ECAC passenger air transport. Table 1 shows a comparative breakdown for intra-ECAC and US domestic scheduled passenger air transport costs in US dollarcents per available seat kilometre.

Not every element in the Table can be manipulated by the airlines. Fuel per gallon/liter is nearly 15% more expensive in Europe than in the US, and fuel costs per available seat-kilometre approx. 20%. In particular years (such as 1984) when the dollar rises appreciably although the oil price does not, the intra-ECAC costs *in local currency* will also rise; of course, this might be undone later. Another point that should be taken into account is the more circuitous routes intra-ECAC flights are forced to take (for defense and air traffic control reasons) and the shorter average stage length (25% shorter in Europe than in the US, with one-third more landings) which drives up several costs elements as calculated per available-seat-kilometre. Probably relatively little of this difference could be squeezed out even under the most radical deregulation that is theoretically conceivable.

Given some irreducable difference in stage length, all other cost elements do depend on regulatory and enterprise behaviour and the structure of the market, including ticket selling and airport charges. But size and density differences will likely cause persistent disparities in costs, if only because on average aircraft in the US have 25% more seats, yet with equal or higher utilisation rates than in Europe. It is extremely difficult to predict how much of this difference could be reduced by attracting more passengers on scheduled routes by prices effects of deregulation.

I.4. Market structure

Both before and (seven years) after deregulation in the US, market structures differ greatly on both sides of the Atlantic. The key difference

– perhaps insufficiently appreciated – is that intra-ECAC flights are international[5] and their US counterparts domestic. Not only does this have a profound impact on the nature, scope and speed of deregulation in Europe (see further), but is also significantly enhances the opportunity for market segmentation and price discrimination, while generating an extremely rigid structure of bilateral regulatory regimes and near perfect (because restrained to be stable) duopolistic market organisations for hundreds of city-pair scheduled routes in the ECAC area. *Together with the greater competition among different transport modes, the fact that intra-ECAC air traffic is international overrides all other considerations in a comparison of US and Western Europe.* Landing rights, the airline designation, route entry and exit, capacity and frequency on city-pair routes, tariffs (and their conditions!), permission or even obligation of revenue or cost pooling on single routes, route creation, more general issues of 'fair' competition among airlines, the relationship between scheduled and non-scheduled (charter) operations as well as the relationship between airlines and public authorities are all largely or solely determined by negotiations on bilateral treaties, and the recurrent consultations between governments, as well as between governments and 'their' airlines and between the airlines directly, both domestically and within IATA. This astounding rigidity is further fortified by the strict vetoes in bilaterals (called the 'double approval system') and by the fact that, of all the trunk carriers in Europe that fly scheduled traffic, only two are private (UTA, of France, and British Caledonian), one is semi-private (Swissair) and all other ones are nearly 100% or fully state-owned. British Airways will be privatized (but not fully) in early 1986.

This rigidity reminds one of the rather conservative policy of the US Civil Aviation Board (CAB) during the 1950's, 1960's and early 1970's, when no new trunk carriers and only a few locals were allowed to enter, many route-monopolies and route-duopolies existed and charters and discounts were strongly discouraged. Yet, it is important to realize that the CAB only approved of inter-carrier agreements (that is, exempted them from anti-trust) upon a public 'interest' test – that was at least roughly objective, irrespective of the merits of such regulatory controls – whereas, in Europe, the higher-cost airline may be protected by its government and carry the day, under veto pressure. In addition, the CAB did not possess regulatory power over capacity and frequencies. Finally, commercial pooling agreements are alien to US air transport, given the nature of anti-trust law in the country, whereas an estimated 75%–80% of the ton-kilometers of scheduled intra-ECAC flights are subject to pooling agreements.[6]

Table 1. Operating costs comparisons; 1983. Cross-border Intra-ECAC scheduled vs. US domestic scheduled.

	Passenger cost (US cents per Available Seat-Kilometre-ASK)		Europe greater than us by percent
	Local Europe trunk	US domestic	
Crew	0.82	0.49	67
Fuel	1.33	1.09	22
Maintenance	0.68	0.41	66
Depreciation	0.39	0.30	30
Route + landing	0.84	0.27 (56)*	211 (50)*
Station + ground	1.09	0.73	49
Passenger service	0.41	0.31	32
Ticketing/sales	1.53	0.71	115
Other	0.43	0.18	139
Totals	7.52	4.49 (4.78)*	67 (57)*

*Due to the 8% ticket tax in the US, and the subsequent lowering of route-and-landing charges, IATA has calculated alternative cost rates (given in parentheses), under certain redistribution assumptions.
Source: IATA, 1984, p. 24.

It is impossible to set out the system fully in a conference paper. In any event, much is unknown about the bilaterals – the lynchpins of the superstructure – because their Annexes are rarely published and letter exchanges between Ministers may remain unknown. Negotiations between governments are largely secret; IATA tariff conferences have only recently been opened up by admitting an EC observer – although one wonders whether this person can detect what will be held hidden for him – and a representative from FATUREC, a business-based consumer organisation in Europe. At present, EC competition rules are not used against air transport, although the Court of Justice of the EC, in a ruling in 1974, implied that they legally apply; at any rate, no implementation rules, ex. art. 87, EEC exist, since air transport is excluded in the famous regulation 17.[7]

An authoritative survey of the market structure, including an exhaustive analysis of the regulatory superstructure – first and foremost, the actual contents of the bilaterals – is badly lacking. Without implementation power, the European Commission cannot enforce the supply of necessary information. ECAC is very unlikely to yield more than the most aggregative and loosely presented data. So, one is compelled to describe the broad features of the regulatory structure, with the inter-carrier agreements tightly fitting in with the varying characteristics of the individual bilaterals. This has been done elsewhere in the literature.[8] The main elements will be discussed when dealing with the EC and bilateral deregulation attempts.

However, it is important to note tht restrictive regulation frequently leads to strong *incentives to exploit mazes in the rules*. This has happened in Europe on a *truly massive scale* in two ways. First, charters take 42% of the total number of international intra-ECAC passengers carried (and even 57% in terms of total international passenger-kilometres).[9] companies are privately-owned, except for the subsidiaries of the major trunk airlines. The regime for charters is unclear. In fact it is improper to speak of one regime, since inclusive tours charters (IT charters; the bulk of the charter market) do not normally fall under bilateral agreements and hence are subject to unilateral approval. Since in Europe, northern-based charter companies sprang up as a by-product of emerging mass-tourism while the bulk of these flights are south-bound, mutual interests were served by a liberal implementation. Thus, a 'non-system' with a potential to throttle any growth actually turned out to yield exceedingly high growth rates, responding to rapidly increasing demand for Mediterranean IT-charters in the spring, summer and autumn. Informal consultations in ECAC and the strong voice of domestic interests have led to well-established traditions guaranteeing market segmentation both functionally (regular charters are under the obligation to offer inclusive tours only or predominantly) and geographically (destinations typically are holiday resorts, far away from major airports). The debate on deregulation generates pressures to start encroaching on hitherto segmented markets, thereby blurring the traditional distinction between scheduled and non-scheduled air traffic.[10]

Second, pressures to increase the load factor and indirect competition for the leisure traveller (train, car, charter, bus) have eventually led to numerous lower fares and discounts for passengers on ordinary scheduled flights in Europe. A number of studies are available on this point.[11] They have clearly shown that average-yield-dilution per passenger increases with distance and that, even on short hauls of ± 500 km average revenue per passenger is substantially lower than the economy fare (for instance, 25% lower in 1975.[12] Lower fares on scheduled routes have restrictive conditions that become increasingly restrictive the greater the discount from the economy fare: they consist of excursion fare, special excursion fare, Apex fare and IT fare. Availability of all or some of them may differ from route to route, and seasonally; the degree of discount may differ from route to route and restrictions may also vary.

In addition, straight group discounts and (usually 50%) spouse discounts are also given, with fewer restrictions. Prorating[16] is not unimportant for business travellers in Europe and also exerts a downward pressure on actually paid air tariffs. Taking a matrix of all routes between the capitals of the EC-Twelve (Frankfurt is assumed to be a 'capital') as well as Oslo, IATA found 648 low and discount fares on 1 April 1984. Comparing low and discount fares on 30 routes in the ECAC area in 1975 and 1984, the average reduction from economy fares was found to have increased from 30% to 50%. It was also found that, in 1981, one out of every two passengers on scheduled intra-ECAC cross-border flights was travelling on such discount fares. It is estimated that, adding discounts on scheduled flights and charter flights, 70% of all passengers and 81% of passenger-kilometres were flown on reduced fares, some of which are very low indeed.[14]

Surely, impressive though it is, the exploitation of the mazes in the rules does not do away with the rigidity in the route structure, the sheltering of economy fares on many routes, and several other anti-competitive features of the European passenger air transport market, but it drastically reduces its inimical effects on consumer welfare and the economy as a whole.

It is still true that, as the study by the European Commission[15] emphasizes, the lack of transparency of the tariffs heightens the transaction costs for travellers to find the best combination of price, service, frequency and attached conditions. Observe that the *international* character of intra-ECAC air transport makes it relatively easy to practice price discrimination by limiting access to discounts in other country markets and by filtering information and computer-booking systems. With such high transaction costs it is not surprising that

- no less than 70% of air tickets in Europe are sold by travel agents (interestingly, the US figure is 26% in 1981 but is increasing because of a strong increase in the number and types of discount fares, that, moreover, change much more frequently than in Europe)
- no less than 20% of the total scheduled airlines' costs are accounted for by sales costs (it is approximately a little less than half of this in the US; see Table 1), partly due to commissions, partly due to the nature of competition between airlines that have fixed routes, capacity, frequency and tariffs already beforehand.

A final point on market structure is the monopolistic or duopolistic position of the European airlines in their own countries. In many ECAC countries there is only one 'flag carrier', having been granted monopoly on many routes and being publicly owned. If they exist at all, fringe competitors are extremely restrained; occasionally, it is not exaggerated to hold that they are at the mercy of the 'flag carrier', both in the market and via the power it can yield through the regulators. The 'flag carrier' phenomenon has emotional-political overtones, deriving its status from a mixture of prestige, employment, national security and foreign currency-earnings considerations. Its being 'untouchable' is greatly facilitated by the unfortunate Chicago Convention of 1944, acknowledging the sovereign rights over a country's airspace with no conditions (say, for periods of durable peace) attached.

I.5. The socio-economic climate

It is well-known that the socio-economic climate in the US and in the EC is somewhat different. However, even climates may alter over time as shown by recent developments in Europe. Three aspects relevant to air transport should be mentioned. First, employee protection is much more respected and expected in Europe than in the US. To a large extent this protection takes legal forms that, being conceived as fundamental 'entitlements', are extremely resistent to adaptation. Thus, radical cutting of labour costs (being 60% higher per available seat-kilometre in Europe than in the US) by lay-offs is more difficult in Europe; changing the work rules is equally hard. Second, the unions in European air transport wield enormous – some would say, excessive – power: unionisation degrees are generally high which is understandable because it tends to pay to organize one-self in a protected, regulated industry where negotiation substitutes for competition. Strikes or the threat of them tend to be effective because societal acceptance of the notion of 'entitlements' usually exclude radical counteraction and because 'solidarity' (by pilots of other airlines, and/or ground personnel) is well respected. Third, state aids to cover losses or subsidize new investments occur on top of the anti-competitive organization of the market. Evey one of the three aspects has become less pronounced recently, but all remain firmly in place.

In Section 5 we shall briefly discuss changes in all these aspects. However, already at this point it should be emphasized that, in Europe, US deregulation is frequently presented as a threat to labour or, stronger, as a typical American whim leading to unacceptable instability as shown by the bankruptcy of Braniff and the 'Lazarus' construction of Continental. In the European socio-economic environment and in politics these arguments tend to go down well.

When comparing deregulation in US and European air transport, two major questions ought to be separated as much as possible. One is, to what extent can one expect economic effects, similar to those having taken place in the US, to occur in Europe in response to comparable measures of deregulation? As the aforegoing suggests, this question implies a number of analytical hurdles that are not easy to take, still apart from the lack of sufficient appropriate data.

The other question is whether European deregulation of air transport can be expected to be similar in nature and scope to deregulation in the US. The closest theoretical equivalent would consist of

- a transfer of air space sovereignty of the twelve EC Member States to the Community, in a permanent form such as by means of an adaptation of the EEC Treaty, and valid for peace-time only
- to empower the Commission as a common civil aviation authority, but limited – again in the Rome Treaty – to matters of competition, air safety and EC-wide bilaterals with third countries (the latter, in conjunction with the Council of Ministers) so that the 'Community sky' becomes comparable to US domestic air transport.
- to conclude liberal EC bilaterals with EFTA countries, so as to extend this 'sky' over the entire ECAC area.

There is no country and no airline in Europe that is forwarding this perspective, not even as a long run optimistic scenario. Observe that British liberalism with respect to bilaterals and privatization of British Airways is squarely based on the national interest.[16] Also the EC Commission accepts bilateralism.[17] Hence, the answer to the second question must be a flat 'no'. In turn, this either complicates the first question even further or renders it irrelevant for analytical purposes. For this reason the present paper takes a descriptive approach, with a cautious dose of casual empiricism.

II. US DEREGULATION, ATLANTIC TURBULENCE AND STABLE EUROPEAN CRUISING

There are at least two important reasons why deregulation in US air transport was followed with apprehension in European air transport circles. One is the general fascination in Europe with the American scene, always inspiring debate at home about the necessity to imitate or reject. Major new strands in American security, foreign or economic policy are perceived in Europe as being introduced much faster in the US due to the functioning of its political institutions, creating testing grounds for similar or compatible ideas in Europe. This 'danger' was quickly perceived in the cluster of interest groups that together constitute the European air transport industry, particularly when parliamentarians and consumer groups (and The Economist) began to pick up some of the arguments about deregulation, imported from over the Atlantic. After nearly six years of back-and-forth between Washington DC and London, Laker finally obtained permission to start his 'Airtrain' over the Atlantic in 1977. The EC Council of Ministers set up a 'priority list' for a future common air transport policy in 1978, the very same year when the US Congress passed the Airline Deregulation Act. The EC Commission came with a first Memorandum in 1979.[18] Hearings on air tariffs were held in the British House of Lords and in the European Parliament. Deregulation quickly became the 'buzz word', helped by severe criticism on loss-covering state aids to airlines in Europe and the activities of the no-frills, no-reservation Laker Airtrain.

The second reason was the US attempt to 'export' deregulation, first of all to Europe (and Canada) of course. The paper will not describe in detail how it was attempted (and largely failed) – this fascinating international political economy of regulation deserves a separate treatment. Three stages with different, though overlapping elements can be distinguished. Undoubtedly the greatest consternation was evoked by the so called Show Cause Order of the CAB in June 1978. The Show Cause Order comprised anti-trust proceedings leading to the conclusion that US carriers could no longer participate in IATA Tariff Conferences. It forced IATA to alter the rules: henceforth, participation in conferences would no longer be compulsory but optional. In exchange the CAB gave interim approval. In 1980 the CAB gave a second interim approval, except for trans-atlantic air transport. Although this decision never took formal effect, it intensified the ongoing price war above the Atlantic with what probably amounted to predatory pricing (especially in the low season) to squeeze Laker Airways out (which happened in February 1982).[19]

Another route consisted of 'liberal' bilateral air transport agreements between the US and (by mid-1984) some 20 other countries. However, only three EC countries could be enticed to conclude them: the Netherlands (already in early 1978), Belgium and Germany; the UK was another special case.[20] According to Haanappel (1984, pp. 43ff) the main characteristics of these liberal bilaterals include:

- unlimited multiple designation of air carriers (both for scheduled and charter traffic)

- open-ended charter authority and increased access to more gateways in the US for scheduled (European) services, in exchange for open-ended scheduled route structure for US airlines (as well as for charters); note that this implies incomplete reciprocity on the part of the US, which is resisted in several (other) EC countries, Canada and Japan.
- no constraints on capacity, type of aircraft and frequency granting of sixth freedoms[21] on scheduled flights, important for KLM and British Airways given their policies to promote 'hubbing' at Schiphol and Heathrow; this may have been the incentive for Germany and Belgium to negotiate with the US for fear of losing traffic to the gateway activities of KLM and British Airways to and from Brussels and German airports.
- encouragement of low tariffs by double *dis*approval systems of country of origin approval, by narrow criteria for rejection, by matching (low prices or other) provisions and by deleting references to IATA conferences (except in the German case).

Compared to the pre-1976 regime for US international flights (the so called Bermuda I based rules) and compared to intra-ECAC bilaterals, these new bilaterals are indeed much more liberal. Obviously, they exert pressure on other European countries to liberalize, if only because unequality of opportunities for European travellers to fly transatlantic will not be easily understood and some transatlantic traffic may deviate via the Benelux, Germany or the UK.

The third stage consisted of a organized response by ECAC. In March 1982 (one month after Laker's demise) the first US–ECAC Memorandum of understanding was signed, followed by several others. For the duration of these Memoranda IATA conferences will be permitted; for the North Atlantic, fares will be free within 'zones of reasonableness' around 'reference fare levels'. But these principles, contained in the Memoranda, have been *applied* bilaterally, in other words, the reference fare levels may still differ substantially between one EC country and another. Politically, the Memoranda constitute a remarkable achievement because they combine elements of two opposed market and pricing regimes. At the airline level – with Laker out of the way and at least some grip on the bottom prices in the market – IATA conferences on the North Atlantic have been successful since and price stability has been restored. It should be noted however, that the Memoranda covered short periods and only in 1985 was the Show Cause Order buried for the next five years.

It is important to see that the Atlantic turbulence has had little effect on the *intra*-ECAC network of bilaterals. US domestic deregulation has certainly helped the EC Commission to solicit attention for its proposals (see Section 3.1) in the broader arena of politics and with more interest groups than those customarily admitted in the tighly closed circuit of European air transport. But the technical obstacles to full comprehension of the sector and the vastly different incentives of the public at large, on the one hand, and the vested interest, on the other, have made it very difficult to sustain the momentum of liberalisation that was in the air in the early 1980's. The worldwide losses of airlines in 1981 and 1982 have also caused prudence, playing into the hands of the opponents of deregulation. Finally, one should not underestimate the power and skills of vested interests with privileged access and political protection, quite irrespective of the merits of more competition and flexible responses to the consumer. Regulated industries can only be understood in terms of their political economy which is especially powerful given the incentives to organize oneself. In the framework of European integration, the political economy of regulated industries such as transport or telecom (and, in some respects, agriculture) has been intertwined with the extremely costly, veto-based modes of decision-making in the Council of Ministers. In this light, even the strong echos of the US deregulation and the noticeable turbulance over the Atlantic have done little to affect European cruising. The recent hearings by the European Parliament in February 1985 laid the basis for what turned out to be a conservative report by the German MEP Klinkenborg.[22] The resolution finally adopted in Strassbourg was only marginally more liberal. The relative immunity of the bilateral regulation and anti-competitive market structure for scheduled operations from public and economic criticism will not be softened by the most conspicuous impact of US deregulation on the Community air transport, fitting the European integration process so well: talking!

III. THE EUROPEAN COMMUNITY: MUCH ADO ABOUT NOTHING?

This section will briefly describe the present policy of the EC Commission and subsequently attempt to survey the positions of the Member States. Policy and positions refer essentially to the talking process, mentioned above. It is followed by a discussion of the only liberalisation decision hitherto made in EC air transport: the EEC Directive for interregional air services of 1983.

III.1. A sketch of the Commission's policy

A necessary condition for any form of market integration in the EC is the removal of any form of national discrimination or obstacle to the free movement of goods or services inside the Community. To the extent that Member States wish to continue to regulate sectors or intervene in them, distortions might remain in existence in the integrated area, but the nature and economic effects of such distortions should in principle be similar over the entire Community. Therefore, a truly Communitarian air transport policy, while substituting national regulation by EC regulation, can be characterized as 'de-regulatory' for individual economic agents, except under very extreme assumptions about the implementation of common regulation. This inference would be strengthened considerably if air transport would become subject to the EEC competition rules, even when exemptions would be decided under art. 85 sub 3, EEC (from restrictive practices, under certain conditions) and arts 92 to 94, EEC (state aids). In this paper, a common air transport policy for the Community is therefore considered as a major step of deregulation.

Early initiatives to set up a common air transport policy had come to nothing. The Spinelli report[23] of October 1975 followed the ruling of the European Court in the French sailors case,[24] holding that the *general* rules of the Rome treaty did apply to air transport (but not – without a special Council decision – the special rules on transport modes as specified in the Treaty for road haulage and inland shipping). For the purposes of this paper, the ruling and the far-reaching consequences that one might deduce from it need not be analysed in full. In brief it would mean that art. 7, EEC (outlawing discrimination among – any – economic agents in the EEC on the grounds of nationality) would apply. That this would have major implication is obvious once it is realized that widespread bilateral single airline designations on citypair scheduled routes as well as frequent exclusions of fifth freedoms[25] for others conflict outright with art. 7, EEC. Other consequences of the ruling include that freedom of establishment (for airlines) would apply (at present usually forbidden in the national air transport laws); that the freedom of trade in services would apply as in art. 59, EEC (which would undermine the Chicago Convention inside the EC); and that the EEC competition rules would apply to air transport. A doubtful element is the freedom of trade in services obtained in this way, since the Court decided that air transport is subject to the general rules of the EEC Treaty *in ways similar to those of other modes of transport*, which points to the necessity of setting up a *special* common policy, following art. 61, EEC.

The Spinnelli report proposed to create one 'European airspace' and a common authority to conclude agreements with third countries. Logically fitting the construction of the EC, the proposals nevertheless foundered on the rocks of unwillingness of the Member States. Despite this setback the new market approach by Laker Airways and US deregulation, including the Show Cause Order, geared the Council into action. Ignoring a few technical proposals (on noise levels, etc.) and an insignificant 'consultation procedure', the following activities could be registered:

(a) the Council set nine priorities in 1978, which are formally still valid; key items include 'provisons regarding aids and competition', 'right of establishment' and 'improvements to inter-regional services'
(b) the Commission issued its so called First Memorandum on Air Transport in 1979[26]
(c) it proposed a draft regulation on scheduled interregional air services[27] in 1980, which was accepted by the Council in much watered-down form in 1983; see Section 3.3
(d) it published a detailed report on air fares[28] which was critical of a number of elements of air tariffs on scheduled intra-European flights
(e) it proposed a draft Directive on air fares[29]
(f) it proposed a draft Council Regulation on implementation rules for the application of EEC composition rules to air transport.[30]

Given the potentially great scope and profound impact of Community solutions, following the Court's ruling, these proposals can be characterized as rather modest. They leave the system of 'bilaterals' among EC countries unaffected, although the contents of the agreements at the government level (including the annexes and additional protocols) and the agreements among airlines with respect to tariffs and pooling would become more constrained, i.e., less restrictive. But even this modesty was considered too ambitious by Member States and airlines alike (with some exceptions) so that a maximum of talking led to a minimum of decision-making. Apart from the watered-down Interregional Air Services Directive, no proposal had been accepted by the Council as late as December 1985.

In March 1984 the Commission published the Second Memorandum[31] which is broader in scope but considerably more prudent in many respects. The Commision maintains that '. . . a number of the underlying conditions which made deregulation possible in the US do not exist in Europe . . . . The issue in realistic terms, therefore, is not whether the Community should deregulate air transport but whether the present system can be made sufficiently flexible so as to contain within itself

Table 2. The Commission's Civil Aviation Memorandum no. 2: major proposals and ideas.

Domain of action	Sub-heading	Key elements proposed/suggested
Competition	Bilaterals	(a) No *requirements* of capacity sharing or revenue pooling for the conclusion of bilaterals.
		(b) No traffic shares guaranteed on citypair routes beyond 25%.
		(c) Air tariffs in 'zones of reasonableness' around 'reference tariffs', with double disapproval or country of origin approval inside the zone (as in the US–ECAC Memorandum; see Section II).
	Inter-carrier Agreements	(d) Permission (but no obligation) for capacity. Sharing, with considerable freedom to opt out.
		(e) Prohibition of complete revenue sharing ('open pools'), being compatible with art. 85, EEC.
		(f) Group exemption possibilities for partial revenue sharing ('limited pools'), dependent on the conditions of art. 85 sub 3, EEC.
		(g) Individual exemption after Commission inspection, of 'joint operations' on thinner routes (ex. art. 85, 3, EEC).
		(g) Group exemption for participation in tariff fixing conferences, tied to the air tariffs proposal (see c.), guarantees for 'an effective right of independent action' and 'freedom to implement' tariffs, and admission of Commission observers.
State aids	Guidelines	(i) Straightforward application of the EC surveillance of state aids (i.e., arts 90–94, EEC) such as notification, transparency, exceptions in art. 92, the 'common interest' condition (since the Philip Morris ruling of 1980); matching aid with that of third countries permitted; prohibition of loss coverage.
		(j) Bringing public enterprises in the air transport sector under the so called 'transparency directive' of 1980*.
Reduction of airline costs	Infra-structure	(k) Efficiency criteria for airports.
		(l) Common principles for user charges at major airports.

Other	Access	(m) Introduce 'multiple designation' of air carriers generally into intra-EC bilaterals, so that unused rights can be assumed by new entrants.
	Charters	(n) Permission for non-schedules services to reserve up to 15% of seats on 'seat-only' basis (i.e., no inclusive tours).
		(o) Permission to carry cargo and mail by charters.

*According to Commission Directive 80/723/EEC (*Official Journal* L 195 of 29 Jully 1980), public enterprises and their governments are obliged to supply adequate information on the financial relations – direct and indirect – between them, if the Commission so requests. Meanwhile the Commission has decided to include, inter alia, transport by means of Commission Directive 85/413/EEC of 24 July 2985; see Official Journal L 229 of 28 August 1985.

enough pressures to ensure that airlines increase their productivity and provide their services at the lowest possible cost' (pp. 26–7). Table 2 contains a summary of the more important proposals and ideas. The presentation should largely speak for itself. If fully accepted and embodied in Community law and actual policy implementation, no doubt substantial improvements could be expected for consumers and some of the cost items in Table 1 would come under pressure in the longer run. As the following section shows this acceptance should *not* be expected.

In addition, a few 'snags' should be emphasized. One is that the proposal with respect to competition represents a package that is difficult to decompose without creating serious (legal and other) inconsistencies that in themselves are unlikely to be compatible with Community law. However, there is a split assignment of decision-making between the Commission (ex. arts 90–94 EEC) and the Council (art. 8; 84 sub 2, EEC, so as to be able to implement arts 85 and 86, EEC by the Commission in a manner consistent with the specific characteristics of air transport) for this package. Thus, the Council can hold the Commission hostage in a way. On the other hand, the Commission may seek for possible Court cases with respect to arts 85 EEC (on restrictive practices) and 86 EEC (abuse of dominant position) and state aids, without waiting for the appropriate implementation legislation. At present there are five grouped cases before the European Court (not brought before it by the Commission but by a French court) that might well lead to a tougher Commision position, dependent, of course, on the outcome.[32] In the course of 1985 EC Commissioner Clinton Davies has repeatedly threatened to go to court if Member States would not take the Second Memorandum seriously. Another snag is that the proposed discretion for the Commission, after legislation will have been enacted, is rather large, leaving in doubt the true extent of liberalization.

III.2 The member states

The tradition of veto-based 'consensus decision-making' in the Council of Ministers of the EC and the tradition of bilateralism in air transport accord well in maximizing the transaction and implementation costs of common decisions. Another way of putting it is that such costs are frequently prohibitive, hence initiatives are throttled and solutions are found on a selective bilateral basis (see also Section 4).

At present (1985) the Council is considering the Commission's second Memorandum. A 'High Level group for Air transport' has confidentially reported to the Ministers in December 1984, formulated a set of guidelines (with close to unanimity, varying on details) and recommended to tackle refinements and proposals/amendments in a Transport Questions Working Group, attached to the Committee of Permanent Representatives (i.e., the Member States' Ambassadors to the Community, preparing Council decisions). It is therefore possible that a watered-down package of mini-reforms might eventually be decided by the Council.

Since the guidelines have not been published, the only possibility is to reconstruct them from interviews (with a risk of distortions and omissions). *With this caveat*, the main strands of the present discussion in Council circles have been recapitulated below, sometimes with positions of individual Member States. The sequence is identical to that in Table 2, column 3.

(a) all Member States *agree* with the Commission that capacity and/or revenue sharing should not be required for the conclusion of bilaterals (but see b, e and f); France, among others, still insists however that equality of capacity should be the leading principle to translate the traditional concept in air law of 'fair and equal opportunity' in bilaterals;

(b) few countries join the Commission in agreeing to a minimum share guarantee of 25% of traffic on a city-pair route; perhaps 45% might be acceptable in the end; it is under consideration at present; however, several Member States (such the Netherlands) prefer to avoid an exact minimum share since they may *add to* rigidities in some cases and will freeze 'entitlements', blocking future progress; the European Parliament has meanwhile floated the idea of revolving increases of capacity shares, but limited to, say, 5% per year or two years – perhaps the Council will accept some such proposal;

(c) it seems that the 'zone of reasonableness' concept for air fares has *not* been *rejected*, but the idea to prescribe it for all scheduled services in the EC is resisted; since the range of the zone (in particular, how far below the reference fare and whether or not to include the economy fare itself in a zone, which would imply *no* restrictions on certain discount fares) is subject to double approval, the need for better arbitration has been recognized but no solutions seem to be in sight; yet, this procedure for dispute settlement is, of course, crucial;

(d) there is *agreement* on the permission (no obligation, see a) for capacity sharing; when there is freedom to opt out, such agreements should qualify for group exemption ex. art. 85, 3, EEC; note that the Commission relates this exemption to less rigid traffic sharing (see b) and to tariff flexibility (see c), whereas several Member States do not seem to accept these linkages;

(e) there is *agreement* that 'open pools' do not automatically qualify for exemption under art. 85, 3 EEC (hence, group exemption is precluded) but – in contrast to the Commission's view – they could qualify for individual exemption. Since it will be within the Commission's power to decide on this, and verification via a Court case would be possible, this item does not present an obstacle;

(f) there is *agreement* on group exemption for partial revenue sharing ('limited pools') but with less stringent conditions; whereas the Commission would wish a ceiling of 1% revenue transfer, most Member States seem to insist on 3%; in individual exemptions it appears to be unclear how the four conditions for exemption in art. 85, 3, EEC would apply (such conditions include, *inter alia*, a reasonable share of the benefits to the consumer; no elimination of competition on a considerable part of the market; etc.);

(g) Member States insist on a special regulation (with criteria) for a group exemption for 'joint operations' on thinner routes; the Commission goes no further than investigation for possible individual exemptions;

(h) There is *agreement* on group exemption for tariff consultation and conferences, provided they are not mandatory (this is current IATA and US rule; not yet so in all EC Member States' bilaterals); however, the Commission ties this in with its tariff proposals (see b) and required guarantees for an 'effective right of independent action' and 'freedom to implement tariffs' as well as admission of Commission observers. About these conditions, I have been unable to register opinions. Probably tariff conferences are not viewed as anti-competitive activities (i.e., against art. 85, 1, EEC) which, in general at least, is an economically untenable position. Hence one could only defend such a view either if the conditions in art. 85, 3, EEC would apply *in general* (which is unlikely, to say the least[33] or if one would maintain that exemptions could be granted under Council regulations, based on art. 84, 2, EEC (on transport policy, and *not* competition as such). Under the latter option, the Council could define conditions for exemptions *different from those* in the competition rules of the Treaty (especially art. 85, 3). The latter would be a remarkable derogation of the well-established competition regime of the Community. It is, nonetheless, the position of the major European trunk carriers, presumably influencing a number of formal Member States' positions;

(i)(j) despite general agreement on action with respect to state aids, the *controversy* between the Council and the Commission relates to whether the present Commission surveillance on aids to industry (based on art. 92/3) should apply – or a special set of (softer?) criteria under a special Council Regulation, ex.art. 94, EEC. The former option is undoubtedly superior with its clear set of guiding criteria and, especially the last four years, increasing effectiveness as well as many infringement procedures before the Court;

(k)(l) unknown; probably because the Commission will soon present proposals on these issues;

(m) there is *agreement* that multiple designation of air carriers should be introduced more generally into intra-EC bilaterals and that another airline *of the same country* (the Commission says: of any of the two countries) should be allowed to operate the route;

(n)(o) no information available.

It would seem that there is sufficient room for agreement to make it possible for the Commission and the Council to act in parallel on the various elements of competitive structure. But there is also ample scope for obstruction on the part of Member States. Much will depend on how restrictive the Council regulations, ex.art. 84, EEC, will be since they could undermine the capacity of the Commission to exercise surveillance and force out restrictive bilaterals or have them adapt. Member States have different views on this. The UK and the Netherlands tend to take liberal positions, but even they squarely remain within the tradition of 'bilaterals'. British policy is based on *deregulation as a means to promote the national interest*. The Civil Aviation Authority's recent report on competition policy[34] emphasizes that the '. . . Authority does not see competition as an end in itself or as one which should be pursued regardless of the impact upon the UK's international competitive strength . . . . The Authority favours competitive solutions . . . . The pursuit of a multi-airline policy can however entail certain costs in terms of the UK's bilateral relationships with many other countries and possibly also in terms of the British industry's overall competitive strength when facing foreign airlines. These fundamental realities must shape and moderate the policies which the UK can adopt'. Thus, it seems that the Irish – usually overly prudent in air transport politics and always insisting on the 'public service' function requiring regulation in the public interest – have proposed to accept fifth freedoms as a right for Community carriers in every case to unused routes (or services) under bilaterals between two EC Member States. In other words, the Irish could fly Dublin–Bordeaux–München if the French–German bilateral gave (unused) possibilities to fly Bordeaux–München. Typically this would tend to undermine the negotiation position of the British who are strictly pushing *bilateral* liberalisation with partner countries so as to strengthen the hubbing system of Heathrow, and perhaps Gatwick and Manchester as well. When pursuing the objective of a free(er) EC Internal Air Transport Market, on the other hand, Britain should have backed the Irish proposals. It is telling, however, that Britain did not.

Many EC countries drag their feet. Greece and Italy and to a lesser extent France are reluctant to liberalize anything. Also, the new Member States Spain and Portugal are expected to take conservative positions. Germany, Denmark and Ireland are a middle group and Belgium occasionally joins forces with the UK and The Netherlands. Undoubtedly, the emergence of a common air transport policy will be slow and its contents anything but radical.

III.3. The Interregional EEC Directive

Since 1 October 1984 an EEC Council Directive on scheduled interregional air services[35] is in force after two-and-a-half years of protracted discussion on a draft proposal (for a Regulation, not a Directive) from the Commission.[36] It is the only material economic decision in EC air transport that has been commonly agreed, yet. It breaks away from the bilateral system and was therefore vigorously opposed by the various vested interests such as the Civil Aviation Labour Unions, the Centre of European Public Enterprises and the major airlines. The opposition has led to a considerable watering down of the proposal but the basic principle of (near-) automaticity of granting licenses to applicants, irrespective of the existing bilaterals has been maintained. The idea of the Directive is to impose common authorization rules on Member States and stipulate common freedoms for air carriers to apply for (any) interregional service, subject to certain conditions. As the Commission[37] puts it, in effect it lifts '. . . a specific and precisely defined segment of the market out of the bilateral structure and thus . . . (gives) . . . opportunities to more airlines to operate certain routes outside the trunk routes'. The services subject to the Directive are suppposed to be complementary to the hubbing systems of the trunk airlines.

Due to the resistance mentioned, nearly complete market segmentation has been imposed and virtually no competition will arise for the 'flag carriers' in their 'spokes' to and from the 'hubs', nor for their established subsidiaries on the domestic routes. The following restrictive conditions circumscribe the freedom to apply and the obligation to authorize:

- airports have been divided into three categories, the first category being the major hubs (mostly capitals), the second major provincial airports (like Stuttgart, Venezia, Lyon, Glasgow) and the third category other airports with facilities for international flights. In the Directive

all 'spokes' to the first category airports (in fact, virtually all the commercially interesting regional markets) are excluded. Only traffic between second and third category airports provides valid reason to apply for authorization. Note that the Commission had proposed to include third-first and second-first category services as well but both were rejected. So, feeder services are impossible.
- maximum size of aircraft is 70 seats (30 ton); the Commission had proposed 130 seats
- minimum stage length is 400 km (shorter when over mountains or seas); the Commission has 200 km
- a licence *can* be refused if another air service also exists from an airport B that is within a radius of 50 km from airport A, being the point of departure in the application; the problem is that this is the more likely if A is the major hub of the 'flag carrier'
- other restrictive conditions with respect to transit times and seasonal flight times have also been included.

Few viable services are expected to be initiated in response to such restrictive regulation. The Directive charges the Commission to report on its functioning before the middle of 1986. The Commission intends to publish a report in January 1986 and attach proposals to relax some provisions and widen the scope of the Directive.

In a recent speech[38] EC Commissioner Clinton Davies announced that the Commission will seek four improvements: (1) a new attempt to have feeder services to category 1 airports included – given the strong growth in new routes and services of this kind *outside* the scope of the Directive, Member States will have some difficulty in arguing sensibly against this proposal; (2) simplifying the Directive by eliminating a number of overly restrictive conditions; (3) inclusion of 'multi-sector journeys' over intra-EC frontiers, i.e., fifth freedom rights for regional carriers inside the Community; (4) (virtually) unrestricted access to the market for very small aircraft (up to 30 seats). One should not venture much hope that all proposals will pass the Council unhampered. The Commissioner went so far as to characterize the proposed amendments as 'a formidable agenda' for the Council. In fact, the proposals are modest and merely refer to a very small segment of the EC air transport market.

IV. BILATERAL LIBERALIZATION

Exerting effective pressure to liberalize the bilaterals inside the Community is only possible for the four big Member States, given the 'diplomatic' tradition of formal and material reciprocity in bilateral negotiations. Even The Netherlands – the largest of the smaller six Member States (before 1986) and, in terms of air transport, tailing after the big four – has difficulties in offering counter concessions of sufficient interest. An example may help to clarify this. It is known that, for a long time already, KLM wants to open a route from Amsterdam to Venice, a service that Lufthansa operates from Frankfurt. If it is known from market research that in the Veneto region the demand for travel to Amsterdam is modest, except for its gateway function to the US (KLM is competitive and holds a strong position on the Atlantic routes), Alitalia will tend to resist such a request. The results might be that (1) most of the demand in North-Western Europe to fly to Venice would be captured by KLM, and not by Alitalia, because of the booking systems and travel agents, while (2) Milan's hubbing function would also be affected negatively, without there being any obvious 'price' that KLM would have to pay to Alitalia (except if they would agree on an 'open pool' revenue sharing!).

At present the UK is practising a policy of *bilateral* liberalization by means of conluding liberal bilaterals. The country has concluded two successive agreements with the Netherlands (in 1984 and 1985), one with Germany (1984), one with Luxembourg and one with Belgium. Its next major target would seem to be France but this would require a roundabout strategy, i.e., attempting to liberalize the bilateral with Switzerland (ECAC member but not an EC member), in addition to the agreements already concluded with Luxembourg and Belgium.

The breakthrough was the Anglo–Dutch Agreement of 20 June 1984.[39] It has four main features:

- on route entry: Any Dutch or British airline can operate scheduled services on any route between the two countries, including routes already served by other airlines
- on capacity: airlines are free to mount whatever capacity they judge appropriate
- on tariffs: there is tariff freedom, no compulsory consultation of other airlines, a country-of-origin tariff approval system[40] and a right to 'match' sixth freedom based tariffs of UK airlines by Dutch airlines (and the other way round)
- on a 'safety net': each government can call for consultation, if its interests or those of the airlines would be affected. In case of route entry the likely threat to 'the economic viability' of an existing service may trigger consultation; in case of capacity, if 'the interests of its own airlines on a particular route . . . were being seriously damaged'

(a much stronger condition); in case of tariffs, the suspicion of 'predatory' or 'excessive' pricing.

The follow-up agreement of 19 June 1985 adds the freedom to combine services to/from any *two* points in any one of the countries but without cabotage rights[41] and a double-disapproval system[42] for tariffs.

It is not to be expected that any other bilateral within the European Community will take such a liberal shape in the near future. Therefore this agreement allows for a brief comparison between US deregulation and the very maximum of *bilateral* deregulation in the EC under the most optimistic scenario. First, the legal security for the economic agents is less than it could be because the official bilateral (Air Services Agreement) has *not* been changed; the 'agreed records of discussion' are policy declarations and can be repealed under art. 12 of the June 1984 Record by simple notice. Given the often fragile financial 'buffer' of new entrants on the new services and the dominance of the major carriers, this insufficient legal security creates a dependence on the political pressures of the day and/or the political colour of the government. Second, the exclusion of cabotage is a fundamental difference between the US and the EC (although *intra*-state transport rules may differ somewhat in the US, preemption renders a *de facto* liberalization likely), be it that the practical importance in air transport is not likely to be great. Third, whether a tariff is predatory or excessive is not judged by (say, Community) anti-trust authorities but during diplomatic negotiations where power considerations might play a role. Finally, since domestic transport is not at issue, no 'adjustment assistance' for communities 'losing' connecting air services has been foreseen, in contrast to the US where changes in the route structure upon deregulation have led to a substantial programme of subsidized, smaller air services. In other words, the 'public service' function of air transport in Europe is strictly interpreted in a domestic sense; whether such a function would not equally (or more forcefully) apply with respect to the Community as a whole, does not seem to have been considered. This demonstrates how important it is that a common EC air transport policy is realized, superseding or obviating the bilateral approach.

The German–British agreement[43] is weaker in serveral respects. There is free access to routes, but two points may only be served 'where traffic may at first be rather light'. There is substantial but incomplete tariff freedom; conditions include a description of 'special fares' (i.e., with restrictive obligations in order to segment the markets) and a bottom of 33% (Germany) and 30% (UK) of the normal economy round trip fare. Tariffs are subject to country-of-origin approval. The strong impression arises that this agreement is nothing more than a cautious match of the Anglo–Dutch agreement of June 1984. It should be noted that exactly in June 1984 the UK and Germany had already agreed on 'a range of attractive low fares' under the double approval system of the existing bilateral, clearly to prevent Dutch, and the British operating in The Netherlands, to succeed in deviating traffic from the airports of Hamburg, Bremen, Dusseldorf, Köln/Bonn and possibly even Frankfurt.

The Luxembourg/UK agreement[44] and the Belgium/UK agreement[45] are closer again to The Netherlands/UK agreements. The one with Luxembourg takes the legal form of a new bilateral. A conspicuous restriction is that 'matching' of tariffs of airlines from the other country (especially relevant for fifth and sixth freedom tariffs) is excluded. Other restrictions include the so-called 'Bermuda capacity rule' (which might cause the authorities to limit capacity in the light of sixth freedom traffic)[46] and a kind of escape clause for disapproval of tariffs (the bilateral stipulates a double disapproval system) of the 'own' companies, even if the journey starts in the other country. The Belgium/UK agreement is slightly more restrictive: it also employs the Bermuda capacity rule; it limits fifth freedom rights under the new agreement to destinations in Europe (and subject to double approval!) and narrows the terms for 'matching'.

While the Belgium/UK agreement is undoubtedly of some importance economically, especially with respect to its indirect effects, the new bilateral between the UK and Luxembourg should be put into perspective: traffic between the two countries proved to be so thin that British Airways had terminated its flight during its restructuring in 1982. It is probably the potential deviation from France (and Germany and Belgium) that renders it significant.

V. ECONOMIC EFFECTS

Ideally, the economic effects of 'deregulation' and liberalization in Europe should be attributed to four different sources of pressures:

- political and consumer pressures to imitate, part or wholly, US deregulation
- the Atlantic price war and the ECAC-US Memoranda or Understanding
- the EEC Directive on Interregional Air Services
- bilateral liberalization.

The author is not aware of systematic studies on any one of these four elements. It should be realized that European air transport statistics are incomparably weaker than US statistics due to omissions (frequently for commercial reasons, or lack of automation, as in the case of charter traffic to some Mediterranean destination) and traditions of secrecy due to too easy attribution in bilateral traffic. Also, the collection of statistics is nowhere centralized although there are a few databanks now. Therefore, the following assessments are based on fragmenting data, interviews and a few informative (but analytically non-rigorous) publications.

V.1. Effects of general pressures for deregulation

The most important effects probably relate to average fare levels, fare structures, route structures, the structure of service quality, industry structure and the position of labour (volume; wages). In Kenneth Boyer's paper in this volume (Boyer, 1985), traffic, costs and financial effects are also mentioned: except where his discussion about costs overlaps with route structures, effects in Europe (if any) are not attributable even intuitively. For example, not only is the splitting out of charter and scheduled services increasingly hazardous in Europe (see below), the slightly higher growth of the charter companies in terms of passengers boarded compared to that of trunk carriers might be atrributable to other factors that 'liberalization' such as increasing tourism to Southern European countries or recessionary business circumstances (causing a downward pressure on the growth of trunk carriers), etc.

The following qualitative assessment can be given:

- *average fare levels* are under pressure, virtually everywhere in Europe, since the late 1970s up to 1983; in 1984, however, the yield per passenger-kilometer of the European trunk carriers and their charter companies was down 5% compared to 1983, when measured in US dollars, but up 8% when measured in local European currencies[47]
- the downward pressure is probably due to changes in the *fare structure*, in particular the increasing use of discounts on scheduled services, as mentioned in Section 1; the European trunk carriers experienced an average discount of 36% in 1984, up from 34% in 1983;[48] about overall price developments in the highly competitive charter market, little is known
- on *route structure*; it seems that charters make increasing use of regional airports with international facilities; this is also encouraged by capacity problems at a number of major European airports, whether for reasons of handling, air traffic control or environment – so in effect, new routes are flown; furthermore, typical charter companies are

beginning to apply for authorizations to fly *scheduled* routes, permitted in the bilaterals but at present unused (example: Manchester–Malaga); in Britain, Germany, Switzerland and The Netherlands, thinner routes have been abandoned by the majors – given their scale-based fleet composition – and taken over by smaller or commuter companies (see further)

- the *structure of service quality* varies in accordance with the use of discounts, the increasing use of smaller (and more bumpy) aircraft on secondary routes, the (high) share of charter services and the (rarely permitted) disparity of frequencies among different suppliers; however, Europe does not possess any no-frills airline à la People Express
- *industry structure* is already changing for at least two decades with respect to the competition between scheduled and non-scheduled airlines; as mentioned before, the latter have taken approximately half of the market and they begin to diversify into scheduled modes in two ways
  - they begin to acquire licences for scheduled operations on routes in the bilaterals that are, at present, unused – this idea is mentioned in the Second Memorandum of the EC Commission
  - they have been selling 'seats-only' tickets, thereby trespassing the dividing line between scheduled and non-scheduled services (the latter must have an 'inclusive tour' character) and competing directly with trunk carriers, be it on routes where the scheduled airlines rarely operate; these legal border-cases have been dubbed 'camping flights' in Germany and The Netherlands; recently, in the UK, charter companies such as Britannia Airways, have obtained permission to sell 15% of their seats as 'seat-only'; interviewing revealed the estimate that, in the UK, 'seat-only' output of charter companies may well have increased from under 10% in 1983 to over 20% in the first half of 1985 (in other words, part of this must still be in the 'grey market')
- the *cost-cutting* exercises of the (allegedly) overstaffed major airlines in the first years of the decade fell largely *on labour*, and less so on route structure (i.e., weeding out unprofitable routes); particularly Sabena and British Airways have implemented impressive efforts of restructuring and rationalization (even by US standards); for instance British Airways has cut its staff by one-third in three years and Sabena by one-fifth; in addition, concessions on the wage front led to wage moderation in both companies (with much greater real effects in the Sabena case). There is little doubt about that US deregulation and its effect of concession barganing have greatly helped to impose these measures in Europe as well and cut the fat, over and above the public budgetary pressures of the governments involved (refusing to continue to cover losses).

All in all, these observations seem to constitute more than just 'straws in the wind' about economic effects of the liberalizing trends in European air transport. However, as Section 2 emphasizes, the main regulatory structure still stands firm. Thus, one important economic effect of US deregulation – restructuring of networks – is but marginally possible in Europe, as long as bilateralism doesn't disappear. Another important economic effect of US deregulation – an enormous increase in discounts and low fares – is only weakly echoed in Europe because European countries already had a much more liberal policy with respect to discount fares while charters played a big role in Europe ever since the late 1960s.

V.2 Effects from Atlantic route competition

Price wars on the Atlantic route, and the no-frills services of Laker Airways, up to February 1982 have had a profound impact on this market segment, even after the ECAC–US Memoranda and successful IATA tariff conferences restored reasonable price stability. Formal IATA statistics about the North Atlantic route[49] show lower-than-inflation, dollar-denominated (average economy) fare increases for 1981 and 1982, a levelling in 1983 and a fall in 1984. In local European currencies fares in 1984 have probably increased roughly with inflation. The key difference between the Laker period (1977–1982) and thereafter is in the share of discount passengers and in secret discounts (or/and secret commissions). Although the latter are unfortunately suggested by mere assertions, the buying-off of Laker's case against British Airways and other trunk carriers in 1985 to the tune of several tens of millions of pounds might be considered as an indication of unfair competition at the time. The share of discount passengers has increased enormously during the Laker period (from 16.9% in 1977 to 41.3% in 1982), but it continues to increase, reaching 48.9% in 1984).[50] Competition on the Atlantic route – the biggest intercontinental route of the world market – is still strong. In the spring of 1984 People Express started a once-a-day no-frill but ordinary-booking service between Newark (its hub airport) and Gatwick airport in London. In November 1984 Virgin Atlantic Airways started flying to New York from Gatwick airport in London at low fares. Due to the great success of People Express's Atlantic service (they claim a 100% load factor, with virtually no exception), the airline requested permission for a greater frequency which was refused. People Express then obtained permission to fly Newark–Brussels and has begun this service on 8 September 1985. After the usual sensational introductory fares (of £70), the regular fare for all seats amounted in

December 1985 to £109, one way. Apart from the downward pressure this may exert on Atlantic fares towards the bottom range of the 'zone of reasonableness' for fares in the liberal bilaterals (US–UK; US–Netherlands; US–Belgium; US–Germany), it might increase possible traffic deviation from Paris as well.

Although there need not be any measurable affect on *intra*-European air traffic, it does increase market and political pressure for liberalization. The case of Virgin Atlantic Airlines is a special one because it exploits a sixth freedom right by bringing passengers from Maastricht to London-Gatwick but the on-line effect for the Atlantic has proved to be marginal.

V.3. Effects of the interregional directive

Recently the European Commission has sent a letter to the Member States requesting information on new companies, new routes and new services under the EEC Interregional Directive that came into force on 1 October 1984. Since the nature of the Directive is restrictive it is certain that no important economic effects will have taken place. The Commission is expected to report in January 1986, but Commissioner Clinton Davies has already revealed that the first year of operation of the Directive comprised 19 applications (15 granted) for new services.[51] This number is small in absolute terms (given the size of the EC) and small compared to the induced applications under bilateral liberalization (see further). The growth in regional air traffic in Europe can be attributed almost entirely to 'spoke' services to and from major hubs, hence those excluded from the Directive (in other words, only possible under bilaterals).

As noted before, this exclusion of feeder services is an important objection to the Directive. Precisely for new companies with fragile finances, it is hazardous to begin with thin routes that – initially – are difficult to market without substantial budgets *and* good access to central booking systems. Therefore companies either start with feeder services domestically (if permitted) and routed under liberal bilaterals or they seek protection otherwise. Thus Netherlines, a new company, hopes to develop Eindhoven Airport as a minor hub, with the initial 'spokes' all geared to the interests of the Philips Electronics Company, which, in turn, has guaranteed reservations of substantial blocks of seats for Philips employees on all these services.

The practical significance of the Directive being insignificant, the Commission should urge Countil to *at least* relax two constraints: permit feeder services to category 1 airports (for small aircraft, still) and allow fifth freedom rights subject to a maximum distance, say 1500 km. So, two or three or four relatively thin routes could be connected, with one major hub somewhere on the route. Failing this, little or nothing will occur in the market.

V.4. Effects of bilateral liberalization

The ECAC report of 1982[52] has revealed how restrictive the bilateral organization of European scheduled air transport really was in the year 1980. The report concentrated on multiple designation, capacity, pooling agreements, fifth freedoms and traffic setting, and ignored route creation and regional cross-boarder traffic. A few examples illustrate the enormous scope for liberalization:

- the report distinguishes the legal designation provisions in the bilaterals studied and the actual carrier designation in practice: in practice, 23% of country pairs under bilaterals are not served by the airline of the responding country, 71% are served by one airline per State and only 6% by two or more airlines per State; on a city-pair basis only 2% (!) of the studied city-pairs have more than one designated airline.
- on capacity, 60% of bilaterals has an '*ex post facto*' review of capacity and 29% of a predetermination of capacity; the method most often used is the fixing of the frequency of flights (including the off-peak hours). It should be noted that, in air transport diplomacy, ex post review boils down to virtually the same as predetermination if the review is regularly held.
- as mentioned before, more than 75% of intra-ECAC tonne-kilometers performed in 1980 were subject to pooling agreements; moreover, where pools don't exist, this is often caused by the fact that only one airline is interested to fly the route.
- the report also distinguishes between the fifth freedom rights granted and those actually exercised; one of the interesting findings is that such rights are relatively frequently granted, but much more seldomly exercised. Unfortunately, no information on separate EC Member States enjoying such rights is supplied; only on those have granted the rights. The following figures give first the number of ECAC *airlines* exercising the fifth freedom rights, granted by the mentioned EC Member State, and in parentheses the total number of ECAC *countries* having been granted such rights: Belgium 2(16); France 8(8); Germany 5(16); Italy 1(18); Netherlands 3(18); United Kingdom 2(9).

The conclusion is inescapable that, *in the present configuration of European air transport regulation, it is bilateral liberalization that has the greatest scope for liberalization.* This process can take forms which are virtually impossible to detect. For example, de facto carrier designation may silently be increased, capacity reviewing may be relaxed in various subtle ways, pools may become less restrictive and the actual exercise of fifth freedoms in Europe may increase (Note that the latter will frequently depend on non-European countries if there is an intercontinental gateway function). Unless a habit of reporting on these matters is developed in ECAC, or until the European Commission obtains the legal right to demand disclosure of necessary data for purposes of competition policy so that some form of aggregated statistics could become available regularly, it is not possible to monitor this road of liberalization. Thus, in a recent statement UK Minister Spicer for Aviation refers to 'some loosening up of arrangements with France'[53] but it is unclear what exactly this means for the market. Mr Spicer probably refers to a recent agreement between France and the UK to deviate from 50%/50% capacity sharing up to 45%/55% both ways. The details of the agreement are however unpublished.

The other method consists of the more conspicuous one of liberalizing bilaterals. Excluding the very recent agreements between the UK and Luxembourg and Belgium, all there is in this category are the UK agreements with The Netherlands and Germany.

What data there is about the economic activity following these agreements points to *a vivid and entrepreneurial response in the market.* According to Mr Stevens of the UK Department of Transport in a letter to the House of Lords,[54] 8 March 1985, no new services between the UK and Germany had been inaugurated in the three months since the agreement but 21 licence applications were outstanding from 14 different airlines (and only one from British Airways). Some of these have very small aircraft (e.g., Birmingham Executive Airways) and it is not clear whether, in fact, such application would not fall under the EEC Directive and qualify automatically, irrespective of the bilateral liberalization (but of course subject to safety and 'economic viability' requirements).

With respect to the first Anglo–Dutch agreement there is data on the first nine months, up to March 1985. The civil aviation authorities of the two countries[55] estimated a 15% traffic increase, compared to 'growth of around 10% in the traffic between London or Amsterdam and other points in Western Europe'. They estimate that the low-fare (off-peak!) capacity has averaged about 2000 seats a week, with ± 75% being diverted from surface traffic or attracted as passengers that would not have travelled otherwise. Table 3 gives the new services: ten new services, six of which are new routes, with a total number of flights of 97 a week. In

Table 3. New services between the UK and the Netherlands*.

Route	Airline	Frequency (per week)
(by UK carriers)		
Exeter–Amsterdam	Air UK	6
Glasgow–Newcastle–Amsterdam	Air UK	12
London(GW)–Maastricht	Virgin Atlantic	7
London(GW)–Rotterdam	British Air Ferries	18
Luton–Amsterdam	London European	11
Newcastle–Amsterdam	Dan-Air	10
(by Dutch carriers)		
Amsterdam–London(GW)	KLM	5
Amsterdam–Newcastle	KLM	6
Rotterdam–Norwich	Holland Aero Leasing	11
Rotterdam–Southend	Holland Aero Leasing	11
(Totals) (10)	(7)	(97)

*At 1 April 1985 (nine months after first agreement).

addition four other licences have been granted already and another 19 (!) are under consideration. Furthermore, price competition on the very busy Amsterdam–London route has altered the fare structure, i.e., low fares are used on off-peak flights (volume inversely related to demand for economy fares), also on regional flights. Also, new types of low fares have been introduced by British Caldenonian on the Amsterdam–London route.

That competition has been invigorated on apparent secondary routes can be illustrated by the Maastrich–London route. This route was traditionally (and still is) served by NLM (a regional-service, 100%-owned subsidiary of KLM), twice a day on working days, with one stop in Eindhoven. Because of the importance of Philips reservations, the tail-end Eindhoven-Maastricht was maltreated and no marketing attempt in the catchment area around Maastricht Airport was undertaken. Observe that the bilateralism is so deeply engrained in Europe that German commercial KLM agents would probably not allow NLM to advertise and promote in the (substantial) German catchment area of Maastricht. Since November 1984 Virgin Atlantic flies London–Maastricht directly, at unconditional low-fares-only, matching the (restrictive) APEX fares of NLM. The result is clearly pointing to the defects of the present, overly rigid business-oriented organization and regulation of the industry.

Over 1984 Maastricht noted 83% growth in its non-domestic European passenger traffic.[56] Since NLM is known not to have suffered traffic deviation – the number of passengers has remained approximately steady – this increase is to be attributed entirely to Virgin Atlantic flights, covering two months only! Further interviewing revealed that Virgin Atlantic has been able to attract more than 30% of the number of passengers flying with NLM to the same city, serving the same airport, in the first half of 1985.[57] Maastricht Airport is now attempting to attract similar traffic from and to other EC countries, be it by exploiting unused routes in bilaterals, be it by persuading companies to apply for new routes, be it under the EEC Interregional Directive.

VI. FINAL REMARKS

Deregulation of air transport in Europe is an uphill struggle. Tangible results after a decade of talking amount to little:

- a (further) increase in the use of discounts and low fares
- a beginning of the blurring between charter modes and scheduled modes
- bilateral liberalization between the UK and the Netherlands, Germany, Belgium and Luxembourg (but *not* among the latter four yet[58])
- a very restrictive EEC Directive for Interregional Service Authorization.

Pressures to deregulate or liberalize further have not decreased. Nor has political attention for the topic diminished. The key problem will remain the bilateral structure of the granting of landing rights, following from the Chicago Convention. It is a phantasy to believe that this solid rock can be removed in the Community before the 21st century. A telling example may illustrate what 'hastening slowly' means in this respect: even the harmless and commercially uninteresting EEC Directive provides for grace periods for airports on the Greek Islands until 1 July 1993, with an extension of another five years, except if the Council would decide otherwise in 1993.[59] Is it difficult to imagine what would happen if *major* decisions on major determinants of the market structure will finally be taken by the Council of Transport Ministers?

It is not impossible that a combination of cases before the European Court, bilateral liberalization and consumer pressures with respect to the Atlantic route might gear the Council into some form of Communitarian action. Hopes should not be set too high as shown by the comparison of the very moderate Commission proposals of 1984 and the present position of the EC Member States, the European Parliament[60] and the Economic and Social Committee of the EC.[61] One should also not forget the power of the labour unions in this regulated sector: they are teaming up with their employers in order to prevent substantial adjustment, a phenomenon also known in other protected industries. Now that European trunk carriers have done some slimming (with tougher measures in a few particularly bad cases) and make profits again, they might well be considered as 'efficient' again. This would strengthen the hand of the labour unions in protesting against the dark sides of the US deregulation.

That allocative efficiency is distorted by the bilateral system of strict regulation and industrial organization – hence, not responding to consumers that are prevented from revealing their preferences more fully – while technical inefficiency is not at issue for the airlines when prices are 'reasonably related to costs', constitute the core arguments to alter the system and deregulate. One wonders what power can be placed behind these arguments in the decisive political economy of the Community's air transport integration.

NOTES

1. See IATA, 1984, *International Air Fares in Europe* (Geneva), p. 28.
2. These examples are taken from Civil Aviation Authority, *Deregulation of air transport, a perspective on the experience in the US*, CAA Paper 84009, London, 1984, pp. 34 and 39.
3. As Section 3.3. will set out, the EEC Directive on interregional air services (see Note 35) classifies European airports into a hierarchy of three categories, category one being the major hubs of the trunk carriers.
4. For a survey and its significance for industrial market integration, see Pelkmans (1984) and (1985) and the Patterson report in the European Parliament on consolidating the Internal Market, 31 May 1985, Doc. A2-50/85/B.
5. If *all* intra-European flights are taken together, only 23% is domestic (mainly inside the big four EC Member States) and 77% is 'cross-border'.
6. See ECAC, *Report on Competition in Intra-European Air Services*, Doc. No 25, Paris, 1982, p. 37.
7. The Court case is the French sailors case (Case 167/73, Commission vs. French Republic), *European Court Reports* 1, pp. 357 ff. A legal treatment is in Close (1980). In Kuyper (1983) a legal comparison is made with the US.
8. See especially P. Haanappel, *Pricing and Capacity Determination in International Air Transport*, Boston/Deventer (Kluwer), 1984; the ECAC report (see Note 6); EC Commission, *Report, Scheduled Passenger Air Fares in the EEC*, COM(81) 389, Brussels, 31 July 1981.
9. IATA, 1984, *op. cit.*, p. 11.
10. Observe that this assertion does not apply to the truly irregular charters. Such ad hoc charters in the ECAC area are governed by the multilateral ECAC *Agreement on Commercial Flights of Non-Scheduled Air Services* of 1956.

11. A survey is in IATA, 1984, *op. cit.* It should be realized that this has caused confusion among consumers about product differentiation. In one airplane many different people may find to have paid many different prices, yet, once being in the air, treatment need not noticeably differ. The following exchange in the House of Lords Hearings makes the key points informally:

    Question:
    I flew back from India last year and on the flight made come enquiries and the range of fares paid for the same flight and the same seating was about four to one. They were on a scheduled flight, by the way.
    Answer:
    Of course, some people may be buying essentially a different product.
    Question:
    You are buying the same seat in the aeroplane.
    Answer:
    You are getting the same seat in the aeroplane but some people may have wished to have complete flexibility to change their flight if their business took them a bit longer. This is something which is an extremely costly freedom for the airlines to provide and a justified reason for a different scale of prices for that sort of person. Somebody else may have been prepared to book at the very last minute and get a standby fare. Again you can see reasons why that should be cheaper. Some people may have been prepared to book a longish period in advance, even paying their money in advance. There are advantages to this. So it does not surprise me at all that people sitting next to one another in the same seats on the same flights could actually have paid different prices, although it may not look like it at the time because they eat the same sandwich, but they are actually getting a very different product'.
    Quoted from Mr H. Stevens, Under-Secretary, International Aviation Directorate, UK Department of Transport, in: House of Lords, Select Committee on the EC, *European Air Transport Policy*, Session 1984–85, 7th Report, (London, 1985), pp. 12/13.

12. See the EC Commission's Tariff Study (see Note 8), p. 26.
13. Prorating is a consequence of the heavy use of 'interlining' in Europe. Interlining refers to the possibility for passengers to switch between companies, for the different stages of one through fare (in other words, the airlines accept each other's tickets in the case of changes or stop-overs). Prorating is a system of sharing revenue between airlines with an interline agreement of a passenger who travels on a multi-stage journey with one ticket. Hence, the (costly) stop-overs are not included in the price and the (lower) throughfare ticket price is distributed among the interlining airlines.
14. See IATA, 1984, *op. cit.*, pp. 8–11.
15. As quoted in Note 8.
16. See, for instance, Civil Aviation Authority, *Airline Competition Policy*, London 184; see also Section 4.
17. See EC Commission, *Civil Aviation Memorandum No 2*, COM(84)72, 15 March 1984; note however that the Commission still aims in the long run, to realize a common air transport policy without bilateralism.
18. EC Commission, Air Transport: A Community Approach, *Bulletin of the EC*, Supplement 5, 1979.

19. An outside observer faces insurmountable obstacles to underpin these assertations. Whether there was predatory pricing during 1980 and 1981 is a matter of legal dispute and whether price stabilization has led to tariffs covering long-run average costs can only be indirectly inferred from general profits; price/cost margins for Atlantic flights only are not available.
20 The US and the UK had concluded the so-called Bermuda II agreement in 1976 which was *more* restrictive than the Bermuda I agreement of 1946, the 'model bilateral' in air law. However, Bermuda II has become de facto liberalized via liberal protocols, added after 1978.
21. In case countries A and B conclude a bilateral, the sixth freedom refers to air traffic from A to C, via the home country B, or (for the other Party) from B to C via home country A.
22. European Parliament, Committee on Transport *Report on Memorandum No 2 from the Commission of the EC on civil aviation* (rapporteur Mr J. Klinkenborg), Doc. A2-86/85/Part A of 7 August 1985, Brussels/Luxembourg.
23. EC Commission, Report and proposed decision on a programme of action for the European aeronautical sector, *Official Journal* C 265 of 19 November 1975.
24. See Note 7.
25. In case countries A and B conclude a bilateral the fifth freedom refers to A's freedom to fly passengers from C via B to A, respectively, to B's freedom to fly passengers from C via A to B; or vice versa.
26. See Note 18.
27. See Note 36.
28. See Note 8.
29. EC Commission, *Proposal for a Council Directive* on Tariffs for Scheduled Air Transport between Member States, COM(81)590, 27 October 1981.
30. EC Commission, *Proposal for a Council Regulation* applying Articles 85 and 86 of the Treaty (rules on competition applying to undertakings) to air transport, COM(81)396 of 31 July 1981.
31. See Note 17.
32. Case 209/84–213/84; upon request for a pre-judicial decision, ex. art. 177, EEC, from the French Tribunal d'Instance de Paris. The Court is expected to give its judgement in the early spring of 1986. In Paris the cases are against KLM, British Airways, Air France and Air Lanka.
33. Even the staunchest defenders of the status quo – the major European trunk carriers – mention only two out of four conditions of Art. 83, 3, EEC; see Association of European Airlines, *EEC Air Transport Policy*, Brussels, July 1984; esp. p. 12 and p. 20.
34. See Note 16.
35. Council Directive, 83/416/EEC, concerning the authorization of scheduled interregional air services of passengers, mail and cargo between Member States, *Official Journal* L 237 of 26 August 1983.
36. EC Commission, Proposal for a Council Regulation concerning the authorization (etc.), COM(80)624, 27 November 1980.
37. In its second Memorandum (see Note 17), p. 15.
38. Speech by Mr Clinton Davies, Conference of airports and airlines interested in interregional air transport, Brussels, 17 December 1985 (mimeo).
39. *Agreed record of discussion*, 20 June 1984, Minister of Transport Mrs Smit-Kroes and Secretary of State for Transport Mr Ridley.

40. A tariff proposal is considered approved if the country of origin (of the airline) accepts it (rather than the traditional 'double approval' system).
41. Cabotage refers to domestic transport carried out by foreign transport firms. Thus, if a Dutch company would fly Manchester–Southend–Rotterdam, no tickets Manchester–Southend could be sold.
42. Apart from full tariff freedom (possibly subject to anti-trust provisions), the double disapproval system is the most liberal system: a filed tariff is considered approved unless both countries' authorities disapprove.
43. Joint Announcement, plus Annexes, on the Liberalization of Air Services between the UK and the FR of Germany, 13 December 1984, *Transport* (UK Department of), *Press Notice* No 564.
44. Agreed record of discussions about scheduled air services arrangements, and, New UK–Luxembourg Air Services Arrangements Announced, in *Transport, Press Notice* No 125 of 26 March 1985.
45. See *Agreed record of discussions* about scheduled air services arrangements between the UK and Belgium, 10 October 1985, Minister of Aviation Michael Spicer and Herman de Croo, Minister of Communications.
46. The Bermuda capacity rule is captured in the clause: '. . . so long as the principal objective of the service is to provide adequate capacity of a reasonable load factor for 3rd/4th freedom traffic'. Dependent on what 'the principal objective' is interpreted to be, it could be used to block (say) capacity enlargement for (sixth freedom) traffic via London to (say) the US.
47. Association of European Airlines, *Yearbook 1984*, Brussels, 1985, p. 9.
48. *Idem.*
49. IATA, *World Air Transport Statistics 1984*, Geneva, 1985, p. 33 (graph).
50. *Idem*, (block diagram). I have taken 'discount passengers' to be 'excursion capacity controlled'.
51. See Note 38.
52. See Note 6.
53. See Comments by Mr Spicer, in: Dep. of Transport, *Press Notice* No 438 of 10 October 1985 (on the Belgium/UK agreement), London.
54. See Report, quoted in Note 11, pp. 294/5.
55. CAA/RLD, *An assessment* of UK/Netherlands Air Services under the liberal arrangements of 20 June 1984, London/The Hague, June 1985.
56. Maastricht Airport, *Verslag over het boekjaar 1984* (Annual Report 1984), Maastricht/Beek, May 1985, p. 11.
57. Observe that, compared to the first half of 1984, NLM suffered no decrease in passengers.
58. Hardly any attention has been paid to *intra*-Benelux air traffic, which ought to be treated rather liberally, following Art. 89 of the Treaty establishing the Benelux Economic Union. See, in this vein, *Advies inzake verdere voortgang* (etc.) (Advice with respect to further progress on the road to liberalization of scheduled international air transport in the EC). Brussels, Economic & Social Council of Benelux, 12 March 1985.
59. Article 15.
60. See the Linkenborg report; note 22. Probably the sharpest, yet reasonable criticism of the Klinkenborg report has come from the European Office of Consumers Unions (BEUC). See BEUC's *Notice* to the Members of the European Parliament of 3 September 1985 (Ref. 153/85) and its *Recommendations* on Air Transport Liberalization, Brussels, 1985.

61. Economic and Social Committee of the EC, *EEC Air Transport Policy*, (Kenna report), Brussels, October 1985.

REFERENCES

Boyer, K., Do we really understand the economics of regulation: the effects of US transport deregulation; in this volume (1985).

Close, G., Art. 84 EEC: The development of transport policy in the sea and air sectors, *European Law Review*, June (Vol. 5, 3) (1980).

Haanappel, P., An analysis of US deregulation of air transport and its inferences for a more liberal air transport in Europe, Council of Europe, Parliamentary Assembly, 21 May 1984 (AS/EC. (36)3) (1984).

Kappetijn, P., (ed.), *The Development of a European Air Transport Policy*, Maastricht, European Institute of Public Administration, Working Documents 83/02 (1983).

Kuyper, P. J., Airline fare-fixing and competition: an English Lord, Commission proposals and US parallels, *Common Market Law Review*, May (Vol. 20, 2) (1983).

Michaud, C. and Thoenig, J. C., *La régulation du transport aerien en Europe*, Fontainebleau/Paris (INSEAD/CNRS) (1982).

Pelkmans, J., *Market integration in the European Community*, Boston/Lancaster/The Hague (Nijhoff) (1984).

Pelkmans, J., *The Internal EC Market for Industrial Products*, The Hague, Staatsuitgeverij, Government Printing Office, for the WRR); in Dutch (1985).

Sichelschmidt, H., Wettbewerb statt staatlicher Regulierung – Wege zu einem besseren Luftverkehrssystem in Europa, *Keil Discussion Papers*, No 100, Keil (August 1984).

16. INDUSTRIAL POLICY IN THEORY AND REALITY

Hiroyuki Odagiri

1. INTRODUCTION

Dennis Mueller once wrote 'The case against conglomerate mergers is that there is not a strong case for them' (Mueller, 1981, p. 71). In the same vein I will argue here: 'The case against industrial policy is that there is no strong case for it'. In fact I believe that such a statement makes even more sense here, because I intend to argue that the government should do little, thus minimizing the cost of policy implementation and bureaucratic discretion, whereas Mueller is arguing that the government should take an action to prevent mergers, thus necessitating such cost.

By no means do I deny that any of the policies usually regarded as constituting the so-called industrial policy can be beneficial. Theoretically one can conceive of cases where governmental intervention improves welfare. Empirically, for instance, from the Japanese experience, one may be able to present cases in whicih governmental intervention seems to have been conducive to industrial development. However, whether such improvement in welfare is quantitatively significant and, in particular, whether it outweighs the cost of implementing the policy may be questioned. Moreover, most of the empirical cases do not seem strong enough to prevent alternative and less sympathetic interpretations. Thus there may be no *strong* case for industrial policy. Meanwhile, there are the political, bureaucratic, and administrative costs of industrial policy. Industrial policy has to be carried out by the government bureaucrats, in contrast to the market allocation that is carried out by the impersonal forces of decentralized markets. In that light, the net benefits of industrial policy are usually negative.

To approach this difficult question, I plan to examine industrial policy from diverse – theoretical, empirical and political – viewpoints, rather than by presenting a specific theory or a particular empirical case. The

de Jong, H. W., Shepherd, W. G. (eds) Mainstreams in Industrial Organization
 ISBN 978-94-017-0495-3

paper starts with examining what is meant by 'industrial policy', because the term is used in so many ways that one may include virtually any governmental action under the term 'industrial policy'. The boundary between industrial policy and regulation is hardly distinct so that advocating both industrial policy and deregulation simultaneously appears contradictory. Section 3 briefly reviews the theoretical arguments in favor of industrial policy, particularly the theory of infant industry. Section 4 examines the Japanese experience, asking if her post-war industrial development really owes much to industrial policy. Section 5 turns to the discussions in the political or public-choice literature and asks if our political system is good or efficient enough to remedy market failure. Section 6 examines a particular field where the necessity for governmental assistance has seldom been questioned, that is, scientific research. Even here I will argue that market-induced R&D is often more efficient than governmental policy. Section 7 summarizes and concludes the discussion.

2. WHAT IS INDUSTRIAL POLICY?

Even though the term 'industrial policy' was virtually nonexistent in English usage ten years ago, the past decade has seen an upsurge of interest in industrial policy, particularly among American economists and politicians. This interest has been aroused partly by the growing recognition that innovation is important in the process of industrial development and international competition, and by the (sometimes superficial) observation that government support and intervention in Japan, loosely referred to as industrial policy, contributed to her development and her catching up (or even surpassing) the United States in quite a few high-technology industries. Nevertheless, what industrial policy is, and how it differs from the other more conventional policies, have been clarified only occasionally. It is a convenient word. Indeed any industry wishing to have some form of governmental support can call it an industrial policy and claim its indispensability for the country.

It is no wonder, therefore, that the definition of industrial policy not only is diverse among authors but also has tended to expand in its scope. Two definitions by Komiya, one of the leading and pioneering Japanese writers on the subject with a basically neoclassical background, well exemplify this tendency. Ten years ago he wrote that 'industrial policy refers to those governmental activities that change interindustry resource allocation and the level of certain economic activities of private firms within each industry from those that should have been attained without such policy' (Komiya, 1975, p. 308, my translation). Now he says that 'today I feel that this definition is rather too limited and needs to be modified to expand the scope somewhat' (Komiya, 1984, p. 3, my translation), and argues that 'the main task of industrial policy is to deal with 'market failure' concerning resource allocation' (*ibid.*, p. 5).

That he felt compelled to expand the scope of industrial policy is not difficult to understand. According to him, industrial policy is classified into four categories: (A) policies on industrial infrastructure, (B) policies on interindustry resource allocation, (C) policies on intraindustry organization, and (D) policies on small- and medium-sized enterprises. Although the major purpose of (A) is probably the provision of public goods and elimination of external effects whereas the major purpose of (D) is income redistribution, these policies yield important consequences to the activities of the firms and inter- or intra-industry resource allocation. The boundary between the policy *primarily* aimed at the provision of public goods, elimination (or internalization) of externalities, and income redistribution on the one hand and the policy *primarily* aimed at changing inter- or intra-industry resource allocation on the other (which Komiya had perhaps in his mind in the 1975 definition) is thus blurred. In fact, any policy that aims to deal with market failure – externalities (such as pollution), public goods (such as infrastructure), inappropriability (such as with technological knowledge), income distribution, economies of scale, and such – is bound to affect industries and, in this sense, is an industrial policy.

Apparently, industrial policy thus defined is hardly separable from other policies. Even fiscal and monetary policies affect interindustry allocation because an expansionary fiscal policy will be beneficial to, say, the construction industry and an expansionary monetary policy, to capital intensive industries. More importantly, industrial policy is indistinguishable from regulation. Both refer to governmental intervention to an industry. Both are viewed necessary due to market failure. See, for instance, Phillips's definition: 'The economics of regulation is the economics of "market failure"' (Phillips, 1975, p. 2).

It is true that, despite this inevitable common definition, most people will take industrial policy and regulation differently. Regulation will mean to most people price regulation in those industries with scale economies (such as in the electricity industry), safety regulation (such as in the pharmaceutical industry), and entry regulation (such as in the transportation industry). Though industrial policy is also concerned with entry, regulation is usually made to deter entry whereas industrial policy is to promote entry (e.g., to promote entry of a domestic producer into an import-dominated market). This difference is not essential, however, because industrial policy has also often worked to deter entry, for instance, by restricting the entry by a foreign dominant firm and by encouraging concentration to a few firms in such an industry where economies of scale allegedly are important (as in fact attempted in the past by the Japanese government).

Thus industrial policy and regulation are hard to distinguish, which suggests that the criticisms against regulation can be also directed to industrial policy. In fact, as the readers will see, many of my criticisms in Section 5 against industrial policy will be those adopted from the literature on regulation. That regulation covers too many industries and interferes with too many corporate activities to maintain an efficient and dynamic economy is now recognized by many and the call for deregulation is heard in many countries. We know that the history of regulation was the history of constantly expanding fields under regulation and of expanding regulatory agencies. Even though theoretically no one would deny the need for regulation in certain industries, we now realize that it may yield more harm than gain to dynamic economic efficiency. We certainly need not repeat the same history with industrial policy.

3. THEORY

Most popular industrial polices are in two categories; to promote entry into an infant, expanding or oligopolistic industry, and to promote exit from a declining industry so as to foster the transfer of its resources to more expanding sectors. The latter is often called the adjustment assistance policy. This section considers the theoretical justification for these two policies.

Those policies under the first category are more or less based on the well-known infant industry argument. This argument applies to an industry where (I) entry to this industry can be made only with substantial cost, in the form of either fixed entry cost (e.g., irreversible investment or R&D expenditures) or loss during the initial periods when learning is being made (e.g., due to the production cost higher than that of the incumbents), and (II) after these periods the entrant is expected to earn positive profits so that governmental support is no more required for its survival. These are but a necessary condition and not sufficient to justify governmental assistance – tariff or subsidy – because the firm will have an incentive to enter without such assistance as long as the present value of the profits in (II) outweighs the cost in (I). Hence, governmental assistance is justified only when (III) the present value of net profits to the entrant firm is negative, and yet the present value of incremental social welfare is positive. This condition, known as the Negishi condition, substantially narrows the range that the infant industry argument can be applied to justify governmental assistance.

To examine in what instances the conditions I to II can be met, a diagramatic device, adapted from Negishi's (1968), is helpful. Suppose, for simplicity, that there are two periods, today and future, everything stays unchanged during each period, and the present value is simply the sum of the values in two periods (e.g., each period is of the same length and the discount rate is zero). Look at figure 1, in which every notation is in a small letter for today and in a capital letter for future. In both today and future, the domestic demand curve, dd′ and DD′, and the import supply curve, ee′ and EE′, are assumed fixed. Most importantly we assume that the supply curve of the domestic firm, ss′, is everywhere above the (non-entry) equilibrium price, denoted by the length oa, satisfying Condition I, and that if it yet produces by oi today, learning takes place to the effect that the future supply curve shifts down to SS′, satisfying Condition II.

With the domestic production of oi today, the total supply curve is e*e*′, obtained by the parallel rightward shift of ee′ by oi, so that the equilibrium takes place at point h with the price of, which is lower than the non-entry equilibrium price oa provided that the import supply curve is upward-sloping (that is, provided that the country is a *large* country). The domestic firm supplies by oi (or equivalently fk) and the foreign producers supply by kh. The loss to the domestic entrant today equals the area shown by sfkj. Alternatively this may be interpreted as the

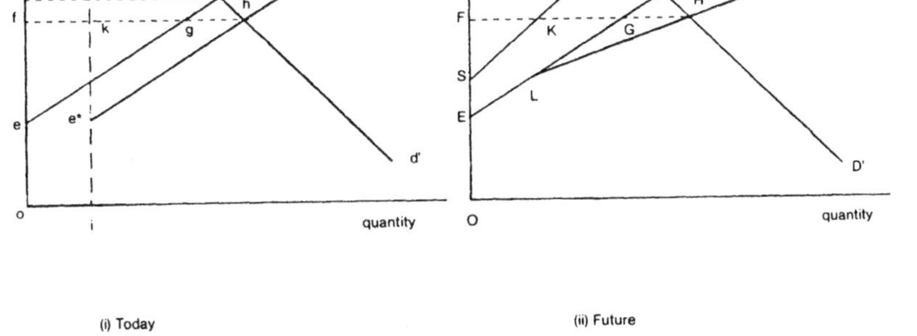

Fig. 1. The theory of infant industry.

irreversible entry or setup cost, such as the cost of establishing a distribution channel or goodwill and R&D expenditures to establish production technology and knowhow.

In the future, given the import supply curve EE′, the total supply curve is the horizontal sum of SS′ and EE′ shown by the kinked curve ELM. The equilibrium takes place at H with the price OF, where were it not for the entry the equilibrium would have been at B with the price OA. The entrant's profit is shown by the area FSK or, equivalently, GLH.

Condition III requires that the present value of the entrant's profits, −sfkj + FSK, is negative and yet the present value of social welfare is positive. Social welfare here refers to the welfare gained by domestic agents, that is, the sum of consumers' surplus gained by the domestic consumers and producers' surplus gained by the domestic firm(s). In other words, the government is supposed not to care about the well-being of foreign consumers or producers.

The present value of consumers' surplus is dab + DAB without entry, and dfh + DFH with entry. Apparently, the latter exceeds the former; that is, entry, by lowering the equilibrium price, increases consumers' surplus in both today and future. Producers' surplus for domestic firm(s) is zero without entry, and −sfkj + FSK with entry. Social welfare, the sum of consumers' and producers' surpluses, is dab + DAB without entry, and dfh − sfkj + DFH + FSK with entry. The increment in welfare due to the entry is the difference between the two, which is afhb − sfkj + AFBH + FSK. Hence as long as afhb + AFHB is greater than sfkj − FSK, this increment is positive, in which case the social welfare is increased by the entry even though it may not be profitable to the firm. Condition III can be thus satisfied, justifying the infant industry argument and supporting the subsidization to a domestic entrant by the amount, sfkj − FSK.

This exposition teaches us that social welfare increases only when the consumer's surplus is increased by a price reduction.[1] Note also that the producers' surplus to foreign firms is decreased by the entry. For this is aeb + AEB without entry, and feg + FEG with entry, implying that it is decreased by afgb + AFGB. This amount, as we have seen, is absorbed by the domestic consumers when entry is made. Therefore, the increment in consumers' surplus is achieved partly by the transfer of surplus from foreign producers to domestic consumers, and partly by the pure creation of such surplus due to price reduction.

The exposition admittedly is elementary and simplistic, for instance, by neglecting the possibility of monopolistic or oligopolistic behavior of domestic or foreign firms and by neglecting the general equilibrium considerations; nevertheless, it is the base of most arguments in favor of entry-promoting tariff or subsidy policy. For example, when the foreign producer is a monopolist, the increase in consumers' surplus is expected to be even larger because the decrease in price will also result from the market structure changing from monopoly to duopoly (i.e., the incumbent and the entrant). In fact, in this case, if the domestic firm also enters the foreign market, the foreign country too will be benefitted provided the foreign consumers' gain by the price decrease outweighs the monopolist's loss. One cannot deny the possibility, therefore, that the industrial policy in one country benefits another country.[2]

Three more sophisticated theories give an additional justification to governmental support on entry in a monopolist situation. First, if the foreign monopolist is initially employing a limit pricing strategy to prevent entry of a domestic firm, a tariff may not raise the consumer price because of the incumbent's fear of entry, in which case the producer price is decreased by the amount of per-unit tariff, enabling the government to exploit a part of the foreign monopolist's profits as tariff revenue (Brander and Spencer, 1981).

Second, if the product is differentiated among firms, the entry should benefit the consumers not only through price reduction but also through the increased variety of products (Spence, 1976, or, as its application to international trade, Curtis, 1983). Third, the announcement of the intention by the government to support R&D of the domestic firm may be taken by the foreign rival(s) as a credible commitment (i.e., not an empty threat), so that the subsidized domestic firm can play the role of a Stackelberg leader to gain larger profits at the expense of the foreign producer(s) (Spencer and Brander, 1983).

The second type of industrial policy is to promote exit from a deteriorating industry. Basically there are two arguments in favor of such a policy. One is that the Cournot-Nash free-entry equilibrium in a homogenous oligopolistic market results in too large a number of firms in the Paretian sense (von Weizsäcker, 1980; Suzumura and Kiyono, 1984), in which case exit of an existing firm is expected to improve social welfare because the loss of consumers' surplus due to the price increase caused by the smaller number of firms is outweighed by the increase in oligopolistic profits. Thus called for is a subsidy to give the marginal firms an incentive to exit. However, this policy of making the market more concentrated so that the remaining firms can charge a higher price benefits the stockholders of these firms at the consumers' expense, causing redistribution of income. Given that the stockholders are usually wealthier, whether such redistribution is socially desirable must be open to question. Whether the theory can be applied to actual markets may be also questioned. For one thing, the assumption of zero-profit equilibrium appears in conflict with the numerous findings that excess profits do exist in oligopolistic markets. For another, actual firms may not behave *a la* Cournot–Nash. Price leadership or tacit collusive behavior may be more common and exit may in fact encourage such non-Cournot behavior.

The other argument emphasizes the cost or delay of intersectoral reallocation of resources due to sticky wages or other market distortions (e.g., Neary, 1982). In this case, unemployment in deteriorating industries may be inevitable and subsidizing these industries may appear useful for the purpose of full utilization of resources. However, this deprives those subsidized of an incentive to leave the sector and slows down the adjustment speed further, hurting dynamic economic efficiency (Lapan, 1976). Essentially what is needed here is to promote the immigration of labor and other resources from a sector to another by means of offering information on job opportunities, retraining workers, and so forth. This is more a labor market policy than what is usually considered an industrial policy, such as subsidizing the industry or protecting it from import competition, though the two policies, as discussed in the previous section, are hardly distinguishable.

The theoretical considerations reviewed here thus indicate that there are instances where governmental intervention, especially to promote entry by domestic firm(s), increases social welfare. Basically, such increase is attained when entry results in price reduction thereby increasing consumer's surplus, or the foreign producers' surplus can be transfered to domestic agents (consumers or producers). It is less likely to take place in a small country (see Note 1), and more likely to take place in markets dominated by foreign monopolists. On the contrary, promoting exit from a deteriorating industry seems more difficult to support except for the general policies, such as labor market policy, to raise the mobility of factors.

That governmental intervention is theoretically justified does not immediately imply that the policy should be actually implemented, for the above argument has not taken into account the cost of implementation. The government, as it were, has been assumed omniscient and almighty. This, we all know, is not real and the cost of implementation can be substantial. For instance, the amount of information required may be enormous. The government has to know how much cost reduction will be attained with learning or R&D, how consumers' surplus and producers' surplus will change, how foreign producers will react, how other industries will be affected, and on and on. It has to know, moreover, not only the present effect of the policy but also its dynamic time path in order to know when to start and when to end the intervention. The cost of collecting this information could be prohibitive and so is the cost of taking a policy on wrong information. More will be said on this topic in Section 5.

4. JAPAN'S EXPERIENCE[3]

The history of what is usually considered the industrial policy in Japan can be separated into four periods. The first period begins immediately after the Second World War and ends before 1950. The keyword for this period was *Keisha Seisan* or priority production, which gives priority to coal-mining and iron and steel industries. The idea was to subsidize coal-mining to have coal supplied at a low price, allocate it heavily to iron and steel production, and in turn allocate the iron and steel thus produced heavily into coal-mining. Subsidies, financing at a low interest rate, and allocating import quotas were the major policy instruments.

The second period is the fifties, when the keyword was *Sangyo Gorika* or industrial rationalization. It was considered necessary to rationalize the industries by, for instance, introducing newer equipment and more efficient production systems, because much of the equipment had not been replaced since the beginning of the war. Special tax treatments and low-interest-rate loans were the major instruments. Also advocated during this period was *Ikusei* or nurturing new industries, the major instrument of which was protection against foreign competitors by means of quotas and tariffs.

The third period is the sixties when the keyword was *Shin Sangyo Taisei* or the new industrial order. It was argued, at the time of trade liberalization, that the scale of production was too small and competition excessive in most industries to compete with other industrial nations. Mergers and investment coordination were encouraged to achieve economies of scale. The major policy instrument was *Gyosei Shido* or administrative guidance – requests, suggestions, warnings, and such – because trade and capital liberalization enforced during this period deprived the government of most of its explicit control devices.

The last period corresponds to the period after the oil crisis of 1973. Here two policies are relevant. One is the promotion of *Chishiki Syuyakuka Sangyo* or knowledge-intensive industries like high-technology, fashion, and information-processing industries, though the government did not do much more than publicly announcing a 'vision'. The other is the adjustment policy to structurally depressed industries. The government, based on the Temporary Measures Law for the Stabilization of Designated Depressed Industries (abbreviated as *Tokuanho*) or its renewed version, *Sankoho*, legalized the formation of cartels in such industries as aluminium, synthetic fiber, and petrochemical industries to coordinate scrapping of facilities, and created a fund to guarantee the firms of the debts needed in scrapping.

To evaluate these policies is not easy. To start with, let us separate two questions. First, how much action did the government really make? Second, did it really contribute to industrial development in Japan? The first question is less formidable because one can quote quantitative evidence such as the amount of government subsidies. The second is formidable because nobody knows what would have happened were it not for the policies.

As for the first question, the answer may be summarized as follows: (1) Even in the early years the amount of government funding to industries – subsidies, tax credits, or loan of low-interest funds – was rather modest, though some of the industries, such as iron and steel, coal-mining, shipping, and electric-power industries, may have gained significantly. (2) There is a clear tendency that such government funding has decreased in its amount and importance over time; in fact, it appears minimal and by no means larger than in other industrialized countries in recent year. (3) Earlier, protection by means of tariffs and other trade barriers may have been important in some industries, say, automobiles and electronics, but this has also been reduced over the years so that Japan now has trade restrictions as small as (if not smaller than) other industrialized countries.

Since the aim of the present paper is not to give a detailed historical account of Japan's industrial policy, I am not going to give quantitative evidences to support these views: Interested readers are advised to see Komiya *et al.* (1984) and Saxonhouse (1983). In addition to this more or less direct government intervention, (4) legalization of cartels and (5) collection and dissemination of information, say, in the form of 'visions' were the policy tools used by the government, especially, the Ministry of International Trade and Industry (MITI).

To evaluate the effectiveness and contribution (or harm?) of these policies is a formidable task. For instance, the fact that from 1946 to 1948 during which the priority production policy was at its peak, coal production increased by 55 percent and steel production more than tripled, and in the entire mining and manufacturing industry the production increased by 60 percent does not necessarily justify the merits of the policy, for nobody knows how much production would have increased without the policy. In fact this was the period immediately after the War so that the return of labor force from battlefields to production cites may have been an important factor for the production recovery. There is also a possibility that the lack of free market mechanisms due, for instance, to the not-yet-completely-abandoned wartime production and allocation controls was itself a cause for another intervention, that is, the priority production policy (Kosai, p. 32). At the same time, the policy seems to have had the unfavorable effects in the following years of causing inflation and slowing the switch from coal to more economical (imported) petroleum as the major energy source.

In comparison, the rationalization and nurturing policies in the fifties with trade protection seem more likely to have helped some of the industries, notably, the automobile, electric and electronic equipments, and petrochemical industries, to take off. That is, many scholars seem to consider that the infant industry argument was successfully applied in these industries. Again, however, we do not know if these industries would have failed to take off to be dominated by foreign competitors had the policy not been adopted. In fact, one may quote examples of firms, such as Sony on transistor radio and Honda on motorcycle, who expanded with little support (or even objection) from the government.

The loss of such explicit policy tools as subsidies and trade barriers in the sixties forced the government to rely more on means that do not carry legal force. Administrative guidance was one such means, in which the MITI requested, suggested, or persuaded the industries and firms of certain actions. Sometimes it seems to have even warned or threatened them of unfavorable consequences. Apparently it worked in some instances but failed in others. For instance, the MITI's promotion of horizontal mergers to attain economies of scale resulted in only a few actual mergers, in most of which the role of the guidance seems to have been no more than to encourage the incentives the firms themselves had and to give a moral support against antimonopoly restriction the Fair Trade Commission might impose.

Another rather implicit role the MITI played was to collect information and reach agreements among interested parties through numerous councils that include as their members those representing not only businesses and the government but also consumers, labor, academia, and so forth. This, some authors argue, such as Komiya (1984) and Ozaki (1984), may have helped the industries in the exchange of information, in reaching compromises among diverse interests, and in attaining consensus on what ought to be the prime national goal, for instance, rapid economic growth through the expansion of the heavy industrial sector in the sixties, and industrial restructuring toward less energy-consuming knowledge-intensive industries in the seventies.

Still two questions remain: First, does the government have better capacity in collecting and disseminating information than the businesses themselves or the business press? The latter naturally have strong incentives and many channels to collect information they need. Whether the government can do better may be an open question. Second, did this information-exchange and consensus-seeking not create an anti-competitive or other unhealthy atmosphere among the industries? For instance, it has often been complained by the businesses that firms engage in excessive competition in recession so that without a temporary cartel a destructive consequence, such as bankruptcy, is inevitable. Some authors believe, however, that they engage in such competition exactly because once in recession a cartel or a MITI's guidance is a possibility so that bankruptcy may be avoided anyway.

As for the adjustment assistance policy, the major policy tools were the legalization of cartels and the credit guarantee. According to Horiuchi (1984), however, the speed of scrapping production facilities was not related to whether the industry formed a cartel or applied for the guarantee. Take, for instance, the case of the aluminium smelting industry which, during the seventies, rapidly lost its competitive edge against the imports because of the sharp increase in electricity cost and the rising value of yen. The industry planned in 1977, under the MITI's approval, to scrap 32 percent of its facilities by 1981. Actually, by 1981, 54 percent had been scrapped. And yet the industry had never formed a cartel or used the credit guarantee. This quite clearly illustrates that market force and not industrial policy was the force behind the industrial restructuring. As a consequence, the proportion of imports in the total supply of aluminium increased from 33 percent to 66 percent during the period.

What was more essential to Japan's development, in my opinion, was strong entrepreneurship and competitive market structure than industrial policy.[4] The Japanese managers have had a strong motive and capability to pursue corporate growth and this, as I have elsewhere argued (Odagiri, 1981), was one of the most important factors of her economc growth. This motive was probably also conducive to the competitive market structure because the firms are keen in attaining larger shares and finding growth opportunities to make entries – not through mergers as usually made by the American firms but through internal expansion, where the latter but not the former contributed to making the market less concentrated. It is perhaps not coincidental that the concentration ratio has been in general lower (the weighted average of the four-firm concentration ratio in 1963 was 35 percent in Japan and 41 percent in the United States, according to Uekusa, 1982, p. 20), and entry activities (not by mergers) appear to have been more rigorous in Japan than in, say, the United States. The industrial policy would have never succeeded in attaining the industrial development were it not for such entrepreneurship and competitiveness, whereas there seems to me little reason to suppose that, without industrial policy, the speed of development would have been much slower.

Although why the Japanese management has such a motive is beyond the scope of this analysis (see Odagiri, 1982), I am tempted to make one remark. This is on the view of the firm as a collection of human resources (see also Odagiri, 1984) than of the firm as a financial means. The accumulation in virtually every employee of firm-specific (rather than job-specific) skills and knowledge and of company-wide perspective through lifetime employment, internal promotion, and frequent and wide-ranging job rotation are common in Japan and yield not only more power in the employees (including management staffs) vis-a-vis the shareholders but also the employee's identification and participation to the company goals. Thus unfriendly takeovers are rare in Japan mainly because they tend to be regarded as intrusion and likely meet the employees' non-cooperation. Consequently, when the Japanese firm pursues growth and/or diversification, it more likely endeavours to attain it by means of internal expansion – physical investment, marketing and R&D – than acquisitions as common in the United States and the United Kingdom. This rare occurrence of unfriendly takeovers and the reflection of the employee interest on corporate decisions, together with the diffusion of share ownership, result in the management preference toward growth, namely, corporate decisions based on a longer time horizon, because the employees are more concerned with the long-run performance of the firm (at least for the period until retirement) than the short-run financial gains, and also because the employee's pecuniary and non-pecuniary gains are closely correlated with the chance of promotion, which is larger the faster the company expands. Such growth preference, I believe, has been the major cause of Japan's rapid economic progress.

In my view, what is deemed as 'trade frictions' has been at least partly caused by this difference in corporate behavior. Even though protection by means of tariffs and import quotas was significant in Japan, say, in the fifties, the process of trade liberalisation has been rapid, probably more rapid than in the history of any other country, and the levels of tariffs and import restrictions in Japan are now among the lowest in the OECD countries.[5] As this fact becomes known, Japan is now blamed for its non-tariff barriers, for instance, that the commercial practices there are so peculiar that foreign firms cannot successfully enter the market. To be sure, the Japanese culture is different from the American or European culture. This, however, implies that the Japanese firms had to suffer in entering into the foreign markets. When they started selling radios, cameras, or automobiles, they did not have any distribution channel or the consumer recognition to their products. Cultural and linguistic barriers were enormous and they had to bear heavy losses for a long time. Yet they kept their efforts, slowly establishing the goodwill to their products and increasing the market share. They did so because they had a long time horizon and realized that unless they go abroad there is little opportunity for corporate growth.

A limited number of foreign firms behave similarly in entering into the Japanese market. A typical example is Braun whose electric shaver is now regarded as a product of superior quality by many Japanese consumers and holds a substantial market share, which was attained only after a long and serious effort in marketing and product improvement. Such a case seems exceptional, however, and many of the American or European firms seem to pursue financial gains in too short a period to successfully penetrate into the Japanese market. Therefore, the so-called 'trade problem' between Japan and other countries is, in my view, the reflection of the different corporate attitudes and goals and, hence, more profound than is usually thought.

5. POLITICAL AND BUREAUCRATIC ISSUES

Theoretically, as we discussed in Section 3, there are instances in which governmental intervention improves social welfare. That is, if there were an omniscient (i.e., with perfect information), omnipotent (i.e., with an ability to make perfectly rational decisions), and neutral (i.e., with perfect balance between the interests of all those concerned) dictator, he/she should be able to make everyone happier or, at least, make someone happier without making anyone else unhappier in these instances. The problem, certainly, is that we do not and have never had such a dictator and we have to live in a world of democracy composed of non-omniscient, non-omnipotent, and opportunistic politicians, bureaucrats, interest groups, and voters. There is little hope that they can seek out the best policy alternative, reach agreement, and implement it without delay. 'Nonmarket failure' (Wolf, 1979) is thus unavoidable and the cost associated with this failure may outweigh the cost of market failure.

As shown in Section 2, industrial policy and regulation both deal with market failure and the boundary between the two, if any, is trifling. Thus the arguments against regulation are, with little modification, applicable to industrial policy except for such specific issues pertinent only to regulation as the Averch–Johnson effect in the rate-of-return regulation. A typical example is the view of 'regulation as a powerful engine of redistribution' by Peltzman (1976, p. 211) who argued that 'the political process does not usually provide the dichotomous treatment of resource allocation and wealth distribution so beloved by welfare economists' (*ibid.*). There is no reason to believe that this argument does not apply to industrial policy, or the argument that 'the common role of regulation . . . is as a fulcrum upon which contending interests seek to exercise leverage in their pursuit of wealth. A common, though not universal, conclusion has become that, as between the two main contending interests in regulatory processes, the producer interest tends to prevail over the consumer interest' (*ibid.*, p. 212). It is in fact seldom that the MITI considers the welfare of consumers as the prime goal of a certain industrial policy. The ministry is composed of many sections, each having jurisdiction over a particular industry. They participate in designing and implementing an industrial policy, evaluate its consequences to the industries they deal with, and frequently defend the interests of these industries, to the effect that the balance among the industries is somewhat taken care of. No section, however, represents consumers' interests.

One reason why regulation and industrial policy leads to redistribution in favor of the producers is the unequal power and influence of interest groups. Since 'oligopolists and other small groups have a greater likelihood of being able to organize for collective action, and can usually organize with less delay, than large groups' (Olson, 1982, p. 41), producers tend to organize active and influential interest groups that consumers do not have. The result is the distributional gain to the former at the latter's sacrifice, in addition to the economically unproductive waste of resources in lobbying and other political activities. Furthermore, as Olson (*ibid.*, p. 65) has argued, these distributional coalitions slow down a society's capacity to adopt new technologies and to reallocate resources in response to changing conditions, and thereby reduce the rate of economic growth'.

The activities of interest groups are not the only reason that regulation or industrial policy can lead to undesirable consequences. Political scientists have also shown that the present political system in democracy, characterized by geographical representation and majority rule in election and legislative decisions, usually results in solutions not in accord with market efficiency. In fact these political solutions could be worse than market solutions under political status quo (Shepsle and Weingast, 1984).

Suppose, that despite these criticisms, political choice could be made optimally. Yet the consequence of governmental intervention may still be undesirable because the bureaucrats in the administrative body may not efficiently or properly carry out what the legislative body has resolved. In implementing the policy they may pursue not economic efficiency but their own interests. The most well-known argument is the so-called Parkinson's law on the rising number of officials with little relation to the volume of work which, Parkinson (1957, p. 4) aruges, stems from two factors: '(1) An official wants to multiply subordinates, not rivals; and (2) Officials make work for each other'. Others argue that bureaucrats seeks to maximize budget, expand personnel, or enjoy leisure and security, all resulting in X-inefficiency *à la* Leibenstein in the administrative body, the cost of which tax-payers have to bear. These arguments on discretionary or managerial behavior and X-inefficiency fit more appropriately to public bureaucrats than to corporate bureaucrats because for public bureaucrats not only is external control weaker but also the evaluation of performance is more difficult owing to the difficulty in measuring the output, and bilateral monopolistic situation they deal with (see Mueller, 1979, Chapter 8).

In a very convenient classification of criticisms of regulation, Noll (quoted in Zimmerman, 1975, p. 370) classified four types: '(1) the "complaint" theory, where regulators respond only to "squeaking wheels"; (2) the "captive" theory, where regulators act to maximize the objectives of the regulated; (3) the "Parkinsonian" theory, where regulators act to maximize the organizational objectives of the regulating agency; and (4) the "muddle-through" theory, where the situation is too complex and subtle for the regulatory agency to be capable of achieving its ostensible goals'. (1) and (2) is bound to lead to distributional inequality and the expanding activity of interest groups that would hamper efficient resource allocation and economic growth, (3) is bound to lead to ever-expanding staffs and budgets of the government as witnessed in every nation, and (4), which refers to bounded rationality and information impactedness to use Williamson's (1975) terms, is bound to result in suboptimal decisions which may in fact worsen resource allocation compared to the market solution, however large is market failure. There is no reason at all that these criticisms should not apply to industrial policy.

Or consider Wolf's (1979) list of four nonmarket failures: (1) internalities and private goals (as opposed to externalities and public goods for market failure), (2) redundant and rising costs (as opposed to increasing returns), (3) derived externalities (as opposed to market imperfections), and (4) distributional inequality in influence and power (as opposed to distributional inequality in income and wealth). (1) refers to the internal standards and goals, which govern the activities of the public agencies, 'that do not bear a very clear or reliable connection with the ostensible public purpose which the agencies were intended to serve' (*ibid.*, p. 117). (2) corresponds to the Parkinson's law, and (3) refers to the side effects that governmental intervention may bring, which could be grave and yet overlooked or neglected due to 'the short time horizon and high time discounts of political actors' and 'the frequently ill-defined nature of both quantity and quality of nonmarket outputs' (*ibid.*, p. 126). Again, these criticisms are perfectly applicable to industrial policy as well.

In short, 'models of bureaucratic, regulatory, and legislative institutions; of self-interested pressure groups, elected politicians, and bureaucrats; and of fiscal illusion and incrementalism all underscore potential biases that may neutralize the anticipated efficiency gains associated with political solutions' (Shepsle and Weingast, 1984, p. 417). An industrial policy should be adopted only if these biases and costs associated with political choice and administrative implementation are exceeded by the economic gains. Otherwise it should not be adopted. In fact, I believe it should not be adopted unless people are really confident of such excess, for any error and the resulting ill consequences of a centralized political system could be bottomless while those of a decentralized market system are not.

With this view, the applicability of industrial policy is much narrower than it may appear with the economic theory discussed in Section 3. In terms of the Japanese experience, therefore, a more interesting question may be why the policy there did not significantly hamper the dynamic reallocation of resources and economic growth than why and how it fostered them. Without clear evidence I am inclined to argue that the market forces in the Japanese economy were overwhelming and many (though certainly not all) of the government bureaucrats were clever enough to be aware of this. The market forces were exercised through strong entrepreneurship with the spirit of independence (from the rivals and from the government) and the preference toward corporate growth, competitive markets with potential or actual entry threat, and the international forces like import competition and political pressure to liberalize trade and capital transactions. It seems that the MITI in many cases were aware of these forces so that they were flexible in changing their targets, and many of the policies were taken with the time limit specified. Yet, there were cases where the political lag caused the policy to take effect at a time when its necessity was no longer obvious, or where the administrative guidance deterred private actions that were reasonable responses to changing environment.

6. THE CASE OF R&D

Research and development is where the need for governmental suport has been taken for granted. Indeed, theoretically, it is easy to argue for such need. All the theoretical arguments in Section 3 apply to R&D: hence, (i) governmental support on R&D may make the entry of a firm feasible, which, after the entry, is expected to decrease the price – by shifting the average and marginal cost curves downward and/or by increasing the number of firms in a monopolistic or oligopolistic market – and thereby increase consumers' welfare; (ii) it may be also expected to transfer profits from the foreign firms to the domestic firms, (iii) with product innovation, the entry is expected to increase the variety of products available to the consumers, and (iv) the mere announcement of governmental intervention to support R&D may be beneficial by making the entry threat credible, thereby lowering the limit price charged by the (often foreign) incumbents or forcing them to act as followers in a Stackelberg situation.

In addition, the public-goods character of information has been emphasized to argue for the governmental support of R&D. That is, it is inappropriable and cannot be used up. Once invented, a new knowledge can be used by however many firms and individuals repeatedly and simultaneously without wearing it out or interfering with each others' use. Thus if the knowledge is made publicly accessible, the external benefits, namely, the benefits accruing to those outside the inventor, can be great which the latter will never take into account in its decisions on R&D. In other words, the private return can be less than the social return so that a private firm may not undertake the research the society needs.[6] In these cases, it is thus argued, governmental support of the research, either by means of subsidies to the research-conducting firms or research by government-sponsored institutions, is needed.

By no means do I deny these arguments. Without doubt, R&D is where governmental support can be most easily defended. Yet there appears some distance from the theoretical discussion to its actual implementation. For one thing, a patent system (which, being a system designed to remedy market failure, is an industrial policy!) may provide sufficient private incentives for R&D, though it is true that the patent system costs the society to the extent the use of invented knowledge is restricted.

For another, as Hirshleifer (1971) argued, the private incentives may be actually quite large (or even excessive) because the private inventor counts a favorable redistribution of income which is of no benefit to the society as a whole. Hence, with or without a patent system, there may be cases for private overinvestment in R&D which make the argument for governmental support less convincing. That R&D may become excessive under rivalry was also recognized by such authors as Kamien and Schwartz (1982, Chapter 4), because the R&D game under the patent system is a rank-order tournament in which the one who succeeds in inventing first captures most of the gains while those who failed capture little.

The efficiency of the government in leading the R&D activity is questioned on many accounts. All the arguments in the previous section on the political and bureauctatic costs certainly apply to any governmental action on R&D as well. In fact there is a reason to believe that these costs could be more serious with technology and science policy. This is the difficulty in correctly foreseeing the long-run consequences of a policy and in making an evaluation and decision on a sufficiently long time horizon. Innovation has far-reaching temporal and spatial consequences. It changes not only the current state of the world but also its future courses. It affects not only the industry in question but also every other sector of the economy to a varying degree. Whether the government is in a better position to foresee these influences than the private sector can be very much questioned. Market mechanisms, with every agent seeking necessary information on self interest, may be more efficient in this regard.

Insofar as perfect forecast is impossible, the policymaker is forced to adapt the policy to changing environment. This adaptability is particularly important with R&D because the advancement of technology itself creates ever-changing dynamic society: Existing technology and information may quickly become obsolete, the need for research in an unforseen field may arise, and some of the research currently undertaken may become no more needed. Thus required are, in addition to keen sensitivity to the changing conditions, flexibility in changing research targets and adaptability of research organization to changing needs. I would never expect the government agency, without a clear performance indicator or competitive threat, to match the private firms in these regards.

In an interesting study of a 'lifecycle in science', Hayashi and Yamada observed a lifecycle in scientific activity in a particular field of research Measuring research activity in either an input to research – R&D expenditures or the number of researchers – or an output – the number of scientific papers, the number of patents, or the number of invented products – they found that it takes at least several years from the conception of the basic idea to the peak in research activity, and that, after a few years of the peak, the activity gradually diminishes. Research activity in every field is governed by such a lifecycle, suggesting the need to transfer research resources from a field in deteriorating phase to one in growing phase.

Also suggested in their study is the lag of governmental reaction to this lifecycle. According to their study of high-polymer chemistry, the number of university departments in Japan majoring in the field gradually increased following the rising interest in the field, but the lag was considerable. In fact, it reached its peak fifteen years after the peak in the R&D expenditures allocated to the field and ten years after the peak in the number of research papers. Note that the significant part of these expenditures were made by the private sector, whereas establishing a university department requires governmental approval. There is probably some lag before the university becomes aware of the need for a new department. Then it has to convince the Ministry of Education of the need for such a department, which may take several more years. If the university is national, as many of the prestige Japanese universities are, it has to then convince the Ministry of Finance of the need to allocate the government budget to this department.

This case of department establishment may not be typical of the government science policy. Perhaps, and hopefully, reallocation of government research funds to an emerging field, and retargeting or reorganizing within a government-sponsored research institution are more prompt. Yet the above case well exemplifies the unavoidable delay in the public sector in adapting to changing environment.

Such reality casts much doubt on the popular notion that the private sector will have an insufficient incentive for R&D and therefore the government should be involved in R&D on a large scale by giving R&D subsidies to the industries or operating government-sponsored research institutions. Even if the private sector in fact has an insufficient incentive, it does not necessarily follow that the government involvement is needed. It is true that much basic research can be made only with governmental support (including research on economics!); however, the extent to which such support is needed appears narrower than is usually thought.

This view is not inconsistent with the Japanese experience, for the involvement of the Japanese government on R&D is smaller and the achievement of such involvement is less spectacular than is often believed. First of all, the proportion of government spending on the total R&D expenditures is smallest among major countries: 23.6 percent in Japan, 46.7 percent in the United States, 48.1 percent in the United Kingdom, 43.1 percent in West Germany, and 57.6 percent in France.[7] The proportion the industries pay is on the contrary largest in Japan. Since the proportion in the R&D expenditures used by the industries does not differ much among these countries, the transfer of the R&D funds from the government to industries must be smallest in Japan.

If the government R&D subsidies to the industries is this small and yet, as some foreign authors believe, the Japanese policy to support R&D has been effective, it must be that the allocation of the limited funds among industries and firms has been appropriate. In fact, in addition to a favorable tax treatment to the incremental R&D expenditures, the major policy tool was the subsidies to selective research topics. In this regard the role of 'research association', an association composed of several firms to pursue a particular research topic, needs to be mentioned. In 1983, for instance, there were forty-four such associations. The total R&D expenditures of these associations were 64 billion yen, of which about half was financed by the firms and the rest by the government. Among the total R&D subsidies by the government to the business sector, nearly half were expected through these associations (Wakasugi and Goto, 1985). Most well-known among the research associations is that on very-large-scale integrated circuits (VLSI), which was composed of five computer producers and active from 1976 to 1979. This association, having yielded numerous patents, is said to have established a foundation for the following Japanese success in the semiconductor industry (Pugel, 1984). This well-publicized 'success', however, is not typical of research associations. In fact, most of the associations did not have any joint research facilities (which the VLSI association had), each member firm receiving its share of research funds (partly financed by the government) and carrying out the research in its own research institution. Thus, they often worked as no more than a channel through which the funds were delivered from the government to the member firms. Furthermore, Wakasugi and Goto (1985) showed that the productivity of research activity as measured by the number of patents as a ratio to the expenditures on R&D was smaller in all the six research associations they investigated than the industrial average.[8] The success of the VLSI association appears thus exceptional.

This finding for the inefficient government expenditures on R&D is also shared by the findings of a few American researchers (Terleckyj, 1980; Link, 1981; and Griliches and Lichtenberg, 1984) that the contribution of government-financed research to productivity increase is less than that of company-financed research. It is true that government-financed research is directed more often to riskier, more difficult, less patentable, or less profitable research projects than that of the private sector, so that the findings may not immediately imply the inefficiency with the use of government funds on R&D. Yet they are not inconsistent with our view that, in terms of both capability and incentive to find out where the research need is and how to carry out the research, the private sector tends to be more flexible and efficient than the government.

7. CONCLUSION

This paper, after pointing out the difficulty in separating industrial policy from regulation, examined the pros and cons of industrial policy. Theoretically there are cases where governmental intervention in an industry is believed to enhance social welfare. The examples are the production of an infant industry and the governmental support of basic R&D. However, political or bureaucratic costs of designing and implementing such intervention can be substantial, partly or wholly negating the benefit the economic theory predicts. Therefore, unless the society confidently agrees that the benefit sufficiently outweighs the cost, any governmental intervention to markets had better be avoided however defective the Invisible Hand is. The experience in Japan, where many foreign scholars seem to emphasize the role of industrial policy, does not provide much evidence of powerful policies or their clear impact on industrial development. More important to her economic growth was the strong entrepreneurship characterized by growth preference and risk-taking decisions, and the competitive markets with active entry activities.

If industrial policy is any policy to deal with market failure, there is no way to deny the need for certain policies. Provision of public goods and infrastructures and the control of pollution come to mind immediately. Even if industrial policy is taken in a narrower sense, there are a few policies the need for which is beyond question. The Japanese experience tells us the importance of entrepreneurship and competitiveness. Hence, antitrust policy to maintain a competitive environment is indispensable. It should be a part of any industrial policy and the view that antitrust policy and industrial policy are conflicting, as evidenced by the past conflict between the MITI and FTC in Japan, is misleading. Also, to enhance entrepreneurship, regulation had better be kept at its minimum (e.g., limiting to such regulations as are really needed for safety considerations).

Also important is the policy on human resources, for the accumulation of human resources and their adequate allocation have become more and more essential to the success and growth of a firm and an economy. Here, too, however, the growing reliance on intrafirm education and training (including on-the-job training) indicates the limited role the government is to play. When the shift from a stagnating sector to an expanding sector was inevitable, many Japanese firms have managed to survive by reallocating and retraining the workers. Such flexibility in the allocation of employed workers benefits not only the firm (or more specifically, the company owners) but also the employees by providing them with steady employment and eventual income increase.

Intrafirm reallocation is not sufficient when the interindustry shift of demand is so fast and drastic that in a declining industry the firms are forced to discharge the workers and/or some of the firms are forced to go bankrupt. The government can then help the transition by retraining the workers and providing information to job-seekers and prospective employers. Such labor policy should be promoted not only for the sake of the worker welfare but also as a part of industrial policy. To avoid the bureaucratic cost and bias, it appears desirable that the policy be general and routinized and not selectively applied to particular industries, local areas, or periods.

I started this essay quoting a phrase of Mueller's. Let me close it with another of Mueller's: 'Those who, like myself, favor democratic, decentralized, market solutions to the fundamental allocation and distribution questions faced by society should favor rules that constrain the growth of both private and public bureaucrats' (Mueller, 1981, p. 93). We had better watch lest industrial policy be used to promote such growth.

NOTES

1. If the country is a small country so that the import supply curve is horizontal, and the learning effect is not so drastic as to lower the future equilibrium price (which requires that all the foreign producers are driven out from the domestic market), the equilibrium price cannot be affected by the entry in either today or future; hence, Condition III is not satisfied and the infant industry argument cannot justify governmental assistance.
2. One may be tempted to raise the Japanese challenge to IBM on computers, to Kodak on photo films, or to the Big Three on automobiles as such an example, though how much the challenge was aided by the industrial policy should remain as another question.
3. My discussion in this section owes to two Japanese books on the subject, Tsuruta (1982) and Komiya *et al.* (1984). The latter, a collection of articles by a number of Japanese researchers, is to be published in English by Macmillan (London).
4. For similar views among American authors, see Hadley (1983) and Trezise (1983).
5. According to *Tsusho Hakusho* (White Paper on International Trade), the Ministry of International Trade and Industry, 1985, pp. 194–195, in 1980 the average tariff rate was lower in Japan in the United States, EC, Canada, and Australia and the number of non-agricultural commodities under import restriction was smaller in Japan than in the United States and France.
6. Mansfield *et al.* (1977) provides an evidence that the social rate of return on R&D exceeds the private rate. Needless to say, the social return on R&D is extremely difficult to measure. Hence it is not surprising that the analysis is based on many limiting assumptions.
7. *Kagaku Gijutsu Hakusho* (White Paper on Science and Technology), Science and Technology Agency, 1983, p. 110. The quoted percentages are for 1982 (Japan and

the United States), 1978 (the United Kingdom), and 1981 (Germany and France). When the government funds for defence R&D are excluded, the difference between Japan and other countries narrows; still, Japan is with the lowest percentage.

8. One reason for this difference may be that their research is directed more toward basic research so that the research outcome is more difficult to patent or, being a semi-public institution, they have a less propensity to apply for patents. As a matter of fact, however, the research in these associations was basically centered on applied research and they have tended to apply for patents whenever possible.

REFERENCES

Brander, James A. and Spencer, Barbara J., 'Tariffs and the Extraction of Foreign Monopoly Rents under Potential Entry', *Canadian Journal of Economics*, 14(3) (August, 1983), pp. 371–389.

Curtis, Douglas C. A., 'Trade Policy to Promote Entry with Scale Economies, Product Variety, and Export Potential', *Canadian Journal of Economics*, 16(1) (February 1983), pp. 109–121.

Griliches, Zvi and Lichtenberg, Frank, 'R&D and Productivity Growth at the Industry Level: Is There Still a Relationship?' in Zvi Griliches (ed.), *R&D, Patents and Productivity*. Chicago: The University of Chicago Press (1984), pp. 465–496.

Hadley, Eleanor, 'The Secret of Japan's Success', *Challenge*, 26(2) (May–June, 1983), pp. 4–10.

Hayashi, Yujiro and Keiichi Yamada (eds.), *Kagaku no Raifu Saikuru* (*Lifecycle of Science*), Tokyo: Chuo Koron Sha (1975).

Hirshleifer, Jack, 'The Private and Social Value of Information and the Reward to Inventive Activity', *American Economic Review*, 61(4) (September, 1971), pp. 561–574.

Horiuchi, Toshihiro, 'Koka Toboshii Sangyo Chosei Saku' (Industrial Adjustment Policy Is Not Effective), *Nihon Keizai Shimbun* (June 7, 1984).

Kamien, Morton I. and Schwartz, Nancy L., *Market Structure and Innovation*, Cambridge: Cambridge University Press (1982).

Komiya, Ryutaro, *Gendai Nihon Keizai Kenkyu* (*Study on the Contemporary Japanese Economy*), Tokyo: Tokyo Daigaku Shuppankai (1975).

Komiya, Ryutaro, Okuno, Masahiro, and Suzumura, Kotaro (eds.), *Nihon no Sangyo Seisaku* (*Industrial Policy in Japan*), Tokyo: Tokyo Daigaku Shuppankai (1984).

Komiya, Ryutaro, 'Josho' [Introduction], in Komiya *et al.* (1984), pp. 1–22.

Kosai, Yasushi, 'Fukkoki' [Recovery Period], in Komiya *et al.* (1984), pp. 25–43.

Lapan, Harvey E., 'International Trade, Factor Market Distortions, and the Optimal Dynamic Subsidy', *American Economic Review*, 66(3) (June, 1976), pp. 335–346.

Link, Albert N., 'Basic Research and Productivity Increase in Manufacturing: Additional Evidence', *American Economic Review*, 71(5) (December, 1981), pp. 1111–1112.

Mansfield, Edwin, Rapoport, John, Romeo, Anthony, Wagner, Samuel, and Beardsley, George, 'Social and Private Rates of Return from Industrial Innovations', *Quarterly Journal of Economics* 91(2) (May, 1977), pp. 221–240.

Mueller, Dennis C., *Public Choice*, Cambridge: Cambridge University Press (1979).

Mueller, Dennis C., 'The Case against Conglomerate Mergers', in Roger D. Blair and Robert F. Lanzillotti (eds.), *The Conglomerate Corporation*. Cambridge: Oelgeschlager, Gunn & Hain (1981), pp. 71–95.

Neary, J. Peter, 'Intersectoral Capital Mobility, Wage Stickiness, and the Case for Adjustment Assistance', in Jagdish N. Bhagwati (ed.), *Import Competition and Response*, Chicago: The University of Chicago Press, (1982), pp. 39–67.

Negishi, Takashi, 'Protection of the Infant Industry and Dynamic Internal Economics', *Economic Record*, 44(1) (March, 1968), pp. 56–67.

Odagiri, Hiroyuki, *The Theory of Growth in a Corporate Economy*, Cambridge: Cambridge University Press (1981).

Odagiri, Hiroyuki, 'Antineoclassical Management Motivation in a Neoclassical Economy', *Kykols*, 35(2) (1982) pp. 223–243.

Odagiri, Hiroyuki, 'The Firm as a Collection of Human Resources', in Peter Wiles and Guy Routh (eds.), *Economics in Disarray*, Oxford: Basil Blackwell, (1984), pp. 190–206.

Olson, Mancur, *The Rise and Decline of Nations*, Nw Haven: Yale University Press (1982).

Ozaki, Robert S., 'How Japanese Industrial Policy Works', in Chalmers Johnson (ed.), *The New Industrial Policy Debate*, San Francisco: ICS Press (1984), 47–70.

Parkinson, C. Northcote, *Parkinson's Law and Other Studies in Administration*, Boston: Houghton Mifflin (1957).

Peltzman, Sam, 'Toward a More General Theory of Regulation', *Journal of Law and Economics*, 19(2) (August, 1976), pp. 211–240.

Philips, Almarin, 'Introduction', in Almarin Phillips (ed.), *Promoting Competition in Regulated Markets*, Washington, D.C.: The Brookings Institution (1975), pp. 1–12.

Pugel, Thomas A., 'Japan's Industrial Policy: Instruments, Trends, and Effects', *Journal of Comparative Economics*, 8(4), (December, 1984), 420–435.

Saxonhouse, Gary R., 'What is All This About "Industrial Targeting" in Japan?' *The World Economy*, 6(3) (September, 1983), pp. 253–273.

Shepsle, Kenneth A. and Weingast, Barry R., 'Political Solutions to Market Problems', *American Political Science Review* 78(2) (June, 1984), pp. 417–434.

Spence, Michael, 'Product Selection, Fixed Costs, and Monopolistic Competition', *Review of Economic Studies*, 43(2) (June, 1976), pp. 217–235.

Spencer, Barbara J. and Brander, James A., 'International R&D Rivalry and Industrial Strategy', *Review of Economic Studies*, 50(4) (October, 1983), pp. 707–722.

Suzumura, Kotaro and Kiyono, Kazuharu, 'On the Concept of Social Barriers to Entry', Discussion Paper, No. 109, Institute of Economic Research, Hitotsubashi University (1984).

Terlecky, Nestor E., 'Direct and Indirect Effects of Industrial Research and Development on the Productivity Growth of Industries', in John W. Kendrick and Beatrice N. Vaccara (eds.), *New Developments in Productivity Measurement and Analysis*, Chicago: The University of Chicago Press, (1980), pp. 359–377.

Trezise, Philip H., 'Industrial Policy Is Not the Major Reason for Japan's Success', *Brookings Review* (Spring, 1983), pp. 13–18.

Tsuruta, Toshimasa, *Sengo Nihon no Sangyo Seisaku* (Industrial Policy in Postwar Japan), Tokyo: Nihon Keizai Shimbun Sha (1982).

Uekusa, Masu, *Sangyo Soshiki Ron* (*Industrial Organization*), Tokyo: Chikuma Shobo (1982).

Wakasugi, Ryuhei and Goto, Akira, 'Kyodo Kenkyu Kaihatsu to Gijutsu Kakushin' (Cooperative R&D and Innovation), mimeo (1985).

Weizsacker, C. C. von, 'A Welfare Analysis of Barriers to Entry', *Bell Journal of Economics* 11(2) (Autumn, 1980), 399–420.

Williamson, Oliver E., *Markets and Hierarchies*, New York: The Free Press (1975).
Wolf, Charles, Jr., 'A Theory of Nonmarket Failure Framework for Implementation Analysis', *Journal of Law and Economics*, 22(1) (April, 1979), pp. 107–139.
Zimmerman, Edwin M., 'The Legal Framework of Competitive Policies toward Regulated Industries', in Almarin Phillips (ed.), *Promoting Competition in Regulated Markets*, Washington, D.C.: The Brookings Institution (1975), pp. 367–383.

17. PUBLIC SUPPORT OF INNOVATIVE ACTIVITY: LESSONS FROM U.S. INDUSTRIAL POLICY

Walter Adams and Stephen Martin

I. INTRODUCTION

In 1859, in the Communist Manifesto, Marx and Engels observed that

> . . . the bourgeosie, during its rule of scarce one hundred years, has created more massive and more colossal productive forces than have all preceding generations together. Subjection of Nature's forces to man, machinery, application of chemistry to industry and agriculture, steam-navigation, railways, electric telegraphs, clearing of whole continents for cultivation, canalisation of rivers, whole populations conjured out of the ground – what earlier century had even a presentiment that such productive forces slumbered in the lap of social labor.[1]

Even the most ardent free-market capitalist would find it difficult to offer a more glowing assessment of the performance of industrial markets with respect to technological progress.[2] Indeed, there has long been a general consensus that technological innovation is the primary engine of long-term economic progress. Despite this, and despite the fact that the nature of public policy toward innovative activity is a perennial topic of lively dispute, economists have only slowly come to grips with the analysis of the process by which technological and engineering knowledge is generated, how it is diffused, and the impact it has on growth and development.

In this paper, we first review the treatment of innovative activity in the economics literature. We then discuss some central issues in the current debate over industrial policy toward innovation. We then contrast the U.S. experience with public support for innovation in two very different industries. In our final section, we summarize and present our conclusions.

de Jong, H. W., Shepherd, W. G. (eds) Mainstreams in Industrial Organization
 ISBN 978-94-017-0495-3

II. ECONOMIC ANALYSIS OF INNOVATION

What is called 'growth theory' in graduate school curricula is an elegant formal analysis of the consequences of growth. The bulk of the field treats technology as 'given', and concentrates on problems of optimum allocation of a fixed stock of resources. As good marginalists, theorists have contemplated, and econometricians have measured, the production function – i.e., the relationship between variations in inputs and associated variations in outputs. They have been fascinated by the problem of factor substitution – the movement along an existing production function in response to changes in factor prices. Only rarely have they shown much interest in explaining *shifts* of the production function, i.e., how 'the existing range of technological alternatives came into existence, and what specific forces generated them.[3] The process by which the nature and rate of technological progress are determined is not, for the most part, a subject of analysis.

Empirical work based on the models of growth theory has measured technological progress as a residual difference between the rate of growth of inputs and the rate of growth of output.[4] But measurement is not explanation. To call this difference a measure of 'resource productivity', says T. W. Schultz, 'gives a name to our ignorance but does not dispel it. If we accept these estimates, the connections between national resources and national income have become loose and tenuous over time. Unless this discrepancy can be resolved, received theory of production applied to inputs and outputs as currently measured is a toy and not a tool for studying economic growth.[5]

As for public policy guidelines to influence the pace and pattern of technological progress, Richard Nelson concludes, we must 'acknowledge, reluctantly, that the general theoretical analyses and empirical observations of economists provide only limited and incomplete guidelines regarding the kinds of policies that pay off under different circumstances. Indeed the economic literature on this subject has grown progressively less conclusive.[6]

Industrial organization economists have done little better. Their efforts have been largely devoted to a seemingly endless debate over the Schumpeterian hypothesis, focusing on what Levin *et al.*[7] term 'the oversimplified propositions that industrial concentration promotes innovative effort and innovative output'. One theoretical view is that it is impossible to rigorously formulate testable hypotheses about the relationship of firm size and research and development,[8] although careful work suggests that this position is extreme.[9] At the same time, empirical tests have been bedeviled by the twin problems of measurement (of both the inputs to and the outputs from the innovative process) and simultaneity.[10] It is a measure of the slowness with which progress in the understanding of progress comes that the final paragraph of a recent comprehensive survey of the Schumpeterian literature contains the observation that 'As this survey of our present state of knowledge discloses, there is still a long way to go before we can rest.'[11] Although Arrow explained the implications of uncertainty and imperfect appropriability for market treatment of innovative activity a quarter of a century ago,[12] these factors have only recently been incorporated in empirical studies.[13]

It is interesting to speculate on the reasons behind the difficulty economists have had with the analysis of the determinants of growth. Without claiming any personal immunity, we suggest that one factor has been the very uncertainty which is inherent in the innovative process. It is extremely difficult to model uncertainty, in a realistic way, in the sort of simple models which have become the backbone of the economics profession.[14] Realistic models of uncertainty are not elegant; elegant models of uncertainty are not realistic.

This may explain the importance of case studies in the economics R&D literature.[15] Case studies are, of course, always open to the objection that the insights which they yield are of limited general validity. But there are always tradeoffs: a narrower focus will often allow a clearer view. It is for this reason that we explore, below, United States' public policy toward innovative activity in two specific, and very different, areas of the economy.

III. POLICY ISSUES

In the United States, the debate on industrial policy generally, and policy with respect to R&D in particular, is hopelessly mired in politics. Advocates of an explicit U.S. industrial policy refer to a perceived deindustrialization of the U.S. economy, and contrast the case-by-case U.S. approach to the Japanese experience. On the high road, advocates of industrial policy call for some form of[16]

Restructuring: the redesign of managerial and labor practices in return for government bnenefits.
Targeting: The overall coordination of government aid to specific industries, whether high-tech or smokestack.
Worker retraining: The education of unemployed workers to perform new tasks.
Infrastructure reconstruction: The rebuilding of roads, bridges and the like.

To the extent that 'infrastructure reconstruction' refers to the maintenance of public goods, it falls within the domain generally accepted for public economic activity. The evidence for a general industrial decline is ambiguous; at least some work suggests that adjustment problems are confined to a few industries.[17]

On the low road, some of the policy proposals touted as industrial policy appear ideally suited as examples of the 'industry capture' theory of regulation:[18, 19]

> One divisive issue has been the impulse on the part of unions and some industries to seek government restrictions on imports. . .
> . . .–corporate managers are not against 'government intervention' in principle; they want more underwriting of research and development and the loosening of antitrust laws. They oppose, however, Federal targeting of specific industries: Government planners might supersede the companies' own strategic plans.

In any event, current policy-makers have specifically rejected calls for industrial policy:[20]

> The best way to deal with the many changes in demand that occur in a dynamic economy is to allow investors and workers to respond to such changes. Because they reap the rewards of their successes and bear the costs of their failures, investors will seek out industries that pay the highest rates of returns. Similarly, workers have incentives to work where they can earn the highest rates. The free movement of capital and labor in response to new profit opportunities and wage differentials increases growth. Government allocation of investment that ignores market signals usually stunts growth by diverting labor and capital from more productive uses.

Distrust of government interference with the market has been a characteristic of economic analysis since (at least) Adam Smith, and most economists will for this reason be instinctively sympathetic to the position outlined above. At the same time, it has been accepted for a somewhat shorter period of time[21] that, at least with respect to innovative activity, the market cannot be expected to provide what are, from the social point of view, the correct signals. Link[22] offers a concise statement of this position.

> Nominally, the federal government justifies expenditures for industrial R&D on three grounds. First, the government is the sole producer of many goods and services with public-good characteristics; therefore, the government should maintain responsibility for providing financial support for technological growth among producers of these goods and services. . . . . Second, federal investments in R&D presumably correct for market failures in the production of products (such as energy) where the social returns from technological advancement are perceived to be greater than the private returns. Finally, the federal government is committed to the general

advancement of technical knowledge and thus supports industrial R&D when the private level is less than socially optimal – that is, where there are positive externalities associated with the creation and distribution of technical knowledge.

As Link makes clear, the United States *has* a policy with respect to industrial R&D, even if ideological positions prevent it being acknowledged as such. Some industries have been protected from foreign competition. Tax legislation induced private R&D spending in some sectors. Patents grant limited monopoly rights to inventors, to increase the appropriability of the output of successful R&D. There is a generally permissive antitrust treatment of joint R&D projects. These measures may be ad hoc and make-shift. They may not be part of a coherent, integrated, long-run 'plan'. But they do add up to a sort of industrial policy.

Moreover, contrary to popular belief, the United States spends more on R&D than Japan, France, and Germany combined. As a percentage of GNP, it spends more on R&D than any one of its international competitors. However, most of its R&D funds (roughly two-thirds) is spent on defence and space programs where any commercial spillover is not a primary objective – and this is the source of much of the current policy debate.

The choice of major research priorities, reflected in Table 1, is largely based on political rather than economic criteria. Perhaps it would be unrealistic to expect that it could ever be otherwise. Moreover, as some critics contend, this allocation of R&D funds reflects the lack of a coordinated industrial policy which, in turn, undermines the international competitiveness of the United States and makes it vulnerable to such

Table 1. Federal R&D funding by function: 1973 and 1983.

Function	Millions of dollars		Percent of total	
	1973	1983	1973	1983
National defense	$ 9,002	$24,936	53.6%	64.3%
Space	2,824	2,134	16.8	5.5
Health	1,585	4,298	9.4	11.1
Energy	630	2,578	3.8	6.6
General science	658	1,502	3.9	3.9
Natural resources/environment	554	952	3.3	2.5
Transportation	572	876	3.4	2.3
Agriculture	308	745	1.8	1.9
Other	667	747	4.0	1.9
Total	16,800	38,768	100.0	100.0

Sources: Statistical Abstract of the United States, 1981, p. 600; 1985, p. 576.

practices as 'targeting', allegedly practiced by Japan and the EEC which do have an industrial policy. This contention is not supported by the evidence. In a landmark study, Gary Saxonhouse found that government industrial policy did not accord Japanese industry and unusual advantages either in the form of direct subsidies or research and development grants:[23]

> In the late 1970s the Japanese government funded no more than 1.9 percent of all research and development undertaken by private sector industry. This contrasts with West Germany funding 15.8 percent of private sector R&D, France funding 25.3 percent, the United Kingdom funding 30.9 percent and with the United States so actively involved in private sector R&D as to fund fully 35.3 percent of all research and development undertaken by the private sector American economy.

Disaggregating these statistics, Saxonhouse reports that the communication and electronic manufacturing industry receives contracts, grants, and subsidies from the Japanese government equal to 1.03 percent of its R&D expenditures, while the comparable figure for pharmaceuticals, machinery, and precision equipment are 0.3, 1.4, and 0.05 percent, respectively. Japanese government expenditures on biotechnology come to no more than $35 million, or one-tenth to one-fifteenth the amount spent by the U.S. government. In 1982, the Japanese government spent $15 million on R&D in flexible manufacturing systems – in contrast to the U.S. Defence Department which alone spends an average of $225 million annually on manufacturing technology innovations like CAD/CAM systems, robotics, and flexible manufacturing systems. Finally, according to Saxonhouse, the Japanese government spent $48 million in 1982 on contracts, grants, and subsidies to the private sector for R&D in computers and semiconductors. By comparison, U.S. government funding for semiconductor research alone averaged $90 million in the early 1980s, while an additional $310 million was spent annually on computer-related research by the Defense Department, the National Science Foundation, and NASA.[24]

Since the United States evidently has, and will undoubtedly continue to have, an industrial policy in support of R&D, we leave the question of whether or not it should have such a policy. We turn now to the issue raised by the putative rationale for such support. If government support for private R&D is designed to correct for market failures due to the uncertainty and imperfect appropriability which are inherent in the innovation process, how should government support be structured to ensure that the public receives the maximum social return for its dollar?

IV. AGRICULTURE

Mansfield[25] has defined technical change as 'the advance of technology, such advance often taken the form of new methods of producing existing products, new designs which enable the production of products with important new characteristics, and new techniques of organization, marketing and management'. If we accept that definition, there can be little doubt that, in the agricultural sector, the investment in research and development had paid handsome dividends, and that government policy has played a cricial role in this success story. Some thirty years ago, for example, T. W. Schultz compared 'the value of agricultural inputs *saved* by the advances in the agricultural arts' during the 1940–50 decade with 'estimates of the cost of all non-profit (public) agricultural research', and found 'a 35 percent rate of return as the lower limit and a 170 percent rate of return as the upper limit per dollar spent on all agricultural research'.[26]

Since then, a plethora of empirical studies – both of the 'imputation' and 'statistical inference' variety[27] – has confirmed Schultz's estimates. (See Table 2 for a sample of the findings.) Based on these studies, one can conclude that:[28] 'Average rates of return to public agricultural research for the aggregate U.S. farm production sector have ranged from near

Table 2. Summary studies of returns to U.S. farm and food system R&D.

Study	Time period	Annual internal rate of return (percent)
Peterson and Fitzharris (1977)	1937–1942	50[a]
	1947–1952	51[a]
	1957–1962	49[a]
	1967–1972	34[a]
Griliches (1964)	1949–1959	35–40
Latimer (1964)	1949–1959	Not significant
Evenson (1968)	1949–1959	47
Cline (1975)	1939–1948	41–50[b]
White, Havlicek and Otto (1978)	1929–1941	55
Lu, Cline and Quance (1979)	1939–1948	30
Davis (1979)	1949–1959	66–100
Evenson, Waggoner and Ruttan (1979)	1868–1926	65

[a]Average annual return per dollar of research investment; all other estimates are annual marginal rates of return.
[b]Lower estimate for a 13-year, and higher estimate for a 16-year time lag between beginning and end of output impact.
All estimates for aggregate U.S. farm sector.
Source: Eddleman Bulletin, 1984, p. 3.

50 percent annually during 1937–52 to 34 percent annually during 1967–72. Marginal rates of return (i.e., returns on incremental investment) to public agricultural R&D have ranged from 30 to 100 percent for the aggregate farm sector in the U.S. and from 18 to 50 percent for the ten USDA major farm production regions. Almost all of these studies indicate rates of return to public investment in agricultural R&D which are well above the 10 to 15 percent (above inflation) that private firms consider adequate to attract new investment'. Put differently, if we examine the yield data of a single crop (soybeans) between the mid-1950s and the mid-1970s, the annual benefit stream attributable to R&D is 'large enough to justify all public and private research expenditures on all commodities at normal returns on investment. Even with some conservative adjustments to the data, the income streams emerging in either corn or soybeans are large enough to justify the entire agricultural research and extension program'.[29] Many other crops show similarly spectacular increases in yields. Livestock production also exhibits major gains in productivity.

It would be tempting to attribute the phenomenal productivity of U.S. agriculture to the production research which has improved crop varieties and breeds of livestock and poultry; or to attribute the spectacular performance to research on purchased inputs which has developed fertilizers with improved nutrient content, new and improved agricultural chemicals, and dramatic improvements in farm machinery and equipment.[30] Such a mechanistic explanation, however, would be misleading. It would ignore the conscious building of institutions which systematically coordinate the creation of knowledge with the diffusion and use of that knowledge in order to extract from it the full potential of productivity. As James T. Bonnen has pointed out,[31] 'Basic science must be interactively linked to various types of applied research and that linked in turn to technology development and ultimately to technology and knowledge transfer mechanisms. If these other activities or the linkage are missing, some basic science knowledge will remain undeveloped . . . and the social return to that investment in basic science [will be] reduced or lost'.

The organization and evolution of the development institutions in U.S. agriculture reflect a conscious effort to promote, in a systematic manner, the interaction between scientific knowledge, investments in human capital, and technology development and use. The public institutions that played a crucial role in this creative process were (1) the land grant college system, (2) the network of state agricultural experiment stations (SAES), (3) the Cooperative Extension Service, and (4) the U.S. Department of Agriculture (USDA). By the 1930s, this web of diverse institutions constituted a coherent, science-based system that subsequently transformed U.S. agriculture.[32] It is a web of institutions that could not have been created by the untrammeled operation of market forces.

The land grant system

Today the United States has a network of some 60 land grant colleges and universities located throughout the 50 states. They trace their origin to the Morrill Act of 1862 which provided an endowment of public land (or its monetary equivalent) to each state that agreed to earmark the income from this endowment for the establishment and support of colleges to teach the agricultural and mechanical arts.[33] In addition to training farmers, farm leaders, and agricultural scientists, these colleges engaged in agricultural research and 'grass roots' extension to bring the fruits of their research to the farming community. Most of them had strong discipline-oriented research programs in the basic sciences (chemistry, botany, physics, etc.) that form the foundation of the biological and physical sciences on which agricultural research is based.

The importance of combining basic and applied research within the same insitution can hardly be exaggerated. In doing research on rice, for example, it is advantageous to provide for close cooperation between specialists in genetics and plant physiology, on the one hand, and specialists in plant breeding on the other. As Hayami and Ruttan explained:[34]

> The geneticist and the physiologist are involved in research designed to advance understanding of the physiological processes by which plant nutrients are transformed into grain yield and of the genetic mechanisms or processes involved in the transmission from parents to progenies of the physiological characterisics of the rice plant which affect grain yield. The rice breeders utilize this knowledge from genetics and plant physiology in the design of crosses and the selection of plants with the desired growth characteristics, agronomic traits, and nutritional value. The work in plant physiology and genetics is responsive to the need of the plant breeder for advances in knowledge related to the mission of breeding more productive varieties of rice.

State agricultural experiment stations

The SAES's owe their origin to the Hatch Act of 1887, which authorized federal funds for direct payment to any state that would establish an

SAES in connection with its land grant college. The Act directed research stations to 'conduct original and other researches, investigations, and experiments bearing directly on and contributing to the establishment and maintenance of a permanent and effective agricultural industry of the United States, including researches basic to the problems of agriculture in its broadest aspects, and such investigations as have for their purpose . . . the maximum contribution by agriculture to the welfare of the consumer'. This law was perhaps the most important legislative step taken in the development of agricultural research in the United States. In one stroke, it not only created the modern network of state experiment stations which are today the principal source of trained agricultural scientists,[35] but it bound the states and the federal government together in a common commitment to agricultural R&D.[36]

Cooperative extension service

The cooperative extension service, the third major component in the land grant complex, was founded in 1914. The Smith–Lever Act of that year authorized federal funds (which had to be matched by state or local units) 'in order to aid in diffusing among the people of the United States useful and practical information on subjects relating to agriculture and home economics, and to encourage the application of the same'. Under this Act, the USDA was able to lend national coordination to a network of state extension staffs that were already in existence and that had been operating for several years. The land grant colleges, in turn, were given major administrative responsibility to take both the products of their teaching and the research of the experiment stations directly to the people who could use them in solving practical problems.

It is noteworthy that the extension service provided a two-way communication link between land grant research and the farm community. On the one hand, the extension system provided a grass roots organization to disseminate new agricultural technologies and knowledge directly to farmers in a systematic and continuing way – triggering the adoption by agriculturists of such major technologies advances as hybrid grain varieties, artificial insemination of cattle, chemical control of agricultural pests, etc. On the other hand, extension programs provided an important feedback system which gave agricultural research a practical, problem-solving, mission oriented flavor. Essentially, the research establishment would say 'here is what we can do for you', and the farm community would reply, 'yes, we want some of those things done, and here are the funds'.[37]

U.S. Department of Agriculture

The USDA was made a cabinet level agency in 1887 – the same year in which the network of agricultural experiment stations was established. 'From the 1880s through World War II, the USDA provided the intellectual and administrative leadership which established national priorities for agricultural sciences, performed most of the basic science research, and made major investments in the long-term intellectual and social capital of agriculture'.[38] Since the 1940s, however, many of these functions have been decentralized. Today USDA performs almost no in-house research, and national priorities for agricultural research are largely determined by an informal process in which the land grant insitutions exercise primary leadership. Nonetheless, aside from serving as the Washington lobby for agricultural interests, USDA still performs an important role in coordinating the decentralized activities of the land grant colleges, the agricultural experiment stations, and the cooperative extension service.

What, then, are the lessons of U.S. experience with government R&D policy in the agricultural sector? First, in the absence of massive government intervention, private R&D activity would have been miniscule or totally non-existent. The reasons are rooted in the structure of the industry. Agricultural firms were typically small – both in absolute and relative terms. Firms did not have the financial wherewithal to invest in R&D, and they had little incentive to do so. R&D entailed considerable risk because the payoff was uncertain; and, even if successful, the fruits of an R&D investment could not be privately appropriated. In short, natural market forces were not sufficient to induce the kind and quantity of R&D effort which was socially advantageous.

Second, the manner in which the government organized its R&D effort tended to assure positive results and handsome returns on investment. From the outset, cost effectiveness was structurally built into the system. An experiment station might want to pursue ambitious (costly) projects, but unless the consumers of that research (i.e., the agricultural community) could see dollars-and-cents benefits from applying the research output, such projects would eventually be aborted for lack of financing. In other words, throughout, there were checks and balances built into the government R&D policy.

Third, each R&D project was of relatively modest proportions. R&D investment in agricultural research was not 'lumpy'. This made it easier, both from a scientific and bureaucratic point of view, to admit failure and reverse course. It counteracted the tendency to continue investing in failure – to continue pouring money down a rat hole.

Fourth, the government confined its role to those segments of agricultural R&D which had to be 'socialized' or not be undertaken at all. It left to the private sector – the industries supplying mechanical and chemical inputs to agriculture – the R&D which the supplier industries had both the incentives and capability to undertake. In other words, where the market worked, government did not try to preempt it.

Finally, the government R&D effort was carefully structured to provide the institutional infrastructure to undergird the R&D effort and to assure its success. Ultimately, as James T. Bonnen has found, 'Man, not science, transformed U.S. agriculture. Men and women, acting through the institutions which they created, developed scientific knowledge, changed human values and aspirations, modified old institutions and created new ones as they saw the need, and step by step transformed the productivity and welfare of U.S. farmers'.[39]

V. NUCLEAR POWER[40]

Nuclear power generation is another sector in which the U.S. government sought to induce innovation by undertaking all the activities – from basic research to invention to development and commercialization – that give rise to a new product or means of production. It was an experiment in industrial policy and industrial targeting which, in contrast to agriculture, has (so far at least) not lived up to its original expectations.

Atomic weaponry and nuclear technology had been developed during World War II as an exclusive monopoly of the government and in utmost secrecy. The safety and health hazards of atomic power were obvious: the public would have to be protected, and regulation would be necessary. But given this, how should the government proceed to determine if nuclear electrical power was commercially viable? Should it limit its role strictly to regulation to protect the public welfare, while making available to private firms the technology that it had developed? Or, should it take the far more significant step of *actively promoting* nuclear electrical power by offering subsidies, financial incentives, and bounties? If the latter, could the government simultaneously promote *and* regulate the field? Or would it, by the very act of promotion, become indissolubly wedded to nuclear power as subsidizer and protector? Once begun, and once investments were made, could the program be stopped if it subsequently proved uneconomic? What of the alchemy between governmental promotionalism and subsidization, on the one hand, and the monopolized public utility environment of electric power production, on the other? What cost constraints, if any, could be expected under these conditions? And, finally, what about the public interest in efficient and safe power?

From the outset, it seemed clear that, if nuclear power generation were to become commercially feasible, the government would have to take an active role in its development. 'If you were to inquire whether Westinghouse might consider putting up its own money to construct [a nuclear power] plant', an official of the firm told a Congressional committee in 1953, 'we would have to say "No". The cost of the plant would be a question mark until after we built it and, by the sole means, found out the answer. We would not be sure of successful plant operation until after we had done all the work and operated successfully. This is still a situation of pyramiding uncertainties'. For the Committee's benefit, he explained: 'There is a distinction between risk-taking and recklessness'.[41]

In response to the urgings of equipment manufacturers and with the prodding of private electric utility companies, the government 'took the leap'. It passed the Atomic Energy Acts of 1946 and 1954, and became an active promoter of nuclear power. It based its decision on an explicit market failure argument:[42]

> We do not believe that the efforts of free enterprise, using its own resources and moneys, are by themselves adequate to achieve the speediest possible attack on the goal of peacetime power. Neither do we believe that maximum progress toward this objective will be afforded by an effort relying exclusively on governmental research and development, using the public's moneys. We believe, rather, that teamwork between Government and industry . . . is the key to optimum progress, efficiency, and economy in this area of atomic endeavor. In other words, our legislative proposals aim at encouraging flourishing research and development programs under both Government and private auspices.

The government thereafter poured billions of dollars into the atomic energy program. It sang the siren song of the 'private' beneficiaries of the program, viz., that commercially viable power was always just around the corner and, with a little more public largesse, would be realized. Together with industry and the utilities, it suppressed safety problems that threatened to raise the costs of nuclear power or to undermine public confidence in the industry. It tolerated constant delay in resolving critical problems, such as the disposal of atomic wastes. And it denigrated competitive alternatives such as conservation and solar power.

Federal support for the development of commercial nuclear power was both massive and multifaceted. First, the government sponsored research and development of military reactors, including nuclear submarine and aircraft carrier propulsion systems, which underlay and directly contributed to the design and construction of civilian atomic power plants.[43]

Second, the Government expended funds directly for the research and development of civilian nuclear reactors. Under various 'rounds' of its Power Reactor Development Program (inaugurated in 1955), for example, the government performed at no charge R&D work requested by industry, made lump sum R&D grants, waived nuclear fuel use charges for utilities, and built reactors whose power was fed into utility power systems while the Government bore the risks attendant on the construction and operation of the plants.[44] By 1979, these subsidies amounted to a cumulative total of nearly $21 billion in constant dollars (see Table 3).

Third, beginning in 1948, the Government put into place financial incentives to create a domestic uranium industry, including guaranteed prices for uranium ores; bonuses paid for discoveries of uranium ore deposits; payment of haulage and development allowances; provision of access to public lands (including the construction of 1500 miles of roads at a cost of $14 million); and guaranteed prices for vanadium (a mineral found together with uranium). In addition, the government carried out extensive exploration programs to locate uranium deposits, developed methods to assay and process raw uranium ore, and prohibited the importation of foreign uranium to protect domestic uranium prices.[45] By 1979, these subsidies amounted to $2.5 billion in constant (1979) dollars.

Fourth, since uranium must be 'enriched' to reactor-grade levels before it is suitable for fueling nuclear reactors, the government chose to provide this enrichment service through three plants located in Kentucky, Ohio, and Tennessee. The prices it charged were a further subsidy to the industry. According to estimates by the Energy Research and Development Administration, a fair value price for Government enrichment services (a price set on the same basis as it would be if operated by a private firm) would be approximately one-third greater than the current and historical fees set by the Government.[46] By 1979, cumulative enrichment subsidies to the industry exceeded $7 billion.

Fifth, the Government subsidized the industry in disposing of nuclear waste by assuming ultimate responsibility for nuclear waste disposal. Under the 'Uranium Mill Tailings Act of 1978', it funded 90 percent of the costs of cleaning up waste tailings at twenty-five abandoned uranium milling sites around the nation. It spent approximately $2.3 billion in researching the management and disposal of nuclear wastes. It sanctioned the failure to incorporate (unknown and unknowable) costs of disposing spent nuclear fuel into utility rates and rate structures. It sanctioned the failure to incorporate (unknown and unknowable) costs of decontaminating and decommissioning nuclear power plants now in operation, at

Table 3. Research and development subsidies, (millions of dollars)

	Fission civilian[a]	Military[b]	Fusion[a]	Total current $	Total[c] constant $ (1979)
1950	3.1	5.1		8.2	25.3
51	5.1	17.7		22.8	66.1
52	6.3	24.5		30.8	87.8
53	10.1	38.8		48.9	137.4
54	18.9	35.5		54.4	150.7
1955	29.9	32.8		62.7	169.9
56	55.1	51.4	7.2	106.5	280.1
57	97.5	99.0	11.6	196.5	501.1
58	148.1	103.6	19.9	251.7	631.8
59	184.7	96.5	36.0	281.2	688.9
1960	243.8	79.3	32.1	323.1	778.7
61	282.5	82.3	30.1	364.8	871.9
62	271.8[d]	47.7	25.0	319.5	747.6
63	265.4	54.5	26.2	319.9	739.0
64	295.8		22.9	318.7	733.0
1965	298.9		23.4	322.3	709.1
66	277.9		24.1	302.0	664.4
67	285.7		25.1	310.8	652.7
68	334.6		27.7	362.3	724.6
69	302.8		30.1	332.9	632.5
1970	280.7		31.6	312.3	562.1
71	301.0		32.5	333.5	567.0
72	356.1		36.1	392.2	666.7
73	417.4		42.5	459.9	735.8
74	600.3[e]		59.0	659.3	923.0
1975	739.1		95.0	834.1	1,084.3
76	959.3		164.0	1,123.3	1,348.0
77	1,217.0		236.0	1,453.0	1,743.6
78	1,237.7		277.0	1,514.7	1,666.2
79	1,266.4		349.0	1,615.4	1,615.4
			Total constant dollars		20,904.7

[a]All figures include operating and construction expenditures.
[b]Includes operating and construction costs through 1959. After 1959, military expenditures exclude construction costs. These numbers are 50 percent of relevant expenditures. See text for explanation. Excludes classified projects, operation of service facilities, general, special nuclear materials consumed, and merchant ship reactors.
[c]Current dollars adjusted to 1979 dollars by applying GNP deflator.
[d]For 1962 to 1975, construction and equipment costs are from Battelle, PNL-2410 Rev.
[e]After 1974, figures include NRC budget obligations.
Source: Nuclear Fuel Cycle Policy and the Future of Nuclear Power: Oversight Hearing Before the Subcomm. on Oversight and Investigations of the House Comm. on Interior and Insular Affairs, 97th Cong., 1st Sess., 583–584 (1982).

the end of their serviceable lives, into utility rates and rate structures. Cumulative waste disposal subsidies are estimated at approximately $6.5 billion.

Sixth, the largest, but least quantifiable, subsidy afforded the industry stems from the Government's assumption of, and limitation of, liability for the damages which would result from a nuclear reactor 'meltdown'. By enacting the Price–Anderson Act of 1957 (re-enacted in later years), the Government limited the liability of reactor manufacturers and operators to $60 million, and assumed liability for any additional damages which might result from a nuclear reactor accident up to a maximum of $500 million.

In spite of these prodigious efforts by the government, nuclear power today is not a viable U.S. industry. According to the Department of Eneryg, 84 percent of operating nuclear plants built during the last thirteen years cost consumers at least twice as much as initial estimates, with final construction costs exceeding initial estimates by four-fold (or more) for 30 percent of these plants (see Table 4). Industry experts, including those in the utility industry itself, estimate that nuclear plants now nearing completion will produce electricity at costs far greater than those of comparable coal-fired plants and, in some cases, at costs equivalent to electricity generated from oil priced at $100 per barrel (i.e., more than triple peak world oil prices of $28 per barrel).[47] 'Any [nuclear] plant which is less than 50 percent complete today should definitely be cancelled', concludes energy analyst Irvin C. Bupp. 'Plants in the 50 to 80 percent range probably should be cancelled'.[48] Abandoned atomic power plants – Marble Hill in Indiana, Midland in Michigan, Washington Public Power Supply System ('Whoops') in Washington, and Zimmer in Ohio – stand silently as monuments to a failed experiment in industrial targeting.

A conservative business magazine concurs in this assessment of the U.S. nuclear energy program: 'Through year after year of cost-overruns on nuclear power, America's electric utilities have added, by some estimates, an extra $100 billion in interest and other costs to the nation's electric power bill and placed ratepayers, shareholders, creditors and taxpayers between the proverbial rock and a hard place. Even at that high price, many customers will be left with nuclear-generated power that is overpriced compared to fossil fuel alternatives and represents more capacity than is necessary to fill power needs into the 1990s. Worse still, a minority of users must help finance multi-billion-dollar shells of nuclear reactors unlikely – at least for the next five-to-ten years – to generate enough power to run a toaster, let alone replace or supplement fossil fuel-based plants'.[49]

Table 4. Nuclear Construction: A Status Report. Cost figures and estimated completion dates are often disputed.

	Under construction			
	Percent complete	Due in service	First cost estimate	Current estimate
Alabama				
Bellefonte 1 (Scottsboro)	83%	4/88–4/89	$725 million	$5.2–5.6 billion
Bellefonte 2	63	4/90–4/91	for both	for both
Arizona				
Palo Verde 1 (Wintersburg)	99	12/84	$2.8 billion	$5.7 billion
Palo Verde 2	98	9/85	for three	for three
Palo Verde 3	81	1987		
California				
Diablo Canyon 1 (Avila Beach)	100	3/84	$620 million	$4.5 billion
Diablo Canyon 2	99	5/85	for both	for both
Connecticut				
Milstone 3 (Waterford)	80	5/86	$400 million	$3.54 billion
Georgia				
Alvin W. Vogtle 1 (Waynesboro)	61	3/87	$2.5 billion	$6.6 billion
Alvin W. Vogtle 2	20	Fall, 1988	for both	for both
Illinois				
Braidwood 1 (Braidwood)	70	4/86	$934 million	$3.575 billion
Braidwood 2	54	4/87	for both	for both
Clinton 1 (Clinton)	82	11/86	$430 million	$2.85 billion
Kansas				
Wolf Creek (Burlington)	90	3/85	$783 million	$2.67 billion

Table 4. (Continued)

	Under construction			
Louisiana				
River Bend 1 (St. Francisvills)	80	12/85	$350 million	$2.5 billion
Waterford 3 (Taft)	99	12/84	$230 million	$2.6 billion
Michigan				
Midland 2 (Midland)	83	Mid-'86	$350 million	$4.43 billion
Enrico Fermi 2 (Newport)	98	12/84	$229 million	$3,075 billion
Missippi				
Grand Gulf 1 (Port Gibson)	100	Late '84	$400–$500 million	$3 billion
Missouri				
Callaway 1 (Callaway Country)	95	12/84	$550 million	$2.85 billion
New Hampshire				
Seabrook 1 (Seabrook)	86	7/85	$900 million	$5.8 billion
(Future of Unit 2 uncertain)			for both	for both
New Jersey				
Hope Creek 1 (Lower Alloways Twp.)	76	12/86	$600 million	$3.79 billion
			for twin units	for one
New York				
Shoreham (Shoreham, L.I.)	100	7/85	$261 million	$4.1 billion
Nine Mile Point 2 (Scriba)	81	10/86	$382 million	$4.2 billion
North Carolina				
Shearon Harris 1 (New Hill)	85	10/86	$1 billion	$2.8 billion
			for four units	for one

Ohio				
Perry 1 (North Perry)	92	5/85	$632 million	$5.2 billion
Perry 2	44	5/88	for both	for both
Pennsylvania				
Beaver Valley 2 (Shipping port)	76	5/86	$321 million	$3.07 billion
Susquehanna 2 (Berwick)	98	12/84	$1.1 billion	$4.1 billion
(Unit 1 in service 6/83)			for two units	for two units
Limerick 1 (Limerick Twp.)	92	4/85	$1.7 billion	$6.45 billion
(Future of Unit 2 uncertain)			for two units	for two units
South Carolina				
Catawba 1 (York County)	99	Early '85	$320 million	$1.95 billion
Catawba 2	65	Early '87	$320 million	$1.95 billion
Tennessee				
Watts Bar 1 (Spring City)	96	Fall '84	$621 million	$3.4 billion
Watts Bar 2	61	Mid- '86	for both	for both
Texas				
South Texas Project 1 (Matagorda Country)	50	6/87	$1 billion	$5.5 billion
South Texas Project 2	25	6/89	for both	for both
Comanchie Peak 1 (Sommervell Country)	97	1985	$780 million	$3.89 billion

Source: M. Wald, 'Millions Face High Rates Because of Nuclear Plants', *New York Times*, February 26, 1984, p. 16.

In our opinion, there are several factors which explain the failure to realize the roseate expectations of the 1940s – the hope of generating electricity 'too cheap to meter'. First, there was a premature concentration on a particular research strategy. In the words of David E. Lilienthal, first chairman of the AEC:[50]

> Not enough time was taken to test reactor ideas and designs that were radically different from the light-water design that quickly preempted the market, alternatives that might have provided us with greater safety and certainly far less complexity.

Second, the movement to large scales of operation was too precipitous:[51]

> In 1969, when utilities had just begun to operate reactors capable of generating more than 200 megawatts of electricity, they rushed ahead with opening the first 650-megawatt plant and with plans to build 38 other plants of more than 600 megawatts, including some up to 1,100 megawatts.

Third, the Atomic Energy Commission found itself in the schizophrenic position of regulating the development of nuclear power while serving as a full, indeed dominant, partner in the development of that power. The familiar bureaucratic affinity for secrecy manifested itself in full force. Full disclosure of technological problems – the sort of disclosure which is essential for successful development of new technologies – was impeded because it was thought that such disclosure might shake public confidence in the government-sponsored program. Because of its dual role, the AEC proved unequal to the task of ensuring that safety considerations were kept in mind as large-scale operations were implemented. For this reason, the AEC was abolished by the Energy Reorganization Act of 1974, and replaced with a single-purpose agency, the Nuclear Regulatory Commission.[52] However, there is some reason to think that this organizational restructuring is more a matter of form than of substance.

Fourth, cost effectiveness tended to be a secondary concern, because the 'customers' for nuclear power generation were public utilities, subject to regulation by state regulatory agencies, and accustomed to the practice of passing along cost-overruns to the public via rate increases. The power of the market to enforce production at minimum cost is weak here; indeed, there is a well-known bias of public utilities toward capital-intensive techniques because the value of capital assets is added to the utility's rate base.[53] In addition, state regulatory agencies have crafted their procedures in such a way as to give a public utility every incentive to complete a nuclear power station, once begun, even if the learning process associated with development suggests that abandonment is the economic course. Most public utilities[54] 'allow stockholders to recoup their investment in a plant and earn a specified return only if it is completed'. Since the size of the investment involved in a nuclear power plant can exceed a utility's equity, this policy creates every incentive for utilities to ignore one of the fundamental precepts of resource allocation: sunk costs are sunk; do not throw good money after bad. Ultimately, of course, it is the public which bears the cost of decisions taken under this cost accounting system.

Finally, the development of nuclear power in the United States was not a policy which evolved gradually in response to demonstrated public needs. It was technology-driven rather than market-driven. The government was intent on perfecting a technology, for whatever reasons, and almost irrespective of cost. The nuclear industry was intent on profiting from the new technology, so long as it did not have to bear the uncertainty risks it entailed.[55] The electric utilities, given their penchant for capital-intensive techniques, and the benefits therefrom to their rate structure, were content to play along. In other words, the symbiotic relationship between government, industry, and the utilities forged a policy which repeatedly ignored market signals and pressed ahead with development even after it became apparent that nuclear power generation was not cost-effective under U.S. market conditions. In this sense, the nuclear power experiment in the United States was not an example of a market failure, but a policy failure. The market was right. The government, which was apparently willing 'to pay any price, and bear any burden' to promote commercial nuclear power, was wrong. It could afford to persist in its policy because the bill for failure did not come due until years later, when the erstwhile decision makers were no longer politically accountable for their misjudgement.

VI. CONCLUSION

Industrial policy, as commonly understood, is a government effort to promote 'sunrise' industries and to protect 'sunset' industries. Ideally, it would be conceived and implemented by Platonic philosopher-Kings – i.e., dedicated public servants, endowed with the requisite expertise, felicitous foresight, and creative imagination to plan a nation's economic future. But, alas, to paraphrase John Dewey, saints dream of great utopias, while burly sinners rule the world.

In reality, especially in a democracy, industrial policy tends to become a football of political economy. Governmental decisions are not necessarily made on the basis of rational economic (rather than political) criteria. Decisions, more often than not, reflect a tug-of-war between organized interest groups, intent on serving their private special interests rather than the public interest. In 'emerging' sectors, therefore, governmental efforts to pick 'winners' or 'national champions' may degenerate into a subsidy scheme for privileged industries and companies – i.e., for chosen instruments. In the 'mature' industries, industrial policy may quickly degenerate into a new form of institutionalized protectionism and lemon socialism. 'One does not have to be a cynic', says Charles Schultze, 'to forecast that the surest way to multiply unwarranted subsidies and protectionist measures is to legitimize their existence under the rubric of industrial policy. The likely outcome of an industrial policy that encompassed some elements of both "protecting the losers" and "picking the winners" is that the losers would back subsidies for the winners in return for the latter's support on issues of trade protection'.[56]

Government R&D policy is a special segment of a nation's industrial policy. Its objective is to target technologies of the future and to implement their development and implantation. In this effort, it must deal with the intractable problem of uncertainty – the uncertainty inherent in new technologies as well as the uncertainty of how commercial markets will assimilate these technologies. It must compensate for the unwillingness or inability of the private sector to invest in R&D projects where the results cannot be privately appropriated, or where the risks are inordinate, or where the payoffs are remote. Nevertheless, government must subject its R&D programs to continuing cost-benefit assessments – except, perhaps, in areas (like national defense, for example) where expenditures are based on political or other non-economic considerations.

The government can do many things. It can create an incentive system – with the right kind of patent laws, e.g. – which will allow private investors to appropriate the fruits of their efforts without enabling them to block technological progress or to slow its pace. It can support investment in human capital and the inevitably gradual accretion of knowledge – quintessential public goods – to correct for the inherent divergence between private and public benefits. In short, it can promote an institutional framework, a hospitable ambiance, a solid infrastructure, to encourage constant interaction between basic and applied research, and the kind of feedback system between R&D producers, R&D users, and ultimate consumers, which are indespensible to technological progress.

The government cannot, however, create certainty where the state of the art is fraught with uncertainty. It may assume liability for potential catastrophe, but it cannot by that act alter the probability that catastrophe will occur. It can push the private sector in directions that market signals deem propitious, but it cannot – by administrative fiat – set the precise course: if there is insufficient information for the private sector to target the most promising line of pursuit, there is little reason to think that the government can do so. As George Stigler recently observed: 'One thing we know about government is that it is not a good entrepreneur'.

The appropriate government industrial policy, we submit, is one which has been given lip service, at least (and sometimes at most), in the United States since 1890: maintain an environment in which markets can work. Let innovators gain from their investment; do not let them use their innovation to interfere with the innovations of rivals. Where the market can work, let it: the record of competition is better than the record of regulation. Where government is necessary, remember: bills must be paid.

NOTES

1. Marx and Engels (1951, Volume 1, p. 37).
2. Although some come close: see the Economic Report of the President, 1984, p. 88, quoted below.
3. Rosenberg, p. 63. Some treatments offer a classification of technological progress as factor-neutral or factor-augmenting, and (for example) explore the consequences of different sorts of progress for shares of different factors in output. Burmeister and Dobell (1970, pp. 136–146).
4. See, for example, Solow (1957).
5. Schultz (1971, p. 6).
6. R. R. Nelson, *Government and Technical Progress: A Cross-Industry Analysis*, Pergamon Press, 1982, p. 2.
7. R. C. Levin, W. M. Cohen, and D. C. Mowery, 'R&D Appropriability, Opportunity, and Market Structure: New Evidence on Some Schumpeterian Hypotheses', *American Economic Review*, Volume 75, Number 2, May 1985, pp. 20–24.
8. Fisher and Temin (1973).
9. Kohn and Scott (1982).
10. J. Lunn and S. Martin, 'Market Structure, Firm Structure, and Research and Development', *Quarterly Review of Economics and Business*, forthcoming, 1986, address the simultaneity problem.
11. Kamien and Schwartz (1982, p. 223).
12. Arrow (1962).
13. Levin, Cohen and Mowery (1985).
14. 'Year after year economic theorists continue to produce sources of mathematical models and to explore in great detail their formal properties; and the econometricians fit algebraic functions of all possible shapes to essentially the same sets of data without being able to advance, in any perceptible way, a systematic understanding of the structure and operations of a real economic system' (Leontief, 1982, p. 107).
15. For example, Nelson (1982).
16. Blumenthal (1983).
17. Robert Z. Lawrence, *Can America Compete?*, Washington: Brookings Institution, 1984.
18. Stigler (1971).

19. Blumenthal (1983).
20. 1984 Economic Report of the President (1984, p. 88).
21. Arrow (1962).
22. 1981, p. 78.
23. 'Tampering with comparative advantage in Japan', Statement of Gary R. Saxonhouse before the U.S. International Trade Commission (332–162), Washington, D.C., June 15, 1983, pp. 4–5.
24. *Ibid.*, pp. 6–8.
25. 1968, pp. 10–11.
26. Schultz, *Investment in Human Capital*, 1971, p. 242.
27. Imputation studies directly relate some measure of productivity change to some measure of R&D input. Statistical studies involve econometric estimation of a production function, the specification of which allows in some way for R&D input.
28. With B. R. Eddlemen, *Bulletin*, 1984, p. 3.
29. R. E. Evenson, 'Agriculture', in R. R. Nelson, editor, *Government and Technical Progress*, New York: Pergamon Press, 1982, p. 265.
30. OTA, United States Food and Agriculture Research Sysatem, 1981, p. 61.
31. J. T. Bonnen, in *United States–Mexico: Agriculture and Rural Development*, Stanford University Press, 1985.
32. Bonnen, 1985.
33. In the 'second' Morrill Act, enacted in 1890, Congress added a 'separate but equal' provision authorizing the establishment of 'land grant' colleges for blacks. Seventeen southern and border states availed themselves of this law to create institutions that are still euphemistically referred to as the 'colleges of 1890'.
34. Hayami and Ruttan, p. 58.
35. OTA, p. 6.
36. OTA, p. 33.
37. Schultz, *Investment in Human Capital*, p. 225.
38. Bonnen.
39. Bonnen.
40. In this section, we draw on the discussion in Walter Adams and James W. Brock, *The Bigness Complex*, New York: Pantheon, 1986.
41. *Atomic Power and Private Enterprise Hearings*, 83rd Congress, 2nd session, 1954, p. 283.
42. U.S Congress, Senate, Rep. No. 1699, 83rd Congress, 2nd session, 1954, p. 9.
43. J. Bowring, 'Federal Subsidies to Nuclear Power: Reactor Design and the Fuel Cycle', printed in *Nuclear Fuel Cycle Policy and the Future of Nuclear Power: Oversight Hearing Before the Subcomm. On Oversight and Investigations of the House Comm. on Interior and Insular Affairs*, 97th Cong., 1st Sess., 569–70 (1982).
44. Id., 573–581.
45. Id., at 592–596; *Development, Growth, and State of the Atomic Energy Industry: Hearings Before the Joint Comm. on Atomic Energy*, part 2, 85th Cong., 1st Sess., 712 (1957).
46. Bowring, supra, at 602–609.
47. Energy Information Administration, Department of Energy, 1983, *Survey of Nuclear Power Plant Construction Costs* (Washington, D.C., 1983), p. 9; *New York Times*, September 3, 1984, pp. 19–20.
48. *New York Times*, January 20, 1985, Section 3, p. 6.
49. *Dunn's Business Month*, 1984.

50. David E. Lilienthal, *Atomic Energy: A New Start*, 1980.
51. J. N. Wilford, 'Safety Regulations Drive Up Expense of Nuclear Reactors', *New York Times*, February 27, 1984, p. 1.
52. The promotional activities once performed by the AEC were eventually taken over by the Department of Energy.
53. Cite the Averch–Johnson piece here.
54. New York State is an exception; Matthew L. Wald, 'Despite high cost, some utilities feel compelled to finish reactors', *New York Times*, February 28, 1984, p. 1.
55. See the statement of the Westinghouse official, quoted above.
56. U.S. Congress, House Subcommittee on Economic Stabilization. 1983. *Hearings on Industrial Policy*, Part 3, 98th Congress, 1st session, pp. 39–40.

REFERENCES

Abromovitz, M., 'Resource and Output Trends in the United States Since 1870', *American Economic Review*, 46 (1956), pp. 5–23.

Adams, W. and Brock, J. W., *The Bigness Complex*, New York: Pantheon (1986).

Adams, W. J., 'Firm Size and Research Activity: France and the United States', *Quarterly Journal of Economics*, 84 (1970), pp. 386–409.

Arrow, K., 'Economic Welfare and the Allocation of Resources for Inventions, in (Nelson, 1962).

Averch, H. and Johnson, L. L., 'Behavior of the Firm under Regulatory Constraint'. *American Economic Review*, 53 (1963), pp. 1052–1069.

Binswanger, H. P., Ruttan, V. W., *et al.*, *Induced Innovation*, Baltimore, Md.: John Hopkins University Press (1978).

Blumenthal, S., 'Drafting a Democractic Industrial Plan', *The New York Times Magazine*, (August 28, 1983), pp. 31–63.

Bonnen, J. T., 'U.S. Agrarian Development: Transforming Human Capital and Institutional Change', in B. Johnson and C. Reynolds (eds.), *United States–Mexico: Agriculture and Rural Development*, Stanford: Stanford University Press (forthcoming) (1985).

Bowring, J., 'Federal Subsidies to Nuclear Power', in (U.S. House Committee on Interior and Insular Affairs, 1982).

Burmeister, E. and Dobell, A. R., *Mathematical Theories of Economic Growth*, New York: Macmillan (1971).

Eddleman, B. R., *Research and Development for the Future Farm and Food System*, East Lansing: Cooperative Extension Service, Michigan State University (1984).

Evenson, R. E., 'Agriculture' in (Nelson, 1982).

Fisher, F. M. and Temin, P., 'Returns to Scale in Research and Development: What Does the Schumpeterian Hypothesis Imply?' *Journal of Politicial Economy*, 81 (1973), pp. 56–70.

Flores, Edmundo, 'Science and Technology in Mexico: Toward Self-Determination', *Science*, 219 (25 March, 1983).

Galbraith, J. K., *American Capitalism*, Boston: Houghton Mifflin (1952).

Griliches, Z., 'Hybrid Corn: An Exploration of the Economics of Technological Change', *Econometrica*, 25 (1957), pp. 501–522.

Hamberg, D., *R&D: Essays on the Economics of Research and Development*, New York: Random House (1966).

Hayami, Yugiro and Ruttan, Vernon, *Agricultural Development: An International Perspective*, Baltimore, The Johns Hopkins Univ. Press (1971).
Hicks, J. R., *The Theory of Wages*, London: Macmillan (1932).
Jewkes, J., Sawers, D. and Stillerman, R., *The Sources of Invention*, New York: Norton, 2nd ed. (1969).
Kamien, M. I. and Schwartz, N. L., *Market Structure and Innovation*, Cambridge: Cambridge University Press (1982).
Kohn, M. and Scott, J. T., 'Scale Economies in Research and Development: The Schumpeterian Hypothesis', *Journal of Industrial Economics* 30 (1982), pp. 239–249.
Lave, L. B., *Technical Change: Its Conception and Measurement*, Englewood Cliffs: Prentice-Hall (1966).
Lawrence, R. Z., *Can America Compete*? Washington: Brookings Institution (1984).
Leontieff, W., 'Academic Economics', *Science* 217 (July 9, 1982), pp. 104–107.
Levin, R. C., Cohen, W. M., and Mowery, D. C., 'R&D Appropriability, Opportunity, and Market Structure: New Evidence on Some Schumpeterian Hypotheses', *American Economic Review*, 75 (1985), pp. 20–24.
Lilienthal, *Atomic Energy: A New Start*, New York: Harper & Row (1980).
Lunn, J. and Martin, S., 'Market Structure, Firm Structure, and Research and Development', *Quarterly Review of Economics and Business* (1986).
Machlup, F., *The Production and Distribution of Knowledge in the U.S.*, Princeton, N.J.: Princeton University Press (1962).
Mansfield, E., *Industrial Research and Technology Innovation – An Econometric Analysis*. New York: Norton (1968a).
Mansfield, E. *The Economics of Technological Change*, New York: Norton (1968b).
Nelson, R. R. (ed.), *The Rate and Direction of Inventive Activity*. Princeton: Princeton University Press (1962).
Nelson, R. R., Peck, M. J., and Kalachek, E. D., *Technology Economic Growth and Public Policy*, Washington, D.C.: The Brookings Institution (1967).
Nelson, R. R. (ed.), *Government and Technical Progress*, New York: Pergamon Press (1982).
Rosenberg, N., *Technology and American Economic Growth*, New York: Harper and Row (1972).
Rosenberg, N., *Perspectives on Technology*, New York: Cambridge University Press (1976).
Rothwell, R. and Zegveld, W., *Industrial Innovation and Public Policy*, Westport, Conn.: Greenwood Press (1981).
Ruttan, Vernon, *Agricultural Research Policy*, Minneopolis, Univ. of Minnesota Press (1982).
Ruttan, Vernon, 'The Global Agricultural Support System'. *Science*, Vol. 222 (October 7, 1983).
Saxonhouse, G. R., 'Tampering with Comparative Advantage in Japan', Statement before the U.S. International Trade Commission. Washington (1983).
Scherer, F. M., *Industrial Market Structure and Economic Performance*, Chicago: Rand McNally, 2nd ed. (1980).
Schmookler, J., *Invention and Economic Growth*, Cambridge, Mass.: Harvard University Press (1966).
Schultz, T. W., *The Economic Organization of Agriculture*, New York: McGraw-Hill Book Co. (1953).
Schultz, T. W., *Investment in Human Capital*, New York: The Free Press (1971).

Schumpeter, J. A., *Capitalism, Socialism and Democracy*, New York: Harper & Row, Harper Colophon Ed. (1975).
Shaffer, J. D., 'On Institutional Obsolescence and Innovation', *American Journal of Agricultural Economics*, 51, (1969), pp. 245–267.
Solow, R., 'Technical Change and the Aggregate Production Function', *Review of Economics and Statistics*, 39, (1957), pp. 312–320.
Stigler, G. J., 'The Theory of Economic Regulation', *Bell Journal of Economics*, 2 (1971), pp. 3–21.
U.S. Congress, House Committee on Interior and Insular Affairs, *Nuclear Fuel Cycle Policy and the Future of Nuclear Power: Oversight Hearings*. 97th Congress, 1st session (1982).
U.S. Congress, Joint Committee on Atomic Energy, *Atomic Power and Private Enterprise Hearings*, 83rd Congress, 2d session (1954).
U.S. Congress, Office of Technology Assessment. 1981. *United States Food and Agricultural Research System*. Washington: U.S. Government Printing Office.
U.S. Congress, Senate, *Senate Report No. 1699*, 83rd Congress, 2d session (1954).
U.S. Council of Economic Advisers, *Economic Report to the President*, Washington: U.S. Government Printing Office (1984).
U.S. Energy Information Administration, *Survey of Nuclear Power Plant Construction Costs*, Washington: U.S. Government Printing Office (1983).
Wald, M., 'Millions Face High Rates Because of Nuclear Plants', *The New York Times* (February 26, 1984).
Wilford, J. N., 'Safety Regulations Drive Up Expense of Nuclear Reactors', *The New York Times* (February 27, 1984).

18. INDUSTRIAL POLICY AND INNOVATION IN EUROPE

William Kingston

INTERVENTION OR LAW?

Every State has a clear choice between Law and Intervention in its economic affairs. That is, one of its options is to legislate, especially in relation to property rights, so as to provide a framework within which independent economic agents are free to act on their own initiative; such legislation will reflect agnosticism on the part of those who run the State, about their ability to know which direction economic activity ought to take, and/or doubt about the possible value of action on their part, when weighed up against its possible harm.

Intervention, or Industrial Policy, on the other hand, reflects a belief on the part of the powers that be, that they do know – and what is more important, understand – what individual sectors of economies should be aiming at; that, left to themselves, the economic agents in these sectors will not act to achieve these ends, or, if they do, will not succeed; and that these same economic agents can be directed into the right paths by suitably devised incentives.

Industrial Policy, it should be noted, is not the same as Socialism, nor is it measurable by the proportion of national disposable income handled by government. Indeed, it responds very much better to study in terms of Mancur Olson's logic of collective action, and particularly his 'distributional coalitions', than it does to conventional Left–Right analysis [1]. Sweden, for example, has been a Socialist state for a very long time. Until recent years, however, it maintained a clear distinction between the creation of wealth and its distribution. Wealth-creation was considered to be very much a matter for entrepreneurs, acting without either interference or assistance from the State; wealth-distribution, on the other hand, was the State's business – hence the heavy taxation, both corporate and personal, and the correspondingly large transfer payments.

de Jong, H. W., Shepherd, W. G. (eds) Mainstreams in Industrial Organization
 ISBN 978-94-017-0495-3

But Industrial Policy does concern itself with the generation of wealth, and in certain European Countries it has a long history. From at least the time of Louis XIV, for example, Ambassadors of France were charged with the duty of seeking out new technology abroad, which might be introduced with advantage at home. Certainly, from the time of the foundation of the Grandes Ecoles by Napoleon, French economic policy has been strongly interventionist. In contrast, the British approach throughout the nineteenth century was wholly sceptical about the power of the State to intervene beneficially in economic matters. The emphasis was upon law to make decentralised action possible, and it is no coincidence that some of the major legal innovations which have shaped the contemporary economic world, took their modern form first in Britain, and in that century.

To begin with, there were the arrangements for rasing and deploying private capital on an unprecedented scale, associated with the financing of railways; these led on to the Companies Acts in the mid-century, with which Limited Liability was closely linked. The modern Corporation everywhere has its origins in these two enormously important social innovations. Then there was the *annus mirabilis* of Industrial Property in 1883. In that single year, Britain passed the first modern Patent Act (building, admittedly, upon a tradition that went back to the Statute of Monopolies of 1624) and the Trade Marks Registration Act, and helped to found the International Convention for the Protection of Intellectual Property. This, otherwise known as the Paris Convention, is the Charter of International Business, since without it neither the Multinational Corporation as we know it, nor the world-wide Brand, could exist [2].

As between the results of the use of law and Industrial Policy respectively, the verdict of history, on the authority of David Landes, is clear: 'Those economies grew fastest that were freest' [3]. Why, then, if law was so successful, did Europe turn away from it, to pursue the new (and, as I think, false) god of intervention? The story is complex, and I do not claim to have unravelled more than a few strands of it as yet.

Firstly, it must be remembered that actual legislation that has a bearing on economic affairs is not conceived (much less passed) by all-wise, disinterested law-makers of Platonic calibre. The initiative generally comes from lobbying, and the most effective lobbying is energetic and therefore self-interested. How did France get Limited Liability, for example? Not by any means because her rulers were convinced by abstract theory that this would be a beneficial measure. It was because a Treaty gave British business men access to certain French markets, via Belgium; Britain had adopted Limited Liability, and French business men claimed that they were thereby put at a competitive disadvantage [4].

Law should not reflect special interests, but frequently (and, indeed, increasingly) it does. Inevitably, too, legislation has effects which are only partially understood, and are very often unforeseen. Trade Mark registration, beginning in France in 1854, came about as a result of pressure from businesses which found that Common Law protection of reputation was inadequate in the wider geographical markets which had been opened up by the transport revolution; no-one envisaged anything of the effects which have changed the whole way of life of the twentieth century. All advertising, most of the media, both print and electronic, and much organised sport today depend upon similar legislation everywhere. By no means all of these effects have been universally approved; much of the emotional basis for the growth of socialism, indeed, is to be found in the new inequalities and rigidities brought about by legislation with an economic purpose. 'The laws of property', as John Stuart Mill noted in 1849, 'have never yet conformed to the principles on which the justification of private property rests' [5]. They conform even less today, as a result of the new kinds of intellectual and industrial property which were brought into being by nineteenth-century legislation. Once law generates vested interests, it becomes correspondingly difficult to reform it, so law almost always fails to change as it should. And every failure of law to generate an economic order which is humane as well as efficient, opens up an opportunity for those who advocate intervention, which they are quick to grasp.

POLITICIANS AND BUREAUCRATS

Those who advocate intervention . . . The most obvious group of these consists of democratically elected politicians, who naturally use their powers in ways that will help them in the vote auction (on which Dan Usher's 'The Economic Prerequisite to Democracy' has not received nearly as much attention as it deserves [6]). In this paper, however, I want to concentrate on a second group, those who actually administer Industrial Policies, the Civil Servants, whose influence has not been adequately studied because it is so much less visible.

The first World War appears as a watershed between the two quite different characteristic types of higher Civil Servant everywhere in Europe. The nineteenth-century Civil Services, which were so good at extracting the pearl of genuine public interest from the oyster of lobbying, were recruited, at the top, from a social class which in terms of property ownership, family connections and eduction, could see little merit in extending the power of the State in economic matters. This class was irreparably damaged by the War and especially by the inflations that followed it. Those who came to staff the higher echelons of European Civil Services in the 1920s and 1930s, depended exclusively on their jobs both for the social standing and for money; consequently, they had a vested interest in intervention, since this, by expanding the system, could augment both.

Moreover, this socially-rooted bias in favour of intervention as opposed to law, received just the intellectual vindication it needed, and with perfect timing, from Keynes's thinking. Buchanan and Wagner have called attention to the way in which this assumed legislators of the Platonic type, and ignored the reality of the world of democratically-elected politicians [7]. It equally ignored the fact that the new Civil Servants also had an axe to grind – and, here, in the *General Theory*, was a magnificent endorsement of their desire to grind it [8]. It can be no coincidence, for example, that a mimeograph translation was circulating inside that citadel of interventionist thinking, the Ministère des Finances, as early as 1937.

It is also interesting that it took so much longer for Keynesian thinking to influence policy in the US than in Europe. But this, too, is more understandable if the self-interest of Civil Servants is taken into account. Initially, the Americans had firmly rejected the European Public Service model, and for a long time, virtually all offices depended upon appointment by electoral victors (as, indeed, many still do). It was only when President Garfield was assassinated by a disappointed office-holder in 1881 that they began to see that a permanent Civil Service could have certain advantages. It has never become as deeply-rooted as in Europe, however, and notwithstanding the boost given to intervention by the New Deal, it is only within the last few decades that the attitudes of mind which favour Industrial Policy have taken root in Washington.

THE DECLINE OF PATENTS

Reference has been made to the way in which every failure of law to bring about hoped-for economic benefits, leaves corresponding scope for the expansion of Industrial Policy. Of all such failures, the most spectacular and harmful has been that of the Patent law, since this has opened the way for Industrial Policy to concern itself with R&D and with innovation.

The Principle of Patenting is a social invention whose value has hardly begun to be tapped. It provides for granting by the State of a monopoly of limited duration, in exchange for the carrying out of something considered to be socially valuable. Originally, this was innovation. A monopoly of two terms of apprenticeship was granted to whoever would introduce 'new manufacture within this realm'. By a series of changes, however, largely explicable in terms of administrative convenience, Patents come to apply to invention, not innovation.

That is, they now purport to protect an idea or a 'teaching', not that idea or teaching *actually turned into concrete reality*. Innovation is now only protected indirectly, and the protection is only as strong as the links to the associated invention. Except for Chemicals, these links are generally weak. Patents also gave up protecting incremental innvoations, and developed a doctrine of 'absolute novelty' which rendered them irrelevant to any firm that was not at the very leading edge of world technology. Their jurisprudence, too, also developed in ways which made settlement of disputes extremely uncertain and expensive. The valid patents of smaller firms could be infringed with impurity, since they could not afford to litigate; whereas invalid patents of large firms still gave *de facto* monopolies, since they would never be tested in the Courts.

The result has been that Patents became little more than a reinforcement of the other types of market power possessed by the largest firms, instead of being an indepedent counterbalance to these. The patent system also became progressively less valuable to firms in the less advanced countries, as a means of getting a foothold in world markets. This is typified by EMI's experience with its invention of computed tomography, or the 'brain-scanner'. It was accepted as being 'the greatest advance in diagnostic technique since X-rays', but blatant infringement in the US market, for which EMI was never adequately compensated, helped the firm to end up as the victim of a take-over bid. Repeated a thousand times, such failures of the Patent system to confer genuine appropriability of rewards on those who invest in innovation in Europe, left a massive vacuum which the advocates of Industrial Policy were only too ready to fill.

They have filled it to the extent that Government support, even of R&D that is described as 'commercial', is now over 30% in Britain, and close to 20% in W. Germany – and these figures understate its importance, because of the contributions from, e.g., Defence R&D. In the aircraft industry, for example, it is virtually impossible to separate what is 'commercial' from what is 'Defence', as recent events in the U.S. have demonstrated. It is probably fair to categorise the French and Belgian approach to Industrial Policy in relation to innovation as enthusiastic, and the German and Dutch as pragmatic. Nelson has recently used the word 'schizophrenic' to describe the British approach, which finds it hard to reconcile so much intervention with its tradition of economic freedom [9].

NATIONAL MEASURES

The latest edition of the Official Directory of Public Measures for Promoting Industrial Research, Development and Innovation in EEC member-states, lists no fewer than 286 separate incentives in the ten countries, excluding tax reliefs. Each of these is an aspect of Industrial Policy. Nor are the sums of money involved in them trivial. Amongst designated areas, French support for Nuclear research is of the order of 0.9 bn ECU a year, German for civil aircraft development 124 m ECU and British for non-nuclear energy R&D, 69 m ECU. (1 ECU = approx. $0.84) Aggregate support which is not tied to a designated field, amounts to about 1.7 bn ECU annually. The most common types of incentives are now discussed.

Collective research

Typical of these are the Fraunhofer Gesellschaft in Germany, with 30 Institutes, and the 11 Sectoral de Groote Centres in Belgium. In France, Italy and Holland, a levy on Trade Association members for their support has legal sanction, and the Government contribution in all countries is typically 50%.

Support for firm's own R&D

In Germany, the Ministry of Research and Technology can provide up to 40% of costs. In 1983, it funded 2,721 projects in 18 broad research areas, at a cost of 2.6 bn DM. In Holland, research in 'priority areas' can obtain 100% Government support. In Belgium, Germany and Holland, subsidies are paid for the employment of R&D personnel. British Government support for innovation in the two years to mid-1984, totalled £342 m for 2,425 projects.

Equity capital and loans

Belgium has SNI, the National Investment Society, as well as similar regional Societies. Soffinova in France is capitalised at Frs. 450 m. In Germany, the Government shares any losses made by 25 financial institutions that invest in innovation. In Holland, a Government Bank, IGF, can take equity up to 50%. 'Private Participation Companies' also have 50% government guarantees as to losses. There is also a Corporation for Industrial Projects for larger schemes.

In France, INNODEV and CEPME can guarantee up to 75% of bank loans as 'last ranked debt'. Germany refinances bank loans for innovation at a fixed interest rate. In Britain, 4 times a bank's loan will be provided by the government at a small premium on the interest rate. In Holland, the government can provide up to 70% of 'launch costs', with interest payable at 5% (but only in the event of success). France has 17 years 'participative' loans, directly from the State.

OTHER INCENTIVES

All countries permit firms to have access to their public research institutes, e.g., the RISØ National Laboratory in Denmark, those of CRNS, CEA, CNET, Space Studies and IFREMER in France, the Max Planck Institutes as well as the Federal Research Institutes in Germany, and TNO in Holland. Most encourage activities at the Industry/University interface. Denmark has Business Research Degrees. Holland has 'project transfer points' in Technical Universities. Belgium is attempting to develop an inter-University micro-electronics laboratory, designed to be 5–10 years ahead of industry's requirements. Germany is running a pilot project, expressly for New-Technology-Based-Firms. This involves grants of up to 90% of pre-establishment investigatory costs, 75% of R&D, and 50% for start-up costs, as well as 50% sharing in bank loan liability.

EUROPEAN COMMUNITY INCENTIVES

In addition to the range of national incentives, the European Community also supports innovation. To a significant extent, the thrust of this is towards compensating for the failure to develop a genuine common market. The position regarding non-tariff barriers to trade is now in fact worse than at any time in the Community's history. There was a 41-fold increase in the number of infringements of the Treaty of Rome in the 10 years to 1982. The cost of 'non-Europe' has been variously estimated at 50 bn ECU or 2% of CDP annually. So bad are things, indeed, that Directive 189/83, which is the primary instrument of an attack on this problem, has the objective of simply preventing new barriers from being erected, not of demolishing those that are already in place.

With regard to innovation, the official view is that 'frequently, no single national market in Europe constitutes more than 5–10% of the market required to justify the investment decision necessary for a major technological innovation' [10]. This is contrasted with the 'continental scale' of the home markets of firms in the two major competitor countries, the US and Japan. Compared with 220 million and 120 million people respectively in these countries, Europe will have 320 millions with the accession of Spain and Portugal. The Commision's efforts in respect of innovation, therefore, can all be seen as surrogates of a kind for the scale of markets which ought to exist in Europe, but do not.

The most important of these is the ESPRIT programme, which has the objective of enabling firms in the Information Technology field 'at least catch up' with the competition within 10 years. It is based on 36 pilot projects and four years' discussion with Governments, and 1.5 m ECU has been budgeted for the first 5-year period, of which half will be paid by industry. The Joint Research Centre at Ispra, Italy, which has been mainly concerned with Nuclear research, has a budget of 700 m ECU for 1984–87. Compared with these, expenditures such as those on biotechnology (15 m ECU between 1982 and 1986) Basic Technological Research (270 m ECU, 1984–87), Measurement (50 m ECU, 1983–87), High Temperature Materials (28 m ECU, 1984–87) Application of New Technologies in Textiles (70 m ECU, 1984–87) and Energy other than Nuclear (43 m ECU, 1984–87) are small. The usual practice is for half of these sums to come from Commission funds. Minor programmes include long range forecasting and machine translation.

A RECORD OF FAILURE

By far the most important fact about this formidable array of polices directed at improving European innovatory capacity, is that *it has not worked.* Zysman, for example, has demonstrated how intervention had partial success in France in areas such as nuclear energy, where the Government could control the market. It failed disastrously in computers and semi-conductors, where it could not [11]. It is widely accepted that the British reactor programme has been an expensive failure. In aircraft, the pattern is obscured by the intrusion of defence requirements, but every commercial aircraft produced in Britain or France under strong government direction lost money. Concorde eventually cost more than 10 times its original budget of $450 m. It is surely significant that the aircraft which brought the world into the passenger jet age, the de Havilland Comet, had no public money or direction in it at all; and that the (comparative) success of Airbus only began when government officials were explicitly cut out of the formulation of design and marketing plans [12].

A valuable global measure of what has been happening has been produced for the European Commission by one of its economists, Brendar, Cardiff [13]. He prepared a series of indices of 'revealed comparative advantage' in high technology in the following way:

1. 28 sectors were selected from the Standard International Trade Classifications as indicative of 'high technology'.
2. For each sector, an index was produced for each country of the EEC, together with the US and Japan, using the following formula:

$$\frac{X_{ij}/\Sigma X_j}{X_i/\Sigma X}$$

where

X_{ij} = exports of product j by country i
X_j = total world exports of product j
X_i = total exports of country i
X = total world exports.

Thus, France had 9.3% of total world trade in 1980, and also had 9.3% of world trade in electrical power machinery (SITC2, item 771) giving it an idex of comparative advantage of exactly 1.00. Calculated in the same way, Japan's index of revealed comparative advantage in recording equipment, is 6.76. A refinement of this approach excludes agricultural trade, which was 21.6% of total trade in 1980. Revised according to this, for example, Japan's revealed comparative advantage in 1980 for SITC 541 (medical and pharmaceutical products) was 0.02, whereas Denmark's was 2.35.

In spite of all the reservations that Cardiff makes, due to differences in definition and in quality of national statistics, the aggregation of these country and sectoral indices shows a clear pattern: Whereas in the 1960s the EEC's revealed comparative advantage was above the OECD average, by 1980 it had fallen considerably below it:

COMPARATIVE ADVANTAGE IN HIGH TECHNOLOGY GOODS.
Total World Manufacturing Exports.
(OECD average = 1.00)

	1963	1970	1980	1983
EEC	1.01	0.94	0.88	0.82
US	1.27	1.18	1.27	1.26
Japan	0.72	1.07	1.27	1.36

The situation as far as the actual financial beneficiaries of innovation are concerned, is probably worse for EEC native firms, and better for US firms, then these indices show. This is because some EEC countries increased their combined share of world high technology trade over the period. However, these changes were overwelmingly attributable to offshore manufacturing subsidiaries, mainly of US parent companies, established in these countries as a result of particular incentives.

PATENT STATISTICS

Crude Patent numbers are a poor indicator of economic activity everywhere. At present, they are particularly difficult to interpret in Europe, because national statistics are being so much affected by the development of the European Patent Office.

However, there must be some significance in the fact that whereas in 1967 the percentage of Patents granted by EEC countries to their own nationals or residents was 37.2, by 1977 this had dropped to 33.9, and this trend is observable in *every one* of the 7 EEC countries that matter as far as Patents are concerned [14]. Also, since most innovations must look towards the US market, it must also be significant that whereas in 1967 applications in the US from EEC countries were 61.6% of all foreign applications, by 1977 this proportion had dropped to 51%. Japan's comparable share increased from 13.9% to 24.4% over the same period [15].

SPECIAL CASES

In Information Technology, the gap separating Europe from its main industrial competitors has widened much faster than most governments and their main IT producers thought possible. Up to 1975, the EEC had a surplus on its international trade in IT goods and services. By 1980, it had a deficit of $5 m, which had increased to $10 m by 1982. Europe provides 30% of the world market for information technology but its firms capture only 15% of it, and this share is being lost at the rate of a percentage point a year [16]. This is in spite of strong protective measures. The common external tariff on semiconductors is 17%, and no less than 98% of telecommunications purchasing is from national champions. European Information Technlogy firms have a return on capital of only 2.5%, compared with 3.75% for Japanese firms, which reduces the resources they have available for R&D.

WHY DON'T THE POLICIES WORK?

The fundamental reason why intervention cannot result in successful innovation, is that innovation, other than the simplest incremental kind, is a matter of uncertainty, not risk. What this means is that the underlying stochastic processes involved in turning ideas into concrete realities, are not regular enough to allow probabilities to be estimated, so that corresponding decisions can be taken. It is not possible to operate on the basis that if you have enough projects, what you lose on some will be more than gained from the successes. Machlup expressed this in the following way:

> 'Contrary to other industries where the probable errors are larger for individual producers than for the industry as a whole, the "invention industry" is apt to present smaller dispersions in the probability distributions for the individual producers' [17].

A discovery which we owe to Scherer's investiagtions of Patents, is that the distribution of their value in the tail is arc-sine, which is characterized by possessing neither finite mean nor variance [18]. Nordhaus commented upon the implications of this, that

> 'a firm faced with the arc-sine distribution or any distribution with $\alpha \leqslant 1$ cannot obtain relief from risk by diversifying among projects. *Dispersion or risk increases as the number of projects increases*, because the law of large numbers does not hold for stable Paretian distributions with $\alpha \leqslant 1$.
>
> Although the statistical findings must be interpreted with caution, the implications of these results are quite striking. Under these perverse conditons, firms should concentrate on a single invention rather than diversifying among projects. Big firms will not possess the alleged advantage of greater certainty over small firms. National policy toward research must be rethought. As we increase the support of research under these conditions, the outcomes will probably become more dispersed . . .' [19].

Nordhaus rightly advocates caution in interpreting the figures. There is now widespread scepticism about the extent to which Patents can act as proxy indicators for innovations. The lastest reinforcement of this comes from Beggs, who reported, from a study of US Patents issued in 20 industries between 1850 and 1940, a *negative* correlation between patent numbers and value added [20]. This fits in with other evidence that patents are no longer being used to protect a large number of innovations that actually make money. We cannot automatically assume, therefore, that the distribution of *innovations* is arc-sine, with the consequences listed by Nordhaus, just because this is the pattern of patented inventions.

At the same time, the Scherer–Nordhaus emphasis on the uncertainty of innovation fits remarkably well with what is known of the innovation process from case-histories. The facts that even in the largest firms, every successful innovation is associated with an identifiable product champion, that concentration on a single objective to the point of obsession is a recurrent characteristic, that conglomerates are the least successful innovators of all, that decisions concerning innovation can only be made at the top of the management hierarchy, that large firms do not automatically innovate more than smaller ones, that so many innovations are carried through by firms from outside the technology in question, that firms which are dominated by accountants (skilled at measuring *risks*) tend to be followers rather than leaders, all testify to the extent to which innovation is only partly the result of rational decision. Where reason is inadequate for decision-making, recourse has to be made to imagination. This is the reason why innovatory activity displays many of the characteristics – albeit at a different level – which are associated with artistic endeavour [21].

Under modern conditions, the creative activity that is most important for innovation is leadership of scientific and technical personnel. An outstanding example is Howard Florey, the innovator of Penicillin. In a quite different context, Norman Borlaug, whose Nobel prize was won for developing plant strains that now feed a significant part of the Third World, asserted that it was leadership that made the whole difference between success and failure in all crop improvement schemes [22].

A characteristic of leadership is single-minded concentration on the immediate task in hand. It is intrinsically a 'micro' activity. The larger the team, the less the creative power of the leader can coordinate the work of every member of it, fill the inevitable gaps, and respond dynamically both to the unforeseen problems and serendipitous bonuses. This is why a well-proven empirical rule for innovatory activity is 'always work with the smallest team possible'. Any shift to the 'macro' level means that creative energy, instead of being concentrated and focussed on a single objective, is diffused over many topics and many targets. Macro-activity is, of its nature, bureaucratic, and bureaucratic creativity consists primarily in reconciling many different objectives; it simply cannot have the single focus that innovation demands.

PROFIT OR 'COVER'?

Industrial policies cannot be handled other than by bureaucrats, who are very poor at dealing with risk, and *cannot deal with uncertainty at all.*

Bureaucratic decisions are invariably committee decisions, and in respect of innovation, will avoid the riskiest projects even more than the individual Committee-members would, if left on their own. The best description of a camel, we should not forget, is that it is 'a horse designed by a Committee'. Further, those who become bureaucrats, either in the large firm or in the public services, do so to some extent because they do not like risk. Those who are promoted in any bureaucracy, are those who like risk least, and who are especially responsive to a learning process that is quite different from that of a typical entrepreneur, still more from that of an innovator. The 'god of Battles' who Napoleon claimed had exclusive responsibility for selecting his Generals, never has them on his short list. If, therefore, bureaucrats are asked to administer interventionist policies for innovation, two factors above all make their task impossible.

1. The search for 'Cover'

An entrepreneur who is spending his own money, or whose remuneration is otherwise closely tied to his firm's success, weighs up a project in terms of 'how much will I make if this succeeds?'. A bureaucrat, who by definition will not share in the rewards of success, must use the criterion, 'How could my career-path within the organisation be affected if it fails?'. 'Cover' replaces 'profit' in selection of projects, with the result that the favoured projects will always be the 'safer' second-grade ones. RCA lost in the video-recorder race because its large-firm bureaucratic structure could not make the decision to move away from a fixed-head scanner. This was much less demanding of mechanical than electronic capability in its anticipated development. Such a trajectory therefore seemed 'safer' for a company which thought of itself as supreme in electronics. But for the future, in fact, was with *rotating* scanners. [23].

2. Reduction in the number of decision-points

If public support for innovation is considered to be necessary, it can only be because firms are unable to finance the innovation from their own resources, or from other, non-Government sources of, e.g., finance. Because innovation involves uncertainty rather than risk, external support has to be provided on the same basis as the innovation is being undertaken, i.e. in reliance on imagination rather than rational assessment. There has to be a 'meeting of imaginations' between the innovator and the investor. But the capacity of any individual to provide such support, is limited by his own imagination. The changes of a fruitful 'meeting' taking place are obviously greater, the more decision points there are which allow diverse imaginations to be brought to bear on a project. Conversely, reduction of these to a single one, as is the case with public support, minimises the chances of the support being given to the 'right' projects.

IMPORTANCE OF AUTO-FINANCING

To the extent that decisions to innovate are taken under uncertainty rather than risk, and are therefore not fully rational, they cannot justify support from external sources, which has to be rationally based. Only the firm's own resources can therefore be brought to bear, and empirical studies of innovation in France show that these are, in fact, the most important source of funds in no less than 87% of cases [24].

Public support of innovation cannot fail to reduce the volume of auto-financing available for innovator, since such support has to be paid for out of taxation. Because the larger firms depend most upon their internally generated funds to finance innovations, the resulting drain on these funds from heavy taxation, probably affects the *quality* of industrial innovation even more than its quantity.

Autofinancing by European fims has declined steadily in recent years, sometimes by as much as 20% [25]. The fact that in 1980 the combined results of the 100 largest companies in Europe showed a profit level of 0%, bodes ill for future innovation from these companies.

But could it not be that where the research project is self-selected, Publicly-funded aid (typically 50%, as has been noted) would correspondingly reduce the risk of undertaking a project? This could be true if projects were genuinely selected only by the applicant firms, i.e., if support were *automatic*. However, in every single case of aid, there is an evaluation of the project by, or on behalf of the Public Authorities. There probably has to be, given the conditions of accountability which apply to public funds, but there is also a strong element of belief on the part of the bureaucrats that they know more than the innovators and industrialists do.

'MICRO' VERSUS 'MACRO'

Inevitably, therefore, the emphasis shifts from the micro- to the macro-level, bureaucratic values take over, 'cover' replaces profit as the criterion of selection, urgency is lost, and creative energy is dissipated.

Firms' own selection of research topics becomes biassed in the direction of topics which will attract State aid, so that bureaucratic values within the firm itself are reinforced. Public support favours those who are good at proposal-writing rather than at actually getting new things done, as the Baruch Report on Technological Innovation in the US recognised [26].

In the nature of things, the projects which are most 'futuristic' and therefore depend most upon imagination, are those which have least supporting data of the type which makes a good proposal. Moreover, public funds for innovation are not generally awarded simply on the basis of written proposals. Lengthy, time-consuming and expensive negotiations are frequently involved, which exasperate the real innovators and entrepreneurs in a firm. Accepting public support, therefore, means giving more power in management to the individuals who are most at home with the bureaucrats with whom it is necessary to deal if that support is to be obtained. These are not the firms' most original spirits, in fact the opposite, so that this development reduces the firm's ability to take decisions under uncertainty, and therefore become involved in innovation.

If firms are not being innovative without State aid, it can only be because there are obstacles which prevent it. Such obstacles could be high taxation, which reduces auto-financing capacity, or inadequate law, for example Patents which fail to confer appropriability of rewards. The State has a choice between policies which are directed towards removing the obstacles, or those which leave them in place, but provide funds, on an interventionist basis, to counter their effect. Modern bureaucrats will always opt for the latter policy since it offers opportunities for expanding the administrative system. In this connection, it is significant that the best means yet devised of using public funds to support innovation – the Small Business Innovation Research Scheme – should have originated in the U.S., and not in Europe. By a law enacted in 1982, the Institutions responsible for 99% of Federal R&D spending, must set aside a very small proportion of these funds (starting at 0.2%, and rising annually by the same amount) to be given in grants to businesses employing less than 500 people, for high-risk research projects. At present these grants are $40,000 for 6 months' work in the first stage and $200,000 for 2 years' work in the second stage. About 10% of applicants received an award at the first stage and one-third to one-half of these obtain a second-stage award. Already, there have been successes.

This Scheme faces up to the problems of both 'cover' and 'centralization' which bedevil other public measures in support of R&D and innovation. The officials of the spending institutions are 'covered', because they are being forced by law to spend money in this way. No blame could possibly attach to them, even if every single grant leads to nothing, since, except for the Department of Defense, assessment is by *external* experts. At the same time, the advantages of decentralized information are obtained, since the initiative comes from a multitude of applicant firms.

The fact that Europe neither invented, nor innovated, nor even (as yet) copied the SBIR scheme, reflects different types of Civil Service, with those in Europe being more committed to intervention.

'POLITICRATIC' THINKING

I have emphasised the role of bureaucrats in retarding innovation, but, of course, the parallel activity of politicians in search of votes has a similar effect. Perhaps our understanding of the problem would be helped by thinking in terms of a hybrid, the 'politicrat'. Politicrats may be politicians or civil servants, or even members of the bureaucracies of large firms, but their common characteristic is that they operate at the 'macro-' level. They consequently tend to benefit from any shift from the micro-level of activity, and from the diffusion of energy which is inevitably associated with this. Inevitably, therefore, and unconsciously as well as consciously, they are biassed towards policies which will bring about such shifts, which are fatal to innovatory power.

Once arrangements for 'throwing money at the problem' are in place, it is easy for the view to become accepted that the State is doing all it can to encourage innovation, and that the problems are altogether intractable, or that nothing need be done about removing them. Then, when the policies fail, this is attributed to inertia, or inadequacy, or sheer perverse refusal to use the incentives which the State has provided for them, on the part of firms.

However, the opportunity for 'politicratic' thinking to become fashionable is primarily due to the failure by intellectuals to develop ways of using law instead of intervention especially in relation to innovation. The obvious place to being to make up for this failure, is with the Principle of Patenting, since this, historically, has been where law and economic innovation have come into intended and explicit contact. The EEC has in fact begun there, by commissioning a study, recently completed, of 'Direct Protection of Innovation'.

INNOVATION PATENTS AND WARRANTS

The stimulus to this came from two proposals which have been circulating in recent years, the 'Innovation Patent' of Dr. Hermann Kronz, and my own 'Innovation Warrant' [27]. Given that these originated quite independently of each other, the extent of their agreement is rather remarkable, including, as it does:

- The Subject-matter of protection to be innovation, not invention.
- Any economic object can be protected, not just technology.
- The novelty criterion is simply 'non-availability in the ordinary course of trade'.
- 'Investment to produce' is therefore a condition of grant.
- Term of monopoly granted is matched to the need for it.
- Examination relies heavily on Third Party involvement.
- Grant is incontestable unless it has been obtained by fraud.
- Terms of grant can differ between regions of a country, or (obviously, by agreement) can apply over more than one country.
- System to be administered by an independent Authority.
- Arbitration is the means used to settle disputes. Appeal to the Courts remains possible, but there is a powerful sanction against this, in that legal aid is then made available to the party who has accepted the arbitrator's decision.

ADVANTAGES OF DIRECT PROTECTION OF INNOVATION

Every attempt at innovation involves obtaining and applying information on the nature of a firm's own relevant capacities, their opportunity costs, the costs of additional research inputs that may be required, the duration of the project, the likelihood of success and its value if it is achieved, and other factors. Uncertainty attaches to each of these aspects of the project. But however inadequate the available information in respect of each of them may be, that of the individual firm which is undertaking the project is incomparably better than a centralised authority can ever have.

Use of the Principle of Patenting not alone taps this decentralised information, but also motivates those who possess it to act upon it, in spite of the associated uncertainty. The classical patent system has become a poor expression of this Principle. It has been offering nominally long (17–20 years) monopoly terms, but these frequently fail to confer any serious element of appropriability of rewards except in the case of Chemicals. Consequently, in many fields, it pays to imitate, rather than to innovate.

Direct protection of innovation, in contrast, would match the monopoly term to the task it has to perform. Terms would generally be shorter than those of classical patents, but within them, genuine appropriability of rewards would be obtained. The arrangements for Arbitration and Legal Aid would substantially erase any differences between small and large firms in terms of resources for litigation. This feature greatly extends the possibility for smaller firms to become involved in innovation.

Shifting from intervention to law, has the following advantages:

1. The information on which an attempt to innovate is based, is better, because decentralised.
2. The criterion for investment is 'profit', not 'cover', so that better projects can be chosen.
3. Creative energy is *concentrated* at the 'micro' level instead of being *diffused* at the 'macro' level.
4. Projects are selected according to market criteria *only*. Politics, whether national or at the intra-departmental level, no longer have a bearing.
5. The mutual antagonism and lack of sympathy between bureaucrat and innovator are no longer a barrier to innovation.
6. The waste involved in collecting funds from firms through taxation, and redistributing part of the same funds to the same firms in the form of grants or subsidies, is eliminated.
7. Consequent lower tax rates leave more cash in firm's reserves that can then be used for R&D and innovation.
8. Size of firm becomes less important (because of the Arbitration provisions).
9. Direct protection of innovation would recover from Japanese firms much of the dominance in incremental innovation which the inadequacy of the classical Patent system handed to them as a free gift.
10. The decentralised decision-making of direct innovation protection is in tune with the intrinsically individualistic tradition of Europe.

ACHIEVING 'EUROPEAN' SCALE

Direct protection of innovation is much more realistic in a *de facto* fragmented 'Europe des Patries' than attempts to compensate for the fragmentation. In the first place, although it does not eliminate the importance of scale altogether, it does reduce it greatly. Empirical studies indicate that scale is not absolutely necessary for carrying through invention to the innovation stage – over a quarter of all innovative industrial break-throughs in the US have been made by firms with less than 100 employees. But scale *is* necessary to protect the innovation and thus to be able to appropriate any rewards there may be from it, *if the patent system is not doing its job.*

Conversely, with Direct Protection of Innovation, which would really confer the power to capture the rewards of innovatory investment, the emphasis of the 'Community Dimension' of innovation could shift away from scale. The relationship between size of a potential market and investment to satisfy it, is evidently a function of the projected achievable market share, which, in turn, reflects the reward-capture mechanism. When, as the new Yale study has discovered, 90% of professional R&D managers think that imitation of a typical patented product would not take more than 3 years and would not cost the imitator more than the innovator, the official Commission view may well be correct [28]. But if imitation is made impossible during the monopoly term by Direct Innovation Protection, so that the innovator can count upon holding 100% of the market for that period, a much smaller total market could justify a given investment in innovation. Individual national markets of EEC member States could then justify such investment.

Moreover, the 'legal' approach has the added attraction that it appears to be more effective at overcoming national barriers than the 'interventionist' approach. As Evenson recently put it,

> 'Ironically, nations do not recognise global rights in non-intellectual property and regularly intervene in commodity and capital trade markets to achieve nationalistic goals. With few exceptions, these same nations have joined international conventions freely granting intellectual property rights to citizens of other countries' [29].

The 'national treatment' provision of the Paris Convention has effectively generated a single world order for Patents and Trade Marks. The value of the latter is vastly greater than the former, as the scale of international brands of consumer- and consumer-durable goods confirms. And the fact that a Patent monopoly secured in a particular country by use of the Paris Convention, can be exploited by *imported* products, testifies to a general readiness to suspend protectionist measures in respect of innovation.

What this all adds up to, therefore, is that by the use of Direct Protection of Innovation, an internal market of Continental scale *for innovatory products* might be able to be achieved independently of such a market for the products of established industries, and irrespective of whether or not the latter proves to be an impossible ideal. The European Commission's effors to compensate for national reluctance to move to a genuine common market have already been costly, and look like costing vastly more, under the Eureka proposals. All that can be claimed for the expenditures so far is that 'non-Europe' might even be worse if they had not been made – although that is not easy to imagine. Nor is there any reason to think that Eureka will be any more successful, since the same underlying misunderstanding of the innovation process inspires it. In contrast, Direct Protection of Innovation would cost virtually nothing.

COULD THE TIDE BE TURNING?

In the mid-nineteenth century, Limited Liability produced a massive upsurge in investment and innovation, by reducing risk as this was perceived by individuals. To-day, Direct Protection could have results of the same order of magnitude, by removing a major element of the uncertainty that is intrinsic to all investment in innovation. As such, it could be the beginning of a movement back towards using law instead of Industrial Policy as means of achieving economic objectives.

The European experience provides ample evidence that if we do not get the law in respect of innovation right, intervention will not work; on the other hand, to the extent that we do get the law right, intervention, in all probability, becomes unnecessary.

REFERENCES

1. Olson, Mancur, 'Ideology and Economic Growth'. In *Proceedings of the Urban Institute Conference*, Sept. 22 and 23, 1983, Washington, D.C. (1984).
2. Kingston, W., *The Political Economy of Innovation*, The Hague: Martinus Nijhoff (1984).
3. Landes, David, *The Unbound Prometheus*, Cambridge (1970), p. 19.
4. Ripert, G., *Aspects Juridique du Capitalisme Moderne*, Paris, (1946), pp. 59–62.
5. Mill, J. S., *Principles of Political Economy*, Book II, Ch. I.
6. Usher, Dan, *The Economic Prerequisite to Democracy*, Oxford (1981).
7. Buchanan, J. MgG. and Wagner, R. E., *Democracy in Deficit: The Political Legacy of Lord Keynes*, New York (1977).
8. Kingston, W., 'Ideas, Civil Servants and Keynes', In *Journal of Economic Affairs* 3, No. 2 (January, 1983), pp. 128–130.
9. Nelson, R. R., *High Technology Policies: A Five-Nation Comparison*, Washington, D.C. (1984), p. 20.
10. Merritt, G., *Industrial Innovation: A Guide to Community Action, Services and Funding*, Brussels, (Nov., 1983), p. viii.
11. Zysman, J. *Political Strategies for Industrial Order: State Power and Industry in France*, Berkeley (1977).
12. Nelson, *op. cit.*
13. Cardiff, Brendan, *High Technology Trade Indicators*, Paper prepared for a Colloquium of the Policy Planning Staff of the Federal Foreign Office, Bonn (11 December, 1984).

14. Grevink, H. and Kronz, H., *Evolution of Patent Filing Activities in the EEC*, EUR 6574 EN, Luxembourg (1980).
15. Grevink, H. and Kronz, H., *Evolution of Patent Filing Activities in the USA*, Report EUR 6575 EN, Luxembourg (1980).
16. E.E.C. Ministerial Conference, Paris (17 July 1985). French proposals.
17. Machlup, F., In R. R. Nelson (ed.), *The Rate and Direction of Inventive Activity*, Princeton Univ. Press. (1962), p. 154.
18. Sherer, F. M., In *American Economic Review* 55 (1965), p. 1098.
19. Nordhaus, W. D., *Invention, Growth and Welfare*, M.I.T. Press, (1969), p. 55.
20. Beggs, J., 'Long Run Trends in Patenting', Washington, D.C. (1982), National Bureau of Economic Research Working Paper No. 952.
21. Kingston, W., *Innovation: The Creative Impulse in Human Progress*, London (1977).
22. Borlaug, Norman, *The Green Revolution, Peace, and Humanity*, Lecture on the Occasion of the Award of the Nobel Peace Prize, 1970, Oslo: The Nobel Foundation (1970), p. 236.
23. Rosenbloom, R. S., *Managing Technology for the Longer Term*, Harvard Business School Paper (22 May, 1984).
24. Piatier, A., *L'Innovation dans l'Industrie*, CPE Etude No 32, Ministère de l'industrie et de la recherche, Paris (May, 1984), p. 59.
25. Merritt, *op. cit.*
26. Report to the President on Technological Innovation in the United States, Washington, D.C., Govmt. Printing Office (1979).
27. An outline of the provisions of both systems can be found in Phillips, Jeremy (ed.), *Patents in Perspective*, Oxford: ESC Publishing (1985).
28. Levin, Klevorick, Nelson and Winter, *Survey Research on R&D Appropriability and Technological Opportunity. Part I: Appropriability*, Yale University Working Paper (July, 1984).
29. Evenson, Robert E., 'International Invention: Implications for Technology Market Analysis', In Zvi Grilliches (ed.), *R&D Patents and Productivity*, Univ. of Chicago Press (1984), pp. 99–122.

BIBLIOGRAPHY

Arndt, H. (1952), *Schöpferischer Wettbewerb und Klassenlose Gesellschaft*, Duncker & Humblot, Berlin.

Arndt, H. (1960/61[1] and 1971[2]), '*Die Konzentration in der Wirtschaft*', Schriften des Vereins für Sozialpolitik, Neue Folge Band 20, Duncker & Humblot, Berlin.

Arndt, H. (1984), *Economic Theory versus Economic Reality*, Michigan State University Press (translated by W. A. Kirby after the original German edition of 1979).

Bienayme, A. (1969), *L'entreprise et le pouvoir économique*, Dunod, Paris.

Böbel, I. (1984), *Wettbewerb und Industriestruktur*, Springer Verlag, Heidelberg.

Chevalier, J. M. (1977), *l'Economie industrielle en question*, Calmann – Lévy, Paris.

van Duyn, J. J. (1979), *De lange golf in de economie*, Stenfert Kroese, Leiden (English translation: *The long wave in economics*, London, 1983).

Clapham, R. (1981), 'Dans Wettbewerbspolitische Konzept der Wettbewerbsfreiheit', in: H. Cox, Jens, K. Markert (eds.), *Handbuch des Wettbewerbs*, F. Vahlen, München.

Dullaart, M. J. H. (1984), *Regulation or freedom, Dutch economic thinking in the interwar period*, Diss., Rotterdam.

Fehl, K. and Oberender, P. (1984), 'Chemie faserindustrie', in: P. Oberender (ed.), *Marktstruktur und Wettbewerb*, F. Vahlen, Müchen.

Hendriks, A. (1984), *De veranderende bouwopgave*, Weesp.

Hennipman, P. (1954), 'Monopoly: impediment or stimulus to economic progress', in: E. H. Chamberlin (ed.), '*Monopoly and Competition and their Regulation*', London.

Heusse, E. (1965), *Allgemeine Markttheorie*, J. C. B. Mohr, Tübingen.

Hoekman, J. M. (1984), *The Role of the Joint Venture in the Strategy of Corporations*, Diss., Amsterdam.

Houssiaux, J. (1958), *Le pouvoir de monopole*, Sirey, Paris.

Houssiaux, J. (1960), *Concurrence et marché commun.*, Génin, Paris.

Houssiaux, J. (1965), 'Les grandes entreprises et les fusions', *Direction* 116, avril 1965.

Jacquemin, A. P. (1967), *L'entreprise et son pouvoir de marché*, P.U.F., Paris.

Jacquemin, A. P. (1975[1], 1979[2]), '*Economie industrielle européenne. Structures de marché et stratégies d'entreprise*, Dunod, Paris.

Jacquemin, A. P. and Geroski, P. (1984), 'Dominant firms and their alleged decline', *International Journal of Industrial Organization.*

Jacquemin, A. P. and de Jong, H. W. (1976), *Markets, Corporate Behaviour and the State*, M. Nijhoff, The Hague.

Jacquemin, A. P. and de Jong, H. W. (1977), *European Industrial Organization*, MacMillan & Co., London.

Jacquemin, A. P. and de Jong, H. W. (1980), *Economia e politica industriale in Europa*, Il Mulino, Bologna.

de Jong, H. W. (1971), *Ondernemingsconcentratie*. de ontwikkelingen in Europa, de Verenigde Staten en Japan, Stenfert Kroese, Leiden.

de Jong, H. W. (1972[1], 1981[2], 1985[3]), *Dynamische markttheorie*, Stenfert Kroese, Leiden.

Kantzenbach, E. (1966), *Die Funktionsfähigkeit des Wettbewerbs*, Vandenhoeck & Ruprecht, Göttingen.

Kantzenbach, E. and Kallfass, H. (1981), 'Dans Konzept des funktionsfähigen Wettbewerbs – workable competition', in: H. Cox, K. Jens, K. Markert (eds), *Handbuch des Wettbewerbs*, F. Vahlen, München.

Kaufer, E. (1980), *Industrieökonomiek*, F. Vahlen, München.

Krüsselberg, H. G. (1969), *Marktwirtschaft und Ökonomische Theorie*, Verlag Rombach, Freiburg im Breisgau.

Lenel, H. O. (1957), 'Walter Eucken's ordnungspolitische Konzeption: die wirtschaftpolitische Lehre in der Bundesrepublik und die Wettbewerbstheorie von heute, *Ordo*, Band 26.

Lenel, H. O. (1968), *Die Bedeutung grosser Unternehmen für den technischen Fortschritt*, J. C. B. Mohr, Tübingen.

Lenel, H. O. (1962[1], 1968[2]), *Die Konzentration in der Wirtschaft*, J. C. B. Mohr, Tübingen.

Lenel, H. O. (1978), 'Zur Problematik der Gemeinschaftsunternehemen', *Tijdschrift voor Vennootschappen, Verenigingen en Stichtingen* (T.V.V.S.), No. 8.

Levy, H. (1911), *Monopoly and Competition. A Study in English Industrial Organization*, MacMillan & Co., London (translated from the German edition of 1909).

Levy, H. (1935), *Industrial Germany*, Cambridge University Press, Cambridge.

Levy, H. (1936), *The New Industrial System. A Study of the Origins, Forms, Finance, and Prospects of Concentration in Industry*, G. Routledge & Sons, London.

Liefmann, R. (1930), *Kartelle, Konzerne und Trusts* (8. Auflage), E. H. Moritz, Stuttgart.

Linda, R. (1969), Il comportamento dei gruppi di sviluppo e delle piccole imprese nella teoria dell' equilibrio dinamico oligopolistico: i profitti, i prezzi, le capacità di produzione e il problema dell' entrata, *Rivista di politica economica*, febr. 1969, anno LIX, serie III.

Linda, R. (1980), 'La division du travail au sein de la communauté européenne et les nouvelles concurrences endogènes', *Revue d'économie industrielle*, Paris.

Linda, R. (1984), 'Crise industrielle européenne', *Bulletin de l'institut international de concurrence commercial*, Nov. 1984.

Marchal, J. (1950–51), 'La crise contemporaine de la science économique', *Annales de l'économie politique*.

Mariti, P. (1977), 'Economia di scala e divisione del lavoro tra imprese', *Rivista di economia e politica industriale*, anno III, No. 1.

Mariti, P. (1983), 'Co-operative agreements and the organization of industry', *Journal of Industrial Economics*, No. 4, June 1984.

Menger, C. (1981), *Principles of Economics*, New York University Press, New York (translated by J. Dingwall and B. F. Hoselitz).

Möller, W. P. (1983), *Der Erfolg von Unternehmenszusammenschlüssen*, Minerva Publikation, München.

Oberender, P. (ed.) (1984), *Marktstruktur und Wettbewerb in der Bundesrepublik Deutschland*, Verlag F. Vahlen, München.

Parent, J. (1970), *La concentration industrielle*, P.U.F., Paris.

Piatier, A. (1984), *Barriers to Innovation*, Francis Pinter, London.

Prodi, R. (1968), *Concorrenza dinamica e potere di mercato*, Milano.

Prodi, R. (1971), '*La diffusione della innovazione dell'industria italiana*', Il Mulino, Bologna.

Ruffolo, C. (1967), *La grande impresa nella società moderna*, Einaudi, Torino.

Salvati, M. (1974), 'Subordinazione o autonomia delle piccole imprese: valutazione politica o economica', *Economia e politica industriale*, No. 7/8.

Schlögl, H. (1972), *Mehrproduktunternehmung, Marktentwicklung und Wettbewerb*, Atheneum Verlag, Frankfurt/M.

Schmidt, I. (1981), *Wettbewerbstheorie und -politik*, G. Fischer verlag, Stuttgart.

Schumpeter, J. (1926), *Theorie der Wirtschaftlichen Entwicklung*, Duncker & Humblot, Berlin (5. Auflage).

Schumpeter, J. (1954), *History of economic analysis*, Oxford University Press, Oxford.

Shepherd, G., Duchène, F., and Saunders, G. (eds.) (1983), *Europe's Industries. Public and Private Strategies for Change*, London Tolksdorf, M. (1971), *Ruinöser Wettbewerb*, Berlin.

Webbink, I. (1984), *Innovatie en het midden- en kleinbedrijf*, EIM publicaties, Zoetermeer.

Weber, A. P. and Jenny F. (1974), *Concentration et politique des structures industrielles*, La documentation française, Paris.

van der Weyden, C. J. (1981), 'Toestaan of verbieden: een beschouwing rond de wet economische mededinging', *Economisch-statistische Berichten*, 23/30-12 1981.

von Weiser, F. (1927), *Theorie der gesellschaftlichen Wirtschaft*, J. C. B. Mohr, Tübingen (2. Auflage).

de Wolff, P. (1982), 'de relatie tussen concentratiegraad den winstgevendheid in Nederlandse bedrijfstakken', *Economisch-statistische Berichten*, 26-12-1982.

Wijers, G. J. (1981), *Industriepolitiek*, Stenfert Kroese, Leiden.